Lecture Notes of the Institute for Computer Sciences, Social Informatics and Telecommunications Engineering 265

More information about this series at http://www.springer.com/series/8197

Anthony L. Brooks · Eva Brooks
Cristina Sylla (Eds.)

Interactivity, Game Creation, Design, Learning, and Innovation

7th EAI International Conference, ArtsIT 2018
and 3rd EAI International Conference, DLI 2018, ICTCC 2018
Braga, Portugal, October 24–26, 2018
Proceedings

 Springer

Editors
Anthony L. Brooks (iD)
Aalborg University
Aalborg, Denmark

Eva Brooks (iD)
Aalborg University
Aalborg, Denmark

Cristina Sylla (iD)
University of Minho
Braga, Portugal

ISSN 1867-8211   ISSN 1867-822X (electronic)
Lecture Notes of the Institute for Computer Sciences, Social Informatics
and Telecommunications Engineering
ISBN 978-3-030-06133-3   ISBN 978-3-030-06134-0 (eBook)
https://doi.org/10.1007/978-3-030-06134-0

Library of Congress Control Number: 2018965503

This Springer imprint is published by the registered company Springer Nature Switzerland AG
The registered company address is: Gewerbestrasse 11, 6330 Cham, Switzerland

ArtsIT + DLI 2018

We are delighted to introduce the proceedings of the 7th European Alliance for Innovation (EAI) International Conference on Arts and Technology, Interactivity, and Game Creation (ArtsIT 2018) and the Third International Conference on Design, Learning and Innovation (DLI 2018), held in Braga, Portugal, October 24–26, 2018.

ArtsIT, Interactivity and Game Creation 2018 was meant to be a place where people in the arts, with a keen interest in modern IT technologies, meet with people in IT, having strong ties to the arts in their works. Since 2009, the event has become a leading scientific forum for dissemination of cutting-edge research results in the area of arts, design, and technology. The event also reflects the advances seen in the open related topics of interactivity (interaction design, virtual reality, augmented reality, robotics, etc.) and game creation (e.g., serious games, gamification, leisure gaming, gameplay, etc.).

ArtsIT has been successfully co-located with the international conference for Design, Learning and Innovation (DLI) since 2016.

Design, learning, and innovation frame the world of IT, opening doors into an increasingly playful world. The DLI 2018 conference was driven by the belief that tools, technologies, and environments, as well as content and approaches, can spark and nurture a passion for learning, transforming domains such as education, rehabilitation/therapy, work places, and cultural institutions. Design, learning, and innovation are a powerful catalyst in empowering individuals to participate, communicate, and create, whereby they can exceed their own limits in a playful way. Making this spirit explicit and visible is crucial for identifying how specific tools, technologies, methodologies and solutions shape opportunities for learning and engaging with the demands of today's world. More than ever, challenges in the fields of design, learning, and innovation are often approached by transdisciplinary teams and solutions that mobilize tools, technologies, methods, and theories from different fields to unlock new frameworks, opening up to partnerships that can enrich learning in formal and informal learning practices. DLI 2018 intended to foster such dynamics.

Preceding the main conferences was a workshop on Playable Cities (October 24) in which participants explored the ways the broad gamut of technologies that make up the smart city infrastructure can be harnessed to incorporate more playfulness into daily life activities that take place within the city. This makes the city not only more efficient, but also more enjoyable to the people who live and work within its confines.

Following the workshop, the welcome reception took place at Paço do Vitorino (http://www.pacodevitorino.com), a heritage hotel located in Ponte de Lima, one of the most characterful and charming towns in northern Portugal. The house, dating back to the XVI century, is a municipal monument that has undergone an innovative architectural intervention. The rehabilitation of Paço de Vitorino emerged out of the desire to enhance the inherited patrimony, seeking to achieve a balance between recovering domestic memories and ensuring its self-sufficiency. The manor house has been in the same family since the mid-sixteenth century and its history is marked by several events that mime and mirror the history of Portugal. Paço de Vitorino impresses the visitor because of the harmonious baroque ensemble that includes the chapel, the battlement wall, the gate, and the expressiveness of the facades entering the yard, richly adorned with elements of dressed granite. The monumental gardens, attributed to the Italian master Nicolau Nasoni, were designed according to the baroque canons and include a sophisticated and unique irrigation system as well as secular camellias.

The technical program of the collocated conferences ArtsIT 2018 and DLI 2018 included 40 full papers and five short papers in oral presentation sessions during the main conference's tracks and 13 poster and demo presentations. Aside from the high-quality technical paper presentations, the technical program also featured three keynote speeches. The three keynote speakers were Prof. Yvonne Rogers from the University College London, Assoc. Prof. Anthony L. Brooks, from Aalborg University, Denmark, and Prof. Anton Nijholt from the University of Twente, The Netherlands. The technical program included three arts performances that were held at the historical Theatro Circo, namely, CO:LATERAL, NaN:Collider and ShellShock.

CO:LATERAL (Né Barros and João Martinho Moura, with Sónia Cunha/ 2016–2018)

CO:LATERAL was developed from the Nuve artwork, a project for performance and digital art. Initially presented in 2010, this solo interpreted by Né Barros was the motif for several national and international publications. In Co:Lateral the body projected and extended itself in a relationship of intimacy with interactive virtual reality. The performative discourse resulting from this connection calls for an extraordinary moment, a poetic moment made of a mixture of realities, made of body, double and images. Co:Lateral evokes moments of the death of the swan immersed in an immaterial space of light and projection: A phantom of the archive of dance now returns to test itself in a reality of illusory imprisonment.

Direction and choreography: Né Barros; Digital creation: João Martinho Moura; Performer: Sónia Cunha; Music: João Martinho Moura; Costume Design: Né Barros; Production: Lucinda Gomes/balleteatro; Research supervision: Paulo Ferreira-Lopes (School of Arts, UCP/CITAR) and Né Barros (Balleteatro).

NaN:Collider (António Rafael, João Martinho Moura and Miguel Pedro. 2016–2018)

NaN:Collider + Miguel Pedro NaN Collider is an audiovisual performance, started in 2016 by João Martinho Moura and António Rafael, devoted to the science, arts, and space exploration. NaN is a numeric data type value representing an undefined or unpresentable value, something impossible to calculate. Collider refers to an opposite concept to that, something very concrete, used as a research tool in particle physics by accelerating particles to very high kinetic energy. On this project they invited Miguel Pedro to work with them with sounds that result from a research process in experimental electronic music developed at the International Iberian Nanotechnology Institute. The artists take the public on a journey into deep space, starting on earth, flying to the moon, passing through a spiral galaxy in formation, facing a black hole and finishing at the nanoscale.

(Music: António Rafael, Miguel Pedro, João Martinho Moura; Visuals: João Martinho Moura)

ShellShock (Doaa Darwish. 2018)

ShellShock is an experimental multimedia performance that explores trauma and PTSD through human movement, by using motion-capture technology to generate audiovisual content in real time. The project aims to explore different approaches to combine digital media with theatre and Performing Arts. ShellShock is developed in the Rhine-Waal University media labs in Kamp-Lintfort (Germany) under the supervision of Prof. Ido Iurgel.

Braga, a city where tradition and innovation meet, was inducted in 2017 into UNESCO's prestigious Creative City of Media Arts network (UCCN), a small selection of 116 cities from 54 countries. Capital of the Minho Province with approximately 182,000 inhabitants, Braga is one of most vibrant technology hubs in north Portugal. In the late twentieth century, the city bore witness to a new generation of artists and entrepreneurs that transformed the local creative ecosystem by combining art with technology and innovation. Ever since, Braga hosts high-profile and international state-of-art tech companies, and media arts is currently the main driver of the local creative economy representing half of the employment in the sector and 40% of the enterprises. For Braga, media arts also provide an opportunity to engage its citizens in re-thinking the city by reinforcing linkages between art, science, technology, and sense of community.

The multidisciplinary GNRation Centre has been established to improve access to new media and cultural activities, with a focus on raising public awareness surrounding the artistic value of digital technologies through interactive workshops. Connecting art with technology, the Braga Semibreve Festival is now an internationally renowned, cross-cutting electronic music and media arts event, featuring avant-garde artists from around the world. Focused on audiovisual performances and experimental live electronic music, the festival offers an immersive visual and sonic experience. The festival also displays works developed by students from the EngageLab of the Minho University; an institution recognized for its advanced ICT-based research.

In recent years, Braga has implemented a strategy aimed at supporting the media arts and creative industries, nurturing an already thriving cultural ecosystem. It aims to generate employment opportunities, to promote and showcase emerging digital talents, and to strengthen the economic impact of the creative field. The city also launched a new media art residency and a start-up hub to provide further support to media arts thinkers and entrepreneurs through regular international roadshows (source: https://en.unesco.org/creative-cities/braga).

As host city, Braga provided the ideal landscape for bringing together artists, designers, and other people working in cutting-edge technologies from a variety of backgrounds from all over the world.

The atmosphere at the events was congenial, comfortable, and friendly. Attendees met like-minded people to engage in fruitful discussions and debates. Great networking was evident from being an active delegate and we understand many close friendships have developed from the event.

December 2018

Cristina Sylla
Eva Brooks

Organization

Steering Committees (*ArtsIT ** DLI)

Imrich Chlamtac (President)   European Alliance for Innovation
*Anthony L. Brooks   CREATE, Aalborg University, Denmark
**Eva I. Brooks   Department of Learning and Philosophy,
                               Aalborg University, Denmark

Organizing Committees

General Chairs

*Cristina Sylla   Centre on Child Studies, University of Minho,
                               Instituto de Educação, Braga, Portugal
**Eva I. Brooks   Department of Learning and Philosophy,
                               Aalborg University, Denmark

General Co-chair

**Cristina Sylla   Research Centre on Child Studies,
                               University of Minho, Instituto de Educação, Braga,
                               Portugal

TPC Chair and Co-chairs

*Ido Iurgel   Rhine-Waal University of Applied Sciences, Germany
*Teresa Romão   Faculty of Science and Technology, New University
                               of Lisboa (FCT/UNL), Lisbon, Portugal
**Wolfgang Müller   University of Education Weingarten, Germany
**Lucia Amante   Universidade Aberta, Portugal

Sponsorship and Exhibit Chairs

*Eva Oliveira   Polytechnic Institute of Cávado e Ave, Portugal
**Sílvia Araújo   University of Minho, Portugal

Workshops Chairs

*Yoram Chisik   .
**Janet Read   University of Central Lancashire, UK

Publicity and Social Media Chairs

*Douglas Menegazzi   Federal University of Santa Catarina,
                               Graphic Expression Department, Brazil
**Douglas Menegazzi   Federal University of Santa Catarina,
                               Graphic Expression Department, Brazil

| **Nelson Zagalo | University of Aveiro,
Communication and Art Department, Portugal |

Publications Chairs

*Thanasis Hadzilacos	Open University of Cyprus, Information Systems, Cyprus
*Taciana Pontual	McGill University – School of Information Studies, Canada
*Isabel Machado Alexandre	University of Lisbon, Portugal
**Taciana Pontual	McGill University – McGill University – School of Information Studies, Canada
**Thanasis Hadzilacos	Open University of Cyprus, Information Systems, Cyprus
**Isabel Machado Alexandre	University of Lisbon, Portugal

Web Chair

| João Martinho Moura | Polytechnic Institute of Cávado e Ave, Portugal |

Posters and PhD Track Chair

| **Alejandro Catala Bolos | University of Twente Research Group Human Media
Interaction (HMI), The Netherlands |

Demos Chairs

*Vitor Carvalho	Polytechnic Institute of Cávado and Ave, School of Technology, Portugal
*Paula Tavares	Polytechnic Institute of Cávado and Ave, School of Design, Portugal
**Pedro Branco	University of Minho, Dep. of Information Systems (DSI), Portugal

Local Chair

| *Carla Antunes | University of Minho, Research Centre for Child Studies
(CIEC), Portugal |
| **Fernanda Leopoldina
Viana | University of Minho, Research Centre for Child Studies
(CIEC), Portugal |

Work-in-Progress Chair

| *Luís Gonzaga | University of Minho, Dep. of Information Systems,
Portugal |

Technical Program Committee

Adérito Fernandes-Marcos	Open University Lisbon, Lisbon, Portugal
António Coelho	Faculty of Engineering, University of Porto, Porto, Portugal
Bruno Cardoso	KU Leuven, Löwen, Belgium
Bruno Herbelin	Ecole Polytechnique Fédérale de Lausanne, Lausanne, Switzerland
Çetin Tüker	Mimar Sinan Fine Arts University, Istanbul, Turkey
Christa Sommerer	Linz Art University Interface Culture Lab, Austria
Christos Gatzidis	Bournemounth University, Bournemounth, UK
Chris Geiger	University of Applied Sciences Düsseldorf, Düsseldorf, Germany
Dan Overholt	Aalborg University, Copenhagen, Denmark
Diogo Cabral	Madeira University, Madeira, Portugal
Eduardo Dias	NOVALincs, University Nova de Lisboa, Lisbon, Portugal
Eva Cerezo	University of Zaragoza, Zaragoza, Spain
Hartmut Könitz	HKU University of the Arts, Utrecht, The Netherlands
Heitor Avelos	European Academy, Portugal
Ian Oakley	UNIST, South Korea
Javier Marco	University of Zaragoza, Spain
Lindsay Grace	American University, Washington DC, USA
Masood Masoodian	Aalto University, Helsinki, Finland
Mel Krokos	School of Creative Technologies, University of Portsmouth, Portsmouth, UK
Miguel Carvalhais	Arts Faculty, University of Porto, Porto, Portugal
Michael Boelstoft Holte	Institut for Arkitekture and Medientechnology, Esbjerg, Denmark
Mónica Mendes	Arts Faculty, University of Lisbon, Portugal
Nikolas Vidakis	TEI of Crete University, Crete, Greece
Nuno Correia	University Nova de Lisboa, Portugal
Oscar Mealha	University of Aveiro, Aveiro, Portugal
Ozge Samanci	Northwestern University, Chicago, USA
Pedro Centieiro	NOVALincs, University Nova de Lisboa, Lisbon, Portugal
Pedro Gamito	Lusófona University of de Humanities and Technologies, Lisbon, Portugal
Rebecca Kane Rouse	Rensselaer Polytechnic Institute Department of the Arts, New York, USA
Rui Nóbrega	University of Porto, Faculty of Engineering, Porto, Portugal
Sercan Şengün	Massachusetts Institute of Technology, Cambridge, USA
Thomas Westin	Stockholm University, Stockholm, Sweden

Ulrike Spierling	Media Design University of RheinMain, Wiesbaden, Germany
Valentina Nisi	University of Madeira, Portugal
Yongsoon Choi	Sogang University, Seoul, South Korea
Yoram Chisik	Independent Researcher, Israel
Alda Pereira	Universidade Aberta, Portugal
Alejandro Moreno	Saxion University of Applied Sciences, The Netherlands
António Quintas Mendes	Universidade Aberta, Portugal
Alke Martens	Institute of Computer Science, University of Rostock, Germany
Ana Amélia Carvalho	University of Coimbra, Portugal
Anna Mavroudi	KTH Royal Institute of Technology, Sweden
Apostolos Kostas	University of the Aegean, Greece
Clara Bonillo Fernandéz	University of Zaragoza, Spain
Clara Coutinho	University of Minho, Portugal
Detlef Krömker	Johann Wolfgang Goethe University, Frankfurt am Main, Germany
Edith Maier	University of Applied Sciences St. Gallen, Switzerland
Elena Márquez Segura	Uppsala University, Sweden
Elsebeth Korsgaard Sorensen	Aalborg University, Denmark
Elvira Popescu	University of Craiova, Romania
Emma Edstrand	University of Gothenburg, Sweden
Eva Cerezo	University of Zaragoza, Spain
Glória Bastos	Universidade Aberta, Portugal
Isabel Dillmann Nunes	Federal University of Rio Grande do Norte, UFRN, Brazil
Javier Marco	University of Zaragoza, Spain
Jeanette Sjöberg	Halmstad University, Sweden
José Lagarto	Catholic University, Porto, Portugal
Jörg Stratmann	University of Education Weingarten, Germany
Laura Farinetti	Politecnico der Torino, Italy
Lina Morgado	Open University, Lisbon
Lorna Arnott	University of Strathclyde, Glasgow, UK
Maiga Chang	Athabasca University, Canada
Marcelo Milrad	Linnaeus University, Sweden
Marco Temperini	Sapienza University of Rome, Italy
María Esther Del Moral	University of Oviedo, Spain
Marko Radeta	Madeira Interactive Technologies Institute, Funchal, Portugal
Mauro Figueiredo	Universidade do Algarve, Portugal
Michael Boelstoft Holte	Aalborg University, Denmark
Nikolas Vidakis	Technological Educational Institute of Crete, Greece
Nikoleta Yiannoutsou	University College London, UK
Nuno Otero	Linnaeus University, Sweden

Paul Libbrecht	German Institute for International Educational Research, Frankfurt am Main, Germany
Pedro Cabral	Universidade Aberta, Portugal
Robby van Delden	Human Media Interaction, University of Twente, The Netherlands
Shuli Gilutz	UX Research, Children's Technology, Tel Aviv University
Teresa Cardoso	Universidade Aberta, Portugal
Tobias Ley	Tallinn University, Estonia
Tomi Kauppinen	Aalto University, Finland
Ulrike Spierling	Media Design University of RheinMain, Wiesbaden, Germany

Contents

ArtsIT - Playable Cities Workshop Track

DLI - Main Track

ArtsIT - Main Track

Why It's Art

Anthony L. Brooks[⊠]

Aalborg University, 9000 Aalborg, Denmark
tb@create.aau.dk

Abstract. Acknowledged as a "great artist" [1, p. 83], a "pioneer" [2], and a third culture thinker [3], the speaker, through his over four decades portfolio of works, in this talk reflects on the question of "Why it's Art?" Such questioning aligns with others who have asked, "What is Art?" [4] "Where is Art?" "Who makes Art?" [5] "What is Art for?" [6] and more. Ongoing discussions abound. However, if the art under scrutiny transcends genres, as in this case, the questioning of "Why it's Art" art becomes multifold and more challenging for third-parties to expertly argue. Aligned to this is that because of its bespoke hybrid synthesized nature, - Performance Art as Human Performance as Performance Art -; the concept in question is posited as one that needs to be self-experienced in order to argue opposition. There are thus few experts with extended involvement given its contemporary and original nature. This keynote talk presents selections from the speaker's works spanning decades either side the turn of the millennium that resulted in European and national awards (across genres). This brief text focuses on extracting from Tolstoy [4] in arguing the author's contemporary position in light of historic argument. These works, awards and text support the positioning, which is further sustained by him achieving numerous national and international multimillion Euro funded projects with various collaborators from industry and public sectors where the work has been central. The work is ongoing.

Keywords: Human · Performance · Art · Life

1 Introduction

The following short paper introduces the concept behind the presented works where foci is upon implementation across artistic creative expression forms (performance, installation, festivals, museums, etc.,) whilst parallel being researched as an original form of rehabilitation training to empower and motivate activity and engagement as a supplement and complement to traditional strategies. The conceiving of the concept arose from the author being born into a family having profoundly disabled members. At an early age he invented alternative means of control of music via the family member's remaining functional ability that resulted in an empowered nuance of life quality. Whilst this activity was private, the speaker's public profile was developing via (as a late teenager) presenting his art at the Institute of Contemporary Art (ICA) in London. This dichotomy of genres had a commonality of creativity and invention and subsequently the speaker's artistic expressivity transcended to be cross informing to his research targeting means of empowerment for those with different abilities. This

A. L. Brooks et al. (Eds.): ArtsIT 2018/DLI 2018, LNICST 265, pp. 3–6, 2019.

research similarly proved enlightening in the artistic works. Advances in technologies offered increased opportunities to the dualism concept that subsequently developed as a bespoke hybrid synthesized sensor-based method and apparatus applicable under both areas. The following outlines the concept and its background.

2   Performance and Conceptual Art and Human Performance

Performance Art has been referred to as "...the most adventurous twentieth-century art"[1] – and as an art form that is "...the chosen medium for articulating 'difference' whether dealing with issues of identity, multiculturalism or globalism"[2]. In questioning 'what is art', Count Lyov (also Lev) Nikolayevich Tolstoy (often in English known as Leo Tolstoy), who is acknowledged in Encyclopedia Britannica[3] as 'a Russian writer who is regarded as one of the greatest authors of all time', defines it as 'an expression of a feeling or experience in such a way that the audience to whom the art is directed can share that feeling or experience' [4]. Tolstoy, in conceptualizing of art as anything that communicates emotion, reflected how "Art begins when a man, with the purpose of communicating to other people a feeling he once experienced, calls it up again within himself and expresses it by certain external signs". Tolstoy also posited how he considered a traditionally recognized work of art as more a piece of life (See footnote 3), Tolstoy, it can thus be argued, supported the author's argument.

The cited literature posits Tolstoy's ability to 'observe the smallest changes of consciousness and to record the slightest movements of the body' [4]. In the presented work therein lies an aspect of the art aligned with the understanding of the technical form to create the interactive environment that promotes, motivates and empowers such nuances of represented behavioral transformations. Correspondingly, there is an art in the learnt comprehension of intervention with the author's developed method and apparatus to evoke engagement. Thus, a subject's desire to express through whatever systemic means is presented is enthused towards realizing human performance attributes previously unattainable. This aligns with how Tolstoy argued that 'true art requires a sensitive appreciation of a particular experience, a highly specific feeling that is communicated to the reader not by propositions but by "infection" [4]. Tolstoy further divided true art into good and bad, depending on the moral sensibility with which a given work infects its audience [4]. Tolstoy also notes that the "sincerity" of the artist—that is, the extent to which the artist "experiences the feeling he conveys"— influences the infection. He further conceptualized art as anything that communicates emotion: "Art begins when a man, with the purpose of communicating to other people a feeling he once experienced, calls it up again within himself and expresses it by certain external signs". Aligned to this is the author's patent titled 'Communication Method and Apparatus' (US6893407) – i.e. an apparatus and methodology that

---

[1] Robert Rosenblum on Performance Art – Goldberg, R. (2001). Performance Art. New York: Thames and Hudson.

[2] Back cover text extract – Goldberg (2001).

[3] https://www.britannica.com/biography/Leo-Tolstoy.

communicates to the self via inter- and intra- subjectivity. The resulting affect on the human performance has been related to Aesthetic Resonance [7]. Tolstoy insisted that art can and should be comprehensible to everyone. Having emphasized that art has a function in the improvement of humanity - capable of expressing man's best sentiment - he finds it offensive that artists should be so willfully and arrogantly abstruse [4].

LeWitt, on Conceptual Art, differentiates between perceptual art that depends on visual forms and conceptual art that is "made to engage the mind of the viewer rather than his eye" [8]. It is the mind of the viewer that is targeted in the author's public works across or within a specific genre.

Two points of art critique are selected in Tolstoy's literature [4] where he posits that at some point recognized art "ceased to be sincere and became artificial and cerebral" (p. 59), which led to millions of works of technical brilliance being created but few of honorable sentiment (p. 144). However, whilst a focus is evident on painted form, and this aligns with the period of Tolstoy's writing, the author claims there is much that analogizes in consideration to arts of today. To elaborate, the following is extracted further from his text "What is Art" [4], which could be interpreted in light of contemporary art, that is, beyond solely painted works as originally stated.

Tolstoy [4] posited that there is no objective definition of art in aesthetics (p. 33) whilst condemning the focus on beauty/pleasure at length, calling aesthetics a discipline:

> according to which the difference between good art, conveying good feelings, and bad art, conveying wicked feelings, was totally obliterated, and one of the lowest manifestations of art, art for mere pleasure - against which all teachers of mankind have warned people - came to be regarded as the highest art. And art became, not the important thing it was intended to be, but the empty amusement of idle people.

Further Tolstoy [4] posits how there is nothing to explain providing an artist – "if he is a true artist, has in his work conveyed to others the feelings he has experienced" (p. 95). In criticizing academia he also reflects how art schools, whilst educating in how to imitate the method of the masters, "cannot teach the sincerity of emotion that is the propellant of great works" as no school "can call up feelings in a man, and still less can it teach a man what is the essence of art: the manifestation of feeling in his own particular fashion" (p. 98).

In evaluating the content of art, again with a delimited focus on painted works – but herein cited as applicable in contemporary works across genres, Tolstoy [4] states his view as to the function of art being aligned to development of humanity positing how:

> just as in the evolution of knowledge - that is, the forcing out and supplanting of mistaken and unnecessary knowledge by truer and more necessary knowledge - so the evolution of feelings takes place by means of art, replacing lower feelings, less kind and less needed for the good of humanity, by kinder feelings, more needed for that good. This is the purpose of art. (pp. 123–4)

3 Conclusion

The subject matter necessitates many more pages than presented herein. It is recognized that others, not versed in the form, will counter the argument of "Why it's art". Further questions may ask 'who is the artist, the creator or the *performer*' - and 'why make an art that cannot be sold'. However, the art has been evaluated positively under its human performance attributes and centrally aligned to human aesthetic resonance [7]. Suffice to state that the interested reader may wish to explore and discuss further and this is encouraged. In closing the author reflects on how Tolstoy's core message is conclusive in that art is recognized as a catalyst that conveys feelings and emotions. Aligned with this, the author briefly positions his argument on his work and "Why it's art" (bias given) as one that targets mind (as [8]) and through the specific art form - the body. Aesthetic Resonance is common through which aspects of humanity difference, and humility is stated through human performance reflected in performance art.

In other words, as Duchamp eloquently stated - "It's Art If I Say So"... [9].

References

1. Haller, M.: Report on ICAT 2006. Int. J. Virtual Reality **6**(1), 83–84 (2007)
2. Williams, C.: The latest on human computer interaction and special needs (TESconnect magazine 7th August) (2013). http://community.tes.co.uk/
3. Brockman, J.: (1991). http://www.edge.org/3rd_culture
4. Tolstoy, L.: What is Art? (Translated by Richard Pevear and Larissa Volokhonsky). Penguin, London (1897, 1995)
5. DeWitte, D.J., Larmann, R.M., Shields, M.K.: Gateways to Art: Understanding the Visual Arts. Thames and Hudson, London (2015)
6. Dissanayake, E.: What is Art For?. University of Washington Press, Washington (1988)
7. Brooks, A.L.: SoundScapes: the evolution of a concept, apparatus and method where ludic engagement in virtual interactive space is a supplemental tool for therapeutic motivation. Ph. D. thesis, Aalborg University Press, Aalborg (2011)
8. LeWitt, S.: Paragraphs on Conceptual Art. Artforum **5**(10), 79–83 (1967)
9. "It's Art If I Say So": Martin Friedman on Marcel Duchamp's 1965 Visit to Minneapolis. https://walkerart.org/magazine/martin-friedman-duchamp-minneapolis

ArtsIT/DLI History, Research and Network Development

Anthony L. Brooks[1(✉)] and Eva Brooks[2]

[1] CREATE, Aalborg University, Rendsburggade 14, 9000 Aalborg, Denmark
tb@create.aau.dk
[2] LEARNING, Aalborg University, Kroghstræde 3, 9220 Aalborg Øst, Denmark

Abstract. The international conference ArtsIT that began in 2009 has grown since its inauguration presentation in Taiwan. Since then it has been hosted twice in Denmark, 2011 and 2016; as well as in Italy 2013; Turkey 2014; and most recently in Crete, Greece in 2017. The international conference Design, Learning and Innovation (DLI) was inaugurated in 2016 as a co-located event to ArtsIT being presented together in Esbjerg, Denmark; in 2017 in Heraklion, Crete, Greece; and in 2018 in Braga, Portugal. The series of conferences has realized over 108000 Springer e-book downloads at September 2018 and numerous special issue journals. This paper presents past aspects of ArtsIT/DLI from the perspective of steering persons having purpose to offer readers a historical framing of the events under the European Alliance for Innovation (EAI). This is supplemented by overviewing the authors' researches, which promoted EAI to invite leadership, alongside a background of the complementary workings, and contextual goals of the partnering.

Keywords: ArtsIT history · DLI history · European Alliance for Innovation

1 Introduction

1.1 History of ArtsIT/DLI Under European Alliance for Innovation (EAI)

ArtsIT, originating as 'The Arts and Technology international conference', began in 2009 when hosted in September in Yi-Lan, Taiwan. The first author was invited to steer the event subsequent to the inaugural edition and this has been ongoing. As of September 2018 the e-book metrics for the resulting Springer book from the 2009 event was 26388 downloads[1].

The event was next hosted in December 2011 at the Aalborg University Esbjerg campus in Denmark. A feature of this event was the showcase of the SensoramaLab complex. The complex was founded, realized, designed, and directed by the first author as a Virtual/Augmented/Mixed Reality, Human behavior, Art and Technology, Game Creation, and Interactivity resource. It also included a green screen laboratory. Foci was on offering students access to explore technologies for creative expression in the arts cross-researched as tools for inclusive well-being in health care – this profile

---

[1] https://www.springer.com/gp/book/9783642115769.

© ICST Institute for Computer Sciences, Social Informatics and Telecommunications Engineering 2019
Published by Springer Nature Switzerland AG 2019. All Rights Reserved
A. L. Brooks et al. (Eds.): ArtsIT 2018/DLI 2018, LNICST 265, pp. 7–16, 2019.

aligned with the first-author's original body of research. Thus, through the Senso-ramaLab complex, Medialogy education students and healthcare research students were offered access to cutting edge technology such as Head Mounted Displays, Gesture controllers, Motion tracking systems, Virtual and Augmented Reality systems, and much more. The Medialogy education started in Esbjerg at Aalborg University in 2002 and the first author was a team member of the originating team that established the education that subsequently grew to Copenhagen and then Aalborg campuses of the University to be the largest intake of students, Danish and Internationals. Serendipi-tously, during ArtsIT 2011, the Center for Design, Learning and Innovation (DLI) was opened at Aalborg University Esbjerg campus. Professor Eva Brooks who now steers the DLI international conference under the European Alliance for Innovation (EAI) established the Center. Keynote for ArtsIT2011 was the first author who was also organizing chair for the event with Professor Imrich Chlamtac, President of Create-NET and leader of EAI co-steering. Integrated into ArtsIT2011 to supplement the traditional academic papers was a demonstration track titled "Creative Showcase & Interactive Art (CSIA)". Additionally, supporting ArtsIT2011 were two related sym-posiums, namely the inaugural "GameAbilitation" symposium and the 6th "ArtAbili-tation" symposium. Also supporting was the 2nd "Ludic Engagement Designs for All" (LEDA) seminar event (see also next section on this event). The two authors were, and ongoing are, active in and across the fields represented by the main conference, the special demonstration track, both symposiums and seminar, thus were originators of these events. Activities under Aalborg University promote external research and stu-dent project relationships with national, regional and local industries and many showcased in a foyer exhibition at the events in 2011. Thus, from these fields and industries associated to the authors' research and project activities, rich networks were on offer to attract submissions and attendance from. Additionally, poster and Ph.D. student tracks supplemented alongside offers for local regional senior student volun-teers to attend to develop further networks and to offer experiences from attendance to such an event. For many in southwest Denmark it was the first such international conference, symposium, seminar they had such a chance to attend specific to the arts. Responses were highly positive following attendance with thanks being received from across the networks of HE educations, industries, establishments and organizations. In this way exemplifying how EAI inspires beyond solely academic audiences. The idea behind opening ArtsIT2011 to a wider audience was that by adding these events that have a history of success (i.e. ArtAbilitation and LEDA) and by adding others that takes advantage of the prolific interest and adoption across disciplines of digital games, creativity with digital technologies, learning, inclusion and accessibility, a major interest would result. This was evident at the time as reported in local and national media. Delegates at ArtsIT2011 were able to visit the other events activities in the form of tutorials, workshops, and presentations, and were invited to participate in the official opening of the Center for DLI and of course the associated celebrations in traditional Danish style with all shouting a loud "Skål" (or cheers in English) many times! A linked exhibition accompanied the events and entertainment and a grand gala dinner in the most famous restaurant in downtown Esbjerg, the multiple winner of 'Danish city of the Year', concluded the offerings. Partners for ArtsIT2011 included "Inspiring Denmark", who collaborated in event organization, and "Visit Denmark" who, as main tourist agency in the region, designed excursions and cultural activities to supplement the academic activities. Delegate evaluations following ArtsIT2011 were "eleven out of ten". As of September 1st 2018 the e-book download metrics for the resulting Springer book was 15950 downloads[2].

Two years later, ArtsIT2013 was hosted by the University of Milano-Bicocca, Italy where a feature was the three different keynote speakers arguing three different points of view over the three days of the event. These were on day one – Austrian media-artist, director/choreographer and composer – Klaus Obermaier (see http://www.exile.at/ko/klaus_bio.html); on day two – Italian art historian and curator Dr Andrea Lissoni; and on day three – Professor Antonio Camurri. As of September 2018 the e-book metrics for the resulting Springer book was 10182 downloads[3].

ArtsIT2014 was held in Istanbul, Turkey, November 2014 with sponsorship by host institute Sabancı University aligned with collaboration with Amber Electronic Arts Festival/Conference. Chairs were Elif Ayiter and Onur Yazicigil from Faculty of Arts and Social Sciences Sabancı University with keynotes by two renowned international artists Murat Germen from Istanbul and Paul Brown from UK. As of September 2018 the e-book metrics for the resulting Springer book was 9739 downloads[4].

There was no event in 2015 due to Danish government dimensioning impacting the authors' workplace. In this break the first author gained permission from EAI to extend the ArtsIT format under the title "ArtsIT, Interactivity & Game Creation". Thus, reflecting the 2011 co-located initiatives and contemporary trending interests in both interactivity & game creation where creativity, art and technology are core. Additionally, he promoted EAI to support a co-located event led by the second author titled as 'The International Conference of Design, Learning and Innovation (DLI)'. This was approved and in 2016 DLI was inaugurated to run parallel alongside ArtsIT when hosted again in Esbjerg at Aalborg University campus. The resulting common publication, again realized as a Springer book stands at 21929 downloads[5].

In 2017 the two events were hosted co-located in Heraklion, with strong local support by Technological Education Institute (TEI) of Crete. The resulting common publication, again realized as a Springer book stands at 23804 downloads[6].

Braga 2018 will be the third edition of DLI as co-located event to ArtsIT and it is notable to mention that we have seen record numbers of paper submissions that have as usual again undergone double blind peer reviews. Demos and posters will also feature and three keynotes are invited.

The next section elaborates on the background and research linkages in line with the purpose of offering readers a historical framing of the ArtsIT and DLI events under the European Alliance for Innovation (EAI) exemplifying why EAI president Imrich Chlamtac selected Brooks and Brooks as ongoing event leaders. It is considered pertinent to mention that in addition to the Springer series of LNICST books realized by

---

[2] https://www.springer.com/gp/book/9783642333286.
[3] https://www.springer.com/gp/book/9783642379819.
[4] https://www.springer.com/gp/book/9783319188355.
[5] https://www.springer.com/gp/book/9783319558332.
[6] https://www.springer.com/gp/book/9783319769073.

the conferences (as outlined in the previous texts with e-book download metrics) are numerous special edition journals of extended papers – for example under the International Journal Arts and Technology[7,8] and at the European Union Digital Library via EAI Endorsed Transactions on Creative Technologies[9,10,11,12]. The proceedings from the Braga event will also realize a Springer book and special issues.

2   Temporal Linkage to ArtAbilitation + LEDA

As mentioned above, one temporal linkage to ArtsIT in its extended form was to the international conference ArtAbilitation. This entity was inaugurated in 2006 by the first author reflecting his cross-sensorial research in the investigations of playful creative expression (as 'art-based') and potentials (e.g. in rehabilitation, well-being, and healthcare quality of life - QOL) of digital technologies, e.g. Extended Realities (VR, AR, MR etc.), alongside advances in interfaces (especially bespoke and adaptive gesture-based non-invasive and worn), signal mappings, and digital multimedia content (including multi-sensorial stimuli, motion-tracking, and robotics). The inaugural ArtAbilitation international conference was held alongside the 6th International Conference on Disability, Virtual Reality & Associated Technologies (ICDVRAT) 18th to 20th September 2006 - Esbjerg, Denmark, where the first author was chair[13]. This event was the first open visit by international delegates to the SensoramaLab (see International Society for Virtual Rehabilitation ISVR - http://isvr.org/wp-content/uploads/ISVR-Newsletter-Issue7-2016-04.pdf). ArtAbilitation 2006 realized a special edition issue of the Journal Digital Creativity Volume 18, 2007 - Issue 2 (see https://www.tandfonline.com/toc/ndcr20/18/2).

The 2nd ArtAbilitation was again co-located, and again hosted in Esbjerg, Denmark, supporting the IEEE 17th International Conference on Artificial Reality and Telexistence (ICAT 2007) when the first author was again chair following being elected to the international board and as committee member of ICAT2006 where he was also keynote. ICAT is the figurehead of the Japanese society for Virtual Reality and ICAT 2007 was the first time ICAT was hosted in Europe (see https://ieeexplore.ieee.org/xpl/mostRecentIssue.jsp?punumber=4414599).

The 3rd ArtAbilitation was held in the Rem Koolhaas' designed Casa Da Música in Porto (see http://www.icdvrat.org/2008/music_special_session.htm) alongside the 7th ICDVRAT, which was held at nearby Maia, Portugal (Sharkey et al. 2008). A feature of ArtAbilitation 2008 was the author's Interpretations showcase with the Portuguese

---

[7] http://www.inderscience.com/info/inarticletoc.php?jcode=ijart&year=2010&vol=3&issue=2/3#issue.

[8] http://www.inderscience.com/info/inarticletoc.php?jcode=ijart&year=2009&vol=2&issue=1/2.

[9] http://eudl.eu/issue/ct/4/13.

[10] http://eudl.eu/issue/ct/4/12.

[11] http://eudl.eu/issue/ct/4/11.

[12] http://eudl.eu/issue/ct/4/10.

[13] 1st ArtAbilitation papers http://www.icdvrat.org/2006/ArtAbilitation/index.htm.

National Symphony Orchestra. This was an event closing ICDVRAT/ArtAbilitation and signifying the opening of the 2nd Art, Brain and Language international conference in Casa Da Música where the first author was co-chair following being keynote in Art, Brain and Language 2007 when hosted in Calouste Gulbenkian foundation in Lisbon[14]. In the Interpretations showcase the Orchestra performed two pieces where the author's bespoke sensor system sourced performance motion data from the conductor and various section musicians. The data was mapped to control stage visuals (lighting, animations, effects, etc.) to complement the musical performance conducted in the large auditorium to a 'sell out audience'. The fourth ArtAbilitation was integrated into ICDVRAT2010 hosted in Viña del Mar, Valparaíso, by the University of Chile[15].

Further temporal linkage includes to the authors' established International Symposium and conference Ludic Engagement Designs for All (LEDA), the first of which took place November 2007 supporting the 2nd ArtAbilitation and the 17th IEEE International Conference for Artificial Reality and Telexistence (ICAT) 2007[16]. Under this symposium a special panel debate took place on the issue Ludic Engagement Designs for All: defining the field. The panel was led by author 2, Professor Eva Brooks, and participants were ICAT keynote speaker Roy Ascott, professor of Technoetic Art, University of Plymouth, UK; Patrice Chazerand, General Secretary of the Interactive Software Federation of Europe, Brussels, Belgium; Phil Ellis, professor in Performance Art, University of Sunderland, UK; Caroline Hummels, professor in Industrial Design, Technische Universiteit Eindhoven, The Netherlands; Lieselotte van Leeuwen, Professor of Psychology, University of Sunderland, UK; Staffan Selander, Professor in Didactics, Stockholm Institute of Education, Sweden; Anthony Brooks (author 1), Associate Professor Medialogy/Art and Technology, Aalborg University, Denmark. Ascott's ICAT keynote titled 'Syncretic Fields: Art, Mind, and the Many Realities' was also cross-referenced in the panel discussions. LEDA2007 realized a special edition issue of the Journal Digital Creativity[17].

The 3rd Ludic Engagement Designs for All (LEDA) was presented under the international conference "Designs for Learning 2012" (DfL 2012) hosted in Copenhagen. This LEDA contribution reported "on a developing 'design for learning' research and application platform that has evolved from two mature bodies of ongoing work. Non-formal learning and (re)habilitation result from exploration of virtual interactive environments that catalyst ludic user-experiences. The created environments are flexible to needs, adaptive, and profile- determined whereby learning goals influence design." The two mature bodies of ongoing research are of the authors – the contribution further details how "Each body of work has emerged models for intervention that transcend and cross-inform in learning and rehabilitation situations." The text posits how "The term Ludic relates to the designed for fun/playful user-experience (UX) for both end-user (learner/disabled person) and facilitator (teacher/healthcare professional). Engagement refers to the targeted immersion of the end-user that is

---

[14] https://www.inderscience.com/info/dl.php?filename=2010/ijart-2062.pdf.

[15] http://centaur.reading.ac.uk/27451/1/ICDVRAT2010_Full_Proceedings_8th_Conf.pdf.

[16] https://ieeexplore.ieee.org/xpl/mostRecentIssue.jsp?punumber=4414599.

[17] Volume 19, 2008 - Issue 3 (see https://www.tandfonline.com/toc/ndcr20/19/3).

achieved through the adaptation of the available environment design parameters so that profile matching is optimized. Designs for All refers to the inclusive iterative inductive strategy where facilitator learning influences subsequent session design, and how the LEDA concept is context independent, thus all encompassing, and applicable across users and fields, i.e. in education, in healthcare, and beyond." The contribution then presents models that questioned existing traditional formal education models that increasingly are reflected upon by contemporary scholars as being redundant as advances in ICT evolve curricula, classroom activities and strategies. Catalyst to this questioning of traditional strategies is a Non-Formal Learning Model (Fig. 1) that aligns to the philosophy behind Ludic Engagement Design for All (Brooks 2013).

Figure 1 illustrates a model emergent from Brooks' body of research – as presented at DfL2012. It posits a holistic overview of a complex situation focused upon qualities integral to the design of user experiences leading to desired learning. The learning within and the design of a learning (or therapeutic) situation constitute a situated activity with inherent actions and interventions. The profile influences the facilitator's decisions on how to set up the attributes of the environment relative to the desired learning process and the expected outcome of that process. The model was developed relative to the development, use and evaluation of interactive environments targeting learning. However, the model has proven to have a more generic value as it has been used in learning situations where other forms of resources and/or methods have been used (Brooks 2013).

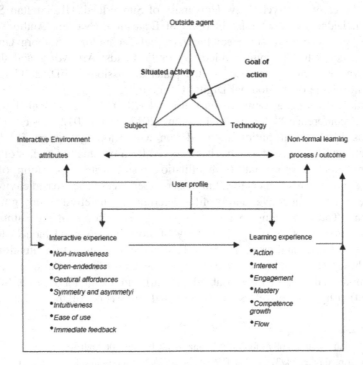

Fig. 1. Non-formal learning model - the composition of learning and design in interactive environments © Petersson 2007/Brooks 2013 – see also PhD thesis (http://muep.mau.se/bitstream/handle/2043/7970/EPHelaboken.pdf?sequence=1.)

From the first author's body of research is another emergent model that complements the Non-Formal Learning Model (Fig. 1). It is titled Zone of Optimized Motivation (ZOOM – see Fig. 2) and was first presented publicly in Busan, South Korea in 2005. This is a synthesized hybrid intervention model where participant/learner ability is ideally matched by a challenge to achieve a tailored idiosyncratic technological supported interactive experience in line with Flow (Csiksczentmihalyi 2002). Challenges are planned according to a dynamic program design to increment participant Microdevelopment and learning pathways (Fisher and Bidell 2007; Battro et al. 2008; Granott and Parziale 2009). The unit of analysis assessing the system is participant action in the designed interactive environment, in this way it is also in line with Vygotsky's Zone of Proximal Development (ZPD 1978); Vygotsky (1978), Leont'ev (1981), and Engeström's (1987) interpretations on Activity Theory (1978) and linked to Wertsch's Mediated Action body of work (1994) that links followed theories of Dewey's thinking on art and learning. A catalyst to the first author's synthesizing of these luminary works into a reflexivity model is Schön's (1983) work informing on reflective practitioners. Notable is that the posited ZOOM model differs from ZPD by the primary inter-subjective entity being the mediating technology in the form of the interactive system supported by a secondary inter- subjective entity, i.e. the facilitator. This dynamic non-formal approach questions facilitator intervention time (t) in respect of parameter change to incremental challenge (δ). Published texts on ZOOM inform how an automated version aligns with the Artificial Intelligent (AI) concept of Dynamic Difficulty Adjustment (DDA), i.e. where change is matched to performance.

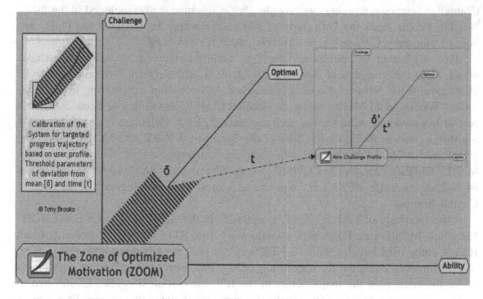

Fig. 2. ZOOM (Zone of Optimized Motivation) © Brooks 2005

3 European Alliance for Innovation (EAI)

EAI was founded in 2010 as a non-profit professional community. EAI person steering ArtsIT and DLI is President Imrich Chalmic. Prof. Chlamtac is the President of EAI, European Alliance for Innovation. Chlamtac pioneered EAI as a global initiative for promoting growth of ICT-based economy and digital society. EAI supports research and innovation worldwide with over hundred and fifty thousand subscribers worldwide through events, publications, and community collaboration. EAI organizes over 70 conferences and summits every year. Additionally, EAI has set up strong collaboration and a strategic partnership with the International Federation of Inventors' Associations (IFIA). Prime foci are Internet of Things, eHealth, Smart city, Applications for future Internet. Prof. Chlamtac's prior positions in Italy included CREATE-NET where he was the Founding President, Bruno Kessler Professor at the University of Trento, among the top ranked ICT institutions in Italy. Prof. Chlamtac also served as Associate Provost for Research and Distinguished Chair in Telecommunications at the University of Texas in Dallas, and Professor at Boston University, University of Massachusetts and Technion. Prof. Chlamtac holds multiple academic and honorary appointments including the University of Trento, the Tel Aviv University, the Beijing University of Posts and Telecommunications, and the Budapest University of Technology and Economics. Prof. Chlamtac's scientific recognitions include IEEE and ACM Fellowship, the ACM Award for Outstanding Contributions to Research on Mobility, the IEEE Award for Outstanding Technical Contributions to Wireless Personal Communications, New Talents in Simulation of SCS, Fulbright Scholarship, IEEE Distinguished Lecturer. He was listed in ISIHighlyCited.Com among the 250 most cited Computer Science researchers worldwide. Prof. Chlamtac is also included in the list of Notable People from the University of Minnesota where he received his Ph.D. and holds a Honorary Citizenship in Slovakia where he was born.

Prof. Chlamtac has published over four hundred refereed articles, and multiple books. He is the co-author of the first textbook on "Local Networks" (Lexington Books 1980), and IEEE Network Editor's choice and Amazon.com engineering books bestseller "Wireless and Mobile Network Architectures" (John Wiley & Sons 2000). As part of his contribution to the research community, Prof. Chlamtac founded the ACM SigMobile, serves as Editor-in-Chief of the Springer WINET and MONET journals, established ACM Mobicom and other leading conferences. Prof. Chlamtac is a co-founder and past President of CONSIP Ltd, the first network emulator company, and of BCN Ltd, currently KFKI Ltd., one of the largest system integrator companies in Central Europe.

Core members of EAI are ICST, Fraunhofer FOKUS, INNOVA, CREATE-NET, Mobicap, Agentúra na Podporu Výskumu a Vývoja, STU, EUREC, Microsoft Israel R&D Center, IBM Israel. CREATE-NET is one of the core members, and main drivers, of the European Alliance for Innovation (EAI), a non-profit organization that brings under the same roof the major actors in the ICT innovation lifecycle. Established in 2003 as a non-profit association with the support of the Autonomous Province of Trento, the Center had been led by Prof. Imrich Chlamtac until the incorporation within Fondazione Bruno Kessler (FBK) in 2017.

The mission of the EAI is to serve as an incubator for fostering innovation in the ICT sectors of society, providing points-of-access at all levels of the innovation cycle. The unique approach of EAI consists of involving active participation of member organizations and empowering their communities through a grassroots approach, thus promoting effective technology transfer, entrepreneurial mindset in education, and increased competitiveness of European companies.

CREATE-NET has been contributing to the formation of this initiative since its active involvement in the European Commission's workshop which took place in Lyon (ICT2008) to analyze and discuss the role of scientific societies in improving the innovation process in Europe, an area where we are informed lags behind the US and other regions.

EAI publishes scientific magazines and journals (Transactions) through its own community-driven publication platform called European Union Digital Library (EUDL). For online publications EAI uses its e-Scripts system, while EUDL houses a database of peer reviewed scientific publications. EAI Transactions are peer-reviewed, community-driven research journals covering the latest specialist topics at the emerging intersections of IT and other fields. Supported by an international network of editorial boards drawn from leading experts in their disciplines, EAI Transactions reach out to an audience of over 150,000 subscribers worldwide. Thanks to the transparent, community-based e-Scripts review system; EAI Transactions are paving the way to the future of open and fair scientific publishing.

Individual members are in the core of the EAI Community, comprising of researchers, innovators, business leaders, venture capitalists, and policy makers. Individual membership is free to ensure the open and equal opportunity nature of EAI Community.

EAI connects members through online tools and international conferences, creating a space to share and discover ideas, while improving their career prospects via equal access to opportunities for professional development and fair recognition. Every member can actively participate in reinventing the governance and economy of research and innovation and get recognized objectively and transparently with EAI Community Awarded Recognition of Excellence (CARE) Index.

EAI Institutional membership: Institutions that join EAI feature leading minds with insight and influence in academia, industry, and government, coming together to engage in the mission of advancing innovation across the world.

The EAI designated team manages and organizes the ArtsIT and DLI events in close liaison with the local host event team/committee. EAI is a non-profit organization and professional community established, in cooperation with the European Commission, to empower global research and innovation, and to promote cooperation between European and International ICT communities. EAI's vision is to foster excellence in research and innovation on the principles of transparency, objectivity, equality, and openness. A guiding principle is community cooperation to create enhancement in research, to provide fair recognition of excellence, and to transform notable ideas into commercial value proposition. EAI's mission is to create an environment that rewards excellence transparently, and builds recognition objectively regardless of age, economic status or country of origin, where no membership fees or closed-door committees stand in the way of research careers. EAI is led by top minds from the highest levels of government, research, industry and academia as well as from the grass roots of the innovation community.

References

Battro, A.M., Fischer, K.W., Léna, P.J.: The Educated Brain: Essays in Neuroeducation. Cambridge University Press, Cambridge (2008)

Brooks, E.P.: Ludic engagement designs: creating spaces for playful learning. In: Stephanidis, C., Antona, M. (eds.) UAHCI 2013. LNCS, vol. 8011, pp. 241–249. Springer, Heidelberg (2013). https://doi.org/10.1007/978-3-642-39194-1_28

Csiksczentmihalyi, M.: Flow: The Psychology of Optimal Experience. Harper Collins Press, New York (2002)

Engeström, Y.: Learning by Expanding: An Activity-Theoretical Approach to Developmental Research. Orienta-Konsultit, Helsinki (1987)

Fisher, K.W., Bidell, T.R.: Dynamic development of action and thought. In: Damon, W., Lerner, R.M., Lerner, R.M. (eds.) Handbook of Child Psychology (2007). https://doi.org/10.1002/9780470147658.chpsy0107

Granott, N., Parziale, J.: Microdevelopment: Transition Processes in Development and Learning (Cambridge Studies in Cognitive and Perceptual Development). Cambridge University Press, Cambridge (2009)

Leont'ev, A.: Problems of the Development of Mind. Progress Press, Moscow (1981). English translation

Schön, D.A.: The Reflective Practitioner - How Professionals Think in Action. Basic Books, New York (1983)

Sharkey, P., Lopes-dos-Santos, P., Weiss, P.L.T., Brooks, T. (eds.): Proceedings of the 7th International Conference on Disability, Virtual Reality and Associated Technologies, with ArtAbilitation (ICDVRAT 2008). Reading University, UK (2008)

Vygotsky, L.S.: Mind and Society: The Development of Higher Psychological Processes. Harvard University Press, Cambridge (1978)

Wertsch, J.: The primacy of mediated action in sociocultural studies. Mind Cult. Act. 1(4), 202–208 (1994)

Interfaces for Science: Conceptualizing an Interactive Graphical Interface

Bruno Azevedo[1]([✉])(iD), Ana Alice Baptista[1](iD),
Jorge Oliveira e Sá[1](iD), Pedro Branco[1](iD), and Rubén Tortosa[2](iD)

[1] ALGORITMI Research Centre, University of Minho, Guimarães, Portugal
brunomiguelam@engagelab.org,
{analice,jos,pbranco}@dsi.uminho.pt
[2] Polytechnic University of Valencia, Valencia, Spain
rtortosa@dib.upv.es

Abstract. 6,849.32 new research journal articles are published every day. The exponential growth of Scientific Knowledge Objects (SKOs) on the Web, makes searches time-consuming. Access to the right and relevant SKOs is vital for research, which calls for several topics, including the visualization of science dynamics. We present an interface model aimed to represent of the relations that emerge in the science social space dynamics, namely through the visualization and navigation of the relational structures between researchers, SKOs, knowledge domains, subdomains, and topics. This interface considers the relationship between the researcher who reads and shares the relevant articles and the researcher who wants to find the most relevant SKOs within a subject matter. This article presents the first iteration of the conceptualization process of the interface layout, its interactivity and visualization structures. It is essential to consider the hierarchical and relational structures/algorithms to represent the science social space dynamics. These structures are not being used as analysis tools, because it is not objective to show the linkage properties of these relationships. Instead, they are used as a means of representing, navigating and exploring these relationships. To sum up, this article provides a framework and fundamental guidelines for an interface layout that explores the social science space dynamics between the researcher who seeks relevant SKOs and the researchers who read and share them.

Keywords: Information visualization · Design · Interface

1 Introduction

Throughout history, the space of information flows supports, simultaneously, the dynamics of social practices and its relations [1] in all sectors and services of society. It equally supports the science dynamics [2] as it emerges in the intangible space infosphere and it is defined by flows of information [1]. Science dynamics is defined by a complex, self-organizing, and evolving relational multi-structure [2] of several axes including researchers, projects, scientific articles, ideas. Science dynamics reveals clutters, patterns and connections among scientific knowledge domains and

A. L. Brooks et al. (Eds.): ArtsIT 2018/DLI 2018, LNICST 265, pp. 17–27, 2019.

sub-domains, collaboration and citation networks [2]. Also, it is characterized by the merging of knowledge domains boundaries which in turn discloses the emergence of new fields of knowledge [2]. Therefore, science dynamics is characterized by a "complex self-organizing and constantly evolving multiscale network" [2–4] of relations, which occurs in the space of information flows.

In this article it is argued that the science dynamics space is also defined by a social dimension, and it is not only characterized by network structures, but also by hierarchical structures. Although networks and hierarchies are distinct and opposing concepts, they coexist and complement each other [5]. These dynamics unveils the main architecture of science space, specifically composed of networks and hierarchies which, in turn, are the basic architecture of information [5–7]. In fact, the expression of the social science space is determined by complex interactions, among researchers and the research they perform. The social science space is the focus of this article, and the goal is to visualize the social dynamics in order to find the most relevant Scientific Knowledge Objects (SKOs; e.g. articles, books, patents, software, disciplines) based on the reader's experience socially shared [8]. This shared experience functions as an organization/ranking mechanism. Thus, the researcher plays two interchangeable roles: First, there is the researcher (seeker), who could be new to some knowledge domain or subdomain, for instance; The second role is defined by the researcher that reads SKOs and shares his experience in the social space dimension. The objective is to design an interface layout that explores the social science space dynamics between the two researcher roles.

The main objective of this article is to present the first iterations of an interface conceptualization aimed to interactively depict the complex and dynamic social science space, based on the referenced interconnectedness and the researcher social experience.

This article is divided in five sections: the first one is this introduction to the problem; the section two describes the information deluge problematic in the context of science and digital libraries; the next section presents a brief description of related work; the section four provides the interface model and the interactivity conceptualization; and the article ends with the final considerations and some directions of future work are presented.

2 The Information Flood Problematics in Science

As a result of a number of factors, including the increased storage and processing capacity, the interconnection between different systems (internet, database) and development of new interfaces [9], accelerated the access, publication, and production of scientific content [5, 10]. 6,849.32 new research journal articles are published every day [11]. The current accelerated pace of scientific and technical discoveries and the emergence of new knowledge domains and subdomains in short periods contributed significantly to increase the number of scientific publications [9, 10].

Currently, the SKOs are stored in digital libraries that are the main repositories of scientific knowledge [9]. Digital libraries are fundamental services for accessing a broad typology of SKOs. Each document returned as a result of a query in a digital library platform is given a relevance score computed from a variety of factors (e.g.

number of citations, the number of word hits). Even though the digital libraries engines allow filtering the results, in many cases the number of results is still unmanageable which calls for improvements at today's refinement and personalization algorithms.

Structuring, framing and filtering content represents an urgent and unceasing challenge [10]. In fact, if in previous times the main concern was to collect and store information or SKOs [5], one of today's digital information society main challenges is to devise and adopt strategies towards the reduction of the so called information deluge [10, 12]. In the scientific domain, the goal is to filter and reduce the volume of results and efficiently frame vast amounts of information in the researcher's cognitive and perceptual field [12, 13]. To efficiently frame a large body of information in the researcher (seeker) cognitive and perceptual field, it is fundamental to design a graphical language. One of the challenges underlying digital libraries is directly related with the information finding, filtering and visualization processes [14]. The application of advanced Information Visualization (InfoVis) techniques to access and depict the digital library as a social/interaction space is an unexplored challenging territory with few approaches. There are currently three approaches aimed at the visualization of science [9]: the first two are the static and interactive visualization which are aimed at the representation of science dynamics (e.g. citation, co-citation and collaboration (co-authorships) networks between researchers, articles, journals, and knowledge domains or subdomains); the third approach is related with exploratory interfaces, as already identified by [8] in the next section. InfoVis constitutes a viable response to several tasks related with information structuring, filtering and finding processes, allowing a greater cognitive and perceptive efficiency [13, 15–17] [13–15, 18, 19]. Succinctly, InfoVis allows to use a graphical syntax to efficiently portray the science social space dimension and its inherent dynamics.

3 Related Work

Most of the former projects are related to the first and second approaches mentioned in the last paragraph, i.e., with static and interactive InfoVis. Some examples are the "Maps of Science", "Hypothetical Model of the Evolutions and Structure of Science", "The Structure of Science", "Map of Scientific Paradigms" or "Citespace" projects. Some projects related to the third approach, exploratory interfaces, are the GTOC, GRIDL, Envision, Antarcti.ca System Inc.'s Visual Map, Citiviz, Active Graph, Result Maps and VIDLS [8]. These projects were innovative and relevant in their time and provided the basis for new approaches more aligned with the approach described in this article. The work proposed by [8] provides a description and comparison of five significant projects with relevant use of information visualization techniques. The following four of these projects are applied to science: Well-Formed Eigenfactor, Apolo, Citeology and PaperQuest. In common these projects aim to develop exploratory interfaces using various techniques to represent and explore the dynamics of science. The remaining project, Mace, also uses a visual exploratory interface not for science but for architecture, it is relevant because it uses social taxonomies to classify topics.

These projects provide solutions for viewing patterns and trends, specifically interfaces aimed at the visualization of scientific network knowledge structures based on citations. Despite their objectives and their remarkable results, they are not well suited to explore SKOs when only a small subset of SKOs is relevant to the seeker researcher.

4 Designing the Interface Layout

The reading and publication of articles, books and other SKOs are part of a researcher's daily life. If a given number of SKOs in a given topic is handled by researchers, it is reasonable to infer that when each researcher reads, shares, comments, tweets, among other interactions, a related informal body of knowledge emerges. Our hypothesis is that this potentially emerging body of knowledge provides evidences about the existence of a social science space dynamics that plays a fundamental role in filtering the most relevant SKOs within a given topic.

In this sense, the equated hypothesis constitutes a new paradigm that determines a change in the focus of the approach, usually centered on the citation metrics and not on the researchers social experience.

The concept of our interface is based on the relationship between researchers, the articles they consider relevant and the subject interests of those who are accessing the interface by consulting this information. Therefore, in the next sections, we discuss the interface layout, its interactivity and its visualization structures. These structures are not being used as analysis tools, since we are not interested in showing the linkage properties of these relationships. Instead, they are used as a means of representing, navigating and exploring these relationships.

The great difference between our approach and other seemingly similar ones is that we relate to the researcher the articles he or she reads and share, while other projects are more focused on the authors and their production (e.g., citation/collaboration networks, co-authorship networks). Our approach is reader-centered while other projects are author-centered.

4.1   Interactivity and Graphical User Interface: Brief Considerations

In this section, a first iteration regarding the interface layout conceptualization, and underline a succinct explanation about the interactivity logic are presented. The interface is constituted by five main views: Global View, Researchers View, Researcher Tree View, Knowledge Subdomain View and Subdomain Researchers View. The graphical layout is subdivided in three main sections (Fig. 1): the top bar (main buttons and the search field box), the visualization section, and the reader researcher's and SKO's metadata section.

The Global View (Fig. 1) provides access to the most relevant SKOs within a knowledge domain. The objective is to visualize the most relevant SKO's that belongs to different knowledge subdomains within a knowledge domain. This view provides various treemaps, where each treemap corresponds to a specific knowledge domain. Nominal information coding [20] is used to label knowledge domains, through the use of the variable color. Therefore, to each knowledge domain corresponds a fixed hue value. Gradients of the same hue provide the distinction between different knowledge

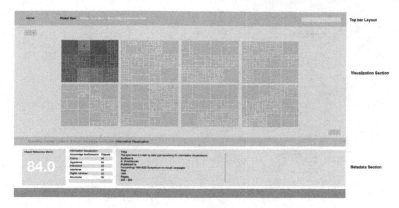

Fig. 1. Global View: a color gradient identifies the SKOs knowledge subdomain (e.g. gradient of blues). By placing the mouse pointer over the SKOs areas, a descriptive tooltip about object metadata emerges in the metadata section. The bottom left rectangle provides the object relevance value (84.0 in this example). The directional buttons inside the visualization section provide the navigation menu, and plus and minus buttons provide the zoom interactivity. (Color figure online)

subdomains within a knowledge domain, through the variation of chroma and luminance of the assigned hue value. It is important to emphasize that the assignment of colors to the different knowledge domains will be a future task and therefore does not fall within the scope of this article.

The variable size provides the quantitative encoding (SKO's relevance). Each squarified area corresponds to a specific SKO. This means that it is possible to visualize in the treemap the most relevant SKOs within a knowledge subdomain. The size of the squarified area will be correlated with a new metric to be developed in the future. A limited number of objects should be defined inside the treemap (e.g. the 25 most relevant SKOs). The hierarchy depth of the treemap will be a subject addressed in future work.

The Researchers View (Fig. 2), portrays graphical information about the most active research readers within a range of knowledge subdomains. This is graphically represented by a ranking of the most active readers within different knowledge subdomains (e.g. the 25 most active readers in Open Data). The circles and the graphical variable color represent different knowledge subdomains, and describe the total number of SKOs based on the relevance metric: the greater the relevance, the larger the diameter of the circumference. By clicking on the reader researcher name the user jumps to the Researcher's Tree View (Fig. 3).

The Researcher Tree View (Fig. 3) depicts the hierarchical relation between the research readers and the knowledge subdomains. The center node represents the researcher and the second layer nodes represent the knowledge subdomain fields (e.g. blue node). The third level of edges/nodes are the SKOs read and shared, which are children of the ancestor knowledge subdomain node (second layer nodes). The edges translate the readers relation between the knowledge subdomain and the various SKOs of that knowledge subdomain. The outer circle visually limits the number of SKOs

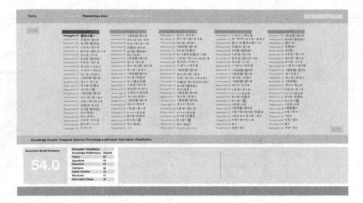

Fig. 2. Researchers View: by placing the mouse pointer over the reader name, a descriptive tooltip about research reader metadata is showed in the bottom section (e.g. ORCID number, researcher's knowledge domain and subdomains or total number of SKOs read and share by a given researcher). Making a rollover over the circles, a descriptive tooltip about SKO knowledge subdomain metadata is presented (bottom section) (e.g. type, total number of SKOs in a given knowledge subdomain). (Color figure online)

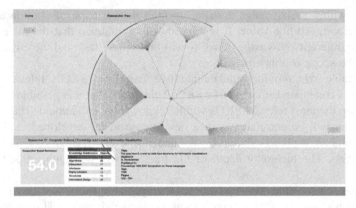

Fig. 3. Researcher Tree View: the metadata section provides a contextualization menu about the different knowledge subdomains related to the research reader. By placing the mouse pointer over the central node, a tooltip (bottom section) is displayed showing the reader metadata. By making a rollover over the second and third level of edges/nodes it is respectively displayed a tooltip (bottom section) describing the knowledge subdomain and the number of children ramification and SKOs metadata (e.g. knowledge domain, subdomain, title, DOI). (Color figure online)

organized by subdomain that a specific reader researcher read and shared. It should be noted that each SKO will act as a direct link to where the SKO is stored.

The Knowledge Subdomain View (Fig. 4) provides the total number of read SKOs within a range of knowledge subdomains. The main objective of this view is to list knowledge sub-subdomains categories within a knowledge subdomain. By clicking on the knowledge subdomain name the user jumps to the Subdomain Researcher's View (Fig. 5).

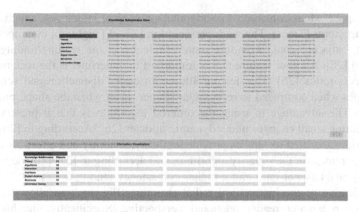

Fig. 4. The Knowledge Subdomain View provides a list of knowledge sub-subdomains categories within a knowledge domain (metadata section).

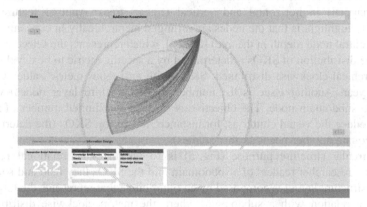

Fig. 5. Subdomain Researchers View: the represented layout reflects the interaction of a single reader. When placing the mouse pointer over the reader and SKO node, a tooltip (bottom section) provides information about the reader and SKO metadata. It also draws the relations between the reader and the SKO's.

The Subdomain Researchers View (Fig. 5) shows the most relevant research readers of a particular subdomain, as well as its relationship with several other sub-domains taking into account the SKOs it reads and shares.

4.2 Objectives and Characteristics of Hierarchical and Relational Structures

The objective of the hierarchical containment structure (treemap algorithm) (Fig. 1) is to provide to the user an overview of the most relevant read/shared SKOs. Treemaps are an algorithm that allows the visualization of large hierarchies [21–24]. The treemap algorithm consists on a rectangular hierarchical structure of containment, aimed at the visualization of data in a compact layout. It is also characterized by an efficient use of the layout space when compared to horizontal or vertical structures, which are very extensive structures (Trees). The work presented in [23, 25] highlight the importance of ordering the adjacent data, providing more efficiency in the reading/finding process (readability) [26]. Another feature that is important to underline, is the rectangles with square aspects ratios [25]. This feature allows an easier distinction and selection of square shapes when compared to rectangular shapes, even when the shape proportions are similar. The advantage in using the ordered algorithm is that it preserves order while presenting small changes under dynamic updates [26]. According to [26] ordered treemaps with squarified rectangles provide legibility, usability and effortless updating. The latest increment in the squarify algorithm, and according to [27] provide rectangles with an improved aspect ratio and a higher consistency among nodes.

The objective of the hierarchical radial structure (Fig. 3) is to allow the user to visualize the researcher reader relational perspective. Specifically, the hierarchical social experience structure that emerges between the researchers and the read/shared SKOs, within various knowledge subdomains. The main characteristic of this algorithm is that it can represent large hierarchies [28] without losing context [28–30], in contrast to what happens in horizontal and vertical (linear) trees. Another feature that is important to highlight is that the nodes are arranged hierarchically in concentric circles around a central node (depth in the tree) [28, 29], which represents the selected research reader. The distribution of SKOs is determined by a specific metric to be developed and it is hierarchical clockwise distributed. SKOs with analogous metric values are organized by year. Another issue is the number of SKOs (third layer nodes) within a knowledge subdomain node. The objective is to display a limited number of relevant nodes to reduce the visual clutter as, for instance, the 25 top SKOs (the determination of the adequate number needs further studies).

The circular structure purpose (Fig. 5) is to visualize the relational panorama between the researcher readers of a subdomain and the SKOs they read and share. The relational structure layout is composed by an outer circle that represents the researchers that have a relation with a subdomain, where the metric clockwise distributes the readers. The inner circle represents the SKOs that are clockwise arranged according to the metric. SKOs with analogous metric values will be organized by year. The edges provide a color gradation [31] between the reader subdomain and the SKO subdomains. The use of transparency is also considered: shorter edges have a higher opacity and, therefore, they are at a higher layer, and the long edges have less opacity and are at a lower layer [31]. The main characteristic of the circular layout algorithm is the reduction of visual clutter in case of a large number of edges. It is also an efficiently aesthetically technique to visualize adjacency relations in relational organized systems. It is important to underline that the work [31] provides important techniques such as the bundling strength and fundamental interaction & usability guidelines.

The next step will be the implementation of the algorithms in Processing programing language. Therefore, and as future work, it is fundamental to perform a literature review to implement both the radial and the relational algorithms.

5 Final Considerations and Future Work

This article conceptualizes an interface model/mock-up based on a previously defined architecture. This interface model/mock-up was designed to validate and guide the visualization and interaction process. The preliminary conceptualization provides a framework of the relational structures that it will be considered in the next developments and implementations.

In what regards the visualization structures, a treemap programed in Processing language was already implemented in order to validate the treemap algorithm [32]. The future work will consist in the improvement of the squarification process based on the work of [27].

One issue that needs to be studied is the dimension of the circles of both the Hierarchical Relational View and the Circular Relational View. The greater the number of SKOs and researcher reader respectively, the greater the diameter of the circles need to be. In this sense, and conditioned by the size of the screen, issues related to managing the number of readers researchers and SKOs will have to be considered.

The next steps will consist in a deep literature review about the radial and circular layout to implement the algorithms in Processing language. It is important to underline that these algorithms are already implemented in D3 javaScript library but not open to the community. Another step will the study and implementation of interaction techniques such as Zoom, the interface validation by conducting usability tests and the validation of navigation steps.

Acknowledgements. This work has been supported by COMPETE: POCI-01-0145-FEDER-007043 and FCT - Fundação para a Ciência e Tecnologia within the Project Scope: (UID/CEC/00319/2013) and the Project IViSSEM: ref: POCI-01-0145-FEDER-28284.

References

1. Castells, M.: The Information Age Economy, Society, and Culture: The Rise of the Network Society, 2nd edn. Wiley-Blackwell Publishing, Hoboken (2010)
2. Fortunato, S., Bergstrom, C.T., Börner, K., et al.: Science of science. Science (80-) **359**, eaao0185 (2018). https://doi.org/10.1126/science.aao0185
3. Barabasi, A., Albert, R.: Emergence of scaling in random networks. Science (80-) **286**, 509–512 (1999). https://doi.org/10.1126/science.286.5439.509
4. Albert, R., Barabasi, A.: Statistical mechanics of complex networks. Rev. Mod. Phys. **74**, 47–97 (2002). https://doi.org/10.1088/1478-3967/1/3/006
5. Wright, A.: Glut: Mastering Information Through the Ages. Cornell University Press, Ithaca (2008)
6. Simon, H.A.: The Sciences of the Artificial. MIT Press, Cambridge (1996)
7. Hidalgo, C.: Why Information Grows: The Evolution of Order, from Atoms to Economies. Basic Books, New York (2015)
8. Azevedo, B.M., e Sa, J.O., Baptista, A.A., Branco, P.: Information visualization: conceptualizing new paths for filtering and navigate in scientific knowledge objects. In: 2017 24º Encontro Português de Computação Gráfica e Interação (EPCGI), pp. 85–92. IEEE, Guimarães (2017). https://doi.org/10.1109/EPCGI.2017.8124310

9. Börner, K., Chen, C.: Visual Interfaces to Digital Libraries. Springer, Heidelberg (2002). https://doi.org/10.1007/3-540-36222-3
10. Thackara, J.: In the Bubble: Designing in a Complex World. MIT Press, Cambridge (2006)
11. Ware, M., Mabe, M.: The STM report: an overview of scientific and scholarly journal publishing (2015). https://www.stm-assoc.org/2015_02_20_STM_Report_2015.pdf. Accessed 14 Feb 2016
12. Wurman, R.S.: Information Anxiety 2, 2nd edn. QUE, London (2001)
13. Card, S., Mackinlay, J., Shneiderman, B.: Readings in Information Visualization: Using Vision to Think. Morgan Kaufmann, Burlington (1999)
14. Marks, L., Hussell, J.A.T., McMahon, T.M., Luce, R.E.: ActiveGraph: a digital library visualization tool. Int. J. Digit. Libr. 5, 57–69 (2005). https://doi.org/10.1007/s00799-004-0110-z
15. Mazza, R.: Introduction to Information Visualization. Springer, London (2009). https://doi.org/10.1007/978-1-84800-219-7
16. Meirelles, I.: Design for Information: An Introduction to the Histories, Theories, and Best Practices Behind Effective Information Visualizations. Rockport Publishers, Beverly (2013)
17. Börner, K., Polley, D.E.: Visual Insights. MIT Press, Cambridge (2014)
18. Börner, K., Chen, C.: Visual interfaces to digital libraries: motivation, utilization, and socio-technical challenges. In: Börner, K., Chen, C. (eds.) Visual Interfaces to Digital Libraries. LNCS, vol. 2539, pp. 1–9. Springer, Heidelberg (2002). https://doi.org/10.1007/3-540-36222-3_1
19. Kim, B., Scott, J., Kim, S.: Exploring digital libraries through visual interfaces. In: Digital Libraries - Methods and Applications, pp 123–137. InTech (2011). https://doi.org/10.5772/14255
20. Ware, C.: Information Visualization: Perception for Design, 3rd edn. Morgan Kaufmann Publishers, Burlington (2012)
21. Johnson, B., Shneiderman, B.: Tree-maps: a space-filling approach to the visualization of hierarchical information structures. In: Proceeding Visualization 1991, pp 284–291. IEEE Computer Society Press (1991). https://doi.org/10.1109/VISUAL.1991.175815
22. Shneiderman, B.: Tree visualization with tree-maps: 2-D space-filling approach. ACM Trans. Graph. 11, 92–99 (1992). https://doi.org/10.1145/102377.115768
23. Bederson, B.B., Shneiderman, B., Wattenberg, M.: Ordered and quantum treemaps: making effective use of 2D space to display hierarchies. ACM Trans. Graph. 21, 833–854 (2002). https://doi.org/10.1145/571647.571649
24. Long, L.K., Hui, L.C., Fook, G.Y., Wan Zainon, W.M.N.: A study on the effectiveness of tree-maps as tree visualization techniques. Procedia Comput. Sci. 124, 108–115 (2017). https://doi.org/10.1016/j.procs.2017.12.136
25. Bruls, M., Huizing, K., van Wijk, J.J.: Squarified treemaps. In: de Leeuw, W.C., van Liere, R. (eds.) Data Visualization 2000. EUROGRAPH, pp. 33–42. Springer, Vienna (2000). https://doi.org/10.1007/978-3-7091-6783-0_4
26. Shneiderman, B., Wattenberg, M.: Ordered treemap layouts. In: 2001 IEEE Symposium on Information Visualization. INFOVIS 2001, pp 73–78. IEEE (2001). https://doi.org/10.1109/INFVIS.2001.963283
27. Cesarano, A., Ferrucci, F., Torre, M.: A heuristic extending the Squarified treemapping algorithm. In: CoRR (2016). https://arxiv.org/pdf/1609.00754.pdf. Accessed 6 Apr 2017
28. Book, G., Keshary, N.: Radial tree graph drawing algorithm for representing large hierarchies, University of Connecticut (2001). http://gbook.org/projects/
29. Ka-Ping, Y., Fisher, D., Dhamija, R., Hearst, M.: Animated exploration of dynamic graphs with radial layout. In: 2001 IEEE Symposium on Information Visualization. INFOVIS 2001, pp. 43–50. IEEE (2001). https://doi.org/10.1109/INFVIS.2001.963279

30. Sheth, N., Cai, Q.: Visualizing MeSH dataset using radial tree layout (2003). http://iv.slis. indiana.edu/sw/papers/radialtree.pdf

31. Holten, D.: Hierarchical edge bundles: visualization of adjacency relations in hierarchical data. IEEE Trans. Vis. Comput. Graph. **12**, 741–748 (2006). https://doi.org/10.1109/TVCG. 2006.147

32. Monteiro, A., Miguel, B.: Harnessing user's knowledge in the construction of rating flows: the design of a collaborative system applied to academic repositories. In: Ortuño, B.H. (ed.) 2016 6th International Forum of Design as a Process: Systems & Design Beyond Processes and Thinking, pp. 780–792. Editorial Universitat Politècnica de València (2016). https://doi. org/10.4995/IFDP.2016.3308

Segmentation of Panels in d-Comics

Xinwei Wang[⊠], Jun Hu, Bart Hengeveld, and Matthias Rauterberg

Eindhoven University of Technology, Eindhoven, The Netherlands
{x.wang, j.hu, b.j.hengeveld, g.w.m.rauterberg}@tue.nl

Abstract. For over a hundred years, comics is presented on paper-based carriers such as magazines and books. With the development of new technologies, the comics industry has the opportunity to embrace a new carrier—the digital environment in electronic devices. However, due to the difference of the carrier, there exist differences between d-Comics (digital comics) and printed comics. One main difference is how the carrier creates segmentation of a sequence of comic panels: the segmentation created by paper is static and exclusive, while the segmentation created by screen-based electronic device may not be static nor exclusive because the same comics can be accessed through electronic devices with different screen sizes. This article describes an online experiment conducted to investigate how panel sequences are segmented in d-Comics. By analyzing the collected data from 80 participants with 4 panel sequences, two types of segmentation of panels in d-Comics were identified and discussed. This finding will further contribute to the design of d-Comics.

Keywords: Digital comics · Segmentation · Panel sequence

1 Introduction

Comics[1] is a storytelling medium. The medium employs a sequence of panels for telling the story [1, 2]. It is commonly seen that comics is printed on paper-based carriers such as books and magazines. Since digital comics started to appear in the 1980s [3], more and more people read comics through electronic devices. According to a recent report from the *All Japan Magazine and Book Publisher's and Editor's Association* [4], the increasing sales of digital comics shared one third of the total estimated sales (about 4 billion US dollar) in Japan, 2016. However, once the same panel sequence can be accessed through electronic devices with different screen sizes, problems may emerge since the size and resolution of a printed page could be different from electronic screens. Many pioneers have tried to overcome this challenge by separating individual panels from printed comic books to display on small screen devices. In the academic area, researchers have studied how to use computer algorithms to distinguish different panels on a page as individual units [5–7].

In the industry, companies like Amazon are working on digitalizing printed comic books both with full page structure and individual panels. The Guided View [8] technology "allows readers to view a comic on a panel-by-panel basis suitable for

---

[1] This article considers comics as one type of the storytelling medium, therefore addresses comics normally with a singular form.

© ICST Institute for Computer Sciences, Social Informatics and Telecommunications Engineering 2019
Published by Springer Nature Switzerland AG 2019. All Rights Reserved
A. L. Brooks et al. (Eds.): ArtsIT 2018/DLI 2018, LNICST 265, pp. 28–37, 2019.

mobile devices in a way that mimics the natural motion of the user's eye through the comic" [9]. Several scholars expressed their concerns regarding breaking the page layout and display comics panel-by-panel. Groensteen [10] claimed that the spatial relation provided by page is a system, and any change of spatial arrangement may jeopardize the narrative and could limit the author's expression. Goodbrey [11] argued that the guided view is "limiting the reader's control" during reading.

These problems reveal that the segmentation of panels in printed comics is normally embodied in the physical pages themselves. In other words, physical pages create segmentations of a panel sequence because one page can contain a limited number of panels. But the current screen-based electronic devices can provide, in McCloud's words, an infinite canvas [12], by displaying images constantly according to the input of the reader. A panel sequence doesn't have to be segmented when being displayed digitally. However, according to Zacks et al. [13], the world is presented to us as a stream of continuous information, but we can perceive this information as a series of discrete units. Thus, this study aims to examine whether there exist panel level units in d-Comics that can be similar to pages in printed comics. The units should meet the perception of the majority of the readers so that the author can take into consideration when designing d-Comics for multiple electronic devices.

2   Experiment Design

2.1   Materials

For the experiment four comic stories were chosen from the web-comics *ZenPencils* [14], shown in Fig. 1. The layout of the comics is altered for the purpose of the experiment to explore how a panel sequence is segmented.

The Lucky Ones   In Spite of Everything   Because It's There   Itaka

Fig. 1. Four short comics from ZenPencils.

The four comics contain different numbers of panels: 9 (*The Lucky Ones*), 18 (*In Spite of Everything*), 35 (*Because It's There*), and 59 (*Ithaka*). *The Lucky Ones* [15] contains a narrative about a profound life reflection, where the moments captured in the panels move backward in time: from the old gentleman visiting his wife's grave to the moment they met. *In Spite of Everything* [16] starts with a grownup man who found his childhood drawing tools. Then a flashback shows his painful childhood experience of being discouraged of drawing. Finally, the narrative is going back to the moment when the man is holding the drawing tools and starts drawing. *Because It's There* [17] tells a story of a mountaineer who conquers many difficulties and finally achieves his goal of being on top of the mountain. The story uses a parallel storyline about a rich couple and the mountaineer, to emphasize the narrator's opinion: to appreciate the mountaineer's spirit and to despise the lifestyle of the rich couple. *Ithaka* [18] is a longer story of a man who receives a map from his father and starts his journey towards Ithaka, he defeats a monster, experiences different cultures, meets the love of his life and finally arrives at Ithaka. When he is reaching the end of his life, he passes a new map indicating the original place he came from to his daughter, and the new adventure of the daughter seems to start, just like her father.

2.2   Panel Display and Interaction

The panels of each story have been placed horizontally, while maintaining the original reading order. The panels have been resized to have equal height (320 pixels on the screen), while the height-width proportion was kept the same with the original. The visual distance between each two panels was equally distributed. The experiment was developed as a web-based application programmed in HTML, CSS, and JavaScript. The participant could scroll the canvas horizontally, either with mouse clicks on a computer or with finger touches on a touch-screen.

Between each two panels, there was a crop icon (represented by the symbol of a pair of scissors), that participant could click or tap to indicate a segmentation. When the icon was clicked or tapped once, a blue line would appear to indicate the segmentation chosen by the participant. When the icon was clicked or tapped again, the placed segmentation would disappear. If the participant created segmentation lines on both sides of a single panel, two selection items would appear, for the participant to indicate the reason of identifying a single group panel. There were two reasons that could be selected: either the panel belonged to both the previous and next panel groups, or the panel could be considered as an independent group. The layout of the panels mentioned above can be found in Fig. 2.

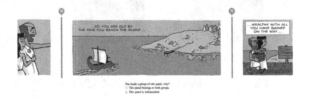

Fig. 2. The layout and interface of the online experiment.

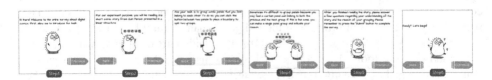

Fig. 3. The introduction interfaces of the online experiment.

2.3   Procedure

Before the experiment was conducted a pilot-study was executed with five participants, with the goal to improve the phrasing of the questions and the flow of the experiment. After the improvements were implemented, an advertisement to recruit participants was posted in groups related to comics on various social network platforms, including Facebook, LinkedIn, and Reddit. The post contained general information including the purpose, the requirements, the risks and the estimated duration of the experiment. After a potential participant read the information and agreed to participate voluntarily, the link for the experiment could be accessed on the device of the participant.

A visual introduction appeared after the participant clicked the link (Fig. 3). The introduction explained the goal and interaction of the experiment. After the introduction, one (of the four comic stories) was presented to the participant. The selection of which comics to show was based on the total amount of participants that completed each story. The system would automatically provide the least submitted story to the next participant. Following this method, each comic story was completed by twenty participants.

The participant read a comic story which was presented linearly on their own electronic device. The total reading time of the comic story was recorded by the system. There was no time limit for the individual reading time. The participant was asked to indicate where there was a segmentation between the panels. This segmentation could be placed based on their understanding by clicking or tapping the icon between the two panels. If the participant placed segmentation lines on both sides of a single panel, the participant needed to select the reason for the decision: whether it is considered as an independent panel or belongs to both the previous and the next panel group.

3   Result

The experiment was published online in November 2015 for two weeks. The results are reported below.

3.1   General Information

Participants

Participants were recruited in online groups related to comics on social networks. The website of the experiment received more than one thousand visits. The experiment received 87 completed responses (finished reading the instruction, the comic story and submitted the questionnaire). Seven responses were excluded from the dataset due to: incomplete answers (n = 4), system error from the device of the participant (n = 1), and two responses were emitted (randomly) to balance the amount of responses for each story (n = 2). The remaining dataset in total had 80 participants including 45 men and 35 women, the average age of which was 29.6 years. The experiment was conducted in English, and all participants were able to read the comics and answer the questions in English: 25% of the participants were native English speakers, 55% were native speakers of European languages, and 20% had other native languages. Out of 80 participants, 75 participants had an education level of a Bachelor degree or higher. Since the participants were mainly recruited from comics related interest groups, 88% of the participants maintained limited comics reading habit. With regard to the experience with comics, 25% of the participants were heavy comics readers, 35% read comics regularly, 27.5% read limited comics from social networks and news, 8.75% read comics only in their childhood, and 3.75% claimed they didn't read comics at all. For accessing the experiment, 72.5% of the participants used a computer, while 27.5% used a tablet device or a cell phone. The range of the screen size was from 980 × 551 pixels to 2160 × 1307 pixels.

Task Time
The average time that a participant required to read all the panels and finish the segmentation tasks was 3.36 min (n = 80, σ = 2.34). The average time of The Lucky Ones was 2.84 min (n = 20, σ = 2.75), In Spite of Everything was 2.39 min (n = 20, σ = 1.53), Because It's There was 4.04 min (n = 20, σ = 2.10), and Ithaka was 4.14 min (n = 20, σ = 2.46). In general, the more panels the story contained, the longer duration was required for reading. However, the average time for reading and segmentation tasks of In Spite of Everything (20 panels) was less than The Lucky Ones (11 panels).

3.2   The Segmentation of Panel Sequence

Overview of Panel Sequence Segmentation
In general, the more panels a story contained, the more panel groups could be perceived (Figs. 4a and b).

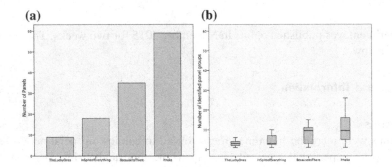

Fig. 4. (Left) a. The number of panels of each comic story. (Right) b. The mean and deviation of identified panel groups of each comic story.

Figure 4a uses a bar chart to visualize the number of panels in each story. Figure 4b uses a box plot to describe the number of segmented panel groups in each story. The more panels a story contains, the more segmentations were identified. The average group number of *The Lucky Ones* is 2.95. The average group number of *In Spite of*

Everything is 4.3. The average group number of *Because It's There* is 7.85. The average group number of *Ithaka* is 10.85. The decision of panel segmentation deviates more when more panels are involved.

The Segmentation Identified by Majority[2]
No gap of *The Lucky Ones* received more than 50% of the identification. Two clear segmentations can be observed in *In Spite of Everything*: Gap 8 (75%) and Gap 17 (70%). Gap 8 is the gap that contains the narrative transition when the story is going backward in time (the adult character starts to recall his childhood memory). Gap 17 bridges the jump from the past to present (the memory ends and the story returns to the adult character). In *Because It's There*, 8 gaps received 50% or more agreement of the participants about the segmentations: Gap 3 (85%), Gap 7 (70%), Gap 12 (55%), Gap 14 (70%), Gap 19 (60%), Gap 21 (n = 13), Gap 24 (65%), and Gap 25 (60%). Gap 3 represents a narrative transition of the main character moving out from his lab to go public. Gap 7 represents the main character finishing his speech then departures with the airplane. Gap 12 represents a transition between the story of the main character in a newspaper and a rich couple walking in a jewelry store, while the clerk was reading the newspaper. Gap 14 represents a transition in narrative from the couple to the main character. Gap 19 represents a transition in narrative to compare the similar actions of the main character with the couple. From the main character digging on top of the snow mountain, to the couple using a fork to eat the meat. Gap 21 represents a transition from the rich couple eating a luxurious meal to the main character climbing the mountain. Gap 24 represents a transition from the main character who found some skeletons on the mountain to the leftover bones on the couple's dining table. Gap 25 represents a transition from the couple back to the main character. Four segmentations were identified in *Ithaka*: Gap 6 (85%), Gap 30 (80%), Gap 37 (55%), and Gap 49 (55%). Gap 6 represents the main character making up his mind and then starting his journey. Gap 30 represents a transition from a red stone dropping on the water (after the main character defeats the monster) to the main character getting older with gray hairs, one wounded eye, and the red stone as a necklace. Gap 37 represents a transition of the main character in a harbor area to an Egyptian city. Gap 49 represents a transition from the main character receiving a newborn, to him getting old and making a map.

3.3 Single Panel Panel-Group

Segmentation lines on both sides of a panel, creating an individual panel, were identified in total 45 times in 4 stories, in which 17 times were identified as "this panel belongs to both groups", and 28 times as "it's an independent panel". Twenty-seven participants (33.75%) identified individual panels in the experiment.

There are nine segmentations in *Because It's There* which are most clearly indicated by the change of characters. This division created two panel groups with only two panels (panel 13 & 14, panel 20 & 21), and two single panel groups (panel 12, panel 25).

---

[2] The images and numbers of the panels and gaps can be found on this website: http://xinweicomics. com/phd_thesis/panel_numbers.html.

4   Discussion

4.1   General Panel Sequence Segmentation Pattern in Each Story

The identified segmentations and panel grouping varied between individual participants. This could be related to age, gender, education, cultural background, and personal experience. The general patterns within the individual stories are reported below.

In *The Lucky Ones*, there is no specific pattern where over 50% of the participants agreed on segmentation lines. An interpretation of this could be that the participants found it hard to make segmentation lines, and therefore formed a group of all the panels.

In Spite of Everything is the clearest example in the four stories where the participants agreed about the segmentation. Three groups were identified by over 70% of the participants. A narrative change (narrative time jumps back or fast forward in this case), combined with visual aids such as changes in environment, character appearance, and color can send a strong signal to the reader about segmentation.

Nine panel groups were identified in *Because It's There* according to the data collected. It is the comic author's intention in this story to use two different perspectives of two were characters to create a comparison. As a result, most of the segmentation lines were based on the switch of characters. This result suggests that even when the narrative structure are two parallel stories (the two character-parties are used as a comparison instead of pushing the narrative forward), the character change combined with environmental change can also generate segmentations.

Ithaka has the longest forward moving narrative time scale among the four stories. There is a life-long transition where the protagonist grows up from young to old, combined with a detailed description of a short duration about the monster slaughtering moment. Four segmentations (Gap 6, 30, 37 & 49) have received over 50% of the recognition rate based on narrative time changes.

4.2   Panel Grouping Categories

Two categories of panel groups can be observed from the experiment. One category are panel groups with a clear segmentation of the panel sequence based on the reader's understanding of the comics. For example, in a three-panel linear sequence, Panel 1 and 2 are segmented from Panel 3. In this case, two panel-groups are identified: Group 1 with Panel 1 and 2, and Group 2 with Panel 3.

Another category is an overlap of two panel-groups based on the understanding of the reader. For example, in a three-panel sequence, Panel 1 and 2 are considered as a group, while Panel 2 and 3 are also considered as a group. In this case, two panel-groups are identified: Group 1 with Panel 1 and 2, and Group 2 with Panel 2 and 3. Panel 2 is the overlap between the two panel-groups. Two examples from *Because It's There* can be used to explain this category further (Fig. 5). Panel 12: Although the connection in the environment is strong with Panel 12, 13 and 14, the connection of character and narrative is strong with Panel 10, 11 and 12. The other example is Panel 25: an identified single-panel-group (both Gap 24 and 25 have received segmentation lines by over 50% of the participants). The difficulty to match a panel to any one of the panel groups could be caused because the characters in Panel 25 changed, but the images and the connection of the text remain very similar.

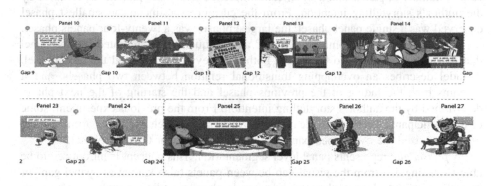

Fig. 5. Identifying panel grouping categories.

Since there are two categories of the segmented panel-group (one is without overlapping of each other, one is with overlapping of each other), it is necessary to create a vocabulary to be able to differentiate between the different categories of panel-grouping.

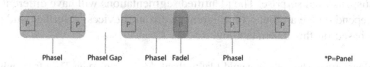

Fig. 6. Demonstration of phasel, fadel and phasel gap.

5 Conclusion

In this experiment, the potential influences of the physical page structure were removed. Such as the complex panel layout, and the different gap size between panels. The fact that participants were still able to make panel grouping—based on linearly presented panels on electronic devices—shows that a panel sequence, without the influence of physical pages, can still be segmented in d-Comics.

To be able to address the units identified in d-Comics, a new vocabulary has been established. There are two types of panel groups that were observed from the previous experiment. One is with a clear segmentation of the panel sequence, the other is with an overlap of two panel-groups both based on the understanding of the reader. The two types of panel groups and the segmentation are shown in the Fig. 6. Based on the experiment results we propose the following vocabulary to be established, in order to discuss the panel level concepts more precisely.

A *phasel* (created by combining "phase" and "sequel") in d-Comics is represented by one panel or multiple panels that belong to each other. The author cannot decompose these further into smaller phasels. A phasel describes a strong relation among a certain number of panels and a significant difference with other phasels, determined by the author's storytelling intention. From the current experiment, the smallest phasel observed was a single panel phasel, the largest phasel was a twenty-four panels phasel.

A *fadel* (created by combining "fade" and "sequel") is represented by one panel that the author considers to be part of both the previous phasel and the next phasel. A fadel describes an overlapping transitional relation between two phasels, and it contains both the fading of the previous phasel and the starting of the next phasel determined by the author's storytelling intention. From the previous experiment, some of the participants were able to identify the overlapped phasels, however, some readers just categorized the overlapped panel(s) into the previous or the next phasel.

A *phasel gap* represents panel level segmentation. This concept is introduced to be able to distinguish from the visual gap between panels (also known as "panel gap" or "panel gutter"). As long as there are two panels, there must be a visual gap. However, the visual gap does not necessarily need to be a phasel gap. Only when two phasels are identified, the visual gap between these two phasels can represent a phasel gap. In the case that a fadel is identified—which means that there are overlapping phasels—there cannot be a phasel gap between the overlapping phasels.

This understanding would change the creation process of d-Comics and help the author to create d-Comics that can adapt to different screens. Instead of using page as the principle of segmentation, the author of d-Comics can define segmentations in the panel sequence based on storytelling purposes such as enhancing reader's curiosity, building suspense and surprise. The identified segmentations will have different display methods depend on the attributes of different electronic devices. A further study will be continued based on this understanding.

Acknowledgements. The authors would like to thank Mr. Gavin Aung Than for kindly giving permission to use his comics for the purpose of this research, and the participants for joining the online experiment. This research is supported by the Chinese Scholarship Council.

References

1. Eisner, W.: Comics and Sequential Art. W. W. Norton & Company Inc, New York (2008)
2. McCloud, S.: Understanding Comics. William Morrow Paperbacks, New York (1993)
3. Garrity, S.: The History of Webcomics The Comics Journal 2011. http://www.tcj.com/the-history-of-webcomics/. Accessed 01 July 2017
4. Association All Japan Magazine and Book Publisher's and Editor's, "紙&電子コミック市場 2016," 2017. http://www.ajpea.or.jp/information/20170224/index.html. Accessed 22 July 2017
5. Li, L., Wang, Y., Tang, Z., Gao, L.: Automatic comic page segmentation based on polygon detection. Multimed. Tools Appl. **69**(1), 171–197 (2014)

6. Stommel, M., Merhej, L.I., Müller, M.G.: Segmentation-free detection of comic panels. In: Bolc, L., Tadeusiewicz, R., Chmielewski, Leszek J., Wojciechowski, K. (eds.) ICCVG 2012. LNCS, vol. 7594, pp. 633–640. Springer, Heidelberg (2012). https://doi.org/10.1007/978-3-642-33564-8_76
7. Yamada, M., Budiarto, R., Mamoru, E., Miyazaki, S.: Comic image decomposition for reading comics on cellular phones. IEICE Trans. Inf. Syst. **87**(6), 1370–1376 (2004)
8. Steinberger, D., Najmabadi, C.: Presenting panels and sub-panels of a document. US9886936B2 (2018)
9. comiXology: What is comiXology's Guided View technology? (2014). https://support.comixology.com/customer/portal/articles/768035-what-is-comixology-s-guided-viewTM-technology. Accessed 22 July 2017
10. Groensteen, T., Beaty, B., Nguyen, N.: The system of comics. University Press of Mississippi, Mississippi (2007)
11. Goodbrey, D.M.: Digital comics–new tools and tropes. Stud. Comics **4**(1), 185–197 (2013)
12. McCloud, S.: Reinventing Comics: How Imagination and Technology Are Revolutionizing an Art Form, vol. 118. Perennial, New York (2000)
13. Zacks, J.M., Speer, N.K., Reynolds, J.R.: Segmentation in reading and film comprehension. J. Exp. Psychol. Gen. **138**(2), 307 (2009)
14. Than, G.A.: Zen Pencils (2012). http://zenpencils.com/. Accessed 01 Sept 2015
15. Than, G.A.: The Lucky Ones (2012). https://zenpencils.com/comic/81-richard-dawkins-the-lucky-ones/. Accessed 01 Jan 2015
16. Than, G.A.: In Spite of Everything (2013). https://zenpencils.com/comic/113-vincent-van-gogh-in-spite-of-everything/. Accessed 01 Jan 2015
17. Than, G.A.: Because It's There (2014). https://zenpencils.com/comic/mallory/. Accessed 01 Jan 2015
18. Than, G.A.: Ithaka (2013). https://zenpencils.com/comic/131-c-p-cavafy-ithaka/. Accessed 01 Jan 2015

Co-designing Gaming Experiences
for Museums with Teenagers

Vanessa Cesário[1,2]($\boxtimes$), António Coelho[2,3], and Valentina Nisi[1]

[1] Madeira Interactive Technologies Institute, 9020-105 Funchal, Portugal
{vanessa.cesario,valentina.nisi}@m-iti.org
[2] Faculty of Engineering, University of Porto, 4200-465 Porto, Portugal
acoelho@fe.up.pt
[3] INESC TEC, 4200-465 Porto, Portugal

Abstract. Museums promote cultural experiences through exhibits and the stories behind them. Nevertheless, museums are not always designed to engage and interest young audiences, especially teenagers. Throughout this paper, we discuss teenagers as an important group to be considered within the Children-Computer Interaction field, and we report some techniques on designing with teens, in particular, arguing that participatory design methods can involve teenagers in the design process of technology for museums. For this purpose, we conceptualized, designed and deployed a co-design activity for teenagers (aged 15–17), where teenagers together with a researcher jointly created and designed a medium fidelity prototype. For this case study, participants were divided into groups and invited to think and create games and story plots for a selected museum. All the prototypes were made by the participants with the support and guidance of the researcher and the Aurasma software, an augmented reality tool.

Keywords: Museums · Games · Visitor experience · Co-design
Teenagers · Cooperative Inquiry · Augmented reality

1 Introduction

There is an increasing concern that the traditional exhibition and communication style of museums often fails to engage children; hence it denies the potencies of museums to be a fundamental institution in a society where cultural heritage is explored [1]. However, according to Roussou and colleagues [2], exhibits and educational initiatives for children are created without involving the children, with some notable exceptions [3, 4]. A systematic path towards making systems truly meaningful and intuitive to visitors is offered by human-centered design [5], together with participatory design methods [4].

Moreover, according to Falk [6], the so-called "one size fits all" experience does not apply to most of the museum visitors. The same can be said about "generation Z" which is seen as quite different from previous generations, particularly regarding beliefs and behaviors [7]. We can mostly verify in museums different guided tours for children and adults, without having any appropriate guidelines for the teens' generation in particular. This generation is identified as an audience group that is often excluded

© ICST Institute for Computer Sciences, Social Informatics and Telecommunications Engineering 2019
Published by Springer Nature Switzerland AG 2019. All Rights Reserved
A. L. Brooks et al. (Eds.): ArtsIT 2018/DLI 2018, LNICST 265, pp. 38–47, 2019.

from a museum's curatorial strategies [8]. In consequence, it is not only museums that seem to ignore a younger audience, but this group itself also appears to be disinterested in what museums might offer.

2 Co-designing with and for Teenagers

The target group of children between 15–19 years old was coined by Prenksy [9] as "digital natives" and critically discussed by Bennett and colleagues [10]. Recent work considers teenagers as being different from both children and adults in their perspectives [11]. Teenagers have collaborative behaviors wherein somehow the opinions of many come together to form a mass opinion [12].

Teenagers are an understudied group within the Interaction Design and Children (IDC) field [12]. The majority of research within this field focuses on children age 4–11, which leaves a gap in the literature for children 12–17. However, because teens represent a rapidly growing group of technology users [13], researchers have sought new ways to involve them more fully in the design process [14]. Methods for undertaking research with teenagers within the scope of interaction design has also been discussed [12].

The expression "co-design" is used because of the importance Cooperative Inquiry places on an equal partnership between children and adults, where designers participate in users' world [15]. In Cooperative Inquiry, children act as full partners helped by adults through the design process where they can share ideas and evaluations alongside with adults [16]. One method to use Cooperative Inquiry is a modified form of participatory design which encompasses sketching ideas with art supplies (paper, cardboard, glue) to create low-tech prototypes during the brainstorming process [16, 17].

Several studies have presented the value of co-designing learning technologies with children aged 7–16 [18, 19]. Participatory Design incorporates several methods and theories while the core philosophy is to include the final users as active participants in the technology design process [20, 21]. Taxén and colleagues [22] pointed out that participatory design is a strategic approach for producing user-oriented information technologies. Druin's seminal work on Cooperative Inquiry [17, 23] and the Scandinavian approach to Participatory Design [24] have gained acceptance within the IDC community. Participatory Design has gained new user groups such as children [17] and teens [25]. Teenagers and participatory design within museum studies are also covered by some papers in the IDC Community, as in the case of the study "Digital Natives" [26] where teens (15–19 years old) collaborated with designers, programmers, anthropologists and museum curators to create four digital installations for an exhibition. The case study "Gaming the Museum" [27] is another example that started from everyday practices where children's (14–15 years old) everyday engagement was strong and thus computers games and online communities were chosen to start a process of creating a game for a museum. However, none of these works incorporates teenagers as the developers of technology. In the study "Digital Natives" [26], the teens' ideas were presented to a team of interaction designers who would be responsible for integrating the voices of the participants into a prototype. Similarly, in the case study "Gaming in the Museum" [27], the participants have not developed a technological prototype.

3 Methodology

The researchers proposed a one-week activity plan to a summer camp in a Junior University. The activity, targeted for teens aged 15–17, consisted in developing gaming experiences for specific museums, and it was deployed for two weeks. The participants, 13 in total, were divided into 5 groups. The first week had 2 groups who worked with the Engineering Museum, and the second had 3 groups who worked with the Medicine Museum, both placed in Porto, Portugal.

The teens were involved in a series of game activities for one week, and two days were reserved for the design and deployment of the experience for the selected museum. The Aurasma software [28] was one of the many easy and free tools out in the market that was chosen to be used within this activity. Aurasma is an Augmented Reality (AR) site which allows us to see and interact with the world through auras. Auras are the digital content which will be unlocked by the Aurasma app. Auras can be as simple as a video and a link to a web page, or as complex as a live 3D animation. For the purpose of simplicity, we chose to make each aura as a video that the participants would create. Over two days, the following activities were organized:

1. *Introduce the Aurasma software.* We stated that participants could unlock small videos with informative content in each artefact of the museum. These auras should enhance the artefacts' scientific information, and they would assemble the videos.
2. *First museum tour.* This tour was made by the museums' curators without any digital support. The participants were then invited to take pictures and notes from the artefacts they thought would best suit their interactive museum experiences through the Aurasma software.
3. *Brainstorming in groups.* This was the time wherein participants were divided into groups and the concept of the experience was defined. To prompt their imagination, they were required to brainstorm their experience as if it was an escape room [29], that is to say that they would have to create a story and riddles to solve within a time limit in order to successfully finish the experience. Participants were free to think of which storytelling plot suited best with the museum as well as which riddles to apply, bearing in mind that an aura would be just a video. Hence, the riddles should appear in the end of the video deployed to create one aura. These videos needed to include information about the artefacts within the story they created and give a clue to the other point of interest. The participants were the ones leading the ideas, while the researcher listened to them and also contributed to the reasoning of the ideas generated.
4. *Script construction I.* After defining the experience, participants started creating scripts for the videos at each point of interest. For each aura, they were required to write: (1) which location the aura is related to; (2) if any image appears; (3) which dialogues, if any; (4) which clue will guide the player to the other point of interest (Figs. 2 and 3). Again, the researcher had a more passive role. The participants led the script while the researcher contributed to it with small details to be added to the text and improve readability.

5. *Second museum tour.* A second tour to the museum was made to clarify some doubts about specific artefacts or points of interest regarding each experience that was being developed.

6. *Script construction II.* Finalization of the script according to the changes made regarding the second tour.

7. *Development of the videos.* With the script finished, the participants started making the video for each aura. The content of these videos was made by the teenage participants on their own. Some of them recorded theatrical performance while others recorded their voices and put together images. The videos and voices were recorded with an iPhone 6, and the manipulation of the video was made in the native video software of their computers (Windows Movie Maker).

8. *Converting videos to auras.* The videos were uploaded to the Aurasma software through a computer. Here the researcher had an active role in guiding and assisting the participants with the technology.

9. *Third museum tour.* This tour was finally made with the Aurasma software. As said in the beginning, the aim of these experiences was to be compared to an escape room. For this, each group experienced the game of others while the researcher was monitoring the time they took in order to check who would be the winning group (Figs. 1 and 2).

10. *Evaluation from the participants.* To end with, all the participants filled out a survey concerning their thoughts about this experience of designing together for a museum (Table 1).

Fig. 1. Images of the interaction of the third moment from the *Bridge Builder* tour.

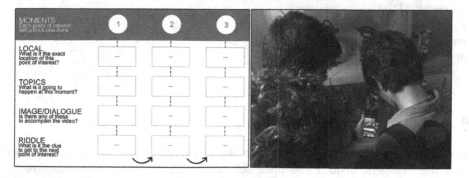

Fig. 2. On the left: graph showed to the participants to help them to construct the script. On the right: one group taking the bridge builder tour throughout the engineering museum, near the topographer no. 21.

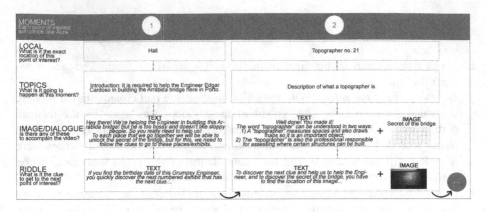

Fig. 3. Example of the first two moments of the *Bridge Builder*'s script.

Table 1. Questions and measures adopted.

Question	Measure	
(Q1) What did you think about the FIRST TOUR to the museum led by its director?	Five degrees of happiness [30]	Teenagers were asked to rate, on a 5-point Likert scale, how much they enjoyed the event. Each smiley was then scored as: 1 = awful, 2 = not very good, 3 = good, 4 = really good, and 5 = brilliant
(Q2) What did you think of the CO-DESIGN activity of a game for the MUSEUM?		
(Q3) What did you think of the activity of EXPLORING THE MUSEUM with the GAMES that your colleagues developed?		
(Q4) Do you think that you will use the AURASMA application in the future?	Again-again table [31]	In the table, users needed to select one of the following options: Yes, Maybe, No
(Q5) Describe all the activity you made for the MUSEUM in one sentence	Writing	
(Q6) On what occasions and for what reasons would you use the AURASMA app?	Writing	

4 Results

In this section, we present the results from the various co-design activities carried out with the teenagers, divided into three sub sections, such as (1) *storytelling plots;* (2) *game mechanics* of each work group; and (3) the *evaluation* of this design activity by all participants. Due to page length constrains, the videos created by the Portuguese participants are accessible online in the following link: https://goo.gl/T2RTZ9.

4.1   Storytelling Plots

The teens created several storytelling plots that can be grouped into five types of stories (Table 2):

(1) *Bridge Builder.* In this plot, throughout 5 points of interest, the player needs to help an Engineer to construct a bridge. At each point of interest reached, the player can unlock several pieces of the puzzle which will uncover the "secret of the bridge". This secret of the bridge is an image of a real bridge in their region coordinated by the engineer featured in the exhibition.

(2) *The Final Landing.* This plot revolves around an astronaut that landed in the earth and need to construct a landing bridge to go to his planet again. In each point of interest (total of 6), the player will find the necessary tools to build the bridge and take off towards his planet.

(3) *Help the Doctor.* In this plot, throughout 5 points of interest, the player needs to help a doctor, who it is in the middle of a surgery, to find a specific tool to complete the surgery.

(4) *Medicine History.* In this plot, throughout 7 points of interest, the player gets to know relevant facts about the history of medicine narrated by a character presented in the museum.

(5) *Visiting the Medicine Museum.* The story plot with 6 points of interest, tells the story of a person that would like to find a specific portrait in the museum and needs the help of the user to find it.

4.2   Game Mechanics

Teens created seven types of game mechanics (Table 2) all revolving around enigmas leading to the next artefact to encounter:

(1) *Calculation* of a number that will lead to the number of the next artefact;

(2) An *image* of an artefact that the player needs to find its location in the museum;

(3) A *name* that the player needs to find to which artefact it is related to;

(4) A *metaphor* in which the players need to find understanding regarding the museum premises;

(5) *Translation* that the players need to make, for example a sentence in other language, or a written phrase from back to front;

(6) *Morse code*, each symbol represents either a text character letter or numeral and is represented by a unique sequence of dots and dashes;

(7) *Binary code*, a coding system using the binary digits 0 and 1 to represent a letter.

4.3   Evaluation

In general, in regards the results from Q4 and Q6 (Table 2), all the participants enjoyed the activity and most would use the Aurasma application in the future in their school's assignments, or even to have fun with their friends. Regarding Q1, 11 participants out of 13 rated the first museum tour, led by the museums' curators, as "really good", and the others as "good". Concerning Q2, 11 participants out of 13 rated the co-design sessions as "brilliant", and 4 rated as "really good". The activity of exploring the museum with the experiences developed by them (Q3) was rated by 9 out of 13 as "brilliant", and as "really good" by 4 out of 13. In overall, the co-design session of a museum experience was referenced by the participants (Q5) as "innovative", "fun", "interesting", "different", and "productive".

Table 2. Game mechanics used per experience.

	Calculation	Image	Name	Metaphor	Translation	Morse code	Binary code
Bridge builder	x	x					
The final landing		x	x	x		x	
Help the doctor		x				x	
Medicine history		x	x	x	x		x
Visiting the museum	x			x		x	x

5 Concluding Remarks

With this study, we contributed to the literature reporting on co-design with teenagers, opening up this area to further exploration [12] by researchers, designers and even curators of museums. Adopting a Cooperative Inquiry strategy, we placed the participants as the main subject throughout the whole design process of the sessions [16]. Teenagers played an active role in the creation and development of ideas, and the researcher had a more passive role in guiding their voices through the predetermined schedule for the sessions, as well as evaluating the logic of their stories and game elements that the young people proposed. According to other studies about participatory design session with teens in museums, such as "Digital Natives" [26] and "Gaming the Museum" [27], it is reported that young people, become enthusiastic and enjoy participating in activities in the museum created by them through paper mockups, or technical prototypes developed by others. However, our study seems to indicate that in terms of engagement, having the chance of realizing their own digital prototype, can be of greater satisfaction than having others do it. These teens visited the museum, took pictures, created a narrative with game elements that they remembered or searched on the Internet. Subsequently, they built the videos using native video programs on their computers. This generation of teens is very fluent in using new technologies and there were no great difficulties in handling this digital content.

From the practical results of this work, young people thought about adventure themes to add to a story plot. In 5 groups out of 6, they embarked on a journey through the museum in search of something to help a greater cause (*Bridge builder*, *The final landing*, *Help the doctor*, *Visiting the medicine museum*). This shows that the teens' everyday engagement in relation to games is mediated through the adventure genre and that a digital interaction in the museum directed to this audience should contain these elements of adventure in order to capture their attention. Regarding game elements, participants thought of clues leading players through a treasure hunt. Clues ranged from basic one, such an *image* or a *name* of an artifact, or even a *metaphor* on how to get to these artifacts, or more complex ones such as to *translate* a sentence from a foreign language, or using *codes*, where participants had to use the internet to know how to decipher the code. We conclude that young people when invited to think of adding clues to the experience, think of several ones that challenge the players. The more difficult, the more challenging, and therefore more involvement from the users.

With this work, we have learned that games can benefit museums by promoting positive attitudes about museum spaces, creating fun destinations in order to promote meaningful informal learning combined with entertainment. Although people could not immediately adopt a game, the positive attitude of implementing technology inside a space cultivates good experiences for visitors, which could help museums achieving greater visitation rates. However, there are some disadvantages with the use of gaming experiences in museums. Players could become fascinated with the screen and fail to observe the physical exhibit in the museum, which is not the goal nor the message museums would like to convey. Clues and escape rooms' experiences in museums have also to be carefully crafted into the logic and purpose of the museum visit, as it could incur into pushing teens through the exhibits too quickly and inviting them to finish the visit rather than enjoying it.

From this study we can confirm that co-design techniques can change the way traditional museum exhibitions are considered by "digital natives" [9]. Teenagers are an important generation of users for museums as they are potential visitors for museums, and their perspectives are vastly different from today's adults [11]. In fact, these perspectives may remain different in the future, therefore it is fundamental to have access to design techniques so that we can anticipate these perspectives and create exhibitions that will attract them. While not all young people will be able or have the interest to take part in these co-design sessions, similarly, not all museums will have the time or resources in hosting these types of sessions. Nevertheless, we observed that from these co-design sessions we can detect patterns of interest (adventurous themes and game elements) that could be later validated through new museum experiences designed by museum designers and curators to be tested with teenagers. By validating and adopting teen-friendly design guidelines for museum exhibits, we believe this group could be encouraged to embrace more interest in museums.

Acknowledgments. ARDITI, project number M14-20-09-5369-FSE-000001.

References

1. Hooper-Greenhill, E.: Communication and communities in the post-museum: from metanarratives to constructed knowledge. University of Leicester, Copenhagen (2001)
2. Roussou, M., Kavalieratou, E., Doulgeridis, M.: Children designers in the museum: applying participatory design for the development of an art education program. In: Proceedings of the 6th International Conference on Interaction Design and Children, pp. 77–80. ACM, New York (2007)

3. Broadbent, J., Marti, P.: Location aware mobile interactive guides: usability issues. In: Fourth International Conference on Hypermedia and Interactivity in Museums, pp. 88–98, Paris (1997)
4. Taxén, G.: Introducing participatory design in museums. In: Proceedings of the Eighth Conference on Participatory Design: Artful Integration: Interweaving Media, Materials and Practices, vol. 1, pp. 204–213. ACM, New York (2004)
5. Kensing, F., Simonsen, J., Bodker, K.: MUST: a method for participatory design. Hum.-Comput. Interact. **13**, 167–198 (1998)
6. Falk, J.H.: Identity and the Museum Visitor Experience. Routledge, Walnut Creek (2009)
7. Wikia: Generation Z: A Look At The Technology And Media Habits Of Today's Teens. http://www.prnewswire.com/news-releases/generation-z-a-look-at-the-technology-and-media-habits-of-todays-teens-198958011.html
8. Tzibazi, V.: Participatory action research with young people in museums. Museum Manag. Curatorship. **28**, 153–171 (2013)
9. Prensky, M.: Digital natives, digital immigrants part 1. Horiz. **9**, 1–6 (2001)
10. Bennett, S., Maton, K., Kervin, L.: The digital natives debate: a critical review of the evidence. British J. Educ. Technol. **39**, 775–786 (2008)
11. Fitton, D., Read, J.C.C., Horton, M.: The challenge of working with teens as participants in interaction design. In: CHI 2013 Extended Abstracts on Human Factors in Computing Systems, pp. 205–210. ACM, New York (2013)
12. Read, J.C.C., Horton, M., Iversen, O., Fitton, D., Little, L.: Methods of working with teenagers in interaction design. In: CHI 2013 Extended Abstracts on Human Factors in Computing Systems, pp. 3243–3246. ACM, New York (2013)
13. Lenhart, A.: Teens, Social Media and Technology Overview (2015). http://www.pewinternet.org/2015/04/09/teens-social-media-technology-2015/
14. Winterburn, N., Gregory, P., Fitton, D.: Designing teenage emotions with a life of their own. In: Little, L., Fitton, D., Bell, B.T., Toth, N. (eds.) Perspectives on HCI Research with Teenagers. HIS, pp. 207–236. Springer, Cham (2016). https://doi.org/10.1007/978-3-319-33450-9_9
15. Muller, M.: A participatory poster of participatory methods. In: CHI 2001 Extended Abstracts on Human Factors in Computing Systems, pp. 99–100. ACM, New York (2001)
16. Druin, A.: The role of children in the design of new technology. Behav. Inf. Technol. **21**, 1–25 (2002)
17. Druin, A.: Cooperative inquiry: developing new technologies for children with children. In: Proceedings of the SIGCHI Conference on Human Factors in Computing Systems, pp. 592–599. ACM, New York (1999)
18. Isomursu, M., Isomursu, P., Still, K.: Capturing tacit knowledge from young girls. Interact. Comput. **16**, 431–449 (2004)
19. Danielsson, K., Wiberg, C.: Participatory design of learning media: Designing educational computer games with and for teenagers. Interact. Technol. Smart Educ. **3**, 275–291 (2006)
20. Muller, M.J.: Participatory design: the third space in HCI. In: Jacko, J.A., Sears, A. (eds.) The Human-computer Interaction Handbook, pp. 1051–1068. L. Erlbaum Associates Inc., Hillsdale (2003)
21. Salen, K.: gaming literacies: a game design study in action. J. Educ. Multimed. Hypermedia **16**, 301–322 (2007)
22. Taxén, G., Bowers, J., Hellström, S.-O., Tobiasson, H.: Designing mixed media artefacts for public settings. In: Darses, F., Dieng, R., Simone, C., Zacklad, M. (eds.) Cooperative Systems Design. Scenario-Based Design of Collaborative Systems, pp. 195–210. IOS Press, Amsterdam (2004)

23. Druin, A. (ed.): The Design of Children's Technology. Morgan Kaufmann Publishers Inc., San Francisco (1998)
24. Robertson, J., Good, J.: Children's narrative development through computer game authoring. In: Proceedings of the 2004 Conference on Interaction Design and Children: Building a Community, pp. 57–64. ACM, New York (2004)
25. Toth, N., Little, L., Read, J., Guo, Y., Fitton, D., Horton, M.: Teenagers talking about energy: using narrative methods to inform design. In: CHI 2012 Extended Abstracts on Human Factors in Computing Systems, pp. 2171–2176. ACM, New York (2012)
26. Iversen, O.S., Smith, R.C.: Scandinavian participatory design: dialogic curation with teenagers. In: Proceedings of the 11th International Conference on Interaction Design and Children, pp. 106–115. ACM, New York (2012)
27. Dindler, C., Iversen, O.S., Smith, R., Veerasawmy, R.: Participatory design at the museum: inquiring into children's everyday engagement in cultural heritage. In: Proceedings of the 22nd Conference of the Computer-Human Interaction Special Interest Group of Australia on Computer-Human Interaction, pp. 72–79. ACM, New York (2010)
28. Aurasma is now HP Reveal. https://www.aurasma.com/
29. Nicholson, S.: Peeking Behind the Locked Door: A Survey of Escape Room Facilities (2015). http://scottnicholson.com/pubs/erfacwhite.pdf
30. Hall, L., Hume, C., Tazzyman, S.: Five degrees of happiness: effective smiley face likert scales for evaluating with children. In: Proceedings of the 15th International Conference on Interaction Design and Children, pp. 311–321. ACM, New York (2016)
31. Read, J.C., MacFarlane, S.: Using the fun toolkit and other survey methods to gather opinions in child computer interaction. In: Proceedings of the 2006 Conference on Interaction Design and Children, pp. 81–88. ACM, New York (2006)

Moderate Recursion: A Digital Artifact of Interactive Dance

Celine Latulipe[1]([✉]), Berto Gonzalez[1], Melissa Word[2], Sybil Huskey[1], and David Wilson[1]

[1] University of North Carolina at Charlotte, Charlotte, NC, USA
{clatulip,agonza32,sdhuskey,davils}@uncc.edu
[2] High Museum of Art, Atlanta, GA, USA
melissa.word@gmail.com

Abstract. In this paper, we describe the process and technology behind the creation of a video art piece, 'Moderate Recursion,' that is a by-product of the dance performance, 'Heavy Recursion.' The original interactive dance work was part of the Dance.Draw project and was a reflection on the role of technology in our lives. The resulting video art piece, 'Moderate Recursion,' uses a combination of recorded videos of the projected visualizations and of the dancers on the stage. This paper presents the emergence of this new visual art piece. This demonstrates how ephemeral instances of interactive performance art can be captured for broader audiences to experience, through a permanent video artifact.

Keywords: Video art · Dance · Interactive performance
Digital artifact

1 Introduction

The Dance.Draw project was an interdisciplinary project spanning four years, in which choreographers, dancers, technologists, and artists worked together to explore how technology could be used to augment dance performances, engage audiences and support the creative process as a whole. One of the interactive dance productions that was created as part of Dance.Draw was called 'Heavy Recursion.' It is out of this particular production that the researchers created a unique artifact that captures the essence and aesthetics of the production.

In a world where our senses are overloaded with information, we can miss an opportunity to capture exquisite art. If not for the attention of a group member, we may not have noticed that the compelling visualizations created by our interactive dance were art pieces in themselves. The video art piece that we describe in this paper, 'Moderate Recursion,' is not just the work of the artist-technologist who designed and programmed the visualizations, but it is also art created by the dancers, who controlled the visualizations with their motion, as well as art created by the choreographer who defined the dance movements. In this paper,

A. L. Brooks et al. (Eds.): ArtsIT 2018/DLI 2018, LNICST 265, pp. 48–57, 2019.
https://doi.org/10.1007/978-3-030-06134-0_6

we explore the idea of using archival video and recordings of interactive visualizations made during a live dance performance to create a form of digital art that stands on its own and subsists as a memory of the live performance.

2 Background

There is a long history of integrating technology into choreographic rehearsal and live performance processes in a wide variety of ways: as a creative process tool, as an audience response measurement or engagement tool, or as a part of live productions either to augment or to make performances interactive.

Some of the earliest work that integrated technology into the dance-making process involved the use of animated figures in the DanceForms system to digitally plan choreography [1,7,8] and the application of systematic notation for choreography [5]. Various tools, such as 'The Choreographer's Notebook', [32] and the 'Creation-Tool' [6] allow choreographers to annotate dances in progress. The Delay Mirror is a digital video system that plays back a video stream of dance movements with a slight delay to allow dancers in a dance studio to pay attention to details of movement [23]. Recently, Ribeiro et al. used 3D data capture and point cloud visualization to capture the dance-making process [27].

There are also technologies for helping to analyze and represent performance, such as in Forsythe's *Synchronous Objects* work [14]. The Synchronous Objects web-site has videos that present visualizations of the performance, many of which have their own artistic merit. BalOnSe is a web-based digital ontology system that allows search, annotation and analysis of existing dance works [11]. Recently, Peeters et al. studied the use of forms to represent the temporal and expressive movement qualities of tango [25].

In addition to understanding the performance, researchers seek to understand how a dance, drama, play or other type of performance might be perceived and understood by an audience. For example, in part of the Dance.Draw project, we used audience sliders to study the effectiveness of a real-time rating system based on galvanic skin response sensors [16]. Other researchers have since developed more sophisticated systems for audience response [20,28,33]. Bio-sensing has also been used with participants in interactive dance performance [29].

As a performing art, there are intriguing issues of presence in dance, and the use of technology can serve to either augment, obscure or diminish the presence of a performer [2]. Interactive dance technology provides new areas of exploratory collaboration between choreographers and technologists [10]. There have been numerous applications of technology to the dance performance [9,12]. In 2001, Faver used live video of dancers behind other dancers [13]. The use of motion capture, silhouettes and video filters in dance can be seen in the work of Mandilian [19] and Meador [21]. Various longitudinal projects have involved bringing technology into multiple dance productions, as in our Dance.Draw project [15], and the Association of Dance and Performance Telematics (ADaPT) Project [3]. Loke has investigated how ritual can be used to design interactive and participatory performance art experiences [17,18]. These examples demonstrate that the use of technology in dance is varied and complex.

Documentation and archiving are topics of discussion within performing arts. A performance can be characterized as being ephemeral [26], existing momentarily before disappearing. We see this paradigm in contemporary post-modern dance, where each night of a live dance performance is thought to be unique and self-contained. Recordings are often made for archival purposes, but they never fully represent the live performance. Interestingly, to some critics, attempting to contain the original performance [30] within transcripts, video, or other forms of archival, declassifies it as a performance [26]. In contrast, Rebecca Schneider challenges us to think beyond the problem of performance and disappearance; to consider how a performance remains different [31], possibly through the 'lived experience' and audience members. If we consider the whole gestalt, the performance is encapsulated not only by the live staging, but by the playbills, video recordings, and personal memories that keep the performance alive. A video art piece created from the videos of a live performance could exist as both a separate art piece and a remnant of the original performance thereby keeping it alive.

Video art is not itself a new art form. In 'The History of Video Art' [22], Meigh-Andrews, a video artist, outlines the progression from early art films and the impact of art movements such as Fluxus on the development of avant-garde cinema. He covers the digitization of video forms, through the increasing availability of digital video editing tools to the mass market, and the increasing use of video in art installations, both interactive and passive. Bizzochi has coined the term 'Ambient Video' referring to video art that is meant to be part of an environment, sustaining, but not requiring audience attention [4].

Our video art piece, 'Moderate Recursion,' is neither ambient video, nor is it interactive or simply an art documentary. It is unique in its generation from a combination of different media streams that were created as part of a live dance performance. Media streams that on their own, are often left tucked away in cabinets and are seldom unsealed except for retrospection by their creators. They exist only as echoes of the original performance. Video art pieces like 'Moderator Recursion' bridge the gap between archive and live performance. They are both an extension of what was and something new.

3   Heavy Recursion

'Heavy Recursion' was staged in 2011 as part of the Fall Dance Concert at the University of North Carolina at Charlotte. The theme of the performance was the relationship and impact that technology can have in our lives. Using an overhead camera and a k-means algorithm, the positions of dancers on the stage are used to control components of visualizations projected behind the dancers (see Fig. 1). Spoken words by the dancers and the musical accompaniment were also used as sources of input to create circles or splashes based on the volume or pitch of the sounds (see Fig. 2). Another dancer-controlled technique was to use a gradient-threshold of movement to determine when dancers made drastic changes in their movements (e.g., stop). This was used to create lingering silhouettes that appeared when dancers slowed down momentarily (see Fig. 3). During

Fig. 1. Photo showing the dancers and the projected visualization of a tree structure branching toward the dancers.

Fig. 2. Visualizations tracking dancers and responding to sound (left) and a dancer putting tape down to create a box around other dancers (right).

Fig. 3. Dancers leaving frozen silhouettes as they move (left) and shadows of the dancers are projected onto the screen (right).

Fig. 4. Splashes of colors responding to dancers crumpling and chewing paper (left) and captured snapshots of the movements of the dancer in the box (right). (Color figure online)

the live performance, the team recognized just how compelling the projected visualizations were and decided to separately record the projected visualizations and musical accompaniment.

As part of the Dance.Draw project, audience surveys were conducted with each performance [15]. Surveys were distributed in the Dance Concert program and an announcement was made about the surveys being part of an ongoing research project, to encourage audiences to respond. Surveys were anonymous and were dropped into boxes in the theater lobby. The surveyed audience for 'Heavy Recursion' found the projected visualizations to be a very compelling component of the performance. Our survey data indicated that 70% of the audience members spent a good portion of their time watching the images of the dancers projected onto the screen with 90% of those people indicating that they enjoyed watching projections of the dancers. The results from audience member survey responses further validated the teams' insights on these very compelling components of the performance.

4 Light Recursion

A recorded video of the visualizations was created using QuickTime Pro's screen-capture feature during three of the five performance nights. Audio of the accompaniment, spoken word of the dancers, and prop noises were recorded from the audio board during two of the performance nights. The audio and video were merged using iMovie to create 'Light Recursion.' In choosing which visualization video from three of the performance nights to use for 'Light Recursion,' several questions were raised: Can we mix together sections of the dance from different nights? Should we trim parts that seem long? Part of the novelty of 'Light Recursion' is that most of the video art content was created by the dancers and their movements. A change in a dancer's footing, stage positioning, or the intensity or cadence of their voice led to interesting and different side-effects. In one instance, the sound-responsive visuals appeared too early because of a noise from the audience. With live performances, there are often nuances that make each night of the performance slightly different, though this usually goes unnoticed by the audience. In the end, we decided to keep the video as unedited as possible and only reduce one section where the visuals were static for nearly 30 s while a dancer was clearing the stage.

As we evaluated and discussed 'Light Recursion,' we recognized that there were portions of the art piece that lost some of their impact or meaning without seeing what the dancers were doing on stage. In order to provide viewers with the contextual information necessary to convey the art's intended purpose, it was suggested that we incorporate footage of the live performance into 'Light Recursion'. We thus created the hybrid video art piece, 'Moderate Recursion.'

5 Moderate Recursion

'Moderate Recursion' is a video art piece created when an interactive dance performance was interlaced with video of the live performance in segments where the context of the stage helps the viewers to understand how the dancers, visuals, and technology fit together. The video is 15 min in length, reflecting the full length of the dance performance. In the terminology of Nam June Paik, we are essentially keeping input-time equal to output-time in our video artifact [24].

'Moderate Recursion' opens with video of four dancers in various static positions. A fifth dancer starts to tape a square around the four static dancers. After she lays the first line, we move to a visualization of grey circles appearing in response to the sound of tape being pulled off the tape roll, with circle size mapped to the volume of the sound of the taping. A white square then appears on screen when the dancers inside the box start to move. As they leave this box, their bodies are represented by white silhouettes. After a short time, one dancer re-enters the white square and begins removing the outline. Two of the other dancers then join her. Every time their movements slow, they leave frozen silhouettes in the space where they dwelled. The term ghosting was sometimes also used, to represent the dancers leaving a part of themselves behind as they moved across the stage.

After the dancers leave, the screen is black until a series of rigid green lines (inspired by printed circuit boards) begins to expand across the screen. After filling the screen, the lines erode away and a series of branches, in shades of blue and green, begin to grow and twist across the screen towards the dancers. These branches were inspired by perfboards, where the wiring isn't as clean as printed boards, especially as an electronic prototype becomes more complex. Eventually everything fades to black.

The dancers emerge as silhouettes, which continue to freeze based on their movements. We fade to video of the live performance. The dancers are kneeling together in the corner with their silhouettes appearing behind and above them on the screen. Shadows of the dancers, from a theatre light downstage-left, are being cast onto the screen. There is a co-existence here between the digital projection, the 'analog' shadow projection, and the live dancers. After the dancers perform gestures on the floor, they make their way to the center of the stage. The theatre light turns off, the dancers stand, and a microphone descends. The live video fades out, and we return to seeing only visualizations. We hear voices that speak in 'programming' language and the visualizations react to the pitch and volume of the voices. As the voices fade, we return to the live video and see the dancers crumpling and chewing paper (see Fig. 4 left). The visuals behind them are bright and large with the noise of the crumpling. After they spit out the paper, we fade to a visualization of five sound responsive dots in a circle. We are then left with one dot that moves and paints along the screen. We briefly return to the live video to see a dancer creating a new square on the stage using blue tape.

There are four dancers on stage, but only one is controlling the visualizations. She explores entering and exiting the taped box, revealing a new white square that appears and disappears in the visuals. As she falls gracefully into the box, the video returns to the visualizations. These visualizations keep a timeline of her movements in the form of color-inverted images (see Fig. 4 right) that are displayed or replaced when there is a dramatic change in the amount of motion occurring within the box. The music changes and the screen goes white with a small rotating ticker, similar to the loading timer on many digital devices.

In the final section, the music picks up and we fade to a live-overhead video feed (unfiltered) with five dots at the top (see Fig. 5). As dancers enter, they 'grab' these dots and begin to paint with them. Every so often, the screen cuts to the rotating ticker, during which the dancers drop to the floor and mimic the 'restarting' ticker movement. After a few seconds, it disappears and the painting is cleared. The dancers stand up and begin painting all over. In the final scenes, we fade to the live video where the stage begins to fade to black. The rotating ticker does not disappear this time, and the dancers are stuck in what appears to be an endless recursion of movement. Upon seeing the spinning ticker, some audience members thought the technology had really failed. Being able to view the dancers during this critical final moment, better enables the viewers of 'Moderate Recursion' to experience the connection between technology and themselves.

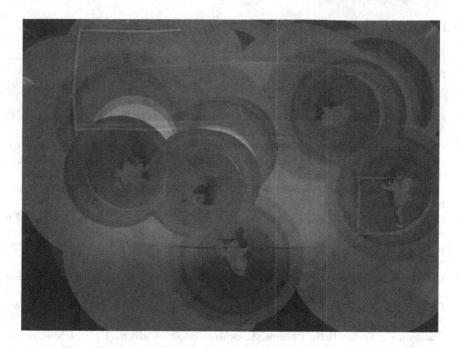

Fig. 5. Sound responsive dots following the dancers.

6 Discussion

'Moderate Recursion' is an artistic artifact through which the community can reflect on the role of technology in our lives, but also experience an interactive dance in a unique presentation format. This is neither live performance nor a filmed dance, but rather a unique art piece created through digital interaction.

It is interesting to consider how other newer technologies could be appropriated to capture live interactive dance and create artifacts that have their own merit. The Delay Mirror, for example, while intended to help dancers study their own movements, could create interesting and thought-provoking artifacts [23]. Current use of social media technologies such as SnapChat could also be used to create stories that become incorporated as new artifacts by both audiences participating and artists involved in the creation of interactive performance.

Acknowledgements. This work was funded by the NSF CreativeIT (#IIS-0855882). We thank the dancers, choreographers, and collaborators who participated in Dance.Draw.

References

1. DanceForms 2.0 - Credo Interactive Inc. http://www.credo-interactive.com/products/danceforms/index.html. Accessed 26 May 2011
2. Birringer, J.: Dance and media technologies. PAJ: J. Perform. Art **24**(1), 84–93 (2002)
3. Birringer, J.: Interactive dance, the body and the internet. J. Vis. Art Pract. **3**(3) (2004)
4. Bizzocchi, J.: Winterscape and ambient video: an intermedia border zone. In: Proceedings of the 16th ACM International Conference on Multimedia, MM 2008, pp. 949–952. ACM, New York (2008)
5. Brown, M.D., Smoliar, S.W.: A graphics editor for labanotation. SIGGRAPH Comput. Graph. **10**(2), 60–65 (1976)
6. Cabral, D., Valente, J.G., Aragão, U., Fernandes, C., Correia, N.: Evaluation of a multimodal video annotator for contemporary dance. In: Proceedings of the International Working Conference on Advanced Visual Interfaces, AVI 2012, pp. 572–579. ACM, New York (2012)
7. Calvert, T.W., Bruderlin, A., Mah, S., Schiphorst, T., Welman, C.: The evolution of an interface for choreographers. In: Proceedings of the INTERACT 1993 and CHI 1993 conference on Human Factors in Computing Systems, pp. 115–122. ACM, New York (1993)
8. Carlson, K., Tsang, H.H., Phillips, J., Schiphorst, T., Calvert, T.: Sketching movement: designing creativity tools for in-situ, whole-body authorship. In: Proceedings of the 2nd International Workshop on Movement and Computing, MOCO 2015, pp. 68–75. ACM, New York (2015)
9. deSpain, K.: Dance and technology: a pas de deux for post-humans. Dance Res. J. **32**(1), 2–17 (2000)
10. El Raheb, K., Ioannidis, Y.: From dance notation to conceptual models: a multi-layer approach. In: Proceedings of the 2014 International Workshop on Movement and Computing, MOCO 2014, pp. 25:25–25:30. ACM, New York (2014)
11. El Raheb, K., Papapetrou, N., Katifori, V., Ioannidis, Y.: BalOnSe: ballet ontology for annotating and searching video performances. In: Proceedings of the 3rd International Symposium on Movement and Computing, MOCO 2016, pp. 5:1–5:8. ACM, New York (2016)
12. Farley, K.: Digital dance theatre: the marriage of computers, choreography and techno/human reactivity. Body Space Technol. **3**(1), 39–46 (2002)
13. Faver, C., Stein, G.: Toward a digital stage architecture: a long-term research agenda in digitally enabled theater. IEEE MultiMedia **4**, 6–9 (2001)
14. Forsythe, W., Palazzi, M., Zuniga Shaw, N., deLahunta, S.: Synchronous objects for one flat thing, reproduced. In: 2009 Website Installation or On Line Resource, Columbus, Ohio. The Ohio State University and The Forsythe Company (2009)
15. Latulipe, C., Carroll, E.A., Lottridge, D.: Evaluating longitudinal projects combining technology with temporal arts. In: Proceedings of the SIGCHI Conference on Human Factors in Computing Systems, CHI 2011, pp. 1835–1844. ACM, New York(2011)
16. Latulipe, C., Carroll, E.A., Lottridge, D.: Love, hate, arousal and engagement: exploring audience responses to performing arts. In: Proceedings of the SIGCHI Conference on Human Factors in Computing Systems, CHI 2011, pp. 1845–1854. ACM, New York (2011)

17. Loke, L., Khut, G.P., Kocaballi, A.B.: Bodily experience and imagination: designing ritual interactions for participatory live-art contexts. In: Proceedings of the Designing Interactive Systems Conference, DIS 2012, pp. 779–788. ACM, New York (2012)

18. Loke, L., Robertson, T.: Studies of dancers: moving from experience to interaction design. Int. J. Des. 4(2) (2010)

19. Mandilian, L.E., Diefenbach, P., Kim, Y.: Information overload: a collaborative dance performance. In: Proceedings of the 1st ACM International Workshop on Semantic Ambient Media Experiences, pp. 57–60. ACM (2008)

20. Martella, C., Gedik, E., Cabrera-Quiros, L., Englebienne, G., Hung, H.: How was it?: Exploiting smartphone sensing to measure implicit audience responses to live performances. In: Proceedings of the 23rd ACM International Conference on Multimedia, MM 2015, pp. 201–210. ACM, New York (2015)

21. Meador, W.S., Rogers, T.J., O'Neal, K., Kurt, E., Cunningham, C.: Mixing dance realities: collaborative development of live-motion capture in a performing arts environment. Comput. Entertain. (CIE) 2(2), 12 (2004)

22. Meigh-Andrews, C.: A History of Video Art. A&C Black (2013)

23. Molina-Tanco, L., García-Berdonés, C., Reyes-Lecuona, A.: The delay mirror: a technological innovation specific to the dance studio. In: Proceedings of the 4th International Conference on Movement Computing, MOCO 2017, pp. 9:1–9:6. ACM, New York (2017)

24. Paik, N.J.: Input-time and output-time. Video art: an anthology, p. 98 (1976)

25. Peeters, J., Trotto, A.: Designing expressions of movement qualities. In: Proceedings of the 2018 Designing Interactive Systems Conference, DIS 2018, pp. 679–690. ACM, New York (2018)

26. Phelan, P.: Unmarked: The Politics of Performance. Routledge, London (1993)

27. Ribeiro, C., dos Anjos, R.K., Fernandes, C.: Capturing and documenting creative processes in contemporary dance. In: Proceedings of the 4th International Conference on Movement Computing, MOCO 2017, pp. 7:1–7:7. ACM, New York (2017)

28. Röggla, T., Wang, C., César, P.S.: Analysing audience response to performing events: a web platform for interactive exploration of physiological sensor data. In: Proceedings of the 23rd ACM International Conference on Multimedia, MM 2015, pp. 749–750. ACM, New York (2015)

29. Rostami, A., McMillan, D., Márquez Segura, E., Rossito, C., Barkhuus, L.: Biosensed and embodied participation in interactive performance. In: Proceedings of the Eleventh International Conference on Tangible, Embedded, and Embodied Interaction, TEI 2017, pp. 197–208. ACM, New York (2017)

30. Schechner, R.: Between Theater & Anthropology. University of Pennsylvania Press, Philadelphia (1985)

31. Schneider, R.: Performance remains. Perform. Res. 6(2), 100–108 (2001)

32. Singh, V., Latulipe, C., Carroll, E., Lottridge, D.: The choreographer's notebook - a video annotation system for dancers and choreographers. In: Proceedings of the 2011 Conference on Creativity & Cognition, C&C 2011, pp. 197–206, New York (2011)

33. Yan, S., et al.: Exploring audience response in performing arts with a brain-adaptive digital performance system. ACM Trans. Interact. Intell. Syst. 7(4), 16:1–16:28 (2017)

Worldmaking: Designing for Audience Participation, Immersion and Interaction in Virtual and Real Spaces

Andreas Siess[1]([⊠]), Daniel Hepperle[1], Matthias Wölfel[1],
and Michael Johansson[2]

[1] Karlsruhe University of Applied Sciences, Moltkestr. 30, 76133 Karlsruhe, Germany
{andreas.siess,daniel.hepperle,matthias.wolfel}@hs-karlsruhe.de
[2] Kristianstad University, Elmetorpsvägen 15, 291 88 Kristianstad, Sweden
michael.johansson@hkr.se

Abstract. Artists often try to open up new experiences for people, challenging them to extend horizons and perception. This becomes particularly relevant when thinking about experiencing built environments: Here, technologies like Cave Automatic Virtual Environments (CAVE) or Head-Mounted Displays (HMD) can be used as a tool to offer richer experiences to the audience in both art installations and exhibitions. We have been developing several exhibitions tackling the challenges that come with exhibiting in (semi -) public spaces: how do we engage visitors in our exhibitions, what role do bystanders play and how can this be considered in the development and design process? The exhibitions were built in a chronological order (2015–2018) and increasing degree of immersion and interaction. For exhibition one ("step-in/Ideal Spaces"), we built a CAVE-like "tryptic" projection showing linear pre-rendered videos of seven different built environments. In exhibition two ("fly-over/Super Nubibus") we build a replica of a hot-air-balloon and let people experience architecture from birds eye view using a HMD. Exhibition three ("cruise/Biketopia") is also an immersive VR using a HMD, but from a very different angle. Here we use a bike to let people actively explore a space by regulating speed and direction of the bike. By using the discreet method of observation, we ensured that the visitors were not disturbed in their experience, which in turn would falsify our findings. So we are able to compare and discuss these three approaches in regards to the above mentioned criteria within this paper.

Keywords: Virtual reality · Spatial perception · Exhibition
(Semi-) public space · Architecture · Museum

1 Introduction

Prototyping and exploring worlds and environments for creating exhibitions with and through technology we sometimes use consumer technology that shortens

A. L. Brooks et al. (Eds.): ArtsIT 2018/DLI 2018, LNICST 265, pp. 58–68, 2019.
https://doi.org/10.1007/978-3-030-06134-0_7

and speeds up our work process, and we can start sketching in hard- and software already early in the conceptual phase of a project. Even consumer products today come with a developing kit and widely open APIs which make them suitable also for experiments and research. One risk although here is that one as an artist, designer and/or researcher gets trapped inside of the presumed future use of this technology, with all limitations that comes with that [9]. Relying on "produced" technology we clearly see a need for a set of tactics to bring our work in our own direction. In our recent practice based work and research, that focuses on exhibition work that spans from 2015 and onwards, we have returned to the idea that if we want to have an audience or a visitor experience 3D spaces of different sorts in an exhibition format, we need to find ways for the visitor to enter, interact and experience these virtual worlds, without too much former knowledge how to enter, navigate and perceive them in order to have the visitor feel both present and immersed by them. Because there is always a risk with new, not seen and experienced technologies that we have the visitor exploring, the technology itself instead rather than the topic of our attention, e.g. spatial constructions. Through our work we gained knowledge that many forms of interaction takes hours of practice to learn and even longer time to master, and therefore are not fit for use directly in an exhibition, but valuable tools for us as artists, designers and technicians to help us create things that have not existed before. In this line of work, we have learned that configuring space via user participation and interaction is not easy, but crucial for an immersed experience to take place. Throughout our work, developing, methods, tools and processes we try to emphasize the importance of a multiperspective view of space and its entities based on the idea to transcend merely scientific or artistic approaches into a more comprehensive and immediate approach and working practice, in which we try to use different forms of interaction and telepresence to create a state of immersion. It is about symbolic objects and entireties (the issue of "Gestalt", not about mere construction and functions). To have the created worlds to stand out as something believable (the issue of "representation") and how through thoughtfully designed user interaction can create an immersive experience for the visitor.

2   Our Three Use Cases: Step in, Fly over and Cruise

The origins of the environments for this article: The used spaces are all derived from the exhibition at the Biennale of Architecture in Venice 2016. Starting from this basis, selected places (i.e. the shown worlds) were made accessible with new media devices in order to explore how the spatial impression is changing as a result of this new approach.

Fig. 1. User's perspective: (a) "step in" (b) "fly over" (c) "cruise" as WiP.

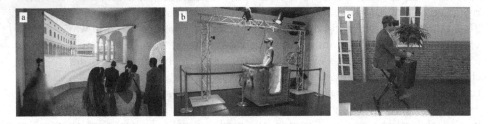

Fig. 2. Setup: (a) "step in" (b) "fly over" (c) "cruise"

2.1   Step in: The CAVE Installation

The installation[1] was shown from May to November as part of the Architectural Biennale 2016 in Venice. The setup consisted of three projectors displaying a seamless image onto a tryptic screen (total size: 3.60 × 6.0 m) (See: Fig. 2(a)). The screen itself consisted of three canvases, each at an angle of 150° to each other. This CAVE-like installation—where also the user's peripheral viewport was covered—allowed each visitor to "dive" into the shown environments and therefore enabled an immersive experience, and to create a bodily notion of that featured space. On this projection screen, pre-rendered movies were shown. Due to the fact that the camera movement was not bound to any (simulated) physical or time constraints free movement in all dimensions was possible: The environments were shown from different perspectives, but always with a constant focal length (35 mm). This approach was chosen in order to offer visitors a realistic size estimation and a feeling of "being there" (dweller/pedestrian).

Findings: A: Size matters, being almost inside of a projection in a cave projection creates a presence of the spaces shown. **B:** Since every visitor individually can approach the cave projection and also share the experience directly with others. **C:** No technical barrier for the users to overcome. **D:** Immediateness: No latency/lag and low-threshold for a majority of users.

---

[1] Created by ideal spaces working group 2016 (Matthias Wölfel, Michael Johansson, Daniel Hepperle, Andreas Siess, Ulrich Gehmann et al.).

2.2   Fly over: The Balloon Installation

For the ZKM—Center for Arts and Media in Karlsruhe, Germany we wanted to set up an installation that is connected to the place where it is exhibited. Because of its special kind of city planning ("fan city") we already presented a version of Karlsruhe in our CAVE Installation and therefore it was of interest for us to make it accessible (here: Karlsruhe from 1834) from another perspective by riding over it via a balloon. In general spaced VR installations have some inherent disadvantages for each individual visitor: The action space available to the user is very limited and any danger of collision must be prevented in advance, e.g. by displaying warnings ("chaperones"). How useful these interventions might be, they strongly interrupt the immersive experience. Therefore, a concept is required that plays creatively with the limitations of VR and simultaneously offers firm support in case of need. Hence we developed an installation that naturally and credibly shapes the playing space without being perceived as a limitation. We chose to build a replica of a balloon-basket that is also mapped 1:1 in the virtual environment (See: Figs. 1(b) and 2(b)). With this setup our installation features: 1. birds-eye perspective for experiencing the special kind of Karlsruhe's architecture 2. slow movements to reduce motion sickness 3. When wanting to ride/fly over a city there currently is a rise in hardware that require users to strap themselves onto it, which might be not perfectly suitable for (semi-) public space and also for physically handicapped or introverted people (see [21] or [17]) and therefore we thought a balloon might suit better. In addition, clinging to the balloons railing also reduces motion sickness and increases immersion [3]. To start the ride, visitors had to enter the nacelle, which is also represented within the virtual environment and pull down the rope (represented in physical and virtual space) to start the ride/virtual burner (See: Fig. 2(b)). The ride took place on a pre-given path with the possibility to change height by pulling down the rope to fuel the burner. In the real environment, the burner was represented by spotlights which radiated enough heat and was augmented with vibrations of the nacelle to foster the illusion. Another trick to further improve the illusion of flying, was to add an airstream using a fan. This, of course, is not correct from a physical point of view, but fits well to most of the visitors (most of them who have not yet experienced a real balloon ride).

Findings: A: One can increase immersion using elements that might not be physically correct (wind in a balloon, vibration when pulling the trigger). **B:** One can regulate viewing direction by implementing spatially located audio files. **C:** Intentionally regulating the given space by using a physical restriction also displayed in the virtual world (nacelle) helps people to orientate oneself within the virtual reality. **D:** Although HMDs are becoming increasingly popular and we added clear instructions next to the exhibition, museum guides still had to attend the exhibition to help out the visitors.

2.3   Cruise: The Bike Installation

The bike installation was shown to a broader public in an art/design performance/exhibition in two cities (Kristianstad and Copenhagen). In this art/design project with the bike we returned to Jeffrey Shaw's original idea from 1986, "Legible City" [18]. The Bike installation was one of five stations in which the visitors could explore different ideas about urban development, here in this installation we had the visitors to visit 15th century Milano to experience a conceptual city space never realized. "As a space, [it] is constructed in such a way that we always have the impression to see only a fragment, a more or less small section of it—because at every meters x, the next structural element can appear, ad infinitum" [5]. For this project we use a VirZoom bike with its speed and direction sensors to explore two of the worlds from the 2016 exhibition. Here we want to see what happens when you take some worlds developed for animation/film and translate that world into real time graphics (Unity3d). What specific qualities get lost and which transfers well?

Findings: A: Direct immersion for the visitor when entering a virtual world with a familiar navigational device such as the bike. They know how to direct themselves almost immediately and there is a low threshold to learn how to navigate oneself. **B:** Biking is not walking, therefore a space needs some adjustment: this was a bit tricky since this world needs to be changed to fit navigation by bicycle rather than by walking, for example have the bicycle go from one floor to the next, using stairs could have been an option, but does not relate very well to cruising—it will be a bumpy ride. We also wanted to keep the original plan of the city and not introducing "modern" or "alien" elements into it. So to keep the flow in constantly biking through Milano, we used ramps as discreet as possible integrated in the original environment to move the visitor on it's bicycle in between the different levels of the city, and at the same time point the biking experience for the visitor into new directions. **C:** The bike soon became an important tool developing the worlds—iterating between modeling/texturing/lighting and the experience of the changes made by bicycling in that area of attention. **D:** It made us aware of the difference between seeing something on the screen (editing) and experience it in full VR [19]. **E:** The bike itself is as we found out also a camera rig and can be used for classical camera work to get camera data out to other 3d programs but also to produce animation paths for Unity3d itself.

3   Thoughts on Audience Participation

One downside that comes with head mounted devices (HMD) in (semi-) public spaces is, that they can only be used by one person at the time. In addition, while experiencing the virtual world, the person who wears the HMD is almost completely isolated from his surrounding although other visitors can easily observe him. This "voyeurism" behavior is quite similar to the one described as one of the first parts of the audience funnel framework by Michelis and Müller 2011 [15]. Their framework is based on observations made in regards to interactions with public displays, but while they argue that visitors either pass by the display or view and react, we would like to add another category: The voyeur implicitly does not want to experience the VR exhibition, but wants to passively observe and find out what is happening. While in general, the term voyeurism has a rather unpleasant notion, in this setting, this behaviour can lead to a honey-pot effect, which then will bring other people to observe and interact with the current user/voyeur or to try it by oneself. There are several possibilities one can come up with to include bystanders into the installation (see Fig. 3): **1.** Directly display the virtual world onto a 2D display placed so that bystanders and voyeurs can see it. **2.** Include the actual user into the 3d world using a greenscreen as described by Intel in 2017 [22]. **3.** (Floor) projections [7,23]. **4.** Project facial expression on the front of the VR headset for bystanders to see it [11,13]. There is also a lot to decide about on how to add auditory cues, but it would extend the scope of this discussion[2]. In our current state, we are considering several possibilities in engaging visitors to interact with the current user. For example: should the visitor be able to see the virtual content on a 2D screen *before* he got fully immersed into the virtual environment via HMD or should one try to only make the content visible for participants *after* they went into the virtual reality itself?

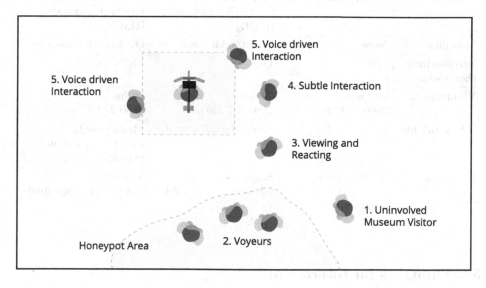

Fig. 3. Audience "funnel" for "Biketopia" VR exhibition.

4   Thoughts on Immersion

By using familiar or at least conventional devices, such as the CAVE, the balloon and the bike, the users' direct physical presence in the virtual environment rein-

---

[2] Kuutti 2014 discusses some of the different possibilities in (semi-) public spaces [10].

forced the sense of physical presence of the virtual world and the interactivity of the respective space or device used in our case studies enhance their sense of immersion. We tried to lay the "focus on the activity, not the technology" and made "the control mechanism obvious" [14] when designing the necessary technical part of our installations. Conversely, this means that immersion cannot be designed directly, but that we have ensured that as many interfering factors as possible are eliminated. As an artist/designer one should always be aware that one never designs the actual immersed experience itself, but only the framework wherein that experience can take place. Since the amount of immersion is not easily measurable, we classify our three works by using the parameters Slater and Wilbur came up with [20]. As one can see in Table 1 the range of sensor modalities (Extensiveness) used, varies. Also the idea on how visitors can interact (Interactability) with the different installations is altered between the exhibitions.

Table 1. Immersion in dependence on to the parameters defined in [20]

	Cave	Balloon	Bike
Extensiveness	Linear audio, video	3D spatial audio, interactive visuals (HMD)	3D spatial audio interactive visuals (HMD)
Matching	None	Vive tracking sensors	Oculus rift sensors
Surroundness (horizontal)	120°	110°	110°
Vividness	30 fps 3600 × 1920 px	60 fps 2160 × 1200 px	30 fps 2160 × 1200 px
Interactability	None	Start, change height	Start, change direction, position, velocity
Experience	Multi person	Single user (observation possible)	Single user (observation possible)

5   Thoughts on Interaction

On interaction we played safe and in each of our examples we deliberately used well familiar forms of interaction by having the visitor, "step into", "fly over" or "cruise" our different environments. We wanted established forms that helped the visitors more directly make the transition from the physical world on a device they already used or at least seen before. Therefore interactivity and navigation used in both the balloon and the bike was directly added to the experience by a tight coupling between display, the movements of the user's body (when maneuvering the device) on which they made the transition from one world to another. In the case of the CAVE example there were no interaction through any technology, here we instead used the design of the physical space itself to have the visitor just step into the worlds showed. Fundamentally, we can state that the concept of affordance [6] from interaction design can also play to its strengths in our context: Although it is ultimately just a sophisticated controller for a virtual environment, the bicycle is clearly recognizable to every visitor. This simplicity and accessibility effectively prevents fears of contact and takes little time to get used to. The balloon can show these strengths even more effectively: The basket restricts the possible degrees of freedom very effectively without actually being perceived as a plain restriction or overruling. We believe that the museal context demands this mixture of strict constraints and clear affordances to be successful. As a designer it is our job to find concepts that integrate these principles into a harmonious environment that plays creatively with these limitations and, at best, uses them as framework for conceptual design.

6 Developing Visual Style and Aesthetics

Developing through iteration is common practice in many art/design disciplines and also for our type of work in which we strive to facilitate an openness towards what happens in-between the design cycles. Similar to the OODA-Loop [2] in which one Observes, Orients, Decides and takes Action, in our case to challenge the machine and software logic and our own limits and conventions, to produce something that is both unexpected and valuable, and in the end will point out possible new directions. So using this loop switching between the state of editing (tweaking the parameters) and experience (being there) help us develop and put forward qualities (that sometimes is produced by errors or wrongdoings) that are hidden from the concept's point of view and by doing so—have the concept redeveloped itself through the results and experiences we achieve by iteration. We try to explore what is being shadowed by the concept itself. Therefore we do not formulate any detailed specification in relation to the concept beforehand, or rather loosely "not photo real" or "do not use textures". But at the same time it is important for us to be able to control or at least understand the in- and outputs of the development environment itself—from bits to spaces. The shortcomings, errors and quirks are vital resources that suddenly can reveal themselves as major feature with specific new qualities. When trying to follow the design intention or concept, the materials/methods and prototypes themselves and when we are "bending" [4] them, can produce qualities not known beforehand. In our line of practice-based work for this to happen, the production needs to reach a certain state of complexity, to be able for all of the possible parameters to be explored thoroughly and have an impact on the details as well as the whole. Therefore a production environment itself is crucial to facilitate practice based research in the area of art and design, where one can game the rules of play [9], otherwise there is a risk that art/design projects are just illustrations of technology, and technology driven projects unreflected use conventions and qualities from art. In the three projects we specifically address this in the visual styles we tried to develop. At present, one of the most important parameters to benchmark an experience in VR is "realism". But realism even technologically advanced is still a cultural construction [12]. And realism in relation to digital simulated ones, is not realism, it is reality seen by the camera lens, as Allen points out "The intention of all technological systems developed since the beginning of the 1950s has been towards reducing the spectators sense of their real world, and replacing it with a fully believable artificial one" [1]. And even if realism would be possible in a perfect replica, it is still a blunt showcase of technological frameworks and not an independent aesthetic quality. If one really wanted to depict physical realism in its original form, then a theoretically infinitely level of detail would be necessary, which not only seems technically impossible, but in particular also not desirable from an artistic perspective. So when designing our environments in the first we have deliberately decided to work in favor of this non realistic approach, to find a level that is believable rather then realistic. For example we used the same light and shaders to develop a common style that connected the seven disparate worlds from our first project with each other, to find a reasonable level to avoid the uncanny valley—a mismatch or break in presence where believability does not clash with falsehood [16]. And it is also important to avoid that, "the virtual environment becomes less immersive since they lose the interest and engagement of the user envision the reconciliation of immersion and interactivity" [15]. During our iterative design process, a visual aesthetic gradually emerged that portrayed the spatial situation in a very minimalistic, reduced yet consistent way. In the context of the "hunt for realism", we constructed just the opposite: a world that deviates completely from this ideal and only shows details where they are indispensable. And that's why we assume these environments worked so well in our use case: because we found that consistent and credible design is not tied to photorealism–although this hypothesis needs empirical foundation in our future user tests.

7   Future Work

Currently we are actively working on *Motopia*—an environment designed by Geoffrey Jellicoe in the 1960ies [8]—to enable this space for the VR-bike as well as for a VR-car simulation. Since this conceptual environment was once meant to be *the* city of motor-mobility we are interested if the 3D bike is able to tap these potentials. For the *Biketopia* installation we are currently thinking about letting the user take pictures from within the virtual environment and only present those pictures to the audience (bystanders, voyeurs etc.). This could improve conversation between the user and the bystanders in such a way, that they want to ask more questions and maybe want to experience the world itself. In addition, the pictures might help the authors to get an idea of what the actual users think might be the most interesting parts of their journey. We then can evaluate this and improve our work based on this feedback. For the balloon flight we implemented an *Immersit Shaker System*, which simulated the vibrations of a balloon's basket and ensured direct haptic feedback for pulling the drawstring.

We expect that the repetitive vibration that occurs when the (virtual) expansion joints of the roadway are passed once again clearly emphasizes the spatial impression as the underlying concept of *Motopia* as a modern era functional city. In regards to our observations on audience participation, the next step will be to monitor visitor-behaviour via top-down camera to generate heat-maps in regards to where they are while they are in the balloon's "sphere of activity" We will continue to further investigate how space in different media is represented via media technology and how it is used.

References

1. Allen, M.: Technology in Contemporary Hollywood Cinema. Taylor & Francis, New York (2013)
2. Boyd, J.: Organic design for command and control (2005). https://www.ausairpower.net/JRB/organic_design.pdf. Accessed 15 July 2018
3. Carrozzino, M., Bergamasco, M.: Beyond virtual museums: experiencing immersive virtual reality in real museums. J. Cult. Herit. **11**, 452–458 (2010)
4. Eagleman, D., Brandt, A.: The Runaway Species: How Human Creativity Remakes the World. Catapult, London (2017)
5. Gehmann, U.: Exhibition Venice 2016–ideal spaces (2016). https://www.idealspaces.org/exhibition-venice-2016/#leonardodivinci. Accessed 29 Sept 2018
6. Hartson, R.: Cognitive, physical, sensory, and functional affordances in interaction design. Behav. Inf. Technol. **22**(5), 315–338 (2003)
7. Ishii, A., et al.: ReverseCAVE. In: ACM SIGGRAPH 2017. ACM Press (2017)
8. Jellicoe, G.: Motopia: A Study in the Evolution of Urban Landscape (1961)
9. Kajo, M., Johansson, M.: Common playground. In: Proceedings of Cast01 (2001)
10. Kuutti, J., Leiwo, J., Sepponen, R.E.: Local control of audio environment: a review of methods and applications. Technologies **2**(1), 31–53 (2014)
11. Kwatra, V., Frueh, C., Sud, A.: Headset "removal" for virtual and mixed reality. https://ai.googleblog.com/2017/02/headset-removal-for-virtual-and-mixed.html. Accessed 15 July 2018
12. Lister, M., Giddings, S., Dovey, J., Grant, I., Kelly, K.: New Media: A Critical Introduction. Routledge, Abingdon (2010)
13. Mai, C., Rambold, L., Khamis, M.: TransparentHMD: revealing the HMD user's face to bystanders. In: Proceedings of the 16th International Conference on Mobile and Ubiquitous Multimedia. MUM 2017, pp. 515–520. ACM (2017)
14. Maynes-Aminzade, D., Pausch, R., Seitz, S.: Techniques for interactive audience participation. In: Proceedings of the 4th IEEE International Conference on Multimodal Interfaces, p. 15. IEEE Computer Society (2002)
15. Michelis, D., Müller, J.: The audience funnel: observations of gesture based interaction with multiple large displays in a city center. Int. J. HCI **27**(6), 562–579 (2011)
16. Mori, M.: Bukimi no tani [the uncanny valley]. Energy **7**, 33–35 (1970)
17. Revresh: Para parachute! http://revresh.com/paraparachute/. Accessed 15 July 2018
18. Shaw, J., Groeneveld, D.: Legible city. https://www.jeffreyshawcompendium.com/portfolio/legible-city/. Accessed 15 Sept 2018
19. Sieß, A., Häffner, N., Wölfel, M.: Color preference differences between head mounted displays and PC screens. IEEE (2018)

20. Slater, M., Wilbur, S.: A framework for immersive virtual environments (FIVE): speculations on the role of presence in virtual environments. Presence-Teleop. Virt. Environ. **6**(6), 603–616 (1997)
21. Somniacs: Birdly - the ultimate dream of flying. http://www.somniacs.co/. Accessed 15 July 2018
22. Tyrrell, J., Bancroft, J., Gerald, M.: Sharing VR through green screen mixed reality video (2017). https://software.intel.com/en-us/articles/sharing-vr-through-green-screen-mixed-reality-video. Accessed 12 June 2018
23. Zenner, A., Kosmalla, F., Speicher, M., Daiber, F., Krüger, A.: A projection-based interface to involve semi-immersed users in substitutional realities. IEEE (2018)

The Development of Băi/摆: An Oscillating Sound Installation

Danyi Liu[1(✉)], Jelger Kroese[2], and Edwin van der Heide[1]

[1] Leiden Institute of Advanced Computer Science, Leiden, The Netherlands
{d.liu.7,e.f.van.der.heide}@liacs.leidenuniv.nl
[2] Leiden University, Leiden, The Netherlands
j.kroese@umail.leidenuniv.nl

Abstract. Băi is an interactive sound installation that uses a pendulum speaker as an interface for audience participation. We track the movement of the hanging speaker with an HTC Vive tracker which allows to use its motion as input for the interactive dialogue. A 6-speaker setup is surrounding the pendulum and reacting to it. While interacting, the behaviour of the installation changes and goes through different states and levels of excitement. This results in a dynamically changing sound environment for the audience to explore. This paper elucidates the design goals we intended to achieve for the audience experience and the behaviour of the installation. We present a comprehensive description of the development process, including physical, software and sound design. Meanwhile, we discus different forms of interacting with the pendulum speaker and the surrounding speakers.

Keywords: Interactive sound installation · Interactive interface
Pendulum speaker

1 Introduction

Since the invention of the loudspeaker researchers, composers and artists have explored various ways of using speakers ranging from multi-channel speaker setups and hemispherical speaker designs to speaker sculptures and wearable speaker-based instruments. While speakers are often used in static positions, Gordon Monahan's *Speaker Swinging*, first performed in 1982, applies a moving speaker as a musical instrument for live performance. The three performers each swing a loudspeaker in circles with a sine or square wave as source signal [2]. The resulting sound is subject to the Doppler effect and the acoustic properties of the space. In his *Pendulum Music* [3], Steve Reich pioneered the pendulum principle. The performance involves phasing feedback tones resulting from suspended microphones swinging above the speakers. *Spatial Sounds* (100 dB *at* 100 km/h) by Marnix de Nijs and Edwin van der Heide (2000, 2001) is an interactive installation using a moving speaker. The installation interprets

A. L. Brooks et al. (Eds.): ArtsIT 2018/DLI 2018, LNICST 265, pp. 69–79, 2019.
https://doi.org/10.1007/978-3-030-06134-0_8

the visitor's position and movement and reacts to it both with its movements and the real-time generated sound. In return, the visitors react to the installation and go through different experiences and emotions [1]. What these works share is that they exploit the physical properties of a moving sound source (or microphone) in their design.

Fig. 1. 3D model of the space setup for Băi: an oscillation sound installation.

We have developed the interactive installation: Băi: an Oscillating Sound Installation. It applies a moving speaker in the form of a pendulum as an interface for the audience to interact with. The pendulum speaker is suspended from the ceiling and is surrounded by a 6-speaker setup standing on the floor (see Fig. 1). The speaker is touched and moved by the audience and reacts to it by means of sound. Furthermore, the surrounding speakers react to the pendulum approaching them resulting in a dynamic sound environment. Like in *Spatial Sounds* (100 dB *at* 100 km/h), the speaker senses the actions of the audience and reacts to them. Therefore there is no distinction between the input and output interface and the audience experiences a direct response from moving the pendulum speaker [1]. For the design of the audience interaction, we make use of the pendulum speaker's physical swinging behaviour. We have developed an algorithm to predict the natural swinging movement so that we can distinguish its self-movement from movement caused by the audience pushing, pulling and rotating the speaker. This allows us to react directly to the audience actions.

This paper describes and reflects on both the technical and artistic decisions that were made during the design and development of the interactive sound installation Băi. It covers the design goals and a short reflection upon what we have achieved so far.

2   The Installation

The name of the installation, Bǎi, is transliterated from the Chinese character "摆", meaning pendulum. The installation consists of a pendulum speaker, hanging on a cable from the ceiling at 2 m above floor height and 6 floor-standing speakers placed in a circle around the pendulum speaker. An HTC Vive base station is mounted on the wall inside the room, and emits infrared signals. An HTC Vive tracker is placed on top of the pendulum speaker, in order to continuously collect the absolute position and orientation data of the speaker in the room. The data is transmitted to a computer running a patch in Pure Data, a real-time graphical programming environment for audio and graphical processing [5]. We have programmed the sensor interpretation, rules for the interactive behaviour and the real-time sound synthesis for the surrounding speakers in Pure Data. Furthermore, Pure Data is controlling a software synthesiser in Ableton Live for the sound generation of the pendulum speaker itself.

2.1   The Pendulum Speaker

A pendulum has a clear inherent behaviour. The natural movement of the pendulum is an oscillating motion that slowly decays because of the friction with the air. This makes interacting with the pendulum speaker (and thereby the installation) not so much a process of having full control over the system, but rather a process of using and directing the behaviour of the pendulum. In order for it to produce swings that would not move too fast or tilt too high, the length, weight and mounting point of the cable that holds the pendulum are important design parameters. We established a minimum cable length of 3 m. The mounting point of the cable is placed 0.5 m above the pendulum's centre of weight, to keep the speaker relatively stable.

We do not want the pendulum speaker to only act as an interface for triggering sounds in the surrounding speakers but intend to give it a form of interactive and expressive behaviour itself as well. In order to achieve this the surrounding speakers not only react to the movement of the pendulum speaker but the pendulum speaker also expresses its own movement in its sound and clearly reacts to people touching and moving the speaker.

2.2   The Space

For the first presentation of the installation we chose to use six surrounding speakers placed in a circle around the pendulum. Each of the surrounding speakers is functioning as a separate entity that individually reacts to the pendulum's movement. The audience can clearly recognise the interaction between the pendulum and the surrounding speakers since the sounds are spatialised around them and therefore easily localised. The installation is not meant to only interact with a single audience member. The swinging movement in space makes it possible for multiple audience members to interact with the installation at the same time. In that case the audience does not only interact with the speaker but

Fig. 2. The audience interacting with Bǎi at NIME 2018.

also interacts with each other through the installation. Furthermore, the audience can play different roles and alternate between engaging with the installation or observing it (See Fig. 2).

3   Interaction Design

Our approach to developing the interaction and behaviour of the installation is such that we interpret the term interaction as a dialogue between the audience and the installation. In such a dialogue the two parties communicate and react to each other while neither of the two parties is fully predictable, nor has full control over the situation. It is therefore important for us to create a surprising but nevertheless easy to understand form of interactive behaviour. The interactive behaviour is not static but develops in order to realise an interesting ongoing dialogue. We have set a number of goals to help us achieve this: (1) use analogies between the physical input and sonic output of the system, (2) give the audience the experience of interacting with a system that reacts to their input but also surprises them with its own unpredictable behaviour, (3) make the audience aware that their actions impact the way the system behaves, without being able to fully control it, and (4) make the audience perceive the system as 'beautiful', but also (potentially) 'upset' or 'dangerous' through the changes of its behaviour (see Sect. 4).

At the core of the design is the choice to use a pendulum speaker as interface to interact with the installation. Through pushing, pulling and rotating the speaker, the audience can set the pendulum into different oscillating motions. The installation does not have a fixed form of interaction but alternates between different rules (and therefore different modes of behaviour) depending on the state the installation is in. At first, it may seem that the environment reacts to the motions predictably. However, the pendulum's self-movement influences the system's behaviour, even when the audience does not directly interact with it, which brings unforeseen results. This, combined with the fact that hard physical labour is needed to restrain the pendulum, leads to a tense dialogue between the participant and object, struggling for control. The movements resulting from this dialogue cause the sounds in the environment to change between different states of stability and chaos.

3.1 Physical Interaction

As we mentioned before the pendulum itself has a strong and clear form of, what we call, natural behaviour. The audience is interacting with this behaviour by accelerating, holding and rotating the speaker. It can swing in a line or a circular way. After touching the speaker, it will continue to oscillate corresponding to the new energy applied to it. We decided to try to distinguish the natural motion of the pendulum from the audience interacting with it. In order to do this, we have developed an algorithm that learns the period, phase and amplitude of the swinging behaviour, we then analyse and compare the current phase and position of the pendulum with the predicted natural movement. This way (human) interruptions of the natural movement can be immediately detected and its energy can be quantified by calculating the amount of deviation. The detected human energy put in to the installation is used to influence the sonic and interactive behaviour of both the pendulum speaker and the surrounding speakers. After interacting with the speaker, the algorithm learns the new swing movement and interprets it as the new natural movement. We believe that this direct form of interaction, realised in this way, gives the audience a feeling that the pendulum is alive and able to respond to the audience's actions. We intent this to result in a playful and physically intensive interactive endeavour.

3.2 Software Development

One of our goals for the experience of the installation was to give the audience the feeling that they are interacting with a system that has a form of autonomous behaviour. The installation was designed to noticeably react to the audience, but also have a certain amount of unpredictability in how it reacts. Furthermore, in order to motivate the audience to interact with the installation for longer periods of time, we chose to let the behaviour evolve as a result of the amount of energy that the audience puts into the installation. To achieve this, a system of rules was developed that was inspired by mathematical models, used to model the dynamics of biological populations. In the process of developing the software, these original models were modified and adapted freely in order to make the interaction with the installation intuitive and fun. The software uses this set of a models to translate the input data from the sensors to parameter values and mappings that control the sound that the installation outputs (see Fig. 3).

Excitement and State. In our system, each of the surrounding speakers forms a separate entity that produces its own characteristic sound. The character of the sound is determined by calculating two main features for each speaker: 'excitement' and 'state'. These features were implemented in order to achieve an evolving form of interactive behaviour. The state determines both the character of

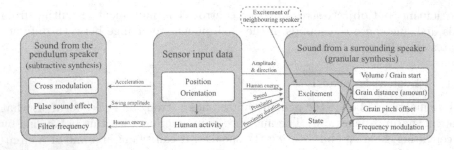

Fig. 3. Diagram with mappings of the input data to the sound output parameters.

the sounds that are produced, and how the speaker reacts to the movement of the pendulum. The level of excitement ranges from 0 to 100. It is a variable to describe how 'excited' a speaker is within its current state. It is continuously updated by an algorithm that uses (1) audience interaction–how much energy has been put on the pendulum speaker, (2) the pendulum's proximity to the speaker, (3) the duration the pendulum is within a certain proximity of the speaker, (4) the pendulum's speed, and (5) the level of excitement of its neighbouring speakers. The excitement level is calculated for each speaker separately. When a speaker's level of excitement reaches 100, it shifts to the next state. When its level of excitement decreases to 0, it falls back to the previous state. There are 10 states in total, starting from 0. Each state has its own mapping strategies. They are designed is such a way that the audience perceives a clear change in sound and interactive behaviour and gets challenged by the new interactive behaviour.

We have added some additional rules to the state changes. A speaker can only switch to a new state when the state difference between the speaker and its neighbouring speakers is less than 3. Otherwise, it will not change state and influence the neighbouring speaker's level of excitement instead and wait for it to get to a higher state. Due to these rules, the system as a whole evolves as a result of the individual speakers' behaviour.

The pendulum speaker also has its state. It is determined by, what we call, the system state. The system state is the average of the states of all surrounding speakers. An important exception to these general rules is that when the system state equals to 8, all of the speakers' states will shift to 9. This state lasts 30 s as a clear stage and builds up to a point where there is no return, because the feedback mechanisms in the system drive it into a state of uncontrollable chaos where all speakers stop being influenced by the audience. We will discuss this special state in detail in Sect. 4.

Growth and Decay of Excitement. The level of excitement increases while the pendulum is close to a surrounding speaker and it slowly decays while the pendulum is further away from it. Furthermore, the growth rate of the excitement varies with the amount of audience interaction. More interaction results in a higher growth rate. When the pendulum is following its natural movement the growth rate will get lower and the speakers start 'cooling down'. Each surrounding speaker has its own growth rate related to the audience interaction. We believe that the implementation of growth rate adds to the intuitive nature of the interaction with the system. We have decided to make the decay rate increase once a surrounding speaker reaches state 4, which means its level of excitement will decline faster and its state will easier fall back to its previous state. Thereby it becomes harder for a surrounding speaker to reach a state higher than 4, especially when there is no continuous human activity detected by the pendulum. To avoid that the states would alternate too fast, a minimum time that a state lasts has been defined.

4   Sound Design

Two different sound synthesis techniques are used to make a clear sonic distinction between the pendulum and the surrounding speakers. While the pendulum generates machine-like (low to mid frequency) sounds, higher frequency sounds are generated from the surrounding speakers. The algorithms that are used to interpret and translate the input data into sound, make the installation react both directly and indirectly to the interaction with the audience. This gives the audience a sense of control, but at the same time makes the sounds that result from the interaction unpredictable. Meanwhile, the sound results of the installation can develop from calm and peaceful to chaotic and aggressive. This was done to make the audience perceive the installation as beautiful and calming when handled carefully, but also dangerous and distressing when handled aggressively.

4.1   Sound from the Pendulum Speaker

We use U-he Diva, a virtual analogue synthesiser in Ableton Live, to generate the sound for the pendulum speaker [4]. The control parameters are calculated in Pure Data and sent to Ableton Live via MIDI. The machine-like sound is produced by two oscillators passing through a voltage-controlled filter (VCF). Using cross-modulation, a sawtooth oscillator and a sine wave oscillator modulate each other's frequencies. The VCF is a low-pass filter, that filters the sounds of both oscillators.

For the sound design of the pendulum speaker we use a mechanical machine as a metaphor. The control parameters for the sound synthesis are derived from the pendulum's own physical behaviour. The amount of human activity is mapped to the amount of the frequency modulation and the filter frequency. The audience can 'power on' this machine by putting energy into the pendulum. The pendulum's position is used to play a single midi note that gets triggered every time the pendulum travels a specific distance in space. Furthermore, the swing amplitude controls the velocity of each midi note. When the pendulum swings, it generates pulse sound effects. The linear acceleration of the pendulum is mapped to cross-modulation between the oscillators, to make it sound like a machine engine is operating and accelerating. Meanwhile, the rotation rate of the speaker is mapped to the pitch of the synthesised sound. The faster the pendulum rotates, the higher the sound. In this way, the amount of human activity is used to create direct feedback when the audience interacts with the pendulum speaker. The more energy the audience is trying to put into the pendulum, the more active and powerful the machine will be, and the more dynamic the sound will be. The parameters decline again when no one touches it. The state of the pendulum speaker is used to make it sound more aggressive. When the pendulum speaker reaches state 9, it stops triggering midi notes but generates a continuous and stable sound. The cross-modulation and low-pass filter are removed, and the pitch goes much lower. The machine turns out to be 'over-excited', and cannot be controlled or influenced by the audience any more.

4.2   Sounds from the Surrounding Speakers

In contrast to the synthetically generated sounds from the pendulum speaker, the surrounding speakers produce a more natural sound. The sounds are generated using a granular synthesiser built in Pure Data. Each of the speakers have their own individual synthesiser that uses the same sound sample but with a pre-edited different pitch. The original sample is a recorded hit of a bell. When the pendulum hangs exactly at its equilibrium point in the centre of the space, the surrounding speakers will not generate any sound at state 0. But when the pendulum moves towards one of the surrounding speakers the sample is played in full length. It sounds like the audience is using the pendulum speaker to hit the surrounding speakers, and 'awake' them.

In a later state, the granular synthesiser is used as a polyphonic sample playback engine. The distance between the pendulum and each surrounding speaker is mapped to the grain distance which sets the rate at which the grains are triggered and results in overlapping grains with a variable density. Currently, up to 100 overlapping grains can be generated resulting in dynamic and rich sonic textures. We believe that this behaviour makes it intuitive for the audience to perceive what kind of effect the pendulum speaker has on each of the surrounding speakers. Next to that, the distance value is also mapped to the start point of each grain player. There is a clear and loud hit at the beginning of the sample. We found that using the start point was an optimal parameter as opposed to the use of volume control since it applies the natural decay of the sound. The closer the pendulum moves towards a surrounding speaker, the louder sound it produces. This behaviour can be easily understood by the audience and is intended to help them to understand the behaviour of the implemented excitement.

We have implemented different mapping strategies for the different states, in order to create distinct sonic characteristics for each state. Initially we implemented 5 states. As the state of a speaker increased, the sound transforms from stable harmonic tones into abstract and unrecognizable synthetic noise. However, the changes between the states were large and sudden. We then decided to implement more states to transform the original sample in a more gradual way. This makes it easier for the audience to perceive changes of the system while navigating through the various states. In order to create more complex dynamics in the playback of the grains, we have added frequency modulation for states above 3 and randomised the start point and pitch within a specific range of each grain. Subsequently, the grains create a more complex, and use a wider sonic range. The original sampled sound gets dispersed because the hits are intensified and blurred as the speaker reaches higher states. The sound becomes more and more chaotic as the speaker gets excited. In state 9, all of the surrounding speakers play the full length of the original sample with frequency modulation and repeat at a random interval. The sounds become more machine-like compared to state 0, and assimilate into the pendulum's synthesised sound. After reaching the highest state the system 'cools down' and needs a little rest before it starts responding again starting in state 0.

5   Experience and Discussion

During a three-day exhibition at the NIME 2018 conference, some observations of the audience interacting with the installation were made. We also had informal conversations about the work with some of the visitors. Although we did not use a strictly defined method for reviewing, our observations gave us some preliminary indications of how the audience reacts to, and interacts with the work. We noticed that, at first, many visitors were mostly observing the installation instead of interacting with it. Some mentioned that 'they were not sure if they were allowed to touch the work'. After interacting with the installation, most of the participants that we observed independently discovered the different forms of movement that the pendulum speaker reacts to, without the need for specific instructions. This seems to indicate that the basic form of interaction is intuitive. Most of the visitors also seemed to quickly notice that moving the pendulum towards a surrounding speaker resulted in this speaker reacting by playing a sound. Some visitors specifically mentioned that the interaction reminded them of handling a bell or wind chimes. Thus, it seems that the direct and noticeable sound results can help the audience understand the interaction and navigate through different types of sound composition. However, it seemed to not always be clear to the audience that the installation's sounds were able to develop from calmly to aggressively sounding and that the effects of the audience's interaction with the sounds would then also change. For some visitors, this was due to them handling the pendulum speaker so gently that the installation would always sound calm and not aggressive. Other visitors did put enough energy in the installation to make it sound aggressive, but seemed to not be fully aware of how their actions altered the sounds. Although we also noticed that with the current setup, visitors needed some explanation before being able to experience the full dynamics and concept of the installation. A clearer distinction between different 'states' of the installation might help visitors to more easily discover the different sounds of the installation independently. Lastly, our observations indicated that visitors had quite varying sensations while experiencing the installation. Some visitors avoided close proximity to the pendulum, but to others purposefully stood right under the pendulum to 'get a rush of it swinging right over their head'. Some visitors experienced the installation while laying on the floor and reported that it was a calming experience to them. This indicates that the audience was able to perceive both sensations of beauty and danger, which we aimed to convey with the installation. We believe that a good interactive installation should explain itself to the audience. In other words: it should steer the audience in such a way that it reveals its behaviour to the audience. Our initial observations indicate that there is still some room for improvement.

6 Conclusion

Băi is an interactive installation that uses a pendulum speaker as an expressive control interface by sensing its position, speed and rotation. Besides performing its own natural movement, the speaker gives both physical and audible feedback to the sensed input. The audience's actions have a direct impact on the sound the speaker produces. Since there is no distinction between the input and output interface we believe that creates is an intuitive way for the audience to interact with the system. The installation tries to challenge the audience when they are playing with, and adapting their behaviour to the interface. We do this in order to give the audience the feeling they are controlling and interacting with a system that noticeably reacts to them, but also has its own behaviour and thereby a certain amount of unpredictability. On its turn, the pendulum speaker interacts with the surrounding speakers. This happens in a bidirectional way. While the pendulum speaker's movement triggers sounds in the surrounding speakers it also influences the excitement and state of the them. The pendulum's state gets affected by their state in return. We have constructed a dynamic relationship where the states of the surrounding speakers shift up and down, depending on the intensity and duration of the audience's input.

There are several options for the audience to be engaged in the installation. One might stand alone and observe the installation, or walk around and move the pendulum speaker. It is possible for others to join simultaneously and either observe or join the interaction.

While our installation is based on a complex system, we believe that the responsive interaction method is easily understandable. The initial observations during the previous exhibition have given us some indications, but for a good review of the interaction of the audience with the installation a thorough study needs to be done. Where the goal of this paper is to describe the development, choices and behaviour of the installation our next step will be a structured evaluation of the interactive behaviour of the installation. The goal of this evaluation is not only to create insight in the current system but will also be used to further develop it.

References

1. van der Heide, E.: Spatial sounds (100 dB at 100 km/h) in the context of human robot personal relationships. In: Lamers, M.H., Verbeek, F.J. (eds.) HRPR 2010. LNICST, vol. 59, pp. 27–33. Springer, Heidelberg (2011). https://doi.org/10.1007/978-3-642-19385-9_4
2. Monahan, G.: Speaker swinging. http://www.gordonmonahan.com/pages/speaker_swinging.html. Accessed 17 May 2018
3. Reich, S.: Pendulum music. http://www.ubu.com/aspen/aspen8/leadPendulum.html. Accessed 17 May 2018
4. Diva Homepage. https://u-he.com/products/diva. Accessed 17 May 2018
5. Pure Data. https://puredata.info. Accessed 17 May 2018

Art-Based User Research: Combining Art-Based Research and User Research to Inform the Design of a Technology to Improve Emotional Wellbeing

Carla Nave[✉], Teresa Romão, and Nuno Correia

NOVALincs, Faculdade de Ciências e Tecnologia, Universidade Nova de Lisboa,
2829-516 Caparica, Portugal
cd.saraiva@campus.fct.unl.pt, {tir,nmc}@fct.unl.pt

Abstract. This paper presents research output from an experiment that combines ideas from User Research and Art-based Research. Artistic processes inspired the study, in which we asked participants to assess and then "paint" their emotions over emotion-eliciting images using an array of materials, such as watercolors and colored pencils. We used a mixed methods approach that included questionnaires, psychometric data from validated scales and informal conversations. Our primary goals were to inform the design of a mobile application meant to improve emotional wellbeing and assess whether creative self-expression can help to engage users when evaluating and exploring their affective states. We conclude by summarizing the results, which we believe to be positive.

Keywords: Art-based research · Design · Emotions
Human-Computer Interaction · Technology · User research · Wellbeing

1 Introduction

This document presents a hands-on research study mainly intended to improve the design of an upcoming mobile application for the self-monitoring of emotional states called PaintMyEmotions. Routinely monitoring our affective states, over prolonged periods of time, can help us to understand how, and why, they vary, which in turn can contribute to enhancing our emotional wellbeing. Self-monitoring is a commonly used activity in clinical settings, but it can also prove useful to those who merely wish to know more about themselves to improve.

Several applications exist to facilitate this activity. However, they frequently present problems of attrition (high drop-out rates or low adherence) [11,12,24]. The lack of user engagement ("the emotional, cognitive and behavioral connection that exists, at any point in time and possibly over time, between a user and a resource" [1]) can lead to the incorrect use of such applications, which can negatively impact its efficacy.

© ICST Institute for Computer Sciences, Social Informatics and Telecommunications Engineering 2019
Published by Springer Nature Switzerland AG 2019. All Rights Reserved
A. L. Brooks et al. (Eds.): ArtsIT 2018/DLI 2018, LNICST 265, pp. 80–90, 2019.
https://doi.org/10.1007/978-3-030-06134-0_9

Our research consists mainly of exploring how the use of artistic expression techniques, such as painting and photography, can be used to enrich interactive experiences and engage people's attention through creative enjoyment. Painting and photography have also been used in therapeutic settings to facilitate emotional expression and healing, in a field called Art Therapy - "the use of art materials for self-expression and reflection in the presence of a trained art therapist" [9]. Art therapy has been found to be an effective treatment by at least two reviews with a short body of quantifiable data [21,23].

We embraced this idea of employing artistic expression to improve users' engagement from the beginning of the design process of PaintMyEmotions, during user research, to inform the future design and lead it in the right direction. For this study, we chose to use a mixed methods approach. We merged a qualitative analysis of participants' paintings of their emotional states and their feedback regarding the activity during group discussions, with the rigor of a psychometric instrument to measure the psychological state of flow. The state of flow happens when activities are so engaging that everything else around seems to "fade away" and is associated with engagement and creativity [7].

We hypothesize that performing creative expression practices can induce a state of flow, which we consider to have the potential to increase engagement with technology and also the level of enjoyment from using it. Furthermore, we deem plausible that the playful nature of painting can make the process more engaging.

1.1 Art-Based User Research

Often seen as a dichotomy, art and science have the potential to enrich each other. As stated in the ArtScience manifesto: everything can be understood through art or science, but both understandings by themselves are incomplete. The manifesto goes on to state that ArtScience serves to attain a richer and universal understanding of phenomena by comprehending the human experience through the union of artistic and scientific modes of exploration and expression [22].

This same idea is shared by what is known as Art-based research - "the systematic use of the artistic process, the actual making of artistic expressions in all of the different forms of the arts, as a primary way of understanding and examining experience by both researchers and the people that they involve in their studies" [16]. Plus, Art-based methods can be helpful in better grasping notions of health and wellbeing [19], which can be especially relevant with complex constructs such as emotional states, since it is difficult to gather this kind of data during user studies, due to its sensitive nature. Moreover, emotions can be difficult to express. To begin with, some individuals might not be able to fully understand what they are feeling at a precise moment, due to a lack of emotional self-awareness or a lack of emotional literacy. Plus, even if they are entirely aware of their own emotions, they might not feel comfortable with sharing them with other people, including researchers. Using methods inspired by the artistic process may help participants to further engage with the study and feel more comfortable expressing their feelings, thus helping in the extraction of phenomenological data.

Human-Computer Interaction (HCI), on the other hand, is an interdisciplinary research domain that intersects technology and computer science with psychology and the social sciences [3]. This field includes several methods aimed to conduct User Research, which focuses on better understanding users and their behaviors, needs, and motivations, to build technologies better suited for them. User Research is a staple of User-Centered Design (UCD) and highly recommended to improve the design and later adoption of the product being designed [13].

We believe that incorporating Art-based methods in User Research can help to enrich the latter, by making participants more engaged with the study and the sharing of personal data, and that is how we came up with the study design presented in this paper, described next.

2   Study Design and Procedure

We designed this study with the concepts of ArtScience, Art-based research and User Research in mind, to obtain answers to the following questions:

1. Does "painting" one's emotional state contribute to induce a state of flow?
2. How do people "paint their emotions" over a photo?

The study was carried out in two phases: a pilot session, to test and optimize the procedure, and three subsequent sessions of a hands-on experimental study, which included psychometric measures and was followed by an informal discussion with the participants.

2.1   Pilot Session

This session's goal was to ascertain whether the devised procedure would generate relevant results. We agreed that it did, and decided to use the knowledge gained from this session to improve the design of the ensuing study sessions. This session involved six participants (two males, with a mean age of 30 years old). In this session, we used three photos and set no time limit for the painting activity. In the end, we asked the participants to fill in the Flow Short Scale [10]. The main conclusions we drew from this session were that participants had a hard time understanding the phrasing of the questions of the Flow Short Scale and that some participants took a long time to paint the photos (one of them painted a single photo for more than 30 min). Because of this, we decided to look for a new flow state measure instrument and to limit the amount of time given to paint each photo. It is also relevant to note that the fact that they took a long time to paint might signify that they were having fun and engaged in the activity. Despite being all seated together at a table, and having to share the painting materials, the participants were concentrated on the painting activity, as illustrated by Fig. 1. Focused attention, to the exclusion of other things and other people, is one characteristic of user engagement [1].

Fig. 1. Participants engaging with the painting activity during sessions one, three and two, respectively.

2.2 Study Sessions

Participants. In total, 19 participants (10 female, mean age: 32 years old) volunteered to take part in the study. All participants signed an informed consent. We distributed participants between three sessions: eight in the first session, six in the second session, and five in the third one. Participants originated from Brazil, Italy, and Portugal. Their professions included: Ph.D. student, software engineer, sound engineer, designer, architect, veterinary, journalist, and teacher. Regarding their acquaintance with mood tracking: 17 participants knew what mood tracking was; 16 said that they believed that mood tracking could be useful; only one of the participants told to had practiced mood tracking (using the app Mood Meter); finally, three participants said to have tried coloring books for adults.

The Self-Assessment Manikin (SAM). SAM [2,17] is a pictorial assessment system that measures (through self-report) the valence, arousal, and dominance associated with an individual's affective reaction to a stimulus. In our study, we only used the valence and arousal dimensions. We excluded the dominance dimension because the stimuli used only provides data for the dimensions of valence and arousal.

The Flow State Scale (FSS). The FSS [15] is a self-report 36-item instrument for the measurement of the flow state. This scale represents all the nine dimensions of flow discussed by Csikszentmihalyi [4,5]: challenge-skill balance, action-awareness merging, clear goals, unambiguous feedback, concentration on the task, sense of control, loss of self-consciousness, time transformation and autotelic experience. Even though the FSS was specifically developed with sport and physical activity in mind, it has been employed before in other settings, namely the relationship between motivation and flow experience to academic procrastination [18], knowledge workers' (mostly engineers and scientists) work experiences (e.g., fixing things like hardware or computer software, assembling prototypes) [20], and also to explore the effect of web-site complexity on flow during web surfing and shopping [14].

Stimuli. We used five printed photos from the Geneva affective picture database (GAPED) [6], which is a collection of visual, emotional stimuli. Two photos had negative contents – spiders and a scene meant to induce emotions related to the violation of moral and legal norms (human rights violation). One photo had neutral content (an empty plant pot), and the other two had positive contents - animal babies and nature scenery. GAPED's photos (Table 2) are rated according to valence and arousal, which we measured in this study through the SAM instrument.

Painting Materials. For the painting activity, we provided the following materials to the participants: tracing paper, crayons, markers, watercolors, colored pencils, and glitter glue.

Procedure. We began the study by explaining to the participants what was going to happen during it and instructing them on how to use the SAM instrument. Then, we handed the participants the consent agreement document, followed by a questionnaire inquiring about demographic data and the participants' familiarity with the concept of mood tracking. The participants were then asked to look at the printed photos from the GAPED database for about 20 s. We distributed the photos in a random order among the participants. After that, the participants filled in the SAM measure. Then, the participants placed a sheet of tracing paper over the photo and started to paint, in whichever way they fancied—three minutes were given to the participants to paint each photo (during the pilot session we observed that this period was the most common among participants). After painting and filling in the FSS questionnaire, we talked with the participants for a while about the meaning of their paintings and the emotions they were trying to express, and also regarding the state of flow experienced (or not) while painting the photos.

3 Results

3.1 Flow State

We measured the flow state using the FSS scale. The internal consistency reliability coefficient for the FSS scale, as indexed by Cronbach alpha, was found to be excellent (alpha = .93). The average score was 125 (out of 180). Table 1 presents the individual scores of the FSS scale. Regarding the nine components of flow, the one with the highest score was "loss of self-consciousness", with a score of 307 out of 380 (19 participants × 5 (maximum score for each question) × 4 questions to access each component). This state occurs when the individual is completely focused on the activity at hands, which was also observable during the sessions. The lowest score was "unambiguous feedback" (232 out of 380), which is understandable, since there was no expected outcome for the activity of painting the photos – they were simply told to try and "paint their emotions", but there was no reference to what would constitute a good, or a bad, outcome.

These results can be seen in Fig. 2. Observable signals of the state of flow, such as focused attention, were also observed during the sessions, as is illustrated by Fig. 1.

Table 1. Individual scores of the FSS questionnaire.

Participant	1	2	3	4	5	6	7	8	9	10	11	12	13	14	15	16	17	18	19
Score	108	94	118	125	120	134	125	134	121	161	166	127	110	109	108	107	148	126	140

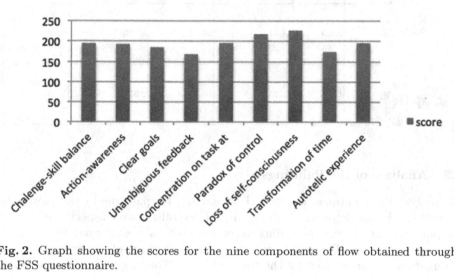

Fig. 2. Graph showing the scores for the nine components of flow obtained through the FSS questionnaire.

3.2 GAPED Vs. SAM

Table 2 compares the standard values from the GAPED images to the SAM scores given by the 19 participants. The GAPED scale goes from 0 = very negative pictures to 100 = very positive pictures, with 50 = neutral. SAM is a 9-point rating scale for each of dimension (arousal and valence). For purposes of comparison, we used the rule of three on the SAM values (e.g., $(4.222 \times 100)/9$). We calculated the Pearson's correlation coefficients between GAPED and SAM values, for the dimensions of arousal and valence. For the arousal dimension, the value of R is 0.8929. This is a strong positive correlation, which means that high X variable scores go with high Y variable scores (and vice versa). For the valence dimension, the value of R is 0.9592. This is also a strong positive correlation.

Table 2. Comparison of GAPED and SAM values obtained during the study.

Photo	Photo code	GAPED - arousal	SAM - arousal	GAPED - valence	SAM - valence
	P072	19.134	46.91	92.978	89.51
	P083	35.561	52.46	78.075	87.65
	Sp069	66.282	62.74	22.636	44.44
	N014	14.34	25.92	59.275	52.46
	H005	72.751	65.43	2.377	16.66

3.3   Analysis of the Paintings

To analyze the paintings, we started by looking for patterns in the paintings created by the participants. Then, we listed several relevant aspects and rated the paintings, one by one, according to those aspects, as yes (the painting reveals this aspect) and no. The results consist of the percentage of the average of the observational ratings given by the three authors. The most interesting aspects we found were: 60% of the participants used the colors present in the photos, or colors in the same hue family (Fig. 3); 84% of the participants were inspired by the form of the subject to paint (Fig. 4); and 47% of the paintings had its subject mostly covered up with ink or other painting material(s) (Fig. 5). It was also interesting to note that, from all the 38 paintings of photos with negative content (photos H005 and Sp069), 61% were painted with dark colors and/or had a negative form (Fig. 6), and 39% covered it with light colors (Fig. 7). When inquired about this matter during the informal conversations, the participants explained that they wanted to cover up the negative subject because it bothered them - the spider provoked fear, disgust and panic, and the little boy evoked emotions such as sadness, shock, and pain. The participants also stated that they wanted to cover the subject in order not to see it, and that the dark color represented their negative feelings toward the photo. The participants that used lighter colors to cover the negative subjects said that they wanted to "cure" the subject (referring to the little boy) and to make "an ugly thing beautiful".

This is consistent with evidences from a study [8] that concluded that for some people making art can serve as a means of releasing negative feelings (catharsis), whereas for others it can work as a distraction from negative rumination and reorient them in a positive direction (redirection), with a result of improved mood in both situations. In our study, when people painted with dark colors to "hide it" might correspond to catharsis, and when participants painted over it with light colors to "heal" and "make it better" it might have been redirection.

Fig. 3. Example of a painting where the participant used the colors present in the photo to paint.

Fig. 4. Example of a painting where the participant was inspired by the form of the photo's subject to paint.

Fig. 5. Example of a painting where the participant covered the photo's subject with ink.

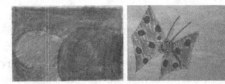

Fig. 6. Example of paintings where participants covered up negative subjects with light colors and forms. The photo painted on the left is H005, and the one on the right is Sp069.

Fig. 7. Example of paintings where participants covered up negative subjects with dark colors and forms. The photo painted on the left is H005, and the one on the right is Sp069.

4   Conclusion

In this study, we collected qualitative (observation, informal discussion) and quantitative (FSS scale) data regarding the flow state of participants while painting "their emotions" (provoked by emotion-eliciting photos). We also analyzed the resulting paintings and discussed the context of their production with the participants.

We are inclined to conclude that painting one's emotional state does contribute to induce a state of flow and might help to engage users when assessing and exploring their emotional states. We also noticed that the form of the photos' subject to paint inspired most participants. Additionally, we observed that a large portion of the participants used the colors present in the photo to paint (or colors in the same hue family) and that some participants covered up the entire subject with ink or other painting material. Furthermore, while some participants painted over the negative subjects using dark colors, others used light colors, which, according to participants' feedback, may be a form of catharsis and redirection, respectively.

In the future, we will apply these insights to the design of PaintMyEmotions. For instance, we will allow users to paint progressively (adding layers on top of each other), so they can "cover" negative subjects, and we will offer users a color palette inspired by the photo being painted. Also, participants were able to successfully assess their emotions using the arousal and valence dimensions, after a brief explanation of the terms, and thus we will use them in the emotion assessment user interface of PaintMyEmotions. Finally, we believe that that merging Art-based methods with User Research enriched the participants' experience and engagement with the study's activities, and provided data that might not be so easily collected otherwise.

Acknowledgements. This work is funded by Fundação para a Ciência e Tecnologia - grant PD/BD/114141/2015 and FCT/MEC NOVA LINCS PEst UID/CEC/04516/ 2013.

References

1. Attfield, S., Kazai, G., Lalmas, M.: Towards a science of user engagement (position paper). In: WSDM Workshop on User Modelling for Web Applications (2011)
2. Bradley, M., Lang, P.J.: Measuring emotion the self-assessment manikin and the semantic differential. J. Behav. Ther. Exp. Psychiatry **25**(1), 49–59 (1994)
3. Carroll, J.M.: Human-computer interaction: psychology as a science of design. Annu. Rev. Psychol. **48**(1), 61–83 (1997)
4. Csikszentmihalyi, M.: Flow: The Psychology of Optimal Experience. Harper, New York (1990)
5. Csikszentmihalyi, M.: The Evolving Self: A Psychology for the Third Millennium. Harper, New York (1993)
6. Dan-Glauser, E.S., Scherer, K.R.: The Geneva affective picture database (GAPED): a new 730-picture database focusing on valence and normative significance. Behav. Res. Methods **43**(2), 468–477 (2011)
7. Gute, D., Gute, G.: How creativity works in the brain. National Endowment for the Arts (2015)
8. De Petrillo, L., Winner, E.: Does art improve mood? A test of a key assumption underlying art therapy. Art Ther. **22**(4), 205–212 (2005)
9. Edwards, D.: Art therapy (2004)
10. Engeser, S., Rheinberg, F.: Flow, performance and moderators of challenge-skill balance. Motiv. Emot. **32**(3), 158–172 (2008)
11. Eysenbach, G.: The law of attrition. J. Med. Internet Res. **7**(1) (2005)
12. Geraghty, A.W.A., Torres, L.D., Leykin, Y., Pérez-Stable, E.J., Muñoz, R.F.: Understanding attrition from international Internet health interventions: a step towards global eHealth. Health Promot. Int. **28**(3), 442–452 (2013)
13. Gulliksen, J., Göransson, B., Boivie, I., Blomkvist, S., Persson, J., Cajander, Å.: Key principles for user-centred systems design. Behav. Inf. Technol. **22**, 397–409 (2003)
14. Guo, Y.M., Poole, M.S.: Antecedents of flow in online environments: the role of website complexity. In: AMCIS 2006 Proceedings, pp. 2933–2941 (2006)
15. Jackson, S.A., Marsh, H.W.: Development and validation of a scale to measure optimal experience: the flow state scale. J. Sport Exerc. Psychol. **18**, 17–35 (1996)
16. Knowles, J., Cole, A.: Handbook of the Arts in Qualitative Research: Perspectives. Examples, and Issues, Methodologies (2008)
17. Lang, P.J.: Behavioral treatment and bio-behavioral assessment: computer applications, in technology in mental health care delivery systems (1980)
18. Lee, E.: The relationship of motivation and flow experience to academic procrastination in university students. J. Genet. Psychol. **166**(1), 5–15 (2005)
19. McNiff, S.: Art-based research. In: Handbook of the Arts in Qualitative Research: Perspectives, Methodologies, Examples, and Issues (1998)

20. Quinn, R.W.: Flow in knowledge work: high performance experience in the design of national security technology. Adm. Sci. Q. **50**, 610–641 (2005)
21. Reynolds, M.W., Nabors, L., Quinlan, A.: The effectiveness of art therapy: does it work? Art Ther. **17**, 207–213 (2000)
22. Root-Bernstein, B., Siler, T., Brown, A., Snelson, K.: ArtScience: integrative collaboration to create a sustainable future. Leonardo **44**(3), 192 (2011)
23. Slayton, S., D'Archer, J., Kaplan, F.: Outcome studies on the efficacy of art therapy: a review of findings. Art Ther.: J. Am. Art Ther. Assoc. **27**(3), 108–118 (2010)
24. Swan, M.: Sensor mania! the internet of things, wearable computing, objective metrics, and the quantified self 2.0. J. Sens. Actuator Netw. **1**(3), 217–253 (2012)

A Framework for Branched Storytelling and Matchmaking in Multiplayer Games

Vitor Pêgas[1](✉), Pedro Santana[1,2], and Pedro Faria Lopes[1,3]

[1] ISCTE-Instituto Universitário de Lisboa, Lisboa, Portugal
{vitor_pegas,pedro.santana,pedro.lopes}@iscte-iul.pt
[2] Instituto de Telecomunicações, Lisboa, Portugal
[3] ISTAR-Instituto Universitário de Lisboa, Lisboa, Portugal

Abstract. Video games often either have good single player campaign modes or good multi-player campaign-less modes. This paper presents a framework aimed at the full game development pipeline, from designers to programmers, to aid in creating multiplayer campaigns by providing components that help singleplayer story modes to be used in multiplayer interaction settings. We also propose a custom matchmaking system capable of matching players so as to intertwine their individual stories. The proposed framework has been validated in a case study. A set of experimental results show that the framework is capable of producing valuable story crossings and proper matchmaking.

Keywords: Video games · Multiplayer · Campaign · Framework

1 Introduction

Currently, there are two main types of commercial video games, SinglePlayer (SP) and MultiPlayer (MP) games. In SP games, a player plays against Non-Player Character (NPC) controlled by Artificial Intelligence (AI), whereas in MP games players can play against each other (Human vs Human) or in cooperative modes (Humans vs NPC).

In 2017 there were five SP games in the top ten sales, with millions of copies sold worldwide [15]. On the other hand, MP games are not only strong in sales, but the revenue of such games surpasses SP revenue, mainly due to micro-transactions. For instance, games like Grand Theft Auto Online (GTA V Online) and League of Legends (LoL) made more than 500 Million USD [13] and 2.1 Billion USD [3] in in-game item sales alone. This shows that although MP games dominate the market in revenue, SP games continue to be bought and played by millions.

A problem that SP games may suffer is that their quality is closely linked to the quality of the AI controlling the NPC. An improper AI may render a game either too easy or too hard to overcome. On the other hand, players in MP games may find themselves immersed in what is known as toxic communities, in which players engage on hostile behavior against each other, a phenomenon known

A. L. Brooks et al. (Eds.): ArtsIT 2018/DLI 2018, LNICST 265, pp. 91–100, 2019.
https://doi.org/10.1007/978-3-030-06134-0_10

to naturally occur in competitive gaming scenarios, such as MP online games [10]. Popular online MP games such as Call of Duty and League of Legends are well known for their community toxicity [7]. To overcome these limitations we propose a generic framework agnostic to the game genre in order to create campaigns with multiplayer interaction that prevent the use of bad AI controlled characters and a matchmaking system that provides a more balanced matching between players to prevent toxicity and ease the learning process of new players.

This paper is organized as follows. A literature review is provided in Sect. 2. In Sect. 3 the proposed framework is described. Then, in Sect. 4, a set of results are presented, followed by conclusions and future work avenues in Sect. 5.

2   Literature Review

2.1   Single Player and Multi-player Crossing

A player engagement study [8] found that players show higher engagement levels when facing humans in a competitive scenario instead of AI controlled characters. This may also be influenced by the fact that AI-based characters quite often produce either too easy or too hard game mechanics. Nevertheless, players do not refrain from playing and enjoying SP games as this type of games often features a well written story (e.g., Until Dawn [4]). For this reason, our framework aims at allowing players to enjoy the flow of a storyline while playing in a MP setting, that is, making use of NPC only when no online players are available.

To improve the lack of engagement or challenge imposed by AI, game developers blurred the line between SP and MP, by having the SP game with its well written and designed story and levels, and occasional MP interactions, such as in Dark Souls and Journey. For instance, in Dark Souls players can be invaded by other human players, which will control NPC's inside the first player story, whereas in Journey players can help each other. Other games, like Absolver, each player's game instance can also host other players to fight, co-operate or ignore one another. There are games with MP campaigns, such as Borderlands and Left4Dead, but these are simply a set of co-op missions that try to create a sense of narrative for each player (friends or random online players).

Our framework was created to allow the possibility for players' individual stories to cross each other at story intersections. In those intersections (hereafter story nodes), players can be on the same or opposite sides. This is possible due to the existence of a list of ideal player profiles for each story node, and the framework uses this to allocate players to nodes in a coherent way.

2.2   Branched Storytelling and Narrative

Replay value is a term used in video game industry that states whether a game is good to play more than once. Usually, due to their linear design, SP games do not hold much replay value. This means that if players complete the story and then try it again, the story (and ending) will be the same. However, there are SP games that try to branch their narrative influenced by player input, thus increasing their replay value. Bearing replay value in mind, our framework handles both linear and non-linear stories.

MP games are quite often repetitive. For instance, First Person Shooters (FPS) usually only have as goals killing the opposite team or capturing a given item or position. In spite of this, players keep playing FPS nonetheless, motivated by [16]: competition, as seen in games like DOTA 2 and CS: GO; socialization, as seen in games like Second Life and Habbo Hotel; and role-playing as seen in games like GTA V, and World of Warcraft.

In SP games, developers must find a way of showing the player that their actions matter and can change the outcome of the game, pushing the player to play the same game several times while producing different outcomes [12]. Procedural Content Generation (PCG) is popular choice to provide the so required in-game diversity (e.g., random levels, fauna, flora). PCG use has increased lately due to the skyrocketing production cost of AAA games [9], for which is difficult to scale up asset production (e.g., 3D models) [6].

Other way to increase replay value is by branching the narrative in non-linear ways. For this to happen, there must be more than one choice of action for the player to perform, and that action must somehow impact the story unfolding. Many games have exploited this ability widely, such as Façade, Witcher 3, and Undertale. These games require some narrative mediation system to ensure the player experiences a coherent story, by creating a path that the player travels according to one choices and the system automatically re-writes the path if the player decides to take a different direction.

Our framework uses multi-dimensional descriptors (hereafter *coherences*) at each story node so as to allow comparing nodes and, as a result, to determine which story node should be visited by the player as soon as it leaves the current one. This implements a form of non-linear procedural story generation whose plot is a result of the story nodes' associated descriptors.

2.3 Matchmaking

A matchmaking system is used in games to connect players in a given match. When a player wants to play online, its game instance (client) sends a request to the Matchmaking Server (MMS), receiving a response with necessary information to establish a connection [1]. A bad matchmaking service is known to be harmful to both skillful and casual players [11].

One of the most popular types of matchmaking, Elo based systems, uses a numeric value, called a Matchmaking Rating (MMR), to match players according to their skill levels and was created for chess competitions, in which the MMR is determined by the results of the player in past games [5]. Matchmaking usually picks players with close MMR values so as to ensure fair and, so, interesting, matches [14]. Match fairness and uniformity can be further enforced by ensuring that the players within a given team have an uniform MMR [2]. By using custom matchmakers, instead of general-purposed matchmaking systems as Elo, games can match players more accurately as a function of the game's mechanics.

This paper proposes a novel matchmaking system that uses multi-dimensional descriptors associated to players (hereafter *Stats*) to more accurately match players and story nodes and, thus, not only by their skill, but for their experience, class, and other in-game statistics.

3   Proposed Framework

The framework has been devised to be agnostic to game genre. Taking into account the typical game development pipeline, the framework is composed of a set of core game components to be handled by designers and artists during the conceptualization phase of the game. Designers and Artists can use a Graphical User Interface (GUI) application to create and manage these components and then pass that information to the programmers which will implement the game in-engine.

For the sake of clarity, let us illustrate an application scenario of the framework to a well-known commercial game, namely, BattleField 1. Battlefield 1 is a game that has a good SP campaign, that suffers from a linear narrative and a good MP part of the game with several modes where players face real human players online. When analyzing the SP campaign, we can identify common areas where the proposed framework could be used to offer aid in a non-linear storyline. In one of the campaign stories, the player is a tank driver whose mission is to conquer key operation posts. While aided by other NPC tanks and infantry, the player fights NPC enemy tanks and infantry. With our framework there could be different roles in this campaign, like the tank driver, the tank gunner and several infantrymen on both sides, each with their back story leading to that particular moment (story node). The tank driver could be playing that battle because he managed to win past missions, or his tank crew got wounded (seen by our framework as a partial mission success) and he found a new crew. To determine which player to allocate to each role in the story node, the players' descriptors (Stats), such as player health, level, experience, weapon information, are matched against the story node's player profiles.

4   Framework Components

Figure 1 depicts the major components involved in the proposed framework. The central component is denominated of *Node*.

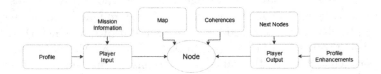

Fig. 1. Overview of the proposed framework's basic components.

Node. The Node is a point in a campaign story, which is a set of linked nodes. It contains engine information such as the assets needed for that node such as a Map (i.e., in Unity it would be associated with a Scene object to be loaded), contains information regarding the ideal profile for players inside the Node and the Node's coherence values, which define that Node in terms of location, appearance, time and story placement. These coherences are used for procedural story generation. In each node there is information for Player Inputs and Player Outputs. The Inputs have the desired player profiles and their roles in that Node, the Outputs have information regarding how the players leave that Node. In a linear story, our framework provides the possibility of near-success missions, this means that there is not a win and lose node, but a list of possible nodes for possible partial successes. Also in the Outputs we have profile enhancements that are used to change the players profiles (increase/decrease stats), for instance a player that wins a Node, deserves to be rewarded with some experience.

Player Information. Each player has a profile defined as a set of Stats. Stats are scalar values that define that player, like *Health, Class, Experience, Ranking*. In each Node, there are multiple ideal Player Profiles which are matched against potential players by the matchmaking system, thus attempting to find the most suited players for that specific node. In a Node, these Profiles have more information about the Objective of the matched player like its role and goal in that Node.

Coherences. Our framework defines Coherences as an one dimensional spectrum. Coherences can be used to define how semantically close are Nodes supposed to be. We defined some example Coherence types, such as Spatial (physical space, i.e., City vs Desert), Temporal (i.e., 1920 vs 2018), Story (Story line flow), and Random (to ensure some stochastic story line flow). These can be added to any Node and defined with a scalar value from 0 to 1. Coherences are used to generate procedural stories (branched storytelling), based on players previous nodes. Each Coherence i has a procedural story generation weight w_i that is used when finding for possible next nodes using a weighted Euclidean Distance. Concretely, if the player is leaving node $\mathbf{N_1}$, the cost of going to node $\mathbf{N_2}$ is

$$\Psi(\mathbf{N_1}, \mathbf{N_2}) = \sqrt{\sum_i w^i (N_2^i - N_1^i)^2}, \tag{1}$$

where $\mathbf{N_k} = (N_k^1, ..., N_k^z)$ corresponds to the z-dimensional coherence vector of node k, and w^i corresponds to the weight of the i-th component of the coherence vector. Weights w_i can be used by the game designer to generate a procedural story. The system compares the Node's coherences vectors to find the one with the least cost. Given that we are at node N_i, we pick, among the set L of the node pool, the node with lowest coherence distance.

$$l = \arg \min_{l^* \in L} \Psi(\mathbf{N_i}, \mathbf{N_{l^*}}). \tag{2}$$

4.1   SP and MP Crossing

The way our framework crosses the two game genres, SP and MP, is due to its architecture for MP campaigns. Designers can use our framework to create tailored linear or non-linear stories for strict player types or create a pool (See Fig. 2 (A)) of unconnected nodes and let the procedural story generator create the story for each individual player as it plays.

To create a procedural story, our framework uses previously defined Coherences to get the closest possible node to a player's current node. Once a close Node has been picked from the node pool (see Fig. 2 (B)), the player will move to that Node and the matchmaking process begins. The system now has to either find players that have a close and similar profile to our player and are set to play in the picked Node or to find any open sessions (a match already on-going) for this player to join (see Fig. 2 (C)). While the system attempts to find a match, a time-fill mission can be played, if previously defined by designers. An example for a time-fill mission could be the an objective to move towards to or the gathering of certain items that can be useful later. For both options, player profiles are compared and matched against each other to allow for balanced matches. In case of failure to find any open sessions, the player starts a game session on the current Node and waits for other players to join later.

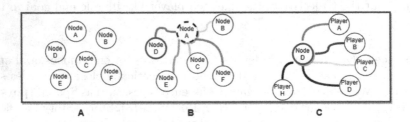

Fig. 2. Framework procedural story generation

4.2   Matchmaking

Usually competitive games base their matchmaking on the skill rating of each player, and the system attempts to match players with a close rating value. Alternatively, we propose a matchmaking system that weighs the several *Stats* included in the player's profile, promoting a more balanced matchmaking. This is attained by computing the Euclidean distance between the multi-dimensional *Stats* vectors composing the profile of the player, $\mathbf{P_p}$, and the required profile set for the Node in question, $\mathbf{P_n}$:

$$d(\mathbf{P_p}, \mathbf{P_n}) = ||\mathbf{P_p} - \mathbf{P_n}||_2, \tag{3}$$

where $\mathbf{P_k} = (p_1^k, \ldots, p_n^k)$ represents a n-dimensional *Stats* vector. The distance between the players Stats is then used to obtain the cost of matching the player and the node requested profile, which favors matches with players waiting longer for a match:

$$\Phi(\mathbf{P_p}, \mathbf{P_n}) = \alpha \cdot d(\mathbf{P_p}, \mathbf{P_n}) + (1 - \alpha) \cdot \gamma e^{-\beta t}, \tag{4}$$

where α and β are empirically defined scalars the game designer can tune to favor, or not, players that are waiting longer for a match, and t represents time. Then, the system computes the cost of matching the player with all available players and uses a threshold to limit the difference between players' Stats.

If a good-enough match is found, then the system sends all the connection information the player needs to join a MP match. While this happens, the player that sent the request can either wait for a match, or play a time fill in mission which is associated to the node in question. When the connection information arrives, the player connects and the matchmaking process ends. If immediate matchmaking is not possible, the server will insert the request on the list for future requests and will set a timeout. When the timeout ends, and no matches are possible, the client or the server can inform the other about giving up the matchmaking process and play with NPCs instead.

4.3 Case Study

To test the implementation of our framework we designed and developed a 2D online web game to be used as case study and for user testings. To fully use the framework we decided to create a Role Playing Game (RPG) as this genre of game usually focus on individual player stories. We designed a story composed of Nodes that would describe a journey across a border of two nations in war, with different missions opposing both countries. Nodes can be played in a linear fashion like most games, but we can also create procedural stories by using Node Coherence components to assign the player's next node. These Nodes were defined by three types of Coherences: *Location*, *Story*, and *Appearance*; for instance, a Node that is physically located in the North of the world would have a *Location* value of $N^{location} = 0$, while a Node physically located in the South would have the value of $N^{location} = 1$.

5   Results and Discussion

Our framework was successfully implemented in the case study game with every component being used like predicted. We used this game to test the matchmaking system by running simulations of concurrent NPCs.

The matchmaking system was tested using simulated players $N = \{10, 50, 200\}$ which were trying to find a match for a given node. We tested our euclidean based system against an elo based system with: one, two, and three Stats with values ranging from 0 to 10. As the elo system only is capable of handling one stat (the rating of the player or MMR), for the two and three stat testing we used the average of the stats as the one defining criterion for matching. We also tested restricting or relaxing the matching threshold (see

Sect. 2.3) to observe how it affects matching. For each test we ran three times and averaged the results.

In each test we used our procedural story generator to generate a story for each NPC based on its current node. We used three Coherences, namely, Story ($w_{story} = 0.8$), Location ($w_{location} = 0.05$), Appearance($w_{appearance} = 0.05$) and Random($w_{random} = 0.1$), so the chance of players going different ways is higher than with a linear story.

Our results for one stat matchmaking are shown in Fig. 3. For N=10, which is a significantly low amount of players, considering our procedural story line and multiple values for one stat, the euclidean based system fails 56% of times for a $\sigma = 3$, meaning that 56% of the total requests for matches, ended up playing with NPCs. Relaxing the value of the matching threshold (σ), we can observe that the system is more successful, as it hits 26% with the same 10 players. It is not ideal, but in a game where there is the possibility of this much deviation, it is no surprise. If we increase the number of players to N=200, the failed matching lowers to 3.8% with the strict threshold and 2.4% with a relaxed σ value. The results show a tendency to lower the failed matching the more players we have. The elo system shows high failed percentage as well for lower player bases but manages to show the same decrease as player base increases. The σ values used for the Elo system were determined to be the same in proportion to the ones used in the Euclidean System, meaning that they limit the same amount of difference between players.

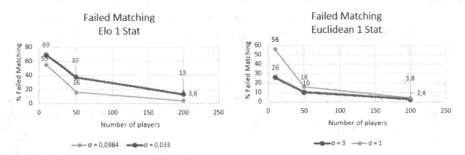

(a) Elo based system Matchmaking Results

(b) Non-Weighted Euclidean based system Matchmaking Results

Fig. 3. Results for one Stat matchmaking. As shown both systems are more successful in matching when the player base increases.

For three Stats however the non-weighted euclidean based system shows more failed matching (14% for $N = 200$ and $\sigma = 3$) due to the increasing difference between possible players, but the weighted system maintains low failed percentages (3.1% for $N = 200$ and $\sigma = 3$ and 80/10/10% weight distribution). The elo based system maintains a low percentage due to the averaging of the stat values with 2.5% for $N = 200$ and $\sigma = 0.0984$.

In terms of failed percentage the elo appears to be able to match players more easily in diverse situations; however this does not prove its total efficacy. Let us imagine an example of a three criterion matching with Stat A,B, and C. Each player can have one of the stats (A,B,C) with value ten and the rest of the values are 0. Player X would have $A = 10, B = 0, C = 0$ and player Y would have $A = 0, B = 10, C = 0$. Now let us try and match Player X and Y. Following the euclidean distance (non-weighted), the system would give a matching value of $m = 14.1$, showing that the players are indeed different. But when we switch over to the elo system, as it only handles one criterion, we have to average the stats giving us a total match value of $m = 0.5$ because the average of the three stats is the same $10/3$. So in conclusion the matching efficacy is not the whole picture as accurate matching is paramount for a good player experience, and Elo based systems cannot guarantee that balance with more than one stat.

The elo works as shown by games such as Rocket League, Overwatch, CS:GO, League of Legends and others, but is limited when given the possibility to match with more than one criterion than just skill, and as demonstrated in the previous example, it can match players but it does not guarantee a balanced match in every situation. However, our framework is not bound to the euclidean based systems, thus being possible to use and implement elo based systems or any more suited system that designers see fit for their game.

6 Conclusion and Future Work

With MP games becoming more common due to their long-run revenue the need for good, story-driven SP games increases. This paper proposed a framework that aims at blurring the line between both genres by allowing developers to connect a good immersive story with the possibility of human vs human interaction. We presented not only a framework that aids the creation of SP games with MP interaction but also proposed a matchmaking system that matches players in a balanced way. Our simulations show that the matchmaking system is capable of balanced player matching. Our case study shows that the framework is generic enough to be used in a story driven game, game-genre independent. As future work, additional testing should be made to validate that with big budget commercial games's player base the efficiency of the matchmaking systems decreases as predicted.

References

1. Agarwal, S., Lorch, J.R.: Matchmaking for online games and other latency-sensitive P2P systems. In: Proceedings of the ACM SIGCOMM Computer Communication Review, vol. 39, pp. 315–326. ACM (2009)
2. Alman, J., McKay, D.: Theoretical foundations of team matchmaking. In: Proceedings of the 16th Conference on Autonomous Agents and MultiAgent Systems, pp. 1073–1081. International Foundation for Autonomous Agents and Multiagent Systems (2017)

3. Altay, O.: Top free to play pc games by revenue 2017 - superdatare-search (2018). https://mmos.com/news/top-free-play-pc-games-revenue-2017-superdataresearch. Accessed 26 April 2018

4. Brew, S.: Until dawn, the interactive movie, and storytelling (2015). http://www.denofgeek.com/games/until-dawn/37259/until-dawn-the-interactive-movie-and-storytelling

5. Glickman, M.E., Jones, A.C.: Rating the chess rating system. Chance **12**, 21–28 (1999)

6. Hendrikx, M., Meijer, S., Van Der Velden, J., Iosup, A.: Procedural content generation for games: a survey. ACM Trans. Multimed. Comput. Commun. Appl. (TOMM) **9**(1), 1 (2013)

7. Kwak, H., Blackburn, J.: Linguistic analysis of toxic behavior in an online video game. In: Aiello, L.M., McFarland, D. (eds.) SocInfo 2014. LNCS, vol. 8852, pp. 209–217. Springer, Cham (2015). https://doi.org/10.1007/978-3-319-15168-7_26

8. Lim, S., Reeves, B.: Computer agents versus avatars: responses to interactive game characters controlled by a computer or other player. Int. J. Hum.-Comput. Stud. **68**(1), 57–68 (2010). https://doi.org/10.1016/j.ijhcs.2009.09.008. http://www.sciencedirect.com/science/article/pii/S107158190900130X

9. McLaughlin, M.: New GTA V release tipped to rake in £1bn in sales (2013). https://www.scotsman.com/lifestyle/gadgets-gaming/new-gta-v-release-tipped-to-rake-in-1bn-in-sales-1-3081943

10. Märtens, M., Shen, S., Iosup, A., Kuipers, F.: Toxicity detection in multiplayer online games. In: Proceedings of the 2015 International Workshop on Network and Systems Support for Games (NetGames), pp. 1–6, Dec 2015. https://doi.org/10.1109/NetGames.2015.7382991

11. Myślak, M., Deja, D.: Developing game-structure sensitive matchmaking system for massive-multiplayer online games. In: Aiello, L.M., McFarland, D. (eds.) SocInfo 2014. LNCS, vol. 8852, pp. 200–208. Springer, Cham (2015). https://doi.org/10.1007/978-3-319-15168-7_25

12. Roth, C., Vermeulen, I., Vorderer, P., Klimmt, C.: Exploring replay value: shifts and continuities in user experiences between first and second exposure to an interactive story. Cyberpsychol. Behav. Soc. Netw. **15**(7), 378–381 (2012)

13. Tassi, P.: GTA online's $500m in microtransactions could mean a very different 'GTA 6' (2016). https://www.forbes.com/sites/insertcoin/2016/04/14/gta-onlines-500m-in-microtransactions-could-mean-a-very-different-gta-6

14. Véron, M., Marin, O., Monnet, S.: Matchmaking in multi-player on-line games: studying user traces to improve the user experience. In: Proceedings of Network and Operating System Support on Digital Audio and Video Workshop, p. 7. ACM (2014)

15. VGChartz: Global yearly chart (2017). http://www.vgchartz.com/yearly/2017/Global/. Accessed 26 April 2018

16. Yee, N.: Motivations for play in online games. CyberPsychol. Behav. **9**(6), 772–775 (2006)

Interactive Evolution of Swarms for the Visualisation of Consumptions

Catarina Maçãs[✉], Nuno Lourenço, and Penousal Machado

CISUC - Department of Informatics Engineering,
University of Coimbra, Coimbra, Portugal
{cmacas,naml,machado}@dei.uc.pt

Abstract. Information Visualisation studies how visual representations can help understanding hidden patterns in large amounts of data. The produced visual artefacts should have both functional and aesthetic dimensions to make the visualisation appealing to the user. However, in the Data Aesthetics field, the process of creation of visualisations is more concerned with aesthetics. Our goal for this project is to develop a framework to explore the aesthetic dimension of a functional visualisation model characterised by a series of parameters, which can make the visualisation more functional or more aesthetically appealing. In concrete, we propose a framework based on Interactive Evolutionary Computation (IEC) to evolve the parameterisation of the visualisation model, enabling the user to explore new possibilities and to create different aesthetics over the data. Our case study will be a dataset with the consumption patterns of the Portuguese people in one retail company. The developed system is able to create a wide diversity of emergent visual artefacts that can be intriguing and aesthetically appealing for the user.

Keywords: Data aesthetics · Genetic algorithms
Evolutionary computation · Swarm systems · Visualisation

1 Introduction

In a partnership with a Portuguese retail company, we had access to a high volume of data about the Portuguese's consumption. This retail company's goal is to communicate with a wider public through aesthetic experiences. For this reason, we aim to create emergent visual artefacts driven by the consumption data, positioning our work in the field of Data Aesthetics [1,2]. The dataset is rich in daily, weekly and monthly repetitions of consumption patterns, offering us the opportunity to transform the consumption of the Portuguese into visual artefacts, while exploring, highlighting and visualizing their periodic nature.

Taking into account a previous project [3], we use a swarm system to create emergent visual artefacts [4]. In the referenced work, the user had to define the parameterisations of the system to create a balance between a more functional or more aesthetically intriguing visualisation. In this project, this parameterisation

© ICST Institute for Computer Sciences, Social Informatics and Telecommunications Engineering 2019
Published by Springer Nature Switzerland AG 2019. All Rights Reserved
A. L. Brooks et al. (Eds.): ArtsIT 2018/DLI 2018, LNICST 265, pp. 101–110, 2019.
https://doi.org/10.1007/978-3-030-06134-0_11

is automatically defined through the use of an evolutionary system, opening the possibilities to create a wider range of visual solutions. Whence, in this project the main concern is to create artefacts that are aesthetically appealing to the user, and not artefacts placed in the functional spectrum.

The result of this exploration is an automatic framework that is able to create a wide and diverse set of solutions. We test the validity of the system through different usage scenarios in which the system relies on the users' preferences as an input to guide the solution towards what they find attractive. We defined three objectives for the user guidance: explore specific parameterisation attributes; guide the evolution to a functional artefact; explore randomly the system.

The remainder of the article is structured as follows. In Sect. 2, we introduce the project, present the dataset used, the project objectives, and the work previously made within this project context. In Sect. 3, we present the visualisation model (Subsect. 3.1), and the Evolutionary Algorithm (Subsect. 3.2) used to generate the visual artefacts. In Sect. 4 we introduce the usage scenarios and discuss the results, effectiveness, and diversity of our approach. Finally, in Sect. 5, we define the future work.

2   Background

This article is part of a larger project developed in association with SONAE, a Portuguese retail company. Our dataset consists of 278 GB of information about customer purchases in 729 Portuguese supermarkets and hypermarkets of the company's retail chains, in a time span of 24 months (from May 2012 to April 2014).

While shopping in the retail stores, costumers tend to use their client cards to accumulate discounts and other benefits. This enables the company to create personalised discounts and to aggregate data by specific geolocations. The dataset comprises approximately 2.86 billions transactions with the following attributes: customer card id, amount spent, product designation, quantity of the purchased product, and date and time of the transaction. Each product is placed within the product hierarchy of the company, which has 6 levels—Department, BizUnit, Category, Sub-Category, Unit Base, Product.

As a guideline for the project, the company was interested in two main dimensions, one related to the analytical analysis of their data and another related to aesthetics, giving us the opportunity to freely explore the last. In the analytical dimension, a set of visualisations were already implemented concerning problems, such as the understanding of how consumption evolves through time in specific regions of Portugal or the identification of potential sites to open new supermarkets, allowing the understanding of seasonal variations [5–9].

In the aesthetic dimension of the project, we have already developed a set of works. Although they are intended to explore the aesthetics of visualisation, they are also concerned with functionality, trying not to overpass the barrier of legibility. In a previous work [10], we explored how the visualisation can morph depending on the data, creating movement and highlighting the rhythm and disruptions of the normal consumption patterns. We also explored the qualitative representations of data, providing an overview of how data behaves through time [3]. In the latter, we apply a swarm based system as a method to create emergent visualisations of the consumption values with the intent to convey meaningful information and, at the same time, explore the boundaries between Information visualisation and Data Aesthetics. The application of swarm systems to visualize data can also be seen in [11–13]. Additionally, in the field of Generative Art, swarm forces were also used in a variety of projects [14–16]. We focused on the ability of this emergent system to communicate information while engaging the viewer with organic visuals [4]. Additionally, with the different parameterisations, we were able to create a set of renderings with different levels of legibility and attractiveness. The approach presented in this article builds on this work, by developing a framework that is able to evolve the configuration of the visualisation model through the use of an Evolutionary Algorithm (EA) [17]. Our goal is to create new, diverse, and surprising visual artefacts, which, in spite of not being completely functional, are engaging and entertaining for the user.

3 Evolutionary Approach

To improve the swarm system detailed in [3], we apply an EA to increase the degrees of freedom in the creation of visual models, enabling a diverse range of solutions. Our intention with this approach is to develop visual artefacts that are continuously readjusting to the intentions of the user and to enable the user to explore artefacts not imagined by him/her. In this way, the company can deploy a system that will evolve and adapt to different audiences' aesthetic preferences.

3.1 Visualisation Model

The visualisation model that serves as the basis for this project, consists of a swarm system that, through different forces of separation, attraction, and cohesion, creates emergent visualisations [4] about the Portuguese's consumption routines. This system is constituted by several boids—artificial objects that simulate the flocking behaviour of birds—in an environment (i.e., the canvas), that react to the changes in consumption over time.

For this project, we aggregate all the transactions of the dataset by the highest level in the hierarchy, i.e., the Department. There are a total of seven different Departments in the dataset: Grocery, Fresh Food, Food & Bakery, Home, Leisure, Textile, and Health. Each transaction has the hour, minute, and second of purchase. However, the representation with this degree of detail would be too subtle to the human eye. Therefore, we aggregate the data in intervals of two hours, resulting in 12 intervals per day. Although the transactions occur only between 8 am and 10 pm, we keep the representation of the 24 h aggregated every two hours so it is easier to distinguish different days of consumption.

Swarming Forces. The swarm system simulates the behaviour of multiple boids [18]. Each boid is represented through a circle and is described by properties such as velocity, position, size, and colour. Only the position and velocity of the boids are affected by the swarming forces.

Based on the work of Reynolds [18], each boid follows three basic rules: (i) cohesion; (ii) separation; and (iii) alignment. To explore the system, we applied different values to each force, so it was possible to create different outputs. If two neighbouring boids are from the same Department, we apply higher forces of attraction and lower forces of separation, but, if they are from different Departments, the attraction force is lower then the previously defined, and the separation force higher.

To prevent the boids from randomly moving on the canvas and to enhance their periodic behaviour, we defined a target that all boids should look for. Hence, in addition to the previously described forces, all boids are under the influence of an attraction force towards this moving target. The target boid, although not represented visually, starts from the centre of the canvas and swirls around, creating a spiral with equal distances between each lap.

Since we want to represent a time-series data, the representation of time must be added to the visual artefacts. We consider that each lap of the swirling boids represents one month of data. Then, depending on the angle of the boid with the center of the canvas, we obtain the day and corresponding hour of the month. To do so, the 360° are divided by the 31 days multiplied by 12 h ($2\Pi \div (31 \times 12)$), since, as previously stated, the data is aggregated in intervals of two hours. Note that all laps have 31 days. By doing so, all months start with the same angle (at the top of the circle), and, if they have less than 31 days, the consumption values are null during those nonexistent days.

| Grocery | Leisure | Food & Backary | House | Fresh Food | Health | Textile |

Fig. 1. Colours used to distinguish the boids representing one of the seven Departments in the company's product hierarchy. (Color figure online)

Rendering. As stated before, each boid is represented through a circle that has a specific size and colour. While colour identifies to which Department the boid belongs to (Fig. 1), the size represents the consumption in a certain time: the bigger the circle, the bigger the consumption value. As the boids wander through the canvas, they leave an imprint of their shape, enabling the user to see its path, and consequently, the consumption values. The boids' size is mapped to a predefined minimum and maximum radii, that can represent the minimum and maximum sale of each individual Department (local normalisation), or the minimum and maximum sale of all Departments (global normalisation). Additionally, we defined three different styles to represent the boids: through a filled circle, through the outline of the circle, and through a line that connects all boids of the same department. Each style is painted with the colour of the corresponding Department (Fig. 1). Additionally, we implemented a mechanism to sort the circles in depth according to their radii. With this, the smaller circles are drawn over the larger ones and are never hidden by the larger ones.

3.2   Evolutionary Algorithm

The visualisation model described above is easy to understand and use, yet it requires the definition of several parameters to create visual artefacts that can be appealing for the user. To aid in this task, we propose a framework based on EAs [19]. To evolve the swarm system, we will be searching for the best combination of the following system's parameters: (i) the separation, alignment, and cohesion forces; (ii) the minimum and maximum radius; (iii) the use of a global or local normalisation; and (iv) the representation modes (lines, circles, transparency, sorted circles). Note that the boids' size is always mapped according to the consumption value on the data. In the following subsections, we present the parameters used to evolve the visual artefacts and the used genetic operators.

Representation. Each EA solution is encoded as a set of values that correspond to the number of parameters needed by the swarm system. In concrete, we have 10 different parameters that are required by the visual model:

- **Separation Force**: a real value between 0 and 3;
- **Alignment Force**: a real value between 0 and 3;
- **Cohesion Force**: a real value between 0 and 3;
- **Boid Render**: one of the following options: lines, circles and filled circles;
- **Transparency**: a boolean value that enables transparency of the boids;
- **Size Ordered**: a boolean value. If this value is true, the visualisation model sorts the boids by radius, i.e., boids with smaller radius will be on top of boids with larger radius;
- **Mapped**: a boolean value. If it is true, it indicates that the separation force is mapped depending on the radius of the boids;
- **Normalisation**: a boolean value that enables normalisation based on the maximum sales values;
- **Maximum Radius**: a real value between 30 and 80 that corresponds to the maximum radius of the boids;
- **Minimum Radius**: a real value between 0.1 and 15 that corresponds to the minimum radius of the boids.

An example of a possible solution alongside with its phenotype representation is depicted in Fig. 2.

Genetic Operators. To promote the evolution and the proper exploration of the search space we rely on two operators: recombination and mutation. The recombination operator is the uniform crossover and combines two solutions by creating a random mask of the same size of the genotype, and then swap the genetic material according to the previously generated mask. Regarding the mutation operator, we apply a per gene mutation to the candidate solutions. This allows the algorithm to change, from generation to generation, a significant percentage of the genes to other valid ones.

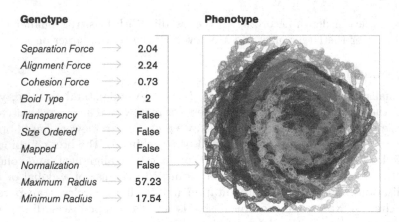

Genotype   **Phenotype**

Separation Force	$\longrightarrow$	2.04
Alignment Force	$\longrightarrow$	2.24
Cohesion Force	$\longrightarrow$	0.73
Boid Type	$\longrightarrow$	2
Transparency	$\longrightarrow$	False
Size Ordered	$\longrightarrow$	False
Mapped	$\longrightarrow$	False
Normalization	$\longrightarrow$	False
Maximum Radius	$\longrightarrow$	57.23
Minimum Radius	$\longrightarrow$	17.54

Fig. 2. On the left, the genotype of a possible solution; On the right, the resulting phenotype, i.e., the visualisation model.

4   Usage Scenarios

Through Interactive Evolutionary Computation (IEC) [20], we explored the evolutionary system based on the user's preferences. We implemented a simple interface to enable the interaction with the system[1]. These explorations were based on three different objectives. In the first exploration, the goal is to evolve solutions with specific parameterisation attributes: the boids must be represented with filled circles, use the local normalisation, and have a zigzagging pattern. In the second, the goal is to attain solutions that must intersect the functional dimension, enabling the readability of the artefacts. Finally, for the third exploration, there is no predefined objective, so the solutions must be diversified according to the user's taste. For the first two explorations, the user must have some experience on how the system works, its parameters and the data. In the last, the user can have no experience with the data nor with the parameterisations, the user only explores the system and creates artefacts suitable for his/her own taste. As the generations evolve, the user chooses the visual artefacts that visually intrigue, amaze, and/or correspond with his/her preferences.

To avoid user fatigue, we used a reduced number of individuals per generation. For each exploration, the number of individuals is set to 20 and the maximum generations to 10 (this value can be increased). Additionally, the user can stop the evolutionary process at any given time if the visual artefacts are in accordance to his/her expectations.

In the first exploration, and as the user has already a target solution in mind, it is possible to perceive that the evolutionary system evolved correctly towards the user predefined goal (Fig. 3). As the individuals are being created, the user selects only the ones with filled circles, and the ones where all colours appeared balanced, corresponding to the local normalisation where the values are

---

[1] A video of this interface can be seen in: https://vimeo.com/289093672.

Fig. 3. Chosen individuals in: (left) first generation, (center) third generation, and (right) sixth generation.

Fig. 4. Chosen individuals in: (left) first generation, (center) third generation, and (right) sixth generation.

normalised by Department. When using the global normalisation, the artefacts colours consist mainly of blues and greens because these colours correspond to the Departments with higher consumption values, and thus, the ones with more visual presence.

For the second exploration, and with the intention to guide the evolutionary system to generate artefacts which can be aesthetic and at the same time functional, the system also proved to be capable of evolving good solutions (Fig. 4). In the last generations, the majority of the individuals were readable. This means that they had less clutter and lower separations forces, which enabled them to have a more strict behaviour as they swirl, not deviating from the spiral path. Additionally, the majority of the generated artefacts are similar to the explorations made in the previous project [3].

For the last exploration, the user had no predefined objective. As the artefacts were being presented, the user chose freely the preferred ones. In the end, the user managed to guide the system through a specific style, which was appealing for him/her—the use of lines to represent the Departments (Fig. 5).

As a summary, we found that the system was capable of discovering artefacts similar to the ones created by human designers, but also to find new ones. Furthermore, the system can be guided by the user, showing artefacts similar to the user choices, but, at the same time, giving to the user others to enhance his/her choice.

Fig. 5. Chosen individuals in: (left) first generation, (center) third generation, and (right) sixth generation.

Fig. 6. Different individuals with similar parameterisations.

4.1 Results' Diversity

One of the important aspects that we looked for in the previous experiments was the capacity of the system to generate and evolve a diversified range of visual artefacts. The random initialisation of the visualisation models creates a wide variety of behaviours. For example, if the forces are too strong, the boids will deviate from the spiral path, creating random zigzagging patterns. In a similar way, these forces can also cause the boids to stagnate at their position in the centre. In Fig. 6, it is possible to see how the system generates a set of individuals, which are different but based on the choices made previously by the user.

As the system evolves the parameters, without the direct intervention of the user, it can generate solutions which the user was not expecting and has not seen before. Even an experienced user, that knows the parameters and the system itself, can be surprised by the solutions found[2].

5   Conclusion

Over the last few years, we have seen an exponential increase in data in all sectors of business. Companies have seen this as an opportunity to improve their operations and increase the satisfaction of their costumers. In previous works, we have proposed, developed, and implemented visualisation models for one of the biggest retail companies in Portugal. We have developed a set of artefacts that refined the way the company looked at their data in order to improve their

---

[2] In https://cdv.dei.uc.pt/ie-of-swarms-in-visualisation it is possible to see other visual solutions.

business strategy. In this article, we extend a previous work [3] and explore an automatic manipulation of a swarm system through the application of an Evolutionary Algorithm. Our main goal was to explore the aesthetic dimension of the consumption data provided by the Portuguese retail company.

As future work, we intend to improve the interactive evolutionary system by enabling it to learn the previous choices of the user and guide the evolution based on those parameters. With this, we can also augment the number of individuals per generations and, in order to diminish user fatigue, show only the fittest (based on previous choices) for the user to choose.

Acknowledgements. The first author is funded by Fundação para a Ciência e Tecnologia (FCT), Portugal, under the grant SFRH/BD/129481/2017.

References

1. Manovich, L.: Information and form (2000). http://manovich.net/index.php/projects/information-and-form
2. Moere, A.V.: Aesthetic data visualization as a resource for educating creative design. In: Dong, A., Moere, A.V., Gero, J.S. (eds.) Computer-Aided Architectural Design Futures, CAADFutures 2007, pp. 71–84. Springer, Dodretch (2007). https://doi.org/10.1007/978-1-4020-6528-6_6
3. Maçãs, C., Cruz, P., Martins, P., Machado, P.: Swarm systems in the visualization of consumption patterns. In: Yang, Q., Wooldridge, M. (eds.) Proceedings of the Twenty-Fourth International Joint Conference on Artificial Intelligence, IJCAI 2015, 25–31 July 2015, Buenos Aires, Argentina, pp. 2466–2472. AAAI Press (2015)
4. Jones, D.: Swarm aesthetics: a critical appraisal of swarming structures in art practice. Master's thesis, MA Sonic Arts (2007)
5. Maçãs, C., Cruz, P., Polisciuc, E., Amaro, H., Machado, P.: ISO-edges for the geovisualization of consumptions. In: Braz, J., Kerren, A., Linsen, L. (eds.) IVAPP 2016 - Proceedings of the 11th Joint Conference on Computer Vision, Imaging and Computer Graphics Theory and Applications, pp. 220–227. SciTePress (2016)
6. Polisciuc, E., et al.: Arc and swarm-based representations of customer's flows among supermarkets. In: Braz, J., Kerren, A., Linsen, L. (eds.) IVAPP 2015 - Proceedings of the 6th International Conference on Information Visualization Theory and Applications, 11–14 March 2015, Berlin, Germany, pp. 300–306. SciTePress (2015)
7. Polisciuc, E., Maçãs, C., Assunção, F., Machado, P.: Hexagonal gridded maps and information layers: a novel approach for the exploration and analysis of retail data. In: SIGGRAPH ASIA 2016 Symposium on Visualization, pp. 6:1–6:8. ACM (2016)
8. Polisciuc, E., Cruz, P., Maçãs, C., Amaro, H., Machado, P.: Flow map of products transported among warehouses and supermarkets. In: Braz, J., Kerren, A., Linsen, L. (eds.) Proceedings of the 11th Joint Conference on Computer Vision, Imaging and Computer Graphics Theory and Applications, vol. 2, pp. 177–186. SciTePress (2016)
9. Maçãs, C., et al.: Time-series application on big data - visualization of consumption in supermarkets. In: Braz, J., Kerren, A., Linsen, L. (eds.) IVAPP 2015 - Proceedings of the 6th International Conference on Information Visualization Theory and Applications, 11–14 March 2015, Berlin, Germany, pp. 239–246. SciTePress (2015)

10. Maçãs, C., Machado, P.: The rhythm of consumptions. In: Expressive 2016 - Proceedings of the Joint Symposium Expressive 2016, co-located with the Eurographics 2016. ACM (2016)
11. Moere, A.V., Lau, A.: In-formation flocking: an approach to data visualization using multi-agent formation behavior. In: Randall, M., Abbass, H.A., Wiles, J. (eds.) Australian Conference on Artificial Life, ACAL 2007. LNCS, vol. 4828, pp. 292–304. Springer, Heidelberg (2007). https://doi.org/10.1007/978-3-540-76931-6_26
12. Ogawa, M., Ma, K.L.: code_swarm: a design study in organic software visualization. IEEE Trans. Vis. Comput. Graph. **15**(6), 1097–1104 (2009)
13. Kamvar, S.D., Harris, J.: We feel fine and searching the emotional web. In: Proceedings of the fourth ACM International Conference on Web Search and Data Mining, pp. 117–126. ACM (2011)
14. Bornhofen, S., Gardeux, V., Machizaud, A.: From swarm art toward ecosystem art. Int. J. Swarm Intell. Res. (IJSIR) **3**(3), 1–18 (2012)
15. Greenfield, G., Machado, P.: Swarm art: Curator's introduction. Leonardo **47**(1), 5–7 (2014)
16. Shiffman, D.: Swarm (2004). http://shiffman.net/projects/swarm/
17. Eiben, A.E., Smith, J.E.: Introduction to Evolutionary Computing. NCS, vol. 53. Springer, Heidelberg (2003). https://doi.org/10.1007/978-3-662-05094-1
18. Reynolds, C.W.: Flocks, herds and schools: a distributed behavioral model. In: ACM SIGGRAPH Computer Graphics, vol. 21, pp. 25–34. ACM (1987)
19. Eiben, A.E., Smith, J.E.: Introduction to Evolutionary Computing. NCS. Springer, Heidelberg (2015). https://doi.org/10.1007/978-3-662-44874-8
20. Takagi, H.: Interactive evolutionary computation: fusion of the capabilities of EC optimization and human evaluation. Proc. IEEE **89**(9), 1275–1296 (2001)

Using Motion Expressiveness and Human Pose Estimation for Collaborative Surveillance Art

Jonas Aksel Billeskov, Tobias Nordvig Møller,
Georgios Triantafyllidis, and George Palamas[⊠]

Aalborg University Copenhagen, Copenhagen, Denmark
{tnma14, jbille14}@student.aau.dk,
{gt,gpa}@create.aau.dk

Abstract. Surveillance art is a contemporary art practice that deals with the notion of human expressiveness in public spaces and how monitoring data can be transformed into more poetic forms, unleashing their creative potential. Surveillance, in a sociopolitical context, is a participatory activity that has changed radically in recent years and could be argued to produce, not only social control but also to contribute to the formation of a collective image of feelings and affects expressed in modern societies. The paper explores a multidisciplinary approach based on tracking human motion from surveillance cameras on New York Time Square. The performed human trajectories were tracked with a real-time machine vision framework and the outcomes were used to feed a generative design algorithm in order to transform the data into emotionally expressive 3D visualizations. Finally, a study was conducted to assess the expressive power of this approach so as to better understand the relationships among perceived affective qualities and human behaviors.

Keywords: Generative art · Surveillance data · Motion expressiveness
Data transformation · Human pose estimation · 3D visualization

1 Introduction

In an age where a large part of an everyday life happens online and mostly everything done online will leave a digital footprint, people are getting increasingly concerned with digital privacy. Some go towards big data and endorse of collecting it for the use in advertisement targeting and scientific research, while others are against, hiding their digital traces by using VPN servers, proxies or boycotting sites such as Facebook. It is a difficult area to maneuver, because it is not certain exactly what data is being saved or how it is being used.

The proposed paper describes a method of how data can serve artistic purposes, in the context of generative art, and how using personalized public data does not have to be intrusive of personal privacy. Data can be used to create art pieces, where the content represented by the data may or may not be apparent. There have been examples of weather data being turned into complex sculptures such as the work of Nathalie Miebach [1] or Laurie Frik's sleep patterns [2] displayed in a non-traditional matter. Recent work in pose recognition allows us to capture pose data by inputting video data

© ICST Institute for Computer Sciences, Social Informatics and Telecommunications Engineering 2019
Published by Springer Nature Switzerland AG 2019. All Rights Reserved
A. L. Brooks et al. (Eds.): ArtsIT 2018/DLI 2018, LNICST 265, pp. 111–120, 2019.

using the software library OpenPose [3, 4]. This project utilise surveillance camera data in order to extract pose information about the people in the footage and interpreting this to create graphical 3D representations. The art pieces should encapsulate the motion expressiveness of the surveillance data and retain this through a transformation into generative art. These art pieces can be viewed as a way of mediating reality to make people ponder about the use of data and surveillance and showing that even ordinary movement can be turned into something aesthetically pleasant.

2   Background

The background section will discuss previous work done in this field and how it relates to this project. It will also discuss other art installations, which inspired this work.

2.1   Motion in Art

Obradović and Marković [5] explore how time can be used to create 3D shapes. They do this by using time as a way of sculpting their shapes. They extrude shapes over time by changing relative scaling and rotation as the object moves through space. The models were visualized in blender and depicted the variety of different shapes that can be obtained with their proposed method. They also suggest that their shapes could be used for decoration and architecture. Using time as a way of sculpting shapes is an interesting idea and this paper will in some ways try to extend this concept.

In traditional art, the Italian painter Giacomo Balla 1871–1958, who is one of the founders of futurism, spent much of his artistic career investigating how art can convey motion. One of his most famous paintings shows a dog where the legs move so fast that they merge together (Fig. 1). Balla was also inspired by technology as seen in paintings such as *"Swifts: Paths of Movement + Dynamic Sequences"*. The shapes in these paintings could seem similar to the shapes procedurally generated in the project by

Fig. 1. Dynamism of a Dog on a Leash (1912) by Giacomo Balla

Obradović and Marković [5] and explores the same concept about extending or duplicating the shape in motion to convey this motion to the viewer.

Takahashi [6] proposed a project called *Voxelman*, where he uses human motion data and presents them using voxels through Unity game engine. There is no apparent transformation to the data, the main purpose was to represent human motion expressiveness but with an altered meaning and significance.

2.2 Surveillance and Data Art

Surveillance art is a commentary on the surveillance happening in society. This could be art both made with surveillance, portraying the effects of surveillance or just exploring the concept. Data art is an art form that generates artistic content based on large data sets with an aim to create an explicit interpretation available to a larger audience [7]. Belgian contemporary artist Dries Depoorter's installation *"Jaywalking"* [8] allow viewers to look at a surveillance camera placed on a street and report jaywalkers to the police at the press of a button (Fig. 2). It is up to the viewer to consider whether reporting the jaywalker is the right thing to do. This is supposed to give the viewer a sense of power and perfectly shows how surveillance can alter social conditions. This approach creates another perspective on surveillance and puts the viewer very close to the new ethical decisions created by surveillance and data gathering.

Fig. 2. (Left) Dries Depoorter's installation *"Jaywalking"* (Right) Nathalie Miebach's artwork *"The Perfect Storm"*.

Laurie Frick is a contemporary data artist working with data visualization [2]. Her art pieces use datasets and visualize them mainly with analog media. Her work *"Sleep Patterns"* are data from sleep schedules made analog with watercolors and pieces of wooden bricks. The data in these artworks retain their qualities and were not transformed into any type of metadata.

Nathalie Miebach makes art based on weather data [1] as for example *"The Perfect Storm"* (Fig. 2). These artworks were created in analog ways and are complex and multilayered, making the original data challenging to interpret.

Seb Lee-Delisle created the project *"Lunar Trails"* as an interactive art installation featured in the Dublin Science Gallery in 2013 [9]. It consists of an arcade machine with the 1979 video game *"Lunar Lander"* and a wall where the game data was rendered onto. Each game played will be rendered as a line on the wall and the final rendering will be a collective art piece of all the player's paths in the game. There is almost no transformation in the data visualization and by simply looking at the final piece the viewer can easily get an idea of how all the different players played the game. Collaborative art such as this is a great way to show trends in data in a visually pleasing way.

2.3 Generative Art

McCormack, et al. [10] writes about open questions regarding generative art. In question 5 he asks *"In what sense is generative art representational, and what is it representing?"*. In this question the representation of generative art based on real life data is discussed. In generative art there is a transformation between the obtained data and the representation of data. This transformation can be of varying size and often depends on the kind of data the artist is working with and the vision of the artist. Another related question proposed is the difference between data visualization and generative art, and how this difference is defined. Edmonds [11] discusses the difference between interaction and influence in generative art. Influence is different from interaction as the influence doesn't have to be direct and can be a prolonged effect. This is relevant to this project as the people influencing the artwork will not know their data is being used and their influence is not a direct interaction with the art piece.

3 Design and Implementation

The design of the proposed generative art workflow (Fig. 3) was influenced by Obradović and Marković [5] and Balla [6] in the way they use time as a way to shape their models and the way complex shapes could be created from a continued shape. OpenPose [3] was used to read data from a surveillance camera looking at Times Square in New York with an aim to extract a sequence of human pose estimations. The pose data was used to create a 3D shape from the motion of the person [4] under

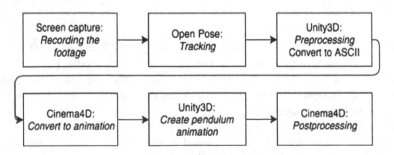

Fig. 3. Flowchart of the implementation process

surveillance. The data then was being processed with a pre-rendering software. Using pre-rendering instead of real-time graphics allowed for better lighting and for a wide variety of materials and textures.

To improve the feeling of having the data in surveillance being used for a different purpose, a simple physics-based transformation were added to the system. This transformation had the form of a double joint pendulum controlled from the human motion under surveillance [12]. The aim of this transformation is to create an artistic representation, rather than a pure data visualization, which retains the human expressiveness of the original data.

3.1 Implementation

This section describes the steps of data collection and the combination of physical pre-processing and conditioning of the motion captured signals.

Data Collection. This step comprises two aspects which are of importance for displaying the human motion expressiveness. First, the method of surveillance camera data collection and second, the data type that was collected. The surveillance camera, which was chosen, is a typical web based camera at Times Square in New York (Fig. 4). The selection of the camera was mainly due to the angle and position provided good data to be analyzed later on. A total of 45 videos captured and saved as individual clips with each of them depicting a single person passing by.

Fig. 4. Screenshot from the surveillance camera from Times Square.

Analyzing Data with OpenPose. The individual clips were fed to the OpenPose software to extract pose information about the person's motion. The software output JSON-files with information regarding 17 two-dimensional key points per person. OpenPose analyzes the data one frame at a time, which means that a 10 s clip at 30 frames per second would output 300 files. JSON-files were used because the data structure makes it easier to transfer the data between different software.

Fig. 5. The performed human trajectories (45 individuals) were used to feed a generative design algorithm in order to transform the data into emotionally expressive 3D visualizations.

Converting the Data. The files exported from OpenPose were then imported into Unity3D using a custom C# script. Each person's trajectory visualized by a single line based on a single point that was calculated as the average of all the key points generated from the human pose estimator. The z-value was then calculated by taking the average length from all key points to the average x- and y- value. This means that the more spread out a person's pose is, the greater the z-value and vice versa. Finally, the data converted into ASCII format and written to a file in order to be used in Cinema4D, using another custom C# script.

Data Transformation. The double-joint pendulum was implemented in Unity3D with 2 spheres connected in a row with hinge joints. Both spheres were equal in size and weight. The data from Cinema4D was then imported into Unity3D as an animation track for the top sphere to follow. The trajectories of the bottom sphere were tracked and then exported back into Cinema4D as ASCII data for final processing and visualization. The pendulum used to transform the data in a way, where the output would be naturally looking with a physically valid motion.

Final Processing and Visualization. In the data visualization stage a number of 3D trajectories produced (Fig. 5) based on the transformed data of the associated human motion. These trajectories were again turned into splines and visualized with a sweep tube following the path generated from the pendulum physical model. Different tubes were rendered with a variety of materials and lighting conditions against a composite ground plane.

4   Evaluation

In order to evaluate the human expressiveness of the visual outcomes, a questionnaire based on the Russel's circumplex model [13] used to assess affective and cognitive properties. The questionnaire based on 5 video clips from a surveillance camera on Times Square, New York with one person passing by at a time. The same 5 video clips were processed in the manner explained in the implementation chapter, and the 5 shapes were presented in the questionnaire. All video clips and shapes were presented in a random order in the questionnaire. The respondents were asked to describe the shape and video clips using a list of 15 different affective states. The Russel's affective model [13] suggests that emotions can be arranged around a circle in a 2D space, with arousal and valence as the dimensions. Based on this model, affective states such as relaxed and calm are related and similar to each other, as they are positioned close to each other in the circle. Affective states such as sad and happy are opposites as seen by their position on each side of the circle. The respondents were asked to choose only one affective state that better describes their feelings in order to evaluate the expressive power of the visuals.

The main idea behind this evaluation was to compare the affective states expressed by the generated shapes to the corresponding video clip, in order to see if a correlation existed or if the generated shapes evoked different affections compared to the original video footage. The reason for researching this correlation was to evaluate whether a transformation of motion data, using a simple physical model, can still contain the same expressiveness of affective states as the actual video data.

5 Results

The questionnaire was completed by 45 respondents. The following section describes the results of this comparative study, where video clips containing single persons walking directly compared to the corresponding 3D representations (shapes).

The first person and the derived shape show almost no similar results. The person was mostly perceived as calm and relaxed while the shape was perceived as nervous and stressed. The reason for this could be the person looking relaxed but walking in a high tempo resulting in a jagged shape with sudden turns formed from his movements. In general, the answers were scattered for both the person and the generated shape. The second person and the derived shape show some similarities as both were perceived as

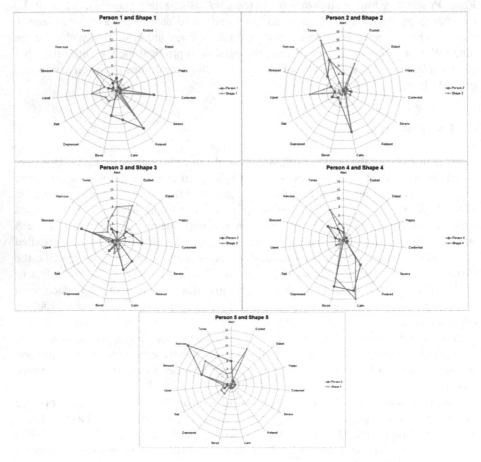

Fig. 6. Respondents' answers for different sets of human motion and generated visuals

tense and nervous. The person was also seen as alert while no one perceived the shape as alert. Despite some perceived the shape as tense, nervous and alert, the video clip is seen as calm, the complete opposite state of affection to the first three affective states.

As the results in the next section show, most generated visuals perceived with almost opposite affective states compared to the corresponding surveillance video (person 1–3). The persons were perceived mostly as calm, relaxed and contented while the corresponding shapes were perceived as mostly alert, exited and tense. The answers were scattered, while the shape was fairly centered on affective states with high arousal. Some pairs of person motion and associated shape (person 4 and 5) were perceived as similar with affection states very close to each other in the model (Fig. 6).

6 Conclusions

The results of the evaluation did not show conclusive results on whether a specific motion expressiveness of affective states could be retained through such a transformation to a 3D shape. This could be due to various conditions and this section will discuss some of these. The video clips used in this evaluation were based on people passing by and given the simple nature of these video clips, the motion of the persons were not very expressive or lacking granularity of expressed affection. For the first three videos, the data pointed in different directions of the circumplex model of affect and no single affective state from a 3D representation was able to describe the person's affective state. However, in the last two clips there was generally more agreement on the expressiveness of the person and this was also the case for the shape. These two clips had both more focused answers and more agreement between respondents, for both the person and the derived shape. From these results can be concluded that a very expressive motion might generate a shape with the same affective state. With the Gestalt law of common fate in mind, it would have been interesting to differentiate the shapes based on their rotations and thus, avoiding participants grouping the shapes because of similar directions. The same principal applies to Gestalt law of good form, because all the shapes in this experiment had the same color.

The aim of this project was to provide new ways to explore human motion expressiveness using generative art as a way to communicate with an audience. Transforming data from surveillance cameras into generative art, while retaining motion expressiveness required a transdisciplinary approach based on state of art human pose estimation technology. Considering the amount of transformation done to the original data, the 3D representations were aesthetically appealing but without conclusive results related to the communication of affectivity.

References

1. Miebach, N.: Weather (2018). http://nathaliemiebach.com/weather.html
2. Frick, L.: Sleep Patterns (2012). http://www.lauriefrick.com/sleep-patterns

3. Cao, Z., Simon, T., Wei, S. E., Sheikh, Y.: Realtime multi-person 2D pose estimation using part affinity fields. In: Proceedings - 30th IEEE Conference on Computer Vision and Pattern Recognition, CVPR 2017 (2017). https://doi.org/10.1109/CVPR.2017.143
4. Qiao, S., Wang, Y., Li, J.: Real-time human gesture grading based on OpenPose. In: Proceedings - 2017 10th International Congress on Image and Signal Processing, BioMedical Engineering and Informatics, CISP-BMEI 2017 (2018). https://doi.org/10.1109/CISP-BMEI.2017.8301910
5. Obradović, M., Marković, S.: Creating 3D shapes by time extrusion of moving objects. In: 20th Generative Art Conference GA 2017 (2017)
6. Takahashi, K.: Voxelman, 30 May 2018. https://github.com/keijiro/Voxelman
7. Carlucci, D., Schiuma, G., Santarsiero, F.: Toward a data-driven world: challenges and opportunities in arts and humanities. In: Big Data in the Arts and the Humanities: Theory and Practice. CRC Press (2018)
8. Depoorter, D.: Jaywalking (2016). https://driesdepoorter.be/jaywalking/
9. Lee-Delisle, S.: Lunar Trails, 25 May 2012. http://seb.ly/work/lunar-trails/
10. McCormack, J., Bown, O., Dorin, A., McCabe, J., Monro, G., Whitelaw, M.: Ten questions concerning generative computer art. Leonardo **47**(2), 135–141 (2014)
11. Edmonds, E.: From interaction to influence: generating form and space. In: GA 2015 – XVIII Generative Art Conference (2015)
12. Bisig, D., Bogner, F.: Pendulum – Exploiting Simple Physics for Generative Art. In: Generative Art Conference GA 2017 (2017)
13. Posner, J., Russell, J.A., Peterson, B.S.: The circumplex model of affect: an integrative approach to affective neuroscience, cognitive development, and psychopathology. Dev. Psychopathol. **17**(3), 715–734 (2005)

Creative Approaches on Interactive Visualization and Characterization at the Nanoscale

João Martinho Moura[1]([⊠]) [iD], Jordi Llobet[2]([⊠]) [iD], Marco Martins[2] [iD], and João Gaspar[2] [iD]

[1] Braga, Portugal
joaomartinhomoura@gmail.com
[2] INL - International Iberian Nanotechnology Laboratory,
Avenida Mestre José Veiga, 4715-330 Braga, Portugal
{jordi.llobet, marco.martins, joao.gaspar}@inl.int

Abstract. Visualizing and characterizing scientific data from observations at the nanoscale is a challenging task. We present creative approaches in the development of an interactive system to visualize and characterize nanopillar structures. This research is a result of a collaboration inside a team of scientists and artists, in the course of an artistic residency that occurred in a scientific institution. Before describing the development approaches, we will present a brief introduction to the thematic of nanotechnologies, media arts, and data visualization. This work arose from the need to observe and present nano visualizations during an artistic presentation, and to provide a software solution, that has been developed. The focus of this paper is to describe the technical and creative processes in the development of a reliable scientific visualization system.

Keywords: Nanoscale · Nanotechnology · Data visualization
Characterization · Nanopillars · Automated SEM characterization
Media art · Creative technologies

1 Introduction

Art offers science an essential store of images, ideas, metaphors, and language while methods of forming and patterning materials at the nano and micro scales are finding increased use as a medium of artistic expression [1]. Many organizations have initiated programs to bring together artists and scientists to stimulate collaboration and encourage the viewing of science as a means of public engagement. We have, as an example, the Leonardo Society, an international society promoting the cross-fertilization among the domains of art, science, and technology since the 60 s [2]. In this paper, we describe the technical and creative approaches developed in the context of an artistic residency at the

---

J. M. Moura—Independent Artist.

A. L. Brooks et al. (Eds.): ArtsIT 2018/DLI 2018, LNICST 265, pp. 121–132, 2019.

International Iberian Nanotechnology Laboratory (INL) [3], in Braga - Portugal, during the last year. In dealing with state-of-the-art technology in nanotechnology, the creative team had to work with large number of observations and obtain visual outcomes to be presented in an interactive performance exhibitions [4, 5]. This process began a set of problem-solving practices while visualizing and understanding data from observations. Within the framework of this collaboration, a software was specifically developed to analyze and characterize patterns in acquired images at the nanoscale, within the manipulation of nanoscale observation instruments. The work took place at the INL's Micro and Nanofabrication Department as practice-based research. In the creative arts, including new media arts, the emphasis is on the creative process and the works that are generated, promoting new understandings that arise about practices, and visual arts training may strengthen such skills and thereby lead to improvements in geometry performance [6]. Therefore, the focus of this paper is the presentation of the visualization results, as well as the practices associated in the course of this development between multi-disciplinary teams. In this sense, practice and research, together, operate in such a way as to generate new knowledge that can be shared and scrutinized [7], and interdisciplinary, transdisciplinary, cross-disciplinary, intermedia, transmedia and multimedia are becoming ever more prominent within the sciences, technology and the arts [8].

2 Nanotechnology and Media Art

One nanometer is a unit of length in the metric system, equal to one U.S. billionth of a meter (0.000000001 m). The idea of nanotechnology first came from the physicist Richard Feynman who imagined the entire Encyclopedia Britannica could be written on the head of a pin [9]. The nanotechnology term was coined by Norio Taniguchi, a Professor of the Tokyo University of Science, to describe semiconductor processes [10]. From the viewpoint of technology and applications, the unique properties of the nanoscale mean that nano design can produce striking results that cannot be produced in any other way [11]. From medicine to computing, to sunscreens, implications of using nanotechnology are present in everyday life. Nanotechnologies play significant role in our life and society, and it spans a range of science and engineering disciplines. Mark Ratner emphasizes its advantages by mentioning that it might allow an aircraft to recover from the sort of fuel tank damage that downed Air France's Concorde flight 4590 or even the space shuttle Challenger [11]. Pioneer media artists Christa Sommerer and Laurent Mignonneau presented the interactive artwork Nano-Scape to bring the theme of nanotechnologies closer to the public awareness [12], by interacting with invisible self-organizing atoms through a magnetic force feedback interface. Victoria Vesna and James Gimzewski demonstrated compelling results when joining groups of scientists and artists outside the academic walls [13], providing a vision that we are all, from the bottom up, molecular in origin. Chris Turmey suggests a neo-cubist spirit for making and seeing nanoscale images [14]. Hawkins and Straughan presented Midas, an artwork that foregrounds the ongoing disassembly and reassembly of matter at the nano-scale [15]. Astrophysicists and nanoscientists, through visualized algorithms, receive pictures out of the depths of the macro-cosmos, and the micro-cosmos, respectively [16], and future applications for nanotechnology seem only to be limited by the creativity of researchers [9].

3   INL Scale Travels – The Context of This Research

INL is the first intergovernmental organization in Europe in the field of nanoscience and nanotechnology [3]. In 2015, the Laboratory launched the Scale Travels initiative, that aims at fostering a multidisciplinary and hybrid approach between science, and one of its goals is to spark the discussion about the social, cultural and ethical impact of nanotechnology through media arts and to create novel media and digital objects based on nanotechnology, leading to original experiences and unexpected products, processes and services. The Scale Travels Residencies aims at bringing media artists and researchers into conversation and convergence embedded in a real laboratory environment inside INL's facilities [17–19]. This creative connection promotes the inclusion of new expert knowledge in the media arts and frames the discussion on the complexities underlying the nanoscience and nanotechnology research. INL is also hosting artistic residencies from the European Commission Starts initiative [20–22]. INL is located in the City of Braga, Portugal, which was included in the UNESCO Creative Cities Network. The title of UNESCO Creative City of Media Arts was attributed to the city of Braga on the 31st of October 2017 [23, 24].

4   Development

Using computer vision technologies [25], and creative programming open-source environments: Openframeworks (C++) [26] and Processing (JAVA) [27], we developed a series of software visualizations which achieve significant advances in the characterization of observations obtained by the Scanning Electron Microscope (SEM), an instrument that produces images of a sample by scanning the surface with a focused beam of electrons. Those visualizations were useful to produce data to understand and present artistic work at the 43rd International Conference on Micro and Nano-Engineering and INL Summit events in 2017 [4], and at the European Researchers Night in 2018 [5]. In the next section we will describe the techniques developed to better acquire, classify and characterize SEM observations in nanofabricated structures, specifically in the case of nanopillar structures, with different scenarios of observation.

4.1   Data Visualization in Nanotechnology

Advanced nanoscale observation instruments and pre-programmed sequential capture techniques offer the possibility of obtaining large amounts of images to analyze. As nowadays our ability to generate information far exceeds our capacity to understand it [28], it is important to have mechanisms to identify, classify and characterize features in those images. Scientists now require more from visualization than a set of results and a tidy showcase in which to display them [29], and because in nanotechnology even a small space measure can represent a lot of data, we based our approach in the principle of reduction and privileging of spatial variables [30], using graphical primitives such as lines, points and simple geometric shapes, focusing on feature-based approaches, very useful to reduce the amount of data which is shown at each instance of time [31]. Visualization research often involve finding innovative graphic and interactive techniques to represent the complexity of information structures [32], and sophisticated technologies of scientific visualization often require a departure from the standards of mimetic representation [33], as researchers constantly tweak them, altering parameters, changing color scales, substituting different algorithms with aesthetic and scientific conventions in mind [34] with the goal of obtaining a better understanding of the generated data, only possible if we collect, organize and characterize it. Artists, scientists and mathematicians are concerned with visualization in many different forms in order to better understand the true nature of reality [35]. Visual data exploration aims at integrating the human in the data exploration process, applying its perceptual abilities to the large datasets available in today's computer systems [36], and interface design for filtering and selecting data is also essential in this process. Eduard Tufte, pioneer in the field of data visualization, says that science and art share intense observing, and postulated principles of analytical design such as comparisons, causality, explanation, evidence, and multivariate analysis, which contributes effectively to a better understanding of a subject by different perspectives and combination of more than one characteristic [37], and suggests that repetition and change promotes comparison and surprise in visual communication [38]. In nano fabrication, observation and characterization, repetition and tiny micro and nanoscale differences are very common, but indeed crucial, and there are many essential variables to compare in repeated samples. Capturing images of nanostructures provided many engaging scientific visualizations with similarities to macroscale life forms and man-made structures [1]. In the next sections we present our approaches developed in the context of visualization and characterization from SEM observations.

4.2 Visualizing Large Arrays of Nanostructures on Large Area Wafers

Nanopillars is a technology within the field of nanostructures placed together in lattice like arrays. Nanopillars set themselves apart from other nanostructures due to their unique shape and get their attributes from being grouped into artificially designed structures that promote different behavior far away from their natural properties. Each nanopillar has a pillar shape at the bottom and a tapered pointy end on top. This shape, in combination with nanopillars' ability to be grouped together, exhibits many useful properties, having many applications including efficient solar panels [39, 40], high resolution analysis [41], antibacterial surfaces [42] and water reduction [43].

Dense and large-area arrays of nanometric scale structures are regularly fabricated at INL Cleanroom (Figs. 1 and 2). The characterization of sub-micron structures (below 500 nm) at large scale and its post data analysis is a very challenging task [44]. The observed subject consists of approximately ten U.S. billion (10.000.000.000) pillars of 1 µm height and 500 nm diameter, with 1 µm period equally distributed among a diameter of 110 mm (Figs. 3, 4 and 5). To have a more real comparative notion, if you imagine a text with 10 U.S. billion words, this would form a book with 18 million A4 pages and with 5 million kilograms in weight. This is a huge amount number of pillar structure to analyze and characterize at a very small size, only possible through challenging and creative tasks with a controlled autonomy. A 110 mm diameter fully nanostructured area has been fabricated by electron beam lithography (EBL) and deep reactive ion etching. Circular pillars of 500 nm diameter have been distributed in 1 μm pitch was patterned. EBL (EBPG 5200 from Raith) exposure using a negative resist was carried out operating at 100 kV. For this EBL experiment, several approaches were used to reduce the exposure time for large-scale nanofabrication process.

Fig. 1. Nanopillar formations, observed from a very far distance.

Automated routines for high and low magnification SEM imaging have been successfully developed. The images have been acquired using a SEM (NanoSEM from FEI) with the IFast scripting software [45], which allows to take large amounts of images from nanometric structures covering multiple regions of the wafer in few hours.

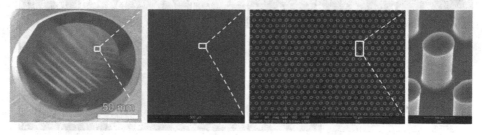

Fig. 2. Photography of the wafer containing the large array of fabricated nanopillars characterized automatically in this work.

Fig. 3. Low magnification SEM image of part of the array.

Fig. 4. High magnification SEM image.

Fig. 5. High resolution 40° SEM image with 1 nanopillar.

With the obtained raw data, geometric parameters were extracted from the images with the development of our custom software using computer vision algorithms. A metrological analysis has been performed to determine the patterning accuracy in the xyz dimensions. A method was developed and established to automatically determine the diameter of each pillar in each observation. For this, a large set of SEM images at high and low magnification were obtained. For low magnification top view images (250 X), more than $2 \cdot 10^8$ pillars (corresponding to $\sim 2\%$) were analyzed revealing the absence of missing or broken silicon pillars.

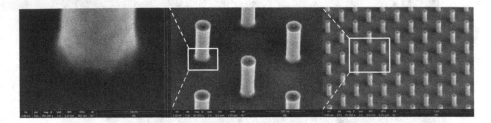

Fig. 6. Tilted SEM nanopillar observations.

High resolution tilted images (75 kX) (Figs. 5 and 6) were analyzed to determine the height of the pillars. More than 1000 SEM images at 5 kX were acquired to characterize the diameter and period along the wafer.

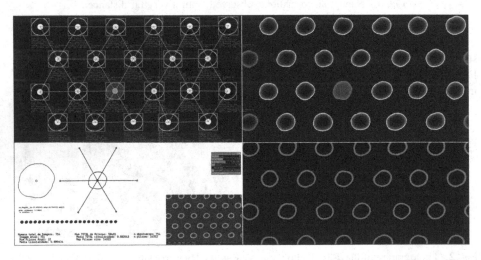

Fig. 7. Computer vision techniques to characterize the nanopillars. Real-time interface to adjust visual parameters. Top-left: neighborhood representation in blue lines, with selected pillar in red; Top-right: in yellow, characterizable pillars inside the image; Bottom-left: information about selected pillar and adjustment controls; Bottom-right: edge detection. (Color figure online)

The period, height and diameter of the fabricated structures were 1.038 ± 0.03 µm, 1.05 ± 0.025 µm and 520 ± 12 nm in the analyzed regions of the wafer demonstrating very little variation of the dimensionality along the wafer. Our code applies the correct contrast and brightness and blurs the image to reduce noise artifacts and have a perfect shape capture (Fig. 7). The software finds contours and selects the fully visible pillars in each observation. Each pillar is classified with its position in the wafer, center of mass, diameter, and a high-resolution circular shape (with more than 150 points) is extracted. Figure 8 shows 60 representations of pillars from the top view in a sequential order, each one with its different forms and sizes, which means that this individual characterization applies to all observed pillars, being thousands or millions, and having this detail for large quantities, in such a fast process, turns possible an efficient and effective large-scale study. Structural analysis of each pillar is performed with shape descriptors [46], including the level of circularity. In this sample, circularity it's important to analyze and get a global idea of the nanofabrication process quality. Neighborhood distance between nearby pillars it's also critical in the analyzed sample. Figure 7 (top left) shows six blue lines for each pillar representing its neighbors' positions.

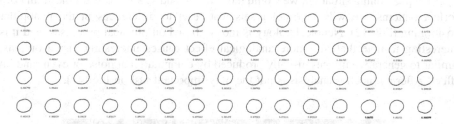

Fig. 8. Representation of pillars from the top view in sequential order of observation. A circularity value (from 0 to 1) is calculated and presented for each nanopillar. 1 means a perfect circularity.

Figure 9 shows an overlayered representation of a large amount (more than 80000) neighborhood positions. A perfect 6-point star would represent perfect equidistant pillar positioning. Histograms of neighborhood distance are also presented (right side bar and gradient graphs) showing that the sample equidistance's level is near perfect values.

Making use of the low opacity, and with the shape superposition, we obtain a good visual reference of the circularity (Fig. 10). As we have a good resolution in the shapes, we can still color the most repeated vertices along all individual observations, and thus have a global notion of the nanofabrication process. This approach visually presents a possible solution to one of the major problems in the area of scientific visualization: the

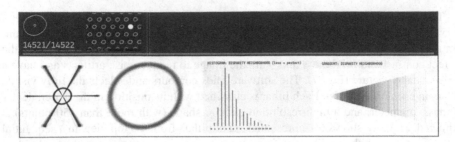

Fig. 9. Neighborhood distances between pillars (0 means the desirable distance in this sample, and greater than 14 goes out of specifications). General circular shape is also presented.

representation of error or uncertainty [29]. Having this result at the level of each pillar, and having calculated its specific position, we can graphically show the variation of the values along the wafer, as shown in Fig. 11, where circularity is plotted in the left and neighborhood equidistance in the right.

After having perfect position patterns, a possible characterization of the equidistance can be achieved if we overlay neighborhood lines by applying negative color effects. In a perfect positioning situation, we would have a clear and straightforward mesh. In non-perfect patterns, we will have color sets that react to differences in the nanopillar positioning (Fig. 12). Nanotechnology is mostly based on physical processes, and it is interesting to note that this more analogical effect causes interesting visual outputs, similar to generative images, usually produced by computational noise or even random effect. After all, neutral analysis is not the only important task in life [47].

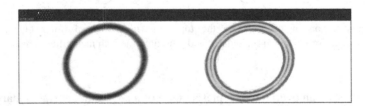

Fig. 10. General view of pillar circularity. In the right-side visualization, color gradients from red to blue represent the most common vertices in each nanopillar in crescent order. Red means less common and blue means most common vertices. (Color figure online)

The proposed visualization system is also interactive, and presented as a software application, meaning that it can characterize different sample sets, and computer vision parameters can be adjusted in real-time. It also stores these configurations for multiple uses over time.

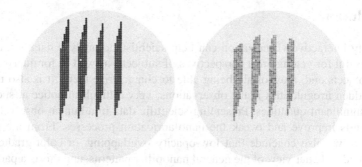

Fig. 11. Circularity and neighborhood equidistance values distributed by position in the wafer. Each point represents one observation and opacity color represents the average value of circularity (left) and average value of neighborhood equidistance (right). Lighter colors mean greater circularity or better equidistance in the neighborhood. (Color figure online)

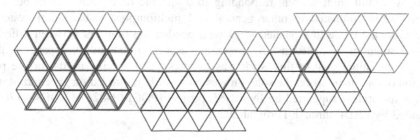

Fig. 12. Overlaying neighborhood distances from different samples and applying color pixel difference (negative overlayered effect) provides a view about the nanopillars positioning disparity. (Color figure online)

A set of visualizations presented in this publication were selected to integrate an interactive installation exhibition (Fig. 13), presented at the European Researchers' Night, in Porto, Portugal [5]. This result was achieved with interdisciplinary work where attention to detail was the most distinctive feature in the process, via creative activity and visual thinking [48]. Innovation happens when convergent thinkers combine forces with divergent thinkers, and art and science – once inextricably linked, both dedicated to finding truth and beauty – are better together than apart [49].

Fig. 13. Image excerpts of the exhibition *Nano Geometries*, at the European Researchers' Night, 28th September 2018, at Palácio das Artes, Porto, Portugal.

5   Conclusion

High-quality interactive visualization can help scientists to analyze data at the nanoscale. It is useful for getting great perspectives of subjects, as well as for querying small details in objects and, most of all, being able to characterize them. It is also useful to uncover hidden irregularities in the observations, very difficult to notice at such small sizes and significant quantities. Presenting scientific data in a human-observable form let the experts improve and tweak the nanofabrication processes. From the point of visualization, we also conclude that low-opacity overlapping, or color-gradient techniques, provide a better view of the general nanopillar patterns, and this is a particularly useful technique when it is critical to analyze tens of thousands, or even million observations. Interactivity is also important in visualization, to change values, conditions and operators during the characterization procedures. The software solution presented in this document can analyze and characterize large quantities of objects at the once, being limited only by the capabilities of hardware machine. Because the system was built from scratch, responding to a specific need, turns out to be quite efficient when compared to other general and multipurpose visualization systems, where tasks are made in separated steps with needed file transfers between different software solutions or platforms. An important aspect to conclude this paper is that although the initial goal of this work was to respond to specific needs for the presentation of an artistic work, the solution was posteriorly improved for specialized use.

This research is supported by INSENSE project (POCI-01-0247-FEDER-017866) co-funded by ERDF through Portugal 2020.

References

1. Yetisen, A.K., et al.: Art on the nanoscale and beyond. In: Advanced Materials, vol. 28, no. 9, pp. 1724–1742. Wiley-Blackwell, Hoboken (2016). https://doi.org/10.1002/adma. 201502382. ISBN 1521-4095, ISSN 15214095
2. Mission - Leonardo/International Society for the Arts, Science and Technology. https://www.leonardo.info/mission. Accessed 25 May 2018
3. International Iberian Nanotechnology Laboratory – INL - Interdisciplinary research in Nanotechnology and Nanoscience. http://inl.int/. Accessed 12 May 2018
4. Moura, J.M., Rafael, A., Mendanha, C., Pedro, M.: Nano abstractions. In: 43rd International Conference on Micro and Nano Engineering, Braga (2017)
5. Moura, J.M., Llobet, J., Martins, M., Gaspar, J.: Nano geometries (2018). http://jmartinho. net/nano-geometries/. Accessed 12 Aug 2018
6. Walker, C.M., Winner, E., Hetland, L., Simmons, S., Goldsmith, L.: Visual thinking: art students have an advantage in geometric reasoning. In: Creative Education, vol. 02, no. 01, pp. 22–26 (2011). https://doi.org/10.4236/ce.2011.21004. ISSN 2151-4755
7. Candy, L., Edmonds, E.: Practice-based research in the creative arts: Foundations and futures from the front line. Leonardo **51**(1), 63–69 (2018). https://doi.org/10.1162/LEON_a_01471. ISBN 9780262019187, ISSN 0024094X
8. Root-Bernstein, B., Brown, A., Siler, T., Snelson, K.: Artscience: integrative collaboration to create a sustainable future. Leonardo **44**(3), 192 (2011). https://doi.org/10.1162/LEON_e_00161. ISSN 0024094X

9. The Royal Society, Why is nanotechnology important? http://invigorate.royalsociety.org/ks5/what-could-nano-do-for-you/why-is-nanotechnology-important.aspx. Accessed 02 June 2018
10. Taniguchi, N.: On the basic concept of nanotechnology. In: Proceedings of the International Conference on Production Engineering, pp. 18–23 (1974)
11. Ratner, B.M., Ratner, D.: Nanotechnology: A Gentle Introduction to the Next Big Idea, vol. 6, no. 2. Prentice Hall (2003). https://doi.org/10.1016/S1369-7021(03)00236-0. ISBN 9780131014008, ISSN 13697021
12. Mignonneau, L., Sommerer, C.: Nano-scape : experiencing aspects of nanotechnology through a magnetic force-feedback interface. In: Proceedings of the 2005 ACM SIGCHI International Conference on Advances in computer entertainment technology, pp. 200–203 (2005). https://doi.org/10.1145/1178477.1178507. ISBN 1-59593-110-4
13. Vesna, V., Gimzewski, J.K.: NANO: an exhibition of scale and senses. Leonardo **38**(4), 310–311 (2005). https://doi.org/10.1162/0024094054762070. ISSN 0024-094X
14. Toumey, C.: Truth and beauty at the nanoscale. Leonardo **42**(2), 151–155 (2009). https://doi.org/10.1162/leon.2009.42.2.151. ISSN 0024-094X
15. Hawkins, H., Straughan, E.R.: Nano-art, dynamic matter and the sight/sound of touch. Geoforum **51**, 130–139 (2014). https://doi.org/10.1016/j.geoforum.2013.10.010. ISSN 00167185
16. Grau, O., Veigl, T.: Imagery in the 21st Century. MIT Press, Cambridge (2011). https://doi.org/10.1016/j.pragma.2013.04.005. ISBN 9780262015721, ISSN 03782166
17. Kurokawa, R.: ad/ab Atom (2017). http://www.ryoichikurokawa.com/project/aaatom.html. Accessed 10 May 2018
18. AGF, Scale Travels: LanguageHack, por AGF. http://www.gnration.pt/agenda/468#.W2HKY9hKids. Accessed 12 June 2018
19. Scale Travels—exposições—Projetos—Braga Media Arts. http://www.bragamediaarts.com/pt/projetos/detalhe/scale-travels/. Accessed 01 June 2018
20. STARTS - (S + T)*ARTS = STARTS Innovation at the nexus of Science, Technology, and the ARTS. https://www.starts.eu/about/. Accessed 23 June 2018
21. CritCat - João Martinho Moura—VERTIGO Starts Residencies. https://vertigo.starts.eu/calls/2017-2/residencies/sci-fi-miners/detail/. Accessed 20 June 2018
22. NANO2WATER - HeHe - VERTIGO Starts Residencies. https://vertigo.starts.eu/calls/2017-2/residencies/ors-orbital-river-station/detail/. Accessed 20 June 2018
23. Braga - UNESCO Creative Cities Network. https://en.unesco.org/creative-cities/braga. Accessed 17 May 2018
24. Braga Media Arts. http://www.bragamediaarts.com/en/. Accessed 12 Apr 2018
25. Bradski, G.: OpenCV (2000). http://www.opencv.org
26. Fry, B., Reas, C.: Processing.org, Processing (2001). https://processing.org/
27. Lieberman, Z., Castro, A., Open Community: Openframeworks (2004). http://openframeworks.cc
28. Lima, M.: Visual Complexity: Mapping Patterns of Information. Princeton Architectural Press, New York City (2011). ISBN 978-1568989365
29. Johnson, C.: Top scientific visualization research problems. IEEE Comput. Graphics Appl. **24**(4), 13–17 (2004). https://doi.org/10.1109/MCG.2004.20. ISBN 0272-1716 VO – 24, ISSN 02721716
30. Manovich, L.: What is visualisation? Vis. Stud. **26**(1), 36–49 (2011). https://doi.org/10.1080/1472586X.2011.548488. ISBN 1472-5878, ISSN 1472586X
31. Doleisch, H., Gasser, M., Hauser, H.: Interactive feature specification for focus + context visualization of complex simulation data. In: VISSYM 2003 Proceedings of the Symposium on Data Visualisation 2003, pp. 239–249 (2003). ISBN 1-58113-698-6

32. Judelman, G.: Aesthetics and inspiration for visualization design: bridging the gap between art and science. In: Proceedings of Eighth International Conference on Information Visualisation 2004, pp. 245–250 (2004). https://doi.org/10.1109/IV.2004.1320152. ISBN 0-7695-2177-0, ISSN 1093-9547

33. Toumey, C., Nerlich, B., Robinson, C.: Technologies of scientific visualization. Leonardo **48** (1), 61–63 (2015). https://doi.org/10.1162/LEON_a_00896. ISSN 0024-094X

34. Burri, R.V., Dumit, J.: Social studies of scientific imaging and visualization. In: Hackett, E. J., Amsterdamska, O., Lynch, M., Wajcman, J. (eds.) The Handbook of Science and Technology Studies, 3rd edn, pp. 297–317. MIT Press, Cambridge (2008). ISBN 978-0-262-08364-5

35. Brisson, H.E.: Visualization in art and science. Leonardo **25**(3/4), 257 (1992). https://doi.org/10.2307/1575847. ISSN 0024094X

36. Keim, D.A.: Information visualization and visual data mining. IEEE Trans. Vis. Comput. Graph. **8**(1), 1–8 (2002). https://doi.org/10.1109/2945.981847. ISBN 1077-2626, ISSN 10772626

37. Tufte, E.R.: Visual Explanations: Images and Quantities. Evidence and Narrative. Graphics Press, Cheshire (1997). ISBN 9781930824157

38. Tufte, E.: Beautiful Evidence. Graphics Press, Cheshire (2006). ISBN 0961392177 9780961392178

39. Faingold, Y., et al.: Efficient light trapping and broadband absorption of the solar spectrum in nanopillar arrays decorated with deep-subwavelength sidewall features. Nanoscale (2018, accepted)

40. Fan, Z., et al.: Three-dimensional nanopillar-array photovoltaics on low-cost and flexible substrates. Nat. Mater. **8**(8), 648–653 (2009). https://doi.org/10.1038/nmat2493. ISBN 1476-1122, ISSN 14764660

41. Kandziolka, M., et al.: Silicon nanopillars as a platform for enhanced fluorescence analysis. Anal. Chem. **85**(19), 9031–9038 (2013). https://doi.org/10.1021/ac401500y. ISSN 00032700

42. Hasan, J., Crawford, R.J., Ivanova, E.P.: Antibacterial surfaces: the quest for a new generation of biomaterials. Trends Biotechnol. **31**(5), 295–304 (2013). https://doi.org/10.1016/j.tibtech.2013.01.017. ISBN 0167-7799, ISSN 01677799

43. Bao, X.Q., et al.: Amorphous oxygen-rich molybdenum oxysulfide decorated p-type silicon microwire arrays for efficient photoelectrochemical water reduction. Nano Energy **16**, 130–142 (2015). https://doi.org/10.1016/j.nanoen.2015.06.014. ISBN 22112855, ISSN 22112855

44. Llobet, J., et al.: Arrays of suspended silicon nanowires defined by ion beam implantation: mechanical coupling and combination with CMOS technology. Nanotechnology **29**(150), 155303 (2018). https://doi.org/10.1088/1361-6528/aaac67. ISSN 13616528

45. Thermo Fisher: Ifast Software. https://www.fei.com/software/ifast/. Accessed 10 June 2018

46. Teh, C.-H., Chin, R.T.: On the detection of dominant points on digital curves. IEEE Trans. Pattern Anal. Mach. Intell. **11**(8), 859–872 (1989). https://doi.org/10.1109/34.31447. ISSN 01628828

47. Viégas, F.B., Wattenberg, M.: Artistic data visualization: beyond visual analytics. In: Schuler, D. (ed.) OCSC 2007. LNCS, vol. 4564, pp. 182–191. Springer, Heidelberg (2007). https://doi.org/10.1007/978-3-540-73257-0_21. ISBN 9783540732563, ISSN 0302-9743

48. Brown, A.G.P.: Visualization as a common design language: connecting art and science. Autom. Constr. **12**(6), 703–713 (2003). https://doi.org/10.1016/S0926-5805(03)00044-X. ISSN 0926-5805

49. Maeda, J.: STEM + Art = STEAM. STEAM (Sci. Technol. Eng. Arts Math.) J. **1**(1), 1–3 (2013). https://doi.org/10.5642/steam.201301.34. ISBN 2327-2074, ISSN 23272074

Contemporary Installation Art and Phenomenon of Digital Interactivity: Aha Experiences – Recognition and Related Creating with and for Affordances

Anthony L. Brooks[(✉)]

Aalborg University, 9000 Aalborg, Denmark
tb@create.aau.dk

Abstract. Observing audience attendance of a student created interactive art installation is posited relating to phenomenon of serendipity, brought about via cumulated conditions and strategies, synchronously resulting in an author-recognized '*Aha experience*'. Identifying of engagement, then disengagement, and subsequent re-engagement informs reflections and critique. Speculation to how multi-affordances in an interactive art installation can combine with perceptual and cognitive pre-knowledge, e.g. pervasiveness of sensors in contemporary society (as audience pre-knowledge), to influence audience expectation, explorations, and engagement experiences. This contextually illustrated in how affordances (false/perceptual/hidden) of the installation became aspects that unwittingly and coincidentally cumulated to establish a *critical incident* moment: A period in time that serendipitously and synchronously involved observation of audience disengagement following initial confrontation immediately followed by a system reset that stimulated (as if playfully) re-engagement. Conclusions question how a strategy of *playful artistic design* that incorporates such audience perceptual and cognitive influencing through affordances can be a potential factor utilized in realizing interactive art installations. Posited thus is a contemporary art strategy goal to engage beyond artless mapping (e.g. one-to-one) toward more stimulating, intellectual, and enjoyable audience experience.

Keywords: Aha experience · Serendipitous synchronicity · Interactive art POPBL · Multi-affordances · Playful design

1 Introduction

1.1 Art and Technology Education, Aalborg University, Denmark

Aalborg University[1] (AAU) has, since its inauguration in 1974, originated, established, nurtured, developed and continuously evolved its Project-Organized Problem-Based Learning teaching model (PBL or POPBL) – see e.g. [1]. Under the Aalborg University PBL model, students study in groups to initially formulate a problem under

---

[1] https://www.en.aau.dk/about-aau.

© ICST Institute for Computer Sciences, Social Informatics and Telecommunications Engineering 2019
Published by Springer Nature Switzerland AG 2019. All Rights Reserved
A. L. Brooks et al. (Eds.): ArtsIT 2018/DLI 2018, LNICST 265, pp. 133–142, 2019.

a dedicated semester project theme that typically carries 15 ECTS. Another 15 ECTS covers semester courses. A group is typically 6–7 students at the start of their under-graduate education and progressively reducing in size to final semester, typically 1–3. Learning goals within a themed project description guide a group's formulation of a problem that then becomes the central focus/catalyst around which research and practical activities are conducted to realize semester objectives. Staff coordination and supervision support student study and project activities. A mixed staff and student study board manage activities of each education.

Art and Technology (ArT) education[2] is a six semester interdisciplinary research- and practice-based education under AAU's Humanistic Faculty. Students are awarded Bachelor of Arts (BA) degree in Art & Technology (Danish title of the degree is "BA i Oplevelsesteknologi"). Research (and to an extent procedure) is exploratory, as stu-dents investigate what they do not know in order, through investigating a problem, to improve their knowledge, skills, and competences aligned with the AAU PBL model.

Spring semester January – June 2018: ArT Exhibition May 8–9.

The author, as semester coordinator for ArT fourth semester spring 2018, selected an outside public space, a municipality-governed park close to AAU's downtown campus in Aalborg, as installation site for the May student semester exhibition. Such places in Denmark are considered "open to all, free of charge" [2]. Justifying selection, a goal was to challenge students with innate site-specific issues e.g. weather, security, power, … whilst offering multiple opportunities for interaction and occasions for sit-uated learning related to the outcome of interactions with the social and physical environment [3]. The public park, whilst generally open grassed areas with shrub encircled divisions separated by meandering pathways, also has numerous stakeholder areas with garden plots, adjacent kindergarten/school with play areas, skater areas, petanque courts, covered gathering spots, and a stage area for live musical perfor-mances. Main stakeholder is the municipality who run the area. An exhibition student committee representative thus had the additional challenge of cooperation with municipality contact and associated service personnel.

By locating the exhibition site away from the university the formal and controlled learning environment is distanced thus challenging students toward emergent and student-led activities targeting learning in a real-world situation outside classroom. Also, and importantly, exposure to public audiences rather than (typically) in-house peers who attend exhibitions within the campus buildings was considered positively impactful. This strategy aligns with promoting contextualized learning experiences through exploration (e.g. by experiencing things at hand in real and authentic settings), interaction (e.g. with more experienced peers and experts in the field), and serendipity (e.g. when "human search for knowledge may occur by chance, or as by-product of the main task" in unplanned, random and unexpected ways) [4, 5].

The author's role, besides coordination, included lecturing courses in interaction design, multimodal perception and cognition, and supervision of two exhibiting ArT student groups. The supervisor role changes to examiner for the students'

---

[2] https://www.en.aau.dk/education/bachelor/art-technology.

examinations. Following this opening framing behind the work, the next section narrows contextualization by introducing an ArT specific student group installation that led to the catalyst of this paper i.e. observed "Aha experience" [6, 7]. NB: Whilst students declined to co-author they agreed citation of their work SCAPE as acknowledged.

2   Places and Spaces of Interaction: SCAPE

Project theme for the fourth semester students in Art and Technology (ArT4) spring 2018 was *Places and Spaces of Interaction* under which student groups were tasked to build temporary public interactive installations in an outside park environment – a city space not associated to any museum or art-based institution or organization. Installations were exhibited over two days (8th and 9th May) and prior consultation with the local municipality as stakeholder-owner was undertaken regarding constraints, rules, use of electricity, etc. A student committee ensured all constrains were adhered.

During the exhibition days each of the student groups collected exhibition data associated to their specific installation, typically, audience reactions using various triangulation of methods and techniques. Such data are subsequently analyzed with final reports written then uploaded for grading alongside a presentation, video reportage, and oral discussion with appointed external censor and examiner.

This paper focuses on one ArT4 student installation, titled SCAPE, realized as a visually static interactive sound installation. Figure 1 illustrates the front of the work that the students changed between exhibition days due to problems as detailed next.

Fig. 1. SCAPE installation with front interface changes – Day 1 (left) Day 2 (right): © + Acknowledgements. SCAPE students: Daniela Bretes Maciel Elneff; Cristina Palo-mares; Christine Hvidt Grønborg; Jonathan Jung Johansen; Lasse Goul Jensen; Sidsel Abrahamsen.

2.1   Installation Detail and Problems

Approximate size of the SCAPE installation was 2.4 m wide × 1.8 m deep × 2 m high. Cover materials were reflective Mylar and black painted plastic on a front wall (see Fig. 1). The design considered various modalities of audience *attractors* including semiotic affordances in the visual design (e.g. vectors, contrast, salience…). Planned main *sustainer* of audience engagement was an interactive sensor-based soundscape perceived via an inbuilt sound system. The soundscapes was designed having two defined zones of interaction – front wall (concrete embedded conductance sensors – via touch) and the perimeter three surrounding walls (Doppler sensors – via proximity). A software algorithm (patch) was created in Cycling74 MAX/MSP, a visual programming language for music and multimedia development. The MAX/MSP patch was planned to receive data from the sensors of sourced human behavior to generate the soundscape. A text document ('info stand') detailed the interactive installation and its elements for audience pre-knowledge, thus in advance of active confrontation. Design influences were cited as [8, 9].

Overview with notes of change interface and interaction:

Day 1: SCAPE front wall interface was thirty-five capacitive sensors mounted within concrete 'blobs' – see Fig. 1 left. Human touch on the concrete blobs incremented audio frequencies. A system algorithm *reset* activated once an auditory threshold had been reached to maintain sounds within a suitable bandwidth for audience listening comfort.

Day 2: The concrete encased capacitive sensors ('blobs') were removed, because of the feedback being considered by the group as 'too ambiguous and unclear'. Students stated "In terms of interaction it should be clear to the participants that they alter the sounds by their interactions and they should receive an immediate real time response." The capacitive sensors were replaced by six 10K potentiometers mounted upon a Mylar shape – see Fig. 1 right. Human audience members thus manually turned each potentiometer to influence the soundscape - so a direct influence on the sound was evident. The *reset* from day one was deactivated as potentiometer control delimited audio frequencies within the comfortable listening range.

Consistent on Both Days: Info-board text document plus five Doppler proximity sensors positioned on side and rear walls of the structure. These sensors were deactivated due to unstable signals but were left uncovered (so visible for audience).

The student group implemented a mixed-method analysis of visitors' behaviors and interactions according to a pre-defined coding scheme established in line with behavioral expressions and gestural meaning [10]. Two group members, in shifts, conducted audience observations. Post exhibition, collected data from observation sheets, recorded videos, and notes were triangulated to determine behavior patterns and standout moments relative to a formulated project problem/question. Results indicated increased engagement on day one (when observations reported audience explorations as curiosity conjoined with confusion) vs. day two when it was perceived as an alternative musical instrument but with observations reflecting less audience interest.

2.2   Audience

People know what they do; they frequently know why they do what they do; but what they don't know is what what they do does... Foucault [11]

The installation attracted satisfactory public attendance across ages and gender as one may predict for a site-specific work in an open public space on two sunny spring days. In the following section, first-hand experience from observing SCAPE audience behavior is shared from one of the author's visits. This analyzed observation led to the posited goal shared via this contribution, which relates to how Foucault's quote [11] can be reflected aligned with artists (and designers) creative use of and thinking about affordances to a higher level in order to stimulate and potentially optimize audience engagement and *Aha experiences* with contemporary interactive installations.

3   Recognition of *Aha Experience* and Reflections on SCAPE

As supervisor, the author visited the installation a number of times during the building day prior to the exhibition as well as at the opening exhibition day. Each discussion and revisit made apparent the students' despair at the installation not working as envisaged. On my final visit, late in the evening of exhibition day one, the student observer informed of the changes planned for day two. Whilst listening I observed audience attendance in the form of a small group of spectators/participants who explored all around SCAPE. They were testing perceived interfaces relative to feedback – likely as associated to the pre-knowledge given as text on the info-board. Following explorations, they disengaged by meeting approximately one meter in front of the main interface (Fig. 1 left) where they discussed their experience. During their discussion the system reset triggered, which changed the auditory feedback. Immediately the group, as one, turned and physically re-engaged with the installation to explore further questioning what had happened. The reset detail is understood as not being noted on the info-board text document. Even though they could not determine what activity they may have influenced, they continued to explore further, clearly with interest but also confusion, eventually leaving, seemingly with stimulating positive experiences but also potentially frustrating. It was not reported if same audience returned for day two.

The author's reaction was to comment to the student that it was interesting to observe such a re-engagement moment – or *Aha experience* - and it could be pertinent to question further. This the students did, to an extent, via a correlation analysis between day one and day two. However the change of installation interface prevented in-depth analysis of the system reset moment, which is herein considered a critical incident toward 'making inferences as to requirements' [12]. Thus, the *Aha experience* – one could say of both audience and observer(s) – is an aspect that could be further questioned and studied in such installations alongside designing with different affordances (false-, perceived-, hidden- etc.,) to impact human traits of audiences. Such work using sensors can thus question contemporary pervasiveness of sensors from a cultural/societal knowledge/experiences perspective to intellectually design for audience experiences via a concept of purposeful playful design with multi-affordances.

4   Discussion and Conclusions

Contemporary pervasiveness of sensor technologies (and especially their wide-spread uses in art installations to attribute interactivity as well as their integration into education and industries) means that audiences are more knowledgeable and aware than ever of how such hardware works e.g. detecting proximity, gestures, actions, etc. In SCAPE, this audience pre-knowledge can be assumed, as well as how resulting sourced data can be mapped to control selected digital output(s), in this case perceived as auditory feedback changeable to touch (capacitive sensors) or physical rotation (potentiometers). By first informing via a text that detailed interactions innate of SCAPE and then openly revealing the Doppler sensors as an apparent 'control mechanism' - but then deactivating (but still revealed) - the group initiated a dialogue with their sensor-aware audience, sending an explicit message. The concealed concrete embedded capacitive sensors offered a different message but one that equally provoked confused exploration – though an understanding is that to some degree these worked but the group declared change required. However, on day one, an understanding was thus shared, motivating engaged audience to question the interaction. The audience was encouraged to choose its own non-reliant interpretation. The open-endedness offered audience authorship and to be generators of their own meaning. The 'critical incident' of *reset* matched to *Aha experience*, according to the author's observation, provoked disruption of interpreted meaning resulting in a serendipitously syncopated happening and positive response activity of re-engagement. Exploration of the system reset moment could have focused and foreshortened video analysis in that a temporal known independent variable could have been targeted with dependent variables according to the cumulated conditions. This should have enabled a more-in-depth analysis leading to a consideration of refinement of research question based upon finding(s) rather than inconclusive outcome as reported. Aligned was the potential for a more in-depth discussion, reflections and critique in the oral examination.

A Prepared Mind: Background Enabling *Aha Experience* Recognition

Observation methods, as utilized in the ArT education, should be open, receptive, and inductive to allow relatively unanticipated aspects and links to emerge in line with Naturalistic Inquiry through utilizing defined coding schema and constant comparison of diverse audience (individual/groups) experiences and interactions [13, 14]. Thus, patterns and outliers can illustrate synchronicity and serendipitous entities within observed behaviors that inform.

Jung, we are informed, defined synchronicity on three occasions as "acausal connecting (togetherness) principle", "meaningful coincidence", and "acausal parallelism" [15, p. 23]. In other words, he defined a conscious reflective linkage between external real-world events (as observed in SCAPE) and momentary subjective state – i.e. the observer's (and possibly the audience's) *prepared mind* [16]. Further, Seifert et al. in [16]), suggested that creativity originates in a *preparation of mind* that allows subsequent recognition of the serendipitous when it is encountered. Relatively, in the literature, serendipity is widely considered an important source of artistic stimulation [17] forming "an integral part of the creative process in the arts and humanities, social sciences and the sciences. In each, however, the experience of serendipity may be different." [18]. Further, serendipity, through being widely recognized in the literature – across disciplines – for its contribution to the generation of new knowledge, can also be impactful via (a) "reinforcing or strengthening the researcher's existing problem conception or solution", or (b) "taking the researcher in a new direction, in which the problem conception or solution is re-configured in some way" [18].

An aspect of the author's background is as an interactive artist exploring sensor-based interactions with an array of digital media. Selected credits include at Olympics and Paralympics culture festivals (Atlanta 1996 and Sydney 2000); European Capitals of Culture (Copenhagen 1996, Thessaloniki 1997, Avignon 2000); Museums of Modern Art (MoMA, numerous venues across years - including in Denmark @Louisiana; @Arken; @Trapholt...); Danish NeWave (Arhus, Copenhagen, and New York city 1999); ... etc. The author's first major showing was at the Institute of Contemporary Art (ICA, https://www.ica.art) in 1978. The majority of the bespoke sensor-based art works were predominantly throughout the last decade of the millennium into the first decade of the twenty-first century. At this time sensor technologies were not as pervasive as now and the designs, whilst intellectual and playful in targeting audience experiences, also targeted inclusive audiences as creative others. Each work built on its antecedent to, in different ways, evoke "Aha experiences".

Aligned with this is the author's parallel (to the above) background history of three decades of applied research into how digital technologies, especially sensor-based, can empower interactive creative expression and playful engagement for children and adults with impairments so as to supplement traditional strategies for rehabilitation. In this work bespoke sensors adapted to best match and source human input that, as signal data, is mapped to digital content to stimulate a motivated optimal experience. Design and intervention of the author-created individual/group/room-size interactive environment (as Inhabited Information Space) are iterative such that behavioral reactions inform re-design and re-intervention until "Aha experience" is identified. Identification involves representation of user self-agency, aesthetic resonance, and efficacy. Further optimization tailors the interactive environment potentializing micro-development for those inhabiting the interactive space (e.g. patients).

To summarize a preparation of mind, in both the author's cross-informing bodies of work, as briefly introduced above, i.e. (1) interactive art installations/performance art, and (2) digital technology in rehabilitation training as technologies of inclusive well being. Elements of inductive coding, constant comparison, serendipity and synchronicity are innate alongside perceptual and cognitive multi-affordance considerations informing affective art design wherefrom research models have developed. From both aspects it can be posited from the author's first-hand artist/designer position that contemporary Aha experiences differ from Aha experiences of audiences from two decades ago as they in turn differed from Aha experiences from two decades previous i.e. around 1978 when the author showcased at the ICA. Learning to recognize differences and changes in order to create for the shifting tide has required applied insightfulness that includes, researching of human attributes, both perceptual, cognitive, affective, and beyond; researching societal and technical advancements; and more. This is believed an ongoing challenge of interactive installation artists.

This paper, through sharing a specific moment in time (the observed installation audience Aha experience) aligns to the targeted learning through exploration, interaction, and serendipity. It speculates on the potential of artistic designs that incorporate variations of affordances to stimulate dynamic balancing to impact human experience. In other words, through considering on the one hand audience investigation, and on the other hand audience perplexity, resulting in targeted engagement, it attempts to inform of potentials that could offer additional insight to interactive art design. Such insight is posited aligned with [19] who reflect how "Interaction is not simply an opportunity to ensure the audience's participation, but instead suggests a creative engagement with the content of the artwork" (p. 46). Aligned with this is how the SCAPE students reported an inconclusive outcome to their research/problem question – however, potentially innate post-exhibition, was an opportunity to refine their question to reflect such an Aha experience that they had unwittingly achieved.

Finally, serendipity relates to chance and coincidence, as synchronicity relates to meaningful coincidence. In the case of SCAPE, the audience was alone in the space and at the right place at the right time of system reset following disengagement when the author was observing with necessary pre-experience engaged with a prepared mind to identify insightfully. Reflection on the observation is that audience pre-knowledge perceived affordances arose from contemporary cultural/societal awareness of pervasive sensor technologies (e.g. smart phones, smart devices, etc.,) aligned with the info-board text detailing designed-for interactions: interactions that were not fully functional. These combined with false affordances of the dysfunctional (clearly visible) Doppler sensors that provided the audience a conceived possibility of discoverability of actions – as expectation - with the SCAPE installation [20–22]. Reflecting the observation, it is posited that the installation's cumulated affordances evoked audience's (societal-cultural) expectations of discoverability of actions.

In closing, and provoking, the author reflects on Maeda's quotation[3] - "Design is a solution to a problem. Art is a question to a problem". Reflecting contextually asking, under the POPBL framework model from within the model's mother lode originating public higher education body and specifically aligned to the context of a selected student project under POPBL, whether, by positing multi-affordances as playful design elements in creating contemporary art installations targeting human traits, a non-answerable question and/or solution is likely given scope of human idiosyncratic. However, not one for shying away from non-answerable questions and, given the framed context as POPBL and higher education of art linked to design, it finally can be concluded that the purpose of this contribution is to argue a case in order to open the subject for conducting research around the problem asking how artists may be able to create (at a higher level?) based upon learnt recognition of affective experiences (e.g. Aha) that are transformed into affordances innate to an interactive installation. Thus, example initial research questions are posited of this unused perspective from a constructivist approach asking - "What data is optimal to be researched and under what design?" "Which methods and theories are ideal to use in this research?" "Who will be researched and under what conditions and strategies?" "How can meaning and knowledge construction in audience affect artistic creativity?" "How feasible is it to create a taxonomy of affordances that can inform design in art under a playful – targeting

---

[3] https://www.interaction-design.org/quote/show/john-maeda-1 (Daily design quote: Jul 13th, 2018).

audience – concept?" – and, finally to ask, "How can interactive art installations be optimized from a contemporary multi-affordance perspective such that synchronous serendipity plays its part as a design variable to optimize audience experiences – and thus entertainment". Here, as an outro, the reader may wish to add their own questions… and/or instead, take a moment to reflect on Kluszczynski's words from almost a decade ago where he states "Long gone are the times of fascination just with the phenomenon of digital interactivity itself" [8].

References

1. Kolmos, A., Fink, F.K., Krogh, L. (eds.): The Aalborg PBL Model – Progress, Diversity and Challenges. Aalborg University Press, Aalborg (2004)
2. Eriksson, E., Hansen, T.R., Lykke-Olesen, A.: Reclaiming public space: designing for public interaction with private devices. In: 1st International Conference on Tangible and Embedded Interaction (TEI 2007), pp. 31–38. ACM, New York (2007)
3. Lave, J., Wenger, E.: Situated Learning: Legitimate Peripheral Participation. Cambridge University Press, Cambridge (1991)
4. Bowles, M.S.: Relearning to E-Learn: Strategies for Electronic Learning and Knowledge. Melbourne University Press, Melbourne (2004)
5. Canova Calori, I., Divitini, M., Eljueidi, M.: A design framework for city-wide collaborative learning systems. In: 8th World Conference on Mobile and Contextual Learning (mLearn 2009), Orlando, Florida, USA (2009)
6. Olsen, P.B., Pedersen, K.: Problem-Oriented Project Work – A Workbook. Roskilde University Press, Roskilde (2005)
7. Topolinski, S., Reber, R.: Gaining insight into the "Aha" experience. Curr. Dir. Psychol. Sci. 19(6), 402–405 (2010)
8. Kluszczynski, R.W.: Strategies of interactive art. J. Aesthet. Cult. 2(1) (2010). https://www.tandfonline.com/doi/abs/10.3402/jac.v2i0.5525
9. Michelis, D., Müller, J.: The audience funnel: observations of gesture based interaction with multiple large displays in a city center. Int. J. Hum.-Comput. Interact. 27(6), 562–579 (2011)
10. Lombard, M.: Intercoder reliability (2010). http://matthewlombard.com/reliability/
11. Foucault, M.: Madness and Civilization: A History of Insanity in the Age of Reason. Vintage Books/Random House, New York (1988). Foucault quoted in Dreyfus, H.L., Rabinow, P.: Michel Foucault: Beyond Structuralism and Hermeneutics, 2nd edn. p. 187. University of Chicago Press, Chicago (1983)
12. Flanagan, J.C.: The critical incident technique. Psychol. Bull. 51(4), 327–358 (1954)
13. Lincoln, Y.S., Guba, E.G.: Naturalistic Inquiry. Sage, Beverly Hills (1985)
14. Glaser, B., Strauss, A.L.: The Discovery of Grounded Theory: Strategies for Qualitative Research. Aldine de Gruyter, New York (1967)
15. Casement, A.: Who Owns Jung?, p. 23. Karnac Books, London (2007)
16. Roberts, R.M.: Serendipity: Accidental Discoveries in Science. Wiley, New York (1989)
17. Cobbledick, S.: The information-seeking behavior of artists: exploratory interviews. Libr. Q. 66(4), 343–372 (1996)
18. Foster, A.E., Ford, N.: Serendipity and information seeking: an empirical study. J. Doc. 59 (3), 321–340 (2003)
19. Oliveira, N., Oxley, N., Petry, M.: Installation Art in the New Millennium. Thames & Hudson, London (2003)

20. Gaver, W.W.: Technology affordances. In: Proceedings of CHI 1991, pp. 79–84 ACM, New York (1991)
21. Gibson, J.: The Ecological Approach to Visual Perception. Houghton Mifflin, Boston, USA (1979)
22. Norman, D.: The Psychology of Everyday Things. Basic Books, New York (1988)

Memorial Design Pattern Catalogue – Design Issues for Digital Remembrance

Susanne Haake[✉], Wolfgang Müller, and Kim-Sina Engelhart

University of Education, Kirchplatz 2, 88250 Weingarten, Germany
{haake,mueller}@md-phw.de,
engelhartkim@stud.ph-weingarten.de

Abstract. The digitalization and commercialization of the Internet have led to a digital culture of remembrance in recent years. This change is difficult; negative examples are subject of ongoing discussions. These discussions are elucidating that the collective remembrance culture, especially within the digital domain, is a sensitive field. Currently there is no guidance available for the development of innovative concepts of digital memory products. "Best practices" collections, which might provide guidance to the development of novel products and services linked commemorative culture, are so far missing. In this paper we will describe the current status of the ongoing project Memorial Design Pattern. The presentation of the theoretical approaches to the culture of collective remembrance, the design patterns concept as well as best-practice researches initiate this work. We present the concept of a catalogue and knowledge base for best practices in the field of digital memorial design pattern. We also present our approach for the identification of patterns and a set of selected examples of design patterns in digital-media based commemorative culture. Finally, the paper provides a discussion on future work for building up a memorial design pattern repository.

Keywords: Digital heritage · Commemorative culture · Design pattern Memorial website · Virtual reality · Interactive maps · Interactive timelines

1 Introduction

The culture of remembrance is subject to a constant transformation process depending on current events as well as social, political and technical changes [1]. For this, each generation remembers differently [2]. The current culture of remembrance 2.0 is characterized by the technical advances and the commercialization of the Internet [3]. The number and diversity of these offers has risen sharply in recent years [4]. These developments require clear didactic concepts and guidance in the development of new multimedia applications and services within the culture of remembrance. Best practices as a guide to design decisions counteract unforeseen and unwanted effects as well as pure "histotainment" offerings.

Against this background, our research targets to extract and gather practice knowledge in terms of best practices, as well as to induce general principles. The objective is to provide identified smart practices in the field of digital memorial and

© ICST Institute for Computer Sciences, Social Informatics and Telecommunications Engineering 2019
Published by Springer Nature Switzerland AG 2019. All Rights Reserved
A. L. Brooks et al. (Eds.): ArtsIT 2018/DLI 2018, LNICST 265, pp. 143–151, 2019.

culture in an online repository, to be furthered and managed in virtual collaborations with international experts in the field. We foresee that the memorial design pattern catalogue will provide a comprehensive reference of best practices for products and media-related artifacts in the field of memorial and culture. It will serve as a knowledge base providing a standard vocabulary to support design debates between experts.

The remainder of this paper is structured as follows: First we will discuss related work, specifically on remembrance in commemorative culture in a media context, then on "best practice" research in general as well as in the field of commemorative culture. Further, we will present our design pattern approach, followed by a presentation and brief discussion of selected patterns from commemorative culture. A short summary and a sketch of further work completes our contribution.

2 Related Work

Our approach mainly relates to the field of commemorative culture studies, but it also applies concepts and methods from the field of Learning from Practice, particularly the theory of design pattern.

2.1 Digital Remembrance in Commemorative Culture Studies

Remembrance represents one of the most important subjects in defining cultural identity [5]. Collective memory, in this field, is typified as a repository of knowledge and information in the memories of social groups or nations. Public memory is often linked to historical places and memorials such as the Holocaust memorial in Berlin (Germany) or Yad Vashem in Jerusalem (Israel). This refers directly to Nora's "lieux de memoire" (places of memory), where collective memory crystallizes [6].

Inside this discourse, remembering the Holocaust represents a well-studied research field from different disciplines: historical science, literature, photography, film and art [7]. Analyzing remembrance culture in digital media was initially neglected. In the last few years, however, first investigations have emerged in this area, in particular on digital media related topics, on commemorative recollection in the social media and with regards to individual websites [8, 9]. In this context, best practices of using new media in commemorative context can be added in the field of Holocaust education [10–12]. Memorial websites, forms of remembrance in social media and applications in a memorial context are described for teaching aspects. They include empirical studies to measure the impact of teaching about the Holocaust with digital media in school context.

In summary, there are rarely described best practices in a non-pedagogical context [8, 13]. An interdisciplinary view on the object of the investigation is missing so far. One main challenge concentrates on the exponential increasing number of web offerings, applications and digital learning objects including new technologies. Hence, a compendium of single studies about the topic was published. What is still missing is an overview with respect to national and international best practices, extracting the ideas and structures behind single examples.

2.2   Learning from Practice

In this paper we refer to research related to work targeted to learn from practice and proven concepts from the field. Best practices research is an approach to extract and gather practice knowledge, as well as to induce principles. It can be defined as "the selective observation of a set of exemplars across different contexts in order to derive more generalizable principles and theories" [14].

Design Patterns [15] represent a recent and very successful approach to the documentation of good practices. Originally developed in the field of architecture to cover elements of environmental design at various levels of scale, design patterns describe reusable forms of solutions to design problems based on a semi-formal approach. Based on a defined pattern structure, corresponding solutions are analyzed with respect to a number of aspects and perspectives. The pattern structure thereby provides both a scaffold for the analysis and a support for the comparison of patterns.

Today, identification of good practice as a source for patterns is usually linked with the metaphor of mining [16]. This involves capturing solutions that are both good and significant [17], while not stating obvious solutions to trivial problems or covering every possible design decision [16]. For pattern mining, two principal approaches can be distinguished: inductive and deductive [18]. Inductive approaches can be considered the most manifest based on the definition of a design pattern, if possible also related to the agreement of a number of experts in this analysis. However, in practice design patterns have been extracted applying deductive thinking methods in a large number of cases. For instance, based on a transfer of attributes and functions of an artifact to another based on a metaphoric perspective (from metaphor to pattern), an expert's analysis of a specific concept and its implications, or based on an expert's analysis of a problem (from experience to pattern) [18].

The Design Patterns approach was successfully adapted to different domains, such as software development, providing descriptions of good practices in context of software design [19], human-computer interaction [20], web programming [21] and education [22]. Design Patterns nowadays are widely accepted to identify, describe, manage and analyze design problems in a structured way.

3   Approach and Concept

The aim of this project is to extract intelligent solutions for hypermedial offers in a commemorative and a remembrance context. In this context the design pattern approach allows best-practice solutions to be documented. These patterns are intended to serve as future orientation for the development and design of media-related artifacts, which is particularly relevant with regard to a heterogeneous memory community [8].

The applied pattern mining process is based on a deductive approach. According to this, our work is more clearly based on theory in related fields to commemorative culture. For this, we reviewed products of collective memory and work related to general and well-known "best practices" in our research fields, not necessarily related to information technology and media. Pierre Nora's theory of collective places of memory represents a good example in this context [6]. Based on the extracted good practices in general, we analyzed how those practices have been transferred to applications in the web and other types of multimedia applications. Thereby an inductive element is introduced to avoid collecting patterns not just by academic invention, but also allowing for a more focused analysis of existing solutions. Further, we also utilized existing expertise in the fields on HCI patterns, media education and visualization, targeting to relate corresponding best practices in commemorative culture to existing design patterns in those fields [23–25].

In our ongoing project we target to develop a catalogue and repository for best contextualized practices for multimedia applications and products in the field of memorial and culture. While there exist various variations of design pattern descriptions, there are on the other hand similarities in the approaches and there exist commonalities in the structural elements. We draw from typical approaches in this field, and our structure provides for the following elements (Table 1):

Table 1. Description of the design pattern structure

Pattern element	Description
A pattern name:	A descriptive name identifying the pattern, also indicating its context and purpose
A problem description:	A description of the concrete problem or challenge requesting for the solution the pattern provides; this is usually written in a brief and user-oriented way
Context:	A thorough description of the specific context where the problem is arising and where the provided solution has proven to be smart and effective; In our case, all patterns are related to the general context of commemorative culture; In addition, we foresee a discussion on the regional (regional what?), since rites in commemorative culture often depict a distribution in local contexts only
Solution:	A description of the general solution strategy and its elements applied to solve the problem based on this pattern
Rationale:	A reasoning why the pattern works, reinforcing the solution; This section provides a separation of rationale information from the proposed solution to make the solution easier to scan and consume
Discussion:	A brief discussion of the pattern, also allowing for a critical analysis
References:	A list of references to related work and approaches, also providing for a relation to theory in the field
Examples:	A brief description of examples depicting this pattern, to illustrate and to substantiate the pattern
Related patterns:	A list of related design patterns, including from other domains, (e.g., human-computer interaction, web-technology, education), as well as from non-digital backgrounds, with a short description and reasoning of the specific relation

Our pattern structure has been extended by necessary elements for managing patterns in a repository, including names and affiliations of authors, the date of the latest version of the pattern, a pattern version history, and a section for general comments on the pattern. These elements have been omitted in the presentation and discussion of pattern examples in the following sections for clarity and space reasons.

4 Memorial Design Patterns

In the following chapter, we present and discuss extracted design patterns from the field of commemorative culture. Three patterns were selected to illustrate our use of the pattern approach in the field. For better ease of reading we will only represent the whole pattern structure of one pattern in detail and add some shorter versions of other examples.

4.1 Pattern "Virtual Tour Based Memory"

Memorial places are fundamental to remembering. The accentuation of places in the culture of remembrance refers to the French historian Pierre Nora [6]. These anchor points of remembrance are often transient. Historical buildings of the Nazi era, such as concentration camps, were converted, expired or are often no longer recognizable as such. Virtual reconstructions of the places of memory enable online-based excursions. Simple virtual tours are possible through 360° shots. The use of interactive 3D technologies, on the other hand, represents an extensive format of the online excursion [26]. The potential is seen in form of an exploration of partly no longer existent or no longer accessible buildings.

The following table shows a short pattern description (Table 2):

Table 2. Memorial design pattern "virtual tour based memory".

Pattern name:	Virtual tour based memory
Problem description:	Historic places are an integral part of the memory and commemoration culture. These places testify to a high degree of historicity that needs to be constructed by users. The visitor needs more background information to understand the historical meaning of the place
Context:	Memorials are an important part of the culture of remembrance because of their inherent historicity. The construction and preservation of memorial sites is one of the most important goals of the culture of remembrance. Visiting a monument is part of a commemoration rite. These memorials offer areas to remember the victims and explain the historical events that have taken place
Solution:	The medial or virtual excursion of a memorial site can be realized by different media. Common solutions are 360-degree images of the memorial rooms. The navigation of the virtual tour is controlled by the user. The solution is to integrate information modules into the excursion. In an international context, 3D representations of the places of remembrance are presented

(continued)

Table 2. (*continued*)

Pattern name:	Virtual tour based memory
Rationale:	Virtual excursions can be considered an optimal complement to a real memorial visit. In addition, ensure the preservation of the Holocaust memorial sites. The advantages are seen especially in the preparation and follow-up of the real memorial visit
Discussion:	Virtual tours cannot replace the real visit of memorial sites. The capture of the memorial site in its complexity and its contextualization is only partially possible. This is justified by the lack of a thorough work on the content of the history of the place. However, it is also possible to explore non-existent sites of memory in the virtual space. Also questionable are the effects of technology use on the memory process. An increased immersion and emotionality is suspected. The navigation of the web applications could be problematic, a good usability of interacting seems to be essential. The effects of virtual excursions on the memory process, in particular on the immersion and emotionality of the user, should also be investigated
References:	Bernsen, D., and Kerber, U. (Hrsg.). (2017). Praxishandbuch Historisches Lernen und Medienbildung im digitalen Zeitalter. Opladen Berlin Toronto: Verlag Barbara Budrich. Gellert (2009) https://www.kz-gedenkstaette-dachau.de/station01.html https://museenkoeln.de/ns-dokumentationszentrum/medien/rundgang.aspx?rnr=0_0_1&lang=de http://www.gedenkstaette-neustadt.de https://web.annefrank.org/de/Subsites/Home/Betritt-das-3D-Haus/#/house/20/
Related pattern:	Interactive floor plans and maps

In the following, two examples of virtual tour based memory databases are presented.

NS Documentation Center Cologne

The NS Documentation Center Cologne offers a virtual tour of the building [6]. The operation of the virtual excursion can be done via mouse interaction. Orientation is provided by green arrows, which serve as guideposts. Further information on the individual stations can be called up in text or audio form. Audio icons provide hints where the user can get additional information.

The Secret Annex Online

Based on Anne Frank's diaries, an online three-dimensional tour was created. The user can navigate her/himself through this "lifelike and colorful visualization" [27] of rooms. When entering the room, the user receives information about the room via the auditory channel and the symbols indicate further sources of information. The virtual 3D reconstruction also includes historical relics that are not present in the real place of remembrance in Amsterdam. Inaccessible real rooms, such as the private office of Otto Frank, can be viewed in the virtual tour.

4.2   Further Memorial Design Patterns

In the following, two more extracted memorial design patterns are briefly described.

Memorial Site Based Memories
This pattern thematizes the memory places of the collective memory [28]. The interactive digital map allows an individual a self-guided exploration of the places of memory. This pattern is a well-suited approach, especially in terms of orientation and integration of extensive content into a small space. A good example is the website "Hotel Silber", with the subtitle "The Virtual History Place" [29]. To make the virtual memorial place accessible, the "memorial site based memories" pattern is used to provide orientation and information to the virtual visitor of the place.

The following paragraph presents the pattern timeline based memories:

Timeline Based Memories
Collecting historical knowledge plays an important role in the memorial context. For a better understanding of historical events a chronological order and contextualization is used and these practices are presented within a timeline. The second Memorial Design Pattern, Timeline Based Memories, includes the classification of historical events in a dynamic and interactive timeline. This pattern provides a solution for individual access to historical events made available through interaction with the system. For this, the timeline supports the comprehension of the impact of single events inside a greater historical coherence. All pattern examples share graphical arrangements along a horizontal line. This line puts all mentioned events into one chronological relationship. Hyperlinks and navigation bars help to navigate and explore the presented digital heritage. Furthermore, presenting content in multimedia context supports learning effects. A good example of this is the timeline of the German historical museum [30].

5   Summary and Future Work

The presented memorial design patterns were extracted on the basis of theoretical research in the fields of memory culture and design patterns, using the method of pattern mining. Patterns give novices a synopsis through the representation of problems, relations and applications in the context of remembrance. Thus, the patterns support the discussion with people who are not among the specialists of the domain. Successful solutions can serve as a template and support for future projects [31].

There are some open research fields, for example memorial design pattern with a connection to web 2.0. technologies. Furthermore, all developed patterns are going to be validated by qualitative interviews with memorial experts. A web-based platform is going to be built up to distribute and discuss these extracted patterns.

The use of reusable patterns may make the development of websites more effective and efficient in the context of memory. In order to secure a long-term quality improvement of the various web offerings the research project should generate comprehensive sample catalogues.

References

1. Assmann, J.: Ma'at: Gerechtigkeit und Unsterblichkeit im alten Ägypten (2. Aufl). Beck, München (1995)
2. Erll, A.: Kollektives Gedächtnis und Erinnerungskulturen. Eine Einführung **2**, 21 (2005)
3. Gellert, M.: Erinnerungskultur 2.0: kommemorative Kommunikation in digitalen Medien; [Basis für den vorliegenden Band bildet die im November 2006 veranstaltete Tagung ... an der Justus-Liebig-Universität Gießen]. (E. Meyer & C. Leggewie, Hrsg.). Campus-Verl, Frankfurt am Main (2009)
4. Meyer, E.: Erinnerungskultur 2.0: kommemorative Kommunikation in digitalen Medien; [Basis für den vorliegenden Band bildet die im November 2006 veranstaltete Tagung ... an der Justus-Liebig-Universität Gießen]. (E. Meyer & C. Leggewie, Hrsg.). Campus-Verl, Frankfurt am Main (2009)
5. Assmann, J., Czaplicka, J.: Collective memory and cultural identity. New Ger. Crit. **65**, 125–133 (1995)
6. Nora, P.: Between memory and history Les lieux de mémoire. Representations **26**, 7–24 (1989)
7. von Keitz, U., Weber, T.: Mediale Transformationen des Holocausts (2013)
8. Hein, D.: Erinnerungskulturen online: Angebote, Kommunikatoren und Nutzer von Websites zu Nationalsozialismus und Holocaust. UVK Verlagsgesellschaft, Konstanz (2009)
9. Neiger, M., Meyers, O., Zandberg, E. (eds.): On Media Memory: Collective Memory in a New Media Age. Springer, London (2011). https://doi.org/10.1057/9780230307070
10. Short, G., Reed, C.A.: Issues in Holocaust Education. Taylor & Francis, Abingdon (2017)
11. Manfra, M.M., Stoddard, J.D.: Powerful and authentic digital media and strategies for teaching about genocide and the Holocaust. Soc. Stud. **99**(6), 260–264 (2008)
12. Riley, K.L., Totten, S.: Understanding matters: Holocaust curricula and the social studies classroom. Theory Res. Soc. Educ. **30**(4), 541–562 (2002)
13. Assmann, A.: The Holocaust—a global memory? Extensions and limits of a new memory community. In: Memory in a Global Age, pp. 97–117. Palgrave Macmillan, London (2010)
14. Overman, E.S., Boyd, K.J.: Best practice research and post bureaucratic reform. J. Public Adm. Res. Theor. **4**(1), 67–84 (1994)
15. Alexander, C.: A Pattern Language. Towns, Buildings, Construction. Oxford University Press, New York (1977)
16. Dearden, A., Finlay, J.: Pattern languages in HCI: a critical review. Hum.-Comput. Interact. **21**(1), 49–102 (2006)
17. Fincher, S., Utting, I.: Pedagogical patterns: their place in the genre. ACM SIGCSE Bull. **34**, 199–202 (2002)
18. Baggetun, R., Rusman, E., Poggi, C.: Design patterns for collaborative learning: from practice to theory and back. In: Proceedings of ED-MEDIA 2004 (2004)
19. Gamma, E., Helm, R., Johnson, R., Vilissides, J.: Design Patterns: Elements of Reusable Object-Oriented Software. Addison-Wesley, Reading (1995)
20. Tidwell, J.: Designing Interfaces - Patterns for Effective Interaction Design. O'Reilly Media, Sebastopol (2011)
21. Vora, P.: Web Application Design Patterns (Interactive Technologies). Morgan Kaufmann Publisher, Burlington (2009)
22. Bergin, J., et al. (Eds.): Pedagogical Patterns: Advice for Educators. Joseph Bergin Software Tools (2012)
23. Aigner, W., Miksch, S., Müller, W., Schumann, H., Tominski, C.: Visual methods for analyzing time-oriented data. IEEE Trans. Vis. Comput. Graph. **14**(1), 47–60 (2008)

24. Müller, W., Schumann, H.: Visualization for modeling and simulation: visualization methods fore time-dependent data-an overview. In: Proceedings of the 35th Conference on Winter Simulation: Driving Innovation, pp. 737–745 (2003)
25. Weber, M., Alexa, M., Müller, W.: Visualizing time-series on spirals. In: Andrews, K., Roth, S.F., Wong, P.C. (Eds.), Proceedings IEEE Symposium on Information Visualization 2001 (InfoVis01), pp. 7–14. IEEE Computer Society (2001)
26. Ahlheim, K.: Erinnern als Chance – auch gegen Rechtsextremismus?: Die Vielfalt der Erinnerungsorte ist eine Chance für wirksame politische Bildung. Erwachsenenbildung 63 (2), 64–66 (2017). https://doi.org/10.13109/erbi.2017.63.2.64
27. NS Dokumentationsszentrum Köln. https://museenkoeln.de/ns-dokumentationszentrum/medien/rundgang.aspx?rnr=0_0_1&lang=de. Accessed 10 Aug 2018
28. Alavi, B. (Hrsg.).: Historisches Lernen im virtuellen Medium: dieser Band … dokumentiert die Ergebnisse einer im März 2009 an der Pädagogischen Hochschule Heidelberg durchgeführten Tagung. Mattes, Heidelberg (2010). https://web.annefrank.org/de/Subsites/Home/Betritt-das-3D-Haus/#/house/20/. Accessed 10 Aug 2018
29. Oggolder, C.: Essay: Das Internet als Ort der Erinnerung. Glob. Media J. 6(2), 8 (2016)
30. Geschichtsort Hotel Silber. http://www.geschichtsort-hotel-silber.de. Accessed 10 Aug 2018
31. Lemo – German Historical Museum. http://www.dhm.de/lemo/. Accessed 10 Aug 2018
32. Riehle, D.: The perfection of informality: tools, templates, and patterns. Cutter IT J. 16(9), 22–26 (2003)

Cyberella – Design Issues for Interactive 360 Degree Film

Susanne Haake[(✉)] and Wolfgang Müller

University of Education, Kirchplatz 2, 88250 Weingarten, Germany
{haake,mueller}@md-phw.de

Abstract. The idea of 360 degree is not a new phenomenon in arts and media. It has its origins in the arts of the early 18th century and later the panoramic view in the field of photography and also in film was adapted. Groundbreaking technological progress has allowed for a new hype in 360 degree videos in recent years, including new possibilities of interaction. In this paper we will describe the current status of the ongoing project Cyberella which focuses on exploring filmmaking and narrating techniques for interactive 360 degree films. Our approach is divided into two steps. Firstly, existing interactive 360 degree videos are examined for their specific film language. A catalogue will summarize important results of the analysis, including research questions, as a basis for our film project. Our second step will comprise of our film project Cyberella, which is testing a variety of film styles to find new ways of filmmaking and defining design guidelines. In summary, this paper aims to contribute to the discussion of how storytelling in relation to traditional film language can or should be adapted in 360 degree interactive video context to formulate first design-issues for practical use.

Keywords: Interactive 360 degree video · Virtual reality · Film language
Design guideline

1 Introduction

The idea of 360 degree in arts and media is not a new phenomenon. In the early 18th century first 360 degree paintings occurred in Great Britain [1]. In this context cycloramas were developed, in which the spectator stands in the middle of a panoramic cylinder. The intended effect is to make spectators feel as if they are standing inside the presented landscapes. Later, the 360 degree idea was adapted in the field of photography and film. In 1897, Raoul Grimoin-Sanson invented the Cinéorama, a panoramic film projection system using ten synchronized projectors [2].

Groundbreaking technological improvements allowed for a new hype in 360 degree videos in the last years. An important achievement was the emergence of virtual reality technologies (VR), for example VR glasses. New interactive video content formats have revolutionized the communication and marketing world in a very short period of time [3]. As a highly immersive visual concept, they are a powerful format to engage with people. This comes along with a changing role of the spectator, especially since interactive 360 degree movies allow spectators to influence narrative plotlines. Due to

© ICST Institute for Computer Sciences, Social Informatics and Telecommunications Engineering 2019
Published by Springer Nature Switzerland AG 2019. All Rights Reserved
A. L. Brooks et al. (Eds.): ArtsIT 2018/DLI 2018, LNICST 265, pp. 152–162, 2019.

this, spectators can be part of the experience and renarrate a story [4]. Further, 360 degree films influenced the film language decisively. Filmmakers have started to experiment with this new medium, particularly in the form of storytelling and an aesthetical point of view. Well known rules such as how to make a film, have to be discussed and redefined in this new context [5].

This is the origin of this project. Our research focuses on how traditional story-telling can or should be adapted in a 360 degree interactive video context to formulate design-issues for practical use. The project is titled Cyberella and transfers the well-known story pattern of Cinderella into 360 degree video format using interactive elements to manipulate the plot line of the film.

The remainder of this paper is structured as follows: At first, the related work according to our research context is presented, focusing on the field of film and new media studies as well as a brief examination of Interactive Digital Storytelling (IDS). In the following chapter, our approach, concept and lessons learned are described. Finally the summary, including our future work will be presented.

2   Related Work

Our approach mainly relates to not only the field of film studies, but also the application of concepts and methods from the field of new media studies and Interactive Digital Storytelling (IDS).

2.1   Film Language in Virtual Reality Context

There exist several standard works on film language yet. For example, the well-known work of James Monaco is often cited in the context of film language and history [6]. "How to read a film" is a good example of the fact that film studies have been opened up to audiovisual forms outside of cinema and television a long time ago. It contains a separate chapter that deals with film language in multimedia. The works of Elsässer and Stam are also part of this research context [7, 8]. There is not only an adaption of film study theories to the new media field, but also the new media field to film study theories. New media studies also increasingly investigate filmic narration [9, 10]. Thus, it becomes clear that an expanding interdisciplinary research field has emerged in the last 15 years.

For our approach, references between film studies and new media studies in the context of virtual reality are particularly important. There are also basic studies in this field [11]. The particular challenge of narration in the field of virtual reality is also being investigated, for example in "The virtual life of film" [12]. Another example is "Towards a narrative theory of virtual reality" [13]. In particularly, the effects of cinematic narratives in the VR context receive greater attention [14]. A basic work, however, is still missing in this context.

2.2   360 Degree Videos and Virtual Reality

360 degree cameras, or the so called "omnidirectional cameras", record a view in every direction at the same time [15]. For this reason, the spectator can change the viewing direction while watching a 360 degree video through a mouse click or other forms of interaction. A high immersion is guaranteed by wearing a headset to increase the feeling to be inside the recorded panoramic shots [16–18]. Virtual Reality and 360 degree video are often used in the same context and are therefore interconnected, for example in the case of using a head-mounted system for the reception. Here, the viewer is completely immersed into the virtual environment - while watching a 360 degree video the outside world is not perceived. In contrast however, we usually term a computer-animated world a Virtual Reality world, particularly in the context of computer games. Of course there also exist numerous 360 degree animation films.

2.3   Interactive Storytelling in 360 Degree Videos

Interactive Storytelling relates to a field of research concerned with the conceptualization, development and evaluation of methods and technologies linked with nonlinear narratives and corresponding mechanisms for user interaction to influence the paths and the outcomes of stories [18, 19]. Corresponding approaches have being investigated in the last years, and lately quite a few of those are being used in the field of interactive entertainment products and computer games, specifically within a sub-genre emphasizing narrative against high degrees of interactivity.

While the number of examples of 360 degree videos is actually high, the lack of interactive storytelling in the market reveals deficits of these approaches. They may not only be linked to technological aspects but also to deficits in finding the right form of how to develop dramaturgical lines in interactive 360 degree films [20]. In addition, while different interaction paradigms have been explored, unfortunately they did not adapt successfully in the 360 degree context.

Accordingly, interactive storytelling with 360 degree videos is still at the early stages and common rules of film language need to be formulated. In the following paragraph the approach and concept of our research project Cyberella, including first results about design-issues, are presented.

3   Approach and Concept

Our project Cyberella focuses on how traditional storytelling can or should be adapted in 360 degree interactive video context to formulate design-issues for practical use.

In our first project phase, existing interactive 360 degree videos were examined for their specific film language. Underlying examination criteria were: Image composition, using of sound, editing and dramaturgical aspects like increasing suspense or establishing plot points. In addition, the analysis of the interaction possibilities played an important role. The results have been collected and tabulated. This catalogue of criteria formed basis for our own 360 degree video project.

Our second project phase includes our practical film project Cyberella that involves testing a variety of film styles in accordance to the catalogue in order to find new ways of film making and gain initial experience. We want to put focus on aspects that have not yet been tried out in this form or that have not been analyzed in detail. Early and regular screenings of sequences in front of test audiences with discussion panels helped to define first design guidelines. Both steps are explained below in more detail.

3.1   Step 1: Examination of 360 Degree Videos

In the following section we will discuss important characteristics of the medium 360 degree video and the corresponding film language. The presented best practice films demonstrate their application. Compared to conventional film, the way of making films is different in a 360 degree context. In traditional video, for example, the user is locked to the angle where the camera is pointing to during the capture of the video. With 360 degree video recording, these boundaries no longer exist. This new freedom of spectators has a significant influence on film language. A film maker cannot limit the details presented to spectators, they choose it them themselves [21]. Pre-defining shots and image composition get difficult to establish, except for the first shot of the film before the user interacts the first time. However, this also means that it must be ensured that the viewer does not miss anything important. Furthermore, usually the camera has a fixed position without moving around. Things or persons cannot be zoomed in well unless they are moving towards the camera on their own. A 360 degree scene is usually told from one setting size. Changing the setting size has to be done through editing the film material which in turn can often lead to new challenges [22].

Cuts are rare in the 360 degree genre and usually mark a change of location. In the field of animated film you can find more experiments with this editing technique. A good example represents PEARL [23]. The short musical from 2017 was created as 360 degree video and can be seen in browser or with virtual reality glasses via Google Spotlight Stories [24]. According to the road movie genre the story is set inside a car, reflecting the relationship between a father and his daughter sharing their love to music. The narrow display window allows close setting sizes and creates a feeling of closeness to the figures. It results in an animated look that is simple and flat, reminding us of the first computer games. This reduced look combined with almost no voice support stresses the music side of the film. Storytelling becomes particularly interesting, using time-leaps forward and backward to narrate. This is realized by the match cutting technique showing the young girl growing up. Besides looking around no further interaction is supported but this technique is used well. Looking back and forth inside the car to the daughter and father lets the audience actively get to know their relationship.

The following 360 degree film uses the technique of film editing in a different way: WELCOME TO ALEPPO represents an example of 360 degree video reporting from 2015 [25, 26]. It combines 360 degree with non-360 degree film material telling the story of the incredible destruction of the city and the numerous victims of the war. A collage of film sequences shows the time before the war and its gruesome consequences. During the film, 360 degree sequences are included, in which the camera is located without any movement in the middle of the ruined city. The viewer now has the opportunity to look around and empathize with the destroyed war scenery, expecting for something to happen.

In many cases the interactivity in 360 degree videos can be reduced in changing the viewing perspective while watching 360 degree videos. Maybe because many platforms, (such as facebook and youTube), do not support further interactivity by default. Google Spotlight Stories offers a solution to integrate interactivity into 360 degree films, particularly for the Google Cardboard. Interactive videos extend boundaries even further allowing to explore the video and to navigate to related information [20]. They are well known in a non-360 degree context. But recently, new forms of interactivity has been recognized in our context. GONE [27] and VR NOIR [28] present two examples that include interactive elements into 360 degree videos to influence the plot line. The mystery thriller series GONE tells the story of Meredith Clover, a mother searching for her missing daughter [29]. Throughout the series the spectator has the ability to use certain hotspots in the scene. These hotspots represent clues and are only available for a limited time. If the user taps on one of these hotspot scenes, the colour saturation will change and a sound will be played. In the meantime, the main scene will not be interrupted. Throughout the series you will also find false hints, a well-used storytelling technique. VR NOIR created by the Australian studio Start VR, builds on the storytelling techniques of GONE, but includes the spectator as a main character by giving him/her freedom to influence the narrative [30]. For example, the user can ask a client further questions or get control of a spy camera as you stake out a mark on a rooftop. The analysis of these films has shown that the 360 degree film language is in a transitional stage.

The following table summarizes important results of the examination of best practices in the field of 360 degree film. Further research questions has also been added as a basis for the second step of our project.

3.2   Step 2: Our Project Cyberella

In the next step, the Cyberella project tests new ways of filming 360 degree videos corresponding to the research questions in the table above. It was important to leave established paths of 360 degree storytelling and to explicitly use new forms of expression.

The story of Cyberella is about a student who moves away from home for the first time and lands in a flat with exploitative roommates. The title "Cyberella" already indicates the adaption of a fairy tale theme, constituting the words cyber and Cinderella. The story includes familiar narrative patterns from the fairy tale Cinderella and applies them to the context of today. This comprises not only figures and objects, but also the setting and the sound. Magical special effects complete the adaptation of the fairy tale theme. The following illustration shows a still from the film CYBERELLA (see Fig. 1).

The non-linear plot line contains interactive elements to manipulate the narration of the film. Once we have installed as many branches as possible, our story tree was gradually reduced during the course of the project.

Fig. 1. Still from the 360 degree film Cyberella

The following graph illustrates the current plot line (see Fig. 2):

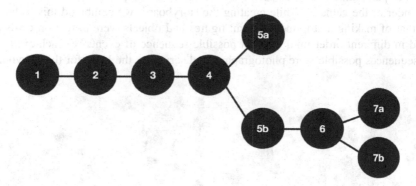

Fig. 2. Branched plot line of Cyberella

The film starts with a linear plot line (step 1 to 4). The character of Cindy, who must work as a servant of her terrible roommates, is introduced. She gets an invitation to a party where she meets a very nice barkeeper. Branching is then used to increase the tension. The protagonist is already there on the way back from a party. Here, the viewer is involved in the course of the story. He/She decides, by using hotspots, what the main character should do and his/her decisions influence the further course of the story. Should the main character go back to the party or go home? In any case, the suspense continues to increase. The first turning point is set up during a chase scene (step 5a and 5b). The second turning point of decision is installed just before the story is triggered (step 7a and 7b).

To integrate the hotspots we experiment with the technique of the frozen image, that is, the image for interaction stands still and the film does not continue until a choice is made. A mix of 360 degree video material and 360 degree photography is generated by this form of editing. The effect of this interruption on the reception of the film has not been clarified yet. For this, it is precisely the form of integration of interactions that is not yet fully completed in our ongoing project.

4   Lessons Learned

The following chapter contains a discussion about design-issues for interactive 360 degree films. Overall, using 360 degree videos should not be used for their own sake and must have a significance for the story through supporting aesthetic issues. The following four main challenges demonstrate our lessons learned in practical use.

4.1   Challenge 1: Storyboard and Image Composition

The storyboard has to be adapted to the special features of 360 degree videos. We used storyboards in the field of virtual reality and game design as a role model. On the one hand, the circular field shows the position of people and objects relative to the camera, which is placed in the middle, represented by a yellow star (see Fig. 3). On the other hand, the panoramic view shows the composition of the persons and objects in the viewfinder of the camera. While creating the storyboard, we combined this technique with that of making a stop motion film: figures and objects were drawn on cards and placed in different order until the best possible sequence of events was achieved. The best sequences possible were photographed and served as the basis for the storyboard.

Fig. 3. Storyboard shots of Cyberella

The following figure shows two examples of the variation of a circle to create the storyboard:

4.2   Challenge 2: Image Composition and User's Attention

360 degree panoramic views can increase the credibility of the feature especially in documentary films because the audience sees the entire picture and is not limited in

his/her field of view through the picture frame. In practical work, however, this also means that the entire area has to be observed by the film maker. Passers-by must be explained that there is no area behind the camera, so they are always in the picture. For the camera operator him/herself, this means that he/she cannot stand in the set to control the shot directly at the camera. Furthermore, if you like, the 360 degree image is always shot from the perspective of the viewer, who automatically feels part of it.

A big challenge is directing the viewer's attention to places where important things were happening to the story, according to the formulated research question in Table 1. Our research has opened different possibilities, clear references and more subtle variations. For example, on the sound level: The character can on the one hand directly ask that one should turn around. On the other hand, a sound that comes from an area that is not focused on at this moment can catch the viewer's attention and encourage him to turn around. Another possibility arises from the fact that the viewer tends to follow movements. If a figure walks by the camera, he/she turns to see where the figure is going. Furthermore, the lighting can also be a good means to direct the viewer's gaze. Brightly lit areas of the setting increase interest. This is a good example of how traditional film language can be used in 360 degree video. The deliberate use of light and shadow, spotlights on striking objects and people are an important element for film drama.

Table 1. First results of the analysis of best practices.

Aspect	Description	Research question
Image composition and sound design:	360 degree videos capture the perspective of the viewer within a panorama shot, which can be freely chosen. It is not possible to install a fixed image composition	How can we direct the viewer's attention? And how can we arrange the composition of a 360 degree setting? Which role is played by sound design?
Editing/dramaturgical aspects:	There are cuts in 360 degree video, but these are rarely used. Their potential remains untapped	How can we cut 360 degree videos without confusing the viewer? How can we create a suspense line using cuts?
Editing/Mixed film formats:	Usually 360 degree films are only cut from 360 degree film material. There are examples that mix 360 degree material with non 360 degree material	How far does it make sense to mix different film formats?
Interactivity:	Interactions are already being used in 360 degree filming, but to a lesser extent in the context of interactive narrative storytelling	How can interactions support the story?

4.3   Challenge 3: Creating Suspense by Editing (Mixed Film Formats)

Usually, many scenes of 360 degree videos resemble those of a theater stage [31]. Cuts are normally implemented by changing a scene, i.e. the change of location. However, montage is an important means of creating dramaturgy in traditional film even within the scene. This refers to our research questions: How can we cut 360 degree videos without confusing the viewer? And how can we create a suspense line using cuts? We are convinced that this is possible in 360 videos too, when you take some rules into consideration. No cuts in sequences with a lot of dialogue. Here, the imagery must be subordinate because the focus is on the dialogue. In visual scenes, however, cuts are easily possible and are mostly accompanied by music. Furthermore, it is a good opportunity to combine a cut with the movement of a camera. These jump cuts as a bridging of space and time are recognized by the viewer deliberately. When connecting different clips, attention must be paid to coherent connections, especially in the area of the 360 degree videos.

Another challenge lies within editing results from the combination of mixed film material according to our research question of how far it makes sense to mix different film formats. This not only applies to the combination of 360 degree and non - 360 degree material, but also 360 degree film material joined by 360 degree static picture material. Irritations occur when the viewer does not notice the change or does not understand the meaning behind it. This can be solved by special effects, for example playing a certain sound when the 360 degree film image freezes. The distinction can also be identified on the visual level without triggering the film's coherent relationship. One possibility is the use of distinct color filters or the differentiation between colorful and black & white pictures. This should be applied in accordance with what is shown in the picture.

4.4   Challenge 4: Interactivity

In addition to just looking around, hotspots embedded in the 360 degree film material are a great way to enhance interactivity. The inclusion of interactivity has a significant impact on the storyline. According to our research question, how interactions can support the story, the usage of hotspots can help branching of the story. An important challenge here is to keep the dramaturgical suspense line, because branching is a challenge in the 360 degree film. Here it is important not to reduce the choices of the story to yes or no decisions. The choices should have a significant impact on the story. An example of this from our 360 degree film CYBERELLA is: The protagonist is being traced by a stranger who is coming closer and closer. Now she is faced with the decision of either to go back to get her lost cell phone to call for help or to find a hideout inside her house. Brave viewers may choose the first variation and then find that the pursuer has no bad intentions, but instead returns the forgotten cell phone to her. This example shows how dramaturgical turning points can be integrated through interaction.

Furthermore, through hotspots, further information that is important for the story can be distributed in the room. Here, the viewer becomes the discoverer of the story.

His understanding of the course of the plot line is revealed through his interaction. Especially in this area we see enormous potential for future enhancements.

5 Summary and Future Work

In this paper we described the current state of our ongoing project Cyberella on exploring narrating techniques for interactive 360 degree films. Making 360 degree videos opens up innovative possibilities as well as challenges for film language and aesthetics. The viewer is granted with more opportunities to discover the cinematic space and becomes a co-narrator of the story. However, this greater freedom also opens up the problem of maintaining the coherent connection of the plot line and telling an exciting story. Not all techniques of conventional film making can be transferred 1:1 to the 360 degree video. This we have briefly described in our challenges in Chap. 4.

In summary, using 360 degree videos should not be used for their own sake and must have a value for the story. Our lessons learned showed first design-issues for interactive 360 degree videos and stressed challenges in the field of making a good storyboard, using new forms of image composition and sound design to direct user's attention, editing sequences and also adding interactivity. Our next steps are the completion of the film and non-public test screenings. At this stage, the research questions described above in Table 1 will be reevaluated. The focus is especially on the interaction with the 360 degree video.

Acknowledgments. We are thankful for the great support of the student project group that was significantly involved in the implementation of Cyberella: Lea Sophie Drees, Simone Koch and Tamara Tromsdorf.

References

1. Oettermann, S., Schneider, D.L.: The Panorama: History of a Mass Medium, vol. 2, pp. 22–33. Zone Books, New York (1997)
2. Nedelcu, M.: Expanded image spaces. From panoramic image to virtual reality, through cinema. Close Up: Film Media Stud. **44** (2013)
3. Alive Film. https://www.alive-film.com/interaktiver-360-grad-film-mit-hotspots/. Accessed 28 July 2018
4. Dolan, D., Parets, M.: Redefining the axiom of story: the VR and 360 video complex. Tech Crunch (2016)
5. Passmore, P.J., Glancy, M., Philpot, A., Fields, B.: 360 cinematic literacy: a case study. International Broadcasting Convention (2017)
6. Monaco, J., Lindroth, D.: How to Read a Film: The World of Movies, Media, and Multimedia: Language, History, Theory. Oxford University Press, Cary (2000)
7. Elsaesser, T., Hagener, M.: Film Theory: An Introduction Through the Senses. Routledge, Abingdon (2015)
8. Stam, R.: Film Theory: An Introduction. Wiley, Hoboken (2017)
9. Manovich, L.: The Language of New Media. MIT Press, Cambridge (2001)

10. Alexander, B.: The New Digital Storytelling: Creating Narratives with New Media–Revised and Updated Edition. ABC-CLIO (2017)
11. Sherman, W.R., Craig, A.B.: Understanding Virtual Reality: Interface, Application, and Design. Elsevier, Amsterdam (2002)
12. Rodowick, D.N., Rodowick, D.N.: The Virtual Life of Film. Harvard University Press, Cambridge (2009)
13. Aylett, R., Louchart, S.: Towards a narrative theory of virtual reality. Virtual Reality 7(1), 2–9 (2003)
14. Shafer, D.M., Carbonara, C.P., Korpi, M.F.: Exploring enjoyment of cinematic narratives in virtual reality: a comparison study. Int. J. Virtual Reality 18(1) (2018)
15. IFI. http://rpg.ifi.uzh.ch/docs/omnidirectional_camera.pdf. Accessed 28 July 2018
16. Neumann, U., Pintaric, T., Rizzo, A.: Immersive panoramic video. In: Proceedings of the Eighth ACM International Conference on Multimedia, pp. 493–494. ACM (2000)
17. Argyriou, L., Economou, D., Bouki, V., Doumanis, I.: Engaging immersive video consumers: challenges regarding 360-degree gamified video applications. In: International Conference on Ubiquitous Computing and Communications and 2016 International Symposium on Cyberspace and Security (IUCC-CSS), pp. 145–152. IEEE (2016)
18. Ryan, M.L.: Narrative as Virtual Reality 2: Revisiting Immersion and Interactivity in Literature and Electronic Media. JHU Press, Baltimore (2015)
19. Crawford, C.: Chris Crawford on Interactive Storytelling. New Riders, San Francisco (2012)
20. Chambel, T., Chhaganlal, M.N., Neng, L.A.: Towards immersive interactive video through 360 hypervideo. In: Proceedings of the 8th International Conference on Advances in Computer Entertainment Technology, p. 78. ACM (2011)
21. Passmore, P.J., Glancy, M., Philpot, A., Fields, B.: 360 cinematic literacy: a case study. In: International Broadcasting Convention, September 2017
22. Berliner, T., Cohen, D.J.: The illusion of continuity: active perception and the classical editing system. J. Film Video 63(1), 44–63 (2011)
23. PEARL, USA (2017)
24. Curtis, C., Eisenmann, D., El Guerrab, R., Stafford, S.: The making of pearl, a 360 degree Google spotlight story. In: ACM SIGGRAPH 2016 Apply Hour, p. 8. ACM (2016)
25. WELCOME TO ALEPPO, USA (2015)
26. Van der Haak, B., Parks, M., Castells, M.: The future of journalism: networked journalism. Int. J. Commun. 6, 16 (2012)
27. GONE, USA (2015)
28. VR NOIR, USA/Australia (2016)
29. Skybound. https://www.skybound.com/tv-film/our-vr-project-gone-is-here/. Accessed 28 July 2018
30. Upload VR. https://uploadvr.com/vr-noir-great-example-virtual-reality-will-change-television/. Accessed 28 July 2018
31. Pope, V.C., Dawes, R., Schweiger, F., Sheikh, A.: The geometry of storytelling: theatrical use of space for 360-degree videos and virtual reality. In: Proceedings of the 2017 CHI Conference on Human Factors in Computing Systems, pp. 4468–4478. ACM (2017)

Smart, Affective, and Playable Cities

Anton Nijholt[(✉)]

Human Media Interaction, University of Twente, Enschede, The Netherlands
a.nijholt@utwente.nl

Abstract. This is a short paper accompanying a keynote talk on playable cities at the 2018 ArtsIT conference in Braga, Portugal. We discuss smart, playable, and affective cities from the viewpoints of on the one hand how a city can be perceived and experienced by its citizens and on the other hand how the city perceives (monitors) its citizens. Both viewpoints assume sensors, actuators and computing systems embedded in urban environments. The viewpoints are illustrated with examples from smart cities, affective cities and playable cities.

Keywords: Playable cities · Smart cities · Sentient cities · Affect-aware cities Human-computer interaction · Sensors · Actuators

1 Introduction

Some cities have nicknames that characterize them. We can talk about Las Vegas as the 'Sin City' because of its casinos and about Amsterdam as the 'Venice of the North' because of its canals. Paris is known as the 'Light City', London as the 'Swinging City' (at least some decades ago) and Detroit used to be the 'Motor City'. Cities evoke certain expectations and sometimes excitement when we visit them. Sometimes we have dear or bad memories of a city because of previous visits and experiences. A city name, or rather where it stands for, can evoke affective reactions.

Less global and more down-to-earth affective reactions can be experienced when we walk, cycle, drive or take public transport in a particular city. How do we experience a city's visual, sound, and smell landscape? How does a city affect our moods, emotions, or mental states that relate to frustration, boredom, alertness or even open-mindedness? Citizens monitor a city, its activities and its changes through their affective feelings. Clearly, there is more to a city than its visual, sound, and smell landscape. As an inhabitant we as well experience a city by its regulations, the taxes we have to pay, its public administration, its local TV stations, its newspapers and how its activities are reflected in social media such as Facebook, Twitter or Instagram.

A city monitors us as well. There are the traditional local councils that represent the citizens and their opinions, there are elections, referendums can be organized, local communities can be consulted when a city plans changes in their immediate environment, citizens or communities need to announce and ask approval of certain public activities, citizens have possibilities to file complaints or report undesired activities, et cetera. The city is assumed to know about opinions and preferences of its inhabitants. Moreover, a city knows about criminal records, professional make-up, income

A. L. Brooks et al. (Eds.): ArtsIT 2018/DLI 2018, LNICST 265, pp. 163–168, 2019.

distributions, family composition, spending of income, consumption of water and energy, traffic behavior, recreational activities and preferences, et cetera. Some of this information is only globally available, there is not always need or possibility to trace it back to an individual citizen.

On the one hand we have the city monitoring its citizens, on the other hand we have citizens monitoring the city. What are the possibilities offered by smart digital technology to on the one hand help the city monitor its inhabitants in order to make the city more efficient, safe, healthy, and attractive, and on the other hand to help the citizen to benefit from the city because it not only makes city life cheaper and more efficient, but also because it makes possible community, family, or personal benefits that make living in a city more attractive.

When talking about smart cities and monitoring citizens' behavior (from energy consumption to attending sports events) the usual starting point is how we can make cities more efficient. Efficiency can decrease costs related to city management, public and company services, and citizens can benefit from it. Smart city technology can also help to decrease more global problems, for example, problems related to health, safety or global warming. From a city's point of view smart city technology helps to collect information about individual citizens and helps to make decisions that benefit all citizens, particular city regions, or particular communities. It is clear that there are no cities that don't want to be smart. Therefore they accept help offered by large information and communication technology companies to reach that goal. City authorities embrace smart city infrastructure offered to them by companies such as Cisco, IBM, Google, Siemens, AT&T and others, that promise to make their city more efficient, whether it is about traffic control, energy consumption, waste management, or safety. Smart city initiatives use smart technology, that is, sensors and actuators that are nodes in an Internet of Things (IoT), where 'things' include living sensors, that is, humans that are known to the IoT because of the data that is collected from monitoring their behavior on social media, in traffic, in public spaces, when and where they recreate or when they are at home.

More efficient use of city and other resources by using smart technology is in the interest of citizens. However, as a counterpoint to this reflective monitoring of the citizens' use of the city, citizens themselves monitor and use the city. They can use their laptop, tablet or smartphone to learn about traffic congestions, busses or trains that depart on time or have delays, construction works in the city, restaurants that still accept reservations for that evening, and whatever a city has to offer to its inhabitants and its visitors. Rather than looking at individual citizens, communities can think about how smart technology can be employed to address their community concerns (independent travel and unsupervised play for their children, safe local air quality, no traffic and associated noise nuisance, no criminal activity, no drug use, no graffiti, no potholes in their streets, etc.). It requires a more active role, a role that goes beyond being monitored and requires learning and making use of digital technology, for instance in DIY and makers communities.

In the next section (Sect. 2) we look at smart city initiatives and how they relate to the two viewpoints mentioned in this introduction. How do citizens experience the city, can we measure such experiences, and can we use them to have impact on what is happening in the city? Obviously, this is not necessarily about real-time adaptations of the environment, it can also concern, once when experiences are collected, designing future changes to traffic, public transport, housing, or entertainment and touristic activities that can be offered by city authorities or that can emerge spontaneously by individuals or communities. Other short subsections will deal with affect-aware cities and citizens that make use of affect-aware city information in their activities.

2 From Smart to Affective and Playable Cities

We start this section with some observations on smart cities. In the previous section we already mentioned some of the benefits that can be foreseen when more information about a city's use of resources and activity on streets and other public spaces becomes available for on- and off-line analysis that makes possible real-time decisions and longer-term strategic decisions. Therefore, in Sect. 2.1 we only mention some initiatives that illustrate the impact smart city technology will have on how we daily perceive and experience the city. In Sect. 2.2 we focus on affect. How do we emotionally experience a city and can the city have access to such experiences using smart city technology? In Sect. 2.3 we look at initiatives to make a city playable, again, using smart city technology.

2.1 Smart Cities: Public Spaces and Public Behavior

Civic authorities start to learn about ubiquitous and pervasive computing and learn about sensors that collect information about their citizens' behavior [1]. Information can be collected about traffic & public transport, presence in public spaces, management of waste, energy consumption, street noise level, air-quality and citizens' presence on social media. Information about our activities can be collected using IoT technology: digital technology embedded in our environments, public spaces, workplaces and in objects and devices that are part of our natural environment.

In smart cities public spaces, roads, lampposts and traffic lights monitor the behavior of its citizens. There are no surfaces in public spaces and street furniture that have no embedded sensors and actuators. A smart city has an urban operating system. In a smart city public space and operating system are under control of companies. At this moment we see that companies offer comprehensive smart city solutions to new cities that have yet to be built. There are many existing cities that plan to implement smart technology in their infrastructure. For example, city and street lighting can be made more efficient when roads and traffic lights know about actual traffic. In my hometown traffic lights give faster green light to cyclists who have a smart app installed on their smart phone. Obviously, the traffic light (and whatever it shares with others in the IoT) therefore knows about the identity of these cyclists. Some US cities start to install company suggested sensors in lampposts that can detect gun violence in the streets and warn the police. Face recognition software makes it possible to match any face in a crowd with those that have been collected in national or international databases. Smart city technology can make use of multimodal and multi-sensory research. Aggressive behavior can be detected from monitoring sound and vision. In New

Zealand we see attempts to use smart technology that helps to detect graffiti by 'smelling' fresh paint, to detect in-appropriate behavior, and rough sleeping.

In addition to introducing smart city technology in existing cities, there are initiatives in Malaysia, China, South Korea and also European countries to build smart cities from 'scratch'. One well-known example that now has been dismissed is the PlanIT Valley near Porto in Portugal. In South Korea the smart city Songdo was planned to be ready to have 300,00 inhabitants in 2015. Presently it has about 70,000 inhabitants, no cultural activities, theatres or museums. Developers are now inciting Korean populations in the USA to return and start living in Songdo.[1] The town of Toronto has given Google's sister company Sidewalk responsibility to design a $50 million smart city neighborhood, making it 'the most measurable community in the world.'[2]

Rather than assuming that smartness can be introduced by digital technology, in [2] it is argued that smartness of a city evolves from lifeways, cultures, and pragmatic local adaptions that evolve in a city. Overspecification using digital technology is another issue that is mentioned in [2]. Some playful applications of overspecification can be found in [3].

2.2   Smart Cities: Affect

Cities, city life and city activities evoke affective feelings. A city is experienced at an emotional level. Obviously, there is more than the city that determines our emotions and mood. Can a city be aware of our moods and emotions and make use of this knowledge? Can a city use smart technology for mood improvement of its citizens? One way to do this is by making city life more enjoyable. This can be done in a global way by the issues we mentioned in the previous subsection. It can also be done by introducing playful and entertaining elements in public spaces that lead to enjoyment. That will be discussed in the next subsection.

In a sentient or affect-aware city citizen sensing can provide information about the affective state of individuals whether they relate to social life, particular city events of being in a particular part of a city. That is, from 'it is great to live here' to feeling stressed because of traffic jams or public transport delays. Does a city part, street or square evoke stress, fear, alienation, intimacy or a sense of security? Information can be obtained from questionnaires, from social media (soft sensors), from sensors embedded in the environment and from wearables. Based on such information changes can be made to logistics or the physical urban environment. Moreover it can be input to urban games and guided audio-visual walks and recommender systems for tourists.

A 2004 example of an affect-aware city is Doetinchem in the Netherlands. Residents can fill in web-based questionnaires and every day their collective affective state is displayed during evening and night by an artistic installation that maps emotions on colors and lights up in one of these colors. Zip codes make it possible to distinguish

---

[1] https://www.scmp.com/week-asia/business/article/2137838/south-koreas-smart-city-songdo-not-quite-smart-enough.

[2] https://sidewalktoronto.ca/.

between different parts of the city. As another example, in 2005 artist Christiaan Nold provided London residents with a 'biomapping' device that recorded their galvanic skin responses during a walk. The recorded data was used to create a map which visualizes points of high and low arousal. More recent research can be found in [4–6] with the introduction of chatty, smelly, and happy city maps. Streets are assigned emotional categories and routing algorithms suggest routes that maximizes the emotional gain. Clearly, 'measurable communities' such as foreseen in Google's plans for Toronto (see the previous subsection) will allow to make cities affect-aware and find applications that exploit this knowledge.

2.3 Smart Cities: Playability

Decades ago the concept of playable cities was introduced in the context of video games and also in some German 'spielbare' (playable) city initiatives. Nowadays playful and playable cities often make references to digital technology that help to introduce playful and entertaining interactive installations in a city. Smart technology can make a city more efficient, but it can also help to make a city more fun to live in. In Bristol (UK) the concept was picked up and several initiatives, including a yearly competition, emerged to design playability in cities using smart technology. There are many reasons why we want to make a city playable [7]. Mood improvement of citizens, make use of play for behavior change, add fun to community activities, collect in a playful way opinions about planned changes in a environment, design attractive urban games, et cetera. The Bristol initiative mentioned *"The Playable City is imagined as a city in which hospitality and openness are key, enabling residents and visitors to reconfigure and rewrite city services, places and stories. The Playable City fosters serendipity and gives permission to be playful in public."* However, in practice the choice of winners in this competition seems to be decided by the possibility to have commercial exploitation of ideas in various cities and countries, leading to a commercialization and a McDonaldization of this playable city concept.

Usually (see also [8, 9]) playable city initiatives are not 'inclusive', they aim at the interests of a city's 'creative class' [10], its authorities, and cultural institutions. Installations have to be robust, so no sophisticated technology is used. Nevertheless there have been a few interesting applications of smart technology, such as 'Shadowing' (infrared cameras attached to lampposts capture shadows of passersby and project one of these shadows for later passersby) and 'Urbanimals' (jumping and crawling virtual animals are projected on walls and floors, inviting passersby to follow or imitate them). A later project was meant to make pedestrian crossings more playful: *"Pressing a traffic light button ignites speakers and a dance floor, bringing the crossing to life. A spotlight will guide you across the road, imitating the lights of a stage performance. ... As further people join the dance floor, more and more of the crossing's surrounding furniture will progressively light up and transform into a disco!"* In practice it turned out to be a primitive camera system hidden in a pedestrian traffic light that was meant to entertain crossers with manipulated pictures of their face, similar to what can be done in photo kiosks, displayed on a small screen attached to the traffic light. But certainly, in many cities there are successful projects: buildings that are lighted in such a way that you can play Pong or Tetris on their walls, pedestrian areas that persuade you by using digital technology to play or exercise, bus stops that entertain you while waiting, interactive billboards that surprise, et cetera.

3 Conclusions

In this paper we surveyed developments in smart, affective, and playable cities. This was done by introducing the many ideas that underlie the development of these cities are otherwise related to living in these cities. Some criticisms on the views on smart and playable cities have been included.

Acknowledgements. I'm grateful to the ArtsIT 2018 organizers for inviting me to give a keynote talk on playable cities. This short paper accompanies this keynote talk.

References

1. Townsend, A.M.: Smart Cities. W.W. Norton & Company, New York, London (2014)
2. Greenfield, A.: Against the Smart City (The City is Here for You to Use Book 1), Kindle edn. Do projects, New York (2013)
3. Jamison, D., Paek, J.Y.: An intentional failure for the near-future: too smart city. In: Shepard, M. (ed.) Sentient City: Ubiquitous Computing, Architecture, and the Future of Urban Space. The MIT Press, Cambridge (2011)
4. Aiello, L.M., Schifanella, R., Quercia, D., Aletta, F.: Chatty maps: constructing sound maps of urban areas from social media data. R. Soc. Open Sci. 3, 150690 (2016)
5. Quercia, D., Aiello, L.M., Schifanella, R.: The emotional and chromatic layers of urban smells. In: Proceedings of the 10th International AAAI Conference on Web and Social Media (ICWSM) (2016)
6. Quercia, D., Schifanella, R., Aiello, L.M.: The shortest path to happiness: recommending beautiful, quiet, and happy routes in the city. In Proceedings of Conference on Hypertext and Social Media (Hypertext) (2014)
7. Nijholt, A.: Towards playful and playable cities. In: Nijholt, A. (ed.) Playable Cities. GMSE, pp. 1–20. Springer, Singapore (2017). https://doi.org/10.1007/978-981-10-1962-3_1
8. Nijholt, A.: Playable cities for children? In: Fukuda, S. (ed.) AHFE 2018. AISC, vol. 774, pp. 14–20. Springer, Cham (2019). https://doi.org/10.1007/978-3-319-94944-4_2
9. Leorke, D.: Location-Based Gaming: Play in Public Space. Palgrave Macmillan, London (2019)
10. Hollands, R.G.: Will the real smart city please stand up? City 12(3), 303–320 (2008)

Serious Game for Teaching Statistics in Higher Education: Storyboard Design

Tiago Barbosa[1(✉)], Sérgio Lopes[1,3], Celina P. Leão[2,3],
Filomena Soares[1,3], and Vitor Carvalho[3,4]

[1] Department of Industrial Electronics, School of Engineering,
University of Minho, Campus of Azurém, 4800-058 Guimarães, Portugal
tijbarbosa@hotmail.com,
{sergio.lopes,fsoares}@dei.uminho.pt
[2] Department of Production and Systems, School of Engineering,
University of Minho, Campus of Azurém, 4800-058 Guimarães, Portugal
cpl@dps.uminho.pt
[3] R&D Algoritmi, Campus of Azurém, 4800-058 Guimarães, Portugal
[4] IPCA-EST-2Ai, Campus of IPCA, 4750-810 Barcelos, Portugal
vcarvalho@ipca.pt

Abstract. Serious games can be used as a way to transmit knowledge to the users/students, playing the role of a pedagogical tool in their learning process. Following this idea, a serious game on Statistics is developed for higher education level, promoting and demonstrating the applicability of statistics concepts in day-to-day life and in the decision-making process. The proposed idea is to create a challenging environment (mystery that needs to be solved), where the clues are contextualized in the statistics area through the practice of probability knowledge, confidence intervals and hypotheses tests. According to the student's answers and choices, the game branches out leading the player to different activities/challenges, guaranteeing that, by the end of the game, the student has a better understanding of the subject. In the present paper, the storyboard and the student competencies are presented and discussed, focusing on the project's main objectives.

Keywords: Serious game · Statistics · Storytelling · Adaptive interaction

1 Introduction and Background

Within the scientific and academic communities, there is no doubt that serious games represent an efficient and engaging tool, used for improvements in the learning process [1–5]. Serious Games (SG) are developed to be used as a learning tool in wide areas and different levels of knowledge [3], being STEM field (Science, Technology, Engineering, and Maths) and health the most common. Higher education has also proved to be another area of concern in the development of SG, presenting positive results and contributions [6–8]. Moreover, serious games benefit skill's development, namely communication, creativity and adaptability competences [6]. Despite the positive features mentioned above, researchers recognize that much improvements remain

© ICST Institute for Computer Sciences, Social Informatics and Telecommunications Engineering 2019
Published by Springer Nature Switzerland AG 2019. All Rights Reserved
A. L. Brooks et al. (Eds.): ArtsIT 2018/DLI 2018, LNICST 265, pp. 169–175, 2019.

to be made, namely in the design phase, in order to not compromise the success of SGs as a learning tool and encouraging the interest of students in specific areas of knowledge [2, 5, 8].

Following these trends and ideas, this work proposes a serious game on Statistics in higher education, an area where engineering students fail and it is still considered by many as not relevant to their courses [9].

Two types of Serious Games that most accurately describe the games related to this paper are Adaptive Serious Games (ASGs) and Sand Box Serious Games (SBSGs).

Motivation is a key element of learning, as it improves student's knowledge retention. Tutors/teachers play a crucial role in captivating and grabbing student's attention, having to provide them with an adaptive and scalable level of challenge, that matches each student's unique profile, competences and progress [10–13]. Serious games growth in popularity led to research on how to include these requirements in a virtual environment, allowing the implementation of personalized learning experience algorithms, where technology takes the role of a "virtual private tutor" [12]. These types of SGs are also known as Adaptive Serious Games. These games provide players with a personalized experience, balancing challenges according to players' needs and difficulties, trying to fill the gaps in their knowledge, motivating them to continue playing. Further research on ASGs led to the formalization of the Competence-based Knowledge Space Theory (CbKST) framework, which tries to provide the basic concepts and strategies to structure and relate a finite set of competences to their respective prerequisites. Following, two SGs that use an adaptive strategy, ELEKTRA [11] and The Journey [12], where the later uses the CdKST framework.

Sandbox, also known as open-world or free-roaming, is a style of video games, characterized by the freedom that players have to explore the virtual world, as well as freely select the various tasks and challenges spread across it. This style inherent freedom and ability for players to choose their own path in the game, presented itself as a perfect scenario to build SGs and explore specific educational domains [10, 13], creating the Sand Box Serious Games. By encouraging players to explore and interact with the environment, by solving different problems or puzzles in the form of quizzes, mini-games or conversations, this type of SG provides a strong basis for configurable software templates that can be easily shaped for various pedagogical intents.

From the conducted literature review, it is possible to conclude that most concepts of Statistics in higher education are not tackled by the serious games found and researchers recognize that much improvements remain to be made, namely in the design phase of serious games.

2 Storyboard

Although some games rely heavily on their mechanics (e.g. Simulations) and their focus solely on the story (e.g. Visual Noves), most try to balance both. The proposed Serious Game tries to achieve just that, providing players with an engaging and personalized storytelling as well as interesting mechanics.

Figure 1 depicts an overview of the structure and flow of the game, which is divided into four main stages: exposition, rising action, climax and falling action. It is usually possible to discern each of these stages in any structured story, either being a novel or a video game storytelling, which makes them guidelines for the writing of a new one. All the examples provided in this topic are sample case scenarios of the proposed Statistics SG.

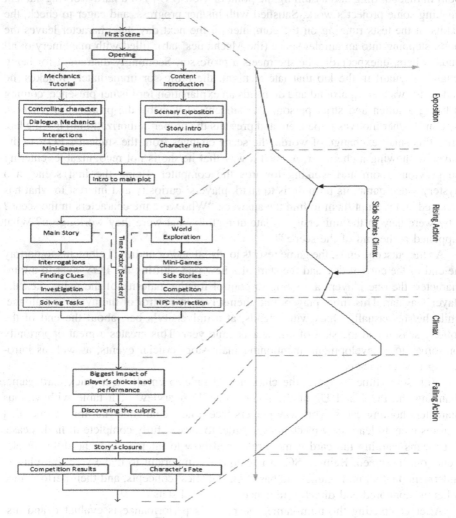

Fig. 1. Serious game structure

2.1 Exposition Phase

Most video games start with an Exposition phase, wherein the player is introduced to the game's story, world and mechanics. It is important, that by the end of this phase, players understand the nature and main scenario of the game, as well as acquired a basic understanding of the game's style and mechanics, like movement, interactions, dialogue and task system. The first scene of the Exposition phase is usually an introductory one that poses questions to catch players' attention and motivates them to keep playing by answering the questions. As an example, the first scene could be a cutscene that starts by showing the context of a university (e.g., a known building facade) and a Mechanics' laboratory, during the night, proceeding to focus on a single room in that building and assuming the point of view (POV) of a hard-working student finishing some project's work. Satisfied with his/her progress, and eager to check, the results of the tests running on the computer on the next day, the character leaves the room, stepping into an ampler space (the Mechanics' lab), filled with machinery of all kinds, where, unexpectedly, he/she meets a professor. Seemingly distraught for being caught off guard in the lab that late at night, the professor immediately rebukes the student for wandering around and demands an explanation for his/her presence, coming as being a sullen and strict person. The student, shaken by the professor's reaction, explains his/her motives to be there and presents the proper authorization to use the lab. After this small exchange of words, the scene changes from the student's POV to the player's, showing a character, in such a way that he/she is not recognizable, entering the previous room and walking towards the computer. Being the first scene in a mystery video game, its purpose is to spark players' curiosity and interest to what has occurred and prompt them to find the answers: "Who were the characters in the scene? Why were they in the university so late at night? What were they working on? What happened at the end of the scene?".

As the cutscene ends, the game resorts to visual and/or audio UI elements to portray the end of the current day and the start of a new one, shifting the POV over to a third character: the one players are going to control for the majority of the game, i.e., the player's avatar. This time, players find themselves in control of the avatar's dialogue, while he/she casually chats with friends, at a university's bar, about the end of the holiday season and the start of a new academic year. This creates a great opportunity for some story development, mentioning main story crucial events, as well as introducing new characters.

With some time to spare, the characters decide to enroll on a quick card game, changing the POV and UI of the game to a 2D overview of a table with various characters holding cards. This way players face a new challenge (i.e. mini-game) that requires them to learn new mechanics in order to successfully complete it. In this case, that means learning the card game's rules and how to interact with the different elements on the screen. Being a SG, it is extremely important to make sure that players understand that all mini-games are based on statistics' concepts, and their performance is being monitored and directly influences their final stats.

After completing the mini-game, the player's performance is evaluated and displayed. Then the game returns to the previous scenario bringing a new character into the scene, the one previously introduced working on the Mechanics lab. This event leads to the discussion about a competition involving some of the present characters, providing some details about it and referencing the influence of the main character on the team's success, even though he/she is not an official member. This transmits the competition's importance, hinting to its big role on the story ahead.

From a technical point of view, the entire scene described above, from the chat in the bar to the characters reaching their classes, is seen as a tutorial to make players comfortable with the game, slowly introducing them to the story and the different mechanics. Although these basic mechanics will be the same throughout the entire game, like the movement of characters and the means of interaction, it is possible to introduce players to different ones later on, mainly through mini-games, providing them with a sense of progression and avoiding the boredom of repetition.

Depending on the complexity of the game, the length of the Exposition Phase may vary. In the example given, this phase should be short, in order to quickly introduce players to the game and make them comfortable playing it, improving knowledge retention.

2.2 Rising Action

The transition between the Exposition Phase and the Rising Action occurs with the introduction to the story's main event, which, in this case happens with the discovery of deleted and modified important documents related to the competition, when both the main character and team members try to check on the progress of the tests mentioned in the first cutscene. This sets the main character on the path to try to discovery the cause of such event and find if someone is trying to sabotage the project's work.

Being the longest phase of the game, the Rising Action encompasses most of the main and side story's events, introducing players to all the mechanics available and different scenarios. Since the example provided is an adaptive serious game built inside a sandbox environment, this phase gives maximum freedom to player's actions, allowing them to interact with the virtual world at their own pace choosing the course of action they desire. More specifically, players are given total control of their avatar and are able to move around the university, interacting with the NPCs to learn more about the current events, engaging in either side stories or mini-games to improve their statistical knowledge and progress in the main story. At this top level, the player (main character), together with some friends, tries to gather as many clues as possible to find the culprit behind the corrupted data. Players' knowledge is gathered during this phase, where the game uses it to understand players' needs and knowledge gaps, in order to provide the necessary tools and activities and to help overcome their difficulties. In some cases, this means blocking the main story progressing, requiring the players to complete more side stories or mini-games, ensuring their readiness for the challenges ahead.

2.3 Climax and Falling Action

All of this effort and progress eventually lead to the climax of the game, where all questions regarding the main story's events are answered and the final most difficult challenge is presented, requesting players to apply all knowledge and skills gathered throughout the entire playthrough, resulting on the most satisfying scene of the game. It is also during this phase that ASGs should handsomely reward players that made good decisions in the story and managed a good performance, giving them a final feel of accomplishment and involvement in the storytelling process.

Finally, at the falling action, players reach the final act of the game, where the game gives some closure to the story and characters.

3 Competencies

Figure 2 represents the map of the pedagogical competencies expected for the players to acquire. After the first introductory concepts are exposed to the player, Bayes theorem and Probability distribution are taught, followed by the central theorem limit and finally inferential statistics. This final topic englobes both confidence intervals, preceded by not only the central theorem limit but also the introductory sampling concepts and the distinction between errors of type 1 and type 2. Throughout the entire game, descriptive statists are presented in a variety of ways.

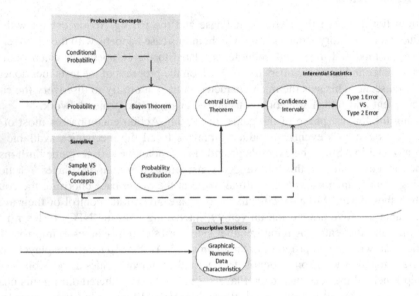

Fig. 2. Learning content structure. Dashed arrows depict dependencies between concepts from different stages of the learning process; straight arrows outline the main learning path. Concepts that can be taught at the same time are represented parallel to each other.

4 Final Remarks

The storyboard of a serious game for statistics learning is given, properly grounded on game theory. The game is designed as a sand box game type with adaptive elements. The player is free to explore a university campus environment in which he/she can carry out multiple activities, and the game reacts to the player achievements on main story's problems. The game reaction consists of additional activities, directly related to the competencies that the player is lacking, which must be completed before progressing in the main story. The next steps are to connect the story with the statists concepts, following both top-down and bottom-up approaches, and develop the game mechanics, always bearing in mind the development of a pedagogical tool that helps students to have a confident attitude towards statistics.

Acknowledgements. The authors would like to express their acknowledgments to COMPETE: POCI-01-0145-FEDER-007043 and FCT – Portuguese Foundation for science and technology within the Project Scope: UID/CEC/00319/2013.

References

1. Popescu, M., et al.: Serious games in formal education: discussing some critical aspects. In: 5th European Conference on Games Based Learning, pp. 486–493 (2011)
2. Girard, C., Ecalle, J., Magnan, A.: Serious games as new educational tools: how effective are they? A meta-analysis of recent studies. J. Comput. Assist. Learn. **29**(3), 207–219 (2013)
3. Boyle, E.A., et al.: An update to the systematic literature review of empirical evidence of the impacts and outcomes of computer games and serious games. Comput. Educ. **94**, 178–192 (2016)
4. Rosyid, H.A., Palmerlee, M., Chen, K.: Deploying learning materials to game content for serious education game development: a case study. Entertain. Comput. **26**, 1–9 (2018)
5. Buchinger, D., Silva Hounsell, M.: Guidelines for designing and using collaborative-competitive serious games. Comput. Educ. **118**, 133–149 (2018)
6. Nadolski, R., et al.: EMERGO: a methodology and toolkit for efficient development of serious games in higher education. Simul. Gaming **39**(3), 338–352 (2017)
7. Barr, M.: Student attitudes to games-based skills development: learning from video games in higher education. Comput. Hum. Behav. **80**, 283–294 (2018)
8. Harackiewicz, J.M., Priniski, S.J.: Improving student outcomes in higher education: the science of targeted intervention. Annu. Rev. Psychol. **69**(1) (2018). https://doi.org/10.1146/annurev-psych-122216-011725
9. Leão, C.P., Soares, F., Carvalho, V., Lopes, S., Gonçalves, I.: A serious game concept to enhance students' learning of statistics. In: Proceedings of the 4th Experiment@ International Conference-Online Experimentation. exp.at 2017, Faro, Portugal. IEEE (2017)
10. Callaghan, M., Savin-Baden, M., McShane, N., Gomez Eguiluz, A.: Mapping learning and game mechanics for serious games analysis in engineering education. IEEE Trans. Emerg. Top. Comput. **5**(1), 77–83 (2017)
11. Kickmeier-Rust, M.D., Albert, D.: Micro-adaptivity: protecting immersion in didactically adaptive digital educational games. J. Comput. Assist. Learn. **26**(2), 95–105 (2010)
12. Dias, J., Santos, P.A., Veltkamp, R.C. (eds.): GALA 2017. LNCS, vol. 10653. Springer, Cham (2017). https://doi.org/10.1007/978-3-319-71940-5
13. Bellotti, F., Berta, R., De Gloria, A., Primavera, L.: A task annotation model for SandBox serious games. In: 2009 IEEE Symposium on Computational Intelligence and Games. CIG 2009, pp. 233–240 (2009)

Speculative Design for Development of Serious Games: A Case Study in the Context of Anorexia Nervosa

Viviane Peçaibes[1(✉)], Pedro Cardoso[2], and Bruno Giesteira[2]

[1] ID+/Faculty of Fine Arts, University of Porto, Porto, Portugal
vivianepecaibes@gmail.com
[2] INESC TEC/Faculty of Fine Arts, University of Porto, Porto, Portugal
{pcardoso,bgiesteira}@fba.up.pt

Abstract. This article presents preliminary findings on the application of both Speculative Design and Game Design towards the conception of two prototypes of serious games with focus on anorexia. The first prototype focuses on psychoeducation of school-age youth, and the second aims to support research and sharing of knowledge about the disease, able to be used in focus groups and interviews. Anorexia is a complex and often fatal disease that has no cure, and by conceiving and playing these first prototypes we were able get a glimpse of the its context, making us more ready for this research's next stages.

Keywords: Speculative Design · Serious games · Psychoeducation Anorexia

1 Introduction

Anorexia affects teenagers and young people around the world, something that has increasingly called the attention of health authorities. People that suffer from this disease behave with excessive concern towards their own weight and body shape [1–3]. This disease is more common in adolescents and young women, being nine times more common in females than males [4, 5], despite the increasing prevalence in males and at progressively younger ages. The beginning of treatment is hard because patients do not assume their own pathology [6, 7].

In Psychology, educational interventions on the knowledge of pathologies are called psychoeducation,[1] which often does not materialize into artefacts, remaining at a level of immaterial clinical strategies or verbalized during sessions with therapists. With that in mind, this short paper aims at exploring, in an initial stage, an alliance between Speculative Design and Game Design for the conception of these serious games as psychoeducational and speculative ludic tools to elevate awareness and to

---

[1] Structured, didactic and systematic intervention in Psychology: Educational, Social and Health. In this type of intervention characteristics about the functioning of diseases people suffer from are explained to them. The point is that if patients have a deeper knowledge about their own illness, they may feel safer in monitoring themselves with increased awareness and conscious, therefore easing their own reflection on their harmful behaviours [9, 10].

A. L. Brooks et al. (Eds.): ArtsIT 2018/DLI 2018, LNICST 265, pp. 176–181, 2019.

take predictive and preventive action regarding the recognition of symptoms of anorexia nervosa. Speculative Design uses objects and prototyping as ways and means to observe and to question the interaction between people and things. Through speculative thinking we can find new answers about behaviours, life models, interactions, needs and knowledge [11].

Since anorexia nervosa is a complex disease, interaction with patients and their families must be thoroughly thought out in order to not adversely affect treatment. Therefore, these preliminary findings are about building knowledge about the disease, behaviours, procedures, and eventual constraints that will shape the social network in which a person that suffers from this disease in enveloped in.

In the next two sections, we present two prototypes that emerged with very different contexts in mind, taking into consideration the fact that their conception and play/testing called our attention to a series of situations we, up until then, had not considered.

2 Prototype 1: ANgame Competitive

This prototype is focused on informing school-aged youth about anorexia. This tool aims to introduce primal concepts about the disease through competitive activities. We believe this mechanism may aid in learning about the disease and in the identification of dangerous recurrent behaviours and initial symptoms. We thought of this game to be useful due to the fact that this disease may or may not be perceived in initial stages, which favors its chronicity and makes treatment more difficult. With this in mind, we conceived this game with the goal to raise awareness about such harmful behaviours (Fig. 1).

Fig. 1. ANgame COMPETITIVE – On the left there is the Package, Question Card (black) and Answer Card (white), and on the right, there the cards are scattered around the table, ready for play.

The package contains: 20 Question Cards,[2] 20 Answer Cards and 1 Instruction Card. Table 1 presents the operation of the game represented by its components and rules.

---

[2] The content of the cards was created from theoretical research [12].

Table 1. ANgame COMPETITIVE – Components and Rules of the game.

Components	Rules
- Restricted time - Punctuation - Cards with questions - Cards with answers	1. Shuffle the Question Cards and set them in a pile with their dark side up at the center of the table, and spread around the Answer Cards with the white side up 2. Turn over the Question Card on top of the pile Players have 1 min to find the corresponding Answer Card and place their choice on the side of the Question Card 3. Players should read aloud the question and their chosen answers 4. Turn over the Question Card to verify the correct answer Who answers correctly gets the Question Card, and players return the Answer Cards to the table to continue playing 5. If no one answers correctly, that Question Card must be removed from the game 6. Wins who gets more Question Cards

The game intent is to articulate healthy behaviours and attitudes like learning about anorexia, perceiving risky situations and understanding the severity of such disease that may manifest itself in adolescence. As for desirable goals, this game may opportune prevention of anorexia nervosa, raise awareness of the topic and break down possible taboos.

By resorting to speculative design methods in conceiving this game, we understood that it may facilitate learning about the disease and be able to create a moment for talking about the disease in the classroom, since it is known that the target audience of this game has predisposition to play, and that motivation through play is a good strategy for effective learning [8].

3   Prototype 2: ANgame COLLAB

This game-instrument focuses on supporting research, since it becomes a conversation tool, while providing visual evidences regarding the knowledge of the themes and the decision-making of the interviewees in focus group[3] sessions and in research interviews (Fig. 2).

ANgame Collab intends to assist in the mapping, management and flow of dialogue through a collaborative process. This is a formative tool for the researcher as it helps him to perceive what the interviewees know about the subject in question, providing a visual data and decision-making resources that can contribute to increments of knowledge about the patient and to the production of resources to aid in patient treatment. Its target audiences are adults, who may be knowledgeable health experts in anorexia nervosa (psychologists, nutritionists, psychiatrists, etc.) and relatives of people with the disease.

---

[3] This research technique guarantees a deep and collaborative discussion of groups from a semi-structured script created by the researcher [13].

Fig. 2. ANgame COLLAB - left is the playset of the game. In the middle is the interviewee writing on the keyword card. On the right is the decision-making moment to put the answer in the right position regarding the question.

To facilitate handling the game, it assumes the format of paper cards,[4] containing the following items: 20 Question Cards, 42 Keyword Chips (30 with printed keywords and 12 blank), 10 Trump Cards, orange and yellow Post-it blocks, and 1 card with instructions. Table 2 shows the functioning of the game through the components and rules.

Table 2. ANgame COLLAB - game operation

Components	Rules
- Restricted time - Question Cards - Trump Cards - Answer Chips: with written keywords and blank	1. Players must shuffle the Question Cards and place them in a pile at the center of the table with the dark side up, and spread across the table the Answer Chips 2. Players have 2 min to answer the question presented in the Question Card that is on top of the pile To answer they need to pick an Answer Chip and write (on the post-it) something (a sentence, keywords, etc.) about the topic present in the Question Card 3. Place the answer at will, but next to the Question Card 4. Players can also use a Trump Card to go back to a previous question or choose a new Question Card 5. Read the Question and the Answers aloud when the time is over 6. At this point and in turns, players must explain the reasons that drove them to such answers and why they placed their Answer Chip where they did 7. There are no winners The goal is to discuss the subject at hand, while creating a conceptual map of discussion/conversation

---

[4] All content of cards was created from theoretical research [12].

This game proposes to build knowledge about anorexia nervosa, by promoting experiences such as collaboration, altruism and self-expression. The ways to achieve these experiences are the creation of dynamics that allow sharing of knowledge and information, qualifying information gathering, mapping the conversation and knowledge, distributing the opportunity for expression, minimizing parallel conversations and/or word monopoly to promote effective collective learning.

For future versions we need develop the content of questions card with more open questions to facilitate the speech of the players, and further research the role of the researcher/interviewer as s/he is the mediator of game and that manages the conversation flow.

By creating an environment that promotes sharing and learning in a ludic fashion, this game has the potential to facilitate the exchange of knowledge as it provides the researcher with another way of understanding the content generated during a given session – the positioning of the cards on the table by the players creates a mental map[5] (or a conversational map).

4   Considerations and Future Studies

We proposed an alliance between Speculative Design and Game Design towards the design of prototypes for psychoeducational and research tools for mental health. These speculative game-instruments act as triggers to capture data, to help us understand what exists and what can exist in the context of anorexia nervosa – Speculative Design is (and was) useful in anticipating behaviours through imagination, creativity, and heavy questioning.

This first exercise is an initial understanding of the theme and context of the research in question, being part of a larger project. It is intended for us to soon to look at these game-instruments in a way to take advantage of their emergence related traits, as that will provide us with new insights and alternative perspectives, in the same way that in the past – when conceiving these first versions of these prototypes – we were able to envision the context of our research through perspectives we were not able to otherwise contemplate so early in this project.

References

1. Kondo, D., Sokol, M.: Perturbações do comportamento alimentar em cuidados de saúde primários. Postgrad Med. (ed. port) **31**(1), 57–62 (2009)
2. Appolinario, J., Claudino, A.: Transtornos alimentares. Rev. Bras. Psiquiatr. - RBP **22** (Suppl. II), 28–31 (2000). ISSN 1809-452X
3. Lock, J., Fitzpatrick, K.: Anorexia nervosa. BMJ Clin. Evid. **pii**, 1011 (2009)
4. Castro, J.M., Goldenstein, S.: Eating attitudes and behaviors of pre and postpubertal females: clues to the etiology of eating disorders. Physiol. Behav. **58**, 15–23 (1995)

---

[5] A mind map is a diagram that is drawn to represent ideas, tasks or other concepts that are related to a keyword or central idea [14].

5. Fleitlich, B.W., et al.: Anorexia nervosa na adolescência. J. Pediatr. **76**, 323–329 (2000). 0021-7557/00/76-Supl.3/S323. Sociedade Brasileira de Pediatria. Brasil
6. Kaplan, A.S.: Psychological treatments for anorexia nervosa: a review of published studies and promising new directions. Can. J. Psychiat. **47**(3), 235–242 (2002)
7. Giordani, R.C.F.: A auto-imagem corporal na anorexia nervosa: uma abordagem sociológica. Psicol. Soc. **18**(2), 81–88 (2006)
8. Huizinga, J.: Homo Ludens. Perspectiva, São Paulo (1998)
9. Wright, J.H., Basco, M.R., Thase, M.E.: Aprendendo a Terapia Cognitivo-Comportamental: Um Guia Ilustrado. Artmed, Porto Alegre (2008)
10. Beck, J.S.: Terapia Cognitiva: Teoria e Prática. Artes Médicas, Porto Alegre (1997)
11. Dunne, A., Raby, F.: Speculative Everything: Design, Fiction, and Social Dreaming. MIT Press Books, Cambridge (2013). Institute of Technology
12. Peçaibes, V., Cardoso, P., Alvelos, H.: UD18 Encontro De Doutoramentos em Design (2018). ud18.web.ua.pt
13. Dresch, A., Lacerda, D., Antunes, J.: Design Science Research: Método de Pesquisa para o avanço da Ciência e Tecnologia. Bookman, Porto Alegre (2015)
14. Buzan, T.E., Griffiths, C.: Mapas Mentais Para Os Negócios: Revolucione Sua Atividade Empresarial e a Maneira Como Você Trabalha. Cultrix Edition, São Paulo (2017)

Multidisciplinary Experience in the Creation of Pervasive Games for Interactive Spaces

Javier Marco[1], Clara Bonillo[2(✉)], Sandra Baldassarri[2],
and Eva Cerezo[2]

[1] Escuela Superior de Diseño de Aragón, C/ María Zambrano 3,
50018 Saragossa, Spain
jmarco@esda.es
[2] Computer Science Department, Universidad de Zaragoza,
María de Luna 1, 50015 Saragossa, Spain
{clarabf, sandra, ecerezo}@unizar.es

Abstract. In this article, a multidisciplinary experience with designers and developers to create pervasive games prototypes for an Interactive Space is presented. The Interactive Space, in which the experience took place, and the toolkit that the developers used in order to implement the games are explained. The different sessions with designers and developers are also described in detail, together with the game prototypes that resulted from the experience.

Keywords: Pervasive games · Interactive spaces
Multidisciplinary experience · Design

1 Introduction and Related Work

Since Weiser first post-WIMP discussion [1], designers of interactive applications are showing a growing interest in creating interfaces that integrate physical manipulation with interactive surfaces and responsive spaces that embody digital information. This is being reflected in the emergence of Interactive Spaces (IS) [2]: Distributed User Interfaces supporting several ways of interactions in digitally augmented rooms. Initially, ISs have been applied to explore new possibilities of collaborative work and meeting rooms [3] but more recently they are being considered as the ideal environment for the creation of pervasive games [4], since IS offer new possibilities to digitally augment the traditional game: on the one hand, ubiquitous technologies embedded in IS allow the identification and tracking of the physical playing pieces as they are manipulated by players; on the other hand, these technologies also allow the system itself to "intervene" in the play space. This is the case of pervasive games, an emerging field in the computer entertainment area that aims to eliminate the gap between traditional games and videogames [5].

During the last years an increasing number of projects and prototypes of pervasive games in ISs [6–8] can be found. However, the progress in the development of pervasive games is slowing down because of the multiple challenges that this kind of games brings to both designers and developers, due to the great variety of interaction paradigms that this kind of games involve and the difficulties of developing applications where so many innovative technologies converge.

A. L. Brooks et al. (Eds.): ArtsIT 2018/DLI 2018, LNICST 265, pp. 182–187, 2019.

In this work, we describe an experience that was carried out with designers and developers in order to create pervasive games for an IS. In Sect. 2 we briefly present our IS. Section 3 presents the software toolkit created to facilitate the prototyping of pervasive games. Section 4 covers the experience that was carried out together with the games that resulted from it. Finally, Sect. 5 is devoted to conclusions and future work.

2 The Juguemos Interactive Space

Our IS consists on a room of 70 m². Embedded on it there is a set of sensor devices that allow different ways of interaction: **four tabletops** for tangible interaction, **three Kinect sensors** for gesture interaction, and **a Real-Time Localization System** (RTLS) for embodied interaction (see Fig. 1).

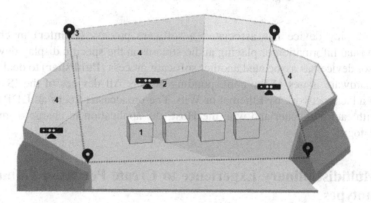

Fig. 1. Interactive Space schema. 1: Tabletops; 2: Kinect; 3: RTLS 4: Video projection on walls.

Regarding the display technologies that are integrated in the IS, there are three video projector screens that cover the surrounding walls, tabletop devices display images on their surface, and audio feedback is provided on all the IS area and on each tabletop device.

This is our current IS configuration, but it is quite flexible and new devices can be added and integrated at any moment as required by the specific pervasive game. This is possible thanks to a software toolkit that has been also developed in parallel, and which is presented in the next section.

3 The Juguemos Toolkit

The Juguemos toolkit has been designed to make it easy the prototyping of applications for IS. It is based on a centralized network architecture in which a software **Broadcaster** is connected with the host application and with each of the hardware devices integrated in the IS (see Fig. 2).

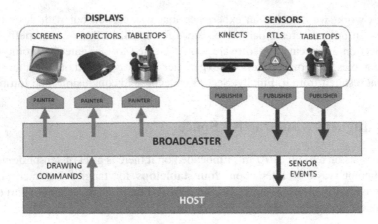

Fig. 2. Schema of the toolkit architecture

Each display device has associated a software process (**Painter**) in charge of painting visual information or playing audio streams in the specific display device, and each sensor device has associated another software process (**Publisher**) to deal with the specific hardware issues of the corresponding device. All devices of the IS are connected to a local network by Ethernet or Wifi. The broadcaster keeps an UDP network socket with each Publisher and with the **Host**, the application in charge of managing the game logic.

4   A Multidisciplinary Experience to Create Pervasive Game Prototypes

Juguemos IS and toolkit have been designed to provide multidisciplinary teams of designers and developers with the adequate tools to foster collaboration and creativity during the ideation, design and prototyping processes of innovative pervasive games [9]. To prove their usefulness, an experience with a multidisciplinary team was carried out in the IS.

The team was composed of five Graphic Design students of the 4th year at the School of Arts in the University of Plymouth (UK) and six Computer Engineering students of the 4th year at the School of Engineering and Architecture (EINA) of the University of Zaragoza (Spain). Neither of them had previous experience on ubiquitous technologies or on the prototyping of pervasive games. The experience was organized in four different sessions that are explained in the following subsections.

4.1   First Session

The six Computer Engineering students attended to a 3 h practical session in the Juguemos IS so that they could familiarize with the ubiquitous technologies involved and with Juguemos toolkit. Each student had to follow a guided exercise in which they had to complete a simple pervasive game by using the Juguemos toolkit. The exercise was divided into four tasks with increased complexity that had to be completed in order to progress to the next one. Only two students completed the last task in three hours, but the main concepts and skills required to prototype a pervasive game in our IS using our toolkit were successfully transmitted to all students, as it was demonstrated in the fourth session.

4.2 Second Session

We organised a 2 h session in the Juguemos IS with the five Graphic Design students. They were introduced to the physical affordances of the ubiquitous technologies integrated in the IS, in order to bring physical interaction to pervasive games. We also showed them different examples of pervasive games developed for our IS.

4.3 Third Session

The third session lasted 3 h and took also place in our IS. This time both computer engineers and design students worked together (see Fig. 3 Left). The eleven participants were disposed in two groups of 5 and 6 people respectively: 2 designers and 3 developers in one group, and 3 designers and 3 developers in another group. The designers were the ones in charge of thinking about the game concept, to choose the interaction paradigms that were going to be used, and to create the graphic resources of the games. Accordingly, the developers listened to the designers' ideas to decide if they were feasible to be developed using the Juguemos IS technologies and toolkit. The ideas that the two groups came up are:

1. **Car races** (group 1): From the start they decided that they wanted to do a car race game for four players, by making the most of the four tabletops of the IS. The group defined the interaction creating two physical objects to control the direction and the velocity of the car. Both designers and developers had many doubts about the physical affordances of the tabletops despite of the explanations of the previous sessions, so it was necessary to show them practical examples so that they understood what kind of interactions the tabletop supported.
2. **Building a car** (group 2): originally, the idea was to make a construction game, without defining yet what was going to be built. The first idea was to build a house but the designers were having many doubts about the pieces that were going to compose it, so they eventually decided to build a car after hearing the concept that the other group had come up with. After some group discussion, the group chose to create a gesture interface based on the Kinect sensor.

At the end of the third session, two perfectly defined concepts of games had been created and the required graphic assets were also developed by graphic designers (see Fig. 3 Right). Since this was going to be the last session in which the designers were going to be present, they gave us their opinion regarding the experience. They all agreed that they have learned about the possibilities of the tangible user interface design, and that they would be interested in continuing working with the Computer Engineering students.

Fig. 3. Different moments of the third session. **Left**: multidisciplinary discussion of concepts. **Right**: graphic designers generating graphic assets with the technical supervision of developers

4.4   Fourth Session

The last session was carried out just with the Computer Engineering students. Neither of them had any particular difficulties to integrate the different sensors necessary for their concept (tabletops for the first group and Kinect for the second group). Figure 4 shows the developed games running in the IS. In the "Car Races" game, players use the tabletops to drive their respective cars with two different objects that control the car's velocity and direction (see Fig. 4 Left). Regarding the "Building a car" game, players use their hands to "grab" the car pieces that appeared on the projection screen to "put" them on their corresponding place of the car shape (see Fig. 4 Right).

Fig. 4. Pervasive games created. **Left**: car races. **Right**: build a car

As a result of this last session, both groups managed to implement completely functional prototypes of the games in three hours. Videos of each concept were recorded and sent to the design students in Plymouth, who showed their satisfaction when seeing their concepts running.

5   Conclusions and Future Work

In this work we have presented a multidisciplinary experience that took place between Graphic Design and Computer Engineering students to create pervasive games. The experience took place in an Interactive Space, equipped with several sensors and displays, and with a toolkit developed to make the coding of pervasive games easier. Both multidisciplinary groups were able to come up with a functional prototype of an IS game. However, this was possible because the ideas presented by the designers were supported by the IS existing hardware: if different physical interactions had been proposed, the complexity would have notably increased, since the design and implementation of applications that include ubiquitous technologies keep being a challenging task that requires advanced qualifications and supporting tools.

Regarding future work, we plan to carry out a more exhaustive and lengthy iterative design experience to see how the space and the toolkit support creative multidisciplinary cooperation in the design of pervasive games.

Acknowledgments. We want to thank Kamal Gohil and the students from "The Agency" (belonging Plymouth School of Arts). Also, we thank the students from University of Zaragoza for participating in the sessions. This work has been partly financed by the Spanish Government through the contract TIN2015-67149-C3-1R.

References

1. Weiser, M.: The computer for the 21st century. Mob. Comput. Commun. Rev. **3**(3), 3–11 (1999)
2. Jetter, H.C., Reiterer, H., Geyer, F.: Blended interaction: understanding natural human–computer interaction in post-WIMP interactive spaces. Pers. Ubiquit. Comput. **18**(5), 1139–1158 (2014)
3. Borchers, J.: The Aachen media space: multiple displays in collaborative interactive environments. In: Workshop Information Visualization and Interaction Techniques for Collaboration Across Multiple Displays in Conjunction with CHI, vol. 6 (2006)
4. Guo, B., Fujimura, R., Zhang, D., Imai, M.: Design-in-play: improving the variability of indoor pervasive games. Multimedia Tools Appl. **59**(1), 259–277 (2012)
5. Magerkurth, C., Cheok, A.D., Nilsen, T.: Pervasive games: bringing computer entertainment back to the real world. ACM Trans. Comput. Entertain. **3**(3), Article 4a (2005)
6. Khoo, E.T., Cheok, A.D.: Age invaders: inter-generational mixed reality family game. Int. J. Virtual Real. **5**(2), 45–50 (2008)
7. Morreale, F., De Angeli, A., Masu, R., Rota, P., Conci, N.: Collaborative creativity: the music room. Pers. Ubiquit. Comput. **18**(5), 1187–1199 (2014)
8. Sherman, L., et al.: StoryKit: tools for children to build room - sized interactive experiences. In: Extended Abstracts of CHI EA 2001 (2001)
9. Marco, J., Bonillo, C., Cerezo, E.: A tangible interactive space odyssey to support children learning of computer programming. In: Proceedings of the 2017 ACM International Conference on Interactive Surfaces and Spaces, pp. 300–305. ACM (2017)

Scentgraphy - Interactive Installation of Scent Communication

Xiaotian Sun[(✉)] and Kiyoshi Tomimatsu

Kyushu University, Fukuoka, Japan
ginasun@foxmail.com, tomimatu@design.kyushu-u.ac.jp

Abstract. This paper presents an analysis on the interactive installation of "Scentgraphy", which could compute, interpret, simulate and store scents behind scenes. It acts like an original camera or gramophone to capture and save pictorial memories. It not only enriches the interactive experiences, but also establishes a closer relationship with the combination of smell, vision and emotion. Meanwhile, Scentgraphy also provide an interesting interaction conducive for immersive experience of breathing aromatherapy. This project explores new experiences about the senses, sensory boundaries, storing and reproducing of the sense of smell. Based on ancient perfumery techniques, a closer bond is developed between memory and sense of smell. Scentgraphy project explored a way for computing, simulation, and telecommunication of odors by visual and olfactory conversion. This is a preliminary exploration on olfactory informationization, and this research ensures that the feasibility of converting visual and olfactory and digital odors can be spread and applied in media and information technology.

Keywords: HCI · Olfaction · Experience design · Digital scent

1 Introduction

One of the prior reasons to the development of cameras and gramophones is that people want to capture and reproduce beautiful memories and moments. Currently, people are no longer satisfied with the sole reproduction of visual and auditory sense and started to wonder if it is possible to find a technological solution in capturing other parts of human senses for scenes, emotions and memories. So far to the current stage, many scientists, engineers and artists have begun to explore the multi-sensory field. However, constrained by the form how smell exists, none significant breakthrough has been made. Currently, the designs of simulated smell can be paired up with a lot of real-life scenarios. However, the full application of scentgraphy still requires further exploration in calculation, storage and reproduction of scents.

At the same time, urban residents in the city confront overwhelming pressure from their rapid lifestyle, putting considerable portion of them into sub-health condition. This abnormal state of health can influence emotion and spirit of people while gases and scents breathed into body can stimulate aberrant change among neurons and cerebral sections. Scentgraphy, in this case, can provide a functional solution similar to that of the ancient aromatherapy that helps people relieve stress and relax. With

A. L. Brooks et al. (Eds.): ArtsIT 2018/DLI 2018, LNICST 265, pp. 188–199, 2019.

development of scent technology, digital scent not only deeply expands multimedia experiences and immersive scenes, but also calculates, reproduces and stores scents. This is closely related with the future wellness of humans. Meanwhile, it is also closely related with marketing and entertainment.

2 Scentgraphy Design

2.1 Smell as Communication

German writer and screenwriter has written in an internationally famous novel *Perfume: The Story of a Murder* that "Odors have a power of persuasion stronger than that of words, appearances, emotions, or will. The persuasive power of an odor cannot be fended off, it enters into us like breath into our lungs, it fills us up, imbues us totally. There is no remedy for it".

Human's sense is infatuated with smell. The emotion and memories of human are tightly correlated with the smell of surroundings. However, with current technology, it is still impossible to store or replicate the scent of encountered environment.

For animals, foraging and breeding serve as the most important two things in life. Most animals rely on smell to differentiate the food and also to identify the position. Performance of animal instincts also relies intensively on the sense of smell. Case in point, the action of mating by a lot of primates is based on the capacity of nose to perceive the possible courtship.

Every creature can breathe. It is a natural performance of metabolic activity by the respiratory system associated with the olfactory system. That is to say, every creature has a sense of smell. Smell is also one of the most important characteristics of a substance and the most representative essence of the substance. Every substance has its own distinct smell while no two different substances with the same smell has been confirmed to exist. The smell of substance does not normally change when the biological components remain the same. It is only through qualitative reactions that changes of smell take part on substances.

As a common language in the world of biology, the sense of smell of every single creature has specific perceptual range. Every creature has its blind area in terms of smell. This specific range of the sense of smell for each creature is only related to its survival needs. It is positively related to its survival benefits while negatively related to its survival harmfulness. There are also special cases, such as oxygen, vapor, carbon dioxide, carbon monoxide, the major components of air in the living spaces on the Earth. People have no specific senses for them because they exist in the air all the time while they don't have to deliberately seek or guard against them. The human olfactory center removes the smell signals. On the other hand, the substances linked to creatures' survival are usually the ones arising sensual reactions. For example, the camel in desert needs to find water. The nose of camels holds the ability to retain its sensitivity to the water vapor. A recent study finds that people who have experienced carbon monoxide poisoning have recovered their sensitivity to carbon monoxide as compared to their previous conditions. The smell of animals also changes temporarily with diet, disease, and mood. The creature can consciously release special smell for use of information exchange, such as offensive and defensive messages.

With the previous studies in biology, it has been testified that humans and animals rely on their past experiences to establish a sense of smell information, which also implies that smell serves as one of the basic ways of biological exchange.

2.2   Sensory Are Interlinked

Five senses of human are interlinked. People can feel the melody inside a room by looking through the window even when you are not actually inside. People can feel the taste of the meal by observing it even when you cannot catch the smell. People can experience different feelings bringing by the warm and cold colors. In real life encounters, connection of senses always takes part, case in point, people associating certain colors with tastes (or flavors). For example, strawberry-flavored candies and strawberry ice-cream can always make people associate it with pink or red coverings while orange-flavored candies and orange-scented pens make people think of orange outliers.

In the study from Department of Psychology, Gettysburg College, people's internalized linkage between scent and color is explored comprehensively by classifying the link into three different levels:

  I. Probability links: if a color and a taste often appear together, they usually would be connected together automatically.
 II. Semantic links: if the color and scent have some common meanings or identities, they might be put together. This can be supported by the example of interconnecting the taste of orange and the orange color.
III. Structural links: If the color and scent are similar in intensity or extensity, they might be linked [1].

Such association relies intensively on the scenarios these two types of stimulus appear together. As it has been testified by the prior study, common identity of color and scent affects the internalized connection across senses. Therefore, we have chosen the common colors often used in basic painting. Through the analysis of scenes and concerning colors, we can simulate the smell behind the scene. In the perfumery industry, the Michael Edwards' fragrance wheel invented by Edwards is taken as the authority in terms of perfume classification. The fragrance classification widely used in the perfume industry is composed by four branches, including floral fragrance, oriental fragrance, woody fragrance and delicate fragrance, and the fragrance has 14 notes. Based on this fragrance wheel, a test regarding the optical and smell senses of users was carried out.

The use value of Scentgraphy can be verified by proving the link between color and smell. Availability of Scentgraphy can in turn be thoroughly manifested. To do so, the research team of ours conducted the following experiment. Smell sense is the feeling mostly close to memory. Therefore, we, the researchers, regarded scene (or object) as the medium in the process of building up the relation between color and odor. Referring to Edward's fragrance wheel, the research team identified 12 colors as the basic colors and meanwhile add the color dark blue, grey, white and black commonly seen in the daily life. We designed an online questionnaire involving relevant 4 or 5 scene pictures in similar colors with only one of the pictures showing up for each time in front of the responding subjects. There was no word appearing in the questionnaire. What respondents needed to do was to quickly choose the picture according to their first impression. The respondents for this test were from 7 countries (China, Japan, Britain, Netherlands, Germany, United States and Brazil). Altogether, they submitted 416 questionnaires. Among all respondents, female accounts for 63% and male accounts for 37%. The eldest respondent is a female aged 42 and the youngest respondent is a male aged 4. Please refer to Table 1 for the statistics of the collected answers from the respondents.

Table 1. Table captions should be placed above the tables.

Color								
Scenes								
smell	red pepper	Berry	rose	orange	lemon	basil	moss	water
Color								
Scenes								
smell	lavender	soil	woods	coffee	tobacco	mysterious	vanilla	Night sky

We, the researchers, used natural fragrance or compound fragrance to choose odor for each scene. However, we also found that the scents of certain kinds of odor was closely related to their smellness. Therefore, we endowed these certain kinds of odor with colors more likely in arousing synesthetic thinking within the respondents' minds. According to prior research, we matched color white with icecream. To echo the scene in dark blue sky at night, blue Lotus Oil was chosen as the color for scents of air with heavy humidity. Because the scene in black corresponds to the sense of mystery, we specifically chose black as representing the smell of Myrrh oil, the one with heavy hints of smoke and bitter taste of traditional Chinese medicine. Likewise, since water corresponds to the light blue, we decided to take light blue as the color standing for water.

2.3 Olfaction and Informationized

From the 1950s to the 1980s, filmmakers were constantly on their tryout in producing relevant scent devices used for the creation of immersive atmosphere. The world of technology, however, was lagged behind as compared to the film-making industry.

iSmell, developed by DigiScents, did not float to the surface until the hatch of the new millennium. This device is a stereo-like speaker that contains a cartridge with 128 "main scents" that can be mixed to replicate natural and artificial scents. DigiScents has indexed thousands of common scents that can be encoded, digitized and embedded in web pages and emails, allowing a wide range of scent exchanges on the electronic network. [3] oPhone, designed Harvard University, allows users to tag scents alongside with their photo from OS-NAP, a smart phone application. Sharing the caught scents behind scenarios via email and social platform has presented new interactive ways through. [4] In recent years, the scent synthesizers for VR devices has also appeared. It is believed that smell is an important factor for the medical treatment, commerce, entertainment and arts, for it not only represents fantasy but also communicates directly with cerebral consciousness and memories, so as to evoke uncontrollable emotions and establish more effective communication.

In fact, smell has now received more and more chances to be fully informationized and pushed to the verge of commercialization. There are already massive business organizations paying great attention to the marketing strategies based on the use of smell. For example, high-end hotels and shopping malls usually choose a set of scents conducive to arising the attentiveness of consumers. The scent might bring customers a sense of belonging, pleasure and more cheerful memories. On the other hand, through the smell, customers may get more excited and more eager to spill their money upon various goods.

2.4 Scentgraphy

This study is conducted with an aim of exploring a new experience connected to the daily breath of people. The study of related works has revealed that there are preset scents in most olfactory devices. Those devices do not have the capability to analyze and formulate scents regarding the change of surroundings. Based on the image recognition technology, a change can be brought to this circumstance. The color distribution of a famous painting, a scene or even a crowd is calculated through the correlations between colors and scents to eventually get the sensually felt emotion underneath each scene. The olfaction calculation of this concerned scene will be, by the end, helping to form the corresponding scents. However, due to the current technical limitations of scent analysis, only the dilute essential oil is used as the "ink" behind each scent. In fact, in our life, there are not only the scents, but also "stench" and "odor". To bring out more realized restoration of scents behind the scenes, future production and digitalization of the scent "ink" should focus on the optimization for a more diversified set of smelling experiences.

3 Prototype

3.1 Design Process

The major design of the whole device adopts the chemical equipment of traditional glass technology, 3D printing and SCM. Regardless of the material, visual or interactive way, it reflects a traditional but modern feeling. Based on the spectrum of color and scent, this system calculates the color pixelated distribution of landscapes, images or even a person, through recognition of landscape and image. According to the quantity of colors, this device controls the concerning air-flowing time of the corresponding (according to Fig. 1: Color and Scent Spectrum) scent "ink" bottle attached to a solenoid valve. With the liquid release being longer, the flow of scent "ink" will be larger, and vice versa. The scent "ink" that is identified when passing through a mixing funnel which has an "ink" electric stirrer that could blend mixing scents evenly. After blending, the mixing funnel will open the solenoid valve to release the mixed scent liquid which has already been smoothly divided into two separate parts.

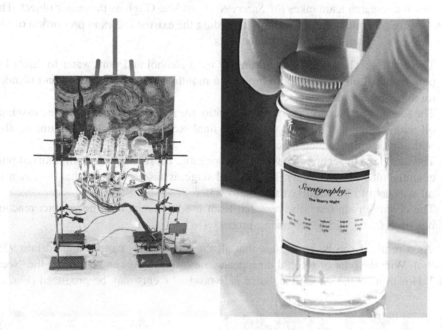

Fig. 1. Prototype and the computed perfume (Color figure online)

One part of the aforementioned two is immediately atomized into a gas atomizer to release into the air so that users smell and experience the scent constantly. The other part could be stored for later release. When running the device, the user can experience the scents changing accordingly with respect to the environment. Besides of this experience, a bottle of "scent liquid" will be generated in analogy to that of a photo taken from a camera. The scent data printed from the printer can be stored for the later building of database and reproduction of pre-existing memories. This process seems like a record for the gramophone, which brings a precious and ritual feeling.

3.2 Scent Ink Production

Scent ink is formulated through a "Color Smell Table", during which a base odor liquid is used. The scent "ink" is produced with the essential oil correspondingly spared from the "Table". When use, the "ink" is stored in the pear- shaped bottle at the top of the aparatus. The "ink" is scentgraphy's source of "energy." In the predictable future, with increased matching precision of scent "ink", Scentgraphy's sensory transformation experiences will be greatly enhanced. During the manufacturing process of the scent "ink", the ancient method used by perfumery has been researched. The research team expected to get "scent ink" to be able to be stored for a long time without being diluted or turned into a messed mixture filled with alcohol taste. When testing the result of the tryouts, the research team takes *the Starry Night* of Van Gogh as the major object. The scents were generated correspondingly regarding the existed colors in proportion on *the Starry Night* during the following three tests.

1. The first test: The research team directly used alcohol and pure water to dilute the pure essential oil. It took approximately a month to get a fully diluted and blended mixture without alcoholic scent.
2. The second test: According to the color ratio, the research team mixed pure essential oil with alcohol and purified water. The final scent of essential oil became weaker with a bit of hint of alcoholic smell.
3. The third test: In accordance with the color ratio, the research team first mixed pure essential oil with well water. By the final stage, it has been found that the essential oil was hard to be dissolved fully into water.
4. The control-group test: The research team used essential oils, no distinct reaction has been found during atomizing process.

As a result, it can be concluded that all the basic scents can be diluted into 95% alcohol. With the odor of alcohol disappears, the resulted gas can be used as the "scent ink". However, at the same time, some side-product scents may be produced (Fig. 2).

Fig. 2. Scent ink

3.3   Hardware

The chemical apparatus serves as the main structure of the product. The interaction among human, machine and environment is adopted through the sensor, solenoid valve, Raspberry Pi, camera, screen, printer and atomizer. The camera gathers the environment (picture) data. Such data are processed and calculated by the Raspberry Pi. The connected computer conducts calculation regarding the captured scenes to achieve pictorial recognition. Subsequently, the permutation and combination of scents correlated with the pixel scale of color are accomplished. The major color can be identified in priority while the corresponding scent "ink" are controlled to be released. All scent "inks" are blended through the rubber pipe. Part of mixed liquids are discharged using the atomizer bottle, which can immediately generate the scene or picture smell, while another part is reserved as a copy for later reproduction. Meanwhile, the printer will print the adhesive label with color data, which could be attached to the bottle of copy for reconfiguration. The user controls the operation of the whole device by controlling the touch screen. Eventually, the user will smell the calculated scents discharged by the atomizer and reproduce the scents with one bottle of liquid mixture. Throughout the whole operation process, a set of interactive systems guiding the user step by step has been achieved to optimize the user experience.

3.4   The Color Detection

The research team of ours have also taken into consideration of the vision recognition functionality involved in the application process of Scentgraphy. The color models, HSL and HSV, are used as the cylindrical coordinators for the color adjustment module. HSL and HSV are the most common color models of cylindrical coordinates. Compared with the previously popular RGB model, these two sets are more visually intuitive. The application of the HSL and HSV models will help the research team to better identify the hue, saturation and brightness of colors under different light conditions. HSL and HSV models for each selected 16 color has been established for the later calculation of their associated values. After being photographed, the captured image will be pixelated and analyzed the computerized system. Each pixel will be matched with the corresponding color value to count the percentage of each pixel in the pixilated image.

With the future establishment of the database, it can be anticipated that more well-founded recognition ability will be achieved.

4   User Study

4.1   Method

To find out whether respondents could correlate specific colors with particular scents among two groups of odors, an exploratory study was conducted by the research team of ours. The research team recorded all experimental procedures through video, including the interviews with the participants after the experiment. In the interview, we asked about the impression of the users on Scentgraphy, including questions regarding the user experience and the value of later development of smell informatization. Experimental data, interview videos, and results from the questionnaires were used as the bases for this later research.

The first experiment: 15 respondents are all aged between 22 and 36. Before the task, the 'Color, Scent and Scenes table' was not exposed to respondents. At the same time, we made a brief introduction to the test flow and conduct a 10-min instruction to every respondent to help them fill in the questionnaire and smell odor. The testers smelled the odor in the numbered bottle. There were 16 scent inks being placed in the bottled and labeled with numbers. Four people are in a group and four scent bottles were provided to each person. The colors are identified by smell correspondingly with the given options. The testers' choices are documented by the research team for later test upon the accuracy. After discerning the odor on the test paper, respondents are required to write down the number of corresponding color on the questionnaire. At the interval between the first and second test, we removed the objects with odor, for obliging the scenario of letting the existing odor affecting the next test. After completing the full tests, we hold a five-minute interview with every respondent and film a video for this.

The results of the first group are listed as below. Among the 15 individuals, 53% of them correctly identified the odors. Scents that frequently appeared in life, such as Floral, Fruity, Purple, Wood Oriental, Citrus, etc., can be easily recognized. Colors with more specific features, such as fog and green, are relatively easy to be identified. In the interview, testers have reflected that understanding of the tested odors will easily be felt in an atmosphere dominated by this color. The color of Fog was created using the smell of Cuban tobacco to produce a feeling of smoke and blemishes. The color of Green was created using Basil smell to create a soothing nerve. As for the colors of Dark Mossy, Navy, Black, White, etc., concerned scent ink were made to inhibit the nerve excitation, making the related odors relatively hard to be identified. It can be explained that people do not have a consensus upon this set colors to relate them to a specific smell in their life. It is only through frequent life encounters, consensual correlation between colors and scents can be established. The results of the second experiment, are listed as followed. The accuracy rate for recognizing the Great Wave off Kanagawa is 54%; the rate for Still Life with Sleeping Woman is 43%; the one for Auspicious Cranes is 36%; the one for Starry night is 27%. As a contrast in terms of this accuracy rate, the color of pumpkin appeared as hard to be identified, the accuracy rate for this color is only 11%. Through the interviews with the testers, a conclusion has been reached that people's sense of smell actually is trained after the birth. Nose has not yet been considered as an organ that can accept information. In regard of this fact, the production of scent ink should also be more specialized. The choice of odor may be correct during the time of test. It is undeniable that the non-specialization of the commissioned essential oils would also affect people's judgment in correlating the odors with real-life colors. However, when the researchers told the testers about the right related color behind the odors, the majority of the testers were able to show an immediate realization and recognized the smell.

The second experiment: There are 15 participants in the second group, whose ages range from 24 to 32. Before the test, all the 15 participants will join the smell test which lasts 40 min at the same time. Through initial learning of the Colour Scent Wheel, elementary memories can be generated. Scents of the five famous paintings generated by Scentgraphy are numbered. The 15 testers smelled the odors in the numbered bottles, and corresponds the smelled scents to the paintings. The accuracy of the tested subjects' verdict was documented to prove the connection between the mixed smell and the scene. By the end of the color recognition test, the respondents all accepted 5-min interview regarding their choices in the prior tests.

During the interview, some of our participants expressed that they had not smelled certain scents that were included beforehand of our test, but those scents did trigger different part of memories related to their personal experiences. For example, one of our participants who is a 25-year-old male going through his graduate study on economics said the woody smell reminded him of the massage shop in the Southeast Asian style. Another 28-year-old architect expressed that the woody smell made him think of the smell of a laser cutting workshop. Most of the participants believed that, despite the differences between the vaguely recalled memories during the two tests, this kind of training can help people establish unified ideas and smell languages. Some testers said it is hard for them to discern the smell of smoke from that of soil as these two smelled extremely similar. However, people believe that they can tell the smells apart after frequent tests for a long time.

Two kinds of conclusions can be reached following the test. After the 40-min training, participants' recognition ability of scents can probably be relatively sharpened to a level higher than the accuracy rate of 42% which is the result we had for the tests. What's more, the scents on the smell wheel's right side is easier to be recognized than those of the smell wheel's left side. As is shown in the Fig. 3, the number of correctly recognized scents decreases following the direction of the arrow (Fig. 4).

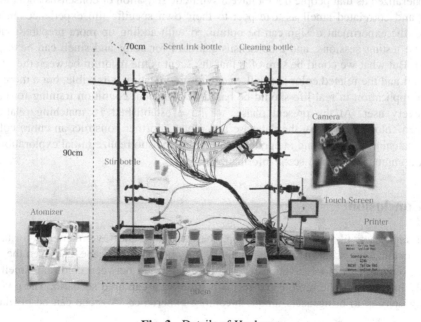

Fig. 3. Details of Hardware

Fig. 4. The user smells and identifies the color. (Color figure online)

4.2 Results

In the experiment process, we, the researchers, also found out that respondents' deviation in color and odor perception is as a result of cultural difference. It could also be generalized as that people do not have a synthetic sensation or consensus about each color and correlated smell as a respect to their own specific life experience. In the future, the experiment design can be optimized with adding up more prepared odors into the testing sessions, and a consensus standard for color and smell can be established. But what we could be sure of is that the scent is the medium between the sense of smell and the related color in mind. Scent communication is feasible, but a more indepth application in real life should be based on the scent cognition training for each and every user. At the present phase, we have established 16 matching relations between color and odor in the database and plan to further construct an entire color-odor matching database and integrate Scentgraphy so as to realize initial exploration in scent communication and scent Informatization.

5   Conclusion

Scentgraphy acts like an original gramophone to capture and save memories for us. It can generalize the scent of specific paintings, the one of a landscape, and even the one of a photograph. A closer relationship can be established between color and smell by simply breathing in the reproduced scents behind each captured scenario. The goal of Scentgraphy is to bring users unique breathing experience. A scene can be pixelated and later calculated to better unveil the relationship between color and scent to help embody the underneath emotion based on the image recognition technology.

Olfactory information can be counted as a kind of sensory data. In the future, such data can be applied to immersive entertainment, multimedia handheld devices, and even medical and beauty industries. The research team truly believes that the future sensory design will permeate into all aspects of life. In addition to obtaining more accurate scent data, the team of Scentgraphy needs to explore deeper to better understand the mechanism for scents to affect the user's emotions, emotions, and memories.

This research will make the media and information technology spread in a more effective way. Making the current device more applicable to immersive entertainment, multimedia handheld devices, and even medical and beauty industries. There is reason to believe that in the near future, this set of sensory input objects will get deep into all aspects of daily life, rather than just stay in the current visual and auditory. In addition to requiring more accurate odor information, the developing team also needs to explore upon the mechanism that how the odor affects the user's emotions, emotions, and memories more than they are now. Scentgraphy serves as the touchstone of the digitization of scents. In the short future, scents can not only be calculate, saved and reproduced, but also can be remotely shared. Controlling people's emotional well-being through nostalgic odors by using certain functional products through odor memory, smell and scent will be applied across the world like any other physical products that have already been widely accepted.

References

1. Gilbert, A.N., Martin, R., Kemp, S.E.: Cross-modal correspondence between vision and olfaction: the color of smells. Am. J. Psychol. **109**(3), 335–351 (1996)
2. Kacmarek, R., Dimas, S.: Essentials of Respiratory Care. Mosby, Maryland Heights (2004)
3. Kaye, J.J.: Making scents: aromatic output for HCI. Interactions **11**(1), 48–61 (2004)
4. Friedmann, D.: EU opens door for sound marks: will scent marks follow? J. Intellect. Prop. Law Pract. **10**(12), 931–939 (2015)

The Use of 360-Degree Video to Provide an Alternative Media Approach to Paralympic Sports

Caroline Delmazo[(✉)]

iNOVA Media Lab/IC NOVA, Faculdade de Ciências Sociais e Humanas,
Universidade Nova de Lisboa, Lisbon, Portugal
caroldelmazo2010@gmail.com

Abstract. This paper describes exploratory research that consists of the production and testing of a 360-degree video-prototype aiming to provide a closer perspective to Paralympic athletes' training universe, exemplified by the wheelchair basketball. Media coverage of Paralympic sports has been changing but still represents athletes as heroes due to the overcoming of odds related to the impairment and not to the sports results. The present work considers immersive journalism and the use of virtual reality (VR) technologies as the path to an alternative framing where the athletes are portrayed as players facing a hard training routine and having sporting goals as the non-disabled ones.

The paper presents a brief description of prototype production and details the user study conducted in the aftermath with four focus groups. Feedback provided by participants indicates the suitability of the 360-degree video, when experienced with a headset and headphones, for the framing proposed and also points out narrative strategies that can be useful not only in Paralympic sports' storytelling but in the conception of diverse narratives for 360-degree video.

Keywords: Paralympic sports · Wheelchair basketball · Virtual reality
360 video

1 Introduction

The Paralympic Games is a multi-sports event organized by the International Paralympic Committee in which athletes with different disabilities participate. It takes place every four years following the Olympic Games. The 2016 Summer Paralympic Games held in Rio de Janeiro had a cumulative audience of more than 4,1 billion people with 5,110 h of broadcast, more than the total hours for the previous editions Beijing 2008 and London 2012 combined [1]. The increasing attention drawn by the event shed light on media representation of impaired people through the coverage of sports. Media portrayal of Paralympic athletes has been changing but still presents a narrative where athletes are framed as heroes that overcome odds related to the disability [2–4].

We hold the position that it is necessary to provide an alternative representation of Paralympic athletes in media coverage, portraying them as athletes - as the non-disabled ones -, without the need to ignore the impairment, but also without hyper-focusing on the histories behind the disability. We consider the immersive journalism

A. L. Brooks et al. (Eds.): ArtsIT 2018/DLI 2018, LNICST 265, pp. 200–205, 2019.

and the use of virtual reality (VR) technologies the path to this alternative framing, giving the audience the illusion of being present in the environment.

In this paper, we describe an exploratory study that consists of the production and testing of a 360-degree video-prototype aiming at giving special access to Paralympic sport's training universe, exemplified by the wheelchair basketball. After the brief description of the prototype's production, we detail the user study conducted with four focus groups to have insights into how participants perceived the Paralympic athletes after watching the prototype with a headset, namely the Samsung Gear VR. Feedback indicates the prototype facilitates the perception of the hard training routine and contribute to seeing the impaired athletes without compassion, just as athletes. The study also suggests the suitability of some narrative strategies for storytelling in 360 video, such as using the first scenes to introduce the audience to the possibility of exploring the 360° and the placement of the character talking directly to the camera.

2   Literature Review

Several scholars have studied the portrayal of disabled people in the coverage of the Paralympic Games. British newspaper's articles about London 2012 and Sochi 2014 (winter edition) show the tendency to promote a "triumph-over-adversity" narrative instead of highlighting the sports results [2]. The Canadian print coverage of London 2012 has a major focus on sports performance. However, almost half of the texts analysed have secondary narratives based on the stereotype "Supercrip" [3]. Berger [5] defines "Supercrips" as "individuals whose inspirational stories of courage, dedication, and hard work prove that it can be done, that one can defy the odds and accomplish the impossible." The "Supercrip" stereotype was not prominent in the Brazilian print coverage of the Rio 2016 Paralympic Games. The photos, nevertheless, are highly focused on the disability [6]. The content provided by broadcasters also uses the "Supercrip" stereotype [4]. Studies centred on the athletes' point of view indicate they prefer the focus on sports performance and felt uncomfortable with the "Supercrip" discourse. However, some of them recognize that this speech attracts broader audience [7].

We hold the position that it is possible to provide a media approach without the use of the "Supercrip" framing, offering an alternative standpoint to the Paralympic world. An immersive experience in journalism aims exactly to provide a "special perspective" to the news. De la Peña et al. [8] explain that the person participates of a virtually re-created scenario representing the news story as a visitor with first-hand access or through the perspective of a character in the story. Two key-concepts about immersive environments are Place Illusion - a strong sense of being in a place even though you know you are not in fact there -, and Plausibility - the illusion that what is happening is actually happening, in a reliable relation to what would happen in reality [9].

The use for news purposes is one of the growing applications of virtual reality (VR), explained by Aronson-Rath et al. [10] as "an immersive media experience that replicates either a real or imagined environment and allows users to interact with this world in ways that feel as if they are there". Immersive narratives have been gaining space in news coverage, especially the 360-degree video, or cinematic VR: the user is in a central position that cannot be altered within the environment, the agency is to look around. It is considered the most accessible type of VR [11]. What turns a 360-degree video into a VR experience is the possibility of seeing the content in a VR headset [12].

Interviews must be captured as they will be experienced by the viewer, with no cuts apart from the beginnings and ends of the scenes [10]. The amount of visual and sound information should be considered to avoid Fear of Missing Out (FOMO) [13]. The voice over should be used attentively: the user needs to look around to check if someone is talking on camera or it is a voice over [14]. Characters can give signals to the viewer, by looking, pointing or walking in a certain direction [15].

3 The Prototype

The shooting for the prototype took place in the High-Performance Centre of Vila Nova de Gaia (Portugal) on December 8th–9th 2017, during the training of the Portuguese wheelchair basketball team. The list of equipment for shooting was the following: 2 Samsung Gear 360 (2016) cameras; 2 Galaxy S7 Edge; tripod; Roland R-44 audio recorder; 5 microphones (four Behringer C-2 and one wireless lavalier mic). Besides the shots with the 360 camera, a linear audio interview was also recorded with the captain and the coach to be used as a voice over on the edited video.

The script for the prototype was designed with nine main scenes, every one lasting at least 25 s to give time to users to immerse themselves in each scene. In the video, the viewers follow the training routine: firstly as if they were with the athletes in the locker room; then in the centre of the court while players are warming up; and in the following scenes in different parts of the court, e.g., from the bench's perspective or below the basket during the exercises. The basic rules and the typical plays of the wheelchair basketball are explained by the captain and the coach. They also highlight the challenges of the athlete's life no matter the disability. We decided to include one scene in which the camera is attached to the athlete's wheelchair, as close as possible to the player's perspective. It's the only part of the video where the camera is in motion. Although shots in movement are considered risky because of motion sickness [16], we pondered that users should evaluate this scene in the user study.

Some narrative strategies were tested. The first scenes are slower and have less intensity, working as an introduction to the possibility of exploring the 360°. On the other hand, in the scene with more amount of information, the character talked directly to the camera, in order to keep the audience's attention. The voice over was another tool used to help users follow the narrative. The video's running time is 5 min (https://youtu.be/eW_e02pSaG4). The shots were automatically stitched with the software *Gear 360 Action Director*. The editing process was done in *Premiere Pro cc 2018*. The software *Reaper* and the *Facebook encoder* were also used for audio editing. The prototype was transferred to smartphones for the user study.

4 User Study

Four focus groups were organized in March 2018 to get insights from people with different levels of familiarity with Paralympic sports and Head-Mounted Displays (HMDs). All-in-all, 23 participants (15 male, 8 female) took part in the study, aged between 23 and 53. Group 1 (participants 1 to 5) was formed by people from organizations related to adapted sports and athlete's family members, all having a strong link to Paralympic sports and no experience with HMDs. Group 2 (participants 6 to 11) was formed by Ph.D. and Master's students with computer engineering and technology background and no/little familiarity with Paralympic sports. For group 3 (participants 12 to 18), Paralympic athletes that play wheelchair basketball were invited, all of them without previous experience with HMD's. Group 4 was formed by people with communication and social sciences background. They had no familiarity with Paralympic sports and no/few previous experiences with HMDs.

The devices used were the headset Samsung Gear VR (2016) plus a Samsung Galaxy S7 (with the Android 6.0 operating system) and headphones. In each group, participants were explained how to wear the devices to watch the prototype. They were allowed to choose if they wanted to experience the video standing or sitting. After all participants saw the video, the moderator initiated the discussion guided by three main open-ended questions about the experience of watching the 360-degree video with the headset; the content/narrative; and the framing of the Paralympic athletes in the video.

4.1 Watching the 360-Degree Video

All groups highlighted the excitement with the possibility of exploring the 360° of the scenes. However, at least two participants in each group said this enthusiasm caused distraction from the voice-over that guides the video. Some of the users also reported Fear of Missing Out (FOMO). Participant 12 said: "I tried to look for as many things as possible, I was really looking for what was happening in the whole scene".

Participants in all groups reported perceptions such as "I felt I was there" (Participant 1); "It put ourselves really inside the video" (Participant 14) or "You feel as if you were part of the group there" (Participant 22). The use of the term "immersion" or the variance "being immersed" came out much more often in group 2 (seven times), formed by students with technology background, than in the other ones (one time in each).

4.2 The Content/The Narrative

In all groups, the scene where the camera was placed in the wheelchair provoked controversy, once it was the only part of the video where the camera was in movement. In group 4, participants 20, 21, and 23 reported discomfort while participant 22 felt excited with the sensation as if he was playing. Group 2 led a more technical debate. Some participants reported feeling a dissonance, as the actions carried out didn't get the expected response by the environment, a break of Plausibility. Participant 11 said: "It was confusing. You turned your head to one side the athlete in the wheelchair did not turn".

Participants in all groups stressed the importance of the first scenes to figure out that is possible to explore the 360°. The scene where the character talked directly to the camera was considered the best example of what helps the user follow the narrative. Users said typical sounds of the sport such as the shock of the wheelchairs should have been more explored. Participant 4 explained she had preferred a lesser use of controlled sounds, as the voice over, and the broader use of environmental sounds.

4.3   The Framing

Participant 20 said the 360-degree video approaches her to the players without feeling compassion, as she managed to see them playing with much energy. Participant 12 (athlete) said: "When I watch television, I do not feel the intensity. Here one really feels the environment, the communion that exists. It is a much closer experience of reality, of being there". As the players were very close to the viewer, the disabilities were clearly visible. Participant 8 explained he paid attention to the impairments only in the beginning. As soon as the athletes started playing hard in training, he stopped being attentive to the disability. Participant 13, who has been playing wheelchair basketball for 28 years, stated: "It (the 360 video) can contribute to push away those clichés that the media outlets traditionally use, in my opinion in a wrong way. We are athletes and, as in the non-adapted sports, there are better and worse players, not all are great stories of overcoming. I hope this technology can potentiate this, but it always depends on the framing. Technology is just technology".

5   Discussion

According to the feedback provided in the user study, the 360 video-prototype, when experienced with a headset and headphones, provides an experience that contributes to framing Paralympic athletes as players that face a hard training routine as the non-disabled ones. The study also suggests that there is no need to hide the impairment, once the disabilities are clearly seen in the video and it didn't provoke feelings such as pity.

This exploratory research has chosen the wheelchair basketball as an example of a Paralympic sport. There are dozens of different ones that include individuals with other impairments such as visual and motor disabilities and cerebral palsy. Future work should create and test 360-video experiences related to other sports, especially the ones with more severely disabled athletes. Paralympic sports played by visually impaired could be subjects of experiences conceived mainly by sounds that also are worth testing.

Our study indicates some narrative strategies for 360-degree video such as the use of introductory scenes not only for presenting the characters but also to introduce the possibility of exploring the 360°; the character as a guide for the audience talking directly to the camera; and the use of the environmental sounds to transmit intensity. However, the excitement with the 360° of the scenes is still a remarkable distraction to the story being told, and it is a narrative challenge not only for Paralympic sport's storytelling, especially when the medium is completely new for users. It is necessary to extend the studies about the elements that direct the participant's attention to the narrative and enhance the feeling of "being there" when designing a journalistic experience to VR and particularly to its first level, the 360-degree video.

References

1. International Paralympic Committee: Annual Report 2016 (2016)
2. Beacom, A., French, L., Kendall, S.: Reframing impairment? Continuity and change in media representations of disability through the paralympic games. Int. J. Sport Commun. **9**, 42–62 (2016)
3. Maika, M., Danylchuk, K.: Representing Paralympians: the 'Other' athletes in Canadian print media coverage of London 2012. Int. J. Hist. Sport **33**, 401–417 (2016)
4. Brittain, I.: Communicating and managing the message: media and media representation of disability and Paralympic sport. In: Darcy, S., Frawley, S., Adair, D. (eds.) Managing the Paralympics, pp. 241–262. Palgrave Macmillan, London (2017)
5. Berger, R.J.: Pushing forward: disability, basketball, and me. Qual. Inq. **10**, 794–810 (2004)
6. Marques, J.C.: Nem Herói, Nem Coitadinho: A Cobertura Dos Jogos Paralímpicos 2016 Nas Páginas Dos Jornais Lance! e Folha de S. Paulo (2017)
7. Marques, R.F.R., Gutierrez, G.L., de Almeida, M.A.B., Nunomura, M., Menezes, R.P.: Media approach to Paralympic sports: the view of Brazilian athletes. Movimento **20**, 989–1012 (2014)
8. de la Peña, N., et al.: Immersive journalism: immersive virtual reality for the first-person experience of news. Presence Teleoperators Virtual Environ. **19**, 291–301 (2010)
9. Slater, M.: Place illusion and plausibility can lead to realistic behaviour in immersive virtual environments. Philos. Trans. R. Soc. B Biol. Sci. **364**, 3549–3557 (2009)
10. Aronson-Rath, R., Owen, T., Milward, J., Pitt, F.: Virtual reality journalism. https://towcenter.gitbooks.io/virtual-reality-journalism/content/
11. Emblematic group: the language of presence: a virtual reality glossary for storytellers, producers, and viewers (2016). https://medium.com/journalism360/the-language-of-presence-a-virtual-reality-glossary-for-storytellers-producers-and-viewers-e6d0413b4ce9
12. Tricart, C.: Virtual Reality Filmmaking: Techniques and Best Practices for VR Filmmakers. Taylor & Francis, Didcot (2017)
13. Newton, K., Soukup, K.: The storyteller's guide to the virtual reality audience (2016). https://medium.com/stanford-d-school/the-storyteller-s-guide-to-the-virtual-reality-audience-19e92da57497
14. Passmore, P.J., Glancy, M., Philpot, A., Roscoe, A., Wood, A., Fields, B.: Effects of viewing condition on user experience of panoramic video (2016)
15. Vosmeer, M., Schouten, B.: Project Orpheus a research study into 360 cinematic VR. In: Proceedings of the 2017 ACM International Conference on Interactive Experiences for TV and Online Video, pp. 85–90. ACM (2017)
16. Jaunt: the cinematic VR field guide (2017). https://www.jauntvr.com/cdn/uploads/jaunt-vr-field-guide.pdf

"I Didn't Know, You Could Do That" - Affordance Signifiers for Touch Gestures on Mobile Devices

Emilie Lind Damkjær, Liv Arleth, and Hendrik Knoche[✉] [iD]

Aalborg University, Rendsburggade 14, 9000 Aalborg, Denmark
{edamkj14,larlet14}@student.aau.dk, hk@create.aau.dk

Abstract. As smartphones have become widely available at low prices, interface designers need to improve accessibility of mobile applications for e.g. illiterate users. We evaluated how effectively and efficiently different signifiers communicated the affordances of dragging and double tapping touch gestures in a text editor environment. We found that spatially represented signifiers for dragging (drag handles and drop shadow) communicated the affordance better than temporal signifiers for double tapping. The latter appeared only for a limited amount of time in the user interface and were less effective and efficient than even a control condition that provided no additional information.

Keywords: Touch interactions · Gesture signifiers · Affordance

1 Introduction

Smartphones with limited touch screen space for user interface controls have become widely adopted by both textually literate and illiterate users. Overloading controls with several affordances (possible actions) allows for leaner and more compact interfaces as several actions can be accessed within the same space through different gestures or sequence of microinteractions. The paper investigates ways to signify the afforded touch gestures of dragging and double tapping through signifiers that have either a lasting spatial representation or only appear for a limited amount of time in the user interface (UI). The gained understanding is relevant for both regular and interfaces for people with special needs.

2 Background

Applications on mobile devices need to be designed for limited screen space. Overloading interface elements and controls with several affordances (possible actions) allows for making more interactions available. Designers employ signifiers to help users at discovering or identifying these affordances. We use Norman's definitions of affordances and signifiers [6] throughout this paper. While

© ICST Institute for Computer Sciences, Social Informatics and Telecommunications Engineering 2019
Published by Springer Nature Switzerland AG 2019. All Rights Reserved
A. L. Brooks et al. (Eds.): ArtsIT 2018/DLI 2018, LNICST 265, pp. 206–212, 2019.
https://doi.org/10.1007/978-3-030-06134-0_23

single-, double-click, right-click, and drag are common in the UIs of desktop operating systems such overloading is less common in the UIs of mobile apps. For example, on a touch screen a button usually gets triggered by a single tap but could narrate its associated function (feedforward) on a long-press [3]. While the question of whether and how to signify affordances of touch gestures on controls is relevant to all touch screen surfaces, we deem the importance of overloading controls particularly valuable in assistive interfaces for users with special needs. We turn our attention to illiterate users and focus on how to use overloading to make text editors on mobile phones accessible to them. While illiterate people can master interactions on smart phones through e.g. rote learning [4] composing text messages represents a desirable skill and challenge [1]. Audio feedback can be used to help illiterate users understand what word(s) a text object in the UI represents [1]. By editor we denote an environment in which users can enter and manipulate some form of data, represented e.g. as text or images.

In a mobile banking application for illiterate users [5] money was represented by pictures of actual bills rather than numbers. Users could drag the desired number of bills into an editor that showed the amount of bills picked so far. Nothing signified the affordance of dragging the bills. Users had to discover this affordance through other means such as introductions or feedback. The editor mainly used swiping and dragging as gestures.

The mobile texting editor for illiterate users by Friscira et al. allowed for listening to complete messages or individual words by tapping on them and provided different options for entering words that did not require typing [1]. The interface overloaded these controls (the word buttons) with two affordances - single and double tap. Displaying words inside a white box on a blue message bubble background, making them visually resemble flat design buttons signified the single tap affordance. The affordance of double tapping words in older messages to add them to the editor had no signifier.

3   Study on Affordance Signifiers

We set up an experiment to investigate how to best signify touch gesture affordances to the user without using text or introductory instructions.

Inspired by Friscira et al.'s text editor [1], we created an SMS (short message service) editor prototype (see Fig. 1) containing a bank of words (rectangles with barcodes in the light blue area) and a grey editor area in which the words were supposed to be assembled to form a message. Single-tapping word elements played out the word as audio. We created a task with a limited set of words to choose which the user had to add to the editor to create the message. Each of the light grey boxes contained one word and the barcode labels on each meant to simulate that participants could not read the words but had to rely on the audio to form the correct message. The editor had no cursor or means for rearranging the words. All words had to be added in the right order. We implemented six different versions of this interface to test a total of four signifiers and two affordances. Two control versions without explicit signifiers served as a baseline.

They were visually identical to Figs. 1A and B, afforded populating the word editor by means of double tapping on or dragging words from the word bank.

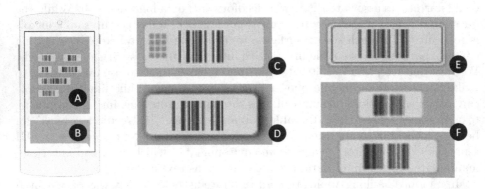

Fig. 1. The study prototype (left) with word bank (A) and editor (B), and magnified the signifiers for dragging (middle) - drag handle (C), and drop shadow (D), and for double tap - border (E) and pulse animation (F).

One signifier for dragging used a common design pattern known as a drag-handle - a cluster of dots - on the word element intended to invoke a textured, "grabbable" surface (see Fig. 1C). The second signifier employed a drop shadow on the word elements (see Fig. 1D) to make them appear to be floating above the blue background.

One signifier for double tapping employed feedback using two borders around the words. On the first tap, the innermost border briefly turned green (see Fig. 1E). On the second tap the outer border became green, too. The second signifier had the words pulsate from small (see Fig. 1F top) to large (bottom) twice, immediately after opening the page mimicking the word buttons being pressed down twice.

3.1   Procedure

The study evaluated the effectiveness and efficiency of the four signifiers - two for each of dragging and double tapping through a balanced between-subjects usability test that measured the participants' completion rates in composing a message. We relied on a proxy population of students, who, however, could not read the symbols, which encoded the words in the editor. While this might raise concerns for the validity of the study, the object of the study was not related to the textual content as such but the understanding of the signifiers of the word objects. Signifiers of affordances are rarely communicated through text in UIs. This approach ensured that the single tap - the primary gesture on mobile devices - provided the audio feedback and the participants had to find other gestures to populate the editor with word objects. We drew on interaction analysis to further the design of UIs to benefit textually illiterate users. In a similar vein, see e.g.

Huenerfauth's approach drawing on task analysis and structured design [2]. The discussion section returns to this topic.

Thirty-six students participated in the test as volunteers, none of whom followed a design oriented education. The test followed a mixed design in which each participant experienced two affordance signifier versions of a smartphone text editor prototype - one for each afforded gesture (dragging and double tapping). The order of gestures was counterbalanced between participants. This resulted in a total of 72 trials from 12 trials for each of the six versions.

After initial explanations, the participant had to compose the phrase "I am very happy" in each version of the prototype. After succeeding or giving up each task, they reported their thought process and reflections about their actions while solving the task. A video camera captured a close-up of the phone screen for subsequent video analysis. We scored task completion for each trial. A subsequent video interaction analysis counted the number of gestures and types (e.g. tap, drag, triple-tap etc.) the participants tried before finding the correct gesture, for cases in which they were successful.

3.2   Results

First, we verified with a Fisher's Exact test that the attempt number (first/ second try) did not affect the participants' success rates (p(two-tailed) = 0.4735). In terms of success rates, participants were better at discovering dragging (see Fig. 2) than double tapping (see Fig. 3). Each figure shows the different signifier conditions. The drag handle was the most effective at signifying its affordance. The least effective signifier was the pulse animation for double tapping. Notably, both double tap signifiers resulted in lower success rates than their no signifier control version.

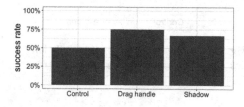
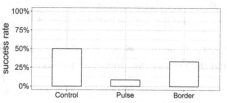

Fig. 2. Success rates for dragging   **Fig. 3.** Success rates for double tapping

Four two-tailed Fisher's Exact tests showed that, compared to their corresponding control, none of the signifiers - *drag handle* ($p = 0.40$), *shadow* ($p = 0.68$), *border* ($p = 0.68$), and *pulse animation* ($p = 0.07$) made the participant perform significantly different. However, one-tailed Fisher's Exact tests of the double tap signifiers showed that the lower success rates of the *pulse animation* was significantly worse (p(one-tailed) = 0.034) than its control version. The pulse animation made finding the right gesture more difficult than when not receiving extra information other than the shape of the word objects.

The video interaction analysis counted the number of gestures the participants tried before finding the correct gesture. We further classified these gestures by type (e.g. tap, drag, and triple-tap). Figures 4 and 5 depict the number of gestures before finding the correct one by signifier for those participants who managed to finish the task successfully. The statistical analysis on the signifiers' efficiency omitted the *pulse* animation, as only one participant found this affordance. Two-tailed T-tests comparing the number of gestures and the number of different types of gestures tried before identifying the correct one against the control conditions found no significant differences ($p > 0.05$). However, the one-tailed T-test comparing *border* to its control was close to significance ($t(4) = 2.1$, $p = 0.051$). On average it took participants twice as many gestures with the border signifier to successfully complete the task than the participants in the control condition. In summary, none of the drag signifiers were more or less efficient than its control in helping the participants to find the correct afforded gesture. But the *border* signifier was less efficient at signalling the double tap affordance than the plain word button objects.

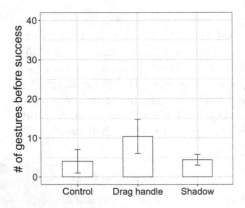

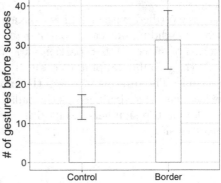

Fig. 4. Dragging signifier efficiencies with 0.95 confidence interval error bars

Fig. 5. Double tapping signifier efficiencies with 0.95 confidence interval error bars

4 Discussion

The signifier with the highest success rate was the drag handle, however, it was not significantly better than the control and required additional space in the UI for each word object more than the similarly performing drop shadow version. A few participants misunderstood our drag handle as a symbol for a number pad or a menu. The pulse animation signifier for double tapping made users find the affordance less often. The most likely interpretation seems that the participants perceived this signifier as a gimmick or artefact of rendering the page and not associated with the individual controls. The green *border* signifier also seemed to lead to confusion as participants required more interactions before successfully completing the task. One possible explanation for the poor signifying performance of *border* and *pulse* animation could be the low temporal availability of the cues. For *border* it was only briefly available after the first tap and could have been partially occluded by the interacting finger.

We used textually literate students, none of whom were experts in user experience design or touch interactions, but who had ample experience with smartphones and other UIs. However, we did not control for their familiarity with double tap or drag gestures on mobile touch device screens. Arguably, dragging gestures are more common in current mobile UIs (Android and iOS) than double tapping but the success rates of their respective control conditions were identical. Technical literacy in terms of exposure to touch gestures might be important as a variable to control for in future studies.

Out of the 36 test participants 24 tried identifying the words based on their barcode length. Illiterate people in non-logographic languages might be to some degree gauge the lengths of the word objects from the duration of a spoken a word to help in such task. While this does not call into question the internal validity of the results on the signifiers it might be helpful for the design of future studies in this area, especially when involving proxy populations.

5   Conclusion

We evaluated signifiers for dragging and double tapping affordances for movable word objects in a touch text editor. The temporally available signifiers for double tapping were either less effective (pulse animation on initial page render) or less efficient (green border after first tap) than a control condition that provided participants with less information. Such signifiers with limited temporal availability (e.g. on page opening) may lead to confusion. Drag handles yielded slightly better performance but required substantial space in the UI.

References

1. Friscira, E., Knoche, H., Huang, J.: Getting in touch with text: designing a mobile phone application for illiterate users to harness SMS. In: Proceedings of the 2nd ACM Symposium on Computing for Development, p. 5. ACM (2012)
2. Huenerfauth, M.: Developing design recommendations for computer interfaces accessible to illiterate users. Master's thesis, University College Dublin (2002)
3. Knoche, H., Rao, P.S., Jamadagni, H.S., Huang, J.: Actions and advice in coli: a mobile social network to support agricultural peer learning. In: Proceedings of the 17th International Conference on Human-Computer Interaction with Mobile Devices and Services Adjunct, pp. 1191–1198. ACM (2015)
4. Knoche, H., Huang, J.: Text is not the enemy - how illiterates use their mobile phones. In: NUIs for New Worlds: New Interaction Forms and Interfaces for Mobile Applications in Developing Countries - CHI 2012 Workshop, Austin (2012)

5. Mesfin, W., Grønli, T.M., Ghinea, G., Younas, M.: A mobile money solution for illiterate users. In: 2015 IEEE International Conference on Mobile Services (MS), pp. 328–335. IEEE (2015)
6. Norman, D.: The Design of Everyday Things: Revised and Expanded Edition. Constellation (2013)

A Social App that Combines Dating and Museum Visiting Experiences

Atakan Akçalı[✉], Ido A. Iurgel, and Tonguç Sezen

Rhine-Waal University of Applied Sciences,
Friedrich-Heinrich-Allee 25, 47475 Kamp-Lintfort, Germany
atakan.akcali@hsrw.org, {ido.iurgel,
tongucibrahim.sezen}@hochschule-rhein-waal.de

Abstract. The use of mobile apps has become a significant part of people's daily life. Mobile apps are used not only to share or have information on social platforms but also to socialise and meet basic human needs. Mobile apps have an incontrovertible potential to provide not only interpersonal communication among users but also help for cultural institutions to communicate and create an attraction for their target audiences. This paper presents the design process of a social mobile app, Acht, which aims to gamify a museum experience with a dating feature.

Keywords: Museum · Dating · Networking · Randomness · Gamification
Design thinking

1 Introduction

The project, Acht, aims to provide a social experience centred around dating by using museum atmosphere as a catalyst for emotional and creative exchange between users. Digital technologies, which shape our social life have changed 'what it is told' as well as 'how it is told' [1]. Dating, which traditionally requires mutual exchange and courtship has become a digitally augmented, fast paced activity. Online dating apps and websites have become a popular way to meet potential partners for around 70% of same-sex couples and around 20% of opposite-sex couples in recent years [2]. This project aims to combine dating with an intellectual and cultural activity—museum visiting. Museums, by definition, are culturally rich and creative places. However, like other cultural institutions they are having difficulties to draw the attention of new and younger audiences [3]. Mobile apps developed for cultural institutions have a high potential in creating attraction for these audiences. By adding a new layer of interactivity, they provide a new museum experience. The Acht project aims both to enhance the quality of dating initiated through mobile apps and to widen the visitor profile of museums. Acht suggests helping potential partners to meet and get acquainted with one-another by setting playful dates in museums and other cultural places.

© ICST Institute for Computer Sciences, Social Informatics and Telecommunications Engineering 2019
Published by Springer Nature Switzerland AG 2019. All Rights Reserved
A. L. Brooks et al. (Eds.): ArtsIT 2018/DLI 2018, LNICST 265, pp. 213–218, 2019.

2   State of the Art

There are many location-based dating apps such as Tinder, Grindr, Happn, and Bumble which are used by different target audiences (i.e. same-sex couples or opposite-sex couples) for entering different types of romantic encounters (i.e. long-term relationship or one-night stands) [4–7]. Despite their popularity, the design of most of these apps tends to dehumanise the romantic experience and underestimates the social expectancies of everyday human interactions [8]. Most location-based dating apps are designed for fast paced matching. The actual physical encounter and the dating process itself are usually left out of the apps' foci. In many cases they do not provide any option to surpass the cyber platform. In this regard Acht aims to provide a dating experience beyond matching.

Mobile apps providing additional information and experiences for visitors have gained immense importance for museums in recent years. While some museums choose to develop their own apps [9, 10], some commercial apps such as Smartify choose to combine different museums under larger digital services and to create wider knowledge pools in order to deepen and personalise the experiences of visitors [11, 12]. The main design strategy of these apps is giving extra information on museums and exhibitions and/or providing a gamified museum experience. However, most of these apps are not designed to create a social community or gather people in the museums. Acht aims to get people meet, share and experience in the museums.

3   Concept and Prototype

The core concept of Acht is to provide a playful date motivation in museums or similar cultural institutions to its users. The interviews conducted with dating app users during concept development of the project show that most of them are not solicitous enough to make the first move to meet in real life and indeterminate meetings put an extra stress on people. In this regard the project suggests a social mobile app that helps people meet, date and get acquainted to one-another in museums.

Target audience of Acht consists of people aged between 18 and 34. This was chosen according to the user statistics of dating, museum, and gallery apps [13, 14]. In addition, interviews with the museum representative of one German museum were conducted and it was pointed out that museums were seeking to increase the number of young and early adult visitors [18]. These findings are in line with US based studies which show drastic declines in art museum or gallery visits in the age group between 18 and 54 [17].

Acht has three phases: Matching through swiping, suggestions for meeting places, and a gamified feature in museums. Matching through swiping concept is a conventional design commonly used by contemporary mobile dating and other apps [15]. In this method, if both users swipe to the right of each other, they match and will be able to start a conversation. If a user swipes to the left, which means that user does not like the person on the screen, there will be no match. Potential matches appear on the screen according to the user's geographical location and their range preferences [16]. After this phase matches should decide at which museum the meeting will take place by choosing it on the map. With the intention of creating a positive experience for both visitors and museums, museums on sensitive topics such as war and crime are excluded on the list of suggested meeting places. When two matches meet at the predetermined museum, they receive a welcome message which informs the users on how to start the gamification phase. During this phase, users receive questions to trigger communication and interaction among themselves. These questions create the spontaneousness of a date in a well-constructed pattern (see Fig. 1). "If this building were a part of your house which room would it be?", "What would you drink by looking at this art piece?", "Choose 3 parts of your body to express this art piece. You have to show". While users enjoy art pieces, they also have the chance to get to know each other with the help of digital question cards that are not directly related to the art pieces but the users' life. These questions are designed to encourage users' creativity, rather than dwelling on their intellectual background and in this way quality of experience is not related to a user's previous knowledge.

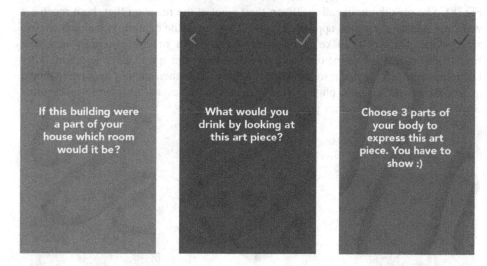

Fig. 1. Digital question cards

To encourage users to move freely and physically, randomness was chosen as the main concept for the digital question cards. Users have flexibility in the museum since these questions are not associated with a specific artwork. Questions are activated when two users shake their phones at the same time in front of the same artwork. This shaking gesture not only serves to make users physically active, but to give the feeling of chance by acting as a dice.

4 Application Scenario

Christina, 27 is a university student who wants to meet new people. She downloads the Acht app to her phone. She opens the app (see Fig. 2) and logs in with Facebook. Facebook takes her profile photo and academic information automatically from her account. She sees a screen where she can change her settings and edit her info. She taps to the "Edit info" button to add more photos and complete her "About me" section. She taps the plus icon to add additional photos (see Figs. 3 and 4). The app asks for her permission to access her photos. She gives permission to the app and then Christina chooses her photos from her phone and she taps the "Done" button to complete her profile. Then, she taps the settings button to change the parameters about age, distance and visibility on Acht. She completes her settings and taps the "Done" button and sees the profile screen again. She taps the Acht icon and begins swiping to find potential matches (see Fig. 5). She can see details about another user when she taps on their cover photo. She swipes to the left if she does not like the person and to the right for the opposite. After viewing a few choices, she matches with Diego. She sees a screen that says she has a match and she is able to send a message to her match or she can continue to swipe. She taps to the "Message to Diego" button (see Figs. 6 and 7). She starts a conversation and Diego suggests to meet at a museum by using the map screen (see Fig. 8). She sees the notification. When they meet at the museum they both receive a welcome message from the app (see Fig. 9). They go to the exhibition hall and choose an artwork. They both shake their phones to reveal a random question card (see Fig. 10). Christina is the first one randomly chosen by the app to ask a question. After Diego answers and they start to break the ice, they shake their phones again revealing a question card on Diego's phone. This process continues as the couple takes turns conversing about different art pieces.

Fig. 2. Opening screen.   **Fig. 3.** Edit info and settings.   **Fig. 4.** Adding photos and info

Fig. 5. Swiping screen.

Fig. 6. Match screen.

Fig. 7. Chat screen.

Fig. 8. Map screen.

Fig. 9. Welcome screen.

Fig. 10. Shaking screen.

5 Conclusion and Future Work

Acht was tested with a limited number of people by using a paper prototype and a prototype app—InVision app. The feedback of these formative tests has had a useful influence on the design process such as; users' reactions to question cards, way of socialising and interacting with artworks. And results were discussed with the museum representatives. The matching concept of this project could be built upon additional selection criteria. For the further steps of this project, interviewees who are in a relationship suggested having an option to use this app with friends, instead of only dating purposes. Since this is an ongoing project to be able to increase the social experience, some other concepts will be included similar to the "shaking" feature which brings people and motivates to act together.

The idea which this project stands on is to create a social experience and a new way of museum visit. Moreover, this idea opens a creative way to use the potential of the museums. Taking this into consideration, this concept is not only for digital platforms and mobile apps, but also provides a unique idea for museums. Although this project seems to focus on dating, museum and experiencing art is the incontrovertible constituent of the project.

Acknowledgement. This project is supported by RheijnLand.Xperiences project and Digital Media Master programme at Rhine-Waal University of Applied Sciences.

References

1. McLuhan, M.: Understanding Media: The Extensions of Man. Routledge, London (2010)
2. Rosenfeld, M.J., Thomas, R.J.: Searching for a mate: the rise of the internet as a social intermediary. Am. Sociol. Rev. **77**(4), 523–547 (2012)
3. The Guardian. https://www.theguardian.com/artanddesign/jonathanjonesblog/2017/feb/02/drop-uk-museum-attendance. Accessed 17 June 2018
4. Grindr. https://www.grindr.com. Accessed 10 May 2018
5. Tinder. https://tinder.com. Accessed 7 Apr 2018
6. Happn. https://www.happn.com/en/. Accessed 10 May 2018
7. Bumble. https://bumble.com/. Accessed 10 May 2018
8. Intel Newsroom. https://newsroom.intel.com/news-releases/future-of-technology-may-be-determined-by-millennial-malaise-female-fans-and-affluent-data-altruists/. Accessed 27 June 2018
9. Staedel Museum. http://www.staedelmuseum.de/de/angebote/staedel-app. Accessed 20 June 2018
10. Rijk Museum. https://www.rijksmuseum.nl/en/guided-tours/multimediatour. Accessed 20 June 2018
11. Economou, M., Meintani, E.: Promising beginning? Evaluating museum mobile phone apps (2011)
12. Smartify. https://smartify.org/. Accessed 17 June 2018
13. Smith, A.W., Duggan, M.: Online Dating & Relationship. Pew Research Center, Washington, DC (2013)
14. Medium. https://medium.com/@_smartify/the-year-in-a-scan-3ef7ff3ee07. Accessed 19 Jan 2018
15. Fast Company. https://www.fastcompany.com/3033319/six-new-apps-that-use-tinders-swipe-theory. Accessed 04 July 2018
16. Junglas, I.A., Watson, R.T.: Location-based services. Commun. ACM **51**(3), 65–69 (2008)
17. Art Museum Attendance. Humanities Indicators. www.humanitiesindicators.org/content/indicatordoc.aspx?i=102#fig417. Accessed 10 Sept 2018
18. Schulze, N.: Head of Arts Education, Museum Scholss Moyland, 11 July 2017. Personal Interview

Effects of Vibrotactile Feedback in Commercial Virtual Reality Systems

Peter Weilgaard Brasen, Mathias Christoffersen, and Martin Kraus[⊠]

Aalborg University, Fredrik Bajers Vej 5, 9000 Aalborg, Denmark
{pbrase14,matchr14}@student.aau.dk, martin@create.aau.dk

Abstract. This study investigates the effects of vibrotactile feedback by motion controllers of a commercial virtual reality (VR) system on immersion, actual and perceived user performance, and perceived difficulty of specific tasks in VR.

To this end, we developed two different tasks in VR with different types of interactions: entering numbers by rotating a number dial and stirring a pot. In a within-subject experiment, 14 participants completed the two tasks with and without vibrotactile feedback.

The results showed that for both tasks self-reported immersion was significantly improved by vibrotactile feedback, while perceived difficulty was significantly reduced for one task, and perceived performance was significantly increased for the other task. These results show that even the limited vibrotactile feedback by motion controllers of commercial VR systems is capable of significantly changing VR experiences.

Keywords: Virtual Reality · Vibrotactile feedback

1 Introduction

Virtual Reality (VR) is a popular platform for emulating reality and creating immersion [5,6]. One of the immersion-enhancing technologies is haptic feedback, which has been used for VR and other platforms for many years [7].

However, the use of vibrotactile feedback in motion controllers of commercial VR systems for haptic rendering has received relatively little attention by the research community. On the other hand, commercial VR games (e.g., Rec Room [1]) provide vibrotactile feedback in many situations, for example, when pulling the (virtual) string of a bow. In this case, the frequency of the vibrotactile feedback is usually scaled with the velocity of the motion controller, which creates an effect that is very similar to haptic rendering.

In this work, we explore the potential of vibrotactile feedback in commercial motion controllers for haptic rendering by adjusting the frequency and amplitude of vibrotactile feedback to the position and velocity of motion controllers. To determine the benefits of this kind of haptic rendering, we implemented a dialing and a stirring task in VR and compared self-reported immersion, actual

© ICST Institute for Computer Sciences, Social Informatics and Telecommunications Engineering 2019
Published by Springer Nature Switzerland AG 2019. All Rights Reserved
A. L. Brooks et al. (Eds.): ArtsIT 2018/DLI 2018, LNICST 265, pp. 219–224, 2019.
https://doi.org/10.1007/978-3-030-06134-0_25

and perceived performance, and perceived difficulty for each task with and without vibrotactile feedback. (Two additional tasks received relatively low presence scores for both conditions—presumably because they both involved virtually touching a virtual wall. Therefore, we are not discussing these two additional tasks.) The dialing and stirring tasks both showed significantly improved immersion with vibrotactile feedback. Furthermore, the stirring task showed significantly improved perceived performance and the dialing task showed significantly reduced perceived difficulty with vibrotactile feedback.

2   Previous Work

A common goal for the use of haptic devices in VR systems is to increase immersion. Similarly to many other haptic devices, the PHANToM Haptic Interface [4] made it possible for users to interact and feel a variety of different virtual objects. To this end, users inserted the tip of an index finger into a thimble. The position of this thimble was measured and a force was applied to it based on collisions with virtual objects. This allowed users to feel virtual surfaces, i.e., it made haptic rendering of virtual surfaces possible. The PHANToM Haptic Interface demonstrated that a low-cost system can provide convincing haptic feedback for interactions with virtual objects, and it showed that users learn to interpret this haptic feedback with relative ease.

More recently, vibrotactile feedback in positionally tracked controllers was used to create the experience of haptic textures. Examples include a vibrating slider by Strohmeier and Hornbæk [8] and the CLAW controller by Choi et al. [2].

Wu et al. [9] used vibrotactile feedback in positionally tracked data gloves to create haptic feedback for a virtual keyboard in VR. A user experiment showed that the virtual keyboard with vibrotactile feedback was considered more realistic by test participants and allowed for faster typing than a virtual keyboard without vibrotactile feedback.

The work by Wu et al. showed that vibrotactile feedback in data gloves has the potential to increase not only immersion of users but also their performance in a specific task. This motivated our study, which investigated whether vibrotactile feedback in commercial motion controllers has a similar potential to increase immersion and task performance.

3   Experiment

Our experiment tried to determine the effect of vibrotactile feedback on immersion, task performance as measured by completion time and amount of errors, as well as perceived performance and difficulty for specific tasks in a VR environment using commercial off-the-shelf components.

Fig. 1. Dialing task.

Fig. 2. Stirring task.

3.1 Materials

For the experiment, we developed a VR application with the Unity game engine for the HTC Vive VR system. The VR application includes a dialing task and a stirring task to provide different forms of vibrotactile feedback. Each participant performed each of the tasks (in a fixed order) with and without vibrotactile feedback (in randomized order), thus, each of the tasks could be considered a separate experiment.

The first task was a dialing task (Fig. 1). Participants were shown a number and were asked to turn a numerated dial to this number by virtually touching the dial with their finger. They had to confirm each number by pressing a button. Each time the dial passed a number, the participant received vibrotactile feedback. After the participant had entered all four numbers, the first task was completed.

The second task required the participants to stir a virtual pot (Fig. 2). The participants were prompted to pick up a large spoon and stir the pot placed right in front of them. When a participant stirred the pot, vibrotactile feedback was provided dependent on the velocity of the spoon. Once the required amount of rotations was met, the task was completed.

3.2 Setup

Apart from the HTC Vive VR system, the experimental setup included a facilitator and an observer. The role of the facilitator was to introduce the participants to the test and inform them about their tasks. The observer took notes during the tests both from how the participant acted and what could be seen on the computer screen, which mirrored what the participants saw in the HTC Vive head-mounted display.

3.3 Procedure

The experiment used a within-subject design, which consisted of an introductory questionnaire to assess previous VR experience and demographics, the tasks with and without vibrotactile feedback, questionnaires about presence and a comparison between the versions with and without vibrotactile feedback, as well as an interview.

The presence questionnaire used a 7-point Likert scale to assess the level of presence experienced by the participant while performing each task. The questionnaire was inspired by a similar questionnaire by Witmer and Singer [3]. The participants answered the presence questionnaire after each version of each task. After participants had completed both versions of a task (with and without vibrotactile feedback), they answered a questionnaire to compare the two versions. After all tasks were completed, an interview was conducted to obtain information regarding the participants' experience of immersion, performance, and VR sickness.

4   Results

The demographic of the test consisted of 14 participants (10 male and 4 female) with ages varying from 21 to 29 years.

Using the Wilcoxon signed rank test with significance level of $\alpha = 0.05$, the presence questionnaire's total scores showed no significant difference between the versions of the tasks with and without vibrotactile feedback. ($p = 0.55$ for the dialing task and $p = 0.86$ for the stirring task.)

A Wilcoxon signed rank test was also performed on the results of the questions directly comparing the versions of each task with and without vibrotactile feedback. The questions were:

1. Which task did you perform better in?
2. Which task did you find more difficult?
3. Which task did you find more immersive?
4. Which task felt more real?

Participants answered by naming either the version without vibrotactile feedback, which was coded as -1, the version with vibrotactile feedback, which was coded as $+1$, or they stated that they saw no difference, which was coded as 0. p values were determined by Wilcoxon signed rank tests comparing the answers to the null hypothesis of no difference. Results for the means and p values are summarized in Table 1.

Participants found the dialing task more difficult without vibrotactile feedback. On the other hand, vibrotactile feedback made the task feel more immersive and real to the participants.

For the stirring task, participants felt that their performance increased with vibrotactile feedback. The task also felt more immersive and real with vibrotactile feedback.

To compare the required time for each task, a Student's t-test was performed, which showed that participants required significantly more time for the dialing with vibrotactile feedback.

Table 1. Mean values (positive for vibrotactile feedback) and p values of Wilcoxon signed rank tests for comparison questions. Significant p values are set in **bold**

Question	Dialing	Stirring
1. Better performance?	$M = 0.21; p = 0.39$	$M = 0.5; p = \mathbf{0.01}$
2. More difficult?	$M = -0.43; p = \mathbf{0.02}$	$M = -0.21; p = 0.15$
3. More immersive?	$M = 0.79; p = \mathbf{0.003}$	$M = 0.79; p = \mathbf{0.001}$
4. More real?	$M = 0.71; p = \mathbf{0.004}$	$M = 0.71; p = \mathbf{0.002}$

The number of errors in the dialing task were analysed with a Wilcoxon signed rank test but showed no significant differences.

The intensity of the vibrotactile feedback was experienced differently by participants. The vibrotactile feedback in the stirring task was found to be either too strong or too weak by 8 participants. 3 participants found the feedback in the dialing task to be too weak.

In the questionnaire that was answered before the test, 5 of 14 participants answered that they had experienced VR sickness while using VR. These participants rated their experience of VR sickness appearing from "rarely" to "sometime." After experiencing the test, 1 of 14 participants said that he or she experienced VR sickness.

5 Discussion

The presence questionnaire showed no significant differences between the versions with and without vibrotactile feedback. One reason for this might be that this questionnaire was not specific enough to show any effect of vibrotactile feedback.

On the other hand, the more specific comparison questions showed that the tasks felt more immersive and real with vibrotactile feedback. Thus, we conclude that vibrotactile feedback can in fact increase immersion in virtual reality.

No significant differences were found in performance errors when comparing conditions with and without vibrotactile feedback. It is possible that the dialing task was not sufficiently well designed to utilize vibrotactile feedback for better performance.

The only significant difference in time was found for the dialing task. This difference showed that participants took longer in completing the task with vibrotactile feedback. One possible reason for this result could be that participants took time to explore the vibrotactile feedback and were not aware that their performance was measured.

The data also suggests that despite the participants not feeling an increased performance in the dialing task with vibrotactile feedback, they found it more difficult without vibrotactile feedback. This might suggest that participants felt that without vibrotactile feedback more effort was necessary to reach the same performance.

The answers to the comparison questions for the stirring task suggest that vibrotactile feedback increased perceived performance. According to the participants, it helped them to know that their interaction had an effect, which might have led them to think that they were performing better.

6   Conclusion

This study showed that vibrotactile feedback by commercial motion controllers can result in higher immersion, increased perceived performance, and decreased perceived difficulty. It also suggests that comparison questions might be preferable to general presence questionnaires to identify these effects with statistical significance.

On the other hand, we did not see a significant effect of vibrotactile feedback in two other tasks that we had tested nor an effect on the actual performance in any of the tasks. This indicates that the tasks were not sufficiently well designed to make use of the vibrotactile feedback and/or that the vibrotactile feedback was not sufficiently well designed to a have a significant effect.

References

1. Against Gravity: Rec Room. https://www.againstgrav.com/rec-room/. Accessed 13 Sept 2018
2. Choi, I., Ofek, E., Benko, H., Sinclair, M., Holz, C.: CLAW: a multifunctional handheld haptic controller for grasping, touching, and triggering in virtual reality. In: Proceedings of the 2018 CHI Conference on Human Factors in Computing Systems, CHI 2018, pp. 654:1–654:13. ACM, New York (2018). https://doi.org/10.1145/3173574.3174228
3. Witmer, B.G., Singer, M.J.: Measuring presence in virtual environments: a presence questionnaire. Presence 7(3), 225–240 (1998)
4. Massie, T.H., Salisbury, J.K.: The PHANToM haptic interface: a device for probing virtual objects. In: Proceedings of the ASME Dynamic Systems and Control Division, pp. 295–301 (1994)
5. Sallnäs, E.L., Rassmus-Gröhn, K., Sjöström, C.: Supporting presence in collaborative environments by haptic force feedback. ACM Trans. Comput.-Hum. Interact. 7, 461–476 (2000). https://doi.org/10.1145/365058.365086
6. Slater, M., Linakis, V., Usoh, M., Kooper, R., Street, G.: Immersion, presence, and performance in virtual environments: an experiment with tri-dimensional chess. In: ACM Virtual Reality Software and Technology (VRST), pp. 163–172 (1996)
7. Stone, R.J.: Haptic feedback: a brief history from telepresence to virtual reality. In: Brewster, S., Murray-Smith, R. (eds.) Haptic HCI 2000. LNCS, vol. 2058, pp. 1–16. Springer, Heidelberg (2001). https://doi.org/10.1007/3-540-44589-7_1
8. Strohmeier, P., Hornbæk, K.: Generating haptic textures with a vibrotactile actuator. In: Proceedings of the 2017 CHI Conference on Human Factors in Computing Systems, CHI 2017, pp. 4994–5005. ACM, New York (2017). https://doi.org/10.1145/3025453.3025812
9. Wu, C.M., Hsu, C.W., Lee, T.K., Smith, S.: A virtual reality keyboard with realistic haptic feedback in a fully immersive virtual environment. Virtual Reality 21(1), 19–29 (2017). https://doi.org/10.1007/s10055-016-0296-6

Evolving Virtual Ecology

Gloriya Gostyaeva[✉], Penousal Machado, and Tiago Martins

CISUC - Department of Informatics Engineering, University of Coimbra,
Coimbra, Portugal
g.gostyaeva@gmail.com, {machado, tiagofm}@dei.uc.pt

Abstract. Within the field of artificial life it has been possible to create numerous virtual models that have allowed the study of the behaviour of living organisms and their interactions within artificially created ecosystems. Whilst the methods employed in this field have been mostly explored by various researchers in their projects, they had not been broadly applied to the entertainment and art fields.

This paper focuses on a system (digital toy) which contains artificial life agents. These agents learn to interpret external audio commands and adapt to their environment using evolutionary computation and machine learning.

Keywords: Artificial life · Video games · Evolutionary computation
Machine learning · Sound recognition

1 Introduction

In this paper, we focus on a 2D virtual ecosystem populated with artificial agents. It utilises Evolutionary Computation (EC) and machine learning (ML) to generate behaviour for agents.

This system is capable of learning the audio spectrum values produced by a user through any external musical instrument and associating actions with them. The sounds can affect the evolutionary process of the agents and can cause either extinction or increase of population. The agents move erratically until they are taught by a user. A user can use the microphone to input sounds and the mouse to indicate correct answers for the neural network. The application can be played with and can be treated as a virtual toy or an artistic experience.

The main inspirations for the project were Polyworld by Larry Yaeger [1] in which he explored the life cycles of artificial agents within a simulated environment, and the evolving creatures by Karl Sims [2]. Additionally Conway's Game of Life [3] and the flocking algorithm by Reynolds [4] showed us that a set of simple rules is capable of generating interesting behaviours.

Steve Grand's Creatures [5] and games such as Nintendogs [6] and Black & White [7] are good examples of artificial life (A-life) within entertainment media and they gave us ideas of how our system could possibly be played or interacted with.

In this paper, we pose a problem of implementation of artificial agents using EC and ML that can be affected by external audio input. The resulting system is directed at

A. L. Brooks et al. (Eds.): ArtsIT 2018/DLI 2018, LNICST 265, pp. 225–230, 2019.

the entertainment and art purposes and serves as a playground for the virtual ecosystem with audio input.

The two contributions presented are: (i) a virtual ecosystem populated with agents that learn to understand sounds produced by a user and evolve their interaction with the environment; and (ii) an exploration of how an EC and ML approach can be applied in art and entertainment.

The remainder of this paper is organised as follows: Sect. 2 describes the proposed system; Sect. 3 includes a practical analysis of the system; and finally, Sect. 4 presents conclusions and directions for future work.

2 Preliminaries

The proposed system is a 2D world populated with various agents. There are three types of agents: pick-ups, core and particles (see Fig. 1).

A user can input various audio spectrum values using the microphone and the core will respond in a way determined by its Deep Q-Network (DQN) [8, 9]. The movements are random by default, but it is possible for a user to manually backpropagate the expected action by dragging the mouse in the desired direction.

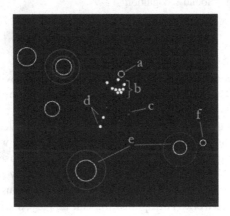

Fig. 1. Screenshot of the system depicting its elements. (a) core; (b) particles; (c) blood visual effect; (d) isolated particles; (e) good and bad pick-ups; (f) pick-up in its growing stage.

Particles are smaller agents clustering around the core. Their interaction with pick-ups is determined by a DQN.

Pick-ups start small but then they grow and start sending audio pings which can be heard by particles and the user if the core is close enough. There are good and bad pick-ups, their sound frequencies differ so that they can be distinguished. When a good pick-up is collected by a particle, this particle produces two similar ones as offspring, however, if it was a bad pick-up, the particle explodes destroying other particles within a certain range.

Because collecting bad objects destroys particles, a low-fitness population reaching for bad pick-ups will soon be exterminated leaving only those particles that ignore or avoid bad pick-ups. When a good pick-up is collected, the particle that collected it will reproduce, creating offspring which copy the weights of their parent's neural network. Sometimes on the reproduction event a mutation of weights can occur which might render a behaviour of an offspring to be different from one of a parent.

In terms of the visual appearance, it was decided to avoid using sharp shapes and instead utilise ellipses because they reflect the biological nature of simulated creatures. The use of circular shapes, in the mind of a user, can relate to the experience of looking through a microscope or observing the night sky. Both cases involve looking at a cosmos, at a micro or macro scale. These experiences are the source of inspiration for the visual appearance. In Fig. 2 the general look of the system is shown.

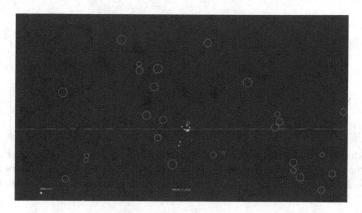

Fig. 2. Screenshot showing the system. The bar at the bottom of the screen controls the audio level input from the microphone.

The following link contains a demonstrational video of the system. It shows a full play through starting with teaching the core and ending with all particles being exterminated: https://cdv.dei.uc.pt/2018/artsit/hive-mind-demo.mp4.

The number of inputs in the DQN of the core is 513. This is the number of values within an audio spectrum transmitted every frame from a microphone. The core receives all spectrum values and then feeds them forward through hidden layers. Hyperbolic tangent (tanh) activation function was used. There are 5 outputs, they correspond to movement directions and a "stand still" action.

Backpropagation of each layer is accomplished by using the Mean Square Error calculation (Eq. 1). Where: Y = vector of the observed values of the variable being predicted; $\hat{Y}$ = vector of n predictions generated from a sample of n data points in all variables.

$$MSE = \frac{1}{n}\sum\nolimits_{i=1}^{n}(Y^i - \hat{Y}_i)^2 \qquad (1)$$

There is a list of the last actions performed by an agent, paired with the audio spectrum input in order to deal with nonconsistent data from the microphone and it is important to make sure that backpropagation is done for all variations of one sound.

DQN of the particles is performing feed forward if there is a sound from a pick-up object that is within the hearing range. Learning is accomplished solely through reproduction and survival over generations.

One of the key problems present throughout the development was how the agents would be able to perceive sounds from their own environment. The solution to this was creating an artificial ear in the form of a grid of sensors around an agent (see Fig. 3).

Because the sounds are being transmitted as pings, it was necessary to implement a temporary memory system for each of the sensors. Whenever a sound is produced, a sensor fires and then keeps the value for several frames, unless it is overwritten with a different value.

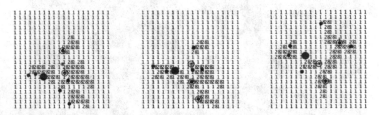

Fig. 3. Each of the three images is a graphical representation of a grid of sensors. Each of the agents on the image is producing sounds. The selected agent has a grid of sensors around it. Numbers on a grid represent detected and memorised audio frequencies. 1 means no frequency detected.

3   Resulting Behaviour

When the application starts a user is faced with a challenge to teach the core agent to respond to sound commands as soon as possible before particles get destroyed by bad pick-ups. Once control is established, the goal of a user shifts into teaching particles to recognise good pick-ups and distinguish them from bad ones. A user will have to rely on particles and their reaction in order to determine which pick-ups are good and which ones are bad.

It is interesting to observe the behaviour of particles when they are reaching towards a pick-up and extending into a line, helping each other to reach further. Sometimes when there are several pick-ups that they want to collect, they can split into two or more "arms" in order to reach them. Some of these interactions are shown in Fig. 4.

The behaviour of particles collecting pick-ups has its own dynamics related to their evolution. Particles that exploded by collecting a bad pick-up will be dead, therefore there will be less particles in the next generation attempting the same action, however, mutations can still cause particles to evolve bad habits. If the particles collect a lot of good pick-ups their population will increase and therefore the chances of lots of particles being caught within the blast radius of an explosion increase. Additionally, more particles can become isolated.

The core itself can learn to respond to audio commands, however, it can often disobey them because of background noise or because a different correct answer was backpropagated through the deep neural network. It can generate unpredictable behaviours that can be interesting to observe.

Particles that were separated from the core remain in place, but whenever a pick-up is moving by, it can be collected by them. As a result, a whole new colony of particles separated from the core can be formed. This can result in an unexpected outcome and emerging behaviour.

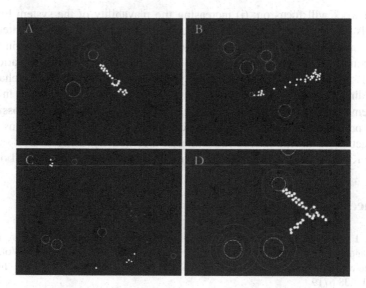

Fig. 4. Screenshots of the system showing interaction between particles and pick-ups. (A) particles are reaching towards a pick-up, trying to collect it; (B) particles are forming a line as they are avoiding two pick-ups on both sides of the line, while trying to get to the core; (C) some particles (bottom of the image) have become isolated from the core and are behaving autonomously, additionally, near the centre of the image, blood can be seen as a result of an explosion of a bad pick-up; (D) particles are splitting into two "arms" as they are trying to reach towards two distinct pick-ups.

4 Conclusion

We have described and tested a virtual environment that contains A-life agents. These are the main contributions: (i) a virtual ecosystem populated with agents that learn to understand sounds introduced by a user and evolve their interaction with the environment; (ii) A-life agents used as key elements in a virtual toy; (iii) use of ML and EC for the behaviour of virtual creatures and their interaction with the environment and a user; (iv) the perception of sounds and the evolution of neural networks through their perception of sound; (v) agents are taught to respond to sounds produced by a user using neural networks, resulting in them being completely controlled by sounds; and (vi) a hierarchy that allows the particle agents to alter their behaviour from the learning that was accomplished by the core agent.

It is not expected from this approach to replace existing techniques used in programming AI behaviour for video games and interactive experiences. It is an exploration of how a ML, EC and sound-based approach can be used in designing a unique behaviour and interaction for virtual agents within art and entertainment directed projects.

The resulting system can be considered a toy because a user can interact (play) with it and the actions of a user affect the state of the environment and the artificial creatures within it.

Future work will focus on: (i) increasing the playability of the system by adding more goals for the user, increasing difficulty and adding more fun interactions; (ii) adding more variants of pick-ups, particle types and effects for them in order to increase complexity; (iii) adding a tutorial for the user and exploring various user interface designs in order to increase usability; (iv) experimenting with the behaviour of agents, adding more possible actions and promoting autonomous behaviour in order to see more emerging mechanics/behaviour as a result; and (v) exploring the possibility of using this project as an interactive experience with more real-life interactions, such as agents reacting to touch, movement and user position by using a tool such as a Microsoft Kinect and projecting the environment of the system onto a wall or floor.

References

1. Yaeger, L.: Computational Genetics, Physiology, Metabolism, Neural Systems, Learning, Vision and Behavior or PolyWorld: Life in a New Context. Artificial Life III, Vol. XVII of SFI Studies in the Sciences of Complexity, Santa Fe Institute, (1), 1–25 (1993). https://doi.org/10.1.1.38.6719
2. Sims, K.: Evolving virtual creatures. In: Proceedings of the 21st Annual Conference on Computer Graphics and Interactive Techniques - SIGGRAPH 1994, pp. 15–22 (1994). https://doi.org/10.1145/192161.192167
3. Conway's game of life on rosettacode. http://rosettacode.org/wiki/Conway%27s_Game_of_Life
4. Reynolds, C.W.: Flocks, herds and schools: a distributed behavioral model. ACM SIGGRAPH Comput. Graph. **21**(4), 25–34 (1987). https://doi.org/10.1145/37402.37406
5. Grand, S., Cliff, D.: Creatures: entertainment software agents with artificial life. Auton. Agents Multi-agent Syst. **57**, 39–57 (1998). https://doi.org/10.1023/A:1010042522104
6. Nintendogs. http://nintendogspluscats.nintendo.com/
7. Wexler, J.: Artificial intelligence in games: a look at the smarts behind lionhead studio's "black and white" and where it can and will go in the future. In: Spring Simulation Multiconference (2008). https://doi.org/10.4018/978-1-60960-567-4.ch007
8. Mnih, V., Silver, D., Riedmiller, M.: Playing atari with deep reinforcement learning (DQN). In: Nips, pp. 1–9 (2013). https://doi.org/10.1038/nature14236
9. Mnih, V., et al.: Human-level control through deep reinforcement learning. Nature **518**(7540), 529–533 (2015). https://doi.org/10.1038/nature14236

A Serious Game for Hemophobia Treatment Phobos: First Insights

João Petersen[1(✉)], Vítor Carvalho[1,2], João Tiago Oliveira[3], and Eva Oliveira[1]

[1] 2Ai Laboratory – School of Technology, IPCA, Barcelos, Portugal
al3996@alunos.ipca.pt, {vcarvalho, eoliveira}@ipca.pt
[2] Algoritmi Research Centre, University of Minho, Guimarães, Portugal
[3] School of Psychology, University of Minho, Guimarães, Portugal
jtoliveira@psi.uminho.pt

Abstract. This paper addresses the development process of a serious game - PHOBOS - for hemophobia treatment. Hemophobia, also known as blood phobia, is the fear of blood, wounds, injuries, amongst others. The game addresses the issue through applied-tension exercise combined with exposure therapy on a virtual reality environment. One of the main challenges was to design a game that reconciliate in a balanced way an immersive narrative and plot with the treatment of a phobia that causes great tensions and find the best mechanics to allow a gradual exposure to blood. Artistically we wanted to create the more realistic environment possible, in tune with the sound design. This process was done with the help of a team of psychologists that in conjunction with the team of game developers created a plot that helps the player to adjust his discomfort and challenge himself in his path to deal with this phobia. We present an early stage development process of a virtual reality phobia game, from the brainstorming concept of the game to the development to the first prototype with its requirements and hardware used.

Keywords: Serious game · Development process · Programming
Game development · Hemophobia

1 Introduction

Blood-injection-injury phobia (also known as Hemophobia), is a specific phobia characterized by an intense fear of being exposed to blood or invasive medical procedures [1]. It is a relatively common disorder [1, 2] where up to 80% of suffers experience a vasovagal response when they face the stimuli [3]. Considering that the intense fear can be generalized to other associated stimuli such like doctors, nurses, hospitals, syringes or dentists, hemophobia can lead to serious effects on individual's health due to the avoidance of these settings [1]. To address this issue, we developed a virtual reality serious game - Phobos – which is a serious game for dealing with hemophobia using as gameplay the exposition method as a way to help the player to adjust his discomfort and challenge himself in his path to deal with this phobia. We also have an educational part to educate its patients on how to control their physical

A. L. Brooks et al. (Eds.): ArtsIT 2018/DLI 2018, LNICST 265, pp. 231–236, 2019.

responses when facing fear. It was built under Unity engine using photorealistic scenery to be played in virtual reality. This paper describes the development process, including the hardware and game design aspects, as well as the artistic aspect of the modelling, lightning and sound design.

2 Related Work

There is evidence suggesting people who suffer from specific phobias tend to be hesitant to seek treatment [4]. Despite this reluctance, research suggests that specific phobia is one of the most treatable of psychological disorders [5]. Along with a wide diverse of treatment approaches, exposure techniques are often considered the first line treatment and widely used with phobic patients [6] presenting robust evidence of efficacy [5].

Therefore, computer-based tools may present an attractive tool to potentiate and amplify the range and effectiveness of psychological treatments and reduce the attrition [7]. Research has been describing the potential effectiveness of using computer games as an adjunct to psychotherapy [8]. One example of this kind of games is based on the model of solution-focused therapy, designed for adolescents to increase their motivation for therapy [9]. Other examples of serious games, grounded on Cognitive-Behavioral Therapy, are the Treasure Hunt [10] or the gNats [5]. In fact, the National Institute for Clinical Excellence has inclusively recommended computer-aided psychotherapy programs [6] targeted for adults suffering from mood and anxiety disorders like Beating the Blues [11] and FearFighter [12].

In the last few years another line of research that uses advanced technology in the service of psychotherapy has been emerging: the development of Virtual Reality (VR) applications, either to use in the assessment or in the treatment of mental health problems [13, 14]. VR is an advanced form of human computer interface that enables the individual to manipulate problematic situations related with his/her problem, in a sheltered setting, without feeling threatened [14]. So, virtual reality exposure therapy (VRET) has become a new medium for exposure therapy presenting good results in terms of efficacy, especially with specific phobias [15, 16] and several advantages over in vivo or imaginal exposure. As Rothbaum et al. say [17], "What distinguishes VR from a mere multimedia system or an interactive computer graphics display is a sense of presence. A sense of presence is also essential to conducting exposure therapy." Hemophobia, being one of the most common phobias and not being addressed in any of the games found on our research, made us want to develop our game to aid phobic patients and ease the costs on their treatments.

3 PHOBOS – A Serious Game for Dealing with Hemophobia

Phobos is a serious game to help with the treatment of hemophobia patients through a controlled VRET. This allows the patients to be exposed to their phobia in a controlled environment, in the psychologist room, that in most phobia cases is impossible. We use Unity engine and the STEAM®VR SDK (Software Development Kit) for the development of the game because it is one of the most used platforms in game development and the background we had on developing on Unity.

3.1 Game Design

We started the game design process by a requirement assessment conference with our peers from the psychology department, where we discussed which types of games could be suitable to this type of phobia, and which mechanics we should explore, as the treatment therapy for hemophobic patients, is the exposure method. After we used the brainstorming technique [18], which allowed the developers to start with a series of ideas narrowing them down to a narrative, some mechanics and a gameplay.

One of our main ideas was that we had to create safe havens and safe cues to our players, this idea was then discarded in conference with the psychology team because it's an avoidance technique that isn't beneficial to the patient. The goal was to create a plot that could put the patient controlling the phobia stimuli but motivating the patient to exceed himself, in a progressive way. The narrative chosen was a detective that is called to a murder scene. The patient is the detective that arrives to a penthouse that has been the scene of a murder, with no body, and has to solve it. He/she has to pick up clues in order to progress in the game, which have phobic stimuli, in this case, blood. In the beginning of the game these phobic stimuli are very few and of small impact to the user, as the detective progresses throughout the crime scene, the phobic stimuli increase gradually leading to more realistic and strong impact blood exposure, so the user gets a paced exposure to his fear. The gameplay is a first person, virtual reality and role-playing genres as the player is in the role of the detective that can freely explore an apartment in virtual reality, can gather clues, read the items gathered, get further knowledge on his phobia and the techniques used to treat it, as well as confront their phobia by controlled phobia exposure, as is the patient who decides if he/she wants to expose himself/herself. The main mechanics are the gather, examining objects/clues, reading their information and the ability to solve puzzles throughout the level until solve the mystery. The more he explores and become closer to the solving, the more he exposes. The patient knows that he needs to expose himself to know the truth but also know that he can control that exposure, which allow the patient to mentally prepare himself to the inner challenge. Concerning this aspect, we developed an educational tutorial to help the patient dealing with his own phobia.

The opinion from our peers from the psychology department was that one of the key features should be a tutorial that can explain to patients all the physical reactions that our bodies feel during the exposition with blood, and how to overcome some of those effects like for example, to apply tension on hands, arms and legs, so that the patient can prevent faint which occurs from exposure to blood due to the increase in blood pressure followed by its the rapid drop [19]. In this tutorial, first we teach the player the basic mechanics on VR controls, which include how to move, how to grab items as well as how to interact with the game inventory system as displayed on Fig. 1 then we incorporated the tutorial with the beginning of the game, the introductory part, example in the suitcase file, in the lobby before entering the house, the user gets access to information about the description of the phobia. The key points of information to be presented are an explanation of the phobia, the natural body reactions, the hypersensitivity, the panic attacks and the treatment process. These key points were chosen and validated by the psychology team, since it was the most relevant information to be passed to the player.

Fig. 1. HUD (Head-Up Display) tutorial on controller mechanics

Our concern related with the artistic aspect of the game, was to simulate a realistic environment. The realism was explored by creating a modern and comfortable apartment exploring the light and sounds and by creating an immersive plot. The goal was not to scare, nor to daunt but to defy the patient to his own fear. All the interaction is made through the HTC Vive as it is ergonomic and easy to learn and can use for example the grip button to grab the interactable objects described above and the trigger button to open the doors, to see the voicemail left in the phone in the lobby and to trigger the puzzle events, for example to turn paintings by 90° until all paintings are in the right order. We designed the game to be played like therapy sessions, so the patient can process the information gathered in that session and feel the accomplishment of passing another stage of the game and of overcoming their phobia as well as the description of each session, for example, the player having grabbed the key in the plant vase, now opens the door and starts searching for clues in the living room, being exposed to the first phobic stimuli a bloodied broken wine glass. The platform, we only chose Windows pc due to its virtual reality support and technology as the Macintosh didn't support virtual reality graphic cards and is more focused for work and not for gaming.

4   Validation

Since the game is still under development, we still haven't done the functionality and usability testing on a large sample. Both tests will first be done on colleagues and afterwards only the usability test will be done on phobic patients to ensure the validity of the project. The functionality tests consist on trying to break the game, using force to see every possible existing bug, while the usability tests consist on seeing if the game doesn't cause motion sickness, if the UI can be read properly without causing strain on the eyes and assess the space required for room-scale virtual reality. After these tests we will test if the game can really help phobic patients in dealing with their phobias.

5 Final Remarks

This project started to be developed for the master's in engineering of Digital Game Development, Project I and Project II classes, which will now be continued for the master's dissertation, where we will test the interaction of biometric sensors for data acquisition on physical responses to the phobia and an AI (artificial intelligence) dynamic control of the phobic stimuli. The development can sometimes be strenuous due to the unknown methods of developing for virtual reality making us go through a series of trial and error implementations to make the game perfect. In the undergoing phases of the development we want to include biometric sensor data acquisition to help us understand the stress inputted on the patient and also to make the phobic stimuli appear gradually and their intensity linked to their blood pressure so that we can warn the user to apply the applied tension method and prevent fainting from happening.

References

1. Puri, B.K.: Blood-injection-injury phobias. Int. J. Clin. Pract. **61**, 358–359 (2007). https://doi.org/10.1111/j.1742-1241.2006.01149.x
2. Pitkin, M.R., Malouff, J.M.: Self-arranged exposure for overcoming blood-injection-injury phobia: a case study. Health Psychol. Behav. Med. **2**(1), 665–669 (2014). https://doi.org/10.1080/21642850.2014.916219
3. Engel, G.L.: Psychologic stress, vasodepressor (vasovagal) syncope, and sudden death. Ann. Intern. Med. **89**(3), 403–412 (1978). https://doi.org/10.7326/0003-4819-89-3-403
4. Wolitzky-Taylor, K.B., Horowitz, J.D., Powers, M.B., Telch, M.J.: Psychological approaches in the treatment of specific phobias: a meta-analysis. Clin. Psychol. Rev. **28**(6), 1021–1037 (2008). https://doi.org/10.1016/j.cpr.2008.02.007
5. O' Reilly, G., McGlade, N., Coyle, D.: David Gnatenborough's Island. A computerised cognitive behavioural therapy-programme for children & adolescents. Version 1.0 (2009)
6. Cuijpers, P., et al.: Computer-aided psychotherapy for anxiety disorders: a meta-analytic review. Cogn. Behav. Ther. **38**(2), 66–82 (2009)
7. Andrews, G., et al.: Computer therapy for the anxiety and depressive disorders is effective, acceptable and practical health care: a meta-analysis. PLoS ONE **5**(10), e13196 (2010)
8. Griffiths, M.: The therapeutic value of videogames. In: Goldstein, J., Raessens, J. (eds.) Handbook of Computer Game Studies, pp. 161–173. MIT Press, Boston (2005)
9. Coyle, D., et al.: Personal investigator: a therapeutic 3D game for adolescent psychotherapy. Interact. Technol. Smart Educ. **2**(2), 73–88 (2005)
10. Brezinka, V.: Treasure hunt-a serious game to support psychotherapeutic treatment of children. In: Andersen, S., et al. (eds.) eHealth Beyond the Horizon—Get iT There, SHTI, pp. 71–76. IOS Press, Amsterdam (2008)
11. Grime, P.R.: Computerized cognitive behavioural therapy at work: a randomized controlled trial in employees with recent stress-related absenteeism. Occup. Med. **54**(5), 353–359 (2004)
12. MacGregor, A.D., et al.: Empirically grounded clinical interventions clients' and referrers' perceptions of computer-guided CBT (FearFighter). Behav. Cogn. Psychother. **37**(01), 1–9 (2009)
13. Powers, M.B., Emmelkamp, P.M.: Virtual reality exposure therapy for anxiety disorders: a meta-analysis. J. Anxiety Disord. **22**(3), 561–569 (2008)

14. Riva, G.: Virtual reality: an experiential tool for clinical psychology. Br. J. Guid. Couns. **37** (3), 337–345 (2009). https://doi.org/10.1080/03069880902957056
15. Krijn, M., et al.: Fear of flying treatment methods: virtual reality exposure vs. cognitive behavioral therapy. Aviat. Space Environ. Med. **78**(2), 121–128 (2007)
16. Meyerbröker, K., Emmelkamp, P.M.G.: Virtual reality exposure therapy in anxiety disorders: a systematic review of process-and-outcomes studies. Depress. Anxiety **27**, 933–944 (2010). https://doi.org/10.1002/da.20734
17. Rothbaum, B.O., Hodges, L., Smith, S., Lee, J.H., Price, L.: A controlled study of virtual reality exposure therapy for the fear of flying. J. Consult. Clin. Psychol. **68**(6), 1020–1026 (2000)
18. Wilson, C.: Brainstorming and Beyond: A User-Centered Design Method. Morgan Kaufmann Publishers Inc., San Francisco (2013)
19. Öst, L., Sterner, U.: Applied tension - a specific behavioral method for treatment of blood phobia. Behav. Resl Ther. **25**(1), 25–29 (1987)
20. The Stonefox, VRTK, April 2016. https://github.com/thestonefox/VRTK

Inside the Geometry - Double Language

Chiara Passa[✉]

Fine Art Academy of Rome, Rome, Italy
chiarapassa@gmail.com

Abstract. Inside the Geometry - Double language is a virtual reality art-project, which takes the form of diverse site-specific video-installations. The project involves the use of various 3D viewers, plus related smartphones playing diverse virtual reality animations.

Keywords: Virtual reality · Video-installation · Art

1 Inside the Geometry – The Concept

For Inside the Geometry - Double language, the 3D viewers are arranged in the exhibition space to orchestrate on wall, or from ceiling, a series of geometric designs conceived site-specific for different occasions. Each geometric design hosts all different animations, the same number, as there are 3D viewers (Google cardboards). So, inside each viewer, the audience can take a journey beyond physical space. The virtual reality animations, completely immersive, are generated by the language of geometry and its unpredictable variations, which, in the liquid dimension, overturn completely Cartesian coordinates. I use Google cardboard as medium to interrogate outer spaces beyond architecture and surface, so challenging the notion of place itself, to render it vibrant and participatory.

The whole virtual reality series (more than thirty-five figures created, and here questioning the artworks: Two Times Four and Earth Spiral) is part of a research project which I began in 2015 and which slots into my artistic journey since 1997. Inside the Geometry - Double language is the fruit of a deep interest in space and how it is transformed and shaped "by" and "in" the language of informatics. In software and electronic devices, I find potential vehicles for the investigation and visualization of my research and theories. Inside the Geometry - Double language led to the materialization of these theories in the most original forms as part of the Live Architectures series (1999-ongoing); artworks designed to behave as if they were alive, to move beyond their own functionality. These are "Super places", a definition coined by me in 1999: dynamic places, which project the spectator into digital and mediated reality, shaking-up the static concept of architecture, as well as virtual milieus.

1.1 Two Times Four, Virtual Reality Video Installation, 2015

Mostly of my virtual reality artworks, as for example: Two Times Four, are based on the idea of the "Super place" explained previously. In Two Times Four we become blind and ultra-seeing at the same time, forced to immerse ourselves into diverse

A. L. Brooks et al. (Eds.): ArtsIT 2018/DLI 2018, LNICST 265, pp. 237–242, 2019.

abstract animations playing with the concept of infinite; including infinitely large and infinitely small (micro and macro dimensions) through minimalist nuances and conceptual degrees, with an apparently icy and impersonal kind of view.

My virtual reality animations playing in Two Times Four, construct a sort of *"mise en abyme"* (droste effect), in which an element shifts the other in depth, merging over these "intangible animations" in continuous transformation, emitting vivid lights turning into super-objects, so mixing geometries, paintings and sculptures praxis, all together.

I use geometry language combined to the virtual reality medium to question real space, exploring it as virtual membrane in order to answer the paradox generated by our contemporary condition, even more diluted in-between physical and liquid space, by searching for the infinity through geometry and abstraction in art (Figs. 1, 2 and 3).

Fig. 1. Two Times Four, virtual reality site-specific installation composed by 12 Google Cardboards and 12 VR animations, performing at Spectra Festival, February 2018.

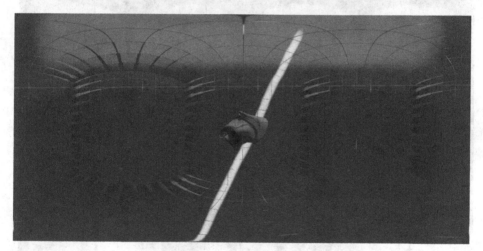

Fig. 2. Frames from two virtual reality animations, part of Two Times Four, 2015.

1.2   From the Series into the Land Art: Earth Spiral, Virtual Reality Video Installation 2016

Earth Spiral is an experimental project which challenges environment to render it fully participating. Spectators through 3D viewers, bow down to nature while kneel to technology and use it to see in depth, just beyond the ontological vision of nature itself. So, in Earth Spiral the underground is animated and lives existing beyond is own functionality. The virtual reality animations show modified versions of Google Earth Maps – bizarre dynamic shapes turning into abstract 3D sculptures (Figs. 4, 5 and 6).

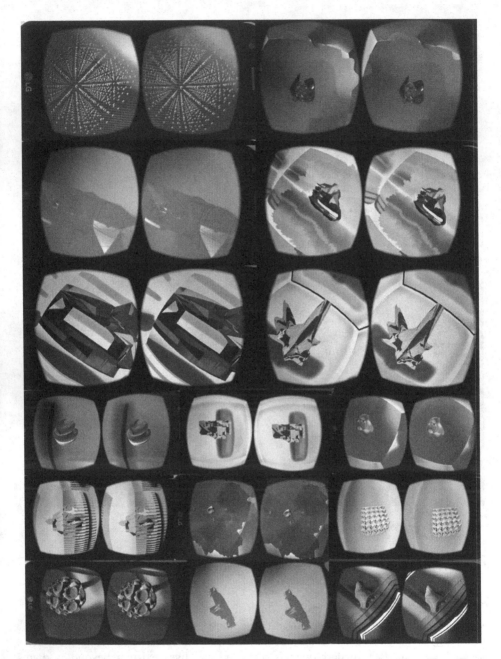

Fig. 3. Some frames playing on smartphones of the virtual reality animations Two Times Four, 2015.

Fig. 4. Earth Spiral, virtual reality video installation composed by 20 Google Cardboards and 20 VR animations, 2016. Performing at Rocciamorgia festival July 2017.

Fig. 5. A Frame from the virtual reality animations Earth Spiral, 2016.

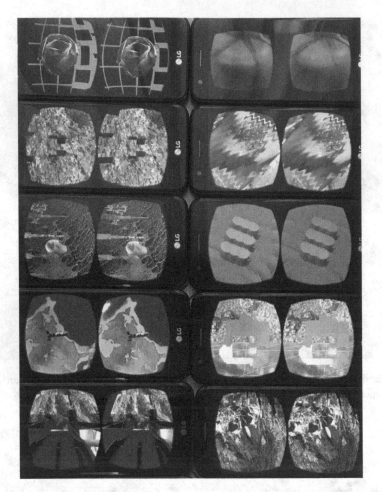

Fig. 6. Some frames playing on smartphones of the virtual reality animations Earth Spiral, 2016.

References

1. Passa, C.: From the series Inside the geometry double language: area between curves, 2015. Performing at MAXXI Museum, Rome, April 2017. https://www.youtube.com/watch?v=_3cjVuK6xLs

2. Passa, C.: From the series Inside the geometry double language: two times four 2015. Performing at Spectra Festival, Aberdeen, February 2018. https://www.youtube.com/watch?v=r7yora7hcfI

3. Passa, C.: From the series Inside the geometry double language: space filling curve 2015. Performing at In-Sonic group show, ZKM Museum Karlsruhe, December 2017. https://www.youtube.com/watch?v=1cPzjhStFrc&t=53s

4. Passa, C.: From the series into the Land art: Earth spiral 2016. Performing at Rocciamorgia Festival, Salcito (2017). https://www.youtube.com/watch?v=xFe6v1lpsyM&t=1s

ArtsIT - Playable Cities Workshop Track

Citizen Science and Game with a Purpose to Foster Biodiversity Awareness and Bioacoustic Data Validation

Pedro Loureiro[1], Catia Prandi[2,3]($\boxtimes$), Nuno Nunes[1,2], and Valentina Nisi[2,4]

[1] Tecnico - University of Lisbon, Lisbon, Portugal
[2] M-ITI/LARSyS, Funchal, Portugal
`{catia.prandi,njn,valentina}@m-iti.org`
[3] University of Bologna, Bologna, Italy
[4] Universidade da Madeira, Funchal, Portugal

Abstract. Biodiversity refers to the variety of life on Earth and its biological diversity. It boosts ecosystem productivity, where each species has a role to play. Unfortunately, human activity is causing massive extinctions and biodiversity losses continue. Because of that, nature conservation efforts and environmental monitoring have become increasingly important to manage natural resources and reacts to changes. Following this line, we designed a game with a purpose (GWAP) aimed to address two emerging issues in this area: (i) engaging citizens in validating bioacoustic samples collected using smart bioacoustics sensors; and (ii) educating and enhancing the user's biodiversity awareness while playing, inspiring them for later reflection and eventually inspire behavioural changes. In this paper, we describe the different design phases and the insights obtained from an early experience prototype session of the game, engaging 14 young-adults. From the prototype session, we collected insightful feedback on the design of the game and its mechanics as well as its interface. Moreover, preliminary positive responses of the users encourage us to refine and continue developing the game.

Keywords: Biodiversity awareness · Biodiversity monitoring Citizen science · Game with a purpose · Bioacoustics sensors

1 Introduction

Over the last 100 year, the abundance of species that exist in our environments has been dramatically affected [5]. Humans have been the main harbingers of environmental destruction and modifications, transforming earth systems, and accelerating climate change [9]. Such activities result in biodiversity losses that affect the ecosystem functions, and impacts the goods/services ecosystems provide [4]. In response to this, different organizations are advocating for urgent actions to undertake to limit the effects of this age of the Anthropocene (a

A. L. Brooks et al. (Eds.): ArtsIT 2018/DLI 2018, LNICST 265, pp. 245–255, 2019.
https://doi.org/10.1007/978-3-030-06134-0_29

relevant example is represented by the 10-years plan developed by the United Nations[1]), requiring the effort of stakeholders, policymakers, and citizens.

In this scenario, monitoring species has become increasingly important. The fluctuation of a species population can indicate the general health of the habitat. This type of monitoring is referred as biodiversity monitoring and through it, we can detect rising problems in a habitat, allowing us to find the source of the problem and mitigate the repercussions on the environment [11]. However, biodiversity monitoring is a complex task, both in collecting and analysing biological data. Involving a group of scientists to manually collect and analyse data is not always feasible, considering the location and size of certain habitats and the number of species that inhabit it. The use of technology in collecting and analysing biological data seemed an apparent and scalable solution [6].

Even though technology is enabling scientists to collect and analyse data more efficiently, if the goal is to globally monitor the environment, creating teams of scientist to do so is still not a scalable solution considering the size of the Earth and the number of species that exist in it. To solve this problem, scientists turned to the general public for help, crowdsourcing the collection and analysis of data (e.g., [1,8,14]). Scientists issue instructions for these "amateur-scientist" to follow, enabling them to collect and analyse data without the need for a specific knowledge, while at the same time improving the reliability of the obtained data. This type of projects is referred to as Citizen Science projects, collaborative process in which volunteers work with professional scientists to study real-world problems [10]. In these projects, the number of people who volunteer strongly influences the project's success, and captivating and engaging the general public becomes a key factor in the project's overall success. Participants in this type of projects are often motivated by contributing to actual scientific research. The entertainment aspect is also relevant in motivating the citizens' participation. In fact, adding gaming elements to these projects proved to be a successful way to increase participation, boosting the number of involved citizen scientists [2].

Taking the above into consideration, we designed a gameful experience, exploiting smart bioacoustics sensors and players' inputs to help monitor biodiversity in a given area, through fun and an exciting game activity. Our final aim is to design a Game with a Purpose (GWAP, [15]) that will contribute in the area of HCI and Environmental Sustainability by exploiting the GWAP framework and Citizens Science paradigm. In particular, we are investigating: (i) if the GWAP will succeed in engaging and eventually educate users, increasing their biodiversity awareness about the environment that surrounds them, and (ii) if we can validate a reliable dataset of animal calls, based on player's inputs, so as to use it to monitor a given species population as well as the environment biodiversity. In this paper, we focus on describing the different design phases of the GWAP and the preliminary results from an experience prototyping validation sessions. Given the positive results emerging from the study and the engagement of the users, we are currently developing the GWAP followed by a user study.

---

[1] https://www.cbd.int/doc/strategic-plan/2011-2020/Aichi-Targets-EN.pdf.

The rest of the paper presents the related work in the context of Citizen Science projects for biodiversity using bioacoustics sensors, the game design process, and insights obtained from an experience prototyping session. Finally, it concludes with final remarks and future work.

2 Related Work

The collection and analysis of biological data have been key challenges for any project focused on biodiversity monitoring. To solve this issue, some projects rely on the citizen science framework (i.e., [2]). Projects like Bat Detective, iBats, and the New Forest Cicada fall into this category, exploiting acoustic sensors to engage citizens in collecting data for biodiversity monitoring. In particular, Bat Detective [15] is an online citizen science project launched in 2012, that relies on volunteers to identify bat calls in audio samples. Those audio samples were recorded during surveys, which were done by teams of volunteers with specific equipment for the effect. The ultimate goal of the project is the creation of a program that automatically extracts the relevant information out recordings to be used by researchers all over the world, simplifying the tracking of bat populations. Another project focusing on bats is the iBats[2] program, established in 2006 through a collaborative effort between the Zoological Society of London (ZSL) and the Bat Conservation Trust (BCT). The aim of this program is to carry out coordinated volunteer-led bat population monitoring on a global scale. This project is powered by citizen scientist. The iBats development team released an iPhone application which can be directly attached to an ultrasonic detector to record grid references, sound files, and other survey data along the route. The New Forest Cicada Project [16] aims to equip the millions of visitors of the New Forest, a national park on the south coast of England, with a smartphone application that can detect and recognise the song of the cicada. This project aims to discover if the cicada is now extinct in the UK or simply migrated to a yet undiscovered site [16].

Building on these inspiring examples, our approach takes advantage of acoustic sensing and Citizen Science to categorise, validate and map local species and biodiversity, exploiting a gameful experience to motivate users in actively be part of and contribute to the community. In fact, different research works have proved that gameful experiences are powerful tools to engage users to participate in crowdsourcing activities, including both digital tasks (e.g., [15]) and real tasks in the urban environment, exploited as a digital playground (e.g., [13]).

3 The Game Design

Aware of the challenges surrounding the collection and analysis of data for project focused on biodiversity monitoring, including cost and problematic scalability in using scientists and professionals, we embraced the GWAP framework

---

[2] http://www.bats.org.uk/pages/ibatsprogram.html.

and the involvement of players as citizen scientists, in categorising and analysing data, aiming at providing fun and knowledge in exchange of time and efficiency. In designing the game, we focus on the specific target audience of young-adults with a developed interest in nature, fauna, and flora.

3.1 Objectives and Methodology

Our aim is to create a GWAP that shares acoustic data collected by strategically placed acoustic sensors in order to engage users in categorising and hence learning about fauna and eventually flora biodiversity while contributing to data classification. The three main objectives that the game addresses are: (1) educating users about environment biodiversity while playing. The user should learn and be informed about biodiversity variety and changes in locations where the sensors are installed. (2) Involving and engaging users in data categorization and analysis through a GWAP. (3) Crowdsourcing the validation of collected data in order to obtain an accurate data set of classified animal calls. These three objectives have driven the design process, composed by different phases: two concept ideation sessions (Sect. 3.2); a focus group session (Sect. 3.3); and an experience prototype (EP, [3]) (Sect. 5).

3.2 Concept Ideation Sessions

To start brainstorming and define some initial game ideas, we conducted two concept ideation sessions, involving two different targets: ten PhD students enrolled in the Interaction Design and HCI course of the Computer Science and Engineering PhD programme (Tecnico, University of Lisbon), and seven experts in game design and multimedia entertainment (M-ITI researchers and PhD students in the digital media programme). The sessions lasted 1 hour and started with a brief introduction to the motivation and goals (objectives) of the game to design. Moreover, to inspire them, we introduced some projects where acoustic sensors are used to monitor biodiversity. Several different game ideas came out from the two sessions. However, several design issues emerged (DI).

DI 1. Developing location-based mobile games versus virtual representation of the locations where the data subsist. This dichotomy highlights the use of different devices, mobile and/or desktop based.

DI 2. Using the sensors as tools for enabling the player to participate in the game (proximity-based game activities) versus using the sensors as a provider of data. This would imply different design and game mechanics.

DI 3. Using real-time data gathered from sensors versus using historical data from sensors. The first scenario implies having animals and event happening during play time, which is very difficult to control, but at the same time gives the game a certain "magic moment" event, when real animals are spotted while capturing and categorizing their sounds, during the game play.

DI 4. Focusing on one specific animal versus the attempt to create game scenarios that can be generalized for different animals. The game can be site specific and can appeal to players because of its uniqueness and ties to a special location, or can be suitable for any location.

DI 5. Creating mini-games to collect points/engage the player versus creating of a complex story. This affects the game design and types of audiences/players interest.

DI 6. Trusting all the users in the same way versus creating a validation model to assess users' credibility, considering the sounds classification. Regarding this latter issue, different models have been investigated in crowdsourcing contexts (i.e., [12]), such as computing the credibility value confronting a defined set of user's answers with a ground truth dataset or assigning the value on the basis of the other users' answers (e.g., exploiting a majority voting model).

Considering the pros and the cons of the different game approaches, and the innovative ideas presented, we developed two game concepts were selected as the more promising in addressing our objectives. The games selected revolved around a future dystopian scenario that could be fixed only with the help of the player. The background story for both the games was based on the following assumption: *a huge catastrophe happened in a far away past (in the year 2050). Human civilization survived. Now (in the year 3050) an agency in possession of time travel technology, focuses in recruiting agents in the past (our present, 2018) to collect samples of original species to restore nature to its former state. The player is part of the agency and he/she is needed to collect samples in the present (2018). A future based scientist guides the players in following the instruction of the game and helping them fix the future.* In this context, the two game scenarios (S) defined are: **S 1.** After the big disaster in 2050, the original nature was completely twisted, warped and original animals (except humans) and plants were not able to adapt and survive. Scientists in the year 3050 a.c. combine the creatures' samples, collected by the player in the past (in 2018, before the big disaster) to obtain several creatures able to survive in the present twisted, warped environments. **S 2.** The original nature was destroyed in 2050 and new creatures (mutants that combine several species together- see, for example, the mutant in the first paper prototyping wireframe in Fig. 2) were able to adapt and live in the twisted present (3050). A scientist from the future shows you (a present time inhabitant of the earth) mutants and asks you to find samples of the original species that compose the mutant, so he can separate the genes of the mutant and recreate the original ones, with the goal to repristinate the original healthy environment.

3.3 Focus Groups

Upon creating the scenarios of the two game concepts, we conducted a focus group session engaging eight researchers, experts in game design, multimedia entertainment, digital media, locative storytelling and HCI and sound with the aim of criticizing and refining the two gameplays. The session lasted one hour, including: the introduction of the context (biodiversity, sensors stations, Citizens Science); motivation behind the creation of a purposeful/persuasive game framework (issues we would like to address); presentation of the two game ideas (concept, goal of the players, gameplay, and so on); discussion/brainstorming on the two game ideas. During the focus group, based on the experts' feedback, some game mechanics were refined and a few added to address the design issues, aimed at better meeting our objectives. After the focused group, the two games were developed into EP sessions in order to be tested and further refined.

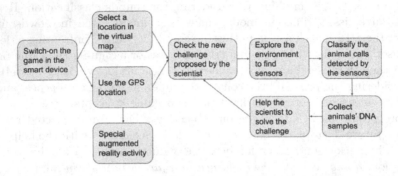

Fig. 1. Gameplay for both the games scenarios (S 1 and S 2).

4   The Resulting GWAP

As we refined the two scenarios and prepare them for testing as an EP, several design issues (DI) emerged from the concept ideation sessions.

DI 1. We hypothesized two game modalities: (i) location-based, where the user needs to be in the park; (ii) remote, with a virtual environment. In this way, we don't penalize users who live in locations without close parks with sensors installed, but we reward (with special contents) users who decide to play in a real park. In both the cases, we decided to exploit mobile devices.

DI 2. With the aim of engaging a large number of users, we opted to use the sensors only as a source of data. This means that, in our games, the sensors are just providers of data, they are not part of the game. This allows us to avoid several complications. Imagine, for example, a game where each sensor represents a virtual kingdom and the player needs to (virtually) "own/conquer" the sensors to be able to play. It is clear how different variables, that the player cannot control, come to play (e.g., the sensor stops working or it doesn't detect any animals calls for a long period).

DI 3. We decided to use historical data, to avoid problems related to the absence of detected animals in a specific period or area. Moreover, this also has the advantage to easily tracking changes on the biodiversity of a specific area, sensitizing the users. In fact, the player can travel in a specific time window in the past, visualizing the evolution (in term of quantity and differences over a specific period, such as a week, month or year) of the specific animals' detection, visualizing a timeline graph.

DI 4. The gameplay has been designed to include different breeds and species in the story, so as to avoid including constraints in the monitored calls and educate the users on biodiversity, in the whole meaning.

DI 5. We defined a game story that motivates the users in playing, moreover, to gain points, he/she needs to correctly classify the animals' calls and solve riddles.

DI 6. To assess the user's credibility, we embedded credibility tests inside the game flow, challenging the user in classifying sounds that have been already correctly labelled. In this way, we can assess the user's credibility and using this value to weight the player's input.

The gameplay (for both the games scenarios) would unfold as shown in Fig. 1. Accordingly, we used the MDA (Mechanics-Dynamics-Aesthetics) framework [7] to design the games in term of mechanisms, dynamics and aesthetics and created wireframes accordingly.

5   The Evaluation

5.1   Methodology

We evaluate our concept ideas through an experience prototyping (EP) session, using a mixed methods approach to collect data during and after the experience, performing observations, personal interviews (qualitative data) and asking participants to answer a questionnaire (quantitative and quantitative data). We only tested the location-based version for the games as the online one was still being designed.

We engaged 14 young-adults ranging from 21 to 30 (7 females and 7 males), 7 participants for each game scenario. We organized the EP session in the local University Biodiversity garden, rich in plants and animals, representing a perfect location for our game experience. In particular, we focused on the animals that inhabit that environment, such as a *Red-footed maderensis* falcon (for sound classification), a *Podarcis muralis* lizard and a *Hipparchia maderensis* butterfly (associated to the specific plants). The experience prototype was constructed as a mix of paper prototypes of the interfaces (see Figs. 2 and 3) and researcher's intervention as a Wizard of Oz style. Each session lasted an average time of 15 min. The researcher conducting the session acted as a storytelling voice (i.e., the scientist) assisting the user while playing. Two further researchers assisted in documenting the session and conducting interviews: one was taking pictures while the other was taking observation notes and performed the interviews, after each user's session.

To test both the gameplays, we defined two tasks to accomplish for both scenarios: (i) wandering in the park to find a certain animal, following the "future scientist character's" hints, and then, classifying its sound (sound samples of that animal were released on location); (ii) finding a specific plant that, in the game was able to attract a specific animals. These activities allow the player to collect animals' sounds samples and accomplish the game goal, accordingly with the game scenario (S 1 or S 2). We randomly assigned one scenario for the experience prototype to each participant, and, in the end, we explained the mechanics of the other scenario.

At the end of each session, we interviewed the participants. We asked them seven questions, regarding the scope, the value, the mechanics, the touchpoints, the visual elements, the language and terminology used in the game experience, and suggestions to improve it. After the experience, we sent participants an online questionnaire. The questionnaire included a few general questions (name, gender, age, education); two questions about their game behaviour (how often they play and motivation for playing); five items related to interest in nature and hiking; three items related to the experience prototype session.

Fig. 2. The paper prototyping wireframes for the experience prototyping of S 2.

Fig. 3. Pictures captured during the experience prototype session.

5.2   Discussion

From the analysis of all the data collected (real-time observations and photographs, the brief interviews and the questionnaires) we can conclude that all the participants have visibly enjoyed the experience prototyping session. This is documented in the pictures taken during the trial, as users' smiles, laughter and having fun expressions (as shown in Fig. 3). Moreover, the written accounts of the observations also support this data, for example, one observer noted: *The player looks amazed and she looks around with enthusiasm ... When she found the animal in the point of interest, she laughed and exclaimed "Awesome!"*. Users found the game interesting, easy to play and with a clear scope, independently from the scenario played. This was documented through the interviews, and questionnaires. Looking into the qualitative data, confirmation of users' enjoyment can be found in the following sentences. A user claimed: *"It felt like a fun way to explore an area and learn about the fauna, and will probably help identify animals after using it"*. Another one affirmed: *"I appreciate the experience, so I'm curious about the final application. I think that was interesting and at the same time didactic"*. Moreover, when queried about the possibility to continue to play with the game, a user answered: *"Yes! Because it keeps me motivated and that is an interesting/different point of view"*. So, overall, we can assume that the game captured quite a majority of not "hard-core game players" in engaging with the game.

50% of users declared that they will like to play the game once fully implemented, while another 35% reported that they are not sure, but if asked they would try it. This information becomes of interest if correlated with the users' personal data, which tell us that the engaged participants are not hard game player (in fact, none of the users plays every day, and the majority of them play one per month or less). In this context, we take encouragement in having engaged non-core players in game activities as this is in line with our overall purpose of influencing biodiversity awareness and care for nature in a general population of young adults.

Regarding the game interactions, the most appreciated features were discovery and the creation of new species. In fact, some users appreciated the *"discovering the animals through sound"*, other appreciated the possibility of *"creating a new species"*. Moreover, the topic of the game itself was greatly appreciate. In fact, one user claimed: *"The topic is very interesting and warns about the consequences of what is happening today"*.

We also collected some players suggestion on how to improve the game. Suggestions range from adding a multiplayer option to making the story more dramatic and/or more challenging.

6   Conclusion and Future Work

This paper presents the design and a preliminary testing of two scenarios for a mobile game with a purpose (GWAP), aimed to: (i) motivate users in classifying animals sounds, collected with bioacoustic sensors; (ii) educate young users about biodiversity. To design the game, we performed an ideation and a concept refinement session with occasional gamers, digital media and engineers Master and Ph.D. students. Exploiting the MDA framework, we defined the mechanics, dynamics, and aesthetics of the game, using wireframes to sketch the screen interactions. Finally, we evaluated the GWAPs with an experience prototyping session, engaging 14 young-adults, considering the primary target of the game. Results show the interest of the participants in playing and contributing to the data classification. Moreover, users being more informed about local fauna after the game session, they immediately realized the importance of the game for education and biodiversity awareness. This outcome represents a first confirmation of the possibility to use this GWAP for data classification and biodiversity awareness, addressing our objectives. We are now implementing the game for Android OS and we will evaluate it in a real-world study, using data from existing remote acoustic sensors present in different parks across Europe.

References

1. Bell, S., et al.: What counts? Volunteers and their organisations in the recording and monitoring of biodiversity. Biodivers. Conserv. **17**(14), 3443–3454 (2008)
2. Bowser, A., Hansen, D., Preece, J., He, Y., Boston, C., Hammock, J.: Gamifying citizen science: a study of two user groups. In: Proceedings of the Companion Publication of the 17th ACM Conference on Computer Supported Cooperative Work & Social Computing, pp. 137–140. ACM (2014)
3. Buchenau, M., Suri, J.F.: Experience prototyping. In: Proceedings of the 3rd Conference on Designing Interactive Systems: Processes, Practices, Methods, and Techniques, pp. 424–433. ACM (2000)
4. Cardinale, B.J., et al.: Biodiversity loss and its impact on humanity. Nature **486**(7401), 59 (2012)
5. Crutzen, P.J.: The "anthropocene". In: Ehlers, E., Krafft, T. (eds.) Earth System Science in the Anthropocene, pp. 13–18. Springer, Heidelberg (2006). https://doi.org/10.1007/3-540-26590-2_3
6. Duro, D.C., Coops, N.C., Wulder, M.A., Han, T.: Development of a large area biodiversity monitoring system driven by remote sensing. Prog. Phys. Geogr. **31**(3), 235–260 (2007)
7. Hunicke, R., LeBlanc, M., Zubek, R.: MDA: a formal approach to game design and game research. In: Proceedings of the AAAI Workshop on Challenges in Game AI, vol. 4, p. 1722 (2004)
8. Joly, A., Goëau, H., Champ, J., Dufour-Kowalski, S., Müller, H., Bonnet, P.: Crowdsourcing biodiversity monitoring: how sharing your photo stream can sustain our planet. In: Proceedings of the 2016 ACM on Multimedia Conference, pp. 958–967. ACM (2016)
9. Moore, J.W.: The capitalocene, part i: on the nature and origins of our ecological crisis. J. Peasant. Stud. **44**(3), 594–630 (2017)
10. Paulos, E., Honicky, R., Hooker, B.: Citizen science: enabling participatory urbanism. In: Handbook of Research on Urban Informatics: The Practice and Promise of the Real-Time City, pp. 414–436. IGI Global (2009)
11. Pereira, H.M., Cooper, H.D.: Towards the global monitoring of biodiversity change. Trends Ecol. Evol. **21**(3), 123–129 (2006)
12. Prandi, C., Mirri, S., Ferretti, S., Salomoni, P.: On the need of trustworthy sensing and crowdsourcing for urban accessibility in smart city. ACM Trans. Internet Technol. (TOIT) **18**(1), 4 (2017)

13. Prandi, C., Roccetti, M., Salomoni, P., Nisi, V., Nunes, N.J.: Fighting exclusion: a multimedia mobile app with zombies and maps as a medium for civic engagement and design. Multimed. Tools Appl. **76**(4), 4951–4979 (2017)
14. Schmeller, D.S., et al.: Advantages of volunteer-based biodiversity monitoring in Europe. Conserv. Biol. **23**(2), 307–316 (2009)
15. Von Ahn, L., Dabbish, L.: Designing games with a purpose. Commun. ACM **51**(8), 58–67 (2008)
16. Zilli, D., Parson, O., Merrett, G.V., Rogers, A.: A hidden Markov model-based acoustic cicada detector for crowdsourced smartphone biodiversity monitoring. J. Artif. Intell. Res. **51**, 805–827 (2014)

To Design with Strings for Playability in Cities

Annika Olofsdotter Bergström[✉][iD]

Blekinge Institute of Technology, 374 35 Pirgatan, Karlshamn, Sweden
aob@bth.se

Abstract. This paper explores how Donna Haraway's "String Figuration" together with Maria Puig de la Bellacasa's concept of "touch" as a design method have worked in the process of an augmented reality (AR) play called Play/ce. The aim of this paper is to propose that designers of playful cities are creating the conditions for playability to show how players can try out and play with responses in a city by different acts of touch. I suggest that responding, which comes from the act of relaying, is part of designing 'games as a social technologies', a concept from Mary Flanagan. I will develop this concept since I think it is especially interesting to take into account when it comes to using cities as playgrounds and turn people into full body players to explore what touch means.

Keywords: Playability · Responding · Social technology · Touch
String figure · City

1 Introduction

This paper explores how Haraway's String Figuration [1] together with Puig de la Bellacasa's concept of touch [2] as a design method has worked in the process of an augmented reality (AR) play called Play/ce. The aim of this paper is to propose that designers of playful cities are creating the conditions for playability of how players can try out and play with responses in a city.

The idea of playability opens up for responding to the city as a self-organized system [3] rather than a fixed entity and asking questions for how to design games (playfulness) as social technologies, a concept from Flanagan [4]. The emphasis on the social is especially interesting to take into account when using cities as playgrounds and turn people into full body players by practicing how cities could become playable when negotiating with its constraints and what might be possible [5].

Play/ce, which is still in progress during 2018, is a collaborative project with focus on playing and exploring an urban space. So far seven design activities, which will be explained in Sect. 5, is the start of forming an AR play for mobile phones. The work with Play/ce is an investigation in how to design a playable city by re-interpreting its system by different technologies of touch and to find the hidden narratives of play and meaning of the place [6]. Puig de la Bellacasa's [2] concept of touch, deepens the knowledge of how bodies can create relations with cities and enhance the concept of play as a social technology. When playing with a city, the playing body is constantly encountering different physical objects and surfaces in the city which the body resists

A. L. Brooks et al. (Eds.): ArtsIT 2018/DLI 2018, LNICST 265, pp. 256–265, 2019.

[7]. In these physical encounters, norms and representations of places transforms into motion and meanings, and patterns of the places are changed or at least challenged. Playability in Play/ce questions fixed meanings of the city spaces. Instead of seeing objects and situations as games we can see them as playable and thereby explore the meaning of the limitations [5] of the physical bodies and the fixed materials of cities.

2 Play Through the String Figure

The cultural theorist Donna Haraway uses the string figure (cat's cradle) as a figuration for knowledge-making and world-making among other practices [1]. To play with string figures is a relaying practice [1], a passing on but also a receiving of threads to stretch or bend. It can be a collective play, with several players passing the string figures back and forth adding something new or proposing something else [1]. In my work the string figure as a practice puts focus on responding, which is an act of giving and receiving and the string figure making often comes from unexpected collaborations of players and combinations of the string [1].

For this paper I will transfer the string into the idea of the indefinite AR play for mobile phones, this is what we had at hand from the start. The string figures that will emerge as soon as the picking and passing of the string are initiated are in the paper transferred into seven different design practices which will later on lead to the final design of the AR play. Utilising Haraway's figuration the'making and analyzing', has resulted in an entangled practice of various positions which are expanding and questioning the public space and changing the perception of it. From working with the figuration it has been clear that relaying is an invitation *to* respond and explore *how* to respond, which can be expressed in various playful ways when using the body as a (touching) sensor. The practice of relaying, to make something to pass on for someone else to perceive and continue, creates a connectedness between players as well as between players and the city.

The response of each design practice which leads to another, is what Haraway calls "response-ability, the collective knowing and doing in an ecology of practices" [8, p. 34]. This ability to respond, which in Play/ce is the collective practices of everyday life and physical matters in a city, becomes a shared experience of rules, behaviors, norms, taboos and possibilities. The response can also become a proposal and invention of new patterns [8] open up for the possibility to connect with a stranger or break a norm for what to do in a place, like walking backwards on the train platform. The response-ability as a collective practice, to play, is to be accountable [8] for relating to a city and its inhabitants and questioning how we can be more connected with one another.

3 The Vision of Touch

Touch is an often neglected sensorial universe since vision has been the dominant conveyor in modern knowledge amassment and concrete conditions [2]. Digitized technology has been focusing on visual experiences where increasingly more advanced graphics cards and resolutions have been the goal, meanwhile touch technologies also have evolved rapidly, something Bill Gates calls "the age of digital senses" [2, p. 302]. Puig de la Bellacasa suggests that the haptic technologies are very much about gadget sprouts expectations of innovation which tends to 'mimic the real thing' [2, p. 32]. Instead she wants to turn to how to enhance everyday experiences which is for me intriguing when designing playable cities. We constantly touch our everyday surroundings with our bodies, both physically but also by feeling the sensations stimulated by all our senses [2].

I see the body as a sensory device which plays with the environmental inputs like buildings, other human bodies, materials of the city, the wind and light. Touching as an activity embody the materials of the city and create reassessments of relationships [2]. In extension this contributes ideas about how we could relate to your world, technology, our bodies and everyday practices [2]. To touch is to relate and to create a relationship with the surrounings.

4   The Everyday Life Technology

A part of designing playability in cities includes how play can be a social technology [4] and how this social technology can help create a relation to a city when perceiving objects and situations as playable [5]. When designing play in the city as a practice or situation, the materials of the city has to be considered as the factor which pushes the development of the play forward [7] and has to take into account the network of humans, non-humans, spacing, timing, contexts and imaginations [9]. Flanagan does not go so much further into how social technology is developed and how it is functioning except that play has the ability to distinguish or abstract everyday actions [4]. The notion of everyday practices is what play designers have to defy to expand the full range of every- day life activities to research the area of playable cities.

Play as social technology embraces the social and cultural networks of a city. How does a city work? What makes a city? Who are in relations with whom, or what? Who are excluded from which networks? The focus of my work is daily life, or to be more precise, the daily movements and the activities which are performed, or not, in public places. What happens with the daily movements and activities when speculating about alternative possible practices and actions in a city? How to get out of the daily routines, like walking to and from the bus station, by the inquisitive question, what if? What if I shake hands with every person I meet on the street? As a designer perceiving players' bodies as sensors I suddenly have a lot of opportunities to play with a whole range of senses and experiences. To be in touch with the city opens up for other ways of playing and being playful. It becomes an embodied experience and moreover embodied knowledge of the city. It is also possible to see these kinds of plays, which Stenros, Montola, and Björk call 'ambient games', like games that are activated when the player wants to play and highlight the players actions in everyday life, which in turn influence the playing [10]. This spatially expanding playfulness uses the city as it is always running in the background, with the possibility to tap in at any moment [10]. To see the city as an ambient playground is to open up to engagement in every day moments and situations and to play with situated responses.

5 Play/ce, a Play in Progress

5.1 Background

Play/ce has the outspoken goal of achieving participation in a city planning process and a set collaboration with the municipality and its city planning office. Even if the project has not finished, it can still show a pattern of the experimental proposal for designing a playable city. The project is a collaboration with Blekinge Institute of Technology, and the municipality of Karlshamn in south east of Sweden. The aim of the project from the municipality perspective is to get more youths to express their opinions about the planning of a city since few young people are involved in the city planning process. The municipality tried summer 2017 together with the youth council, a Minecraft camp, to get more engagement in the city planning process. The initiative was not very successful due to technical issues the youths faced when adapting a real city area into the engine. The participants also had problems working independently to find motivation for problem solving and they experienced working with Minecraft dull and monotonous. The fact that the youths did not explore the physical area until very late in the project, created a distance to the environment and how it was experienced. There were no female participants in the project.

Since I am interested in what designing playfulness in public places actually mean and what these kinds of play do to the players, non-players and the city, my approach to the Play/ce project was to combine the physical world with the digital to explore how these two approaches could benefit from each other. Rather than focusing on building Karlshamn in a digital game like Minecraft, which require a lot of time and focus in front of a computer, I wanted to consider another technological solution, to approach a mix of different technologies, both physical and digital, to explore the physical city. During a conversation with a technically skilled colleague, who also became part of the project, he saw that an AR solution for the smart phone could be the solution we were looking for to get away from a to fixed computerized world. To sit in front of a computer to plan a future city is contradictory when relating to playability, touch and body as a sensor. Smartphones are also under development to become "prime loci for digital mapping practices" and the creation of spatial stories to pattern the everyday movements [11]. To this mapping other practices can be added, which is not only about locations but about sensations and touching. The mobility of the phone gives the possibility to combine both digital and physical technologies influenced by touching and responding with the digital and the physical world.

5.2 String and String Figures in Playce

The string loop for Play/ce is the idea of the AR play. We do not know how the play, the final combination, at the moment made from seven design practices, will be experienced or how it will work out but we do have this string to figure it out. When draping the string over the hands the design process starts. The idea is to let the play design emerge from different design practices to follow up on each one to see what emerges. It is a slow and sometimes frustrating process since the eagerness to know or at least imagine the final result can sometimes take over. It is not about me as a designer

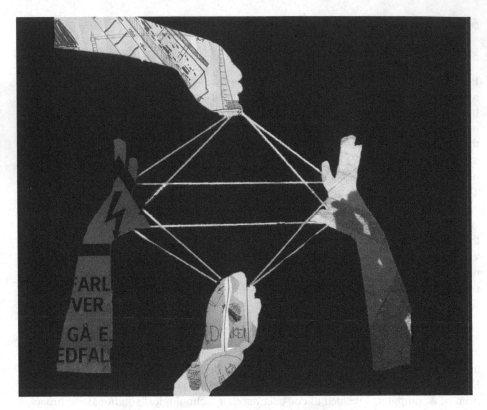

Fig. 1. String figure game Picture by the author.

or researcher but about the collective "knowing and making" [8] slowly becoming a part of the city through everyday practices and experiences.

The seven different design practices/string figures, so far, which has started to shape the combination for Play/ce, have been a practice of relaying in the sense that different players, in different constellations have participated from time to time. It was not planned from the beginning but since all the players (young women in the age 15–17) have been busy with school and sport activities, it turned out to be the best solution for the project. In the next Section I will explain the seven design practices with different technologies of touch and how they follow on each other.

5.3 Mapping

When a city is the playground a convenient start could be to take a map to see its shape and structure of streets, buildings and in between spaces.

In order to situate ourselves in the city of Karlshamn, the first string figure to emerge when picking up the string was to jointly draw a map over the city. By mapping important places like home, school, library, café, and how each and every one of us moved around in the city on a daily basis, an emotional map appeared. Usually maps are used to understand and grasp a city but when drawing your own map it becomes more emotional and not just a graphic representation of the spatial understanding [12]. Maps are a set of codes and conventions that follow cultural, political and even ideological interests, and for a map to be useful it must offer a categorization of the real world [12]. To draw your own map is a highly subjective but nonetheless situated act to get an image of how young women perceive their city, disrupting the coherence of the planned city and open up for possibilities which showed an alternative taxonomy [12]. The drawing did not only become a pattern of young women's movements, orientations and what places they found valuable for their daily life and socializing, but the drawing also broke the conventions of what a map looks like and how it represent a city. Now the map showed favorite places like the library, the shopping mall and home in a non - representational way and added an invisible story about the issues between youths and their communities, which was marked as symbols for telling about for example a big fight outside the MacDonald restaurant. The vivid storytelling about everyday life through the drawing gave a new layer of experiencing a more sensorial map of embodied knowledge.

5.4 Walking

The experience of the mapping was not enough, so to be more in touch with the map the new pull of the string gave an alternative drawing of the map, this time with the body, by walking. Walking as an act to explore a city is well known from Baudelaire with his idea of the 'flaneur' and from the Situationists with their 'derivé'. The concepts have during decades been widely used by artists and game developers [4]. When becoming aware of our surroundings the walk can generate an embodied engagement with the surroundings [13], a sensing of the physical resistance as surfaces, traces, and marks that the body creates. Walking creates an active engagement through the perceptual and the material in the landscape [13]. From drawing a representation of the spatial understanding to an embodied action, the drawn lines expanded the spatiality of the city. To move through the physical environment, which on the map is plotted in various lines in different colors, is like turning its symbols into lived experiences by using the body as a sensor. Our first place to visit was a secret spot upon the big tunnel leading in to town, through a rock, sheltered but also vulnerable because of its distance to people. When reaching the top, it was obvious that from above the rather small town gave the impression of being bigger through a bird's eye view. One of the players recorded the sound and we all agreed that the traffic noise below, from a distance gave the impression of a far bigger city. Shifting from looking to listening the experience of the city expanded our embodied knowledge.

5.5 Placing

The combination of mapping and walking, gave the feeling of too much drifting, and to not risk to lose the players' interest, I took the decision to choose one site to work closer with. The municipality had in earlier meetings expressed an interest in the train station, which was undergoing plans for a combined housing and station development.

A train station is a transfer of people and when spending time there it was obvious that the area in many ways was a non- place, a place which is not relational, have no identity or is historical [14]. People pass it to depart or arrive with trains or busses, coming and going. By inviting two architects to come and have a conversation about the station area my idea was to see how they wanted to continue the relay of the non-place which had emerged. One of the architects told us how she had when commuting, continually photographed her feet leaning on the bench while waiting for the train. A photo sequence showing different shoes, different lights. From the story the waiting as an activity emerged, and sparked us to think what kind of touching activities could be possible to do while waiting.

5.6   Photographing

When asking ourselves how to turn a non-place to a place of content, to sense it differently, while waiting, the starting point was to pay attention to all the details of the area, details that at first did not seem to matter at all but when noticing began to come into play. By taking photos with our phones, details were traced and caught. First some of the players thought it was odd to take photos of the station but when a player suddenly saw themes like shadows, squares, green colors, trash, writings, and circles, the act of photographing turned the eye sight into touch to get the experience of the materials in the area [2]. The countless chewing gums traded into the asphalt became secret marks leading to somewhere specific. The close up details of things that otherwise had been invisible now emerged with its fabrics, outlines, colors, and importance of giving the station area its specifics. Very soon the feeling of familiar became more noticeable and we ended up with hundreds of pictures.

5.7   Combining

The photographs opened up to a place of new emotions and meanings [15] but the pictures were scattered pieces of the station with no internal coherence. How to put the place together again but this time with emotions rather than representation? One player suggested a collage to fit the pictures together as a jigsaw and by putting the pictures together while asking what each picture does to the other, a pattern of the station area emerged. Obviously, it was a rather grey area with only some solitary color dots like the red ticket machine, the yellow post box and the green grass growing between the paving-stones. There were not many circles in the station area except from the manhole covers, the big pots with planted flowers, signs, and buttons on the ticket machine. There were more squares, like doors, boxes, house, windows, and ventilation gaps and straight lines showing directions. The string figure was a collage over the station area with details that have been unseen and untouched until now. The details did not reveal much activity.

5.8   Adding

From the absence of activity in the station the following discussion was about actions and practices. What if activities were added to the collage? We started to cut out pictures from different magazines of people and animals doing things, like running, cooking, gardening, kissing, caring, drinking, sporting, washing, talking, cheering and even slaughtering a sheep. When adding these pictures into the silent and still collage, the train station now turned into a far more exciting place, more livable and active. A space of potentials and speculations. Could it be possible to play sports in front of the station house? What if people washed their clothes and hanged them on strings? Could strangers meet on the staircase over a cup of coffee and share their dreams and desires? All possible activities were raised from the new collage as an alternative world-making process [2].

5.9 Acting

The adding and speculating of activities reminded us that places have rules in themselves which could possibly be linked to different activities. What practices were already waiting for the player to activate? When returning to the area we found the rules dominating the train station were the visual signs of prohibitions or warnings like, 'don't smoke', 'watch out for trains.' There were also invisible rules, 'how to sit on a bench', 'how to wait in the lounge'. What if our group cheered people as a welcome when arriving with the train? When the train arrived, we cheered the passengers and got responses of surprise or confusion. We discussed what it felt like breaking an invisible rule and the common reaction was that as a collective it felt much easier to do so. After tweaking other invisible rules like walking backwards back and forth on the platform and start talking to strangers, we discussed what new rules to add. One player from Syria wanted a rule which says: 'Speak Swedish with me', since she never got the chance to learn Swedish. The embodied experience of making new rules opened up for opinions of how to expand the relation with the station to create more encounters.

6 Play as a Social Technology

In this paper I have proposed that designers of playful cities are creating the conditions for playability in which players can try out and play with responses in a city and its materials. By using Haraway's 'string figure' together with Puig de la Bellacasa's concept 'touch', as a design method I have shown how the practice of responding in the process of Play/ce opens up for multiple technologies, behaviors, wishes and practices.

These responding connections craft conditions [1] where different experiences and knowledges can expand and shape various possible cities. The city means different things to different people, or even further, have no meaning at all, for example some of the players from Syria and Somalia did not even know what city they lived in since they mostly stay in their housing area when not being in school. There are women of all ages and nationalities who do not want to walk in cities when its dark and after the stores are closed. Cities are often depicted to counter women's needs and desires [16]. To play with only women reveals what is not working in a city, that women in all ages do very often feel insecure in public places, that men take bigger part in public and that some places excludes women in fear of sexual harassments [16]. The city is not an open playground, it is very much predefined by city planners, imposed by hierarchies and various social relations.

How can playability in a city become "respons-ability", playing with relaying practices where the collective knowing and doing [8] but also previous experiences, are generating new string figures for others to respond to? The process of Play/ce has shown several examples of how play is a way of testing the city's unknown and hidden systems, and how to speculate about responses while trying them out. For example, the player who wanted a sign in the station, which says "Talk Swedish with me" made her desire outspoken but also pointed to the fact that very few people talked Swedish with her. This in turn led to another player to sit down with a stranger on a bench and start talking.

Relaying is a constantly changing practice which do not preserve one player's ideas or concerns but connects combinations of experiences and desires which creates unexpected responses. Playing in the city becomes a way to negotiate with what already is there and to consider alternative relations by re-configuring rules and behaviors in an urban area. To design playability with the embodied player is undoubtedly to challenge the principles of how to live, behave, relate, move, share and connect in an everyday city [17]. Play as a social technology is to enable relaying. It is to design for giving and receiving of manifold collective responses for learning how to live with others and become able to respond for the becoming of a city [2] as a playful and flexible system of belonging.

The process of Play/ce will continue in the autumn of 2018.

Acknowledgments. I want to thank everyone involved in the making of Play/ce so far, my co-researchers Pirjo Elovaara and Cecilia Barry, Jonas Svegland for technical expertise, the municipality of Karlshamn, the youth council and in particular the players who have contributed with their time and ideas to make the best out of the work.

References

1. Haraway, D.: A game of cat's cradle: science studies, feminist theory, cultural studies. Configurations **2**(1), 59–71 (1994)
2. Puig de la Bellacasa, M.: Touching technologies, touching visions. The reclaiming of sensorial experience and the politics of speculative thinking. Subjectivity **28**(1), 297–315 (2009)
3. Tan, E.: Play the City. Jap Sam Books, Heijningen (2017)
4. Flanagan, M.: Critical Play: Radical Game Design. MIT Press, Cambridge (2009)
5. Bogost, I.: Play Anything: The Pleasure of Limits, the Uses of Boredom, and the Secrets of Games. Basic Books, New York (2016)
6. Walther, B.K.: Pervasive game spaces. Gameplay out in the open. In: Space, Time Play. Computer Games, Architecture and Urbanism: The Next Level, pp. 290–304. Birkhäuser, Basel (2007)
7. Nilsson, E.: Arkitekturens kroppslighet. Staden som terräng. Ph.D. thesis, Lund University, Lund, Sweden (2010)
8. Haraway, D.: Staying with the Trouble: Making Kin in the Chthulucene. Duke University Press, Durham (2016)

9. Mackenzie, A.: Transduction: intervention, innovation and collective life (2003). http://www.lancaster.ac.uk/staff/mackenza/papers/transduction.pdf. Accessed 12 May 2018
10. Stenros, J., Montola, M., Björk, S.: Designing temporal expansion. In: Pervasive Games, pp. 97–110. Morgan Kaufmann, San Francisco (2009)
11. Lammes, S.: Digital cartographies as playful practices. In: Playful Identities: The Ludification of Digital Media Cultures, pp. 199–211. Amsterdam University Press (2015)
12. Harley, J.B., Woodward, D.: The History of Cartography 1, xvi (1987)
13. Ingold, T.: Lines: A Brief History. Routledge, Abingdon (2007)
14. Augé, M.: Non-places an introduction to the anthropology of supermodernity. Verso, London/New York (1995)
15. Bell, V.: Photo-image. In: Inventing Methods. The Happening of the Social, pp. 147–163. Paperback, London, New York (2014)
16. Listerborn, C.: Trygg stad: diskurser om kvinnors rädsla i forskning, policyveckling och lokal praktik. Chalmers tekniska högskola, Thesis. Chalmers tekniska högskola. Göteborg (2002)
17. Montola, M., Stenros, J., Waern, A.: Designing spatial expansion. In: Pervasive Games, pp. 77–90. Morgan Kaufman, San Francisco (2009)

A Storytelling Smart-City Approach to Further Cross-Regional Tourism

Nicolas Fischöder[1]([⊠]), Ido A. Iurgel[1], Tonguç I. Sezen[1], and Koen van Turnhout[2]

[1] Rhine-Waal University, 47475 Kamp-Lintfort, Germany
nfo@hochschule-rhein-waal.de
[2] HAN University of Applied Sciences, 6826 CC Arnhem, Netherlands
Koen.vanTurnhout@han.nl

Abstract. Museums are crucial elements of regional and local cultural offerings and can play a major role in tourism-related, educational, economical and urban-planning policies. To increase visitor numbers and thus further cultural exchange between regions and economical profit, we provide insight to a storytelling-based smart-city approach that routes users between the age of 14–25 years across 8 museums along the Dutch-German border using both Informations and communications technology (ICT) and gamification as part of the Rhhijnland.Xperiences project. Creating an appealing user-experience is a key-objective as the users motivation to continue his journey between the museums will highly depend on it. Each visit at one location facilitates the longing for visiting the next museum in the network. This approach is applicable to various other sets of institutions or points-of-interest (POI). The project itself is yet in a development stage and its product will be released by 2020.

Keywords: Museum digitalization · Smart-cities
Intercultural exchange · Mobile technology · Museum devices
Story-telling

1 Introduction

Engaging citizens and fostering educational and cultural offerings among cities using ICT can be described as a Smart-City's key-objectives. In 2010, 41 % of all estimated 9.92 million foreign tourists that traveled to the Netherlands have visited at least one museum [2]. With a total of 14 Million visitors expected in 2020, museums play a key role in city's tourism and thus economical policies up to marketing and urban planning strategies [2]. Since the increase and preservation of visitor numbers has beneficial effects on a cities' cultural awareness and economy [2], the attraction of visitors is desirable. As part of the Rhijnland.Xperiences (RLX) project [4,6], we provide a smart-city approach that aspires to boost visitor numbers by routing visitors between a set of 8 museums

A. L. Brooks et al. (Eds.): ArtsIT 2018/DLI 2018, LNICST 265, pp. 266–275, 2019.
https://doi.org/10.1007/978-3-030-06134-0_31

across the Dutch-German borders using ICT paired with challenges in forms of riddles and mini-games. This approach can be applied to other public sectors as well. Applying digital technology to enhance museum visits itself is not a novel approach. Especially in the current decade, with the rise of high-performance mobile-computing public institutions such as museums already provide digital experiences to successfully engage a wider audience [3]. However, utilizing digital technologies to draw users across interregional POIs using ICT raises specific issues as themes and experiences of POIs may vary as well as the expectations and skills of a broad audience. To escalate the motivation to visit multiple locations, story-telling methodologies are being established and applied to maintain an engaging experience. However, the thematic diversity and the user-determined sequence of museum visits requires the creation of an flexible narrative structure. A focus on the target audience, which primarily aims at youngsters between the age of 14 to 25 years, requires additional consideration, as well. Therefore, user research must be conducted and both the story and the game-play of the individual games have to meet the interests of those that match the target audience. Since smart-phones are a wide-spread ICT among youngsters in western cultures [7] it appears coherent to deploy the story and games on smart-phone devices in form of a mobile-application. Aside an engaging story, the experience is also defined by the games and visual design that is used to keep the user motivated [10]. For each museum, the system can include interaction with stationary devices to supply the user with a more diverse amount of challenges or screen-based and AR-based games. This paper focuses primarily on tackling the challenges mentioned above and describing the designated smart-phone implementation, whose games can range from puzzle games, up to Beat-Em-Up mechanics and beacon-controlled events as stationary devices are still in conception. The project is mainly financed by the European Union's Interreg program and the project's partners. Together with Erfgoed Gelderland, Rhine-Waal University of Applied Sciences in Germany, HAN University of Applied Sciences in Holland and the 8 participating museums:

- Museum Arnhem (Arnhem, Netherlands)
- Openlucht Museum (Arnhem, Netherlands)
- National Bevrijdings Museum (Groesbeek, Netherlands)
- Geldersch Lanschap Kasteelen (Ammerzoden, Netherlands)
- Museum Schloss Moyland (Bedburg-Hau, Germany)
- Museum Kurhaus Kleve (Kleve, Germany)
- Museum Goch (Goch, Germany)
- Archeologischer Park Xanten (Xanten, Germany).

Due to the large amount of stakeholders, clear and constant communication remains a mandatory feature during the conception and the development, as well as during marketing. Therefore, constant meetings are held to ensure the state of knowledge regarding the projects state, goals and concepts.

2   Related Work

Over the current decade ICT has become more prominent in the cultural sector. Ranging from applications that route users between regional points of interest up to VR-museum tours for home usage, mobile- and CG-technology has been successfully used to peak people's interest in visiting cultural institutions.

In 2013, the National museum of Scotland launched its *Capture the museum* application. Within that application visitors can join one of two teams who's goal is to claim virtual territory by solving puzzles and other virtual challenges within the museum space using AR-technologies.

In the scope of the RLX project Jacobs et al. have previously outlined vital aspects of the designated application to provide enhanced museum experiences, such as mixed-reality blended experiences [4], co-creation with the stakeholders, story-lines to connect museums, museum infrastructure and visitors devices. Moreover, Jacobs et al. present its novel 1-10-100 method for concept creation involving multiple stakeholders [4]. Additionally, Kahl et al. have already described the Rhijnland.Xperiences project at an earlier stage, outlining user- and business requirements, as well as requirements to the storyline [6].

The CHESS project, conducted extensive research in the application of mobile technologies and storytelling in the museum sector. One of the main focus points of the project was the attempt to prioritize the focus from "exhibit-centric, information-loaded descriptions, to story-centric narrations with references to the exhibits" [6]. One of the difficulties to overcome during the project was to create appealing mobile applications through the use of exploratory activities, an adaptive game-experience and AR-representations of cultural artifacts wrapped in a drama-based storytelling approach. As the visitor enters one of the enhanced museums, an introduction to the story is revealed and exhibit- and theme based episodes are presented to direct the user towards exhibits using narration and on-screen instructions on the users' devices. After all exhibits have been visited, the experiences closes with an end to the story. Based on an earlier paper [6] which is describing this project in an earlier stage, we present a more accurate outline of the content or storytelling-aspects that are being applied within the project.

3   Requirements

3.1   General Requirements

One of the project's main factors to consider is the target audience. Therefore, user-centered design methodologies such as design thinking, prototypes, user-surveys and focus groups have been applied. Based on existing research we already determined that to enhance the museum experience for youngsters our application should include non-monotonous experiences, games and location based technologies. In addition during prototyping, we found that participants enjoy the possibility to scan for objects as part of a trial, while some did not approve of traversing the museum by literally jumping back and forth between different floors. Therefore we found that the user's route has to be linear, in a manner that no exhibition has to be visited twice. In focus-group sessions with the stakeholders, we found that although the designated audience consists of 14–25 year-olds, we should not loose sight of older and more-experienced visitors, as well. While the implementation of a cartoon-like and futuristic-looking core-design and mini-games clearly addresses younger visitors, the incorporation of a stimulating storyline might aid in creating an appealing experience for visitors above the target age as well. Finding the right balance in the difficulty and complexity inside the mini-games is a major challenge. While younger visitors might easily understand complex game-mechanics from games that they played on video-consoles, older visitors would find these mechanics possibly not as intuitive [11]. The audience should have the possibility to start from every museum, which requires a modular storyline approach that is yet linear. Ideas of an interactive storyline have been suspended due to the complexity of 8 museums that are diversely themed and the tight project life-span. Within our user requirements we found that stories dialogs should be context-sensitive and incorporate the route of the user inside the museum.

3.2 Technical Requirements

The wide spread of smart-phones especially amongst youngsters along with the increasing performance, high mobility and ICT capabilities convinces us to choose a mobile-application as our main-platform. The application is complemented by a set of stationary installations such as interactive kiosks. Each of the 8 locations raised different technical challenges: For example, the Museum Schloss Moyland does not provide any internet-access while Archeologischer Park Xanten does not qualify for the use of beacons [12]. Another technical but not yet as obvious limitation is the spatial size of the exhibition and the battery capacity of mobile devices. Especially the computational efforts of AR-Based games can rapidly deplete energy resources. Without any additional power-supply, the duration of these particular experiences may not be overextended. The time of game-play has been limited to maximum of 1 hour, in order to conserve the power of the player's cellphone.

Also, the size of the application on the device must be taken into account as many youngsters can not afford consuming large bandwidths and most museums do not offer free internet-access. We consider implementing a modular location-based data-structure in combination with pre-download features for that matter. These limitations must be kept in consideration to meet the requirement of accessibility at every location. Another technical key-aspect is interchangeable content that goes hand in hand with a modular structure: In case one exhibit has to be replaced with another one modularity and specialized authoring software is required for the museum administration to adept the experience. As a fall-back, it is possible to restrict the application to permanent exhibition pieces.

Performance of smart-phones is a key-factor that is crucial to the application accessibility. High resolution 3D-Models combined with expensive game-mechanics and AR-features can overburden the device's capabilities which results in a poor user-experience. For the release date in January 2020 we consider smartphones such as the currently wide-spread Samsung Galaxy S7 as *prev-gen* and will gear up to its specifications to provide a balance between graphically appealing and yet slightly backwards-compatible graphics without oversizing the application.

4   Story-Framework

4.1   Storymodules

As stated earlier, the story is kept in a modular fashion allowing a linear storyline which adepts according to the order in which the user visits a museum. The main events stay the same at the end of each chapter, while the location differs. Our framework can be subdivided into three module-types. The overall linear story of the game is divided into story fragments that we name Universal-Story-Modules (USM). All USMs are however, fairly unrelated to the currently visited museum. To connect the story with the locations we utilize Local-Story-Modules (LSM) that tell a location-specific story that triggers progression of the USMs upon completion. Each LSM consists of Mission-Modules (MM) which are puzzles and games that are tied to exhibits and other POIs inside a museum.

4.2   Narrative Design and Challenges

As stated earlier, creating an appealing and applicable storyline raises several narrative challenges:

- **Thematic diversity of museums:**
  The museum network that includes 8 local museums bears a vast variety of themes, ranging from local art up to historic events of different time-frames. Therefore the story must at least address all of those diverse themes. Our approach of using distinct local story-modules for each module that connect to an overall story-line is one way to tackle this challenge. A selection of entities that are displayed in the museum, either as part of an exhibition or location must be made to create a pool of portals. Each of the portals shall reference the current museums theme and also a theme of its target museum.
- **Multiple entry points:**
  The fact the sequence of museum visits shall be user-defined and therefore allow the user to tackle each museum without any restrictions in order requires a flexible story-pattern. We propose a linear narrative design to reduce complexity in reduction in which details differ according to the order of museum visits. Whereas the dramatic events remain the same the location of the plot changes. As a result, despite a linear storyline each player will achieve a different version of the same story.
- **Irregular progress of the story:**
  Since the challenges to progress in the story are bound to the museum locations, it is conceivable that, depending on the visitors motivation, the continuation of the story will not succeed in regular intervals. This may cause the user

to forget about story-content which might widely affect the user-experience. Therefore, we aim to implement journals in which the player can revise content from past visits. Moreover, the possibility to reset a local story-module's progress also enables the player to repeat the latest events.

For a narrative design we aim to establish a universal structure that can be applied to every museum. A structured and intuitive design structure is vital to the applications user-experience.

In the first step that is processed after the user opens the mobile application inside the museum, a simple check is performed whether the user has already started a local mission in that particular place. If not, the application will check for the current USM and will provide the user with a USM-cut-scene to understand the current context of his museum visit to the global story. Right after the first cut-scene the user is introduced to the current LSM by an additional cut-scene. Subsequently, the user is introduced to an explicit mission module which starts with a short dialogue that is explaining the possible interactions and whereabouts of his next target location which he has to approach. Once the visitor has reached the vicinity of a location, a query is performed whether the location matches the target location of a current mission module. If the correct location has been reached, the mini-game or challenge starts. Upon completion of the challenge the user is introduced to the next mission module (4). If the user has already started a mission module in the current context, he is asked to choose between resetting or continuing his progress. Once the user has completed all the challenges a final cut-scene of the local story module appears and the user is presented with a hyper-portal which directs him to the next museum where the story would continue (Fig. 1).

Fig. 1. An overview of our story-module structure

4.3   Main Plot

In order to utilize the described framework, we established a plot that can be outlined as follows:

The player is invited to become the apprentice of a mysterious women called the trader. The trader is immortal and has the ability to access a hidden layer of reality in museums which is an amalgam of emotion, ideas, and memories left by humans on artistic or historical artifacts and locations. The trader provides an app to the player to interact with this reality and asks her to do missions for her. The earlier missions are legal trade work and require interactions with museum mascots, i.e. helping them, trading with them etc. Later missions seem to be somewhat illegal. The museum mascots warn the player that the trader might have a dangerous hidden agenda. The player is given the mission to track the trader. The player finds out that the trader has been collecting powerful personal memories which may give her the power to destroy the hidden reality. When the trader learns that the player has been spying on her she fires her. The museum mascots start to give The player missions to stop the trader. When competing to collect the final memory it's revealed that the trader actually wanted to end her immortality in a human manner. The museum mascots on the other hand filled with negative emotion from the anger about the trader's plannings now want to obtain all the memories to gain power. The player and the trader face the mascots filled with negative emotions. The trader uses her memories to cleanse the mascots from negativity but in doing so sacrifices herself and dies. As she dies the app slowly looses the ability to access the hidden reality and the player gives his/her farewells to the now healed mascots for the last time.

4.4 Hyperportals

Within the scope of our project, Hyperportals are a key-feature to encourage the user to visit another museum in the network. Hyperportals provide a short but meaningful insight to another museums location and local story-module to promote the user's awareness and interest of other location in the network and thus encouraging further visits. These insights can be provided through real-time video streaming, computer-generated animations and AR-based windows or stationary-devices with video-output. To integrate Hyperportals into the story and the locations in a meaningful manner references both to the story and the locations are imperative. Thus choosing the right object/space to view through the portal is one of the main challenges to further the cause of the user being routed between the museums. For the visual design we aim to create dark-themed portals that provide a sense of mystery that shall spark the user's interest.

4.5 Culture-Caching

Analogically to Geo-caching [13], Culture-caching requires the user to visit various locations and collect virtual objects of cultural significance. With the rise of GPS-capable mobile-technology, app-based geo-caching games have gained prominence. One of the most prominent examples from the current decade is Pokemon-GO in which players can collect virtual creatures and trophies by traveling to points of interest in the real-world. Likewise, editable Geo-Caching applications that enables the implementation of custom stories and trips for hiking events are a wide-spread phenomenon that delight numerous players [13]. For the purpose of our app we adapt the concept of Geo-caching and alter the objects to collect and find to something thematically fitting (e.g. cultural-meaningful). Therefore, instead of being routed between random POIs and collecting virtual monsters and such, the player is supposed to collect virtual historical artifacts from museums that provide a meaning to the cultural and historical background of the location.

5   Game-Mechanics

Throughout the game the player is faced with several challenges in form of mini-games. Those can be enumerated as:

- **Scan for the object (revealing or identifying mechanics):**
  The player has to locate a certain object (e.g. a picture) within a museum space. This is usually aided by a vague description about the object's background. Once the player has located the right object, AR-technology is used to scan the object to finish the challenge. Upon detection "hidden", object-related 3D-content would be revealed to improve the experience. The player then may have the opportunity to interact with the revealed content. During field-testing of prototypes, we have received positive responses by the audience (3 students, age 20–27) and between the age of concerning the enjoyment of these mechanics.
- **Collect or catch the object:**
  One possible interaction would be the collection or catching of an item. For instance, the scan of the right object would reveal a treasure box that emits coins that the player would have to catch in a certain amount of time. Similar mechanics have already been successfully applied in 'Moorhuhn'. A German shooting-game, that captivated millions of players from various generations.
- **Carry and drop the object (object movement mechanics):**
  Another possible interaction mechanic would be the physical moving of an virtual object by oneself. The challenge would be the task to balance the object onto a virtual plate that is hooked into the smart-phones gyroscope. Once the object slides off the plate, the challenge is lost, if the object reaches the destination point, the next challenge, in which the object has to be placed would arise. For instance, the player would have to use swipe-gestures to throw the coins into another container, similar to the popular mechanics of PokemonGO [15].
- **AR-Beat 'em up:**
  Beat 'em ups have been a popular and yet simplistic genre since the 1980s for young and old [8]. Thus, famous games like *Streetfighter*, *Tekken:* or *Dead or Alive* still count as the most famous console franchise. We adopt and combine these mechanics with AR-technology allowing the player to experience a Streetfighter-like experience on any arbitrary real-world surface. Beat 'em Ups, can be described as fighting-games, in which a player controls an avatar that has to defeat his opponents with martial-arts.

- **Pac-Man:**
  As a screen-based solution, we decide to create Pac-Man abbreviations that
  fit into a museum's theme due to its simplicity and popularity. The player
  has to escape from his/her foes on a two-dimensional grid while reaching a
  target aera to win [9].
- **Color-the-Frame:**
  An AR-based game, which is an abbreviation of the revealing or identifying
  mechanics. The player has to find an object via AR such as described above
  and paint is going to shoot out while a museum-themed frame appears around
  the player's screen. Each half is painted in two different colors. Catching the
  color causes the second color to change through mixing the existing color with
  the caught one. Once the player managed to match the first color the player
  has won.
- **Draw-the-silhouette:**
  The player needs to draw a silhouette of an object on the mobile-screen
  with its finger. If done correctly, the player wins. We assume that this game
  mechanic is easy to understand and its mechanic can be reused in every
  museum. Prototypes have proven to be fun during testing.
- **Classic riddles:**
  Riddles with location-themed multiple-choice questions will also be a part of
  our framework. We are not clear yet to provide multiple-choice riddles or allow
  the user to type in results on its own which impacts the riddle's difficulty.

6   Conclusion and Discussion

This paper provides a first glimpse on a smart-city approach that may have
the potential to create a cross-boarder museum experience and thus enhancing
a city's economical and educational state. The usage of mini-games and storytelling (in this case museums) should foster the motivation of youngsters to
traverse places. Games such as *PokemonGO*, have already proven the high potential in that matter. We do not yet have a clear concept on the interface design,
as to the project's early development stage. However, iterative, user-centered
design methodologies are being applied to elaborate on an appealing and intuitive product. The large diversity in technical restrictions between each POI,
requires extensive planning and testing and may cause some game-mechanics to
be left unimplemented at a particular region. The fact that some of the POIs
do not provide any form of internet-connection will require the conceptions of
workarounds. All-in-all, we believe that the foundation on terms of early prototypes and an established framework will provide us with a solid base to build an
appealing and successful product.

References

1. Cesario, V., Matos, S., Redeta, M., Valentina, N.: Designing interactive technologies for interpretive exhibitions: enabling teen participation through user-driven innovation. In: Bernhaupt, R., Dalvi, G., Joshi, A., K. Balkrishan, D., O'Neill, J., Winckler, M. (eds.) INTERACT 2017. LNCS, vol. 10513, pp. 232–241. Springer, Cham (2017). https://doi.org/10.1007/978-3-319-67744-6_16
2. Raemaekers, D.: The Social Significance of Museums, 1st edn. Netherlands Museums Association, Amsterdam (2011)
3. Museums and the Web. https://mw2016.museumsandtheweb.com/paper/virtual-reality-at-the-british-museum-what-is-the-value-of-virtual-reality-environments-for-learning-by-children-and-young-people-schools-and-families/. Accessed 13 July 2018
4. Jacobs, M., van Turnhout, K., Jeurensm, J., Bakker, R.: Two countries, eight museums: aiming for cross-cultural experience blend. In: Lukowicz, P., Krüger, A., Bulling, A., Lim Y., Patel, S. (eds.) Proceedings of the 2016 ACM International Joint Conference on Pervasive and Ubiquitous Computing: Adjunct, pp. 1498–1502. ACM, New York (2016). https://doi.org/10.1145/2968219.2974046
5. Dorward, L., Mittermeier, J., Sandbrook, C., Spooner, F.: Pokémon go: benefits, costs, and lessons for the conservation movement. In: Game, E. (ed.) Conservation Letters, vol. 10, pp. 160–165. Wiley Periodicals (2016). https://doi.org/10.1111/conl.12326
6. Kahl, T., Iurgel, I., Zimmer, F., Bakker, R., van Turnhout, K.: Rheijn-Land.Xperiences – a storytelling framework for cross-museum experiences. In: Nunes, N., Oakley, I., Nisi, V. (eds.) ICIDS 2017. LNCS, vol. 10690, pp. 3–11. Springer, Cham (2017). https://doi.org/10.1007/978-3-319-71027-3_1
7. Campbell, M.: The Impact of the Mobile Phone on Young People's Social Life. Queensland University of Technology, Queensland (2005)
8. Adamo, T.: The Life, Death, and Rebirth of the Beat 'Em Up Genre. https://tiltingatpixels.com/post/beat-em-up-history/. Accessed 3 Sept 2018
9. Riskenm, S.: Pac-Mania: How Pac-Man and Friends Became Pop Culture Icons. Stanford University, Stanford (2002)
10. Røtne, O., Kaptelinin, V.: Design choices and museum experience: a design-based study of a mobile museum app. In: Collazos, C., Liborio, A., Rusu, C. (eds.) CLIHC 2013. LNCS, vol. 8278, pp. 9–13. Springer, Cham (2013). https://doi.org/10.1007/978-3-319-03068-5_3
11. Chesham, A., Wyss, P., Müri, R., Mosimann, U., Nef, T.: What older people like to play: genre preferences and acceptance of casual games. JMIR Serious Games J. 2(5) (2017)
12. Using beacons effectively in museums. http://innovation.mubaloo.com/news/using-beacons-effectively-museums/. Accessed 13 July 2018
13. Ihamäki, P.: Geocaching: interactive communication channels around the game. Eludamos. J. Comput. Game Cult. 2(5), 133–152 (2012)
14. Roussou, M.: Flow, staging, wayfinding, personalization: evaluating user experience with mobile museum narratives. Multimodal Technol. Interact 2(5), 32 (2016)
15. PokemonGO. https://www.pokemongo.com/de-de/. Accessed 13 July 2018

Re-interpreting Cities with Play Urban Semiotics and Gamification

Mattia Thibault[(✉)] [ID]

Tampere University of Technology, 33720 Tampere, Finland
mattia.thibault@tut.fi

Abstract. This paper aims to propose a semiotic perspective on how play can be used to change the citizens' perception of the city. The paper propose a meaning-centered understanding both of play activities (seen as resemantisations of the surrounding environment) and of urban spaces (seen as complex meaning-making machines) and attempts to show how the first ones can be used to re-interpret the second ones. Finally, a few examples such as *parkour* and flash mobs are analyses in order to test the efficacy of the approach.

Keywords: Urban play · Gamification · Semiotics · Parkour · Flash mobs

1 Urban Play: An Introduction

Nowadays, the idea that cities shouldn't just be smart but also playable is gaining more and more recognition. This paper aims to propose a semiotic perspective for studying urban play in the wider frame of gamification, in order to deepen our understanding on how we can use play to affect the urban spaces and on what effects this might have on the citizens and their practices. In particular this paper focuses on outlining a meaning-centred approach to urban areas and to analyse how playful activities of reading and rewriting the city can influence the citizens' perception and interpretation of the urban environment.

Urban areas are not new to becoming playgrounds. Everybody has, at least once, played at "don't walk on the pavement lines", or encountered an hopscotch chalk drawing on a side-walk. But the city is also home of new forms of play, such as Pokémon Go, or new playful performances like flash-mobs.

Playing in the city, however, is not simply a matter of entertainment or having fun. Situationism was maybe the first movement to point it out, even if not in these terms. Ivain, in his *Formoulaire pour un urbanisme nouveau* [9], underlines how a situationsit approach might save the city from the modern "mental illness" of a banality driven by production and comfort. Places devoted to playfulness, argues Ivain, are able to influence strongly the citizens' behaviour and have a great force of attraction.

Nowadays the social importance of city-play is recognised again: it is seen, more and more, as an antidote to the anonymity of the urban environment. The inhabitants of cities feel increasingly powerless and disconnected in face of the changes brought by globalisation and by the ICT revolution. This is even more critical to vulnerable populations in a moment where the right to the city of lower classes, minorities and

A. L. Brooks et al. (Eds.): ArtsIT 2018/DLI 2018, LNICST 265, pp. 276–285, 2019.

immigrants is often questioned. Urban play, on the other hand, reinforces the perception of "city ownership": it is an activity that requires immersion and light-hearted engagement and is able to build communities around a shared experience.

In Europe, for example, as around 75% of the EU population lives in urban areas, it is not surprising that the Union itself financed several projects that address the societal challenges related to cities by promoting the use of play and game-like activities – such as GIFT (exploring hybrid playful forms of virtual museum experiences) or City-Zen (using games to illustrate to citizens the benefits of a clean energy transition) – and recognises "Optimal and cost-effective use of behavioural games" as one of the main strategies in the forthcoming H2020 call "Visionary and integrated solutions to improve well-being and health in cities".

2 Play and Interpretation

But, what is play? This is, of course, a tricky question. The debate on how to define play – and even if this endeavour is possible at all – is still open, and produces many arguments and counter-arguments. The most convincing perspectives, however, are those considering the concept of "play" more like an operational tool that an ontological definition. Wittgenstein's claim that there is nothing actually in common between all the activities that we label as play if not a *family resemblance* [25] means that any attempt of defining play is actually an attempt to *re*-define it. It is an attempt to create a new concept while keeping the same label. Which is what Brian Sutton-Smith states when he speaks of the rhetorics *of play* [18]. These are the different ways of conceptualising playfulness in order to use it either to explain or to control society around us.

In this paper, then, I will not attempt to propose a general definition of play, but only to define what is the rhetoric of play as semiosis [20]. The idea that play spurs from a different set of *meaning* has been advanced and described by several scholars, but its best conceptualization is to be found in the works of Lotman. In the article "The place of art among other modelling systems" [12] which, as the title suggests, deals mainly with the cultural role of art, Lotman, exposes a restricted theory of playfulness. According to Lotman play involves the dynamic constant awareness of the possibility of alternate meanings to the one that is currently being perceived. These different meanings of the same element do not appear in static coexistence but "twinkle" while each interpretation makes up a separate synchronic slice, yet retains a memory of earlier meanings and the awareness of the possibility of future ones.

Basically, Lotman suggests that play involves a *resemantisation* of the world—i.e. a systemic shift of its meaning. This resemantisation gives to the world a second, additional and fictional meaning, that the players perceive and interpret as such. The players, then, oscillate between two different systems of interpretation, between two different ways to *make sense* of the same physical reality. On the one hand, the players never give up completely their awareness of the "ordinary reality", but, on the other hand, they *almost* act as if the playful situation was real. From a semiotic standpoint, thus, the starting point of any playful activity is the systematic resemantisation of objects and actions, that translate the whole world (or better, a portion of it delimited by the borders of play) into the semiotic domain of play. This resemantisation, however, does not entail any serious confusion between the two domains, that are perfectly separated in the mind of the player.

Play's ability to resemantise our surroundings without the need to modify them, can be a rather important asset in any action that attempt to reappropriate alienated public spaces. The limits that citizens have in regard of their ability to act and change the urban spaces they inhabit, can be somewhat dismissed, if we act on our perception of the city and therefore our behaviour within it. We shall call this playful resemantisations of the urban spaces as acts of *urban gamification*.

The term "gamification" generally indicates the attempt of using game design elements and inducing a playful behaviour in order to boost user engagement and increase the efficacy of non-game activities, both digital and not. Gamification can be implemented in a vast range of activities, from promoting exercising to conditioning driving behaviours (the Swedish Speed Camera Lottery). The concept (born in the digital media industry between 2008 and 2010) has been applied especially to education and learning [17], business [24] and health [15].

Analytic approaches and theoretical frameworks are quite recent in the field and are articulated around a perspective focusing mainly on defining "game elements" and their efficacy [5] or on redefining gamification on the basis of the participant responses [8]. This second approach seems to be most efficient: as a recent study [7] points out, gamification's positive effects are greatly dependent on the context and on the final users of the activity.

3   Cities as Texts

We have claimed that play can be a tool for making sense of the city in a way that is alternative to that of ordinary life. In order to understand how, however, we need to engage the semiotic properties of urban areas.

Already in 1980 Michel de Certeau in *his L'invention du quotidien* [3] proposed to consider the city as a textual form. This parallelism – metaphorically already implicit in the expression "urban fabric" – leads de Certeau to consider the city as a real texts, actualised (and transformed) by the practices of interaction and crossing of their inhabitants. The journey of the latter through the urban space, then, is nothing but an *enunciation*, by which the individuals take possession of the places and transforms them by introducing their own subjectivity. The city, then, is a text anything but fixed: it emerges as the result of practices of enunciation that, at the same time, actualise and deeply modify the urban spaces. In the same years, Marshall Berman, from another perspective, elaborated the idea of the city as a machine that produces meaning, a "multimedia presentation whose audience is the whole world" [2, p. 288].

The metaphor of urban space as a text, as well as that of the city as a producer of meaning, can be found, whit some distinctions, in urban semiotics. In one of the founding works of urban semiotics Volli [22] writes that from the semiotic point of view, an expressive reality that is renewed and continually redefines itself such as the city, is defined a discourse: a signifying practice which, however, at all times projected behind itself a text. The city is alive, it changes materially and in the sense that it projects; but in every time it is stable and legible as a book.

The city, therefore, is not *really* a text, but rather acts as a text – as a text it can be read, but also approached, analysed and understood [14, 23].

The city, just like a text, is both an organic whole – that can be understood and labelled as a unique thing – and characterized by an irreducible structural heterogeneity – a city encompasses numerous texts of smaller scale (neighbourhoods, streets, buildings, signs, street furniture, graffiti ...). All these smaller texts are interconnected by their simultaneous presence within the city, which then becomes a web of meaningful elements connected to each other [22]. This is obviously an unstable and uncertain mingling, whose metamorphoses follow different times and rhythms, from the slow construction of new neighbourhoods to the quick work of street-writers and the ephemeral presence of advertising posters. This dual nature, of homogeneous text and of container of textualities of a smaller scale, is recognised by authors semioticians such as Lotman [11] and Cervelli and Sedda [4] and leads to a fundamental disappearance of a clear distinction between text and context. If, on the one hand, the elements of larger size can become the context for those, incorporated, of smaller size (a neighbourhood becomes the context of a building, a square that of a monument), the relationship between text and context is not limited to a simple relationship of incorporation, and therefore, on the other hand, it is possible that the objects of a smaller size, but with a greater symbolic efficacy, can become the context for larger-scale objects: "iconic" buildings and monuments are able to lessen the meaning of all that it is around them, creating a semiotic void that allows them to "shine". Urban areas, then, appear as a polilogical set to which we have to add also all the objects moving thought it: goods, trucks, cars and the inhabitants of the city themselves, which cross its spaces and are distributed in different parts of the city giving meaning to the metropolitan landscapes.

Text-cities, as already implied by de Certeau, are inevitably *polyphonic* texts, which elude any attempt of standardization by the political, economic or religious powers. The city-enunciated is the product of countless authors, eras and conceptions of urban spaces, to which correspond a great number of different strategies – sometimes even conflicting – which meet, collide, mingle and overwrite each other in the city. The urban areas, then, become places whose elements are pervaded by an antagonistic tension: competing to obtain dominant positions (centrality, verticality, passages), attention (traffic) and prestige. This tension, however, is petrified in the buildings and streets of the city, which freeze them in a spatial arrangement. This incessant internal tension of urban spaces entails a constant transformation: the city is a variable text, alive, never identical to itself, a text that retains elements of its past (text as *testis*, Latin for witness) and interweaves them with those of the present (text as *textus*, Latin for fabric) in a set often heavily layered and ontologically complex [23].

This kaleidoscopic web of meaningful elements features also its own hierarchy: an ideological stratification that gives greater emphasis and meaning to the buildings of the political and religious power, to monuments and "landmarks" and, instead, relegates to a marginal role the communicative traces of most of the inhabitants, which can only count on their ephemeral presence, or recur to billboards, signs, graffiti.

This ideological stratification is accompanied by a historical one, which moves at different speeds: some elements of the city can last for thousands of years (the topography, the orientation of the street map), other for centuries (buildings, streets and monuments), other for years (signs and elements of street furniture) or weeks (posters and display cases), down to the momentary presence of the inhabitants themselves: every look at the city, then, essentially captures just a section of it.

If the city is certainly the product of a culture, on the other hand it is itself also a *producer of culture*. There is a city-enunciated, but also a city-enunciator, which produces meaning and tells about the society and the people who inhabit it.

Focusing on this specific characteristic of urban spaces, allows us to emphasize the ways in which they convey meaning, they communicate with those who inhabit them, walk them, live them. On the one hand, the meanings conveyed by a city profoundly influence the actions of their inhabitants, through obligations, prohibitions and directions. On the other hand, cities transform people into citizens: they make them *urban* and *polite* – words that come respectively from the Latin and Greek words for "city".

The city, then, can be considered as a complex communicating machine [14], object of discourses and analysis that interpret it providing identity and consistency, but, at the same time, it is itself the subject of discourses and an important producer of meaning and culture.

4   Interpreting and Re-interpreting Urban Spaces

To live and move through the city means, first of all, to be able to read and to interpret it. The experiential aspect of the city becomes even more important if, as in our case, we want to focus on the relationship between playfulness and urban spaces: gamifying city spaces is, first of all, an operation of interpretation and reinterpretation. In this paragraph, we will focus briefly on how the city is read by its inhabitants and which mechanisms and actions are necessary to re-write it.

If we take in consideration the movement through the city, the constitutive heterogeneity of the city can be reduced to a basic axiological opposition between the continuation and interruption. The range of possibilities of movement and reading in the urban space, then, can be articulated four combinations: the continuation of the continuation (the fluid and uninterrupted movement), the interruption of the continuation (the insurmountable obstacle), the interruption of the interruption (temporary obstacle) and the continuation of the interruption (the impossibility of moving). From these combinations we can outline two classes of urban objects: the passage (the road, the entrance, the side-walk, the pedestrian crossing, subway, but also the car door) and the obstacle (the wall, enclosure, barrier, the closed gate, but also the passer-by, the policeman directing traffic and the traffic lights) [19]. These two classes of objects regulate the actions of whoever moves into the urban space through a series of possibilities and prohibitions.

On the one hand, passages and obstacles are, above all, signs of their possible uses – they convey the possibility or impossibility to cross them – while, on the other hand, they are also significant surfaces. The palaces of the city – their representing and communicating aesthetic surfaces – at the same time prevent and direct the gaze, according to projects of strategic manipulation, intended to steer and guide those who live and move through the city. These meaningful surfaces simultaneously block the view and become a surface on which to engrave messages, whether architectural (decorations), symbols (flags, logos), commercial (advertising), social (mortuaries), identity (commemorative plaques) or ideological (political posters, graffiti) [14]. The passages, on the other hand, direct, regulate and guide the reading of the urban text and therefore they become the place where citizens can make sense of it, through the selection and a reading order determined by the path.

A famous example of the different practices of city crossing is the work of Floch [6] outlining a typology of the users of the *metro* of Paris. As his work accurately highlights, the different ways of reading the city vary also according to what the "reader" selects as significant and meaningful within the "jungle of signs" that is the urban space.

To read a rich text such as a city, it is necessary to choose some *saliences* – which items are significant, and which are trivial – and then to draw isotopies between them, in order to give a unique and organic meaning to the heterogeneous whole in which these diverse elements are immersed. Selecting the saliences, however, is not enough to be able to move consciously within the city. If it is true that in a social environment everything becomes a sign of its possible use, on the other hand, many objects are used differently by different individuals or at different times. Some objects may even be "reinvented" through practices contradictory of their constituent strategic purpose. We should talk, then, of possible *uses*, in the plural form, thus implying the need for a second operation of selection and interpretation. The selection of a specific use between many possibilities is guided by a "urban semiotic competence" [22]: the ability to correctly interpret what the city tells us. This competence is rather pragmatic, as it will guide the inhabitants in their tasks for experiencing the city. The city itself can hinder or facilitate the use of this competence in virtue of its legibility – the urban characteristic of assisting people in creating their mental maps and fostering wayfinding [13], which is nonetheless that the exercise of the urban semiotic competence.

The two classes of urban object that we discussed above, obstacles and passages, are products and objects of *writing* practices. Tracing a path, whether physically (building a bridge, a road, a tunnel), whether as a strategic choice to move through the city – including the choice to leave the track (climbing a fence, crossing the street where forbidden, ignoring a traffic light) – are all acts of writing.

It is writing also any act on and with surfaces: building, affixing, smearing, demolishing, uprooting, colouring the objects of the city. "Writing the city" assumes often a character of *re*writing, of superimposing new writing to an existing text. Writing the city means adding layers of meaning, removing and filling gaps, rectifying what already exists in an environment that is then continuously modified. It is, therefore, a form of *bricolage* that re-works already existing elements and materials. The city, in a nutshell, is formed by a material substrate produced by the superposition of multiple inscriptions which, in turn, become the substrate and support of new writings, whether they are strategic or simply the traces of the human activities that take place in the urban space.

We can distinguish two polarities of city-writing: one close to the idea of the *palimpsest* (a medieval manuscript from which the writing has been scraped off so that the page could be reused for another document), involving the removal, at least partial, of the pre-existing substrate and the construction of something new, and one characterized by a kind of *maquillage* in the name of recovery, based on the transformation or *resemantisation* of existing urban objects. This second, more common, form of rewriting is exercised both by the power – for example with regard to the transformation of a convent in a hospital or in an ancient palace into a town hall – and by peripheral social actors – which occupy buildings, become squatters, camp in parks, write on the walls, and so on. These rewritings, even when with practical purposes, cannot be regarded as exclusively functional: instead, they always have a highly communicative character. On the one hand, they affect the general meaning of the object that is resemantised, and, on the other hand, they become a way for individuals or for social political or religious groups, to engrave themselves *within* the city-text, to leave a trace, to represent their existence within the universe that the city represents.

5   Ludicisation and Playable Cities

We have claimed that cities are also a mean through which a culture represents itself and its own understanding of the universe. It is not surprising, then, if urban spaces are one of the areas touched by the *ludicisation of culture* – the cultural trend that sees games and play occupying a more and more central place in our society.

The city, then, becomes a playground, host of playful activities and interactions that escape from the places traditionally devoted to them. The very enunciation of these cities – the way we live them, cross them, interact with them – is becoming more and more playful. Urban practices that used to be absolutely "serious" are now reformulated or modified in order to follow this cultural change. These activities generally take the form of pervasive play practices, as they involve a widening of the boundaries (spatial, temporal and social) of the play activity, which will then involve large portions of public space, moments not institutionally devoted to play and unsuspecting passers-by [16].

The choices that lie behind the use of strategies of urban gamification may vary. Some of them are bottom-up actions fuelled by the desire of (re)appropriating public spaces or to send a political message, while others are merely marketing techniques put in place by fashion-following companies. What all they all have in common, however, is the desire to rewrite the city, to reshape it, to engrave oneself in it, to renew it by resorting to the energy and the ability to motivate people that emanates from play. Let's engage a few examples.

5.1   Flash Mobs

Flash mobs are probably one of the most widespread practices of urban play. They take place at the hearth of the city, in squares, streets or train stations and involve the sudden gathering of a crowd of people executing an unusual performance with a playful flavour. Flash mobs invade the space of traditional events: they have the same purposes and settings of protest marches, sit-ins, and fairs and they often replace them [21]. We have flash mobs used for political protest, and others promoting moments of sociability (e.g. the "dinners in white"). Flash mobs that have commercial purposes and advertise some product, while others are purely recreational (as are "zombie walks"). They all work in the same way: during the performance, the spaces of the city are transformed in improvised stages for shows that involve masking, carnivalesque features, and surrealisms.

Flash mobs, then, are a semiotic device aiming at acting on the border between everyday reality and play: viewers of a flash mob become players without their knowledge. The communicative effectiveness of these practices is based on this interpretative disorientation: the temporary inability to distinguish between semiotic domains. Flash mobs play with the status of playfulness, they omit the message "this is play" [1] and entrust it to an implicit metacommunication: passers-by have to activate their competence in the semiotic domain of play in order to be able to correctly interpret the scene unfolding before their eyes.

5.2   Parkour

Another interesting case of playful rewriting of urban spaces, this time concerning the reinterpretation of its obstacles, is that of parkour. Parkour was born in the degraded suburbs of Paris, and in particular in Evry. This practice started as a form of rebellion against the power and its writings of the city. Evry, as many other French suburbs, is an artificial city inaugurated in the 1970s for hosting immigrants. It was the product of a top-down urbanist ideology that did imagine the city as a space completely regulated by the power, at whose centre, functional and symbolic, stand the *prefecture* [10]. This project, therefore, failed spectacularly at constructing that polyphonic and plural character that we have identified as a constituent of a city able to transform its inhabitants into citizens.

The urban writing in Evry, unsurprisingly, was perceived by its own inhabitants as an imposition, a vexation. Some of them, however, reacted in an unusual way: with a practice of rewriting that had a strong playful component: *parkour*.

Parkour is an acrobatic alternative to the traditional ways of crossing the city spaces, those prescribed by the power. It defines a new way of moving within the city [10] and, therefore, a new way of enunciating it and making it meaningful. Parkour is characterized, on the one hand, by speed (symbolic fruit of the conflicting relationship between the *traceurs* – the people which traces these new paths – and the power, which often results in them escaping from of the police) and on the other by an unusual way to relate to the obstacle. The obstacle is an element used to coerce, and it has a dual nature: symbolic and concrete – in indicates a route and it prescribes it. The *traceurs*, however, refuse the path imposed by the obstacle – which in Evry often prevents a fluid movement in space, forcing its inhabitants to long zigzagging – and replace it with an alternative route, which overcomes the obstacles with stunt jumps, transforming them into an opportunity to test physical and mental abilities.

Parkour has clearly a playful component: it can be interpreted as an attempt to resemantise in a playful way the urban space, it is manifested as a desire to turn the entire city into a huge playground, where all the elements of urban architecture are resemantised and re-functionalised in for urban entertainment, stripped of their practical functionality and covered with a playful functionality. This is not because traceurs are particularly playful, but because play appears as the only alternative to the interpretation of the city imposed by the power.

5.3   Other

There are of course many other examples that will have to be taken into consideration and that here we can only mention. The fact that the practice of city rewriting *par excellence*, graffiti, is often contained by video games (see the work of famous French street-artist Invader) and, more recently, by internet memes, is rather interesting. Some activities have a clearer aim at reappropriation, as *Park(ing) day*, a civil bottom-up festivity in which people from around the World rent parking spots but, instead of parking their car, they unroll some clods of grass, position some plants and create a small, green, park instead. There are coordinated projects such as *Fun Theory* from Volkswagen, that employ a more "classic" take on gamification trying to devise ways of influencing people's behaviour through play, such as *Piano Stairs, The World's deepest bin* or the *Speed camera lottery*. Finally, platforms such as *Playable cities* promote projects that make high use of technology in order to rewrite city experiences, for example recording the shadows of passers-by and projecting them a few minutes late (*Shadowing*) or allowing citizens to exchange texts with street-furniture (*Hello Lamp post*).

6   Conclusions

In this paper we have seen how the city, a semiotic machine stupendously complex, as well as its innovative digital representations, is increasingly subject of playful rese-mantisations. Play is able to infiltrate several contexts and spaces, and propose new meanings, new constraints, new strategies and new motivations.

This sort of meaning-centred approach to urban areas, can be rather useful to conceptualise the types of actions that can be undertaken in order to use play and to describe how they can influence the readings and interpretations of said spaces. Its descriptive capability, however, does not immediately translate in a prescriptive capability. In others words, if it helps us understand how urban gamification works, it is not enough to help us design activities of urban gamification, nor to assess them.

Acknowledgements. This project has received funding from the European Union's Horizon 2020 research and innovation programme under the Marie Sklodowska-Curie grant agreement No. 793835.

Marie Skłodowska-Curie
Actions

References

1. Bateson, G.: A theory of play and fantasy. Psychiatric Research Reports (1955)
2. Berman, M.: All that is Solid Melts in the Air. The Experience of Modernity. Simon and Schuster, New York (1982)
3. De Certeau, M.: L'invention du quotidien, 1. Arts de faire. Union générale d'éditions, Paris (1980)
4. Cervelli, P., Sedda, F.: Zone, frontiere, confini: la città come spazio culturale. In: Marrone, G., Pezzini, I. (eds.) Senso e metropoli. Per una semiotica posturbana, pp. 171–192. Meltemi, Roma (2006)
5. Deterding, S., Kahled, R., Nacke, L.E., Dixon, D.: Gamification: toward a definition. In: CHI 2011, 7–12 May 2011, Vancouver (2011)
6. Floch, J.M.: Sémiotique, marketing et communication: Sous les signes, les stratégies. PUF, Paris (1990)
7. Hamari, J., Koivisto, J., Sarsa, H.: Does gamification work? A literature review of empirical studies on gamification. In: 2014 47th Hawaii International Conference on System Sciences, pp. 3025–3034 (2014)
8. Huotari, J., Hamari, K.: A definition for gamification: anchoring gamification in the service marketing literature. Electron. Markets 27(1), 21–31 (2015)
9. Ivain, G.: Formoulaire pour un urbanisme nouveau. Internationale situationiste 1, Bulletrin céntral, Paris (1958)
10. Leone, M.: Le Parkour sémiotique. Pratiche urbane di invenzione della naturalità. In: Bonadei, R. (ed.) NaturaleArtificiale: Il palinsesto urbano. Lubrina, Bergamo (2009)
11. Lotman, J.M.: L'architettura nel contesto della cultura. In: Burini, S. (ed.) Il girotondo delle muse: Saggi sulla semiotica delle arti e della rappresentazione. Moretti and Vitali Editori, Bergamo (1998)
12. Lotman, J.M.: The place of art among other modelling systems. Sign Syst. Stud. 39(2/4), 251–270 (2011)
13. Lynch, K.: The Image of the City. MIT Press, Cambridge (1960)
14. Mastroianni, R.: Writing the City. I Saggi di Lexia. Aracne, Rome (2013)
15. McGonigal, J.: Reality is Broken: Why Games Make us Better and How They Can Change the World. Penguin Books, London (2011)
16. Montola, M., Stenros, J., Waern, A.: Pervasive Games Theory and Design. Morgan Kaufmann Game Design Books. Morgan Kaufmann, San Francisco (2009)
17. Salen, K.: The Ecology of Games: Connecting Youth, Games, and Learning. MIT Press, Cambridge (2007)
18. Sutton-Smith, B.: The Ambiguity of Play. Harvard University Press, Cambridge (1997)
19. Thibault, M. (ed.): Gamification Urbana: Letture e Riscritture ludiche degli spazi cittadini. I Saggi di Lexia. Aracne, Rome (2016)
20. Thibault, M.: The meaning of play - a theory of playfulness, toys and games as cultural semiotic devices. Doctoral dissertation, University of Turin, Turin (2017)
21. Turco, F.: Flash mob: quando la performance diventa strumento di protesta. In: Lexia, vol. 13–14, pp. 305–319. Aracne, Rome (2012)
22. Volli, U.: Laboratorio di semiotica. Laterza, Bari-Roma (2005)
23. Volli, U.: Il testo della città—problemi metodologici e teorici. In: Leone, M. (ed.) Lexia, vol. 1–2, pp. 9–12. Aracne, Rome (2008)
24. Werbach, K., Hunter, D.: For the Win: How Game Thinking Can Revolutionize Your Business. Wharton Digital Press, Philadelphia (2012)
25. Wittgenstein, L.: Philosophical Investigations, E. Anscombe (trans.). Palgrave Macmillan, New York (1953)

Fostering Social Interaction in Playful Cities

Xavier Fonseca(✉) ⓘ, Stephan Lukosch(✉) ⓘ,
and Frances Brazier(✉)

Faculty of Technology, Policy and Management,
Delft University of Technology, Delft, Netherlands
{f.x.fonseca, s.g.lukosch, f.m.brazier}@tudelft.nl

Abstract. This paper describes different types of activities/challenges designed for social interaction, while discussing the performance of such challenges using the mobile digital game "Secrets of the South" (http://secretsofthesouth.tbm.tudelft.nl/, Secrets of the South). The game was played as part of a scientific meeting, with participants from 25 to 62 years of age and a varying degree of cultural differences. The presentation and discussion of the results of the gameplay provide insights on the appropriateness of the different challenges for social interaction in a playful city. Directions for future work for such challenge designs are presented.

Keywords: Serious games · Social interaction · Playable cities

1 Introduction

To achieve greater social inclusion, to make people feel they belong to a society, and to value diversity is a difficulty that today's humanity is facing [20, 23]. Games can foster play and participation in playful cities, support citizen communication, social inclusion and coordination, and develop capital in social relationships [1, 9, 10, 17]. Mobile outdoor games in particular promote significant social interaction via physical activity, engagement, face-to-face interaction, mobility, health benefits, and extra motivation and enjoyment [3, 4, 11, 22]. In urban environments games can bring people with different social, cultural and emotional backgrounds [18] and behaviours [6] together.

This paper explores the design of challenges for social interaction between participants of a scientific conference. The game framework[1] in which these challenges are implemented has been designed for (1) meaningful interaction in the public space/neighbourhood, (2) with a smartphone, (3) with the potential to engage as many people as possible, and (4) in a fun way, criteria for a playable city [15].

In the following sections, this paper explores how serious games can support the concept of playable cities, and briefly describes the game framework. Further sections focus on the experiment, report on 5 different types of challenges played by strangers in a new environment, and discusses the lessons learned on the appropriateness of these challenges for a playful city. This paper closes with overall remarks and future steps.

---

[1] http://secretsofthesouth.tbm.tudelft.nl/, Secrets of the South.

A. L. Brooks et al. (Eds.): ArtsIT 2018/DLI 2018, LNICST 265, pp. 286–295, 2019.

2 Related Work

Playful technology embedded in urban environments can make life more enjoyable, in particular when such technology supports collaboration, enabling people to work/play together [14]. Common places for the use of technology range from home, work environment, and public places such as musea and city festivals, while technology typically explored ranges from street furniture (e.g. lamp posts, mail boxes, or trash bins), smart chromogenic materials, LEDs, brain-computer interfaces, movement cameras, sensors and actuators (e.g. in smart watches/phones), and augmented reality devices (e.g. Kinect or similar devices) [15].

Playable cities can be supported with games that can range from (1) playgrounds without any technology, to (2) games predominantly played with smartphones, and (3) other types of technology and custom-made installations. An example of (1) is "A playful street", a project that sets up several traditional playgrounds on the streets of Dublin without technology, and invites open play behaviour from the young and the elderly with objects put on scene[2]. An example of (2) is "Koppelkiek"[3], a game created to stimulate playful encounters and interactions in public spaces, using smartphones' cameras to take pictures of players with random people, and placing those pictures in a neighbourhood centre to encourage conversation between neighbours. "Hello Lamp Post" is a game designed for city dwellers to converse with urban objects in Bristol, where a playable city app allows communication with chatbots via text messages and can answer questions about the environment[4]. With regard to example projects of type (3), a well-known game for playful cities is "Social Stairs", a subway staircase that has been turned into a giant live piano as a way to seduce travellers to climb the stairs instead of taking the escalator [16]. Other examples include "Shadowing" that uses infrared cameras to record shadows of passers-bys and provokes humorous situations by impacting people's awareness of other people's shadows[5]; "Urbanimals" that uses projectors to cast tailored images of animals onto the physical environment[6]; and "ActiWait", with a set of pedestrian semaphores equipped with devices that allow the play of Pong game between people waiting for a green light[7]. Smart's "Dancing Light" ad campaign installed a dancing booth and connected it to pedestrian semaphores. While not being a game, it also invites playful behaviour via performative dance acts displayed in the semaphore[8]. While the three mentioned types of games for playable cities (1), (2) and (3) are not exhaustive, they indicate the nature of work done on turning cities into playful scenes.

---

[2] https://www.aplayfulcity.com/the-lab, "A playful Street" project.

[3] https://whatsthehubbub.nl/projects/koppelkiek/, Koppelkiek, 'couple snapshot' in Dutch.

[4] http://panstudio.co.uk/, "Hello Lamp Post" project.

[5] http://shadowing.cc/, "Shadowing" project.

[6] http://urbanimals.eu/, "Urbananimals" project.

[7] http://urban-invention.com/, "ActiWait" project.

[8] https://www.youtube.com/watch?v=SB_0vRnkeOk, "The Dancing Traffic Light by smart".

3   Game, and Challenge Designs

The "Secrets of the South" (see footnote 1) (SotS) is a mobile outdoor serious game that lets players walk around their neighbourhood and other public spaces, engage with people they (might) have never seen or spoken to before, go to places that they might have never been or seen before, and solve challenges together with other people (actively playing the game or not) to advance throughout the game. It is designed to support people playing together, hunting for QR codes that other people have, perform in multiplayer challenges, and solving single player quiz challenges designed for face-to-face interaction in the neighbourhood (Table 1).

Table 1. The Secrets of the South serious game

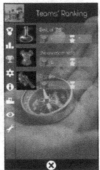

Challenges within the game framework are purposefully placed in specific places to expose players to unnoticed details of a neighbourhood, to other people in public spaces, and to promote playful behaviour and fun. These places can be related for e.g. to the history of a city (e.g. the birth of a legend, the biggest port in the world, a local star) or to local activities. The game framework currently supports two different types of challenges, quiz and multiplayer: quizzes are designed for single player gameplay, and multiplayer challenges for groups of people playing together in teams (teams against teams). This paper explores multiplayer challenges in which teams solve a challenge, get points/rewards for the quality of their performance, and compete with other teams.

3.1   Challenge Designs

To foster social interaction in urban environments this paper explores the impact of 5 different challenges for scenarios in which people (most likely) do not know each other beforehand (common fact in public spaces). It explores the goal of fostering social interaction, and uses several factors from the social cohesion framework [9] to design these challenges. This framework distinguishes 3 factors that influence social cohesion with regard to an individual (in contrast to communities and formal institutions): (1) self-motivation, (2) perceptions, norms and values, and (3) participation and performance. Social interaction, a means to acquire social cohesion [8, 12, 19], is influenced by aspects such as for e.g. intimate face-to-face communication [5], quality of intimate topics shared [21], degree of like-dislike [13], sense of belonging [7], individual participation [2], and task competence [8]. Table 2 lists both the factors linked to social interaction in this framework, and aspects of influence.

Table 2. Main goals for challenge designs, and aspects that can achieve them

Factors fostering social interaction	Aspect influencing the factors
Self-motivation	1. Intimate face-to-face communication [5]
	2. Quality of intimate topics shared [21]
Perceptions, norms and values	3. Degree of like-dislike [13]
	4. Sense of belonging [7]
Participation and performance	5. Individual participation [2]
	6. Task competence [8]

The following challenges for social interaction in playful cities are designed to explore the influence of these factors in practice.

Challenge 1: Guess If You Can. The objective of this challenge is to introduce players of a team with each other to jointly solve in a collective problem solving task. It consists of estimating the precise volume of a big and complex building at a given location, while stipulating a time limit of 5 min. This exercise is designed to require the least effort and act as ice breaker. It addresses the aspects in Table 2 by initiating communication and collaboration in the same location (aspects 4, 5) without need for intimacy, and making people solve a common problem with time pressure (aspect 6).

Challenge 2: Shape In. The objective of this challenge is to interact in a fun and different way, and to tap into each other's creativity. It consists of having all team members putting on blindfolds and forming a large circle with a rope on the floor. Together they must create a geometric shape with the rope by communicating. It addresses the aspects in Table 2 by requiring imagination (aspect 6), using blindfolds (aspects 1, 4, 5), and implementing intercommunication to coordinate the task (aspects 1, 3, 4) in close body proximity (aspect 1, 2, 4).

Challenge 3: Creative Dance. This challenge is designed to stretch comfort zones, and foster the thrill of creative effort in an engaging and fun way. The team can earn rewards by uniting as a group and making a performance of the three musketeers fighting for a princess (they choose the princess). This entails placing a speaker on the floor, playing music of choice, and team performance. It addresses Table 2 by creating memorable experiences via a joint dance (aspects 1, 3, 5, 6), and stretching comfort zones in close body proximity (aspects 1, 2, 3).

Challenge 4: Creative Talk. This challenge is designed to overcome communication barriers through creativity, to build on each other's knowledge and consider other perspectives. This is done by making the team coordinate without speaking out loud. A unique secret number is whispered to each person, and the team has to line itself up in a numerical order without talking. Difficulty can be added by using numbers from 11 to 99. It addresses the aspects in Table 2 by deploying blindfolds (aspects 1, 4, 5), requiring creativity in new ways of communication (aspects 5, 6), inviting communication through gestures and close proximity (aspects 1, 2), and inviting touching between players (aspects 3, 4).

Challenge 5: Knot. This challenge seeks to enable team members to provide support to each other to solve a problem. It requires players to create a knot with their own hands, and untangle themselves. To do so, they are asked to form a circle, stretch their right arm forward and grab a random hand. They then do the same with their left arms. It addresses Table 2 by deploying touching (aspects 1, 2, 4), mutual support (aspect 4), and close body proximity (aspects 1, 2, 3, 4).

Below, the suitability of these challenges for playful social interaction are explored, within the mentioned existent game framework, and targeting strangers within a playful city. The order of the challenges is relevant, because there are challenges that require levels of intimacy (due to blindfolds, touching, and dancing acts) to be played, and build on top of previous interactions. The following section explores whether these challenges foster interaction between strangers attending a scientific meeting, via reported levels of (1) self-motivation, (2) perceptions, norms and values, and (3) participation and performance.

4 Experiment

An experiment was conducted to assess the validity of the proposed challenges introduced in the game framework SotS. It was executed within the context of the TMP graduate consortium[9] in The Hague, an annual meeting for doctoral candidates, their direct supervisors, and faculty member representatives from around the world. This meeting provided an opportunity to test the challenge designs with people in a (for most) new location, whom belong to a varied age group, do not know each other, and are in the city for a 2-day visit.

4.1 Participants

Of the 26 participants of the workshop, 14 people participated in the experiment: 6 women, and 8 men. The participants' ages were within the range of 25 to 62 years of age, and only 2 had been to The Hague before. Of the 14, 1 is a male full professor aged 62, 3 professors/researchers aged 35 (2 males, 1 female), 2 female researchers aged 31 and 32, 4 researchers aged between 28–29 (1 male, 3 females), and 4 younger male researchers aged between 25–27.

---

[9] https://www.tudelft.nl/en/tpm/current/tmp-consortium/technology-management-policy-consortium/, Technology, Management and Policy graduate consortium.

4.2 Procedure

The gameplay was executed between two points A and B in the centre of The Hague, where A is the consortium's venue, and B the restaurant where all the participants had a joint dinner on the first evening of the event. Participants signed consent forms for data collection, and when possible installed the game on their own phones or phone provided (not all phones met the specific requirements of the game).

Participants were divided into 3 groups of up to 5 people with at least 2 smartphones with the game running per group. The geographical position of the 5 challenges provided the context of the activities involved. Each position was also marked by a facilitator whose task was to oversee and rate each team's performances. After 30 min of gameplay, the winning team was rewarded with free drinks at the restaurant.

4.3 Method

Each group was followed by one or two observers whom did not interfere with the gameplay. Each observer collected video recordings of his/her group's gameplay, for each challenge and across all challenges. The three groups of participants, the 5 facilitators and 4 observers were interviewed at the end of the gameplay. The interviews were semi-structured, addressing what the participants thought of the game itself, their overall game experience, whether they had noticed any difference in social interaction resultant from having played the game and the challenges, and which challenges worked best. The results reported below are based on the transcriptions of these interviews. The transcriptions label all the participants as PX (being X the number of participant; e.g. P1, P5), and these labels are used when citing what a participant has stated. The video recordings are used to better understand both the gameplay and the feedback from the interviews.

4.4 Results

Game Experience: In general, players said that the game experience was positive, it did not take much effort to play, the challenges were within a comfortable walking distance, the overall game mechanics of collaboration and meeting other people in and out of the group was appreciated, and that it was overall a repeatable experience. The challenges were reported to be good ice breakers and good to create experiences with people on the street that they can remember later on. They also mentioned enjoying particular challenges that had a nice themed description (for e.g., prisoners back in the era did...), as a powerful means to learn about the history of the place. They said that not all participants were as active as others (some refused to play certain challenges), and that leadership behaviour was noticed in some teams.

Challenges: Challenge 1 was reported to be a positive warming up experience that provided limited opportunity for communication. Challenge 2 was reported to be very positive because they were blindfolded and that it required a bit of imagination while still being achievable. Challenge 3 was reported to be weird, with the dancing and singing being too much. They said that role playing is nice and should be kept, but that more appropriate music, in line with the history of the place, should be used. Players thought challenge 4 was too difficult and frustrating. Challenge 5 was too easy to solve (mostly solvable within 10 s) and groups did not have strong opinions except that holding hands at that stage was already within their comfort zone. In general, they reported that themed challenges should be used. The use of rope in the challenge 2 was named as a prime example of disconnection between the places and the challenge. They also reported that two blindfolded challenges were too much, even though they felt comfortable performing these tasks.

Impact of Game: Players recognize that the game with the challenges was designed for social interaction and that it did that. They argued that, if they would not have played the game, they would not have had the chance to talk as much as they did with other players. They reported that the gameplay forced them to collaborate, and that this provided them with circumstances to have natural conversations outside the scope of the game. They also reported that some of the activities ended up being fun, but that the overall experience could have been better if technical difficulties had not occurred. They also referred to a good build-up of the comfort zone within the group across the challenges: the first ones did not require touching but the last ones did.

Gameplay With/Out Smartphone: Team players without a smartphone with the game running reported a more frustrating and mixed overall experience than those with phones with the game. These players communicated a greater difficulty to participate, lower engagement, perceived the existence of bigger technical difficulties when reported by other players with the game as compared to the reports of the players that actually played (for e.g., "…every time we tried to do something, it was, like, it didn't really work…" (P5)).

4.5 Discussion

The challenges were reported to be good ice breakers and good at creating memorable experiences with people on the street. All groups commented on the high difficulty level of challenge 4, but none commented on how easy a challenge was (namely, challenge 5, where all groups took less than 10 s to solve). This raises the question on the level of difficulty that is the most appropriate to facilitate social interaction and gradual participation and performance to occur. On the one hand, harder challenges might imply a bigger barrier for participation than easier challenges, but an easier challenge might fail to mediate observable face-to-face social interaction. On the other hand, a harder challenge does not necessarily imply lack of self-motivation to play, as all participants performed challenge 4 (allegedly the hardest) but not all of them performed challenge 3 (which has a lower level of complexity than challenge 4).

The challenges were designed to promote participants' self-motivation to interact, by influencing their levels of intimacy (intimate face-to-face communication and quality of intimate topics shared). In and between challenges, players had plenty of opportunities to have natural conversations outside the scope of the game, which might have led to certain levels of bonding observed at the end of the gameplay. The order of the challenges proved to be relevant: challenges requiring intimacy due to specific requirements (e.g. blindfolds, touching other people, and dancing in public space) were built on top of previous interactions, which also helped to provide with circumstances to initiate dialogue. Results from the execution of challenge 3 show that, when players are faced with a task that demands too much intimacy, their degree of like-dislike is negatively affected and they end up not participating. It was observed and reported during the interviews that groups behaved friendlier and closer after the gameplay, being an anecdotal remark that a WhatsApp group was created with the participants of the winning team, which is something that would otherwise not have happened ("this happened because of the game" (P3)). The impact of the group's cohesion of the winning team was also observed through the act of taking selfies of the group when they were announced as the winners, which shows a certain pride and happiness in their overall performance.

The degree of like-dislike seems to be affected by the players' perceptions of how good or bad they think they will perform, which could be observed by seeing certain players purposefully avoiding doing certain challenges that could be perceived as rendering them more exposed to the public eye (e.g. dancing). Players also mentioned liking particular challenges that had a nice themed description, and this might indicate that having challenge designs that take the physical space more into consideration can be appreciated by the players and even affect engagement.

5 Conclusion

This paper explored the suitability of 5 different challenges purposefully designed for playful social interaction in urban environments, within the SotS game framework, and targeting strangers within the context of a conference. The results from the executed experiment provide insights on the appropriateness of the proposed challenge designs for the fostering of (1) self-motivation, (2) perceptions, norms and values, and (3) participation and performance between team members: they show that the overall experience of the players was pleasant, that there was a desire to keep playing these types of challenges and games in the future, and that levels of comfort were apparent during and after the gameplay, both between players and in regard to the challenges themselves. This indicates that the proposed challenges within the used game framework were appreciated and appropriate for these participants.

The results show that participants of a scientific conference that (mostly) do not know each other are willing to play a game with challenges designed for a fun and collaborative gameplay experience with others, that the build-up of the comfort zone of players within groups is noticeable and appreciated, and that the game also promotes circumstances to have natural conversations outside the scope of the game. This indicates that face-to-face social interaction between strangers in a scientific conference can be fostered by the proposed challenge designs within the SotS game framework.

Direction for future work start with the study of different levels of engagement that can stem from further challenge designs, divided in different categories, and designed for different types of players of diverse target ages. Different types of categories can be based on, for e.g., augmented reality, puzzles, or sensors/actuators from the internet of things, which can provide different levels of immersion in the overall intended experience. Further research will also seek to understand whether social interaction via these and other challenge designs within the SotS game framework can be fostered in other urban environments from different countries. Such research across different societies can provide added value insights on the heterogeneity of the provided gameplay experience, which can inform other researchers on designs for digital mobile gameplay experiences that promote social interaction in playful cities.

Acknowledgement. Acknowledgements are due to Amir Fard, Hendrik Engelbrecht, Isabelle Kniestedt, Kusnandar Kusnandar, Daniel Broca, Chun Cheung, Bramka Jafino, Els van Daalen, and to the research project that supported this research[10].

References

1. Ball, K., Cleland, V.J., Timperio, A.F., et al.: Love thy neighbour? Associations of social capital and crime with physical activity amongst women. Soc. Sci. Med. **71**, 807–814 (2010)
2. Braaten, L.J.: Group cohesion: a new multidimensional model. Group **15**, 39–55 (1991)
3. Cheok, A.D., et al.: Human Pacman: a mobile entertainment system with ubiquitous computing and tangible interaction over a wide outdoor area. In: Chittaro, L. (ed.) Mobile HCI 2003. LNCS, vol. 2795, pp. 209–223. Springer, Heidelberg (2003). https://doi.org/10.1007/978-3-540-45233-1_16
4. Chittaro, L., Sioni, R.: Turning the Classic Snake Mobile Game into a Location-Based Exergame that Encourages Walking, vol. 7284. Springer, Heidelberg (2012). https://doi.org/10.1007/978-3-642-31037-9_4
5. Cooley, C.H.: Primary groups. In: Social Organization: A Study of the Larger Mind, pp. 23–31. Charles Scribner's Sons, New York (1909)
6. Cox, T.H., Lobel, S.A., McLeod, P.L.: Effects of ethnic group cultural differences on cooperative and competitive behavior on a group task. Acad. Manag. **34**(4), 827–847 (1991)
7. Council of Europe: Report of High-Level Task Force on Social Cohesion: Towards an Active, Fair and Socially Cohesive Europe (2008). Accessed 28 Jan 2008
8. Festinger, L., Back, K.W., Schachter, S.: Social Pressures in Informal Groups: A Study of Human Factors in Housing. Stanford University Press, Palo Alto (1950)
9. Fonseca, X., Lukosch, S., Brazier, F.: Social cohesion revisited: a new definition and how to characterize it. Innov.: Eur. J. Soc. Sci. Res. (2018). https://doi.org/10.1080/13511610.2018.1497480
10. Galinsky, A.D., Ku, G., Wang, C.S.: Perspective-taking and self-other overlap: fostering social bonds and facilitating social coordination. Group Process. Intergroup Relat. **8**(2), 109–124 (2005)
11. Görgü, L., Campbell, A.G., McCusker, K., et al.: Freegaming: mobile, collaborative, adaptive and augmented exergaming. Mob. Inf. Syst. **8**(4), 287–301 (2012)
12. Groenewegen, P.P., van den Berg, A.E., de Vries, S., et al.: Vitamin G: effects of green space on health, well-being, and social safety. BMC Public Health **6**, 149 (2006)
13. Lott, A.J., Lott, B.E.: Group cohesiveness and individual learning. J. Educ. Psychol. **57**, 61–73 (1966)
14. Nijholt, A.: How to make cities more fun. Wall Str. J. (Eastern Edition) (2017). ISSN: 0099-9660

---

[10] https://www.tudelft.nl/tbm/onderzoek/projecten/engineering-social-technologies-for-a-responsible-digital-future/, Engineering Social Technologies for a Responsible Digital Future.

15. Nijholt, A.: Playable cities: a short survey (Keynote Paper). In: 2017 6th International Conference on Informatics, Electronics and Vision & 2017 7th International Symposium in Computational Medical and Health Technology (ICIEV-ISCMHT), Himeji, Japan (2017)
16. Peeters, M., Megens, C., Hoven, E.V.D., et al.: Social stairs: taking the piano staircase towards long-term behavioral change. In: PERSUASIVE: International Conference on Persuasive Technology. 8th International Conference, PERSUASIVE 2013, Sydney, NSW, Australia (2013)
17. Peters, K., Elands, B., Buijs, A.: Social interactions in urban parks: stimulating social cohesion? Urban For. Urban Green. **9**(2), 93–100 (2010)
18. Peters, K., Elands, B., Buijs, A.: Social interactions in urban parks: stimulating social cohesion? Urban For. Urban Green. **9**, 93–100 (2010)
19. Polansky, N., Lippitt, R., Redl, F.: An investigation of behavioral contagion in groups. Hum. Relat. **3**, 319–348 (1950)
20. Sharp, J., Pollock, V., Paddison, R.: Just art for a just city: public art and social inclusion in urban regeneration. Urban Stud. **42**(5–6), 1001–1023 (2005)
21. Stokes, J.P.: Components of group cohesion intermember attraction, instrumental value, and risk taking. Small Group Res. **14**, 163–173 (1983)
22. Verhaegh, J., Soute, I., Kessels, A., et al.: On the design of Camelot, an outdoor game for children. In: Proceeding IDC 2006 Proceedings of the 2006 Conference on Interaction Design and Children, pp. 9–16. ACM, New York (2006)
23. Winden, W.V.: The end of social exclusion? On information technology policy as a key to social inclusion in large European cities. Reg. Stud. **35**(9), 861–877 (2001)

Saving Face: Playful Design for Social Engagement, in Public Smart City Spaces

Karen Lancel[1,2(✉)], Hermen Maat[2], and Frances Brazier[1]

[1] Delft University of Technology, Delft, The Netherlands
lancel@xs4all.nl
[2] Artists duo Lancel/Maat, Amsterdam, The Netherlands

Abstract. Can social engagement and reflection be designed through social touch in today's smart city's public spaces? This paper explores ludic, playful design for shared engagement and reflection in public spaces through social touch. In two Artistic Social Labs (ASL), internationally presented in public spaces, a radically unfamiliar sensory synthesis is acquired, for which perception of 'who sees and who is being seen, who touches and who is being touched' is disrupted. Participants playfully 'touch themselves and feel being touched, to connect with others on a screen'. On the basis of the findings in the ASLs, guidelines are proposed for orchestrating social engagement and reflection, through social touch as play.

Keywords: Social engagement · Digital art in city spaces · Playful social touch

1 Introduction

Can social engagement and reflection be designed in smart city's public spaces through social touch? This paper explores ludic, playful design for social engagement and reflection in public spaces through social touch, between person to person and person to city.

Playfulness in digital interactive art in public spaces ambiguously combines aspects of physical and virtual presence, familiarity and unfamiliarity, predictability and unpredictability, seriousness and fun [2, 7, 9]. Sensory and social interaction is disrupted to evoke the participants' ambivalence between action and reception, between observation and identification or immersion, for engagement and reflection to emerge [10]. Playful social and haptic disruption have been pursued in many digital art works [1, 13, 16], to promote new sensory connections and relational spaces [2, 8] embedded in the smart cities' networked information flows [4, 14]. However, playful social touching in public spaces has been subject of little art nor research [11].

This paper presents two experiments 'Saving Face' [12], from a series of Artistic Social Labs (ASL). These ASLs are fact mixed reality, multi modal public interfaces. The ASLs are firstly designed to disrupt perception of 'who sees and who is being seen, who touches and who is being touched' among public participants. Participants are asked to publically touch themselves and feel being touched to connect with others on a city public screen. The ASLs have been performed in various cultural contexts and

A. L. Brooks et al. (Eds.): ArtsIT 2018/DLI 2018, LNICST 265, pp. 296–305, 2019.

geographical city public spaces (Venice Biennale (2015), Utrecht (2012), Amsterdam (2015), Berlin-Dessau (2013), Beijing (2013, 2015-16)).

Combining artistic insights and academic analysis, this paper presents results of two ASLs called 'Saving Face' and proposes guidelines for social engagement and reflection design in city public spaces, through social touch as play.

2 Method

This paper describes and analyses two experiments in outdoor city public spaces to explore the effect of the interface design choices through research through design [17]. Two experiments explore the design choices, based on (1) observations (by a Host, see below) of participants' actions and reactions; (2) thick descriptions of open ended interviews with participants; (3) photo and short video documentation that support these observations, when available (Fig. 1).

Fig. 1. Actors participating in the ASL caress their faces in Amsterdam and Utrecht

3 ASL Interaction Design: Caress to Mirror and Merge

Saving Face is a 'city interface' designed to provoke social engagement and reflection in smart city public spaces, through social touch as play. Citizens are invited to meet in a playful, networked social system. In front of a city public screen, enhanced with face recognition technology system, participants caress their own faces, to connect with others in the physical public space, on the public screen and in the digital network, guided by a Host.

By caressing their faces, participants 'paint' their portraits on the screen. Their portraits appear and slowly merge with the portraits of previous visitors. These portraits merge further through every face-caressing act of following participants, co-creating untraceable networked 'identities'. Each composed identity is saved in a user generated database, to be printed, provokingly, for a Saving Face Passport.

Spatially, Actors' intimate caressing gestures are publically staged both in the physical space and on the *screen*. In front of the screen, the intimate, slow and vulnerable character of caressing gestures is designed to contrast with common public dynamics of the city public space, to visually articulate an 'aesthetic distance' [10]. Such aesthetic distance has been designed to frame the intimate gesture of caressing as an invitation to play.

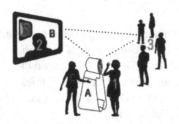

Fig. 2. Interaction Model for Artistic Social Lab (Interaction Model for City Interface: Artistic Social Lab 'Saving Face'. © Lancel/Maat 2015.). (A) Aluminium City Sculpture (Camera, face recognition technologies), (B) City Public Screen, (C) Host. (1) Actor, (2) Virtual Persona, (3) Spectators (potential Actors).

3.1   Actors and Spectators

Technically, the multi-modal interface consists of an interactive, aluminium sculpture with a camera and a small, in-built mirroring screen with face-recognition technology (A in Fig. 2), connected to a city public screen (B in Fig. 2).

Socially, the interface invites participants to interact with each other in various possible roles: that of Actor (this notion is used to describe an active rather than passive role of audience), Spectator and Virtual Persona. As Actors[1] (1 in Fig. 2), people from the public are invited to caress their faces in front of the camera and publically 'paint' their portraits on the city public screen. Actors can then choose to save their portraits and merge them with the portraits of previous Actors, people they have often never met before. The merging process of portraits into Virtual Personae is visible on the screen, for Actors and Spectators (3 in Fig. 2).

Spectators (3 in Fig. 2) view from a distance (and can become Actors themselves).

3.2   Virtual Personae

The merged portraits are described as Virtual Personae (2 in Fig. 2). These Virtual Personae are designed to 'virtually gaze' into the public domain, as contemporary 'fellow men and women'. They emerge from the interplay between Actors, Spectators, the technological system and caressing gestures as described above. All Actors'

---

[1] The Actors' participation exposed to the Spectators [15] can be described as 'performative'. Instead of referring to the notion on *performance* as a form of 'role-playing', *performativity* [3] is, in this context, considered to be a repetitive act designed for public spaces, to share reflection on social engagement.

caressing gestures are visualized real-time on a city public screen. The gestures are translated into visual, slowly emerging 'data traces'. While caressing, only the caressed part of the face is highlighted as 'data trace', building up to a (full) portrait. These data traces then merge with previous participants' portraits from a database[2]. When no Actors participate, the Virtual Personae morph auto-play from the database, displaying the process of merging with others (Fig. 3).

Fig. 3. Excerpt of online, generative database collection: merged portraits ('Virtual Personas'). (Generative database collection of merged portraits © Lancel/Maat, 2015. Each merged persona is automatically uploaded to Flickr, for public use: https://www.flickr.com/photos/savingfaceportraits/page1/)

3.3 The Host

A *Host* (C in Fig. 2) is part of the interface design, often performed by the artists or by volunteers. In all Saving Face ASLs the Host explains (a) the project researching social engagement through mediated touch and (b) the physical interaction. The ASL is explained to people using words such as 'mobile phone', 'connect', 'meeting', 'touch' 'digital', that are internationally understood. Through both words and body language words such as 'caressing', and 'being close' are visualized. The explanation serves both as a spoken manual and as contextualization. The Host then (c) witnesses the performativity of the Actor from a distance, ensures a safe space for concentration when necessary and (d) mediates reflection through open ended interview afterwards. In this way, the Host mediates between physical and virtual presence, between public space and intimate space. The Host, in fact, mediates the mediation.

4 Two ASL Experiments in Public Spaces

Below two experiments, in outdoor city public spaces, are described and analysed, to explore the effects of the interface design choices addressing two research questions: Does disrupted touch lead to playful exploration and engagement in smart public

---

[2] In this way, each Virtual Persona exists of data traces generated by many caressing acts. The last portrait layer contains 50% of the previous portrait, to enhance the Actor's self-recognition and connection. Colours of skin merge, but the last colour is dominant.

spaces? and Does the ASL's sensory orchestration of social touch lead to playful engagement and reflection in smart public spaces?

4.1 Festival aan de Werf, 2012, Neude, Utrecht

ASL 1 took place during 10 days between 10 am and 11 pm, on a dynamic square in the middle of Utrecht, during the art festival Festival aan de Werf. During this period, streams of people passed from all directions: men and women off to work, youngsters strolling along, families exploring the festival, girls shopping, tourists dwelling. In this context, the ASL addresses the question: Does disrupted touch lead to playful exploration and engagement in smart public spaces?

The Host stands near the sculpture and observes people's actions and reactions when they pass. As people pass, they often stop to watch the ASL from a certain distance.

Most Spectators are first attracted by the screen, but only stay to watch if they also see an Actor caressing his or her face. In these cases, they turn to the screen, look back at the caressing act and back to the screen again, relating the caressing gestures and the virtual faces on the screen, immersed in a disrupted, two-fold gaze.

When Spectators see Actors emerging on the screen, they show interest, come close and ask the Host what's going on. When the virtual faces merge and partly disappear into composite faces, many Spectators take pictures of the image on screen. Often, they then take on the role of the caressing Actor. Lively discussions with Actors about the use of social media and sensory connections, often follow.

The Host observes that once one Actor starts caressing, more follow. At first, Actors often express to feel socially uncomfortable and strangely exposed to be observed while caressing in public space. This feeling seems to disappear once they are absorbed in the interaction between themselves and the screen, losing touch with their surroundings. This unique experience of touch in public space is often stated to be a totally different experience, often described as disturbing, involving co-location of oneself. This experience is not described as such when no Spectators are around.

The Host observes many ways of caressing practiced over time: Actors show body language of immersion, intensity, alienation, stillness, and unfamiliarity. Their faces express disbelief, pleasure, wonder, joy, concentration, and sensory involvement. Often Actors are fascinated by caressing their face and tell the Host that they have never had this experience before. Instead of caressing, some mimic putting crème on their faces or 'shave' their faces. Others just softly touch one spot on their face and then another. Some hesitantly caress their faces partially, some eagerly grasp their full faces. The Host directs Actors to caress: 'Caress your face as if it was your lover's face' and 'Take your time'. Actors strongly respond to this intimate reference, smile, giggle and concentrate. Various video captures show people slowly and intensively caressing their faces, again and again.

During the first days, the position of the sculpture was tested. It was placed at various distances and visual angles to the screen. It became clear to the Host that if both the act of caressing and the screen cannot be seen from the same position by both Actors and Spectators, they all express less connection with the merged, Virtual Personae on screen – they 'lose touch'.

Often, the Host observes participants' engagement and reflection. For example, three young men caress each other's faces. While caressing, their increasing concentration and tenderness is observed by the Host. During caressing, they talk with each other about how it feels to appear on the screen though touching their faces. Another example is a father who wanted to surprise his daughter by 'painting' his moustache in her portrait that she previously created on the screen. While starting the caressing act as instrumental to surprise his daughter, the Host witnesses a transition to a shared experience of exploring the effects and the feeling of caressing his moustache in the ASL, visible to all. The Host observes that many Actors come back to merge with friends and family, to embrace the visual effects and co-creation of the shared Virtual Personae over time. For example, a girl having participated comes back the next day with her parents and her brother to co-create merging portraits as a family.

4.2   Findings

The ASL synthesis is activated by a Host, Actors and Spectators. Relations between caressing gestures, gesture tracing on screen and a resulting shared Virtual Persona, incite playful immersion for both Actors and Spectators. This immersion is established only when both screen and caressing gestures can be seen or experienced from one spatial position. The Hosting design creates conditions for all kinds of caressing and allows Actors to fully concentrate on this process. People experiment with acts and experiences of caressing, while expressing and sharing pleasure and joy. Even when acts of caressing result in merely 'losing touch with surrounding Spectators', Actors still need the witnessing presence of the Spectators' gazes around them, to experience their gestures as socially engaging. Moreover, the unpredictable results of merging portraits, becomes exciting only when witnessed and discussed by others. Co-creation of the Virtual Personae on screen seems to incite participation (Fig. 4).

Fig. 4. Participants exploring in the Artistic Social Lab. Connecting Cities, 2015.

The unfamiliarity with this role creates a safe space to embrace interdependency, experiment and sharing conversations both with the Host and Spectators around. People of all ages, social cultures and geographical backgrounds participate. Participants share expression of reflection among each other, to accompany each other when caressing and seduced by the unpredictable outcome of merging portraits.

4.3   Connected Cities Network Berlin: Dessau

Connecting Cities Network invited the ASL around the historical Bauhaus Architecture (1919, W. Gropius), now housing the Academy for Architecture Dessau. In this context, this second ASL addresses the question: Does the ASL's sensory orchestration of social touch lead to playful engagement and reflection in smart public spaces?

During two days, from late afternoon until midnight, people came along wondering. In between the Dessau buildings, the sculpture's silvery aluminium mirrors the fading daylight. It seems to be floating without gravity, connected to the digital network. A video device with the ASL documentation was added to the sculpture (an extension of ASL 1). More than 130 Actors caress their faces.

The Actors' small, caressing gestures were counter-parted by a huge wall high quality projection. The projection on the wall (instead of an electronic screen as in ASL 1) provided a very 'clean' visual environment, in which the projected, Virtual Persona seemed to appear as a loose, floating Gestalt.

The Host observes people of all ages, in small social groups or families, crowding the space. The Spectators' gazes, between (a) *mirroring the caressing gestures and (b) watching at a distant screen the corresponding visual traces, is disrupted.* The emerging traces on screen direct the Spectators' dwelling eyes.

After participation, Actors are challenged by the Host to reflect and answer questions about their experiences. They often stated that it felt strange, and that they do not have words to describe this experience as a sense of touch. And yet they try. It often leads to stuttering and to finding new words and images, expressing their experiences, as a form of reflection. For example, for many, the installation appears to be an incentive for the gesture to caress their faces, to mirror and be part of a coded system. One Actor commented: "When I closed my eyes caressing in front of this technology, knowing that that my caressing act was exposed, it seemed as if a hand outside caressed me, as if it was not my hand but the hand of God." Some told that they felt like giving away a piece of themselves to a 'digital grid'. Others would be immersed in a twofold, disrupted experience of seeing and feeling their faces, for a long time - and then stop, as if awakening.

4.4   Findings

The Host mediates the mediation and challenges Actors and Spectators to describe their experiences on the ASL's disrupted synthesis. All participants reflect on an embodied sense of mirroring versus the scanning, tracing and emerging information on screen. They reflect on their experiences of caressing themselves in order to appropriate a Virtual Persona, shared with others. Their aim to reflect leads to stuttering, to finding new words and images, as a shared form of playful reflection. The Actors expressed unfamiliarity with the visual-haptic experience of *caressing-and-feeling-caressed* intertwined with visually emerging on screen (Fig. 5).

Fig. 5. Participants exploring in the Artistic Social Lab. Connecting Cities, 2015.

5 Conclusion

City interface Saving Face is designed for playful engagement and reflection, through social touch. Technically, the smart cities infrastructure is reconfigured to accommodate participants to play with a city public screen, a generative database system and face-recognition technologies. A novel, social touch interface has been designed in which the familiar relation between 'who you see, who you touch and who is being touched' is disrupted. The ASL is orchestrated to experience a socio-technical synthesis on the basis of 'caressing your face to connect with others on a screen'. Design impacts of two experiments are analysed below, to propose guidelines for designing social engagement and reflection, through social touch as play.

Social Touch. People of various ages play, from diverse geographical backgrounds and cultures. Playful exploration and reflection emerge from both self-referential exploration and from relations with others. Both experiments have shown to provoke participants' joyful experiment and shared pleasure. Many people perform and observe face caressing, in concentrated and touching ways, as if for the first time. They interact with others who are previously, virtually, actually and potentially present, in various time relations.

Ambivalent Design. Vital to the design are aesthetic principles of unfamiliarity, unpredictability and disruption, to engage in playful exploration, interaction, immersion and reflection. Experiment 1 shows that Actors and Spectators interact in co-dependency, relating simultaneously in the physical space and via their bodies as signifiers on a city public screen. Their acts of physical caressing must be mirrored real-time as emerging data traces on the screen. The unfamiliar, ambivalent design of both physical and virtually mirroring is crucial to engage shared immersive, playful exploration. The ambivalence occurs when all participants can perceive both acts of caressing a face and data traces from the same spatial position. The unpredictable results of merging portraits with previous participants becomes exciting only when witnessed by others.

Reflection Through Play. The acts of caressing need to be visually staged, counterparted by social city dynamics and exposure on city public screens, to evoke an aesthetical distance from which playful reflection and dialogue can emerge. Hosting is conditional to involve the Actors and Spectators in shared expression of reflection, as became clear in experiment 1. The Host invites Actors to participate, mediates the mediation and frames the public space as a lively agora. Actors describe their experiences to the Host in new words and images, as found in experiment 2, as a new form of 'embodied sense of knowing' [6] and express a sense of shared embodiment with others, 'through technology'.

Both Artistic Social Labs show that the social touch interface design evokes social engagement and reflection, in smart cities' public spaces, through social touch as play.

Acknowledgements. *Saving Face* (2012) was developed by artists-scientists duo Lancel/Maat (Karen Lancel, Hermen Maat) as an art work, artistic research and case study (http://www.lancel.nl/work/saving-face/). It was generously supported by Media Fund, Mondriaan Fonds, Festival aan de Werf Utrecht, MediaFonds@Sandberg, Cultural Consulate Beijing, BCAF Beijing, Beam Systems Amsterdam, Dutch Embassy Berlin, SICA NLTR 400 and technically developed in collaboration with Sylvain Vriens, Tim Olden, Matthijs ten Berge, Mart van Bree, Beamsystems, using Jason Saragih's open source Facetracker library.

References

1. Blast Theory: Can You See Me Now? (2007). https://www.blasttheory.co.uk/projects/can-you-see-me-now/. Accessed 12 July 2018
2. Benford, S., Giannachi, G.: Interaction as Performance. Interactions **19**(3), 38–43 (2012)
3. Butler, J.: Gender Trouble, Feminism and the Subversion of Identity. Routledge, London (1990)
4. Castells, M.: Informationalism and the Network Society. In: Himanen, P. (ed.) The Hacker Ethic and the Spirit of the Information Age, pp. 155–178. Random House, NY (2001)
5. Ga, Z.: People's Portrait (2004). http://www.medienkunstnetz.de/works/peoples-portrait/images/3. Accessed 3 Sept 2018
6. Gill, S.: Tacit engagement, beyond Interaction. Springer International Publishing, New York (2015)
7. Gould, C., Sermon P.: Occupy the screen: a case study of open artworks for urban screens. In: Armstrong, K. (ed.) The 21st International Symposium of Electronic Art Proceedings of ISEA 2015, New Forms Art Press, artists and writers, Vancouver (2015)
8. Gsöllpointner, K., Schnell, R., Schuler, K.S.: Digital synesthesia, a model for the aesthetics of digital art. De Gruyter, series: Edition Angewandte, Berlin/Boston (2016)
9. Huizinga, J.: Homo Ludens. H. D. Tjeenk Willink & Zn., Haarlem (1940)
10. Kwastek, K.: Aesthetics of Interaction in Digital Art. MIT press, Cambridge (2013)

11. Lancel, K., Maat, H., Brazier, F.M.: Kissing data, distributed haptic connections through social touch. In: Acoustic Space volume No 17. Riga's Center for New Media Culture RIXC/Art Research Laboratory of Liepaja University (2018)
12. Lancel/Maat: Saving Face (2012). http://lancelmaat.nl/work/saving-face/. Accessed 31 Aug 2018
13. Lozano-Hemmer, R.: Body Movies, Relational Architecture 6 (2001). http://www.lozano-hemmer.com/body_movies.php. Accessed 12 July 2018
14. Nijholt, A.: Playable Cities: The City as a Digital Playground. Springer, Singapore (2017)
15. Reeves, S., Benford, S., O'Malley, C., Fraser, M.: Designing the Spectator Experience In: CHI 2005 Proceedings of the SIGCHI Conference on Human Factors in Computing Systems, pp. 741–750. ACM, New York (2005)
16. Sermon, P.: Occupy the screen (2014). http://www.paulsermon.org/occupy/. Accessed 3 Sept 2018
17. Zimmerman, J., Forlizzi, J.: Research through Design in HCI. In: Olson, J.S., Kellog, W.A. (eds.) Ways of Knowing in HCI, pp. 167–189. Springer, New York (2014). https://doi.org/10.1007/978-1-4939-0378-8_8

Exploring Requirements for Joint Information Sharing in Neighbourhoods: Local Playgrounds in The Hague

Geertje Slingerland(✉), Stephan Lukosch, Tina Comes,
and Frances Brazier

Delft University of Technology, Delft, The Netherlands
g.slingerland@tudelft.nl

Abstract. Resilient communities are an important prerequisite to reach urban resilience. In such communities, citizens need to be able to participate for improving liveability and safety of their environment. The playable city, where participation is key, provides the environment for this process to unfold. This paper researches requirements for the design of playgrounds: environments for open interaction and collaboration, as part of the playable city. Two workshops were organised in two neighbourhoods in The Hague to explore specific citizen preferences for playground design. Neighbourhood locations and the type of information citizens would like to discover, share, and create are identified, in particular with respect to healthcare, safety and social engagement. The implications of these requirements are presented and discussed with design options which exemplify how playgrounds in the city enable joined information sharing, creation, interaction, and collaboration.

Keywords: Community resilience · Interaction design
Playable cities · Playgrounds

1 Introduction

Cities are confronted with major transitions, ranging from the energy transition to the digital transition, from migration to poverty. These transitions mandate the ability of individuals and communities to survive despite the challenges with which they are faced [20]. This ability, referred to as *urban resilience* by the Rockefeller Foundation, is core to their "100 Resilient Cities Network" (100RC). This network helps cities around the world to become more resilient, and explicitly includes social inclusion and cohesion [1] in its goals. As fragmentation of neighbourhoods is one of the major challenges faced by cities [11], this paper focuses on The Hague[1], one of the 100 RC and the most fragmented city in the Netherlands [12, p. 52].

---

[1] This paper reports on research performed within the context of the project BART!, that aims to improve coordination and collaboration between citizens, municipality, and police through co-creation, to increase safety and liveability of The Hague.

© ICST Institute for Computer Sciences, Social Informatics and Telecommunications Engineering 2019
Published by Springer Nature Switzerland AG 2019. All Rights Reserved
A. L. Brooks et al. (Eds.): ArtsIT 2018/DLI 2018, LNICST 265, pp. 306–315, 2019.
https://doi.org/10.1007/978-3-030-06134-0_35

An important part of The Hague's Resilience Agenda [2] is to empower citizens to engage in finding solutions for the liveability and safety challenges of the city. To this end, citizens need to be able to participate and to jointly share and create solutions for the neighbourhood. The Playable City [15,16], where residents are empowered to participate, is considered to provide the setting for such local engagement. This paper proposes the design of "playgrounds" as part of the playable city: physical and virtual environments where open interaction and collaboration can take place, engaging residents with their local community. On these playgrounds, information sharing, co-creation, and spontaneous social interaction enable citizens to learn about and engage with their surroundings, empowering them to take action to improve their own situation.

2   Related Work

Communities are considered to be one of the core aspects of urban resilience. Their ability to "take collective actions, and to use the available resources to self-organise, respond to, withstand, and recover from crises [8]" is thus a more specific approach to urban resilience.[2] Such *community resilience* is not only supported by the connectedness between neighbours [17], but also by the ability of citizens to influence change or decision-making on local issues of concern [4,14].

In a playable city, technology is often used to offer playful interactions between citizens or with the environment [15] to evoke participatory initiatives from bottom up [16]. Technology, however, is repeatedly used in city making to increase efficiency, leading to less spontaneous encounters and involvement with the direct environment [5,14]. This paper explores whether playgrounds, as part of the playable city, can be created for collaboration and interaction, to open up the opportunity for citizens to participate in the development of their community.

Playful interactions within these particular environments concern citizens jointly sharing and creating local information and stories, aiming to lead to increased involvement for the community well-being [10]. Other types of interactions, such as co-creating the current mood of the neighbourhood [18], tagging specific locations to share with other residents [3,7,13], or gamified social interactions taking place at particular neighbourhood locations [5,7,9], are also potential enablers of a playground. This research explores the requirements for the design of playgrounds for joined information sharing and creation, as an enabler of the playable city.

3   Method

As this research aims to find requirements for open, interactive environments for participation, a playful and participatory approach was used in this exploratory

---

[2] Note that this paper does not focus on resilience towards crises as in shocks, but rather on the ability of communities to respond to long-term crises/challenges and trends as they emerge.

case study. Two neighbourhoods in The Hague were selected and residents were actively approached for participation, to make sure the identified requirements would be suitable to their specific situation. Two workshops were organised with citizens in these two neighbourhoods, to investigate which information they would like to share, receive, and create, on which topics. They also explored which locations would be most appropriate for open interaction and collaboration. The aim of these workshops was to acquire insight in requirements for the design of a playground, as the initial basis for the design of an intervention in these neighbourhoods.

3.1 Participants

Purposive sampling [19] was used to find citizens for the workshops. The criteria deployed specified that citizens needed to live in one of the two neighbourhoods and be interested in contributing to the quality of life and safety in their own neighbourhood. Six citizens from one neighbourhood attended the first workshop, and 22 citizens from both neighbourhoods attended the second. Citizens for the first workshop were recruited through gatekeepers, such as the community centre. Citizens for the second workshop were recruited through gatekeepers and "Burgernet", a government-run safety alert platform.

3.2 Workshop Procedure

Workshop 1: Identifying Locations and Information. The aim of the first workshop was to identify which locations in the neighbourhood are most appropriate for sharing and creating specific types of information. Two playful prototypes were developed and used as the basis for discussion during the workshop, see Figs. 1 and 2.

Fig. 1. Participants read stories about their neighbourhood.

Fig. 2. Participants are adding locations on the map.

The first prototype, Fig. 1, was a wooden box with sticks on which various stories from the neighbourhoods were displayed. These stories were based on information shared on local social media pages, and both pictures and written text were used to communicate the narratives. Empty sticks were available as well so that participants were able to add their own stories. Participants could first freely explore the stories and after 10 minutes, discussion was started to focus on the specific neighbourhood needs, expressed by the participants, in relation to the prototype. Thus, which narratives participants found intriguing, with whom they would share these stories and what other stories they would be interested in.

The second prototype was a printed map of the neighbourhoods, see Fig. 2. On the map, specific locations and information were already marked for participants to consider. Materials were provided for them to mark other locations as well. As in the first prototype, participants first worked on this task within the prototype, and discussion followed on which locations were still missing on the map, and why these locations were considered to be appropriate.

Workshop 2: Identifying Scenarios and Information. The aim of the second workshop was to identify which information needs to be shared when and where. In other words, when do citizens want to share information with each other and where. In particular, for example, the question was addressed whether the need for information sharing depends on specific circumstances such as a neighbour asking for help. A digital prototype was developed to explore the influence of context: if and how different scenarios lead, or do not lead, to the need for information exchange between neighbours.

The prototype for this workshop was a digital interactive website, see Fig. 3, and displayed various questions, problems or stories of citizens. These pieces of information relate to the themes of safety, healthcare, and social engagement, and were based on actual challenges and developments in these neighbourhoods, some identified during the first workshop. This information could be sorted by the participants on the basis of specific citizen (personal), topics (theme), or position on a map (location). In addition to being able to view information, participants could also create new information or respond to one of the questions or problems stated on the website.

Fig. 3. Participants are reading and responding to the stories in the digital prototype.

The workshop took place in two rounds with 10 and 12 citizens respectively. Citizens took place behind a laptop in groups of two, and received a brief instruction on the functionality of the prototype. For about 20 minutes, citizens could interact with the prototype, viewing different questions, stories, and problems of neighbours prepared by the designers, and respond to these online. After that, participants were asked to fill out a questionnaire on the relevance of the information provided.

3.3 Data Collection and Analysis

The discussions during the first workshop were recorded and transcribed for analysis. The transcript was analysed using thematic content analysis [6], by selecting and interpreting quotes that said something about which locations participants found suitable as playgrounds, and what information they perceived appropriate to share. During the second workshop, data was collected through the questionnaire and from the responses written in the website. Each response was interpreted and coded, and the resulting codes were clustered to identify the influence of context on the need for information exchange between citizens.

4 Results

The aim of the workshops was to explore the requirements for playground design: in particular with respect to locations, information, and topics needed to transform neighbourhood streets into playgrounds for participation. These requirements are to provide the basis for the design of an intervention that enables citizens to playfully interact in the playgrounds of their neighbourhood. This section describes the results with regard to locations, information and topics.

4.1 Relevant Locations for Information Sharing

Building on the locations already on the map, participants proposed several other locations to be included: a local theatre, three churches, two mosques, a school, a sports club, the Salvation Army, and a community centre. These were suggested for two reasons. First, these locations have a history - neighbours already gather at these locations for activities of which some are aware. Such location-based information on activities could be shared with more neighbours. Second, the location itself could be of interest to other neighbours. All participants in workshop 1 agreed that this would lower the barrier to explore new neighbourhood places or to meet new people.

Interestingly, three participants mentioned not only wanting to interact with others in locations from their own direct neighbourhood, but also in neighbourhoods they often frequent. For example, neighbourhoods in which their children's schools are situated, neighbourhoods they traverse on an almost daily basis: participants expressed interest in knowing more about these neighbourhoods and their local activities. Therefore, the first requirement for the playground design is that at least two types of locations have to be included: *gathering locations*, where people are already meeting for activities, and *discovering locations*, where an interesting story could be told about.

4.2 Appropriate Information for Participation

The selected quotes about appropriate information to share and create indicated three different types of information. Activities, i.e. information about activities or places for activities (such as community centre), were mentioned 15 times during the discussion. History, i.e. information about the history of the neighbourhood, was mentioned in 7 quotes. Finally, local people, i.e. information about people from the neighbourhood, was mentioned 8 times. All participants from the first workshop agreed that such information contributes to neighbourhood pride, as citizens need to know something about their local area to be proud of it.

During the workshop, the facilitator asked the participants about which stories they would like to add. All participants were reluctant to add something, and needed to be convinced to share their own story or piece of information. The second requirement for the playground is thus that it needs to be inviting for citizens to share, create, and add information on topics such as: activities, history and people.

4.3 Relevant Use Scenarios

Seven different use scenarios were evaluated during the second workshop, and in the themes *safety*, *healthcare*, and *social engagement*. The scenario on safety evoked most responses, 8 reactions. Scenarios about healthcare and social engagement led to less interaction, varying between 3 to 7 reactions per scenario. One researcher analysed the responses and distinguished four main clusters: refer to institutions, offering help, providing tips, and linking residents. Scenarios about healthcare mainly provoked responses belonging to the "refer to institutions" (5 reactions) and "offering help" (5 reactions) category, while social engagement scenarios led to "linking residents" responses. For the safety scenario, participants mainly provided tips (5 reactions) to increase safety and prevent burglaries.

In the survey, 13 participants choose the safety scenario to increase citizen engagement the most in their neighbourhood, 9 mentioned one of the social engagement use scenarios, and only 4 mentioned one of the healthcare use scenarios. To this end, the third requirement for the platform is that local issues or questions, in particular related to safety and social engagement, have to be included to evoke interaction between neighbours.

5 Design Proposal: Playgrounds in the Neighbourhood

The results were translated to three requirements concerning the design of playgrounds for interactive information sharing and creation. This section proposes design options based on the requirements identified in the workshops described above, to be integrated into the playgrounds and that enable neighbours to interact, meet, and share information about the area.

At least two types of physical locations were identified to be suitable for playgrounds: places where people normally come together, and places where

something interesting can be shared (Requirement 1). Second, a need was identified for an inviting playground where citizens are seduced to multiple ways
of sharing and creating information: historical, personal, and information about
neighbourhood activities (Requirement 2). To evoke interaction, specific local
issues or questions need to be addressed, in addition to open-ended narratives
about the neighbourhood (Requirement 3).

5.1   Design Option: Augmented Playgrounds with Mobile App

A design option is to enable citizens to connect to local information using their
mobile phones. Figure 4 shows an example design: a mobile application that
reveals neighbourhood playgrounds when citizens arrive at that particular location. Citizens can interact in the digital environment, by viewing and responding
to information and narratives left by others. In this design, they can interact
with neighbours who have been at the same geographical location previously or
who are still to come. The playgrounds are thus partially physical and partially
digital, as the application allows citizens to both interact with people whom
are physically present, or with the information they have placed in the digital
environment.

Fig. 4. Citizens are persuaded to interact with other visitors of the community centre.

This designs stimulates citizens to explore their own neighbourhood and find
playgrounds with information or other opportunities for interaction. For example, at locations where neighbours already gather, citizens could be persuaded to
go inside the community centre, learn about the activity programme and interact with neighbours. This playground could thus focus on creating interaction
in the physical space with the people currently present.

5.2 Design Option: Physical Playgrounds with Interactive Installations

Another design option is to transform physical locations into playgrounds, by placing an interactive installation at a particular location. Such playgrounds are easily recognised by citizens passing by, and evoke interaction with the people around. Figure 5 shows an example of such an installation, which aims to stimulate playful interaction with provoking questions or statements that residents can respond to by interacting with the machine, or discuss about with others around.

Fig. 5. An interactive, multi-modal installation stimulates playful interaction between citizens.

To provide for playful encounters, the installation offers multi-modal means for interaction. Citizens do not only get a visual representation of opinions of others, but can also listen to the speaker to interact in another way. To input their own opinion, citizens can use touch or record their story with the microphones.

These design options illustrate how playgrounds could be designed to stimulate open information sharing and social interaction between neighbours that usually are not engaged in such activities. These options will be further elaborated in a third citizen workshop, which especially focuses on the interactive installation design, since that was not covered in the current workshops. In the following research phases, the design proposal is further developed and prototyped to be discussed and evaluated with participants from the case study neighbourhoods. The main aim is to create a design that supports participation and engagement to increase community resilience in particular with respect to the well-being and safety of the local neighbourhood.

6 Conclusion

The aim of this paper is to explore the design of playgrounds that stimulate interaction and collaboration for community resilience. In two workshops with citizens from The Hague, several requirements were identified, concerning suitable locations, information, and topics to convert neighbourhood locations into playgrounds for participation. The results of the workshops illustrate the potential of playgrounds to be places for open discussion, information sharing, and interaction between neighbours, increasing engagement and community resilience. Design options are proposed that fulfil these requirements. In the next stages of this research project, a design that incorporates these options will be detailed and prototyped for evaluation with citizens.

Acknowledgements. This research is part of the project BART! and received funding from the Municipality of The Hague and the National Police.

References

1. 100 Resilient Cities: What is Urban Resilience? (2018). http://www.100resilientcities.org/resources/#section-4
2. AECOM: The Hague 100 Resilient Cities: Preliminary Resilience Assessment. Technical report, Resilient The Hague, Den Haag (2018). http://100resilientcities.org/wp-content/uploads/2018/03/The-Hague-PRA-English.pdf
3. Angus, A., et al.: Urban social tapestries. IEEE Pervasive Comput. **7**(4), 44–51 (2008). https://doi.org/10.1109/MPRV.2008.84
4. Asad, M., Le Dantec, C.A.: Illegitimate civic participation: supporting community activists on the ground. In: Proceedings of the 18th ACM Conference on Computer Supported Cooperative Work and Social Computing, pp. 1694–1703. ACM (2015)
5. Balestrini, M., Marshall, P., Cornejo, R., Tentori, M., Bird, J., Rogers, Y.: Jokebox: coordinating shared encounters in public spaces. In: Proceedings of the 19th ACM Conference on Computer-Supported Cooperative Work and Social Computing, pp. 38–49. ACM (2016). https://doi.org/10.1145/2818048.2835203
6. Braun, V., Clarke, V.: Using thematic analysis in psychology. Qual. Res. Psychol. **3**(2), 77–101 (2006). https://doi.org/10.1191/1478088706qp063oa
7. Cila, N., Jansen, G., den Broeder, L., Groen, M., Meys, W., Kröse, B.: Look! a healthy neighbourhood: means to motivate participants in using an app for monitoring community health. In: Proceedings of the 2016 CHI Conference Extended Abstracts on Human Factors in Computing Systems, pp. 889–898. ACM (2016). https://doi.org/10.1145/2851581.2851591
8. Comes, T.: Designing for networked community resilience. Procedia Eng. **159**, 6–11 (2016). https://doi.org/10.1016/j.proeng.2016.08.057
9. Fonseca, X., Lukosch, S., Lukosch, H., Tiemersma, S., Brazier, F.: Requirements and game ideas for social interaction in mobile outdoor games. In: CHI PLAY 2017 Extended Abstracts, pp. 331–337. ACM Press, Amsterdam (2017). https://doi.org/10.1145/3130859.3131304

10. Foth, M., Choi, J.H., Satchell, C.: Urban informatics. In: Proceedings of the ACM 2011 Conference on Computer Supported Cooperative Work, pp. 1–8. ACM, Hangzhou (2011). https://eprints.qut.edu.au/39159/1/39159.pdf
11. Gaventa, J.: Representation, community leadership and participation: citizen involvement in neighbourhood renewal and local governance. Technical report, July, Office of Deputy Prime Minister (2004)
12. Jennissen, R., Engbersen, G., Bokhorst, M., Bovens, M.: De nieuwe verscheidenheid. Toenemende diversiteit naar herkomst in Nederland. Technical report, Wetenschappelijke Raad voor het Regeringsbeleid, Den Haag (2018). https://www.wrr.nl/publicaties/verkenningen/2018/05/29/de-nieuwe-verscheidenheid
13. Kleinhans, R., Van Ham, M., Evans-Cowley, J.: Using social media and mobile technologies to foster engagement and self-organization in participatory urban planning and neighbourhood governance. Plan. Pract. Res. 30(3), 237–247 (2015). https://doi.org/10.1080/02697459.2015.1051320
14. de Lange, M., de Waal, M.: Owning the city: new media and citizen engagement in urban design. First Monday 18(11) (2013)
15. Nijholt, A.: Designing humor for playable cities. Procedia Manufact. 3, 2175–2182 (2015). https://doi.org/10.1016/j.promfg.2015.07.358
16. Nijholt, A.: Playable Cities: The City as a Digital Playground. Springer, Singapore (2017). https://doi.org/10.1007/978-981-10-1962-3
17. Putnam, R.D.: Bowling alone. J. Democr. 6, 65–78 (1995)
18. Scolere, L.M., Baumer, E.P.S., Reynolds, L., Gay, G.: Building mood, building community: usage patterns of an interactive art installation. In: Proceedings of the 19th International Conference on Supporting Group Work, pp. 201–212 (2016). https://doi.org/10.1145/2957276.2957291
19. Teddlie, C., Yu, F.: Mixed methods sampling: a typology with examples. J. Mixed Methods Res. 1(1), 77–100 (2007). https://doi.org/10.1177/1558689806292430
20. The Rockefeller Foundation, Arup: City Resilience Framework. Technical report, The Rockefeller Foundation, Arup (2014). https://assets.rockefellerfoundation.org/app/uploads/20140410162455/City-Resilience-Framework-2015.pdf

DLI - Main Track

Infusing Creativity and Technology Through Repurposing Existing Digital Tools and Social Media Apps for Educational Purposes

Sama'a Al Hashimi[✉], Yasmina Zaki, Ameena Al Muwali, and Nasser Mahdi

University of Bahrain, P.O Box: 32038 Sakheer, Zallaq, Kingdom of Bahrain
samaa.alhashimi@gmail.com, yasminazaki7@gmail.com, ameena.almuwali@gmail.com, abuabulla00@gmail.com

Abstract. As an emerging technological and communication form of this century, digital and social media applications are gaining acceptance as platforms for creativity and inspiration in fine arts and graphic design. However, despite the proliferation of social media platforms and digital manipulation and painting apps, repurposing them for pedagogical purposes is yet to be explored as an educational strategy in the traditional painting studio or computer graphics classroom. The essence of this paper is to employ qualitative as well as quantitative research methods to explore the capabilities of digital and social media applications as a technological apparatus for creativity and expressivity in art and design education and practice. The research involves an empirical investigation of the potential offered by digital media applications and social media platforms to enhance the creative learning experience in art and design. The methodological procedures that are discussed in this paper are the result of two experimental studies; the first study explores the use of a digital painting technique – Phone Art– in the fine arts studio, while the second study investigates the use of social media applications in the graphic design classroom. The investigation is undertaken in an experimental educational setting in an attempt to determine how technology can be utilized by educators in order to optimize the creative performance of students.

Keywords: Creativity · Social media · Pedagogy · Innovation

1 Introduction

A growing trend is emerging toward the use of social media in the learning environment. Researchers started looking at specific technological interventions to the creative process involved in various domains in an attempt to improve creative outcomes. Some of them argued that influencing the creative process can change creative outcomes [7], but it is still unclear how to incorporate the emerging social media technologies to improve the creative outcomes in art and design pedagogy and practice. As no other studies appear to exist in the area of repurposing digital and social media for educational purposes, this paper comprises two preliminary experiments that aim to investigate the effectiveness of utilizing digital and social media in enhancing creativity. It

A. L. Brooks et al. (Eds.): ArtsIT 2018/DLI 2018, LNICST 265, pp. 319–330, 2019.

also aims to prompt an enquiry that could potentially uncover the preferences and patterns of interaction with these social media platforms in art and design educational contexts. In the first section, the paper presents a general overview of the key concepts discussed in the subsequent sections. In the second section, it situates its topic in the context of previous research and relevant literature related to the employment of multimedia-based learning strategies and supportive digital and social media applications in the stimulation and enhancement of student creativity. In the third section, it discusses the experimental procedures and presents the findings and their implications in an attempt to lay the ground for future research on this topic. The eventual aim is for these findings to be used in order to provide valuable insights to educators and aid them in their selection of the most effective applications to utilize during the creative processes involved in graphic design or fine arts. The findings and conclusions, which are discussed in the last section, have implications for future research in better understanding how digital and social media applications can aid students in enhancing their creativity. This research attempts to find answers to the following questions through surveying students at the University of Bahrain, and conducting empirical experiments in the classroom;

1. How can digital applications and social media platforms be repurposed and harnessed to promote a creative mindset in art and design students?
2. To what extent can repurposing these applications have an impact on fostering student innovation and creativity?
3. What are students' preferences and patterns of interaction with social media platforms in art and design educational contexts?

The next section presents the literature review that lays the ground for investigating and propelling a wave of inquiry into the experiences, preferences and interaction patterns of students during the use of social networks and digital applications to foster their creativity in art and design educational practices.

2   Supportive Digital and Social Media Applications for Creative Learning

Previous work has looked at various technological interventions to the creative process to try to improve creative outcomes [7, p. 1]. Tiryakioglu and Erzurum [13] investigated the utilization of Facebook to support learning, and the attitudes of academics towards the use of Facebook for educational purposes. They found that instructors mostly use Facebook to communicate with their students and that *"social networks improve communication skills, enhance participation and social commitment, reinforce peer support, and ensure realization of education based on collaboration. Moreover, social networking sites can be easily and inexpensively used without a substantial support from universities so that they can be integrated into educational process of students"* [13, p. 40]. They argue that educational environments that involve the utilization of social networks will better attract students' attention and lead to more effective educational experiences. In an attempt to design an online environment that enables social interactions adapted to creative processes between artists, Kim,

Agrawala, and Bernstein [7] created Mosaic: an online social platform for artists to share their artworks-in-progress. Mosaic, which can be visited at http://www.artsaic. com, allows artists to enhance their own creative processes as well those of others through sharing their failures and their successes. It also allows them to reflect on the various creative possibilities and options, and give and receive feedback from each other. On the other hand, Igarashi [6] believes that current user interfaces are crowded with buttons and menus, and therefore interfere with creativity and exploration. He designed three systems, which contain fluent user interfaces that can facilitate the early exploratory stages of the creative process; *"Pegasus interactively beautifies freeform drawings satisfying possible geometric constraints. Teddy allows the user to design freeform three-dimensional objects by drawing their silhouette shapes. Flatland provides various computational supports for simple note-taking activity on an office whiteboard"*. Chai and Fan [2] investigated the influence of social media technologies on the creative achievements of students in design education. This body of literature shows that using digital and social media applications purposefully to influence the creative process can change creative outcomes, but it is still unclear how to incorporate these applications effectively and strategically into students' learning in order to help them gain creative inspiration. Deeper knowledge of these topics and further exploration of such endeavors is critical in framing the research methods, findings, and the conclusions discussed later in this paper.

3 Experiments and Results

This paper engaged two purposive samples in two experimental settings. In Study 1, a group of seventeen fine arts and graphic design students undertook a digital painting workshop in Phone Art in order to explore the effectiveness of digital tools in fostering creativity in the art classroom. In Study 2, the effectiveness of repurposing digital and social media applications in enhancing creativity were explored in a more natural classroom setting with forty-two students engaged in character design learning activities. The two studies and their results are discussed in this section.

3.1 First Experimental Design and Setting

This part of the study examines the effectiveness of Phone Art in fostering students' creativity. According to Dr. Salman Al Hajiri, an assistant professor who uses this technique with his students at the University of Sultan Qaboos, *"Phone Art is an artistic practice that involves using smart phone apps to create graphic illustrations and designs"*. In addition to interviewing Dr. Al Hajiri, data was collected from multiple sources, including questionnaires, interviews, and empirical observation and analysis. The integration of technology with fine arts was explored in a field setting with students engaged in Phone Art. In order to complement the empirical research with quantitative analysis, online questionnaire were distributed to a purposeful sample of participants who were trained to employ Phone Art by Dr. Al Hajiri. Twenty-three participants, fifteen female and eight male, participated in the survey. The experiment combined digital art with classic art and part of it was conducted in an art studio before participants painted their artworks outdoors at the University. The participants used mobile phones to take photos and were then taught how to digitally manipulate these photos using the following apps: WeTransfer, ArtRage, Sketches, Prisma, Adobe Capture, Adobe Clip, Adobe Draw, Adobe Sketch, Adobe Scan, Adobe Comp, PS Express, AutoDraw, PaintCan, PicsArt, Layout, and CamScanner. The students then printed their artworks on 40 × 60 cm canvases, and used acrylic paint to add color layers and brush stroke effects and treatments. According to Dr. Al Hajiri this technique, which integrates digital art and classical art, was interesting to the participants who indicated that they were impressed by the idea. He stated that the students have learned how to install a wooden frame for the canvas and how the cloth is pulled on this wooden frame. All these skills are performed by the classical artist, and using the various apps which they have used enabled them to produce attractive results despite the fact that some of them are not artists.

Many respondents (52%, N = 11) indicated that using digital applications helped them in drawing creatively. When asked about the obstacles that they have encountered during their Phone Art experience, 52% (N = 11) of the students indicated that they did not face any obstacles, 24% (N = 5) mentioned that they encountered technical difficulties, while 14% (N = 3) of them indicated that the use of the apps distracted their attention, and also 14% (N = 3) indicated that the time was short. In addition, one of them stated: *"Some applications are specific to the Android system and cannot be installed on the IOS system"*. On the other hand, Dr. Al Hajiri suggested that not only students may face obstacles, but even he faced obstacles while trying to employ and promote this technique. He stated that he faced some resistance due to the lack of understanding of this technique, but he started writing about it and explaining it in various news articles and through conducting many workshops until people gained awareness and started to request these workshops in Oman and abroad. He also added, *"I strongly encourage professors to employ digital painting applications and experiment with them as they can open many possibilities. It is very important to introduce these techniques to students and make them part of the curriculum. The most important starting point is for professors to start using these apps and become experienced in using them and once they do, they shall be able transfer their skills to their students and employ a more digital dimension in teaching fine arts."* Some art instructors, however, are skeptic about the usefulness of digital tools in fine art practice. According to Annum [1], *"There is documentary evidence to show that some critics expressed skepticism about the validity of using computer as a multimedia apparatus for executing paintings during its early period of inception in the 1960's. The rejection was based on the premise that the art of painting cannot be done on a computer since the device only generates digital graphical images, which are superficial, without depth and of limited artistic value [5]. To most traditional artists, computer art is solely a technological craft that is informatively and aesthetically deficient. To them computer generated art is for commercial considerations, dull in outlook, lack innovation and quality hence could not be given a place in fine arts [12]"* [1, p. 2]. Yet, Annum [1] implied that digital painters can influence public acceptance and alter the negative perceptions about digital paintings through the creation of artworks that reflect aesthetic values which are consistent with the aesthetic values of spectators. Dr. Al Hajiri, however, does not think that digital art poses a threat to traditional studio painting techniques or that Phone Art will put an end to manual hand drawing. He stated that hand painting existed since the beginning of civilization when the primitive man drew on caves. According to him, *"Despite the evolution of civilization, the human never stopped hand drawing. Drawing, just like writing, is an intrinsic behavior which the human can never stop. Traditional and contemporary artists draw in order to express their ideas towards various aspects of life. Phone Art is also a form of drawing, but instead of using paper as a drawing surface, an electronic surface is used by the artist, which allows for faster production of artworks"*.

In addition, 52% (N = 11) of students indicated that there are advantages from using digital applications during the drawing process. One of the students mentioned that among the advantages of using digital applications in drawing is that anyone can use them through their mobile phones in order to create artworks in a very short time. Another student stated that *"the use of digital applications in the design process is easy and helpful"*. Most of the participants (76%, N = 16) indicated that they benefited from the Phone Art experiment. One student stated that he *"learned something new and enjoyable"*. Another student added, *"I benefited a lot, and learned how to use many digital applications, each of which has different features"*. When asked to rank the digital apps according to their effectiveness in enhancing creativity during the experiment, most students considered Sketches and Prisma to be the most effective, followed by PicsArt, Adobe Draw, Adobe Sketch, AutoDraw, and ArtRage. They considered the rest of the apps to be significantly less effective in enhancing their creativity (Fig. 1).

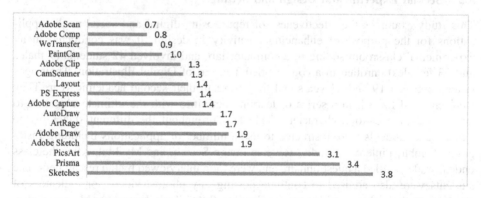

Fig. 1. Rankings of the digital apps according to their effectiveness in enhancing creativity during the Phone Art experiment

Most of the students (57%, N = 12) supported the integration of art and digital applications, thus stressing Dr. Al Hajiri's statement that Phone Art is a new means of practicing art and is considered very close to the younger generation of artists due to their proximity to smart devices and constant use of technology. He believes that these devices allow them to get inspirational ideas at all times and to practice art beyond the limited space of the art studio; while they are in waiting areas, on their way out of lectures, or while they are in restaurants with their friends they can still record their ideas and save their plans in their devices. They can then access this data anytime and anywhere. In the next study, the same advantage of saving and storing data is also suggested by some of the participants, who expressed their preference to use digital apps rather than papers to sketch their ideas. Furthermore, Annum [1] suggested additional advantages for the use of digital tools for art practice: *"it has most importantly the advantage of the ability to undo and redo applied strokes. The digital painter also has at his or her disposal several tools not available to the traditional painter. The virtual palette for example consists of millions of colour shades from which to choose. He also has the ability to obtain any size of canvas on which to paint [...] Studio painters who are not comfortable with acrylics and also suffer allergic reactions to turpentine, a major solvent for oils, can now heave a sigh of relieve since the computer multi-medium apparatus offers a positive alternative for artistic exploration."* [1, p. 7]

As a result of all the above-mentioned advantages, Dr. Al Hajiri believes that Phone Art enhances students' creativity and their ability to invent technical and artistic solutions through the employment of the various tools provided in digital apps. He suggests that these tools and features encourage the artist to propose and try many ideas, and to draw and paint recurrently and comfortably without calculating the expenses, and without fear of the loss that may result from spoiling the canvas, or damaging the paper as in the case of painting. Thus, Phone Art enhances creativity through allowing for recurrent exploration and production, and also through allowing these digital artworks to be published through social media.

3.2   Second Experimental Design and Setting

This study examines the effectiveness of repurposing digital and social media applications for the purpose of enhancing creativity in design. It was conducted in an experimental classroom setting in a computer lab, and involved 42 students (9 males and 33 females) enrolled in a course titled The Art of Digital Illustration. Their ages ranged between 19 and 23 years and they were in their second academic year. They were engaged for 4 h in a series of learning activities with the ultimate objective to design a unique cartoon character (Table 1). Throughout the different stages of the experiment, students were instructed to use a number of applications including Instagram, Tumblr, Pinterest, Mindly, Reverse Image Search, and My Idol. After the class ended, students filled a questionnaire and were then interviewed by the researchers. The students were also advised to continue posting any photos, videos, or indicators of progress in their character designs, in Tumblr (https://uob-funoon.tumblr.com), after the classroom. In tandem, content analysis was conducted of their engagement (posts, comments, and likes), which was observed and analyzed by the researchers for two months until they submitted their character designs as part of the final project for the course. These were then correlated to the survey findings.

When asked to brainstorm at the beginning of the experiment, most respondents (94%, n = 30) indicated that they used Pinterest to draw inspiration. Instagram (41%, n = 13) and Google Images (41%, n = 13) were used by some, followed by Tumblr (31%, n = 10). Only few students used Google+ (16%, n = 5), Mind Map (13%, n = 4), You Tube (9%, n = 3), Whatsapp (6%, n = 2), Behance (3%, n = 1), and Facebook (3%, n = 1) respectively (Fig. 2). This greater preference score for Pinterest is again emphasized by the survey results when students were asked about the

Table 1. The stages of the experiment, which involved a series of learning activities

Activities	Duration	Description
Non-directed brainstorming	10 min	Students use a digital app of their choice to get inspired and generate ideas for the character
Mind-mapping	4 min	Students use **Mindly** to choose a name for their character and write the traits and features
Directed brainstorming	10 min	Students use **Pinterest** to get inspired
Sharing mind maps	5 min	Students share their mind maps through **Tumblr**
Peer feedback on mind maps	5 min	Students write their suggestions and feedback on their peers' mind maps through **Tumblr**
Sketching	15 min	Students sketch their characters on paper
Sharing sketches	5 min	Students share their sketches through **Tumblr**
Peer feedback on sketches	10 min	Students write their suggestions and feedback on their peers' sketches through **Tumblr**
Searching for a source	5 min	Students use **ReverseImageSearch** to get a source similar to their character
Drawing	1 h	Students draw characters on paper or on Adobe Illustrator
Sharing drawings	5 min	Students share their character drawings through **Tumblr**
Peer feedback on drawings	10 min	Students write their suggestions and feedback on their peers' drawings through **Tumblr**
Drawing expressions and actions	1 h	Students use **MyIdol** to draw the expressions, movements and actions of their characters
Sharing expressions and actions	5 min	Students share their character expressions, turnarounds, and actions with their peers through **Tumblr**

applications they will use again in the future; (97%, n = 31) indicated that they will use Pinterest, (67%, n = 21) will use Tumblr, and (44%, n = 14) will use Mindy. Only few students indicated that they will use Myidol (16%, n = 5) or Reverse Image Search (13%, n = 4) again.

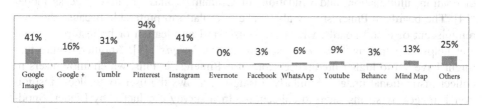

Fig. 2. Rankings of the applications that students used to get inspiration when asked to brainstorm in the beginning of the experiment (respondents were allowed to choose more than one app).

It is worthy to note that students considered Pinterest and Instagram to be the most effective in getting ideas, followed by Tumbler and Mindly, respectively (Fig. 3). Other apps were considered less effective in stimulating creative ideas in drawing characters. Apparently, students have a preference to look for new ideas in a collaborative environment like Pinterest because *"It creates spaces for lightweight social engagement and collaboration that simultaneously enable independent work and access to others' ideas"* [10, p. 9]. Moreover, Pinterest allows a variety of activities such as collecting, discovering, collaborating and publishing, which make it popular and social.

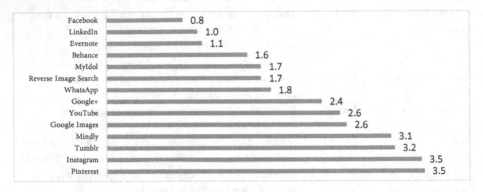

Fig. 3. Rankings of apps according to their effectiveness in generating creative ideas for character design

This idea is emphasized by Linder, Snodgrass, and Kerne [10, p. 9] who consider Pinterest as a social and collaborative platform which enhances creativity due to its "secret" boards that can be seen only by the user, which remove fear of evaluation, while enabling positive feedback; *"Pinterest provides a sense of unevaluated workspace. In curating, our participants ironically felt nearly anonymous. Users feel free to work on Pinterest without judgement, in contrast to social networks like Facebook and Twitter."* This anonymity and sense of privacy in generating and incubating ideas is similar to "incubation", which is the second stage of the four stages (preparation, incubation, illumination, and validation) of Graham Wallas' creative process model [14]. The boards in Pinterest may also make this platform preferable because they are reminiscent of mood boards, which are considered an ideation or brainstorming tool that helps in gathering *"aesthetic cues for future designs"* [3]. Another feature that might have led to higher preference scores for Pinterest is Pins, which allow users to collect inspirational images. Similarly, Instagram allows the user to "collect" inspirational images by saving them to collections. In a survey conducted by Linder, Snodgrass, and Kerne [10], the majority of participants, saw pins as ideas and referred to collecting Pins into boards as "ideas". This finding is interpreted by the researchers to mean *"that forming and presenting ideas is essential to how everyday ideators use Pinterest as a social medium of curation [...] Pins enable ideation, revealing previously unknown concepts and approaches. Everyday ideators use Pinterest to be inspired, not only by newfound ideas, but also by others engaged in everyday design in unexpected ways"* [10, p. 5]. This is also suggested in a study by Langefels [8, p. 30] where participants uniquely preferred Pinterest in comparison to other social media platforms. The participants expressed, in reference to the pins in Pinterest, *"that they enjoyed the ability to search more easily and collect images to be able to re-visit later"* [8, p. 30]. Langefels also suggested that allowing for the quick and easy search, collection, organization, retention, and sharing of ideas is considered a "unique functionality" in Pinterest [8].

Another factor which might have affected the students' preferences is that Pinterest and Instagram have a "picture-dominant" interface. Langefels' study [8] suggested that an image-dominant interface was a key driver in users' preference to browse through Pinterest instead of other social media. This also applies to Instagram, which relies mainly on visuals and has little menus and buttons. This minimizes distraction and increases the fluidity of interaction as emphasized by Igarashi [6] who indicated that *"Nested menus, arrays of buttons, and dialog boxes interfere with the flexible exploration"* (p. 1). The predominance of visuals seems to be a common feature among Instagram and Pinterest, which the students considered most preferable in generating creative ideas. Other common features among these apps are the social aspects which include sharing, getting feedback, likes, and comments. According to Langefels [8] picture-dominant interfaces could be perceived as more social. This is also emphasized by Lee [9] who suggests that social aspects play an important role in driving loyalty, and that Pinterest has some social aspects that allow users to connect with people who inspire them. Sheldon and Bryant [11, p. 95] seem to agree with Langefels [8] and Lee [9] as they also refer to picture-dominance and link it to creativity: *"There are ample opportunities for users to portray their creative talents on Instagram. Instagram allows users to apply filters to pictures in order to make their posts appear "artsy." Also, Instagram users have the option to post creative captions and hashtags. One potential reason that "Creativity" as a motive came about in this study is due to the fact that Instagram is a visually-based social networking site. While other forms of SNSs have many different features such as status updates, video sharing, and more, Instagram primarily focuses on pictures."* Among the social aspects specified by Lee [9], sharing seems to be especially noteworthy as 43.75% (n = 14) of the surveyed students in this study indicated that there are advantages for sharing their designs through social media, and 43.75% (n = 14) indicated that there are advantages to a certain extent, while 12.50% (n = 4) indicated that there are no advantages. This reflects an increasing awareness among students of the importance of sharing their artworks in enhancing their creativity, and stresses the findings of prior studies, which have noted the importance of sharing work in enhancing creativity. Kim, Agrawala, and Bernstein [7] attempted to promote the idea of designing creative communities that allow creators to share their work in progress rather than just sharing finished work; *"By designing an environment that rewards sharing early work and clear explanations, instead of just rewarding good outcomes, we may create opportunities for creators to not only learn specific techniques from each other but also enable them to reflect more effectively on their own work"* [7, p. 1]. In addition to the sharing feature, the "explore" feature in Instagram and Pinterest may also explain the students' preference scores because this features allows for *"the rapid exploration of alternatives"*, which Gross and Do [4, p. 1] mentioned in their research as an important feature in creative interfaces.

When the surveyed students were asked about the extent to which multimedia applications help generate creative ideas for cartoon character design, 46.88% (n = 15) of them answered "To a great extent", 53.13% (n = 17) answered "To some extent", and nobody answered "not at all". However, the majority of students (84.38%, N = 27) generally think that technology enhances creativity, and also the majority of them (78%, N = 25) found the experiment useful. Despite the aforementioned role of technology and multimedia-based pedagogical approaches in enhancing creativity, there are some obstacles which may be encountered either by the students or their instructors while implementing these approaches. When the students were asked if they encountered obstacles while trying to generate creative ideas through multimedia-supported learning, only two students stated that they faced obstacles. Some students (41.18%, n = 7) stated that the dispersion of attention and shortage of time hindered their work, and only one student stated that technical difficulties hindered his work during the experiment. Another remark which some of the students mentioned is that *"they found it easier to compose hand-written mind maps because using their hands does not obstruct the flow of their creative thoughts"*. However, the rest of the students said that they preferred using Mind Map, because it allows them to save their mind maps without having to worry about losing them. However, due to the exposure to others' ideas while using social media platforms to get inspired, there are increased chances of plagiarism. Concurrently, however, there are increased chances for instructors to detect plagiarism through the same platforms. Pinterest, and many image search apps allow instructors to capture a student's artwork or design and search for similar images on the internet. Regardless of the aforementioned obstacles, there are a number of advantages related to repurposing social media for educational purposes. Through an interpretive analysis of the engagement (posts, likes, comments) on Tumblr in addition to field notes and transcripts of the interviews, the researchers observed that the use of Tumblr to share and provide peer feedback introduces new affordances for peer-supported learning and enables more effective collaboration and improvement of students' work-in-progress. Students were able to reflect on their works and creative processes with their peers through feedback, which enabled them to identify gaps between their creative ideas and plans and how others perceive their execution of these ideas. Moreover, the use of Tumblr to post students' work-in-progress allows them to document their creative processes and artistic journeys. Some of the students, for instance, posted video break-downs that displayed their progress. This documentation helps other students learn from other students' processes, experiences, and the feedback received online either from followers, peers, or the instructor. It also helps the instructor guarantee that the student did not get the assignment done by another person.

4   Conclusion

The main research question, "How can digital applications and social media platforms be repurposed and harnessed to promote a creative mindset in art and design students?" was investigated deeply and meaningful findings and conclusions were extracted from the information provided by fine arts and graphic design students who were involved in two multimedia-based experimental settings. The paper developed a new understanding of how social and digital media can support art and design educators in their pedagogical endeavors and leverage students' creativity. It demonstrated the potential benefits of repurposing social and digital media applications for educational purposes, and discovered that social and collaborative platforms can foster students' creativity due to a number of factors and features that are imbedded in these platforms including sharing, exploring, commenting, and collecting inspirational images. Therefore, students particularly preferred using Pinterest and Instagram while brainstorming possibly because these applications contain all the previously mentioned features in addition to their interface, which is "picture-dominant". On the other hand, students' use of a number of digital painting applications as a complementary technique to hand-painting, allowed them not to only enhance their creativity but also reflect on their creative artmaking process. The preferences of the participants and their patterns of interaction with a number of digital and social media applications in art and design educational contexts, which were interpreted through this study, can offer several considerations for educators and students in the future. First, by providing educators with insights to the most effective digital applications that they can employ to enhance their students' creativity. Second, by providing ways in which students can repurpose these applications to aid them in the creative process of producing their artworks. This paper focused specifically on illustration and painting, but the discussed preferences and patterns may generalize to learning environments centered around many creative domains including media, film, photography, animation, interior design, and architecture. Further follow-up studies would provide additional ways of approaching the research topic to discover the visual, technological, social, or educational factors that influence the participant's usage and preferences of social media platforms and various digital tools in creative tasks and contexts. Valuable insight could be gained by looking deeper into the ways students and even artists and graphic designers connect and interact with social media, and with the potential to suggest ways to improve these apps or develop new ones that may reach increased or even specific usage by designers and artists.

References

1. Annum, G.: Digital painting evolution: a multimedia technological platform for expressivity in fine art painting. J. Fine Stud. Art **4**(1), 1–8 (2014)
2. Chai, J., Fan, K.: Constructing creativity: social media and creative expression in design education. Eurasia J. Math. Sci. Technol. Educ. **14**(1), 33–43 (2018)
3. Gentes, A., Valentin, F., Brulé, E.: Mood Boards as a Tool for the "In-Discipline" of Design. Brisbane, Australia (2015)
4. Gross, M.D.: Do EY-L Ambiguous intentions—a paper-like interface for creative design. In: Proceedings of Ninth Annual Symposium for User Interface Software and Technology, pp. 183–192 (1996)
5. Helmick, R.: Virtues of verisimilitude in design and art. Comput. Graph. **19**(4), 505–507 (1995). http://wiki.commres.org/pds/Project_7eNrf2010/Virtues%20of%20verisimilitude%20in%20design%20and%20art.pdf. Accessed 19 Dec 2018
6. Igarashi, T.: Supportive interfaces for creative visual thinking. In: Collective Creativity Workshop, Nara, Japan (2000)

S. Al Hashimi et al.

7. Kim, J., Agrawala, M., Bernstein, M.S.: Mosaic: designing online creative communities for sharing works-in-progress computer supported cooperative work (CSCW), pp. 246–258 (2017)
8. Langefels, E.: Millennial Women's Use and Perception of Pinterest. University of Minnesota, Minnesota (2016)
9. Lee, Y.C.: m-Brand loyalty and post-adoption variations for the mobile data; services: gender differences. Comput. Hum. Behav. **27**, 2364–2371 (2011)
10. Linder, R., Snodgrass, C., Kerne, A.: Everyday Ideation: All of my ideas are on Pinterest. Toronto, Canada (2014). http://dx.doi.org/10.1145.25556288.2557273. Accessed 12 May 2018
11. Sheldon, P., Bryant, K.: Instagram: motives for its use and relationship to narcissism and contextual age. Comput. Hum. Behav. **58**, 89–97 (2016)
12. Smith, B.R.: Beyond computer art. In: Computer Art in Context, Leonardo Supplemental Issue, pp. 39–41 (1989). Journal of the International Society for the Arts, Sciences and Technology
13. Tiryakioglu, F., Erzurum, F.: Use of social networks as an educational tool. Contemp. Educ. Technol. **2**(2), 135–150 (2011)
14. Wallas, G.: The Art of Thought. London, Johnathan Cape (1926). (Republished in 1931)

GLOBE – Cognitive and Social Competence Development by Virtual Collaboration and Simulation Games

Markus Bresinsky and Sophia Willner[✉]

Department of General Science and Microsystems Engineering,
Ostbayerische Technische Hochschule Regensburg (OTH-R),
University of Applied Sciences, Galgenbergstraße 30,
93053 Regensburg, Germany
markus.bresinsky@oth-regensburg.de,
sophia.willner@web.de

Abstract. This paper first examines a variety of conceptual contemporary challenges and cognitive shortcomings of public policy makers, entrepreneurs and other practitioners in Germany as a knowledge-based economy. Systems thinking, digital competencies and several modern leadership skills are identified as possibilities to meet contemporary challenges in fast changing and complex environments. Modern leadership skills and promising working styles imply the ability to manage agile processes, flexibility and diversity, and the modus operandi as self-organizing networks. After that, the simulation game GLOBE Exercise at the OTH Regensburg is introduced as an innovative and transformative learning method. In its concept, the GLOBE Exercise combines virtual collaboration with Action Learning, and thus contributes to skills development and transfer both concerning digital competencies and analytical skills.

Keywords: Virtual collaboration · Action learning · Problem-based learning
Interactive and collaborative learning · Systems thinking · Leadership
Digitization · ICT · Simulation games

1 Introduction

Globalization and digitization and their respective consequences have created an unpredictable and more than ever complex world [1]. Forecasts become increasingly unreliable and growing dynamics and intertwined processes further reduce predictability. Different organizations, corporations or public institutes react in similar ways to these changing external conditions. Therefore, certain general implications for young professionals can be derived and have to be incorporated in higher education systems.

A. L. Brooks et al. (Eds.): ArtsIT 2018/DLI 2018, LNICST 265, pp. 331–342, 2019.

2 Contemporary Challenges and Cognitive Shortcomings

Among scholars and practitioners there is a consensus concerning contemporary challenges and the respective shortcomings in competencies that organizations and individuals on the international level show [1, 3, 7, 10]. Challenges range from cognitive abilities to grasp complex systems, to lacking digital skills and competencies, and insufficient leadership capabilities.

2.1 Systems Thinking and Wicked Problems

A system is generally defined as a set of elements that are related or interconnected and interact in such a way that they can be considered as a task, sense, or purpose unit, a structured, systematic whole [1].

The twentieth-century philosopher and professor Karl Popper, whose theory of critical realism made a major contribution to scientific philosophy, provides a clarification of the nature of complex systems that policy makers confront [2]. Popper introduced the concept of a continuum that illustrates different types of systems. At one end he imagined a clock with regular and predictable features, similar to the mechanics of a bike for example. The functioning of such a mechanical entity is linear and clear, whereas at the other end, Popper imagined a cloud that had neither regular nor predictable properties. Many of today's problems faced by public policy makers, as well as corporations, are more like a cloud system [3]. These kinds of problems, situations or systems are characterized by multi-layered, complex interdependencies, mutual influences and fast-changing underlying dynamics that make such phenomena immensely difficult to grasp.

The notion of situations or problems that are dynamic, intractable, unpredictable and open-ended, was already introduced by Churchman (1967) [4] and by Rittel and Webber [5] in the field of urban planning (1973). What they refer to as "wicked problems" constitutes a *"class of social system problems which are ill-formulated, where the information is confusing, where there are many clients and decision makers with conflicting values, and where the ramifications in the whole system are thoroughly confusing."* [4]. Furthermore, suggested solutions which are mostly based on conventional problem-solving often worsen the situation [6]. Innovative thinking and a comprehensive approach are necessary to meet the challenges of modern world problems. In the perspective of systems theory, dealing with one aspect of a wicked problem only is as ineffective as tackling solely one part of a complex system [4, 7]. Therefore, system thinking combined with the notion of a wicked problem pose a promising and practical approach to current issues faced by practitioners in complex environments.

System thinking as a tool to make sense of a situation with intertwined processes has been recognized by multiple actors and organizations ranging from policy makers to military instructors, scholars or entrepreneurs.

In February 2010 NATO replaced its "Allied Command Operations Guidelines for Operational Planning" (GOP) [8] with a trial version of "Allied Command Operations Comprehensive Operations Planning Directive" (COPD) [9] and paved the way for a more holistic method in international operations. This renewal emphasized the comprehension that military means must be accompanied by the inclusion of all involved actors in a conflict or a crisis [10]. Collaboration is thus the key to meet the challenging requirements of complex planning processes outlined in the COPD manual. However, it can be argued that these processes are overall orientated towards systems theory since the revised planning methods in the manual are intended to be used to manage volatile fast changing systems by means of comprehensive and collaborative operations. Consequently, a cognitive gap between conventional planning processes in the military and the conceptually different methods in the COPD can be observed, as several practitioners face challenges in applying the manual. Thus, an effective way to tackle shortcomings in conceptual understanding is to equip students and young professionals with adequate cognitive competencies to manage complex planning processes.

Also in the peacebuilding domain, systems thinking is perceived as a necessary approach to achieve long-lasting change. Among peacebuilding practitioners, adaptive ways of managing projects in conflict transformation are emphasized, which promotes systems thinking as an essential method when engaging in interventions [7].

Concerning complex systems in which peacebuilding missions in international environments operate, certain characteristics have been detected:

- *"The whole is greater than the sum of its parts.*
- *Relationships between the parts of complex systems are nonlinear and therefore unpredictable.*
- *Complex systems "self-organize" in response to systemic problems.*
- *Complex systems are "emergent"; local-level changes can produce global effects.*
- *There is no one objective reality of a system."* [7].

Bearing these characteristics in mind, systems thinking in peacebuilding focuses on taking complexity into account when working towards long lasting conflict transformation. Especially in fast changing contexts and dynamic conflicts with convoluted underlying root causes, no single aspect can be understood detached from the others [11]. However, complex systems and in particular changing circumstances can, by their very nature, in no way be completely captured and depicted in a static way as the human mind would prefer it [7]. Thus, incompleteness, imperfection and fragmentariness of the analysis result in the risk of retreating into the illusion of certainty instead of actively dealing with the unease generated by the complexity.

Nevertheless, the ability to make sense of fast changing environments and intertwined systems is strongly needed in the context of a globalized world, be it at government level, in non-governmental organizations, military forces or in the corporate landscape. Thus, innovative and transformational learning approaches are essential to equip the next generation of managers, analysts and leaders with the cognitive abilities to grapple with modern day challenges.

2.2   Information and Communication Technologies Skills

Not only the changing international order and the increasing complexity, but also new technological developments illustrate the need for digital capacity building.

The European Union encourages its members to actively work towards the accomplishment of digital literacy as adequate knowledge of and skills concerning information and communication technologies (ICT) are vitally important for multiple aspects within the European Union [12]. Especially concerning socio-economic growth and competitiveness for Europe as a knowledge-based economy, e-skills constitute a crucial factor, as the Europe 2020 strategy highlights [13].

Shortages and gaps in digital competencies pose a great risk to economic development, innovation and social cohesion, and must be addressed urgently. Not only must digital key competencies be provided, but e-skills also have to be kept up-to-date constantly. Technological development tends to outpace individuals who do not further educate themselves permanently [12]. Hence, innovation and creativity with regards to the development of new concepts to face this challenge are essential. This has also been identified by a recent study carried out for the European Commission [14] which emphasizes that *"As part of the new global sourcing models, different skill sets are required in different regions, and new technologies keep demanding changes in the type of skills required. These new technological trends are likely to act as further drivers of increased demand for ICT practitioners over the coming years."* Digital literacy therefore serves as an essential mean to utilize the full potential of ICT in the European Union and must be included in the educational curriculum to ensure smart growth [14]. However, a conceptual change can be observed within the European Framework for Key Competences as it highlights the provision of competencies in contrast to teaching knowledge [15]. This must be taken into consideration when designing innovative digital learning methods.

2.3 Successful Organizations and Leadership Skills

Organizations and corporations active in international multi-cultural contexts are confronted with dynamic environments, fast changing conditions, and rapidly developing technology. Globalization with all its symptoms already engenders profound transformations in these organization in every aspect [12].

Governments and public institutions for instance succeed at pursuing policies and providing public services as long as the activities are to a certain extent standardized, high-volume and part of a routine [16]. However, public institutions appear to be less well prepared when they face unexpected, nonroutine and more complex challenges, as several public officials confirm [16].

Not unexpectedly, organizations (corporations, public employers, associations, etc.) almost never fail due to external problems. Most of them fail because of internal conflicts, leadership problems and their inability to effectively react to changing conditions [1]. According to multiple recent studies, leaders are usually insufficiently prepared for their tasks [1].

In Germany, multiple studies on how organizations in highly dynamic environments can be successful have been conducted. One of the most recent is "Führungskultur im Wandel" (Leadership Culture in Transition) of the "Neue Qualität der Arbeit" initiative, funded by the Federal Ministry of Labor and Social Affairs in 2013 [17]. The aim of the survey was to make the immanent knowledge of managers visible and to show which value patterns influence their leadership. The results show that most executives recognize the need for change and confirm that there is a deficit in implementing novel leadership and working methods. Executives face a dynamic and interconnected working environment that requires high levels of autonomy and cooperation but in many cases individuals in leadership positions do not feel capable to meet the challenge.

Thus, several parameters to render future leadership concepts more successful have been identified in the study, and the ones with the greatest potential for innovative learning and to be integrated in the framework of higher education will be elaborated in the following [1, 18].

2.3.1 Competence to Manage Agile Processes

Process competence constitutes a form of agile professional ability [17]. The vast majority of the interviewed executives consider the ability to effectively design open-ended processes and to utilize agile methods a key competency. In view of unstable market dynamics and decreasing predictability, a gradual step-by-step approach and adapting processes quickly to changing external conditions promises more success than following rigid procedures that might not be adequate to the new environment anymore.

2.3.2 Flexibility and Diversity

Flexibility in its essence means adaptability [17]. Being able to quickly and easily adapt oneself and the work force to changing circumstances and thus to respond to new requirements.

Diversity describes the ability to constantly acquire new knowledge. As stated by the interviewed executives, a wide applicability of knowledge and not the restriction to a special field is required. Few professionals are able to provide this mental adaptability, but it is essential for a working environment characterized by dynamic changes.

2.3.3 Self-organizing Networks

Self-organizing networks are the favored future model to meet the challenges of the modern professional world [17]. The collective intelligence of self-organizing network structures fosters creative impulses, innovation, simplification of processes and thus complexity can be reduced. Self-organizing networks are characterized by the fact that they continue to work even without further specifications on tasks by superordinate entities. The communication between the parts occurs in a direct way and resources and tasks are managed collaboratively.

Self-organizing networks are furthermore characterized by several aspects [17]:

1. Autonomy: there is little or no external control.
2. Dynamic Operation: resources and tasks can be added, modified or removed in a dynamic way without disturbing operating processes. Also, the behavior of the participants and the structure of the network are modifiable.
3. Adaptivity and self-maintenance: the network is able to react to disturbances and to repair itself.
4. Feedback: between the elements occur positive (effect-enhancing) and negative (effect-weakening) reactions.
5. Emergence: the whole is more than the sum of its parts (Aristotle). The interaction of the elements leads to the formation of new properties or structures within the system. The emerging properties of the system cannot be traced back to the characteristics of isolated elements.

6. Criticality: this term describes the critical state of the system, which can lead to a chain reaction. Even small changes can then have a big impact.
7. Stigmergy: this is a method of indirect communication in a decentralized system with a large number of individuals with the environment being modified. An example for this is could be ants. What has been created in a collaborative way becomes the trigger (see emergence) of follow-up activities and general instructions for how to proceed with them.

These characteristics account for of well-equipped organizations and leaders able to understand a complex environment and to respond effectively to drastic changes [1]. However, it can be assessed as highly critical that the development of personal characteristics and qualities of a human being is currently not a part of the German educational system [1].

3 Practical Approaches at Innovative and Transformative Learning

Consequently, the development of effective ways to foster learning which harness innovative, interactive and technology-based methods must be encouraged. This article argues that one possible concept of innovative and transformative learning can be achieved using Action Learning developed by REVANS [19] and simulation games [20] with respect to training of digital competencies.

Action Learning constitutes a method initially introduced by Reginald Revans in 1980 [19]. The term describes a concept where an individual or a group of individuals within a corporation or organization develop concrete and relevant products for existing projects. Simultaneously or shortly after, participants reflect on their own learning process. Action Learning is based on the assumption that practitioners best learn while developing solution approaches to challenges that actually exist within the organization. Furthermore, the method aims at enabling participants to access the knowledge and the competences that they already possess, thus encouraging them to change their perspective and use their abilities in an innovative way.

3.1 GLOBE Exercise as an Innovative and Transformative Learning Method

As part of the study program 'International Relations and Management' at the University of Applied Sciences OTH Regensburg, the GLOBE Series is a unique set of exercises in cooperation with the Federal University of Applied Administrative Sciences in Mannheim. It consists of a series of simulation games, where several teams of students are responsible for both the organization and the participation of the exercise. In 2013, the concept has been introduced to the academic context by Professor Dr. Markus Bresinsky and has since then taken place bi-annually with various additional partners, for example the Technical Educational Institute of Crete, Libertas International University in Dubrovnik, or the Charles University in Prague, as it can be observed regarding the preceding editions of the simulation:

- Address GLOBE (2013)
- Byways GLOBE (2013)
- Collaborate GLOBE (2014)
- Deployed GLOBE (2014)
- Engaged GLOBE (2015)

- Facilitate GLOBE (2015)
- Go GLOBE (2016)
- Horizon GLOBE (2016)
- Impact GLOBE (2017)
- Joint GLOBE (2017)
- Key GLOBE (2018)

The scenario in the simulation is based on the ongoing conflict in Afghanistan with focus on the United Nations Assistance Mission in Afghanistan (UNAMA) and the NATO-led Resolute Support Mission (RSM) in which German troops take part with up to 1,300 soldiers [21].

3.2 Training Objectives

This article argues that the concept and the methodology of the GLOBE Exercise accomplishes to impart competencies that enable students to cope with previously described challenges of the modern working environment. This is achieved by utilizing and adapting the principle of Action Learning [19] and conveying competencies within the framework of a simulation game. The practical approach of a simulation game harnesses the potential of both the students' already existing skills and serves as an experience-oriented form of teaching and learning, which is rather marginally used higher education or schools in Germany [20]. Furthermore, the learning outcomes of the simulation exercise, are oriented towards level 6 of the European Qualifications Framework (EQF) to ensure international comparability [21].

(1) Knowledge	(2) Skills	(3) Responsibility and autonomy
Advanced knowledge of a field of work or study, involving a critical understanding of theories and principles.	Advanced skills, demonstrating mastery and innovation, required to solve complex and unpredictable problems in a specialised field of work or study.	Manage complex technical or professional activities or projects, taking responsibility for decision-making in unpredictable work or study contexts; take responsibility for managing professional development of individuals and groups.

3.2.1 Systems Thinking

Considering the structure of the exercise and the elaboration of the real-world scenario, the simulation game fosters the ability to better comprehend volatile complex systems. Both the training audience consisting of participating students, the whole structure of the simulation game including the organizing entities and the partners, and the corresponding elements within the scenario represent systems in which individual parts interact in a highly dynamic and mutually influencing way. The students find themselves in an environment where they represent parts of a collective entity, where influence can be exerted only through collaboration and cooperation with other parts of the system. In accordance with the scenario, the students learn that even small changes on a local level can entail large-scale consequences. Thus, in case of changing environments, the characteristics of the team must be adapted accordingly, e.g. restructuring of the team, prioritizing of different tasks, etc., all while maintaining the functioning of the system.

3.2.2 Digital and ICT Competencies

The use of ICT runs through the entire concept and all stages of the GLOBE Exercise. Starting with the planning phase, successful virtual collaboration between the different international partners is essential for a sound preparation of the simulation game. Also, during the actual run of the exercise and the evaluation afterwards, acquiring and applying e-skills represent substantial success factors to make the simulation game a valuable experience for all participants.

In a previous analysis of the GLOBE Exercise [23] several digital competencies that are deepened within the simulation game have been identified: (a) communication and collaboration, (b) situational awareness, (c) information and knowledge management, and (d) data analytics. Possible examples of knowledge and digital skills include:

(a) Communication and virtual collaboration:

- Synchronous and asynchronous digital communication methods; Prioritize, sustain, and moderate communication channels; Use of innovative soft- and hardware to foster collaboration.

(b) Situational awareness based on the domain of communication:

- Implementing and administrating alert and warning systems; Prediction of developments.

(c) Information and knowledge management:

- Platform management; Data storage management.

(d) Data analytics:

- Management of search algorithms; Assessment of references and research results; Critical thinking and analysis; Use of data analysis tools.

Due to the exemplary involvement of ICT within the simulation game, the GLOBE exercise has been included in the Digital Learning Map [24] where educational learning scenarios that explicitly use digital tools are collected and publicly displayed. A wide variety of interactive information-management instruments (e.g. an interactive map), adaptive management tools (e.g. a constantly self-updating collection of tasks) and communication technologies (e.g. video transmission to share information) is used extensively during the exercise. This enables the students to acquire digital competencies under real-world working conditions and to test various digital tools in the context of a simulation game.

3.2.3   Leadership Skills and Modern Working Styles

Concerning the leadership skills and working concept with a high success potential as they have been defined by the study "Führungskultur im Wandel", the GLOBE Exercise achieves to impart and train management and leadership competences on multiple levels.

During the organization and planning phase of the exercise, the students in the steering and in the scripting committee can encounter multiple obstacles, be it in the recruiting of possible participants, the development of the scenario, or when acquiring partners. Depending on the characteristics of each situation, the next steps in organizing the exercise must be adapted accordingly. Agile management of the processes to effectively plan the whole exercise must be implemented. Students constantly learn how to react to dynamic external conditions and how to create innovative processes to still be able to continue their work.

Also, during the run of the exercise itself, students in the training audience are permanently confronted with the symptoms of highly volatile conflicts within the scenario. Especially in emergency situations, the continuation of working processes and the functioning of the team is of upmost importance. Thus, students learn how to create new processes if the prevailing conditions do not permit a continuation by conventional means anymore.

Flexibility as one of the essential competencies to face complex challenges is highly stimulated before and during the exercise as the students may face changing circumstances and consequently new requirements. Diversity as the ability to constantly acquire new knowledge is trained both during the preparation, especially during the scripting of the scenario, and during the exercise. As several tasks consist of gathering information and presenting them in customized way for the demands of the recipient, students acquire and train the competency to look for reliable sources and to process high amounts of previously unknown information.

Particularly during the exercise, students learn how to form self-organizing networks and how to sustain their network, as it can be observed in the following examples:

1. Autonomy: The team of students is entirely controlled by itself, there is no outside source of control.
2. Dynamic Operation: Constant modification and adaption of tasks (prioritizing in times of crisis) and resources (students might be missing due to other mandatory lectures) takes places without disturbing working processes.
3. Adaptivity and self-maintenance: The team is able to react to disturbances in a protective way and recover from disruptions of the operating processes.
4. Feedback: Individual sub teams support each other, e.g. by dividing the work or by protecting the working elements from outside disturbances.
5. Emergence: The interaction of sub teams leads to the formation of new properties or structures within the whole team, e.g. the team structures intend briefings twice per day to the head of the team, or every product must be checked and adapted by a research sub team before being submitted to the head of the team.
6. Criticality: An essential part of the team (e.g. head of the team, large amount of team members) ceases due to unforeseen circumstances, which results in a

drastically reduced working capacity of the team as a whole. this term describes the critical state of the system, which can lead to a chain reaction.

7. Stigmergie: Operating processes in case of emergency have been created and have to be internalized by every member of the team. In case of an occurring emergency, the team follows the instructions that it has created beforehand.

4   Conclusion

The potential of simulation games that particularly aim at teaching competencies rather than solely knowledge is still not fully exploited in the German higher education system [1, 20].

Concerning the provision of analytical competencies, deeper understanding of complex real-world international processes, and leadership skills consistent with new requirements of the modern working world, the GLOBE Exercise continues to make large contribution in the education of young professionals.

With regards to the technical aspects, conceptual research shows that there is still no common understanding of terms but that the versatile aspects of digitization are reflected in colorful diversity of notions surrounding digitization [25]. Thus, despite the immense potential of technological developments, a systematic approach to digitization in the German higher education system still has to be generated [26]. However, there is a general consensus among German policy makers that the potentials of new technologies in the context of higher education can only be seized if practitioners are even better prepared and equipped with adequate digital skills – achieved through initial training as well as in lifelong learning [27].

With the GLOBE Exercise the OTH Regensburg contributes to fostering innovative and transformative learning, combining theoretical knowledge and practical competencies. In the domain of virtual collaboration, participants acquire digital competencies and practice successful leadership in a multicultural context. Due to the classification of the learning outcomes in the EQF, the possibility of international expansion of the exercise is ensured, which further contributes to the sustainability of the exercise.

In every round of the exercise, an evaluation is implemented where multiple aspects of the exercise are covered. Participants' performance, personal improvement and the organization and implementation of the exercise are evaluated by a team of students who observe all aspects of interest during the run of the simulation game. Thus, before-and-after states can be compared within one round of the simulation, and the respective conclusions can be drawn, which differ from exercise to exercise.

In September 2018, a general management concept which can be used in each future run of the GLOBE exercise has been developed. This general concept can be applied by participants, establishing a basis of comparability between different rounds of the simulation game. Consequently, future evaluation of the effects of the GLOBE exercises can be conducted based on a consistent exercise concept ensuring constant improvement and a sound basis for further research.

References

1. Finckler, P.: Transformationale Führung. Wegweiser für nachhaltigen Führungs- und Unternehmenserfolg. Springer, Berlin (2017). https://doi.org/10.1007/978-3-662-50292-1
2. Popper, K.: Objective Knowledge: An Evolutionary Approach, Rev edn. Oxford University Press, Oxford (1979)
3. Termeer, C., Dewulf, A., Breeman, G., Stiller, S.: Governance capabilities for dealing wisely with wicked problems. Adm. Soc. **47**(6), 680–710 (2015)
4. Churchman, W.: Guest editorial: wicked problems. Manag. Sci. **14**(4), 141–142 (1967)
5. Rittel, H., Webber, M.M.: Dilemmas in a general theory of planning. Policy Sci. **4**, 155–169 (1973)
6. Hauss, C.: Security 2.0. Dealing with Global Wicked Problems. Rowman & Littlefield, London (2015)
7. Leroux-Martin, P., O'Connor, V.: Systems Thinking for Peacebuilding and Rule of Law: Supporting Complex Reforms in Conflict-Affected Environments. United States Institute of Peace, Washington, DC (2017)
8. NATO: Guidelines for Operational Planning (GOP) Final Revision 1. Supreme Headquarters Allied Powers Europe, Mons (2005)
9. NATO: Allied Command Operations Comprehensive Operations Planning Directive, COPD Interim V1.0. Supreme Headquarters Allied Powers Europe, Mons (2010)
10. Lundqvist, S.: Why teaching comprehensive operations planning requires transformational learning. Def. Stud. **15**(2), 175–201 (2015)
11. Garred, M., et al.: Making Sense of Turbulent Contexts: Local Perspectives on Large-Scale Conflict. World Vision International, New York (2015)
12. Rossignoli, C., Virili, F., Za, S.: Digital Technology and Organizational Change: Reshaping Technology, People, and Organizations Towards a Global Society. Springer, Heidelberg (2017). https://doi.org/10.1007/978-3-319-62051-0
13. European Commission: Europe 2020 a strategy for smart, sustainable and inclusive growth, Com(2010) 2020 final. http://eur-lex.europa.eu/LexUriServ/LexUriServ.do?uri=COM:2010:2020:FIN:EN:PDF. Accessed 27 May 2018
14. European Commission: e-Skill: the international dimension and the impact of globalisation (2014). http://ec.europa.eu/DocsRoom/documents/7040. Accessed 27 May 2018
15. European Commission: A digital agenda for Europe, COM(2010), p. 245 final/2 (2010b). http://eur-lex.europa.eu/LexUriServ/LexUriServ.do?uri=COM:2010:0245:FIN:EN:PDF. Accessed 27 May 2018
16. Head, B., Alford, J.: Wicked problems: implications for public policy and management. Adm. Soc. **47**(6), 711–739 (2015)
17. Kruse, P., Greve, A.: Führungskultur im Wandel. Initiative Neue Qualität der Arbeit, Berlin (2013)
18. Brodbeck, F.: Internationale Führung: Das GLOBE-Brevier in der Praxis. Die Wirtschaftspsychologie. Springer, Berlin (2016). https://doi.org/10.1007/978-3-662-43361-4
19. Revans, R.: Action Learning: New Techniques for Management. Blond and Briggs, London (1980)
20. Rappenglück, S.: Handbuch Planspiele in der politischen Bildung (Reihe Politik und Bildung, Band 81). Wochenschau Verlag, Schwalbach (2017)
21. European Commission: Descriptors defining levels in the European Qualifications Framework (EQF) (2018). https://ec.europa.eu/ploteus/en/content/descriptors-page. Accessed 01 Jul 2018

22. Resolute Support NATO: RS Commands. https://www.rs.nato.int/rs-commands.aspx. Accessed 26 May 2018
23. Bresinsky, M., von Reusner, F.: GLOBE – learn and innovate digitization by a virtual collaboration exercise and living lab. In: Brooks, A.L., Brooks, E., Vidakis, N. (eds.) ArtsIT/DLI-2017. LNICST, vol. 229, pp. 273–281. Springer, Cham (2018). https://doi.org/10.1007/978-3-319-76908-0_26
24. Digital Learning Map: GLOBE – Praxisorientierte Kompetenzausbildung in der virtuellen Zusammenarbeit (2018). https://www.e-teaching.org/community/digital-learning-map/globe-praxisorientiert-kompetenzausbildung-in-der-virtuellen-zusammenarbeit. Accessed 27 Sept 2018
25. Von der Heyde, M., Auth, G., Hartmann, A., Erfurth, C.: Hochschulentwicklung im Kontext der Digitalisierung - Bestandsaufnahme, Perspektiven, Thesen. Gesellschaft für Informatik, Bonn (2017)
26. Bundesregierung: Bundeswehr bleibt in Afghanistan (2018). https://www.bundesregierung.de/Content/DE/Artikel/2018/03/2018-03-07-bundeswehrmandat-fuer-afghanistan-verlaengert.html;jsessionid=DBE68048846A086966E691A5F1DEC881.s3t2. Accessed 26 May 2018
27. Bundesministerium für Bildung und Forschung (ed.): Digitale Chancen nutzen. Die Zukunft gestalten. Zwischenbericht der Plattform "Digitalisierung in Bildung und Wissenschaft". Repa Druck GmbH, Saarbrücken (2016)

Makerspaces Promoting Students' Design Thinking and Collective Knowledge Creation: Examples from Canada and Finland

Janette Hughes[1]([⊠]), Laura Morrison[1], Anu Kajamaa[2],
and Kristiina Kumpulainen[2]

[1] Faculty of Education, University of Ontario Institute of Technology,
11 Simcoe Street North, Oshawa, ON L1H7L7, Canada
{janette.hughes,laura.morrison}@uoit.ca
[2] Faculty of Educational Sciences, University of Helsinki,
P.O. Box 9, 00014 Helsinki, Finland
{anu.kajamaa,kristiina.kumpulainen}@helsinki.fi

Abstract. Despite the growing popularity of makerspaces in education, we currently have little understanding of the conditions and processes that promote students' design thinking and knowledge creation in these digitally-enriched learning environments. To address these research gaps in current research knowledge, we draw on two ethnographic case studies on students' maker activities situated in Canada and Finland. In the Canadian study, the focus is directed to analysing students' design actions carried out in a five day long "microcycle" of learning by individual students in a Maker Lab. In the Finnish study, attention is directed to investigating forms of students' collective knowledge creation during an elective course in a makerspace, The Fuse Studio. This paper shows that design thinking is a potentially fruitful way to build students' global competencies and to approach knowledge creation in a makerspace environment as students engage in interest-driven making, requiring various levels of instructor/peer support, from independent making to guided inquiry.

Keywords: Makerspaces · Design thinking · Knowledge creation
Digital learning environment

1 Introduction

Makerspaces are collaborative and creative spaces where people come together to hack, build, innovate and ultimately, to learn—either formally or informally. Maker pedagogies are generally associated with STEM or STEAM (where the Arts are integrated into Science, Technology, Engineering and Math) education; however, making is inherently interdisciplinary, hands-on, inquiry-based, and driven by student interests and passion. Educators in Canada and Finland are now increasingly harnessing makerspaces as learning environments to promote inquiry, imagination, creativity, curiosity, and perseverance in STEAM learning and beyond. Most notably, making is considered to promote the development of important global competencies and

© ICST Institute for Computer Sciences, Social Informatics and Telecommunications Engineering 2019
Published by Springer Nature Switzerland AG 2019. All Rights Reserved
A. L. Brooks et al. (Eds.): ArtsIT 2018/DLI 2018, LNICST 265, pp. 343–352, 2019.

transferable skills, such as creative and critical thinking, problem solving, collaboration, leadership, and innovation.

Despite the growing popularity of makerspaces in education (Honey and Kanter
2013; Kumpulainen 2017), we have currently little understanding of the conditions and
processes that promote students' design thinking and knowledge creation in these novel
digitally-enriched learning environments. Furthermore, what accounts as a makerspace
in formal education deserves further attention. In this paper, we address these gaps in
research knowledge by introducing and combining, in a novel way, two theoretical
lenses, namely design thinking and knowledge creation in the study of makerspaces in
Canada and Finland. The makerspaces in the two research sites are largely similar. Yet,
the pedagogical approaches of the making and design activities in these two research
sites are slightly different: The Canadian Maker Lab emphasizes design thinking, a
fluid and non-linear methodology that typically involves tackling complex problems in
local and global communities. Using design thinking, learners are considered to be able
to exercise their agency to define real world problems that they are passionate about by
first empathizing and trying to understand the human needs involved. They brainstorm
to generate multiple solutions and begin to prototype and test their solutions. The
Finnish site underscores students' interest-driven engagement in STEAM design
challenges that are introduced to them in a digital infrastructure for learning, The FUSE
Studio. The STEAM challenges of the FUSE Studio (named *Keychain Customiser,
Electric Apparel, Coaster Boss* and *Solar Roller etc.*) that students can choose from
have been structured to introduce students with new ideas and to support them through
more complex iterations of those ideas. The challenges 'level up' in difficulty like video
games and are accompanied by various tools, such as computers, 3D printers and other
materials (e.g., foam rubber, a marble, tape and scissors, which we refer to as "artifacts"), as well as instructions on how to process the challenges (Stevens and Jona
2017).

In sum, our paper addresses the following research questions:

- How does a theoretical design challenge support students in the design process of
  their own personal passion project? What specific global skills and competencies
  are developed in the theoretical challenge and in the personal passion project?
- How do students engage in collective knowledge creation through STEAM design
  challenges?

2   Theoretical Framework

The theoretical framing of our work is informed by design thinking (Doppelt 2009;
Kafai and Peppler 2011; Gobble 2014) and knowledge creation approaches (Paavola,
Lipponen and Hakkarainen 2004; Kajamaa, Kumpulainen and Rajala forthcoming).
We consider these two approaches useful as they represent the core elements entailed in
makerspaces and making.

2.1 Design Thinking

Social demands for certain skill sets are changing and with the implementation of maker pedagogies, students are given the opportunity to develop those foundational skills that are necessary for success. Design disciplines are those which provide open-ended ways that students can approach problem solving through authentic, real world applications (Kafai and Peppler 2011). Makerspaces are rooted in design disciplines, so they align with the concept of problem solving through open-ended approaches to create unique learning opportunities for students. It is in these opportunities that the skillsets necessary for success are developed.

Over the years, as our society has evolved from one of consumer to one of creators in many aspects, the concept of design thinking has emerged as a critical aspect of our everyday lives (Gobble 2014). Many people align design thinking with the aesthetics of something, however in reality it encompasses much more than just how something looks (Gobble 2014). Different models that are used in design thinking utilize different tools and frameworks as vehicles to create a more human centred approach to problem solving (Gobble 2014; Brown 2009; Cahn et al. 2016). Creating authentic applications of real world situations elicits design thinking, which promotes collaboration and communication, as well as empathy and citizenship, which are commonly used in real-world problem solving.

2.2 Knowledge Creation

In makerspaces, based on the principles of design thinking students are encouraged to make their knowledge explicit in their innovation processes by constructing novel solutions to the challenges and problems in question. Knowledge creation takes place in the social activity of students and teachers and it is a crucial process for students' learning and knowledge advancement (Engeström 1999; Engeström, Engeström and Suntio 2002; Paavola et al. 2004; Kajamaa, Kumpulainen and Rajala forthcoming). Knowledge creation is mediated by various tools embedded in the activity. These tools can entail both conceptual (signs, language) and material artefacts (Vygotsky 1978). Similarly, the results of knowledge creation processes are often tangible objects (e.g. creation of an artefact or a completion of a challenge presented on a computer screen), but they may also result in "conceptual artifacts" (Wartofsky 1979; Engeström 1999; Paavola et al. 2004; Kajamaa, Kumpulainen and Rajala forthcoming).

Our previous study shows that in a makerspace context, knowledge creation may take place in different, and often intertwined forms (vertical knowledge maintaining). It can also manifest as students making their own initiatives to creatively break away from the given situation and instructions (horizontal knowledge breaking). In some cases, it may evolve into an innovative process where the student groups and some-times also students together with their teachers collectively challenge and question one another and the existing knowledge to co-create future-oriented learning activity (knowledge expansion) (Kajamaa, Kumpulainen and Rajala forthcoming).

3   Methodology

To answer our research questions, we used two approaches. To analyze the data from the Canadian context, we used a design-based research (DBR) approach that focused on the design thinking processes of individual students (Barab and Squire 2004). To analyze the data from the Finnish context we applied a new framework developed by Kajamaa, Kumpulainen and Rajala (forthcoming) for the study of different forms of knowledge creation in technologically enhanced makerspaces.

3.1   Setting

In Canada and Finland, the research took place in STEAM-focused makerspaces [links will be added]. In Canada, the makerspace was situated in the Faculty of Education at [university name] and in Finland the makerspace was both online and in a city-run comprehensive school with 535 students and 28 teachers at the primary level. In 2016, as a response to the new curriculum requirements, the school introduced the FUSE Studio (www.fusestudio.net) - a design and making environment - as one of its elective courses. The Canadian Maker Lab was established to conduct research into production pedagogies in general, and maker pedagogies in particular.

3.2   Participants

At the Canadian site, the researchers worked with a group of fifteen students ranging in age between 7 and 14 years old. Eight of the students were male and seven were female - 11 of whom had no identified exceptionalities and four of whom had exceptionalities that included giftedness, anxiety, ADHD, ASD and other learning challenges. The students had a range of experience with, and access to, technology and different digital tools both at home and in school from previous grades. The students participated in a March Break Camp to spend five full days using the design thinking process to work on a personal project in the Maker Lab.

In the Finnish site, the research focused on 94 students aged between 9 and 12 years old. Due to the elective nature of the FUSE course, the groups consisted of students from several classes. Group 1 consisted of 32 students (22 boys and 10 girls), Group 2 consisted of 30 students (19 boys and 11 girls) and Group 3 consisted of 32 students (19 boys and 13 girls). Each group was supported by two to four teachers and teaching assistants.

3.3   Research Design

In Canada, the design process was used in two ways during the March Break Camp – first, it was used in a daily theoretical exercise with the students (responding to the challenges of training a new puppy) and second, it was used to frame the participants' week-long design project. At the Ontario site we adhered to the following cyclical five-stage design framework adapted from the Engineering is Elementary website (Museum of Science, Boston) (Fig. 1):

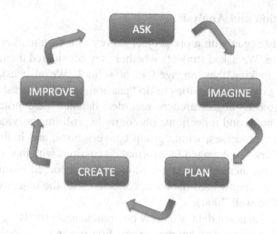

Fig. 1. The design framework used at the Ontario site.

The framework included: 1. Ask (what is a personal project or problem that needs to be solved); 2. Imagine (what already exists that could solve this problem or could be hacked or re-mixed to better respond to the problem); 3. Plan (what resources are needed, what steps will be involved in realizing the end product); 4. Create (a prototype of the product for testing with others); 5. Improve (what worked, what could have been improved). Each day of the camp was devoted to a different (and sequential) stage of this design process

In Finland, we investigated students' maker activities in a novel "makerspace", the FUSE Studio—a digital learning environment focused on enhancing student- and interest-driven science, technology, engineering, arts and mathematics (STEAM) learning. In the FUSE Studio, students were free to select which 'challenges' to pursue, who with (or alone) and when to move on. The core idea was to promote young learners' STEAM learning and to cultivate STEAM ideas and practices among those who are not already affiliated with them, and by so doing broadening the access to participation in STEAM learning (Stevens and Jona 2017). Figure 2 shows a student interface (view) of the FUSE challenges on a computer screen.

Fig. 2. 'My challenges' student interface

3.4 Data Collection and Analysis

In Canada, the study began with a pre-project survey as a base marker of the students' beliefs about making. We asked students whether they considered themselves "makers" and what kind of making they engaged in at school. We also asked the students whether they were given opportunities to do "passion-based" (interest driven) making. Throughout the project, the researchers recorded detailed field notes, collected the students' planning notes and reflections, photographs, still images/video recordings of their design thinking processes, whole group conversations, and individual exit interviews. The researchers also engaged in informal discussions with the students, of which noteworthy comments, themes, ideas or feedback were recorded through text or voice recorder. This type of open-ended data was collected with the objective of developing common themes (Creswell 2004).

In analyzing the Canadian data, we drew on content analysis (Berg 2007) and as we combed through the various data sources in our first reading, we looked for emergent codes. On the second reading, we looked for patterns and grouped similar codes into categories. On the third reading, we narrowed our focus to examine how design thinking led to the development of a series of global competencies, and in this paper, we specifically focus on problem solving.

In Finland, the primary data was comprised of 111 h of transcribed video recordings and field notes of students (N = 94) aged between 9 and 12 years old and their teachers carrying out making and design activities in the FUSE Studio. The video recordings were collected intermittently over a period of one academic year.

The video data and field notes were transcribed and analyzed using interaction analysis methods (Jordan and Henderson 1995). Our analytic approach can be defined as abductive, involving repeated iterations between theory and data. Our analysis was based on Kajamaa, Kumpulainen and Rajala (forthcoming) framework of the different forms of students' knowledge creation. We inductively analyzed the discursive acts from the students' and teachers' talk, depicting forms of knowledge creation.

4 Findings

4.1 Individual Students Design Thinking in the Maker Lab

Framing the Passion Projects Through Focused Problem-Solving. To help participants develop the problem-solving skills they would need during the creation of their passion projects over the course of the week, they were guided through focused and intentional problem-solving activities each day of camp. The challenges were thematically centered around the training of a new puppy and required participants to think creatively and to persevere in finding solutions to their puppy training problems. As the students worked through their first 'puppy challenge', they were stretched to conceive of realistic and humane ways to train their new puppy. Beginning ideas included low-tech and easy to implement, yet impractical, solutions such as building a box in which the puppy would live and relieve him/herself, thus removing the issue of focused training altogether. Other solutions included the use of more elaborate, futuristic technology. One participant designed a jet-pack for the puppy that would sense when s/he needed to relieve him/herself and would fly the puppy to a designated area of the backyard. While this idea was certainly more creative and innovative, it was again less practical and raised ethical issues, such as animal cruelty. As the group shared their working solutions (drawing on collaboration and communication skills), discussion arose surrounding the well-being of the dog in at least a few of the scenarios. One boy raised the question, "which [of these] could put a lot of strain on the dog?" He pointed to the jet-pack example and explained that this would put "a lot of strain on his organs". So, this was identified at the beginning of the week as an area for development and improvement. While most of the ideas theoretically provided a solution to the problem posed, they each required feedback, reflection and revision to generate viable solutions. Each day, a new challenge connected to training the puppy was introduced and encouraged the campers to continue to use the design process in order to refine their solutions. As a result, the students' problem-solving skills were developed by drawing on some of the other global competencies such as collaboration (i.e. asking peers for assistance in their making process and input in their designs and final products), perseverance (i.e. continuing to troubleshoot and problem-solve when faced with technological and/or design challenges), empathy/citizenship (i.e. in the development of an artefact in response to real-world or imagined problems) and creativity (i.e. in their innovative/unique solutions).

Problem-Solving in the Design Process. As they worked through the stages of their designs, each camper was forced to pause at crucial moments to consider the feasibility of their designs and how they might need to reconsider and refine their choices of direction or materials (similar to the theoretical puppy training challenge). One pair that was working together on Harry Potter wands as their passion projects (the main design projects separate from the theoretical puppy-training design challenges posed each day) decided they wanted to create wands that light up at the tip when they cast their spell. They planned out their week and articulated the steps they would take to achieve their end goal (verbally and in their design planning notebooks). Continuing on in their design process, they used sewing and Lilypad - a codable E-textile tool - to create a prototype of their wands. To complete their prototypes, they were required to learn about circuitry and a traditional skill that many find frustrating - sewing. To complete this task, both students went through a number of problem solving tasks, from learning how to thread a needle to how to wire the circuit to ensure that it worked the way they wanted. This process was not easy for the pair and they encountered many challenges along the way; however, with support from one another, leaders and other campers, they persevered and succeeded in this portion of their project.

Following their prototype creation, the pair were required to modify their design multiple times, adapting their prototypes each time. The problem-solving aspect of the design process became very evident at this point in the project as the duo used TinkerCAD to create the 3D model file of each of their wands. It was quite simple creating the wand shape; however, when they realized that they had to make the inside hollow, they ran into the problem of how to make sure there was enough space inside the wand to fit all of the wiring. The most challenging aspect of the project for them was creating the circuits and although they became frustrated and were close to quitting, through collaboration, patience and hard work, they were able to add the illumination element to their wands.

4.2 Students' Collective Knowledge Creation in the FUSE Studio

Our analysis of the students' knowledge creation processes in the FUSE Studio revealed the dynamic interplay of three forms of knowledge creation: Namely, vertical knowledge maintaining, horizontal knowledge breaking and knowledge expansion. Below, we illuminate one example of the dynamic interplay of these three forms of knowledge creation.

The vignette shown below highlights the exchange between two students and their teacher during the FUSE challenge titled, "Keychain customizer". During this exchange, the boys—about to save their work on the computer programme—are approached by the teacher to check in. Although the boys express that they want to design their artefact in such a way that it could hang the right way up, the teacher explains to the boys that it would be better to hang it upside down. The teacher also tells them how thick or thin to make the ring. The students then question the teacher by attaching the ring to the top of the letters, nevertheless. Despite this effort, the teacher overrides the students' perceptions on what a 'nice' keychain would look like and how it should be hung (pseudonyms are given to the students in the excerpts):

Teacher: I think that this ring is too weakly attached to the letter I. It's too much on the edge.
Eetu (student): But Onni (student) said it was ok.
Onni: But isn't this ok?
Teacher: I would like it to be a lot more firmly attached. I would, in fact, attach it (the ring) to the letters (referring to their initials) and probably from the bottom maybe.
Eetu: But then this name would be upside down.
Teacher: Then it would hang from the bottom, but the keychain is not always hanging from somewhere.

The student attaches the ring to the top of the letters nevertheless.

Teacher: And I would also use the "tube" – tool to make it thinner.
Eetu: It's already as small as it can be.
Teacher: No it's not. Carefully adjust it so that it can be used as a keychain (student uses the tool). Now that's better than the previous one (student keeps adjusting) Not that narrow, that's as it doesn't exist at all. It's not firm enough so that it will hold.

In this example, the students were enthusiastically focused on their joint activity of designing keychains and made active use of the artefacts available in the FUSE Studio. The students' attempted to use their agency and knowledge in their making activity: the activity was initiated by a FUSE challenge, but the students started to follow their own ideas and ways of working. We interpreted this as horizontal knowledge breaking, as it provided evidence of the students' breaking away and expanding their activity from traditional schooling towards design and creativity. The student-driven activity was then interrupted by the well-framed instructions given to them by the teacher. The teacher disregarded the student's initiative. This tension could have potentially triggered opportunities for knowledge expansion, if the teachers and the students had started to negotiate and make attempts to create collective solutions to guide their future actions.

5 Discussion and Conclusions

In this study, we investigated students' design thinking and forms of knowledge creation in two educational makerspaces in Finland and in Canada. In terms of design thinking, the Canadian case revealed that the makerspace is a space where students can develop global competencies such as problem-solving, collaboration, empathy and communication. Both of the studied makerspaces provided useful material conditions supporting students' design thinking and knowledge creation. They provided the students with a rich variety of digital tools and more traditional (craft) materials that the students actively, and often creatively, utilized within these contexts.

In the Canadian Maker Lab, design thinking was introduced through the engineering design process framework (adapted from the Engineering is Elementary website). In the findings section we presented an example of the theoretical puppy training challenge the participants engaged with at the beginning of each design day. The competencies developed through this challenge supported the students in their own, personal design projects. The theoretical challenge also assisted them in considering the real-world application and/or practicality of some of the components of their designs. In the findings, we also discussed some of the skills the students developed and the challenges the students encountered in their personal projects which ranged from learning and debugging the technology (i.e. constructing circuits) to engaging in iterative attempts to add to and improve their final products (i.e. the Harry Potter wand).

The FUSE Studio in the Finnish context included a unique design and making infrastructure and a social context, which enhanced different forms of the students' collective knowledge creation. Overall, in our data, the students' strict following of the structures and instructions given by the FUSE computer program and the facilitating teachers (i.e. knowledge maintaining) dominated the design and making activity. Yet, relatively often, the students exercised horizontal knowledge breaking and used their own initiatives to break away from the situation creatively. Sometimes this created tensions as the students questioned the customary ways of making and designing. The challenging and questioning of the existing knowledge led in some rare cases to knowledge expansion where groups of students, sometimes also with their teachers, encountered the tensions, negotiated, and thereafter co-configured novel, future-oriented learning activities. In the Finnish context, the flexible intertwining of the multiple forms of knowledge creation is a current pedagogical challenge for educators and conscious efforts are needed to improve the processes and conditions giving rise to qualitative different forms of knowledge creation in the students' maker activities.

Our analysis provides novel findings also in connecting design thinking to the theoretical notion of knowledge creation. Our research shows that the main difference between these approaches relates to the initial level of agency of the students in determining what kinds of making they will engage in. However, these approaches also importantly add to one another as teachers grapple to understand what kinds of pedagogical supports to provide students during the design/making process. In both cases, the participants were given varying levels of guided inquiry support from others, both instructors and peers.

References

Kajamaa, K., Kumpulainen, K., Rajala, A.: Digital learning environment mediating students' funds of knowledge and knowledge creation. Stud. Paedagog. **23**(4) (forthcoming)

Kumpulainen, K.: Makerspaces: why they are important for digital literacy education. In: Marsh, J., et al. (eds.) Makerspaces in the Early Years: A Literature Review, pp. 12–16. University of Sheffield, Sheffield (2017). Makey Project

Barab, S., Squire, K.: Design-based research: putting a stake in the ground. J. Learn. Sci. **13**(1), 1–14 (2004). https://doi.org/10.1207/s15327809jls1301_1

Berg, B.L.: Qualitative Research Methods for the Social Sciences, 6th edn. Allyn & Bacon, Boston (2007)

Brown, T.: Change by Design: How Design Thinking Transforms Organizations and Inspires Innovation. HarperBusiness, New York (2009)

Cahn, P.S., et al.: A design thinking approach to evaluating interprofessional education. J. Interprof. Care **30**(3), 378–380 (2016). https://doi.org/10.3109/13561820.2015.1122582

Creswell, J.W.: Educational Research: Planning, Conducting, and Evaluating Quantitative and Qualitative Research, 2nd edn. Pearson Education Inc., Upper Saddle River (2004)

Doppelt, Y.: Assessing creative thinking in design-based learning. Int. J. Technol. Des. Educ. **19**(1), 55–65 (2009)

Engeström, Y.: Innovative learning in work teams: analyzing cycles of knowledge creation in practice. In: Engeström, Y., Miettinen, R., Punamäki, R.-L. (eds.) Perspectives on Activity Theory, pp. 377–404. Cambridge University Press, Cambridge (1999)

Engeström, Y., Engeström, R., Suntio, A.: Can a school community learn to master its own future? An activity-theoretical study of expansive learning among middle school teachers. In: Wells, G., Claxton, G. (eds.) Learning for Life in the 21st Century, pp. 211–224. Blackwell, Oxford (2002)

Gobble, M.M.: Design thinking. Res. Technol. Manag. **57**(3), 59 (2014). https://doi.org/10.5437/08956308X5703005

Honey, M., Kanter, D.: Design, Make, Play: Growing the Next Generation of STEM Innovators. Routledge, New York (2013)

Jordan, B., Henderson, A.: Interaction analysis: foundations and practice. J. Learn. Sci. **4**(1), 39–103 (1995)

Kafai, Y., Peppler, K.: Youth, technology, and DIY: developing participatory competencies in creative media. Rev. Res. Educ. **35**(1), 89–119 (2011)

Paavola, S., Lipponen, L., Hakkarainen, K.: Models of innovative knowledge communities and three metaphors of learning. Rev. Educ. Res. **74**(4), 557–576 (2004)

Stevens, R., Jona, K.: Program design. FUSE studio website. https://www.fusestudio.net/program-design. Accessed 20 May 2017

Vygotsky, L.S.: Mind in Society: The Development of Higher Mental Processes. Harvard University Press, Cambridge (1978)

Wartofsky, M.: Models, Representation, and the Scientific Understanding. Reidel, Boston (1979)

Spatial Asynchronous Visuo-Tactile Stimuli Influence Ownership of Virtual Wings

Anastassia Andreasen$^{(\boxtimes)}$ (ID), Niels Christian Nilsson (ID), and Stefania Serafin (ID)

Multisensory Experience Lab, Aalborg University, Copenhagen,
A. C. Meyers Vaenge 15, 2450 Copenhagen, Denmark
{asta,ncn,sts}@create.aau.dk,
https://melcph.create.aau.dk/

Abstract. Previous studies revealed that a compelling illusion of virtual body ownership (VBO) might be achieved under a condition of recognizable anatomical and morphological similarities to human body. Though certain deviations from morphology might be acceptable (e.g. virtual tails, longer arm or larger belly), if external limbs are responsible for specific functions in conjunction with a certain virtual scenario. Thus, this study aims at showing a possibility to achieve a compelling VBO illusion over a non-human avatar in a virtual environment. The paper describes a within-subjects study exploring if immersed users could achieve a compelling VBO illusion when inhabiting a virtual body of a bat. Test subjects experienced visuo-tactile stimulation of their arms while seeing an object touching their virtual wings. The mapping between the real and virtual touch points varied across three conditions: no offset between the visual and the tactile input, 50% offset, and 70% offset from the tactile input. The results revealed variations in the degree of experienced VBO across the conditions. The illusion was broken in the absence of visuo-tactile stimulation.

Keywords: Virtual and augmented realities · Novel applications Interactive environments

1 Introduction

While Virtual Reality (VR) has been developing for more than half a century, its purpose largely remains the same – to create a sense of presence in virtual environment (VE); that is make to our brain believe that we are actually inside the VE, even though physically we are not. VR has the potential to providing compelling experiences of being not only other humans, but even other species. In order to create a believable illusion of being a flying creature inside the VE there are some considerations to ruminate – primary how would the virtual

© ICST Institute for Computer Sciences, Social Informatics and Telecommunications Engineering 2019
Published by Springer Nature Switzerland AG 2019. All Rights Reserved
A. L. Brooks et al. (Eds.): ArtsIT 2018/DLI 2018, LNICST 265, pp. 353–362, 2019.
https://doi.org/10.1007/978-3-030-06134-0_39

body look like in terms of size and shape. In fact having an artificial body inside VE might increase the sense of presence [7]. Previous research showed that similarity between the real and the virtual body is one of the important factors of creating and sustaining a compelling illusion of virtual body-ownership (VBO) [14]. VR allows users to inhabit avatars that differ from their own by altering the morphology of the virtual body [11,16], or even adding extra limbs [19]. Nevertheless researchers were less successful in their attempts to establish VBO over non-corporeal objects [17] and mostly failed to provide a compelling illusion of owning the virtual body.

To the authors' knowledge there have been no studies conducted, where individuals could experience a compelling illusion of ownership over anatomically similar but morphologically different virtual body. That is the virtual body that has a different form, size and shape from a human structure that could be perceived as the users' own body in VR. Out of all flying creatures bats are the only existing flying mammals in nature with the similar anatomy of their wings to a human hands. Very often their wings are also called "hand–wings" [5]. Thus the study will focus on the attempt to generate a compelling illusion of owning the virtual body of a bat.

This experiment is a part of ongoing research about agency and ownership in VR. This paper expands upon our previous work [1]. In an attempt to study the influence of morphologically different virtual shape on users' acceptance of the virtual body we need to take into consideration several combinational factors, such as touch though tactile stimulation, proprioception through passive movements and actions with intentions through active movements, as these are the constituent parts of embodiment. Therefore in this research we address several questions, such as: (1) To which extent might anatomically similar but morphologically different virtual body influence users' experience of VBO and (2) To what degree is it possible to achieve and sustain the sense of ownership of the virtual bat's body using visuo-tactile stimulation.

2   Background

2.1   Body Ownership and VBO

Realizing that someone has a body is a complex cognitive process. Self-attribution to a body is the main identification factor of owning the body that is your "own" [20]. Both agency – intentions and executing actions [22] and body ownership (BO) – awareness of one's movements and self-recognition [20] are two consistent parts of a cognitive self-attribution process. Knowing that your body has been moved, by sensing it and not creating action yourself (during the involuntary movement), would infer only BO but not agency [22]. Varela [23] points out that it is problematic to dissociate the body from one's self, therefore it is challenging to replicate this experience. Cognitive psychology clearly distinguishes between agency and BO that together constituting embodiment, described by Varela [23]. Though in relation to VR there might be some confusion, due to the usage of term "VBO", which relates more to embodiment rather than BO as a separate sense from agency. VBO, described by Maselli et al. [14] is integration of different senses, including vestibular sensation and motor control. Furthermore, it has also been defined that VBO should include not only 1st person perspective including humanoid-shaped avatar, but also synchronous visuo-tactile information and synchronous visuomotor correlations [16]. Visuo-tactile information should be understood as belonging to BO, whereas visuomotor correlation – belonging to agency. The problem of embodiment (out-of-body experience) has been further reviewed in VR [3]. VBO illusion is an illusion, where healthy test subjects believe that artificial body is their own physical body [14]. Kilteni et al. [10] defined the sense of embodiment as "being inside, having and controlling" the body, which has spatial representational characteristics: location inside the body, self-attribution and intentions together with actions. This leads to several components that are essential in VE – sense of self-location, sense of BO and sense of agency [10]. Biocca et al. [3] discussed that self-presence is the main factor of embodiment of one's self representation. Self-presence is a psychological matter, as it is a perceptual sense of being inside the body. Based on the coordinate system self-location and presence might be described as complimentary concepts, characterizing spatial representation, as either being located inside the virtual body (egocentric or internal space) or inside VE (allocentric or external space). While inhabiting a virtual avatar our skin acts as a border to the external environment, that is why tactile input plays another significant role in self-location [10]. According to VR research human-shaped avatar enhances VBO illusion as VBO might be highly susceptible to individual differences due to the fact that virtual body obeys certain structural and morphological constrains, like similarities between the biological body and its virtual avatar. Several researchers even speculate if individualized avatars might strengthen ownership by increasing body and self-recognition [10]. The current paper adheres to the concept of embodiment that defines BO and agency as two separate concepts theoretically, though practically mostly inseparable.

2.2 Related Work

The feeling of BO is possible to study through multisensory stimulation by shifting body experience from BO present to BO absent [20]. The original study of Rubber Hand Illusion (RHI) is a perfect example of interaction between vision, touch and proprioception, which manipulates BO experience in a controlled environment [4]. Seeing the tactile stimulation on the rubber hand and detecting the sensation on the real hand results in the displacement of the felt location towards the spatial location of visually induced observation. Different manipulations of BO illusion using RHI modifications could also be seen in other studies [8,9,18]. Longo et al. [13] could distinguish between BO, agency and location. In a further study [12] they suggested that similarities between the rubber hand and the real hand only elicits ownership under the condition when strokes were applied synchronously to both hands. The results of one study suggested that BO illusion could be established only for corporeal objects. For example, a wooden block (a non-corporeal object) could not support the illusion, while the wooden hand, having structural similarities to the real hand, could [21]. However, the view of the human-shaped manikin experiment did not completely dampened the illusion, due to visuo-tactile component present in the experiment [17]. The results of the recent study indicate that BO increases when virtual human hand looks realistic, though during active movement [2]. Furthermore, Steptoe et al. [19] tested acceptance of an extra virtual limb (a tail) as belonging to the virtual body. The experiment showed that the correct gestural input (controlled through active participants' movement) of the extended limb combined with a game context, a 3PP, humanoid looking avatar and synchronous movements are necessary, in order to accept an external virtual limb as belonging to the body and to get the sense of VBO [19].

3   Methods

The aim of this study is to test if it is possible to achieve a VBO illusion over bat's avatar with the help of visuo-tactile stimulation, presented in Fig. 1. Since apart from visuo-tactile sensory input, BO could also be elicited during passive movements it is essential to test the influence of passive movements on VBO illusion. Instead of delivering proprioceptive input to the physical body we will move the virtual body by moving body's object together with the camera in the scene, which might induce the illusion of passive movement in VE. Due to subjective matter of VBO illusion in regards to self-location mentioned in Sect. 2.1 it has also been decided to measure if test subjects felt present inside the VE and/or inside the body.

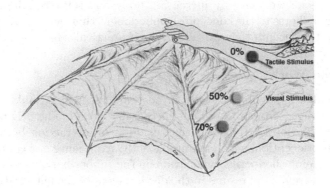

Fig. 1. Visuo-tactile stimulation in test conditions. Green ball represents "offset-0" condition, where the real and the virtual touch points were mapped at the same location, Yellow ball – "offset-50", where the virtual touch point mapped with 50% displacement from the real location, Red Ball – "offset-70", where the virtual touch point mapped with 70% displacement from the real location (Color figure online)

3.1 Study Design

For this purpose we applied a within-subject study design (n = 22) involving three conditions, visualized in Fig. 1, followed by a questionnaire and interview. In the first condition the mapping between the real and virtual touch points were 1:1, that is when viewed from the user's point of view they appeared to be co-located. Mapping was called "offset-0". In the second condition the virtual touch point was mapped with 50% displacement from the real location with respect to the outermost point of the wing. Mapping was called "offset-50". In the third condition the virtual touch point was mapped with 70% displacement from the real location. Mapping was called "offset-70". "offset-70" displacement was adapted after a pilot test, where test subjects reported the least visual spot on the wings. There was no difference between 70% and 90% displacement. All the conditions were applied in randomized order.

3.2 Participants

Twenty two test subjects (13 males and 9 females) with age between 15–54 (M = 32.86, SD = 12.24) took part in the study. The majority of test subjects were recruited from Aalborg University and had no prior experience with VR (18/22). All test subjects had normal vision and no sensitivity disorders.

3.3 Procedure

Test subjects were exposed to the VE for approximately two minutes per condition. During the test, participants were asked to lay down on the floor with their hands stretched in front of them, matching the virtual bat's position. Their head was placed on a pillow to eliminate HMD weight on the neck. Test subjects were asked to place their hands on a predefined position, marked on the floor to ensure the correct placement of their arms. Their virtual wings were visible at the location of their physical hands (shown in Fig. 2).

Fig. 2. Virtual bat's position from first person perspective (Color figure online)

The wings were twice as long and wide than the test subjects' hands. Tapping on test subjects' hand was performed by a physical wand. The tip of wand was presented by a yellow ball in the VE. When the conductor finished tapping the bat's body was moved forward towards animated lattice with knives in order to test involuntary movements and the reaction of the body towards the threat. When the body stopped moving before reaching the knives, the last touch was performed on the thumb area and was visually presented by the hammer instead of a yellow ball, simulating a threat to the virtual limbs. Finally interview was conducted at the end of the test.

The visual feedback was delivered through HMD (nVisor SX60 with a resolution of 1280×1024 pixels, diagonal eye FOV of $60°$). Both HMD and wand positions with attached markers were tracked by OptiTrack motion capture system with 13 cameras that captured the transformed position of these two markers in space. Headphones (Sennheiser HD570) provided audio feedback of the touch sound and surrounding soundscape. The virtual scene was developed in Unity 3D.

3.4 Measures

VBO was measured using a questionnaire, involving series of Likert scale items, ranging from '1' (totally disagree) to '7' (totally agree), adapted from [6,11,15, 16,18]. After each test, participants were asked to fill in the questionnaire shown in Fig. 3. Personal interview questions, tailed by explanations and discussion, included presence (as being there – inside VE), feeling of VBO (as the body was test subject's own), questions about movement (if participant felt that his/hers virtual body was moved, if participant was only observing the movement of a virtual body, if participant controlled the movement).

1. During the experiment, there were moments where I felt as if the virtual wings belonged to me, despite the differences in physical shape between the wing and the hand.
2. During the experiment, I felt that my physical hand was located at the same spot where the virtual wing was.
3. During the experiment, there were moments when I felt as if the virtual wing was my own hand.
4. During the experiment, there moments when I felt as if I was located inside the bat's body.
5. Even though the virtual body I saw in the environment might not have had the same physical shape that I have, I felt as if the virtual body belonged to me.
6. There were moments during the experiment when I felt that the touches on my arm were caused by the yellow ball I saw on the screen.
7. I felt that the touch of the yellow ball on the wing corresponded to the same place as the touched I felt on my arm.
8. There were moments during the experiment when I felt hits on my physical body, when the virtual wing was hit with the yellow ball.

Fig. 3. Questionnaire

4   Results

Analysis of the data focused on aggregate scores, calculating VBO score per condition. Results obtained from the questionnaire was not normally distributed according to Kolmogorov-Smirnov test (p > .05). Consequently, the data was treated as ordinal. Friedman's test showed significant difference of scaling factor on VBO at p < .05 level for three conditions [$F(12, 780) = 138.95, p < .01$]. Results are presented through boxplots of three conditions in Fig. 4. Collected mean and median per condition can be seen in Table 1.

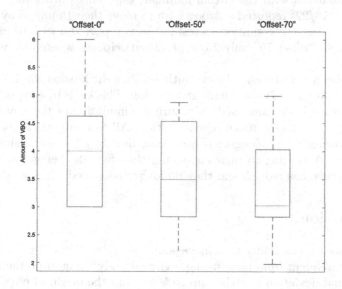

Fig. 4. Boxplot of VBO of three conditions's grand means, reviewing 7-point Likert scale, presenting medians, interquartile ranges, minimum and maximum ratings. The higher the results are on scale the more is VBO achieved.

Table 1. Table of collected mean and median per condition

Conditions	Mean	Median
(1) "offset-0"	3.96	4
(2) "offset-50"	3.8	3.5
(3) "offset-70"	3.59	3

The higher the answers were rated the more VBO illusion test subjects got in regards to Likert scale. Pairwise comparison using Mann-Whitney-Wilcoxon rank sum test (p < .05) revealed difference between "offset-0" and "offset-70", but no difference was found between "offset-0" and "offset-50". Significant difference of the results imply the influence of morphological differences between the human and the virtual bodies. Furthermore, no difference between "offset-0" and "offset-50" might indicate that the same amount of VBO could be perceived with 50% visual deviation from the primary touching point without noticeable implications.

During the interview test subjects reported a strong wish to move away from the threats. Some of them (17/22) tried to move their head away, even though it was difficult, as the head was placed on a pillow. When test subjects' thumb area was stimulated with the virtual hammer, especially during the "offset-0", the majority (18/22) reported a strong wish to move their thumb away from the hammer. In "offset-50" condition 15 test subjects reported a wish to move away their thumb. In "offset-70" only 2 out of 22 participants wanted to move away their thumb.

During the interview test subjects outlined that the illusion was immediately broken in the absence of visuo-tactile stimulation. This leads to a hypothesis that VBO illusion might be sustained only during stimulation of the physical body and visually synchronized touch representation. All test subjects reported unintentional movement as belonging to presence, but they lost ownership of their virtual wings. According to their comments they felt like being "an observer" while bat's body was moved, and they no longer perceived wings as their own.

5   Discussion

Results showed a possibility to achieve some degree of VBO illusion over morphologically different from human-shape virtual body using visuo-tactile stimulus with visual deviation stretched up to 50% from the origin of physical touch point. Even though no significant difference was found between the first and the second conditions, degree of ownership decreased based on mapping. Unfortunately, it was difficult to sustain the illusion as soon as stimulus was absent, which indicates a strong connection between physical body and it's virtual representation.

Visual simulation of passive movements without vestibular and proprioceptive inputs did not provide the same effect as when performing involuntary body movements in the real world (e.g. lifting user's finger or arm), therefore test subjects felt as being observers of a virtual body while being moved during the experiment. Camera movement together with the virtual body might have created only an illusory self-motion effect, which was not enough for achieving the sense of VBO.

Results from the interview, including self-reported fear of the threats, revealed a strong sensation of presence in the environment. However, during presence of threats test subjects reported a strong wish to move away from it. Stimulation around thumb area was noticed as giving the best VBO sensation. Albeit test subjects reported absence of VBO feeling during the interview, results show the highest score, especially in "offset-0" mapping condition. This might have happened due to results' subjectivity and post-interview timing (as they were interviewed only after trying all three conditions). Nevertheless, above mentioned indicates that certain deviations from human morphology might still be acceptable even without voluntary movements involved. Reducing the size of the wing area (too large wings in comparison to hands) by matching test subjects' hand length might possibly improve the illusion.

6 Conclusion

Friedman's test revealed a significant difference between the three conditions during visuo-tactile stimulation and presence of the threats, indicating that the highest VBO amount belonged to "offset-0" condition. However, synchronous visuo-tactile stimulus needs to be permanently present in order to sustain the illusion. Apart from visuo-tactile stimulus VBO might involve passive movements, which should activate vestibular and proprioceptive input of the physical body and might strengthen the illusion. Watching virtual body being moved was not enough. Illusory self-motion is not able to simulate the mentioned input and therefore made test subjects' feel as observers of a virtual body inside the VE. Proprioceptive awareness of the physical body plays a significant role and should not be underestimated.

The influence of agency on VBO illusion should be studied in the future, as active movements were disregarded in this experiment. Furthermore, participants expressed that they missed movements and speculated if they might have achieved a higher VBO illusion if they were allowed to move, which suggests a need for agency for a sustainable illusion over anatomically similar but morphologically different virtual body.

References

1. Andreasen, A., Nilsson, N.Chr., Serafin, S.: Spatial asynchronous visuo-tactile stimuli influence ownership of virtual wings. In: IEEE Virtual Reality 2018. IEEE Press (2018)
2. Argelaguet, F., Hoyet, L., Trico, M., Lécuyer, A.: The role of interaction in virtual embodiment: effects of the virtual hand representation. In: 2016 IEEE Virtual Reality (VR), pp. 3–10. IEEE (2016)
3. Biocca, F.: The cyborg's dilemma: progressive embodiment in virtual environments. J. Comput.-Mediat. Commun. 3(2) (1997)
4. Botvinick, M., Cohen, J.: Rubber hands' feel'touch that eyes see. Nature 391(6669), 756 (1998)
5. Fenton, M.B., Simmons, N.B.: Bats: A World of Science and Mystery. University of Chicago Press, Chicago (2015)
6. Gonzalez-Franco, M., Perez-Marcos, D., Spanlang, B., Slater, M.: The contribution of real-time mirror reflections of motor actions on virtual body ownership in an immersive virtual environment. In: 2010 IEEE Virtual Reality Conference (VR), pp. 111–114. IEEE (2010)
7. Heeter, C.: Being there: the subjective experience of presence. Presence: Teleoperators Virtual Environ. 1(2), 262–271 (1992)
8. IJsselsteijn, W.A., de Kort, Y.A.W., Haans, A.: Is this my hand I see before me? The rubber hand illusion in reality virtual reality and mixed reality. Presence: Teleoperators Virtual Environ. 15(4), 455–464 (2006)

9. Kalckert, A., Ehrsson, H.H.: Moving a rubber hand that feels like your own: a dissociation of ownership and agency. Front. Hum. Neurosci. **6**, 40 (2012)
10. Kilteni, K., Groten, R., Slater, M.: The sense of embodiment in virtual reality. Presence: Teleoperators Virtual Environ. **21**(4), 373–387 (2012)
11. Kilteni, K., Normand, J.-M., Sanchez-Vives, M.V., Slater, M.: Extending body space in immersive virtual reality: a very long arm illusion. PLoS One **7**(7), e40867 (2012)
12. Longo, M.R., Kammers, M.P.M., Gomi, H., Tsakiris, M., Haggard, P.: Contraction of body representation induced by proprioceptive conflict. Curr. Biol. **19**(17), R727–R728 (2009)
13. Longo, M.R., Schüür, F., Kammers, M.P.M., Tsakiris, M., Haggard, P.: What is embodiment? A psychometric approach. Cognition **107**(3), 978–998 (2008)
14. Maselli, A., Slater, M.: The building blocks of the full body ownership illusion. Front. Hum. Neurosci. **7**, 83 (2013)
15. Maselli, A., Slater, M.: Sliding perspectives: dissociating ownership from self-location during full body illusions in virtual reality. Front. Hum. Neurosci. **8**, 693 (2014)
16. Normand, J.-M., Giannopoulos, E., Spanlang, B., Slater, M.: Multisensory stimulation can induce an illusion of larger belly size in immersive virtual reality. PLoS One **6**(1), e16128 (2011)
17. Petkova, V.I., Ehrsson, H.H.: If I were you: perceptual illusion of body swapping. PLoS One **3**(12), e3832 (2008)
18. Slater, M., Perez-Marcos, D., Ehrsson, H.H., Sanchez-Vives, M.V.: Towards a digital body: the virtual arm illusion. Front. Hum. Neurosci. **2**, 6 (2008)
19. Steptoe, W., Steed, A., Slater, M.: Human tails: ownership and control of extended humanoid avatars. IEEE Trans. Vis. Comput. Graph. **19**(4), 583–590 (2013)
20. Tsakiris, M.: My body in the brain: a neurocognitive model of body-ownership. Neuropsychologia **48**(3), 703–712 (2010)
21. Tsakiris, M., Carpenter, L., James, D., Fotopoulou, A.: Hands only illusion: multisensory integration elicits sense of ownership for body parts but not for noncorporeal objects. Exp. Brain Res. **204**(3), 343–352 (2010)
22. Tsakiris, M., Schütz-Bosbach, S., Gallagher, S.: On agency and body-ownership: phenomenological and neurocognitive reflections. Conscious. Cogn. **16**(3), 645–660 (2007)
23. Varela, F.J., Thompson, E., Rosch, E.: The Embodied Mind: Cognitive Science and Human Experience. MIT Press, Cambridge (2017)

Developing Production-Oriented, Problem-Based and Project-Work Courses - The Case of Game Development in a Video Conference Setting

Henrik Schoenau-Fog[✉], Lise Busk Kofoed,
Nanna Svarre Kristensen, and Lars Reng

Aalborg University, Copenhagen, Copenhagen, Denmark
{hsf,lk,nsk,lre}@create.aau.dk

Abstract. There is a growing need to develop new types of learning environments using different kinds of digital support to improve learning. Aalborg University which is based on problem based learning (PBL), has for several years tried to rethink the traditional courses to optimize and enhance the quality of the learning processes, e.g. when using video conference systems (VCS). In order to develop a new format of VCS courses we have used the course "Theory and Practice of Game Design and Development" as a foundation for experimenting with a new structure based on blended synchronous learning environments. This paper will introduce the learning environment concept of this course, the structure and students' opinions of the new course concept and structure using VCS.

Keywords: Theory and development of games · Video conference teaching
Playcentric approach · Problem based learning · Production-oriented learning
Design based learning

1 Introduction

In many universities, there is a strong focus on establishing new learning environments using digital support to improve the learning process. Aalborg University (AAU) has as a Problem Based Learning (PBL) university for several years tried to rethink the traditional courses to optimize teaching resources and enhance the quality of the learning processes, e.g. flipped classroom pedagogy, integration of Massive Open Online Courses (MOOCs), ICT tools for communication, Google drive/docs, Moodle and video conference systems (VCS). AAU is spread over three campuses, located in three regions in Denmark, and some of the programs are located on two or three campuses having the same curriculum e.g. at Medialogy (The Study Board for Media Technology 2017). When a course has to be carried out in two or three campuses, there has been a need to optimize the teacher resources in a way so courses could be running simultaneously using VCS.

There are only limited experiences using VCS in classes with more than 60 students e.g. divided into two classes. However, there are studies indicating some major

A. L. Brooks et al. (Eds.): ArtsIT 2018/DLI 2018. LNICST 265, pp. 363–373, 2019.

problems using VCS (Brower et al. 2015). One of the main problems seems to be connected to existing VCS technology (Irvine et al. 2013). Another problem is the physical learning environments that are not properly designed as VCS learning environments (Park and Bonk 2007). Finally, it can be very difficult to keep the students motivated when the teacher is not present in the same location as the students (Bower et al. 2015).

In order to overcome the above-mentioned problems, we have developed a new format using VCS on the 5 ECTS elective course "Theory and Practice of Game Design and Development" (a 6th semester course at Medialogy, Aalborg University) as a foundation for experimenting with a new course structure.

There is already various literature on courses in a game-based learning environment (Schoenau-Fog et al. 2018), however there are less studies of game based learning courses using VCS learning environments (Timcenko et al. 2017). The combination of teaching in a Game Production-Oriented, Problem-Based and Project-organized approach using VCS seems to be a challenge for both teachers and students. This challenge we wanted to address by developing a VCS university course in production-oriented game development including the basis of theories and literature on game development. In 2018, the course had to run on two campuses simultaneously with 82 students (in 2017 it ran on three campuses with over 120 students). Our aim was to use VCS in a way so students would get the necessary hands-on experience together with the theoretical knowledge and at the same time keeping students' motivations high. In this paper, we present the theoretical and pedagogical background of the new course, the description of the course, the experiences and results as well as a conclusion with future perspectives.

2   Pedagogic Approach: A Blended Synchronous Learning Environment

When designing a university course with a focus on both the theoretical part but also the practical design and development of games, we are using various pedagogical approaches and theories. The pedagogical background is based on AAU's approach of Problem Based Learning and project organized group work (PBL) (Askehave et al. 2015). In order to establish a new course using VCS we will integrate experiences from a design-based learning approach founded on a production-oriented game development (Schønau-Fog et al. 2015). The design based approach has shown successful results for students developing skills and understanding, when they needed to undertake solutions of complex and sometime ill-structured problems (Ke 2013). According to theories of problem-based learning and situated learning, designing creates contextualized and authentic learning, because design tasks force students to understand and work in an environment that demands skills and domain knowledge close to real work environment (Savin-Baden 2014), and it fit very well with the PBL approach. Digital game *development* has furthermore been considered and examined as a "powerful learning environment" to stimulate active, autonomous learning via rich contexts and authentic tasks of composition and construction (Robertson and Howells 2008; Schoenau-Fog et al. 2018).

However, there is a need to develop experience in how to integrate the VCS in practical course design such as in the game production course. The students at the 6th semester have not yet any experience using VCS in a course, but are familiar with the Moodle platform, Flipped Classroom, and to some kind of Blended Learning activities as well as project organized teamwork (Reng and Kofoed 2016). Blended learning has various definitions. In a study (Finn and Bucceri 2004) it is defined as the combination of the best features of traditional learning and online learning. According to Skylar (2009) blended learning environments integrate the advantage of e-learning methods with traditional learning methods such as face-to-face (F2F) interaction. However, the definition has evolved to encompass combinations of various models to combine F2F education and online education in an efficient way in which students can engage in interactive experiences (Bower et al. 2015). Blended synchronous learning approaches might be a solution where one course has to run simultaneously in two campuses.

We thus define blended synchronous learning as *Learning and teaching combining F2F teaching with online possibilities for students to engage in interactive learning experiences where remote students participate in F2F classes by means of media-rich synchronous technologies such as video conference systems.*

Evidence from several studies find that blended synchronous learning can lead both groups of students to attain similar learning outcomes (Szeto 2014) and to develop a similar sense of community (Atweh et al. 2005). Creating an enhanced sense of community among both F2F students and remote students might be one of the main educational advantages of blended synchronous learning (Lidstone and Shield 2010). It has been claimed that students in a blended synchronous learning interventions experience high level of social presence (Garrison et al. 2000) which might partially be because of immediacy that real-time communication offers and the spontaneous nature of interaction and feedback (Cunningham 2014). However, several studies also argue that social and emotional connectedness cannot be taken for granted. It has to be actively encouraged and supported by teachers in a blended synchronous learning environment (Butz et al. 2014; Szeto and Cheng 2014).

The design of the course has to consider the organization of the course plan to combine a fair share of F2F teaching for the two classes, planning the hands-on work, planning the assignments, students' presentation of their games, giving feedback. Finally, the teachers have to find a strategy how to present and act in front of the camera(s) so both the remote and present students get the sense of being part of the same course.

3 Methods and Data Collection

Before conducting a larger scale implementation, we found it essential to test the course using VCS. A pilot of the course was launched in 2016 and a full course was implemented and rolled out simultaneous at three campuses in 2017. The experiences from those courses have given valuable knowledge and ideas, which has been the basis for the course presented in this paper. Furthermore, the 2018 course have developed during the process as a developing experiment with several reflection loops during the process. We have used an explorative case approach (Stebbins 2001; Remenyi 2013) in combination with a descriptive, mixed-method study (Stake 1995; Yin 2008) to investigate especially students' experiences. In 2018, the course took place simultaneously in two campuses: Aalborg and Copenhagen. The parameters of the study are reflected in a student survey questionnaire (with qualitative and quantitative questions) and are elaborated in interviews. Researchers not involved in the course have made six observations of the course, conducting content analysis of the observation data supplemented with the findings from students' survey, and weekly feedback sessions with the students. The hand-in frequency of assignments, the exam and students' final game production have also been analyzed. This study addressed the following research questions:

(1) How was the course of Theory and Practice of Game Design and Development structured and organized?
(2) How did the blended synchronous learning environment function?
(3) How did students experience their learning process?
(4) What was the student's final exam/learning results?

4   Overview of the Course Concept

In this chapter, we will introduce the curriculum of the course content and the learning environment concept.

4.1   Course Content and Curriculum

The study plan curriculum describes the course as an activity, which "[…] provides students with the knowledge and skills required to use game design and development theories to design, prototype, develop, playtest and evaluate games and game-like media experiences" (The Study Board for Media Technology 2017). We designed the course with a focus on practical design and development of games, however, we also made sure that students would be introduced to the literature and that they had to revisit it to solve the weekly assignments at the workshops, during the course.

4.2   The Learning Environment Concept

In order to use the curriculum above as a foundation to create a blended synchronous learning environment, where students from several campuses were motivated and involved through video conference and online tools, we needed to develop a novel way to organize the course.

Based on the former experiences (the 2016 pilot and the 2017 roll-out), we were inspired to make a more efficient course, while still maintaining motivation among students.

In 2018, we thus decided to minimize the use of lecturing through VCS, and instead use the system as a communication tool, to give introductions in the mornings of each course day, and then make follow ups and afternoon kick-offs before lunch. This also helped to establish a community across campuses.

The teacher role thus changed from being a lecturer to a course "facilitator", where the main task was to make sure that the learning was organized in a way so that students learned the practical aspects of the course (to conceptualize, develop and playtest a game) as well as the theoretical content of the main course literature. Table 1 is showing the structure of the learning environment concept

Table 1. The learning environment concept

VCS kick-offs, status and lectures:
- Short face-to-face VCS morning kick-offs, with inspirational short videos (e.g. examples of innovative games), feedback from students and planning the next steps.
- Plan of the day introduced at the VCS kick-off and always available and updated on Moodle (a learning management system).
- In the beginning of the course, a few brief sum-up/status, VCS meetings with both campuses before lunch and at the end of the day.
- A few short one hour VCS lectures with additional "inspirational" topics, new ideas, literature and guest lecturers.
Assignments:
- Assignments formulated as challenges which were part of the stages of the development of the games (e.g. paper prototypes)
- Assignments uploaded to Moodle and gamified as "Experience Points" (XP), counting 5% of the final grade.
- Assignments uploaded to common online Google Drive portfolio (visible to all students)
Conceptualizing, Designing and Developing the game:
- Hands-on work with assistance from TAs and mentoring from course teachers.
- A lot of brainstorming, practical prototyping and playtesting.
Evaluation, Feedback and Exam:
- A mandatory final "PlayDay" game festival, where teachers, teaching assistants and all students had the opportunity to watch presentations, teaser videos and play the games while giving feedback.
- The written exam hand-in included questions, where students should individually reflect, evaluate and grade their own games with arguments based on the main literature (with deep references to page numbers)
Digital tools:
- The VCS was a generic solution developed for AAU.
- Moodle was used to organize preparations, plans for the days, assignments and communication with all involved
- Google Drive was used for the main online portfolio with links to hand-in assignments, playable prototypes etc.
- YouTube was used for game teaser videos, which were presented at the final PlayDay.

Based on the curriculum, we designed the course to consist of 9 full days (spread over the months February to April) with VCS introductions in the mornings, assignments, design and development during the rest of the days. In addition to this, students needed to prepare for the course days, and develop a final game.

5 Experiences and Results

The blended synchronous learning environment has been the framework of teaching and learning, and below the students' experiences of how this structure worked in practice are presented. Observations were conducted during the course from campus

Copenhagen in both lecture time and while students have been working on exercises/producing their game in their groups. Thereby the observations gave insight into students' practice of working problem based and product-oriented in their team work. Furthermore, the observations have shown the challenges for the lecturers using VCS, while they were lecturing and facilitating game based learning in F2F and remote classes.

The findings are based on the overall question: How has the structure of the course as a blended synchronous learning environment worked?

5.1 How Did VCS Affect the Teaching and Learning Opportunities?

In the following, we present the students opinion on VCS. Compared with the 2017 course, where the VCS did not work optimally half of the time, the 2018 course had the benefit of the system working better. 70% of the students didn't find VCS directly destructive for their learning, but still 30% of the students indicate that the course would have been much better without the use of VCS (N = 54, out of 82 attending the course). This feedback show that there are still problems using VCS though observations show that there were no technical problems related to the VCS and no unexpected interruptions in the lecturing, kick-offs, status and feedback done using VCS at both campuses.

The observations also showed that the students were concentrated when the lecturing was transmitted from Aalborg and students in Copenhagen were remote. The setting of the video transmission was zoomed on the teacher which gave a high degree of visual connection to the teacher for both groups. However, some problems related to the physical setup were observed. The setup and the teachers' use of the screens is very important for the communication among the teacher and the two groups of students. The setup was made with two screens in Aalborg; one showing the video transmission of the lecturer (if he was in Copenhagen), the other showing the online elements such as Google docs (which students could update synchronously from both campuses), Power Point slides etc. In Copenhagen, there were two screens; one with the online elements presentations and one in the back end of the classroom showing the students in Aalborg. This setting made communication possible between the teacher and the remote students, but there were some problems, both in the teacher-remote student's interaction and in the student-student interaction between campuses. The observation of a student presentation in Aalborg show how this in practice became a problem:

The students in Copenhagen are facing the front screen they have been using during the lecture and do not turn their view to see the students in Aalborg presenting, but they hear them from the speakers and look ahead. Another situation is to stay within the camera's recording view when presenting their work.

After the presentation, the students in Aalborg have moved away from the camera but are still connected via the sound system. If a teacher or student want to communicate with the presenting group, they can hear but not see them (because they walked away from the view of the camera after the presentation).

The physical limitations of both communicating to a camera that might not catch the interaction because people move around, and the physical setting of the transmitting screen creates barriers for communication. This problem was mostly seen under student presentations while the more traditional lecture time was not affected by these barriers. This also affects the opportunities for working problem- and project based while using VCS. The pedagogical strategy of active learning is thus limited because of the communication and interaction barriers. The setting of the VCS limits the student-student activities between the two campuses because they cannot see each other, and activities between teacher and remote student become troubled when students move in and out of the camera view. Those problems can be solved with another screen setup, but it was also experienced that the use of teaching assistants became very important as long as the current VCS screen set-up was not changed. Teaching assistants (TA's) usually are a valuable resource to help students while doing exercises and working "hands on" with their problems. The TA's at this course also had another important role, they were technical support for the remote students and they made it possible to zoom, change video settings and create the light settings so the remote student could follow the transmitted teaching. In the survey, 53% answered that support from the TA's was needed during the development of the game, while 17% did not need help and 30% were indifferent which confirm that TA's support is a valuable asset in blended synchronous learning.

5.2   How Did the Facilitation and Communication on Google Drive Affect the Teaching and Learning Opportunities?

The use of Google Drive became a facilitation platform for the teacher to interact with the students in an equal way no matter if the student were F2F or remote. The teacher used a Google Doc for choosing group presentations from the online portfolio made in the group work time. The student presentations (Google Slides) were shown on the screen in both campus. The students did then present and discuss what they had been working on and the teacher could give instant feedback. The students were confident about using Google Drive tools and they did not use a lot of time around the platform. The students from the two campuses alternately presented their work (assignments etc.), and the teacher facilitated the presentations. Thereby the students were activated equally and were given feedback on their own material to their continuous work. This gave opportunities for the student-centered learning using elements from problem based and project organized learning.

5.3   How Did the Structure of Exercises and Production-Oriented Work in a PBL Environment Affect the Teaching and Learning Opportunities?

The lecture time is one thing in the course, but most of the time were - as mentioned in the above description - given for the students to work "hands on" with the production of their game in the group-rooms, where there was more space than in the lecture room. This production-based learning in the groups own workspace showed a motivated and engaged work effort. Survey data shows that 81% of the students found that the course made them more motivated for learning technical topics such as programming, and 57% of the students become more motivated to continue studying at the Medialogy Master.

The group work observations also showed that students used their experience from PBL work methods. While the students gathered around tables and whiteboards creating a physical playground they also created the non-physical rules, modus and narrative characters. Theoretical and complex work were slowly developed in a constructive discussion using both theories and methods learned in the course.

We experienced that students were both working together in the complexity of power and solidarity and working problem-oriented to solve the continuing problems that they run into when creating and deciding on a whole game design. When working with physical products the visual development seems to provide the basis for working problem-oriented. The visual "argument" (understood as physical movements of play objects or drawings) for a problem or a solution in creating the game, gives all in the group the same visual foundations to understand and solve the problem. The product-oriented learning environment thereby create the opportunities to work problem oriented from a visual and physical framework that are equal for the group. In the future, it could be interesting to experiment with the visual argument approach in a VCS setting.

5.4   How Did Students Perform at the Final Exam?

At the final presentation of the group's games - the "PlayDay" - it was observed that students were very motivated to show off their games. In 2017, groups only showed a video of their games, but according to negative feedback this was changed in 2018, so that teachers, teaching assistants and all teams had the opportunity to play each other's games and give feedback.

According to the survey (N = 54), 95% of students agreed that the PlayDay was a good event, and 60% agreed that they acquired new knowledge at the day, while 78% became more motivated to make their game better due to the PlayDay.

At the exam, the students handed in their playable games (40% of the grade), a report with answers to theoretical questions (50% of the grade), an extra assignment (5% of the grade), and finally the quality and quantity of the handed-in "experience-point" assignments were used for the last 5% of the grade. The resulting games turned out to be of a high standard, and it was obvious that students had used the course content and theories to make unique and engaging games. At the Aalborg campus (where the lecturers only visited three times) the games had a bit higher quality than in Copenhagen. A major reason for this might be that all groups in Aalborg had good programmers on board, and that the TA was very dedicated and invested time during development of the games.

Over 90% of the non-mandatory Experience-Point ("XP") assignments were handed in on Moodle. On other courses, this rate is usually much less, so it might have been due to the "gamified" concept that the amount/quality of the handed-in assignments was high. The "XP" system thus seems to work when motivating students to hand in their assignments, even though students were not "forced" to hand in.

All students, who signed up, passed the exam and many of the written hand-ins were of a high quality. All students used the main course literature, and the best students had up to 80 deep references to exact page numbers in the literature. We have tried to create an exam format, which motivates students to go deeper into the literature; because they need to understand, the theories before they can critical evaluate their own game.

6 Discussion

The experiences with the practical/theoretical production-oriented blended synchronous learning environment has shown that it is challenging to use VCS for teaching a practical oriented course for students in two campuses. However, the concept with short kickoffs, plans on Moodle, shared documents on Google Drive, assignments and teaching assistants has proven to work for both teachers and students – but with some technical adjustments of physical environments. The teachers and students has to be introduced in the staging and choreography connected to using VCS in the specific physical environments. The VCS creates some barriers for students discussions across campuses, but working with Google Drive to facilitate student centered presentations and working problem oriented in groups on the hands - on exercises that activates students learning process. Furthermore, the PBL experience of the (6th semester) students might have helped them a lot during the implementation and assignment during the different parts of the course.

This course can be effectively used in students' semester PBL projects, since it almost gives the perfect plan for working on the design and implementation for their project (but with no demands of formulating a problem). The lack of problem is one of the things the students like about the course. So, adding a problem to get it closer to the semester project might not be a good idea. However, the way students have worked on their game project has been very close to a PBL approach.

When making teaching more efficient and using the resources in the best way – e.g. teaching the same course in two different locations, this kind of learning environment could beneficially be used in other topics. As the very tight assignments, fast feedback, continuous hands-on work on a single project, and good amount of time to work on assignments should work on a wide range of topics.

7 Conclusion and Perspectives

We have experienced that it is possible to create and implement a practical production-oriented blended synchronous learning environment with the use of video conference system, learning management systems (Moodle), online tools (Google Drive) and teaching assistants

The main findings are that it is important to minimize the usual long lectures, as they do not work as well with VCS and many lectuers do not give the framework for working problem oriented the necessary time for "hands-on" assignments and production of the game. Instead it is advisable to organize the course content around these more practical assignments, and give the teachers the role as facilitators while giving students more responsibilities throughout the course. The design of this course requires a lot from both teachers' capability to handle the technical systems and their capability to act in and use the VCS environment (cameras, screens, sound etc.) and facilitate teaching. A common kick-off in the beginning of each learning activity and "plans for the day" with assignments works as a framework, which keep students informed and motivated throughout the course. The observations, evaluations and survey support our experience as students were motivated and the exam results were also satisfying.

In the future, we plan to experiment with having external consultants from the industry to give feedback to students' concept during the production phase as well, this to increase the relation and work with real world problems. We would also like to experiment with even more collaboration between campuses focusing on game productions with a purpose/message, and not only "engaging" games, in order to hone students' skills in using games as a communication/ persuasive medium.

To prevent some of the problems concerning the use of VCS, we need to look at the physical settings of transmitting the teaching. By putting up one or more transmitting screens in both campus where students can see each other from a front view it might open up new opportunities for both student-student communication and student-teacher communication. This communication opportunity is of great importance in a PBL environment where knowledge and methods learned in courses is meant to be integrated in students' project work.

References

Atweh, B., Shield, P., Godat, M.: The bumpy road of collaborative innovation in online delivery: how to negotiate it? In: proceeding of the Online Learning and Teaching Conference, pp. 10–18. Queensland University of Technology, Brisbane (2005)

Butz, N.T., Stupnisky, R.H., Peterson, E.S., Majerus, M.M.: Motivation in synchronous hybrid graduate business programs: a self-determination approach to contrasting online and on-campus students. MERLOT J. Online Learn. Teach. 10(2), 211–227 (2014)

Bower, M., Dalgarno, B., Kennedy, G.E., Lee, M.J.W., Kenney, J.: Comput. Educ. 86, 1–17 (2015)

Askehave, I., Linnemann Prehn, H., Pedersen, J., Thorsø Pedersen, M. (red.): PBL: Problem Baseret Læring. Aalborg universitet. Rektorsekretariatet (n.d.) (2015). http://www.aau.dk/digitalAssets/148/148026_pbl

Cunningham, U.: Teaching the disembodied; othering and activity systems in a blended synchronous learning situation. Int. Rev. Res. Open Distance Learn. 15(6), 34–51 (2014)

Finn, A., Bycceri, M.: A case study approach to blended learning. In: A Study of Student's Perception in a Blended Learning Environment Based on Different Learning Styles. International Forum of Educational Technology and Society (IFETS) (2004)

Garrison, D.R., Anderson, T., Archer, W.: Critical inquiry in a text-based environment: computer conferencing in higher education. Internet High. Educ. 2, 87–105 (2000)

Irvine, V., Code, J., Richards, L.: Realigning higher education for the 21st-century learner through multi-access learning. MERLOT J. Online Learn. Teach. 9(2), 172 (2013)

Ke, F.: An implementation of design-based learning through creating educational computer games: a case study on mathematics learning during design and computing. Comput. Educ. 73, 26–39 (2013)

Lidstone, J., Shields, P.: Virtual reality or virtual real: blended teaching and learning in a master's level research methods class. In: Inoue, Y. (ed.) Cases on Online and Blended Learning Technologies in Higher Education: Concepts and Practices, pp. 91–111. Hershey, Derry Township (2010)

Park, Y.J., Bonk, C.J.: Is online life a breeze? A case study for promoting synchronous learning in a blended graduate course. MERLOT J. Online Learn. Teach. 3(3), 307–323 (2007)

Reng, L., Kofoed, L.: New teaching strategies for engineering students: new challenges for the teachers. In: Proceedings of International Conference on Engineering Education and Research. Western Sydney University (2016)

Remenyi, D.: Case Study Research. Academic Conferences and Publishing International Limited, Reading (2013)

Robertson, J., Howells, C.: Computer game design: opportunities for successful learning. Comput. Educ. **50**(2), 559–578 (2008)

Savin-Barden, M.: Using problem-based learning: new constellations for the 21st century. J. Excell. Coll. Teach. **25**, 197–219 (2014)

Schoenau-Fog, H., Reng, L., Kofoed, L.B.: Fabrication of games and learning: a purposive game production. In: European Conference on Games Based Learning, p. 480. Academic Conferences International Limited, October 2015

Schoenau-Fog, H., Kofoed, L.B., Olga Timcenko, O., Reng, L.: Motivated learning through production-oriented game development. In: Games and Education: Designs in and for Learning. Sense Publishers (2018, forthcoming)

Skylar, A.A.: A comparison of asynchronous online text-based lectures and synchronous interactive web conferencing lectures. Issues Teach. Educ. **18**(2), 69–84 (2009). Fall 2009

Stake, R.: The Art of Case Study Research. SAGE Publications (1995)

Stebbins, R.A.: Exploratory Research in the Social Sciences. Sage Publications, Thousand Oaks (2001)

The Study Board for Media Technology: Curriculum for the Bachelor's Programme in Medialogy. Aalborg University (2017)

Szeto, E.: A comparison of online/F2F students' and instructors experiences: examining blended synchronous learning effects. Procedia-Soc. Behav. Sci. **116**, 4250–4254 (2014)

Szeto, E., Cheng, A.Y.: Towards a framework of interactions in blended synchronous learning environment: what effects are there on students' social presence experience? Interact. Learn. Environ. (2014). Advance online publication

Timcenko, O., Kofoed, L.B., Schoenau-Fog, H., Reng, L.: Purposive game production in educational setup: investigating team collaboration in virtual reality. In: Stephanidis, C. (ed.) HCI 2017. CCIS, vol. 714, pp. 184–191. Springer, Cham (2017). https://doi.org/10.1007/978-3-319-58753-0_29

Yin, V.K.: Case Study Research: Design and Methods. Sage Publications, Thousand Oaks (2008)

Dynamic Lighting in Classrooms:
A New Interactive Tool for Teaching

Kathrine Schledermann[1], Henrika Pihlajaniemi[1,2], Sumit Sen[1],
and Ellen Kathrine Hansen[1(✉)]

[1] Lighting Design, Department of Architecture, Design and Media Technology,
Aalborg University, A. C. Meyers Vænge 15, 2450 Copenhagen, SV, Denmark
kathrine@schleder.dk, sumit.sen571@gmail.com,
ekh@create.aau.dk
[2] Oulu School of Architecture, University of Oulu, Pentti Kaiteran Katu 1,
90014 Oulu, Finland
henrika.pihlajaniemi@oulu.fi

Abstract. This paper presents the results of a field study on the use of lighting as a tool to structure and support teaching and learning activities by teachers. In a Danish elementary school, a dynamic lighting technology with the option of choosing four different lighting scenarios was installed in classrooms. The teachers' use of the lighting was studied combining qualitative research material from observations and interviews and quantitative data from the lighting control system which indicated the teachers' choices for lighting scenarios. As a result, different types of motivations for interacting with lighting emerged in the analysis: Supporting and structuring learning activities; Communicating with lighting and involving students; Affecting students' activity level and behavior; Creating atmosphere; and Supporting visual task and visual comfort. All these motivational aspects should be considered when designing dynamic lighting systems for learning environments, thus creating a new interactive tool for teachers.

Keywords: Interactive lighting · Dynamic lighting · Lighting design
Learning environment · Teaching tool · Field study · Interaction
User-centric design

1 Introduction

According to the Danish Ministry of Education, students will have spent 13.000 h at school by the end of the 9th grade [1], most of which in classrooms designed before the development of dynamic lighting technologies and digital devices such as smart boards and IPads. Neither the classrooms nor their lighting has been designed for the rapidly changing activities entailed by the different pedagogical approaches. Although this indicates the potential for tailor-made lighting scenarios for various learning situations, there still is a lack of knowledge on how teachers will adopt these dynamic lighting applications as interactive tools for teaching.

© ICST Institute for Computer Sciences, Social Informatics and Telecommunications Engineering 2019
Published by Springer Nature Switzerland AG 2019. All Rights Reserved
A. L. Brooks et al. (Eds.): ArtsIT 2018/DLI 2018, LNICST 265, pp. 374–384, 2019.

1.1   Light for Learning

Previous studies conclude that long-term exposure to blue-enriched light especially during morning lessons increases the students' academic performance, concentration and progression [3–8]. However, the studies using academic performance as a test parameter showed a contradiction between findings from field studies and the controlled experiments [2]. Other studies indicate that exposure to warm light can reduce aggression and positively affect social behavior [7–9]. The review points out the need to focus on users' needs through more holistic field research approach. Therefore, this field study uses a holistic methodology where several factors and the relation between them are studied to indicate how teachers interact with light in classrooms and what the motivations for interactions are.

This paper presents the results of a case-study of interactive lighting in classrooms. In a Danish elementary school, a new lighting system with possibilities of choosing different lighting scenarios was installed in three case-study classrooms. An analysis of the classroom environment was carried out in 2016, prior to the evaluation, investigating the teachers' and students' needs and the effects of the existing lighting on the students' behavior [10]. Based on this analysis, four different dynamic lighting scenarios were defined, which were subsequently implemented in the classrooms and evaluated as the last test phase of the research project in 2017. It was hypothesized that the lighting scenarios would support the teacher in structuring the teaching.

The objective of this paper is to present and discuss the results of how dynamic lighting can be used as a tool for teachers to "set the scene" and thereby support different learning activities by asking: *Is there a relationship between the teachers' usage of lighting and the classroom activities? Moreover, what motivations are indicated for using the lighting scenarios?*

2   Methods and Materials

The research focuses on light as experienced in the classroom, meaning that both the daylight and the electrical light are considered together. A field study was carried out using a mixed-methods approach [11, 12] combining quantitative data with qualitative data, creating a holistic understanding of the teachers' interaction with the lighting. While the non-participatory observations and structured datalog information of the lighting control system provided a view of the teachers' interactions with the new lighting system, the interviews provided an insight into the teachers' personal experience.

2.1   Research Setting and Lighting Scenarios

The field study setting consists of three classrooms with windows on one side of the room. The renovation of the rooms replaced florescent tube ceiling luminaires with controllable LED lighting. The lighting scenarios were designated as Standard, Smart Board, Fresh, and Relax.

Teachers could select these scenarios, or switch off the lights entirely, as well as manually adjust the CCT (Correlated Color Temperature) and illuminance (lux) of each scenario. The Standard scenario was designed to fulfill the requirements of standard DS/EN 12464-1 DKNA. The primary aim of the Smart Board scenario was to prevent the artificial lighting from reducing the contrast of the projected image, yet at the same time to allow the students to perform tasks on their desks. The Fresh scenario was designed to "freshen up" the students, and to increase their alertness while focusing on the teacher or on the task. Finally, the Relax scenario was designed to create a relaxing and informal atmosphere in the classroom by providing dim and warm lighting (Fig. 1).

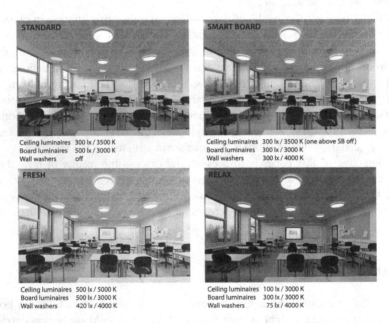

Fig. 1. The illuminance level and correlated color temperatures of different luminaire groups used in the four lighting scenarios

2.2 Data Collection and Analysis Methods

The data was collected over a 3.5-month period from 4. September to 15. December and consisted of quantitative data from the lighting system's datalog, and qualitative data from interviews and observations conducted over two shorter periods consisting of a few weeks each. The participants were teachers and school children of three classes, X, Y and Z. Each classroom consisted of 22 to 24 children in the age group 11 to 12. The three classes had each a main teacher, all female, with an additional five rotating teachers, two females and three males. With the exception of one female, who was in her fifties, all the teachers were in their thirties.

2.2.1 Quantitative Data: Lighting Control Data Log

Quantitative data was collected from the lighting system's datalog over the period 04/09/2017-15/12/2017 in which absent data, day trips and holidays were left out of the analysis. The datalog tracked the choice of lighting scenario and manual adjustments of the lighting. The analyses used the durations of lighting scenarios, calculated in minutes, as well as the instances of choice, calculated as the number of times a setting occurred. The break periods were not factored into the analysis of durations, but they were included in the count of instances. The total count was plotted against week numbers to assess the trend of usage. Due to holidays, absence from classrooms and missing data, the week 42 and some single days have been left out of the analyses.

2.2.2 Qualitative Data: Interviews and Observations

The first observations were carried out in 2017 in weeks 37 and 38, the second round in weeks 48, 49 and 50. The observers focused on specific themes that were derived from the pre-refurbishment observations, but with the option to add additional information if relevant. Whereas the datalog provided information of the teacher's interactions with the lighting system, the observations elucidated the reasons and motivations for their choice of scenario and how this affected the students' behavior. The focus of the observations was on the teachers' interaction with the lighting during their lessons, and on mapping activities taking place and the students' behavior.

Semi-structured interviews [12] were conducted during September and repeated again in December with the same teachers to track their progress and experiences. These interviews addressed the teachers' experience with the new lighting, their motivations for using the scenarios, the changes in students' behavior, and how they adapted the lighting to their teaching strategies. Within the span of research, eight teachers were observed, and six participated in group interviews which were conducted with two and four teachers at a time. Group interviews (20–30 min) were conducted to allow the teachers to share their usage of the scenarios and experiences with each other, generating a discussion [12].

2.2.3 Combining Quantitative and Qualitative Data

The data from the observations were thematised through content analysis [12] into the main categories of the teaching and learning activities and organized into timelines, specific to each teacher, where their lighting scenario choices were added from the data log. Within this, the durations of each lighting scenario and a certain activity could be counted side by side. These timelines enabled a comparison of the teachers' individual patterns of usage of lighting scenarios and their corresponding activities. The timelines of three teachers (T1, T2 and T3) were chosen for further analysis, and the relative amount of each lighting situation for certain activities were calculated in percentages. The choice of these teachers was based on the fact that their lessons had been observed both in the autumn and winter, and their lessons contained all the activities of interest. While explaining the findings from the analysis of the interviews, some examples of also other teachers' habits of using lighting as a tool have been presented.

3   Results

On average, lighting scenarios were chosen four times a day in a classroom, including the option to switch lights off and adjust them manually. Only lessons before lunch were included in the count. The usage rose in the beginning and came gradually down to a steady level, but peaked in the last week. The increased use of the lighting scenarios in the first weeks of the study was due to a curiosity towards the new technology and a will to play with it, after which the novelty wore off. This was equally reflected in the interviews by a teacher: *"I am not aware of the light anymore. In the beginning it was exciting, but light does not play as big role now. [...] There are 10.000 other things"* [T2: 18/12/2017]. Deciding a scene was not an automatic part of every teaching routine, nor their first priority. Rather, the teachers had to adapt the lighting scenes to their teaching strategies, students' needs and lessons (Fig. 2).

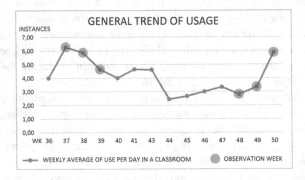

Fig. 2. Weekly averages of daily use of lighting scenarios in a classroom. Repetitive rapid changes of lighting with only 1–60 s interval were counted as one instance.

The analysis identified that the usages of lighting scenarios was related to five different types of motivations.

3.1   Supporting and Structuring Learning Activities

The analysis of the classroom activities and teachers' usage of lighting scenarios in parallel, indicate that the change of a lighting scenario often happened with a change in activity during the lessons. This was confirmed in the interviews with T3 who explained that the choice of lighting depended on the learning situation. On the other hand, T4 explained that he only changed the lighting to suit the activity when he entered the classroom, and mostly only changed this during the lesson if they had to watch a video on the Smartboard, or if someone had changed the lighting while he was out of the class. A general finding which emerges from the data is the individual nature of interaction that the teachers have with the lighting. A good example is the reading session (Fig. 3), which involved students either reading themselves or the teacher reading aloud. The graph indicates that T1 preferred to use the Relax scenario, whereas

T2 only used the Fresh scenario and T3 mostly used the Standard scenario. T3, however, changed his preference towards the end of the year and started to use the Relax scenario for the Christmas stories.

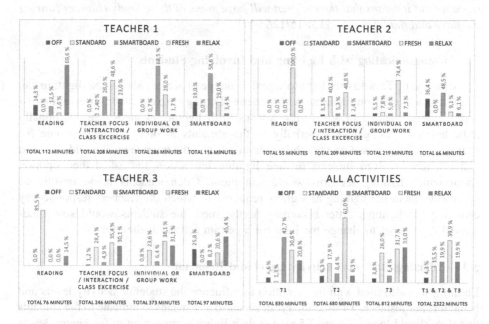

Fig. 3. Relative amounts of lighting scenarios used by teachers during selected activities and all activities

In the interview, T3 explained that his choices were related to a difference in learning situation. During the subject of religion, the students are allowed to leave the classroom to work on their assignment somewhere else, and come in again, which can lead to lots of interruptions. In these situations, T3 preferred to use either the Standard or the Fresh scenarios, as he found them activating. He explained that the Relax scenario, which he uses during mathematics during which the students remain in the classroom working either alone or in groups, would be ill-suited for these kinds of active sessions, because the students have adapted to the idea that mathematics entails a calm uninterrupted learning environment. The teacher described the interactive relation of learning activities and lighting as followed: *"Each activity has their scenarios. [...] the [learning] scenarios influence the lighting and the lighting influences [learning] scenarios to take place."* [T3: 15/12/2017]. Besides the motivation of supporting a certain activity with an adequate lighting scenario, there was equally an incentive to use lighting as a tool to structure the learning activities. In the interview, T3 explained that he also uses the lighting to signal the start of a new activity, for example, when they need to read. As such, the choice of lighting scenarios depended on the learning activity and not so much on the subject being taught. T3 also referred this to the new peda-gogical approach in teaching which promotes dynamism in school work with changing activities and working methods: "*A lot of the improvement results in a teaching that becomes more dynamic and is not uniform and boring for the children. That you also are able to change the lighting scenes at the same time, do not result in that the children sit still that day, and it is not the great acoustic panels that make the children sit calm, but it means that the children will have some of these funny changes [during the day] and that matters.*" [T3: 15/12/2017]

3.2   Communicating with Lighting and Involving Students

The example of T3 who uses light to signal a change of activity shows that lighting can be used as a tool to communicate with students. During the September observations T4 had a similar manner of structuring lessons with lighting changes. He additionally indicated his lighting choice verbally to the students in order to create a cue for changing activity. Based on both the observations and the interviews, it could be stated that teachers involved students in their lighting interaction and asked their opinion about which lighting scenario would suit them. Often students made unsolicited comments about the lighting as well as requests, to which the teachers responded by changing the lighting. After becoming accustomed, the students would sometimes remind the teacher to change the light for a certain activity if they forgot.

3.3   Affecting Students' Activity Level and Behavior

Lighting was also used with the intention to influence the students' activity levels and behavior. For instance, T4 used the Fresh scenario as a means to indicate to the students that they should focus. T2 and T5 related their lighting interaction to the energy levels of students: they told that if the classroom was too energized, they would switch to the Relax scenario to tone it down which, according to their experience, worked. T3 said that he did not use the lighting to make students calmer when they were noisy and explained that the students only see the light and not hear it, and that only what they heard could stop them from off-topic behavior. In addition, the interviews in December with T3 and T4 indicated that it was very difficult to see what the effect of lighting was, and what the effect of other factors were in the refurbished classrooms such as for example the new acoustic panels. In addition, the students had matured by one year, and there had equally been a change in the way the groups were formed.

3.4   Creating Atmospheres

One specific motivation in using lighting as a tool was to create an adequate atmosphere for the learning situation or activity, which sometimes related to the maturity level of the group. T3 explained in the second interview that during the Christmas reading sessions, when reading the story to the class, he chose the Relax scenario and manually adjusted it to make it even dimmer with the intention to create a cozy atmosphere. In the second interview, T4 explained that he considered the maturity level of the class rather than the specific learning situation. For this, warm toned light was chosen to create a cozy atmosphere, thus a comfortable learning environment for the students who were lagging behind. T4 used the manual adjustment to try and create a lighting situation with sufficient amount of illuminance but with a warm CCT, as this kind of scenario was missing in the choices. The analysis revealed a seasonal variation with respects to the preferred scenarios. When approaching the winter, the preferred CCT shifts towards warmer tones, and illuminance levels decrease as the natural light coming from outdoors becomes scarcer. As an example, the use of the Relax scenario increases. Both T3 and T4 explained in the winter interviews that their usage had changed towards warmer settings, which they sometimes tried to manually adjust to even lower settings. T4 related this choice of warm scenario to the situation of natural light outside, and to the high contrast between inside and outside which occurs during the dark season. Although it was outside the scope of this study, this relation between the use of scenarios and seasonally changing daylight conditions is an interesting preliminary finding and worth studying more accurately and with the use of statistical methods.

3.5 Supporting Visual Tasks and Visual Comfort

Finally, teachers interacted with lighting in order to create suitable lighting conditions to support visual tasks and to maintain visual comfort. Most of the time this was achieved by using the manual override of shades or by drawing the curtains to reduce glare from the direct sun light, or to increase the visibility of the smartboard.

The graph in Fig. 3 illustrates that the Smart board scenario was used prominently when the smart board was used as part of the activities. However, in the interviews the teachers were critical about this scenario. Several teachers mentioned that the scenario was not sufficient enough for smart board visibility: in the programming, all the round ceiling lights should have been turned off and not only the middle light fixture. Teachers had solved the visibility issue by either choosing the Relax scenario (T3), which generally has lower lighting levels, or by turning the lights off (T2, T4).

4 Discussion and Conclusion

By applying mixed methods, the findings of this study elucidate how the visual effects related to coziness and visibility play a large role in both the teachers' and students' sense of well-being and comfort. Whereas preferences of lighting scenes have previously been studied in lab-tests [2], this study contributes to the existing field [2, 4, 5, 14] by conducting it in a field-study where daylight is a co-founding factor.

In the preliminary study prior to the refurbishment, the light was subconsciously a part of the teachers' everyday practice of the classroom. By contrast, the evaluation of the teachers' interaction with the dynamic lighting revealed that the teachers had become aware of the possibilities and their usage of the lighting.

A comparison between the chosen lighting scenarios and the learning activities revealed a relation between them, indicating that teachers used lighting scenarios as a tool to both support activities and structure lessons through changes in lighting. However, the manner in which the lighting scenarios were used i.e. which scenario for which activity, was individual and teacher specific, and was based on their own pedagogical approaches.

Our sample size in this study was small including three case study teachers and five other teachers which were observed over five weeks; further studies with larger sample of teachers and a longer observation period combined with statistical analysis might also reveal some general patterns and correlations between chosen lighting scenarios and teaching activities, besides the individual patterns.

The analysis of the interviews and observations showed that different strategies were employed. The teachers were aware of which scenes to choose to affect a particular behavior, and according to their experience, lighting had an effect. Additionally, the analysis also showed that the teachers were motivated to affect the students' behavior throughout the day, by creating a dynamic variation of the lit surrounding to accompany the dynamically changing activities. As the findings show, also seasonal changes are a co-founding factor in the teachers' practice of creating atmospheres. This is seen by the increased use of the Relax scene while reading Christmas stories, or by the amount of times the lighting was switched off while watching Christmas shows.

The observations revealed that the students were partly decision-makers in the choice of lighting scenarios. Either the teachers involved them actively when they chose a scenario, or the students would make unsolicited suggestions. As such the students became co-creators in defining suitable classroom spaces and decision-makers in deciding what they considered as the optimal learning environment for the task. In this way, the four lighting scenarios are a tool that promote the interaction between students and teachers. Becoming participants in the design of learning environments affects motivation to learn: *"Improving the congruence between the perspectives of students and those creating the learning environment (i.e., teachers and instructional designers), thus, is likely to improve student learning"* [13].

As indicated in the interviews, one of the reasons that the lighting system was used less after the initial period can be related to the busy schedules during teaching sessions. Naturally, lighting is not necessarily the main priority, and was not part of the planning of the lessons but was used rather spontaneously. As such it is worth re-thinking the design by considering a more autonomous lighting system. However, previous research argues that a hybrid between full autonomous systems and manual user control are most desirable, because providing the users with the possibility to manually change the lighting has a positive effect on their well-being and comfort [15]. Therefore, the balance between a complete automated system and interactive control must be considered.

In conclusion, this research has illustrated how lighting can be an integrated part of future pedagogic approaches. Five motivations for using lighting as a tool to support teaching were identified:

- Supporting and structuring learning activities
- Communicating with lighting and involving students
- Affecting students' activity level and behavior
- Creating atmosphere
- Supporting visual task and visual comfort

We argue that these motivations should be considered while designing interactive systems for dynamic control of lighting in classrooms. Results show that teachers generate individual patterns and manners in using lighting as a tool, thus, the systems should allow this versatility. Besides interaction possibilities, a more developed automatization and a self-learning system could ease the use for less-motivated teachers and also take into account the seasonal variation of daylight availability.

These findings raise the issue whether classroom lighting in the future should be designed not only according to the DS/EN standards for Lighting, but to a larger extent aligned with the users' needs for different lighting in a classroom. This could imply for example designing lighting typologies that would enable teachers to orchestrate space and atmosphere in their daily practices with the use of lighting scenarios. This study also elucidates the importance of conducting evaluations after implementations of lighting to create lighting designs that meet users' needs.

Acknowledgement. We warmly thank children and teachers of the 6th grade at Herstedlund School and Albertslund Municipality, Zumtobel and Sweco, our project partners in the Interreg project, Lighting Metropolis. Thanks to the Academy of Finland for the funding which enabled H. Pihlajaniemi to work in the project as a visiting researcher at the Aalborg University.

References

1. Undervisningsministeriet.   https://www.uvm.dk/statistik/grundskolen/elever/elevtal-i-grundskolen, https://www.uvm.dk/folkeskolen/fag-timetal-og-overgange/undervisningens-samlede-laengde. Accessed 14 Dec 2017
2. Hansen, E.K., Nielsen, S.M.L., Georgieva, D., Schledermann, K.M.: The impact of dynamic lighting in classrooms. a review on methods. In: Brooks, A., Brooks, E., Vidakis, N. (eds.) ArtsIT/DLI -2017. LNICST, vol. 229, pp. 479–489. Springer, Cham (2018). https://doi.org/10.1007/978-3-319-76908-0_46
3. Barkmann, C., Wessolowski, N., Schulte-Markwort, M.: Applicability and efficacy of variable light in schools. Physiol. Behav. **105**, 621–627 (2012)
4. Mott, M.S., Robinson, D.H., Walden, A., Burnette, J., Rutherford, A.S.: Illuminating the effects of dynamic lighting on student learning. SAGE Open **2012**, 1–9 (2012)
5. Sleegers, P.J.C., Moolenaar, N.M., Galetzka, M., Pruyn, A., Sarroukh, B.E., van der Zande, B.: Lighting affects students' concentration positively: findings from three Dutch studies. Light. Res. Technol. **45**, 159–175 (2013)
6. Keis, O., Helbig, H., Streb, J., Hille, K.: Influence of blue-enriched classroom lighting on students' cognitive performance. Trends Neurosci. Educ. **3**, 8–92 (2014)
7. Choi, K., Suk, H.J.: Dynamic lighting system for the learning environment: performance of elementary students. Opt. Soc. Am. (OSA) **24**(10), A907–A916 (2016)
8. Wessolowski, N., Koenig, H., Schulte-Markwort, M., Barkmann, C.: The effect of variable light on the fidgetiness and social behavior of pupils in school. J. Environ. Psychol. **39**, 101–108 (2014)
9. BRANZ Ltd.: Designing Quality Learning Spaces: Lighting. New Zealand: Ministry of Education (2007). ISBN 0-478-13619-6; WEB ISBN 0-478-13624-2
10. Georgieva, D., Schledermann, K.M., Nielsen, S.M.L., Hansen, E.K.: Designing user centred intelligent classroom lighting. In: Brooks, Anthony L., Brooks, E., Vidakis, N. (eds.) ArtsIT/DLI -2017. LNICST, vol. 229, pp. 314–323. Springer, Cham (2018). https://doi.org/10.1007/978-3-319-76908-0_30
11. Creswell, J.W.: Research Design: Qualitative, Quantitative, and Mixed Methods Approaches, 4th edn. SAGE Publications Inc., USA (2014)

12. Bryman, A.: Social Research Methods, 4th edn. Oxford University Press, New York (2012)
13. Könings, K.D., Seidel, T., van Merriënboer, J.J.G.: Participatory design of learning environments: integrating perspectives of students, teachers, and designers. Instr. Sci. **42**, 1–9 (2014)
14. van Someren, K.L., Beaman, C.P., Shao, L.: Users' experience of lighting controls: a case-study. Light. Res. Technol. **2017**, 1–16 (2017)
15. van Essen, H., Offermans, S., Eggen, B.: Exploring the role of autonomous system behavior in lighting control. In: Proceedings of Designing Interactive Lighting workshop at DIS 12, Newcastle, Great Britain (2012)

Designing a Playful Robot Application
for Second Language Learning

Gijs Verhoeven[1], Alejandro Catala[2(✉)], and Mariët Theune[1]

[1] Human Media Interaction, University of Twente, Enschede, The Netherlands
g.a.g.verhoeven@student.utwente.nl,
m.theune@utwente.nl
[2] Centro Singular de Investigación En Tecnoloxías da Información (CiTIUS),
University of Santiago de Compostela, Santiago de Compostela, Spain
alejandro.catala@usc.es

Abstract. Both *storytelling* and *learning by teaching* approaches have shown to be beneficial separately when integrating robots into learning settings. This paper discusses how to combine them, based on principles found in the literature, and presents the design and implementation of a playful robot application for second language (L2) learning targeted at primary school children. Our first tests showed that the robot kept the children engaged throughout the learning activity. It appears to be a promising approach as some vocabulary gain is observed in children, but there can be several factors involved that were not controlled in the trials and that will require further work.

Keywords: Interaction design · Robot · Second language learning
Playful

1 Introduction

In educational technology, robots are being introduced to facilitate learning and improve educational performance. Among the very different ways that robots can be integrated into learning settings, we are especially interested in exploring *learning by teaching* and *storytelling*. The former is a powerful approach as the stress is put on the children's activity, requesting them to perform some action that involves showing or explaining concepts to others. There is rich evidence for the effectiveness of this pedagogical approach, both in terms of learning outcomes and motivational effects [11]. In this approach, technology can be implemented as a teachable agent (TA), which plays the role of an entity that needs to be taught by the child. Initial research on learning by teaching with a TA was carried out with virtual TAs instead of robots. According to Chase et al. [5], students from 10 to 14 years old seemed to take responsibility for their (virtual) teachable agents and spent more time on their learning activities than when they learned by themselves. In recent years, there is growing interest in having a robot as TA [6, 7, 11, 13, 15]. Robots, being physical entities, might have a greater impact on children than virtual TAs [12]. This can help in the acceptance of the robot by the children and increase engagement and focus. More research is needed to explore potential advantages of a robot TA over a virtual TA.

A. L. Brooks et al. (Eds.): ArtsIT 2018/DLI 2018, LNICST 265, pp. 385–394, 2019.

Storytelling has been shown to be valuable in the development of children's skills such as linguistic skills, communication, logical thinking and creativity [8]. Robots have been used successfully to bring general exploratory storytelling activities (e.g. [2, 3, 10]). Concerning language learning, Kory and Breazeal [9] argue that children's language development is not just about exposure to words, it is also about embedding them in the context of a social interaction in which words are used to communicate meaning (a "dialogic context"). A storytelling activity can be a reason for such a dialogic context to arise. Besides this, they argue that robots can be beneficial as an intuitive physical interface for interaction, using easy interpretable social cues such as speech, movement and gaze. In addition, students can practice with a robot as often as they want [4].

In our work we combine learning by teaching and storytelling in a playful robot application for children's second language learning. Based on the previous points, this seems like a worthwhile approach, which to our knowledge has not been previously explored. The main question we address in this work is how to design a suitable language learning setting that combines a teachable robot and storytelling. Relevant issues to be addressed include how to integrate the content into a meaningful story, how to design the teachable agent in such a way that encourages children to teach the robot, and how to manage collaboration between children and the robot. This paper contributes to the design rationale of a robot application to support second-language learning (L2), and reports on preliminary tests carried out at school. The rest of the paper is organized as follows. Section 2 describes related work. Section 3 describes the design and development of the robot application. Section 4 reports preliminary user tests of the system, and Sect. 5 concludes by giving directions for future work.

2   Related Work

2.1   Robots in Storytelling Activities

Robots in storytelling activities for children have been used for diverse purposes. Kory and Breazeal [9] adapted the robot's language level to the children's level in a shared storytelling game and found that matching the robot's language skills improved native language learning outcomes for the child. Their research shows the benefit of a social and interactive environment, created via storytelling, for language learning. Giving the robot a slightly lower level possibly triggers learning by teaching.

The successful use of tangibles in a storytelling activity with a robot is shown in [10] and [14]. Krzywinski and Chen [10] designed a collaborative, tabletop storytelling activity with a robot as main character. Their small robot on wheels could be pushed and pulled by the children with tangible tiles, and successfully enhanced collaboration among students while telling a story together, passing tangibles and having discussions about the plot. However, due to technological constraints the robot was not advanced enough to fluently support the narrative. The children wanted the robot to express more behavior and emotions than it could. A possible solution to such technological constraints in research contexts is the use of a Wizard-of-Oz approach. This means that the robot is controlled by a person from a distance, which reduces the need for advanced and/or autonomous technology to allow a smooth interaction, as shown in [9]. The child is not aware of this, unless the effect of telling it is part of the experiment.

2.2   Second Language Learning

Some research has focused on second language learning (also called L2 learning) targeted at children. The effect of so-called word-word learning versus image-word learning has been investigated by Tonzar et al. [16]. Word-word learning means learning L2 words by being shown the first language (L1) translation. Image-word learning means learning L2 words by being shown an image of the meaning. Tonzar et al. conclude that image-word L2 language learning is more effective. It appears that this way, learned words stay longer in memory because they are coupled to the concept they express, instead of to the L1 word. They also confirmed that cognate words are easier to learn than non-cognate words. An L2 cognate word is a word which is similar to the L1 word in meaning and way of writing and/or pronunciation. For example, in English-French: *letter* and *lettre* or *adorable* and *adorable*.

A popular research topic in L2 learning for primary school children is the implementation of a social robot as tutor. Belpaeme et al. [1] provide an overview of such robots and present some guidelines for designing them. They argue that words should be taught in groups of the same subject (e.g. supermarket products or animals in the zoo) and within an appropriate context (e.g., an imaginary visit to the supermarket). In addition, they show the importance of repetition to learn an L2 word and its pronunciation. Finally, they state that introducing the robot as a peer could reduce anxiety and make sub-optimal interactions due to technical constraints more accepted by the child. Moreover, introducing the robot as a peer who needs to learn the language could lead to learning by teaching.

2.3   Robot as a Teachable Agent in a Learning by Teaching Activity

So far, there has not been much research on the effectiveness of robots used as teachable agents in learning by teaching. The main challenge is how to design the robot in such a way that it best helps learning for the student. Recent studies on robots as teachable agents in writing and reading activities have explored the effects of various design choices such as spatial placement and gesture use of the robot [7, 17]. Jacq et al. [6] investigated how to achieve a "protégé effect", making the child feel responsible for the robot's learning. Keys to this were having an appealing scenario and the robot convincing the child of being a beginner who needed the child's help.

An important discussion among researchers in the field of teachable agents is whether a robot as TA is better than a virtual TA. Lindberg et al. investigate this in [11]. They conclude that both options work. The robot TA used in their experiment elicited more attention and enthusiasm amongst the students, compared to the virtual TA. However this enthusiasm decreased as the activity progressed. Also, compared to the virtual TA the robot was more limited in its behaviours due to technical and physical constraints. Increased enthusiasm for a robot compared to a virtual TA was also mentioned by Rosenthal et al. [13]. They did not find any differences between the different TAs in terms of perception of the system and linguistic alignment by children.

3 Design Overview

Below we discuss the design of our playful robot application for second language learning. As the basis for our design we used a so-called surfacebot, developed as an affordable social robot for use in schools [2]. The robot consists of two parts: a round base on wheels (about 20 cm diameter), and a tablet on top of it that forms the face and "brain" of the robot. We iteratively designed and tested a number of lofi prototypes before developing the final hifi prototype that was tested in a classroom experiment.

3.1 Lo-Fi Paper Prototype

From the works discussed in Sect. 2 we took several ideas that we incorporated in our design. To encourage learning by teaching, we framed the robot as a peer in need of help. To ensure that words are taught in coherent packages, we provided a context in the form of a storytelling activity with the robot as protagonist. We gave the robot emotions to increase the children's engagement with the robot. Since the use of tangibles is intuitive and appealing for children, we combined this with the image-word learning method. These ideas led us to a design in which the robot is an elephant who is visiting France, but does not know the language. Guided by the child, the elephant can visit different locations, represented by images on the tabletop (farm, beach, city, supermarket, mountains). At each location, the elephant finds three objects, represented by tangible tiles with images, which he can use in his adventures if he learns the French words for them (e.g., gold found in the mountains can be used to buy cheese in the supermarket).

We opted for a limited form of learning by teaching where the child does not need to have prior knowledge about the French words. Instead, the child sees the words displayed on a graphical interface, together with their corresponding image, and can "teach" them to the elephant by dragging them to an image of the elephant on the interface. When the elephant is taught a word he repeats it (in French) with a happy exclamation and a happy facial expression. After a while the elephant forgets the words (making him sad) to invite repeated teaching by the children, and thus repeated learning for the child.

To quickly check for pitfalls and potential design improvements, we created a lofi paper prototype of the application (see Fig. 1) and tested it with children in a local daycare centre. Our main target group are children aged between 7 and 8. They are old enough to read and to make up a structured story, and young enough to still use toys in their stories. A first pilot test with one child (aged 9) revealed that we needed to provide more guidance and opportunities for storytelling. To this end, we changed some of the objects or put them in different locations. We also revised the sentences to be spoken by the elephant, so that they provided suggestions on what to do with the various objects. To set a clear end goal, the number of words to be taught to the elephant was restricted to eight. A second test with eight children (between 6–11 years old, average 8) showed that these revisions worked reasonably well, leaving the children with enough freedom to come up with their own story by deciding where to go and with what object to interact. We only needed to make some minor adjustments to the story-related sentences before finalizing the prototype. Because it was not fully clear to the children how they could interact with the tangible objects, in the hifi prototype we provided a way for the robot to physically carry a tile and move it around between locations.

Fig. 1. (Left) Lofi paper prototype; (Right) Word-learning progression mock-up.

3.2 Hi-Fi Prototype Implementation

The hifi prototype implementation is based on three Android apps that are connected via wifi. One is for the surfacebot which implements the character (see Fig. 2-Left). It is able to show the elephant's emotional responses and play out the spoken utterances. Additionally, it provides a visual feedback reward by means of a colorful animation when a word is taught to the robot by children, and it displays the words that are learned. The robot has a mechanism to simulate the elephant forgetting a word and to request children to remind him, and reinforce learning this way. The word that is being forgotten is progressively being faded away on screen, and children should teach the word again to keep the elephant happy.

Fig. 2. (Left) Elephant in a surfacebot; (Right) Screen of the Child UI app.

The second app is the Child UI, which is the panel controlled by the child (see Fig. 2-Right). On the left it has an array of tiles containing the word-image pairs in French, which can be dragged into the onscreen elephant on the right, in order to teach them to him and hear the word. The robot is intended to move autonomously within the physical playground, containing five different places. However, due to technical difficulties found in tracking the robot among the locations, we decided to remove this functionality for now. This required the child to move the robot physically between locations, but the core language learning activity could still be carried out.

Finally, we opted for tele-operation to prevent any adverse effects of technological constraints on the final evaluation. The Teleop app supports the activity manager (e.g. teacher or researcher) to operate and coordinate the responses of the robot following the Wizard-of-Oz approach. The utterances were pre-recorded in Dutch by an actor. They were specially designed to mediate interaction with the robot and support the story-telling and the learning by teaching strategy that was implemented. For example, there are sentences to ask the children to teach the robot (e.g. "X, can you teach me what that is in French?", where X is the teachable word in Dutch), to give feedback on the teaching and pronounce the French word (e.g. "Aha, so X is Y in French! Thank you!"), to request repetition (e.g. "X, what was that again in French? Could you teach me again?"), or to mediate and regulate the pace of the activity so that children discuss and make decisions on the story instead of just systematically trying to teach words (e.g. "Wait, I cannot learn words so fast").

The workflow of the activity is as follows. The robot introduces himself and his need to learn some French with the children's help on his way to the beach in France. Then children can explore going from one location to another, using the objects, and listening to the story suggestions given by the elephant. The objects can be used in the story by physically transporting the object tiles between locations using a tray fixed on the robot (see Fig. 2-Left). When children teach a word to the robot or fail to reteach on time, emotional responses and utterances are properly provided by the robot, controlled by the teleop in our implementation.

4 First Classroom Experiences

We carried out a preliminary classroom experiment to test how the elements implemented in the prototype fit the purpose of second language learning. After getting approval from the Ethics Committee of our faculty and informed consent from the children's legal tutors/parents, 22 children with a mean age close to eight years old (13 male, 9 female) participated in an experimental playful activity at school with the developed prototype.

The method included a pre-test language questionnaire, participation in the activity with the prototype, and a post-test, carried out one day after. The language questionnaire was designed to easily gauge the children's pre-knowledge, filter initial guesses, and assess language gain by comparing the results between post- and pre-tests. It listed the French words that were available in the playful activity, showing the corresponding Dutch image-word pairs (in random order) on the sides (see Fig. 3-Left). It included five French distractor words that were not considered in the activity in any way. To prevent issues such as spelling mistakes, children did not have to write but just connect words by drawing lines between them. They were clearly informed that the results would not count for their actual grades, and that they were not required to connect any words they did not know. The post-test questionnaire also included a few open questions to gather feedback on aspects of the activity the children liked and disliked. Pre- and post-test questionnaires were taken in the classroom for all children at the same time.

Fig. 3. (Left) Language questionnaire. (Right) groups playing during the learning activity, child putting the honey on the robot and discussing the action with the child behind the tablet.

Children participated in the activity in pairs in a separate room. One child was the tablet operator, who was responsible for teaching the words to the robot. The other one was the robot operator, who had to move the robot to the right physical location on the tabletop and handle the tangible object tiles. Both roles remained unchanged during the activity. They had to cooperate, but their responsibilities and the way they experienced the materials were slightly different (see Fig. 3-Right). The activity lasted ten minutes. Video recordings were made during the activity to facilitate the review of any remarkable behavior. Children were informed after the post-test that tele-operation had taken place.

The results of the language questionnaires showed that the children did not have any real knowledge of French prior to the activity. This was expected, as they did not have any formal education in that language yet. Even though the activity was short, it still had some positive effect in terms of language gain. On average, there was an overall gain of 2.05 words (sd = 1.93, mode = median = 2, min = 0, max = 9) in the post-test compared to the pre-test. Figure 4 shows the frequency of the words marked correctly by the children, split by their roles. Based on the findings about cognate words in the literature [16], it is very likely that this is the reason that *le bebe* and *le cactus* were learned so many times. This is probably also the reason that they were often already done correctly in the pretest.

We expected children operating the tablet, who had to teach the words to the robot, to have shown a higher gain than the robot operators, because of their more active role and increased exposure to the French words (which they could see on the tablet). However, both roles had similar gains (m_{tablet} = 2.1, sd = 1.4, median = 2; m_{robot} = 2, sd = 1.09, median = 2). Firstly, we hypothesize that the learning activity was too short as to lead to differences in mean gain, as children in both roles remained highly

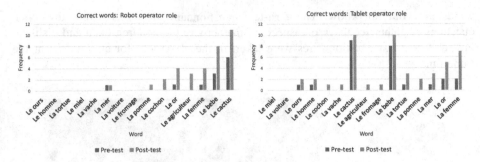

Fig. 4. Words correctly marked by children in the pre- and post-tests, by operator role: (Left) robot operator; (Right) tablet operator.

engaged throughout the activity. This issue is something to be explored in a long-term intervention as discussed in the future work. We also noticed that the tablet operators had more words correct and exhibited a wider range of vocabulary in both the pre-test and the post-test. This may have been caused by the fact that children were allowed to choose freely which role they wanted to adopt. It is not unlikely that children with stronger language skills were more eager to adopt the tablet (active teaching) role.

The overall learning gain displayed by both groups cannot be strictly and fully explained by the words taught to the robot, because not all of the gained words had been chosen by children to be taught. Possibly, some extra informal learning took place outside the learning activity. Afterwards, we overheard some children talking about the words, and the activity may also have triggered some additional discussion at home with parents, when the children explained what they did at school. Such extra informal learning cannot be reliably confirmed, but it is a plausible explanation. It would be in line with findings from Tanaka and Matsuzoe, who let children teach English words to a robot in the classroom. The children's parents reported that the children enjoyed the experience so much that they continued learning at home [15].

Regarding the questions to gather feedback, children showed positive responses overall. In many cases, they started with an unspecific *everything* (was liked). Typical specific responses for what they liked the most included 'learning new words', 'teaching the elephant new words', 'solving the tile puzzle', 'working with the robot', 'the French pronunciation by the robot', 'the elephant', and 'the robot'. It clearly shows that having a teachable robot was a focus of attention. Concerning dislike, just a few comments were made such as 'that you thought you had to control the elephant via the tablet', 'teaching the elephant again each time', 'dragging the circle to the elephant' and 'French'. Note that all these single more specific answers for both questions were given only once or twice.

In general, children seemed to be having fun while doing the activity. Smiles were often triggered when the robot started to talk "autonomously". Especially the French pronunciation of the robot made the children laugh or smile often. The children also said (some of the) French words themselves, either before or after teaching them to the robot. Communication between children often took place in the form of discussing where to go and what object the elephant should carry. Interaction with the system was performed similarly for all sessions; no single duo interpreted the activity significantly different from the others. Many different words were taught to the robot in different orders. There was no trend in which words were taught.

The clear affordance that the robot could carry an object, combined with the explanation that this was possible, changed the way the children did the activity, compared to the tests with the lofi prototype. Many children now perceived the activity as a puzzle where the objects needed to be moved to their correct location. Moving tiles to other locations was done constantly and was a major form of interaction with the application. The children perceived the robot's utterances as hints to where an object needed to go. This puzzle-like experience had a positive effect on the engagement with the activity. The re-teaching mechanic of the activity worked as expected. Many children noticed the sad face of the elephant and/or the fading away of a word before the elephant started to talk about this. They said things like "Quick, quick, quick, otherwise he will cry" or "He forgot something" or "He is crying!".

The children generally waited until the robot would say something, especially in the beginning. They let themselves be guided by the robot's hints. When the activity progressed, this waiting reduced and free play took over more. The children still listened to what the robot said, but interpreted this more freely.

5 Conclusion and Future Work

We have developed a playful robot application for second language learning at primary schools. Our design relies on combining storytelling with the learning by teaching approach. It led us to consider spoken utterances as hints, which are part of the story. A strategy was implemented in the robot to forget words and request help from children to remember. The tests suggested there was some gain in words learned by children. However, it cannot be strictly and fully explained by the design of the activity, in particular with respect to the learning by teaching aspect, since not all the learning gains related to words that had been taught to the robot. A possible explanation is that some additional informal learning happened outside the classroom as a result of the activity at school. Also individual differences in children could have had an effect. For this reason, future work will focus on deploying a long-term intervention in such a way that we can explore the evolution of learning and robot interaction. Specific design aspects to be further explored are ways to strengthen the learning by teaching side of the application, e.g., by having this tie in with classroom activities giving the children prior exposure to the learning content to be taught to the robot and by giving the children a more active way of teaching, such as having to say more words or sentences themselves as part of a dialogue with the robot. It is also interesting to explore how learning can be supported more strongly by the puzzle behaviour that the children showed.

Acknowledgement. Research partially funded by H2020 MSCA-IF grant No. 701991 coBOTnity, European Regional Development Fund and Consellería de Cultura, Educación e Ordenación Universitaria (acc. 2016-2019, ED431G/08).

References

1. Belpaeme, T., Vogt, P., van den Berghe, R., et al.: Guidelines for designing social robots as second language tutors. Int. J. Soc. Robot. **10**(3), 325–341 (2018)
2. Catala, A., Theune, M., Gijlers, H., Heylen, D.: Storytelling as a creative activity in the classroom. In: Proceedings of the 2017 ACM SIGCHI Conference on Creativity and Cognition (C&C 2017), pp. 237–242. ACM, New York (2017)
3. Catala, A., Theune, M., Reidsma, D., ter Stal, S., Heylen, D.: Exploring children's use of a remotely controlled surfacebot character for storytelling. In: Chisik, Y., Holopainen, J., Khaled, R., Luis Silva, J., Alexandra Silva, P. (eds.) INTETAIN 2017. LNICST, vol. 215, pp. 120–129. Springer, Cham (2018). https://doi.org/10.1007/978-3-319-73062-2_9
4. Chang, C., Lee, J., Chao, P., Wang, C., Gwo-Dong, C.: Exploring the possibility of using humanoid robots as instructional tools for teaching a second language in primary school. Educ. Technol. Soc. **13**(2), 13–24 (2010)
5. Chase, C.C., Chin, D.B., Oppezzo, M.A., Schwartz, D.L.: Teachable agents and the protégé effect: increasing the effort towards learning. J. Sci. Educ. Technol. **18**(4), 334–352 (2009)
6. Jacq, A., Lemaignan, S., Garcia, F., Dillenbourg, P., Paiva, A.: Building successful long child-robot interactions in a learning context. In: 11th ACM/IEEE International Conference on Human-Robot Interaction (HRI), pp. 239–246 (2016)
7. Johal, W., Jacq, A., Paiva, A., Dillenbourg, P.: Child-robot spatial arrangement in a learning by teaching activity. In: 25th International Symposium on Robot and Human Interactive Communication (RO-MAN 2016), pp. 533–538. IEEE (2016)
8. Kocaman-Karoglu, A.: Telling stories digitally: an experiment with preschool children. Educ. Media Int. **52**(4), 340–352 (2015)
9. Kory, J., Breazeal, C.: Storytelling with robots: learning companions for preschool children's language development. In: The 23rd IEEE International Symposium on Robot and Human Interactive Communication, Edinburgh, pp. 643–648 (2014)
10. Krzywinski A., Chen, W.: Hi robot: evaluating Robotale. In: Proceedings of the 2015 ACM International Conference on Interactive Tabletops and Surfaces, ITS 2015, pp. 367–372 (2015)
11. Lindberg, M., Masson, K., Johansson, B., Gulz, A., Balkenius, C.: Does a robot tutee increase children's engagement in a learning-by-teaching situation? In: Intelligent Virtual Agents, pp. 243–246 (2017)
12. Mubin, O., Stevens, C.J., Shadid, S., Al Mahmud, A., Dong, J.J.: A review of the applicability of robots in education. Technol. Educ. Learn. **1**, 1–7 (2013)
13. Rosenthal-von der Pütten, A.M., Straßmann, C., Krämer, N.C.: Robots or agents – neither helps you more or less during second language acquisition. In: Traum, D., Swartout, W., Khooshabeh, P., Kopp, S., Scherer, S., Leuski, A. (eds.) IVA 2016. LNCS (LNAI), vol. 10011, pp. 256–268. Springer, Cham (2016). https://doi.org/10.1007/978-3-319-47665-0_23
14. Sylla, C., Coutinho, C., Branco, P.: A digital manipulative for embodied "stage-narrative" creation. Entertain. Comput. **5**(4), 495–507 (2014)
15. Tanaka, F., Matsuzoe, S.: Children teach a care-receiving robot to promote their learning: field experiments in a classroom for vocabulary learning. J. Hum.-Robot. Interact. **1**(1), 78–95 (2012)
16. Tonzar, C., Lotto, L., Job, R.: L2 vocabulary acquisition in children: effects of learning method and cognate status. Lang. Learn. **59**(3), 623–646 (2009)
17. Yadollahi, E., Johal, W., Paiva, A., Dillenbourg, P.: When deictic gestures in a robot can harm child-robot collaboration. In: 17th Conference on Interaction Design and Children (IDC 2018), pp. 195–206. ACM (2018)

Study on the Optimal Usage of Active and Passive Technology-Based Teaching Resources

Valentina Terzieva$^{(\boxtimes)}$, Yuri Pavlov, Katia Todorova, and Petia Kademova-Katzarova

Institute of Information and Communication Technologies, Bulgarian Academy of Sciences, Acad. G. Bonchev St., Block 2, 1113 Sofia, Bulgaria
{valia, yupavlov15, katia, petia}@isdip.bas.bg

Abstract. Today's digital age is redesigning the educational process significantly, so the researchers have conducted a survey to explore the practice of teachers in the integration of contemporary information and communication technologies (ICT) at school level in Bulgaria. The paper presents and analyses findings of the teachers' views on the frequency of use and usefulness of passive and active teaching resources – presentations, simulations, virtual laboratories, and learning games. Furthermore, based on a mathematical approach grounded in the utility theory and stochastic approximation the researchers develop a quantitative model. This model presents a utility function that reflects the teachers' preferences for employing ICT tools and their impact on two of teaching approaches – passive and active. The derived utility functions help to reveal the sub-optimal proportions of the considered technological resources in the classroom education. The authors also provide some discussions, suggestions, and conclusions.

Keywords: Active and passive teaching · ICT-based resources
Teachers preferences · Utility function

1 Contemporary View on Teaching Methods

In today's highly digitized era, people around the world are already using ICT for a variety of activities, and for the younger generation, this is a daily routine. Education and technology are the two fundamental themes that shape our society. More innovations are being promoted in schooling for knowledge acquisition and practice, and students are increasingly using their digital culture in education. Modern technologies can make lessons more attractive, and motivate both students and teachers [1]. They can increase the chances of gaining new skills and achieving learning goals while reducing the number of dropouts.

The challenge of contemporary education is the adaptation to the digital generation. It is a difficult task because the traditional teaching methods have to be implemented by means of modern technologies. The innovative tools enable to perform various scenarios in an attractive and engaging manner. However, they should be used in the right

A. L. Brooks et al. (Eds.): ArtsIT 2018/DLI 2018, LNICST 265, pp. 395–405, 2019.

situation, in the right way and in an appropriate amount thus to improve the teaching-learning process and make it efficient.

The basic ideas of the constructivist theory claim that people learn from both their own experience and the new knowledge they meet [2]. Modern technologies offer tools for implementing these active and passive learning methods (e.g., interactive learning content, virtual labs, simulations, videos, presentation, and computer games) [1, 3]. Thus, teachers have the opportunity to blend both approaches according to their views as well as to flexibly change the teaching method as per the specific situation. During lessons, this manner enables various interactions and effective communications both among students and with the teacher. Thus, a positive attitude of learners to the educational process can be established. Innovative teaching is based on the integration of contemporary pedagogical experience and ICT tools. It provokes curiosity and motivation in students; engages them in self-seeking information, learning by doing and through an emotional experience. In this way, students, besides being trained, have the opportunity for self-studying, exploring and investigating.

In this paper ICT-based resources are considered as passive (knowledge delivery through e-texts, presentations, animations, and videos) and active (experiments, virtual laboratories, process simulations and educational games). The research issue is to define what should be their optimal usage in the teaching process. For the aim of this exploration, the authors use the findings of a conducted survey revealing how often Bulgarian teachers implement ICT resources in the active and passive approaches as well as teachers' assessment of the usefulness of various technology-based resources [4]. Moreover, an analysis of what should be the best proportion of used digital resources in active and passive teaching to make the educational process more effective is a matter of consideration in the current paper.

2   Survey Findings

Respondents of the considered survey are among Bulgarian teachers who take part in events focused on innovative and technology-enhanced teaching. Above the half of all participants (190) are primary teachers, a quarter and nearly 20% are from low and high secondary schools respectively; in each group prevail more experienced teachers with more than 15 years of practice. They are distributed relatively evenly across the country. More details about the survey are available at [4]. Some results concerning learning activities in which ICT tools are employed, different types of digital resources used, and effects of their application, are already presented in [5]. This paper explores and analyses in-depth the findings concerning the use of various ICT resources in both passive and active pedagogical methods. The authors focus not only on the quantity (frequency of use) but also on the assessment of the educational value of technological resources (how teachers evaluate their usefulness).

Figure 1 illustrates how often teachers use diverse types of ICT tools respectively in passive and active educational context. The majority (60%) most often uses passive ones as a substitute for traditional textbooks and workbooks, as a source of information, for sharing content, etc. Those who are technology proficient exploit the power of ICT for creating animations, multimedia as well as virtual and augmented reality. Most teachers use active training tools (virtual labs, experiments, and process simulations) only occasionally, despite the shared belief that to perform an experiment by yourself and to have a chance to test variants while doing it without any risk is exciting. Surprisingly, the highest frequency of the active tools is for educational games – 43%, which can be explained by the prevailed number of primary school teachers. An interesting observation is that almost the half (47%) of teachers have never employed active e-training tools.

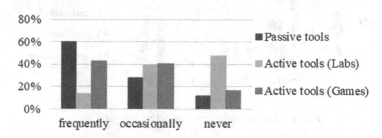

Fig. 1. Frequency of usage of passive and active ICT teaching tools

The most appreciated passive teaching tools are videos and presentations as Fig. 2 indicates. Undoubtedly, those easily attract students' attention and are convenient to put into practice. There are almost no negative assessments for each of the passive instruments.

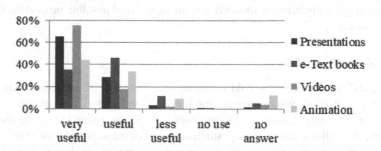

Fig. 2. Average usefulness of passive teaching tools

Respondents use active tools in the process of teaching through lesson presentations with interactive learning content and assignments, for individual and group projects, interactive online testing, discussions, etc. The survey findings show that considerable part of the respondents estimate each of the active teaching tools as very useful or useful (see Fig. 3). These resources often have equal value in the learning context, and in some cases are interchangeable.

The survey results displayed in both statistical graphics (Figs. 2 and 3) are an outcome of the recent increase in the availability and variety of e-learning resources for knowledge delivery. It is noteworthy that the resources for active training like virtual laboratories, software for experiments, etc. are still scarce or not so widespread; even many teachers have never used such in their practice. This is probably the reason for a relatively high percentage of respondents that do not give any assessment of the usefulness of the active teaching resources.

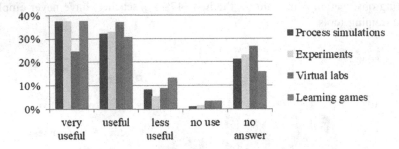

Fig. 3. Average usefulness of active teaching tools

3 Mathematical Modelling

The authors apply an evaluation methodology for modelling an aggregate opinion of surveyed teachers about using ICT-based resources in classrooms. It concerns the respondents' preferences to the employed resources respectively in passive (knowledge delivery through e-texts, presentations, animations, and videos) and active approaches (experiments, virtual laboratories, process simulations and educational games). The estimation of these preferences allows determining the best possible proportion of these teaching resources.

3.1 Mathematical Theory

Term "utility" in the decision-making refers to a property of an object that can be measured quantitatively through measuring human's preferences regarding the primary objective of the study. Utility evaluation methodology is grounded in the theory of measurement (scaling), utility theory, stochastic approximation and probability theory. Based on utility theory it is possible to develop complex models that analytically represent human preferences and allow the analytical inclusion of decision maker (DM) in mathematical modelling. The individual utility functions allow developing mathematical models of complex processes with human participation.

Until recently, procedures for an evaluation of the utility function have been mostly empirical and based on so-called lottery approach [6]. Lately, a mathematical approach and numerical methods for analytical evaluation of utility functions based on stochastic approximation as machine learning and pattern recognition are developed. Here, the utility evaluation approach is based on the potential function method [7]. By its nature, the evaluation is stochastic pattern recognition of two different sets that express positive and negative decision maker's preferences.

The mathematical implementation of evaluation methodology is carried out through a prototype of a decision support system for assessment of an individual's utility functions. The specialized software based on the numerical methods assess these functions. The evaluated utility functions correspond to the concepts of von Neumann [8]. Thus, a polynomial approximation of the utility function is made in Visual Studio and MATLAB environment. Assessment procedure has several steps, depending on the number of attributes of the utility function and their decomposition.

3.2 Method of Evaluation

The authors apply the abovementioned evaluation methodology for modelling an aggregate opinion of surveyed teachers about using ICT-based resources in classrooms. It concerns the respondents' preferences to the employed resources respectively in passive (knowledge delivery through e-texts, presentations, animations, and videos) and active approaches (experiments, virtual laboratories, process simulations and educational games). The estimation of these preferences allows determining the best possible proportion of these teaching resources. The value of the utility function shows if the use of considered tools in teaching practice is reasonable and if so what the appropriate proportion of ICT resources is.

The preferences about results of any potential choice under conditions of uncertainty are used to construct a multi-attribute utility function in frames of the normative approach of decision-making theory [6]. The first step in designing a quantitative utility model is a description and structuring the main objective and sub-objectives. In this study, the main objective is „Evaluation and analytical utility representation of the effectiveness of teaching methods." The sub-objectives are "Subjective preferences of the passive/active ratio in teaching" and "practical training/games ratio within active teaching." Figure 4 presents the structure of the problem.

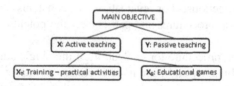

Fig. 4. Structure of the problem

This structure determines the multi-attribute utility function as a function of three variables. As criteria for a quantitative evaluation are used percentage of each variable: $x_T \in [0–18]\%$, $x_G \in [0 – 36]\%$, $y \in [0–46]\%$. The empirical results from the survey help to derive these intervals. The most convenient way to evaluate the multi-attribute utility is to decompose the function into functions of fewer variables according to the structure of the problem. This decomposition base on utility theory and it uses notion as utility independence and lotteries. A "lottery" is called every discrete finite probability distribution over Cartesian product $X_G \times X_T \times Y$, where respectively the sets are $\mathbf{X_T} = [0–18]\%$, $\mathbf{X_G} = [0–36]\%$ and $\mathbf{Y} = [0–46]\%$. Let $z_1 = (x_{G1}, x_{T1}, y_1)$, $z_2 = (x_{T2},$

x_{G2}, y_2) and $z = (x_T, x_G, y)$ are randomly distributed selected vectors. The lottery is denoted as $<z_1, z_2, \alpha>$; here α is the probability of appearance of the alternative z_1 and $(1 - \alpha)$ is the probability of the alternative z_2. The most widely used evaluation approach is the assessments described in [6, 9] as follows:

$$z \underset{\sim}{\overset{\curlyvee}{\approx}} <z_1, z_2, \alpha> , \text{where } z_1, z_2, z \in \mathbf{X_G} \times \mathbf{X_T} \times \mathbf{Y}, \alpha \in [0, 1]$$

Definition of utility independence is following: attribute 1 is utility-independent of attribute 2, if conditional preferences on lotteries on attribute 1, given a fixed value of attribute 2, do not depend on that constant. Note that utility independence is not symmetrical: it is possible that attribute 1 is utility-independent of attribute 2 and not vice versa. If attribute 1 is utility-independent of attribute 2, the utility function in respect of attribute 1, for every value of attribute 2 is a linear transformation of the utility function for every other value of attribute 2. In the process of investigation, independence by the utility, determined by the decision maker, is among the following factors:

$$X = \mathbf{X_G} \times \mathbf{X_T} \text{ from Y and vice versa; } \mathbf{X_G} \text{ from } \mathbf{X_T} \text{ and vice versa;}$$

Since the teacher assumes that the factors $\mathbf{X}$ and $\mathbf{Y}$ are mutually utility independent, the multi-attribute utility function is presented by the following equations as it follows from the utility theory [6]:

$$U_{12}(x_G, x_T) = k_1 f_1(x_G) + k_2 f_2(x_T) + k_{12} f_1(x_G) f_2(x_T), \tag{1}$$

$$U_{123}(x_G, x_T, y) = b_1 f_3(y) + b_2 U_{12}(x_G, x_T) + b_{12} U_{12}(x_G, x_T) f_3(y) \tag{2}$$

In these formulas, k_1, k_2, k_{12}, b_1, b_2, and b_{12} are constants whereas $f_1(.)$, $f_2(.)$, $f_3(.)$ are single attribute functions. For evaluation of constants and utility functions, stochastic approximation procedures and particularly the potential function method are used.

The main stochastic procedure for evaluation of the single attribute utility function $f_1(.)$ is as follows [9]. First, $\mathbf{x_T}$ and $\mathbf{y}$ are fixed at chosen points, as long as it varies only $\mathbf{x_G}$. The DM compares the "lottery" $<x, y, \alpha>$ with the simple alternative z, the other variables $x, y, z \in X_G, \alpha \in [0, 1]$ are fixed at values $\mathbf{x_T}$ and $\mathbf{y}$. The choices are: ("better $-\}$, $f(x, y, z, \alpha) = 1$", "worse $-\}$ $f(x, y, z, \alpha) = (-1)$" or "can't answer/equivalent $-\sim$, $f(x, y, z, \alpha) = 0$"; $f(.)$ denotes the qualitative DM's answer). This determines a learning point $((x, y, z, \alpha), f(x, y, z, \alpha))$. The following recurrent stochastic procedure constructs the utility polynomial approximation:

$$u(x) = \sum_i c_i \Phi_i(x)$$

$$c_i^{n+1} = c_i^n + \gamma_n \left[f(t^{n+1}) - \overline{(c^n, \Psi(t^{n+1}))} \right] \Psi_i(t^{n+1}),$$

$$\sum_n \gamma_n = +\infty, \quad \sum_n \gamma_n^2 < +\infty, \quad \forall n, \gamma_n > 0.$$

Following notations are used in the formulas: $t = (x, y, z, \alpha)$, $x, y, z \in X_G$, $\alpha \in [0, 1]$, and $\psi_i(t) = \psi_i(x, y, z, \alpha) = \alpha\Phi_i(x) + (1 - \alpha)\Phi_i(y) - \Phi_i(z)$ where $\{\Phi_i(x)\}$ is a family of polynomials. The line above the scalar product $\bar{v} = \overline{(c^n, \Psi(t))}$ means: $(\bar{v} = 1)$, if $(v > 1)$, $(\bar{v} = -1)$ if $(v < -1)$ and $(\bar{v} = v)$ if $(-1 < v < 1)$. The coefficients c_i^n take part in the polynomials:

$$g^n(x) = \sum_{i=1}^{n} c_i^n\Phi_i(x), \quad G^n(x, y, z, \alpha) = \sum_{i=1}^{n} (c_i^n\Psi_i(t)),$$

$$(c^n, \Psi(t)) = \sum_{i=1}^{n} (c_i^n\Psi_i(t)) = \alpha g^n(x) + (1 - \alpha)g^n(y) - g^n(z)$$

The procedure is, in fact, a pattern recognition through function $G^n(x, y, z)$ of positive and negative preferences, expressed by DM's comparisons of lotteries. Evaluated polynomial approximation of the utility $f_1(.)$ is $g(.)$. The same procedure is used for evaluation of the utility $f_2(.)$ and $f_3(.)$. Learning points (lotteries) are set with a pseudo-random sequence. The next section shows the results: seesaw lines in figures depict pattern recognition whereas smooth lines are the von Neumann utility function approximations.

3.3   Mathematical Processing of Survey Findings

The implementation of the above-described procedure for evaluation of utility function shows that the most used teaching tools are the passive ones – the usage frequency reaches 46%. Figure 5 presents the constructed normalized utility function of passive teaching tools. After an initial increase (up to approximately 12% usage), a plateau-like section of the utility function is noticeable – up to 25% usage. This steep section represents the fact that the increase in the usage of the passive method causes the rapid

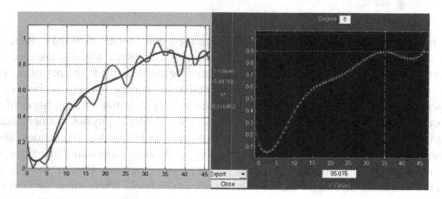

Fig. 5. Utility function of passive learning $f_3(y)$: left part – without (seesaw line, red) and with approximation (smooth line, blue); right part – confidence range (dashed line, red), spline approximated (smooth line, green) and polynomial (least square – line with crosses, yellow). (Color figure online)

growth of its utility. The plateau section indicates a possibility for combining with other types of resources without diminishing the effectiveness of this one. The maximum of utility function lies at 36% usage frequency (which equals to 78% of the total frequency scale) after that follows a decrease of the utility function. Border values at the beginning and the end of graphics have to be discarded because of the calculations' uncertainty.

The mathematical representation of teachers' assessments of the usefulness of both active teaching methods – practical exercises and games – is similar (see Fig. 6). The derived utility functions are normalized. The maximum of the utility function lies approximately at 13% for active training (X_T) and at 27% for educational games (X_G) (which respectively equal to 72% and 75% of the corresponding total frequency scales). There are plateau-like sections (between 4% and 8.5% for X_T and between 7.5% and 20% for X_G), the latter is more noticeable. As mentioned above, the plateau sections indicate possibilities for combination with other types of resources without compromise with the effectiveness of the considered ones. Boundary values at the beginning and the end of graphics should not be taken into account because of the algorithm uncertainty.

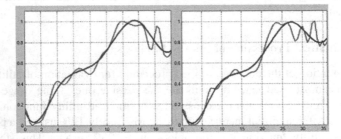

Fig. 6. The utility function of active learning through training $f_1(X_T)$ (left) and games $f_2(X_G)$ (right): without approximation (seesaw line, red) and with approximation (smooth line, blue). (Color figure online)

It is noteworthy that the learning games are used twice more often than practical tools like virtual laboratories. The authors see various reasons for this unexpected finding. Considering these particularities, results of the study on the frequency of use of active learning tools are not surprising. Digital tools cannot entirely replace real experiments and laboratory – software instruments only can make a simulation of a process. What is more, the school subject matters too. Biology, physics, mathematics, and chemistry can often use active learning tools such as laboratory, simulations, and experiments. Other subjects – geography, history, philosophy, literature, languages or arts are more probably to use educational games as active training. Further, the school level of education also make a difference. In primary schools where the same teacher teaches almost all subjects, educational games occupy a great deal of the active learning. In the secondary, school subjects are of a very diverse nature so are taught by different teachers and the teaching methods and tools are fundamentally dissimilar.

The authors apply the above-described mathematical procedure to evaluate the multi-attribute utility over both single-variable functions for passive and active teaching tools. Following formulas (1 and 2), two surfaces presenting multi-attribute utility functions are constructed (see Figs. 7 and 8). Figure 7 shows the teachers' preferences regarding the sub-optimal allocation of ICT-based active teaching tools X_G (games) and X_T (training).

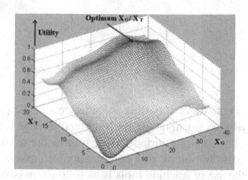

Fig. 7. The utility of active teaching: relation of educational games to e-training

The utility function has a definite maximum and a quite noticeable plateau-like area in which the proportions of these teaching tools can vary and yet be equally successful employed. The overall utility function has relatively high value.

Figure 8(a) displays the teachers' preferences concerning the sub-optimal allocation of ICT-based passive teaching in relation to the active one through X_G (games). The value of the active training tool X_T is set approximately at its maximum utility (X_T = const. and is 13% of overall teaching activities).

The teacher selects the appropriate means according to the specifics of the considered students' group – most likely the combination will vary for different classes. The new technology delivers just those characteristics – flexibility and speed in choosing and applying the specific tools and approaches.

It is not necessarily only to use the optimal point (function's maximum). A sub-optimal area with an amply high utility (e.g., over 70% or 80%) is large enough and allows for multiple combinations and variants.

Figure 8(b) depicts teachers' preferences regarding the sub-optimal allocation of ICT-based passive teaching in relation to the active one through X_T tool (e-training). In this case, the value of active tool X_G (games) is constant, approximately fixed at the maximum of its utility function (X_G = 27% of the overall teaching process).

Both multi-attribute utility functions presented in Fig. 8 are very similar, which is understandable because of the similarity of the single-parameter functions and the reasons given above (see in Fig. 6). There is a plateau-like area in which the proportions of active and passive teaching methods can vary, so several different types of tools (educational games, electronic simulations, virtual labs, e-experiments, etc.) can be successfully mixed as needed.

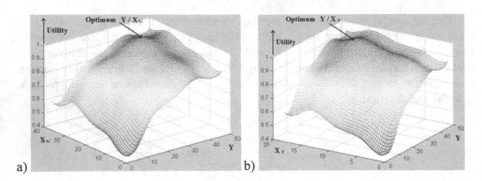

Fig. 8. The utility of passive in relation to active teaching through: (a) games; (b) e-training

The graphics (see Figs. 7 and 8) outline some aspects of the proportion of passive and active technology-based teaching approach derived through a utility evaluation of teachers' preferences. The resulting surfaces clearly show the relatively high benefit of ICT-based teaching tools. The utility of a combination of passive and active teaching lays over 80% when the use of teaching tools is as follows: passive is over 27%, an e-training is over 22% and a game – over 10.5% respectively. In fact, this utility function is an indicator of the considerable pedagogical value of innovative instruments, which is already appreciated by teachers.

4   Conclusion

This paper explores the employment of technology tools in the educational process in Bulgarian schools. The authors suggest a scientifically grounded approach to determine the usefulness of digital resources in the schooling context recognizing their frequency of usage. For this purpose, the researchers considering teachers' opinions obtained by a survey implement a mathematical procedure to define the utility of examined passive and active teaching tools. The resulting utility functions give a clear mathematical evaluation of the effectiveness of different combinations of technology-supported teaching approaches. They have practical application in developing reasoned recommendations to the integration of technology tools in teachers' practice.

These guidelines can serve teachers and school authorities to construct sub-optimal combinations of diverse active and passive ICT-based educational resources to increase the effectivity of the teaching process. Besides the indisputable balance between both passive and active teaching approaches, a balance must also be struck between the used various technology-based tools. There is no one fit-for-all teaching method, so the implemented approaches have to be flexible and manifold to meet the specifics of each student and learning subject. ICT gives the opportunity for application of high quality, modifiable, adaptable and easy-to-use teaching resources to build an effective teaching-learning process.

References

1. Hennessy, S., Ruthven, K., Brindley, S.: Teacher perspectives on integrating ICT into subject teaching: commitment, constraints, caution, and change. J. Curric. Stud. **37**(2), 155–192 (2005)
2. Dycre, G.: Constructivist approaches: application and perspectives in the field of education perspectives, vol. 31, no 2, pp. 109–125 (2001)
3. Bontchev, B. Customizable 3D video games as educational software. In: Proceedings of EDULEARN15, pp. 6943–6950, IATED, Barcelona (2015)
4. Survey: ICT in the Bulgarian Schools. https://docs.google.com/forms/d/e/1FAIpQLSejz86 E16vsYik6mo0wzE085uYgNsmKOeGwCCvMiA6Oc6o1Og/viewform. Accessed 09 Aug 2018
5. Terzieva, V., Todorova, K., Kademova-Katzarova, P., Andreev, R.: Teachers' attitudes towards technology rich education in Bulgaria. In: Proceedings of EDULEARN 2016, pp. 1232–1241, IATED, Barcelona (2016)
6. Keeney, R., Raiffa, H.: Decision with Multiple Objectives: Preferences and Value Trade-offs. Cambridge University Press, Cambridge (1999)
7. Pavlov, Y., Andreev, R.: Decision Control, Management, and Support in Adaptive and Complex Systems: Quantitative Models. IGI Global, Hershey (2013)
8. Fishburn, P.: Utility Theory for Decision-Making. Wiley, New York (1970)
9. Pavlov, Y.: Subjective preferences, values and decisions: stochastic approximation approach. Comptes Rendus L'Académie Bulg. Sci. **58**(4), 367–372 (2005)

An Interactive Multisensory Virtual Environment for Developmentally Disabled

Alexandru Diaconu, Flaviu Vreme, Henrik Sæderup,
Hans Pauli Arnoldson, Patrick Stolc, Anthony L. Brooks[✉],
and Michael Boelstoft Holte

Department of Architecture, Design and Media Technology,
Aalborg University Esbjerg, Niels Bohrs Vej 8, 6700 Esbjerg, Denmark
{adiaco14, fvreme14, hsader14, holsen11}@student.aau.dk,
{psto, tb, mbh}@create.aau.dk

Abstract. This paper investigates the interaction of developmentally disabled adults with a mediated multisensory virtual reality experience within a familiar social context. This was done as part of an exploratory case study. To this end, a media technological artefact was derived from the Snoezelen concept, a multisensory environment for stimulation and relaxation. This system is comprised of an HTC Vive based virtual reality environment tailored to the specific requirements of the case and its stakeholders. Play sessions were conducted at Udviklingscenter Ribe, a residence and development centre for the disabled. After compiling passive and participant observations from the sessions, and interviews with key staff, a series of guidelines were proposed. These guidelines encapsulate the project's concerns and overarching trends and provide a future basis of study when designing and developing an interactive multisensory virtual environment.

Keywords: Virtual Reality · Snoezelen · Multisensory environment
Interaction · Recreation · Developmental disability

1 Introduction

With consumer Virtual Reality (VR) devices becoming more and more affordable every year, it is becoming increasingly possible for them to be used as alternatives for traditional, more expensive setups and experiences. One such example is the Snoezelen, used for sensory stimulation [1]. In place of the multi-room setup requiring a prohibitively expensive set of equipment, VR could provide a low-cost, low-maintenance alternative while offering a similar Multi-Sensory Environment (MSE) experience [2]. Institutions such as Udviklingscenter Ribe, a residence and development centre for the disabled, are looking towards VR-based MSE, as a way to supplement the daily activities of their developmentally disabled citizens. The centre offers its facilities to people from the Ribe area through its social club, Club Pil. The club caters to the social difficulties of its members, as every individual has their own goals and aspirations within the club. Exhibiting a mental age of roughly 5 years, often with severe reading and writing impairments, as well as battling psychological issues,

A. L. Brooks et al. (Eds.): ArtsIT 2018/DLI 2018, LNICST 265, pp. 406–417, 2019.

the citizens at Udviklingscenter Ribe require a custom-built VR experience to fulfil their requirements. With all this in mind, this project's research team designed and developed a Multi-Sensory Virtual Environment (MSVE) starting from a Snoezelen concept and building it up with the help of an exploratory case study.

The unit of analysis for this case study is to investigate how developmentally disabled adults interact with a mediated multisensory VR experience within a familiar social context, for recreational purposes. To support the study of this case, the following research questions were established:

1. What impact does the mediation have on the experience?
2. How does the MSVE compare to other activities within the social context of Club Pil?
3. What is the biggest obstacle in experiencing the MSVE?

This paper is organised as follows. Section 2 presents the theoretical background and related work of Snoezelen, MSE, VR and interaction. In Sect. 3, the adopted methods are detailed, and Sect. 4 describes the design and implementation of the MSVE. Section 5 presents the obtaining results, which are discussed in Sect. 6. Finally, in Sect. 7, concluding remarks are given.

2 Theoretical Background and Related Work

Multisensory environments are spaces tailored to match the sensory needs of a user and designed to enable them to utilise their existing, remaining or preferred senses in a more purposeful way [1]. Snoezelen was created in the 1970s in The Netherlands as a form of multisensory environment combining play equipment with an audio-visual ambience [1]. In this paper, Snoezelen and MSE may be used interchangeably. However, the predominant use will be MSE, as Snoezelen is a registered trademark [1]. There are several traits that define MSE, including sensory stimulation; choice of opportunities; possibility of exploration; offering a sense of refreshment or invigoration; allowing for both active and passive interaction; and being a controlled environment [1–3]. However, one notable aspect connecting these attributes is that an MSE is not specifically designed for teaching skills or simply being a 'quiet' room; although therapeutic results may occur [2, 3]. Overall, MSEs are seen as a pleasant activity, and they can be purposefully used to aid in therapy with mixed therapeutic results [3]. MSEs are nonetheless a popular approach for staff and therapists that usually work with people with developmental disabilities and dementia [1, 3, 4]. This may be due to the very tailored nature of MSE, allowing and requiring preference screening by a facilitator that has a close relationship with the user, which is being guided throughout the experience [1, 3].

MSEs are relatively accessible across Europe and North America. However, they are prohibitively expensive in terms of arrangement and furnishing, as they require not only a dedicated space, but also various technical resources to offer stimulation across all the sensory channels. This can approach several thousands of dollars in cost even for a minimal setup [3]. The cost can increase exponentially when setting up multiple rooms, each with their own experiences provided by a wide range of technological artefacts. Possibilities of lower scale, lower cost solutions have been explored [3], including the use of virtual reality systems [2]. Virtual reality has been shown to be able to artificially induce immersion through embodiment [5–8], opening up the area of possibility for MSE inspired experiences. A VR solution seems even more attractive with the consumer availability of VR systems on the market [5, 6], especially in contrast with the high cost of traditional MSE.

Virtual Reality is defined by [5] as "a computer-generated digital environment that can be experienced and interacted with as if that environment were real" (p. 9). With technological advancements, computers step out of their secondary position as tools, to being windows to different worlds, to stepping into the real world, bringing the site of the interaction from the abstract cyberspace to the world of the user [9]. Originally reserved to governments and scientists in research laboratories, VR arrived at first in the public view, and within less than two decades into consumer homes [5, 6, 10]. VR is now used not only for leisure and entertainment, but also in education, communication, simulation, scientific visualization, as well as in therapy [5], such as in helping patients suffering from phobias, anxiety [11, 12] and autism spectrum disorder [2].

Murphy [8] investigates which virtual avatar body parts are present in the top 200 consumer VR applications for the HTC Vive VR headset, as well as the impact that avatar bodily coherence has on the senses of body ownership, agency and perceived embodiment. Their results indicate that users may experience these illusions of embodiment even when virtual avatar body parts are not visible. Hence, such representations may not be essential, and instead users are affected more by sensorial immersion and interaction with smooth real time feedback [8]. Full body ownership illusions through technological immersion is also indicated to be possible through the guidelines of [6].

Gerling et al. [13] present a set of guidelines for full-body motion control with accessibility concerns for age-related impairments. Notably among these principles lies the notion of exertion management, as well as that of adaptability for different ranges of motion. Exertion management is the principle of offering plenty of relaxing tasks in-between more challenging ones, whereas individual range of motion adaptability reminds the designer to calibrate full-body interfaces to individual user abilities [13]. Additionally, a study conducted by [14] investigated how the discrepancy between virtual objects and their physical counterparts affects interaction and suspension of disbelief in substitutional virtual environments. The resulting guidelines include indications of materials and proprioceptive feedback do matter, but that users are capable of engaging with substitutes as much as with high-fidelity replicas.

3   Methods

This research work uses the case study approach for investigation, due to the benefits offered, which will be explained in detail in this section. A case study is a type of qualitative research commonly defined as an in-depth analysis of a complex phenomenon, an event, or a group of people, within its environmental context [15–17]. By investigating from multiple angles, and collecting data through varied methods [16], case studies allow researchers to make sense of a topic that would otherwise be too complex for a different qualitative research approach [17]. Unlike in controlled experiments, in case studies, the context in which an event or phenomenon occurs is part of the research because the line between the two cannot be clearly drawn [15, 16].

The following recount and detail the methods used in this research case study. The first stage is preliminary research and documentation. The research team conducted several meetings with the staff at Udviklingscenter Ribe, in which data was gathered about the way the centre operates, the nature of disabilities affecting residents, as well as the general level of activities they participate in. This continued at later stages through written communication, and regular visits to Udviklingscenter Ribe. As a result, a list of requirements for the virtual reality experience was established.

Next, several interviews were conducted both with key staff at Udviklingscenter Ribe, and a therapist at a local kindergarten, which has its own Snoezelen (MSE). A visit to the local kindergarten occurred early in the study with the explicit goal of witnessing an MSE first-hand. During this visit, a guided tour took place, led by the resident therapist who had been working with children there in the MSE for over 20 years. For ethical reasons the research team could not observe the Snoezelen in active use.

After multiple sessions in which residents experienced the MSVE, approx. 20-minute-long interviews with staff at Udviklingscenter Ribe were conducted, collecting opinions and impressions of the facilitators (pedagogues). Due to their often severe disabilities, interviewing the residents directly was not feasible. The interviews were semi-structured and conducted based on guidelines and frameworks laid out by [15, pp. 89–92] [16, pp. 39–44]. The focus on the interviews were on the enjoyment experienced by the residents, as well as how the MSVE compared to their regular activities. Specifically, the interviews aimed to obtain information in three issues of interest: Background information on the facilitator, information on how the MSVE experience compares to the regular leisure activities the citizens perform, and the facilitators' own opinions and observations on the experience. The exact nature and number of follow-up questions asked differed for each interviewee, as is often the case in open-ended semi-structured interviews [15, 16].

Observations, both from passive observers and participant observers were taken. Over the course of multiple sessions, the researchers observed residents at Ribe Udviklingscenter, as they experienced the MSVE (see Fig. 1). During these sessions, one member of the research team acted as facilitator for the residents, guiding them through the experience, while the others observed and took notes, photos and video recordings. The observers were also able to observe what the participants were seeing in VR, due to a digital mirror set up on a nearby monitor. This means that the observers were able to correlate the real-world and VR actions of the participants.

Separately from the play sessions, observations were gathered as participant observers [18] by visiting Udviklingscenter Ribe during regular club opening hours and spending time with the residents there, while they were going about their usual activities. This provided valuable insight into the interactions between residents and pedagogues, as well as how they approached various activities.

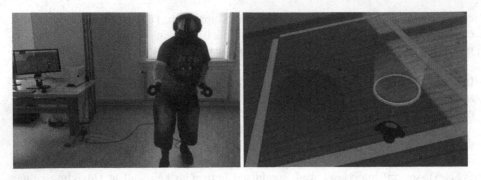

Fig. 1. Resident at Udviklingscenter Ribe trying out the MSVE during the second play session. (Color figure online)

4   Design and Implementation

A virtual reality environment has been developed for the purpose of this study. The equipment used was an HTC Vive head-mounted display with HTC Vive controllers (See Fig. 1). The implementation was done in Unity Engine, using the SteamVR software development kit (SDK) and was facilitated by employing the Virtual Reality Toolkit (VRTK), which is a free collection of software solutions to aid in VR development. These plugins contain a series of premade scripts and prefabs specifically for Unity 3D development. The direct input method, aside from head-tracked vision, is found within the HTC Vive controllers. Most notably, the SteamVR SDK allows the controllers to have identical counterparts in the virtual world. The controllers support 6 degrees of freedom (three axes for position and three axes for orientation). This helps with the suspension of disbelief in the virtual environment by providing accurate visual and proprioceptive feedback [14].

Each of these controllers have several analogue and digital buttons. Following the stakeholder meetings and observations outlined in the methods section, the main control scheme was implemented. The control scheme distinguishes between the two virtual controllers by painting them in distinct colours: green and orange. The use of colours was motivated by the target user group's inability to either read or distinguish left from right. Thus, any instructions would have to reference a familiar concept, such as colours. A different behaviour is then tied to the main analogue trigger of each controller. The green controller became responsible for navigation, while the orange controller was responsible for interaction. This distinction avoids problems caused by duplicate inputs on both controllers. The decision was made because in early test sessions the target users often pressed multiple buttons at the same time, with both hands.

The setup of the VR system includes a play area of up to 5 meters in diagonal (approx. 3.5 m by 3.5 m), which allows for natural locomotion to a certain degree. However, the virtual environments quickly become much larger, and an artificial means of locomotion is necessary. This means of locomotion is most commonly a form of teleportation, which bypasses the issue of motion sickness [5, pp. 303–304]. In this way, the user can cast a trajectory to a target destination by holding the trigger and teleporting there upon release. The player remains in the same position relative to the play area, which is in turn moved to a different location in the digital world. Players alternate between natural and artificial locomotion as they navigate the digital space, walking to cover short distances and teleporting over long ones.

The interaction control, utilised on the orange controller, is similarly performed solely with the analogue trigger on the controller. When the virtual controller enters the proximity of an interactable object, the object is highlighted with an orange aura, indicating that it can be picked up. If the trigger on the controller is held down, the object will replace the controller in the "hand" of the user and can be move around. As soon as the trigger is released, the object is dropped or thrown (depending on the velocity of the controller at the moment of release) and the controller reappears.

The environment consists of a main scene and three secondary scenes. The main scene is the most complex one, as it contains multiple type of interaction that are introduced gradually. Although the first element that is encountered is non-interactable (passive), most of the elements are predominantly aimed at active interaction. The non-interactable element is a dynamic column of coloured floating bubbles that is intended to be aesthetically pleasing. The three types of active interaction present in the main scene are manipulation of cubes, a bouncy ball and spheres that orbit in the air. Baskettargets are placed at specific points to encourage throwing interactions. Figure 2 shows a map and images of the main scene.

After going through the entirety of the main environment, users can remain there and interact with all the elements, but there is also the possibility of visiting the secondary environments. Each of these environments can be accessed by pressing one of three large buttons, each corresponding to a different destination. The destinations are indicated by large framed pictures above the buttons (to accommodate the users' illiteracy). All destinations contain buttons of their own for returning (see Fig. 2). Each of the secondary environments is themed according to a single type of interaction encountered in the main environment. As such, the secondary environments are: the cubes room, the balls room and the orbiter room.

The cubes room focuses on interaction with throwable and stackable cubes of various colours and sizes. The appearance of the room is rather bright and emphasises right angles. The interactable cubes are generally littered across the floor. A small stack of them can be seen in one side of the room, encouraging its destruction or further construction. The cubes can be manipulated in the same way as the ones in the main room: picked up, examined, thrown and stacked. These cubes are set apart by a particularly bouncy behaviour, which enables this environment's special feature. The special feature is an additional input method on the Vive controller (the grip button) that can be held to deactivate gravity. In the absence of a gravitational force, the bouncy cubes can create a spectacle of moving colour within the room if engaged correctly (see Fig. 3).

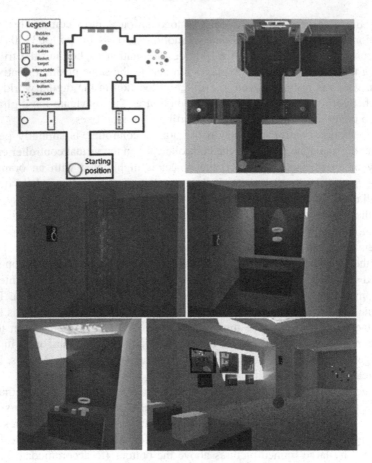

Fig. 2. Main scene map and images showing the non-interactable dynamic column of coloured floating bubbles; three types of interactables: cubes, bouncy balls, and orbiting spheres; and navigation buttons on wall to enter the secondary scenes. (Color figure online)

The balls room is a relatively small, well-lit environment. The salient element is a collection of several red bouncy balls of different sizes. Target baskets are mounted on the walls, reminding the user of the interactions in the main room. Two of the walls contain angled recessions that add variety to the rebound behaviour (see Fig. 3).

The orbiter room is named after the behaviour of the central interactable component, a collection of spheres hovering in mid-air. Once disturbed form their original positions by a user interaction, the spheres will attempt to return. However, due to their antigravitational properties and bouncy surface, they will instead travel around the large environment at the speed at which they were displaced. The user can pick these coloured spheres up, some of them luminescent, and explore the side-corridors or add to the dynamic spectacle (see Fig. 3).

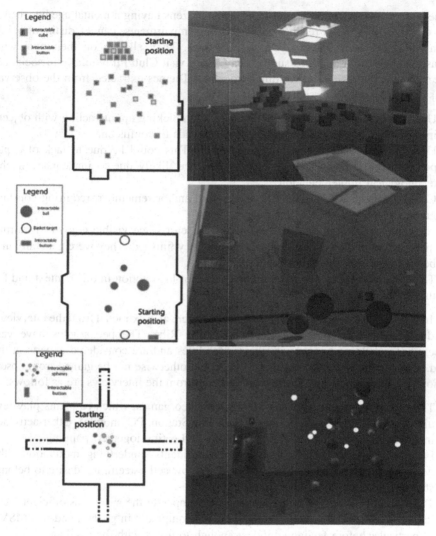

Fig. 3. Maps and images of the three secondary scenes: the cubes room, the balls room and the orbiter room. (Color figure online)

5 Results

The results section presents the trends and themes extracted from two different play sessions at Udviklingscenter Ribe, where residents tried out the MSVE. A total of ten residents (three female) participated in the sessions: five in the first and six in the second, with one individual taking part in both sessions. For privacy and ethical reasons, the research team was not given detailed information about each specific resident that took part in the two sessions, but instead presented with an overview of the group as a whole. Their ages range between 18 and 75. They exhibit various stages of developmental disabilities, with most of the citizens having a mental age between 5 and 6 years. Most have reading and/or writing impairments, cannot distinguish left from right, and some have psychological issues. They all live on their own with occasional help from qualified support staff. They visit Club Pil regularly to socialize, take part in activities and to eat dinner together. Themes extracted from the observations during these two sessions are:

- Users expect to be able to use both hands when picking up/interacting with objects in the virtual world. This inability to do so leads to confusion.
- Users grasp at objects that are out of reach. This could be due to lack of depth perception within the virtual reality experience, likely due to inadequacy in the technological implementation.
- Control scheme is too difficult to understand and/or remember, requiring constant guidance.
- All participants were observed expressing at least some visible enjoyment during the sessions, and vocalized enthusiasm after they finished. They were generally in a better mood after the play session than before.
- Teleportation may not be the optimal choice for locomotion in this context and for this specific user group.

In addition to the above observations, themes were also extracted from the interviews conducted with pedagogues at Udviklingscenter Ribe. The pedagogues have vast experience in helping people with these disabilities and are considered experts in the field. The interviews provide insight which could otherwise not be gained from observations by outside persons. The themes gathered from the interviews are as follows:

- The closest experiences to this MSVE are video games, which residents play regularly at Club Pil (named devices include PlayStation, PC, mobile). Other activities include board games, card games, cooking and eating together, painting.
- Facilitators shared their insights into the residents' underlying motivations: the desire to improve social skills and overcome low self-esteem, the desire to belong, striving to be like their respective role models.
- The staff anticipates difficulties in learning to operate the system as efficient facilitators. They would require training with VR equipment in general and this MSVE in particular before feeling confident enough to use it with the residents.
- Symbolism and colours are recommended in terms of visual cues, due to general illiteracy and the nature of developmental disabilities among residents.
- Overall, the experience was fun and engaging for the residents. Consensus among the pedagogues interviewed was that it left a lasting positive impression on those who participated.

6   Discussion

The data collected as part of this case study revealed several overarching trends regarding the usage of the MSVE in the social activities context of Udviklingscenter Ribe, specifically during Club Pil hours. This section will elaborate on these matters from the theoretical perspective, and ultimately propose a set of considerations addressing the framing of the case.

The first question that was investigated in this case regards the impact of mediation on the MSVE. The user interaction with the system was mediated; however, the mediation was heavily focused on getting the users accustomed to the system. In contrast, a typical MSE mediated session focuses on the individual's sensory sensibilities, under guidance from a facilitator that has a close relationship with the user [1, 3]. As such, a definitive answer implies a facilitator that is both familiar with the individual user, as well as well-versed in the full extent of the possibilities the system offers.

The second question that was investigated in this case refers to a comparison between the MSVE and other activities that are being run in the same social context at the location (Club Pil). The collected data revealed that a VR system is not completely foreign to the users and facilitators, as it is thematically related to video games. As indicated previously, the participants are familiar with using personal computers, video game consoles and mobile devices for leisure activities. Nevertheless, they have not experienced a VR environment before, which led to a high novelty factor experience. Consequently, another prevalent theme was that the participation was fun, exciting and enjoyable. Participants had positive comments and reactions both during interaction and afterwards.

As per the staff interviews (detailed above, in Sect. 5. Results), the experience is comparable to the other leisure activities at Club Pil. Specifically, they are similar with regards to providing the escapism that many residents seek due to their low self-esteem and feeling of being different. Games of all kinds allow residents to practice their social skills in a safe environment together. At the same time, games also enable them to step in the shoes of their respective role models (such as superheroes). However, the proposed MSVE experience differs from the usual Club Pil activities as follows: It is a much more personal experience, as they step alone into the virtual world; It is a physically intensive activity; They interact one-on-one with a facilitator for extended periods of time, allowing for a better mutual understanding.

The last and maybe most fruitful inquiry pertains to the biggest obstacle in the engagement with the MSVE. This has been identified as being the control scheme. There are several facets to this consideration. To begin with, it was noted that controls were simply not intuitive enough for most of the users. This is reflected most notably in their attempts at grabbing objects with both of their hands, which the implementation did not fulfil. Furthermore, several shortcomings were observed as participants grasped at objects beyond their reach, indicating issues with spatial and depth cues [5, 6]. Conversely, the visual cues provided semantic separations that were received positively, at least according to the experts interviewed. Given that users can experience illusions of embodiment even when virtual body parts are not present [8], it seems that the sense of agency and/or bodily coherence overtook the functional capacity of the control scheme. In other words, the existing sense of embodiment characteristic of the human nature [7, 9] inhabits the virtual experience in the lack of any other element to simulate it. As presented by [5] and [6], properly implementing an embodied VR experience is a challenging and sophisticated task. When such fundamental problems arise for the users, the technical design side is the primary suspect. Moreover, as seen in the data, all participants had the ability to achieve some of the interactions in the MSVE, despite their varying degrees of physical impairments. It is concluded that the main issue resides not necessarily in the physical accessibility of the interaction scheme, as much as in the application of an embodied interaction perspective in the design procedure.

The shortcomings in the control scheme also influence the mediation aspect. As a facilitator is a principal requirement for the MSVE, difficulties on their side affect the experience for the user. During the stakeholder interviews, their concern towards a potentially steep learning curve regarding VR for themselves as facilitators was noted. Even though the stakeholders agree that the MSVE experience was pleasant for the users and expressed their clear interest in it, a training period with the system will be helpful when working with their residents. This raises questions, which can be addressed through a usability-oriented design process.

Having reviewed the results from this case study, we propose the following guidelines for researchers and facilitators:

- The facilitator should be both familiar with the individual user, and well-versed in the full extent of the possibilities the system offers. This would ensure the best mediated experience.
- Extra attention is necessary in making the controls as simple and intuitive as possible, to ensure that the controls are understandable, usable, and memorable for the user regardless of their developmental level.
- The system must be reliable and flexible, in order to adapt to the wide range of needs of this target group. Disruptions should not require a session to stop or restart.

7 Conclusion

This study set out to explore how developmentally disabled adults interact with a mediated multisensory VR experience within a familiar social context, for recreational purposes. It did so by designing and implementing an interactive MSVE, which was evaluated through observations of play sessions and interviews with pedagogues at Udviklingscenter Ribe. The compiled data was used to extract themes, from which design guidelines were derived. In summary, the most important findings, which should be taking into account when designing and implementing an interactive MSVE: the facilitator should be familiar with the individual user, the MSVE and associated VR technology; the controls should be simple and intuitive; and the system should be reliable and flexible.

Acknowledgments. The authors would like to thank Udviklingscenter Ribe for their collaboration on this project.

References

1. Pagliano, P.: Using a Multisensory Environment: A Practical Guide for Teachers. Routledge, London (2013)
2. Zaman, H.B., et al. (eds.): Advances in Visual Informatics, vol. 9429. Springer, Cham (2015). https://doi.org/10.1007/978-3-319-25939-0
3. Lancioni, G.E., Cuvo, A.J., O'Reilly, M.F.: Snoezelen: an overview of research with people with developmental disabilities and dementia. Disabil. Rehabil. **24**(4), 175–184 (2002)
4. Staal, J.A., Pinkney, L., Roane, D.M.: Assessment of stimulus preferences in multisensory environment therapy for older people with dementia. Br. J. Occup. Ther. **66**(12), 542–550 (2003)
5. Jerald, J.: The VR Book: Human-Centered Design for Virtual Reality, 1st edn. Association for Computing Machinery, New York (2016)
6. Spanlang, B., et al.: How to build an embodiment lab: achieving body representation illusions in virtual reality. Front. Robot. AI **1** (2014)
7. Kilteni, K., Groten, R., Slater, M.: The sense of embodiment in virtual reality. Presence: Teleoperators Virtual Environ. **21**(4), 373–387 (2012)
8. Murphy, D.: Bodiless embodiment: a descriptive survey of avatar bodily coherence in first-wave consumer VR applications. In: IEEE Virtual Reality, pp. 265–266 (2017)
9. Dourish, P.: Where the Action is: The Foundations of Embodied Interaction. MIT Press, Cambridge (2001)
10. Ryan, M.-L.: Narrative as Virtual Reality: Immersion and Interactivity in Literature and Electronic Media. Johns Hopkins University Press, Baltimore (2001)
11. Juan, M.C., Pérez, D.: Using augmented and virtual reality for the development of acrophobic scenarios. Comparison of the levels of presence and anxiety. Comput. Graph. **34**(6), 756–766 (2010)
12. Kwon, J.H., Powell, J., Chalmers, A.: How level of realism influences anxiety in virtual reality environments for a job interview. Int. J. Hum.-Comput. Stud. **71**(10), 978–987 (2013)
13. Gerling, K., Livingston, I., Nacke, L., Mandryk, R.: Full-body motion-based game interaction for older adults. In: Proceedings of the SIGCHI Conference on Human Factors in Computing Systems, pp. 1873–1882 (2012)
14. Simeone, A.L., Velloso, E., Gellersen, H.: Substitutional reality: using the physical environment to design virtual reality experiences. In: Proceedings of the 33rd Annual ACM Conference on Human Factors in Computing Systems, pp. 3307–3316, ACM, New York (2015)
15. Yin, R.K.: Case Study Research: Design and Methods, 5th edn. SAGE, Thousand Oaks (2014)
16. Hancock, D.R., Algozzine, R.: Doing Case Study Research: A Practical Guide for Beginning Researchers, 3rd edn. Teachers College Press, New York (2017)
17. Baxter, P.: Qualitative case study methodology: study design and implementation for novice researchers. Qual. Rep. **13**(4), 544–559 (2008)
18. Bernard, H.R. (ed.): Handbook of methods in Cultural Anthropology, 2nd edn. Rowman & Littlefield, Lanham (2015)

Making Puppet Circuits

Michael Nitsche(✉) and Crystal Eng

Georgia Institute of Technology, Atlanta, GA 30308, USA
{michael.nitsche,c.eng5}@gatech.edu

Abstract. The *Prototyping Puppets* project presents a craft-based prototyping project for STEM education of early middle school level students in informal learning. The project combines crafting and performing of hybrid puppets. It was pilot tested in two expert workshops (n = 6 and n = 10), which focused on crafting practices and materials and two student workshops (n = 8 and n = 9), which included performance elements. The resulting data back the main design concept to combine craft and performance in a STEM-focused maker project. They suggest particular focus on key elements of our educational scaffolding that focus on material performance in combination with crafting. We close with an outlook toward emerging changes as references for related work.

Keywords: Craft · Design · Performance · Puppetry · STEM

1 Introduction

Affordable microcontrollers, accessible APIs, sensors, and prototyping materials have invited a range of hybrid approaches in STEM education that combine material crafting with tangible interaction design. This combination tries to reach new students who might not identify with electronics or engineering but are interested in crafting and making. The *Prototyping Puppets* project extends these efforts as it adds Performance Art to the design of craft-inspired STEM approaches. Craft and performance are both applied as practical methods for personal engagement and expression.

The paper reports on the design stage of this project. It will sketch out the background for the craft-based design space, then it will describe core elements of the project at hand, it will discuss this design through four workshops held during the design phase of *Prototyping Puppets*, report on the workshop results, and conclude with a summary of the resulting design changes to point toward an increased awareness for and role of the adaptation of performance in making-related design.

Prototyping Puppets is centered around a workshop design to teach middle school level students basic circuit building techniques in an informal setting. Key concepts that informed this approach are educational theories on "learning-by-making" [1] and embodied interaction design [2]. In some of this work, performance and expression are already noted as active components: "as an extension of themselves [= the users']; they act *through* it rather than *on* it" [3]. Applied effectively, agency remains in the hands of the student and the embodied learning stretches from a crafted making to an actual performance setting. To achieve this, our project combines making mechanical puppets with the construction of simple circuits included in the puppet designs. Key learning

A. L. Brooks et al. (Eds.): ArtsIT 2018/DLI 2018, LNICST 265, pp. 418–428, 2019.

objectives were modeled after the CSTA and NGSS and touch on translation of computational thinking into collaboration with peers and design thinking. Workshops unfold over 4 stages: (1) Learn underlying technology, (2) Create a shared story, (3) Create customized puppets, (4) Rehearse and Perform. Students encounter the technology, contextualize it with their own story, and build hybrid puppets to perform them in a shared puppetry show, which also serves as a technical dissemination.

1.1   Craft

Craft and a renewed interest in materiality have evolved into key themes in interaction design and how to apply it to education. Buechley and Eisenberg built on soft circuits [4] to realize the educational potential "of new and accessible materials and programming platforms [that] permits the growth of a new educational subculture" [5]. Berzowska also focuses on wearables to potentially "convey personal identity information" [6]. The role of crafting as a personal creative practice, rooted in cultural and social context, continues in tangible design [7] leading to notions of hybrid craft [8]. This has led to initial discussions bridging HCI, making, and performance art [9] and work on "how technology and craftsmanship can be reconciled to enable diverse forms of expressive practice" [10]. This turn to craft as expressive practice led to new toolkits aimed to circumvent black-boxing of technology. These approaches emphasize "creative expression, diversity, manual skill, and individual autonomy" [11].

There are two key challenges among many existing tangible design projects in this area: first, the way interaction design has included craft in STEM education. Craft served as a means to reach new audiences through a "personal" [6] approach that attracts new "subcultures" [5] to learn STEM material. However, the danger is that craft becomes only an access point and its creative practice replaced by e.g. Computer Science or Math curricula. Second, many STEM-related projects use black-boxed technology through commercially available kits. They hide the material encounter that is central to crafting. To counter this black-boxing, Mellis et al. propose an "untoolkit" [11] and Perner-Wilson et al. introduce "a kit-of-no-parts" [12]. Both approaches combine craft materials with electronics in basic kits that emphasize novel encounters with technology. Particularly Perner-Wilson's approach does not simplify the task but focuses on a direct encounter with the technology at hand through a craft-driven approach. The concept of an open, material-based kit, thus, guided *Prototyping Puppets* to counter possible black-boxing of technology through a sharpened focus on craft.

1.2   Puppets and Tangibles

Puppetry as performance art and puppet making as crafting are directly connected creative practices that allow for personal and shared expression on both levels outlined above. *Prototyping Puppets* follows this approach, connecting the materiality of the puppet-as-crafted-object to the expression of the puppet-as-performance-object. Expression, here, is realized first through craft practice and in the encounter with mixed materials and controllers. It manifests not only through technical skill but also individual expression of identity through the manipulation of the finished puppet.

Some hybrid crafting approaches already use puppets for educational purposes [13]. Yet, puppetry's potential still holds much more promise, providing manifold ways for personal expression through structured interaction between human and objects as it plays with the interdependency of the two. Because the art form is so old, puppets are liminal objects [14] shifting through time and technology. As cultural artifacts they are "powerful conservators of social values, but also political subversives" [15] and they take countless forms. Thus, Posner steps away from a pre-conceived notion of a puppet object and suggests the term "material performance" [16].

Through this material encounter puppets are understood as "something with which we are deeply connected, and through which we strive to express, understand, and negotiate our interrelationship with each other and with the non-human world." [23] With the notion of material performance as a bridge between making and performing, a new look at the challenges in the domain is possible. The negotiation with the material that is typical for a crafter can be expanded to a negotiation with a performative object. Design, making, puppet performance are combined in the *Prototyping Puppets* project.

2 Project

2.1 Project Goals and Motivation

Prototyping Puppets aims to attract and engage new audiences by countering black-boxing through the use of accessible materials and innovative educational design. The combination of tangibles with collaborative performance and story-making has been successful in related context [17]. In our case, it targets early middle school students to teach them basic prototyping and circuitry skills. Mirroring related projects [5, 11, 18], the method to develop this approach works through iterative workshops that explore feasible materials, practices, and modifications. In addition to this iterative approach on making and crafting, *Prototyping Puppets* also covers the creation of a story and its live performance. Participants realize, test, and ultimately evaluate their products in a concluding puppet show that combines technical validation with individual performative expression of a shared storyline.

The project is a collaboration with the Center for Puppetry Arts, which has extensive on-site and off-site educational programming. Their *build your own puppet* workshops served as an initial reference. Here, audiences are invited to build their own puppets from pre-designed kits that relate to a current show. These kits feature basic materials, such as popsicle sticks, paper, or thread, and a step-by-step explanation how to create the particular puppet. *Prototyping Puppets* mirrors this approach but integrates the construction of a simple circuit in the puppet design. This circuit is operated through the manipulation of the puppet and combines mechanical and electronic design. It shows students that if one can create a puppet, one can also create a basic circuit. The design constraints follow the limitations that the original kits at the *Center for Puppetry Arts* face: focus on easily accessible materials, on affordable supplies, avoid dangerous components or practices such as hot glue guns or needles, and limited complexity to allow for a quick construction time.

2.2 Development

Keeping the design feasible for informal education in terms of cost, framing, technology, and scope remained defining criteria. That is why we conducted expert workshops to test different puppet designs before presenting the most suitable one to students. In the expert workshops we evaluated different components as well as teaching methodologies. They served as feasibility studies for our design and its approach.

To create feasible designs, we consulted directly with the *Center for Puppetry Arts*, their educational director, Aretta Baumgartner, and puppet designer Jeff Domke. Based on these discussions, we developed multiple hybrid puppet designs, ranging from sock puppets to marionettes to rod puppets. All puppets shared the basic design criteria of simple and affordable materials, a combination of basic circuit building with mechanical puppet construction, simple and safe assembly practices, and short assembly time.

Two *expert workshops* tested the feasibility of these designs and informed further improvements. Participants consisted of teachers, puppeteers, and informal educators. In each workshop, participants were divided into small groups (2–4) and had to follow instructors to individually build consecutively three different puppet designs each. After each build, we collected immediate feedback on the design, the teaching methodology, and the materials. In addition, each expert workshop included an initial demographic questionnaire, a final assessment questionnaire, and a concluding reflective discussion. Expert workshops lasted approximately 4 h and were held at the *Center for Puppetry Arts* and a local charter school.

The *student workshops* tested the iterated puppet designs with the target audience of early middle school students. Unlike the design-focused expert workshops, these events featured the full educational scaffolding including story-making and final performance. Based on the feedback from the expert workshops, the format for the student workshops settled on a four-step approach:

(1) *Learn Technology*; students familiarize themselves with the materials and designs at hand (∼20 min)
(2) *Create a shared story*; students outline a shared story they want to perform (∼45 min)
(3) *Create customized puppets*; based on the provided puppet designs, students build their customized puppets, props, and stages for their story (∼60 min)
(4) *Rehearse and Perform*; students rehearse their performance together and adjust their shared storyline (∼30 min)

Each experimental student workshop also included collecting student's assent (in addition to the parent's consent) an initial demographic questionnaire, a final questionnaire, and a reflective discussion of the whole group after the workshop. Student workshops lasted 3–3.5 h and were held at the *Georgia Institute of Technology* and a local charter school.

Data collected from all four workshops included video and sound recordings, field notes, photos, questionnaires filled out by the participants before and after the workshops, and the puppets constructed during the workshops. Video recordings were reviewed and partially transcribed before key points were identified in close reading. We will report on results that relate to our main question on how to include the performative component in the design of a craft-inspired STEM workshop. The results draw from the feedback regarding this question from both experts and students.

2.3 Piloting Puppet Designs: Expert Workshops

Workshop Design and Goals. We conducted two expert workshops in the winter 2016/17. The first (n = 6; 1 female/5 male) included puppeteers in the *Center for Puppetry Arts*. All of them had extensive experience with puppetry (15–37 years professional experience) and the use of puppets in education. The second expert workshop (n = 10; 9 female/1 male) included teachers of various subjects from a local charter school. Their expertise was in teaching (9–34 years professional experience) with no expertise in puppetry. In the demographic questionnaire both expert populations self-identified as knowledgeable in "making" and "performing" and reported less experience with "electronics and prototyping."

During the workshops, all participants were guided through three hybrid puppet designs which combined basic electronics with puppet types. These included a sock-puppet design using conductive thread, a LED, and a 3V battery to include a basic circuit to light up a LED (see Fig. 1); a rod puppet using conductive copper tape and paper puppets; and a mixed marionette style format. The goal was to identify the most feasible design in terms of materials, technical difficulty, and puppet control. Because these workshops focused on the technical puppet designs they did not include a performance.

Fig. 1. Participants of the expert workshop spontaneously break into play.

Workshop Observations and Feedback. The expert workshops did not include a performance condition but especially participants of the first workshop at the *Center for Puppetry Arts* "broke into play" even without being prompted.

These puppet experts emphasized the role of the puppet as an active performative object in context even though no specific context was developed. The role of the puppets' expressive roles were emphasized as motivating for the construction: "it had a goal, it had a reason and that made us want to complete it even if it got hard and frustrating."

The experts approached the simple puppets as valid expressive units in themselves. This became obvious not only in their feedback and their immediate engagement but also through customization and individual adjustments. Notably, this close engagement changed once they took the puppets off to move on to the next design. Bringing the objects to life was a natural continuation of their construction process but once that purpose was fulfilled, the puppet experts did not show any further connection to the puppets. For example, they did not ask to keep them.

During the second expert workshop, teachers voiced interest in the educational approach to engage students "hands on" and across different disciplines. "To be able to create them and reenact a story, write originally to begin with." They already envisioned possible inter-subject use of the overall approach to work between different subjects (e.g. writing, math, art). Interdisciplinary connections and kinesthetic engagement stood out as indicators for a performative turn. As one noted: "My kinesthetic learners would just flip out to be able to use – at any level - anyone of these types of puppets." The design was also seen as a possible fit for at-risk students.

The experts worked with three different puppet designs to test for feasibility of materials and techniques. Based on the concluding discussion and the experts' performance during making, the clothe pin rod puppet emerged as best suited (see also Fig. 2). It was favored by the experts as the best introductory level design and details for improved teaching of that design were added to strengthen the educational approach.

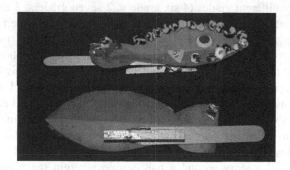

Fig. 2. Rod style puppet (created in student workshop 1) front and back; the LED is attached to the clothe pin.

Workshop Impact. Both workshops included a retrospective survey to assess changes in participants' attitudes towards electronics as well as arts and craft. Participants rated questions from 0 (lowest) to 5 (highest) which cumulatively allowed assessment of six key attributes. These did not show any notable changes in the arts and craft perception but indicated improvements in the electronics assessment (Table 1).

The biggest effect is an increase in the perceived "creativity" in relation to electronics (+1.3/+1.6) followed by increased "confidence" in handling them (+1/+1.2). In combination, these effects indicate a growing self-confidence of the experts to adopt this kind of electronics as they realize the creative range they provide.

Table 1. Attribute changes to electronics in workshop for teachers (left) and puppeteers (right).

Item	Before	After	Change	Before	After	Change
	Teacher WS (n = 10)			Puppeteer WS (n = 5)		
Confidence	2.9	3.9	1	2.4	3.6	1.2
Enjoyment	3.65	4.4	0.75	2.8	4.1	1.3
Importance and perceived usefulness	3.4	4.3	0.9	3.4	3.6	0.2
Identity and belonging	3	3.5	0.5	2	2.8	0.8
Intent to persist	3.25	4.15	0.9	2.5	3.3	0.8
Creativity	3.3	4.6	1.3	3	4.6	1.6

2.4   Piloting Craft with Performance: Student Workshops

Workshop Design and Goals. Taking the findings of the expert workshops into consideration, the student workshops followed in spring 2017. The experts had rated a rod puppet style design as the most feasible entry level approach. It uses copper tape to integrate the circuit to light up a LED using a clothes pin as a switch. This design was adapted for the students next to the narrative and performance components.

The first student workshop (n = 8; mean age: 12.1 years) featured only female participants from seventh grade classes and two different after school clubs. The second (n = 9; mean age: 12.8) was more gender balanced (5 female, 4 male) and had a wider distribution across different grades (4 six graders, 2 seven graders, 3 eight graders). In both events students were recruited from local schools. Overall, the participants represented a diverse racial background: 9 white, 5 black, 1 Hispanic, 1 multi-racial, with 1 undisclosed. Instructors from the students' schools were present in both workshops to help facilitate and their feedback was recorded but did not affect this argument.

Both workshops followed the 4-step structure outlined above. Unlike the expert workshops, they included shared story construction, rehearsal, and final performance. The creative process was collaborative. Students constructed a shared storyline, self-assigned work on the acting puppets, and organized the rehearsal and performance without any dedicated director or single author. Storylines differed widely. The first workshop developed a story around a fish couple wherein the male fish fell for a trickster shark and needed to be rescued by his partner. The performance and story of the second workshop was inspired by a local disaster. A hurricane had hit the city months ago and students built their piece around a storm throwing sea animals on land where they merged with land beings.

Workshop Observations and Feedback. Student participants showed the expected range of differing interests in the domains involved. This ranged from students who readily experimented with technology to students focused on the aesthetic design of their puppet. Even though the participants were not recruited from a single class or unit and had clearly differing interests, they collaborated throughout and helped each other out during the construction process. Some puppets and props had more than one student working on them from the start, others were shared during the process.

Participants of the first student workshop were recruited from a local school's robotics club and its *Odyssey of the Mind* after school program (a creative thinking and problem solving program). Before the workshop, they self-identified as interested mainly in "making and crafting" (4.38 out of 5), secondly in "performing and art" (4.25 of 5), and lastly in "electronics and prototyping" (3.56 of 5).

Participants of the second student workshop were more diverse in their grade and age groups as well as their interest: "Making and crafting" was rated 4.44; "performing and art" 3.67; "electronics and prototyping" 3.56 out of 5. All students of both workshops successfully participated in the exercise from the making of individual puppets to a shared story construction, to building customized puppets, to a final performance.

Workshop Impact. In the concluding questionnaire, students from the first workshop showed that they liked the workshop (4.75 out of 5) and they perceived the performance part as a "fun part" of the workshop. Some emphasized the teamwork aspect of it: "I wasn't really good friends with some of these people [=other participants] before this, but now I feel like we are bonded." They also noted that the multi-modal approach of the workshop appealed to their different learning styles.

All students of the second workshop appreciated the workshop (5 out of 5) but for a wider range of reasons. On the one hand, a student noted during the final discussion that "doing the play!" was the best aspect of the workshop and another stated that "I like this activity because I get to profess in my artistic skills." On the other hand, a more technical inclined participant "really liked the technology part: making things light up."

Technically inclined students' interest also reached beyond the idea of puppets as one noted that "I would not necessarily do puppets, I would do other stuff with LEDs." In practice, these students realized their interest as they experimented with the set up to add additional LED in their own version of a "sun" object for the puppet performance (see Fig. 3) while the artistic expressions drove much of the storyline in the puppet play (Table 2).

Fig. 3. Student experimenting with multiple LEDs (left) to build a "sun" object (right).

All participants reported improved attitudes toward electronics with the "intent to persist" (+1.44/+1.11), "identity and belonging" (+1.25/+1.11), and "creativity" (+1.44/+0.94) as the highest improvements. As one student noted: "[t]he best aspect of this workshop was getting to use our creativity without restrictions."

Table 2. Student attribute changes to electronics workshop 1 (left) and workshop 2 (right).

Item	Before	After	Change	Before	After	Change
	Student WS 1 (n = 8)			Student WS 2 (n = 9)		
Confidence	3.13	4.13	1	3.11	4.22	1.11
Enjoyment	3.44	4.5	1.06	3.94	4.83	0.89
Importance and perceived usefulness	3.57	4.57	1	3.89	4.78	0.89
Motivation to succeed	3.38	4.25	0.88	3.22	4.44	1.22
Identity and belonging	2.63	3.88	1.25	2.89	4	1.11
Intent to persist	2.56	4	1.44	3.17	4.28	1.11
Creativity	3	4.44	1.44	3.72	4.67	0.94

3 Discussion and Outlook

This paper reported on work during the pilot phase of the *Prototyping Puppets* project that relate the role of performance to our craft-based approach to STEM education and tested the feasibility of the material design components. The workshops were part of an iterative design process to inform two main questions: The expert workshops were conducted to assess the technical design and its feasibility; the student workshops aimed to test a 4-step educational framing in combination with those craft-hybrid designs. The pilot data are limited to tentative findings but overall supported the feasibility of the main craft designs. The increase of all participants' attitudes towards the electronic components in the workshop indicates a successful inclusion of the electronic components no matter whether the event included a performance or not. The expert workshops informed a final selection of puppet designs that was then re-tested with students and combined with the performance components in the following workshops.

The performance condition proved to support collaboration between different (and differently motivated) students. The educational scaffolding and the 4-step approach aimed to connect student to the exercise - see the improvement of their "belonging" ratings; they felt motivated to engage - see the improvement of their "intent to persist" ratings; and they noted increased "creativity" to the electronics/making components. We argue that these effects are interconnected. Through the inclusion of the puppet performance, technical maker ingenuity stood next to performance art. Differences between students were not avoided but included along a range of material forms of expression from the typical puppetry performance (animation and voice during the performance) to the technical improvisation in making (customization and experimenting with the materials). At the same time, the collaborative work toward a shared performance allowed students to self-position themselves in a role they saw fit. We argue that it is due to this increased positioning, that students expressed a strong feeling of ownership and pride for their constructions. As one student emphasized: "If I could take it home, I would put it in a glass frame [...] I would look at it every day." This indicates strong engagement and personal investment [19]. We argue that the stronger feeling of ownership in the student workshops, compared to the expert workshops which did not show this effect, is connected to the framing of a shared story and performance.

Forward going, a key challenge is to design documentation and educational material so that the workshops can be handed off to educators. The goal is to empower formal and informal educators to conduct the workshops without any help from the researchers and test them again in this condition. This first stage confirmed the focus on performative elements in the design of a craft-based prototyping workshop and *Prototyping Puppets* presents specific solutions that emerged during our project's design phase.

Acknowledgments. This material is based upon work supported by the National Science Foundation under Grant No. #1612686 (NSF AISL program).

References

1. Papert, S., Harel, I.: Constructionism. Ablex Publishing Corporation, Norwood (1991)
2. Dourish, P.: Where the Action Is: The Foundations of Embodied Interaction. MIT Press, Cambridge (2001)
3. Klemmer, S.R., Hartmann, B., Takayama, L.: How bodies matter: five themes for interaction design. In: Proceedings of DIS 2006, University Park, PA, pp. 140–149. ACM (2006)
4. Buechley, L., Eisenberg, M.: Fabric PCBs, electronic sequins, and socket buttons: techniques for e-textile craft. Pers. Ubiquit. Comput. **13**, 133–150 (2009)
5. Buechley, L., Eisenberg, M., Elumeze, N.: Towards a curriculum for electronic textiles in the high school classroom. SIGCSE Bull. **39**, 28–32 (2007)
6. Berzowska, J.: Personal technologies: memory and intimacy through physical computing. AI Soc. **20**, 446–461 (2006)
7. Rosner, D.K.: Mediated crafts: digital practices around creative handwork. In: CHI 2010 Extended Abstracts, Atlanta, GA, pp. 2955–2958. ACM (2010)
8. Rosner, D.K., Ikemiya, M., Regan, T.: Resisting alignment: code and clay. In: Proceedings of the 9th International Conference on TEI, pp. 181–188. ACM, New York (2015)
9. Devendorf, L., Rosner, D.K.: Reimagining digital fabrication as performance art. In: CHI 2015 Extended Abstracts, Seoul, Republic of Korea, pp. 555–566. ACM (2015)
10. Jacobs, J., et al.: Digital craftsmanship: HCI takes on technology as an expressive medium. In: Proceedings of DIS 2016, pp. 57–60. ACM, New York (2016)
11. Mellis, D.A., Jacoby, S., Buechley, L., Perner-Wilson, H., Qi, J., et al.: Microcontrollers as material: crafting circuits with paper, conductive ink, electronic components, and an "untoolkit". In: Proceedings of the 7th International Conference on TEI, pp. 83–90. ACM, New York (2013)
12. Perner-Wilson, H., Buechley, L., Satomi, M.: Handcrafting textile interfaces from a kit-of-no-parts. In: Proceedings of the 5th International Conference on TEI, pp. 61–68. ACM, New York (2011)
13. Peppler, K., Tekinbas, K.S., Gresalfi, M., Santo, R.: Short Circuits: Crafting e-Puppets with DIY Electronics. MIT Press, London (2014)
14. Tillis, S.: The Appeal of the Puppet: God of Toy? In: Kominz, L.R., Levenson, M. (eds.) The Language of the Puppet, pp. 11–16. Pacific Puppetry Press, Seattle (1990)
15. Blumenthal, E.: Puppetry: A World History. Harry N. Abrams, New York (2005)

16. Posner, D.N., Orenstein, C., Bell, J. (eds.): Routledge Companion to Puppetry and Material Performance. Routledge, Florence (2014)
17. Sylla, C., Coutinho, C., Branco, P.: A digital manipulative for embodied "stage-narrative" creation. Entertainment Comput. **5**, 495–507 (2014)
18. Rosner, D.K.: Craft, computing and culture. In: Proceedings of the ACM 2012 Conference on CSCW Companion, Seattle, Washington, USA, pp. 319–322. ACM (2012)
19. O'Neill, T.: Uncovering student ownership in science learning: the making of a student created mini-documentary. School Sci. Math. **105**, 292–301 (2005)

From Stigma to Objects of Desire: Participatory Design of Interactive Jewellery for Deaf Women

Patrizia Marti[1(✉)], Michele Tittarelli[2], Matteo Sirizzotti[1], Iolanda Iacono[2], and Riccardo Zambon[1]

[1] University of Siena, Siena 52100, Italy
{marti,matteo.sirizzotti,
riccardo.zambon}@unisi.it
[2] Glitch Factory S.r.l., Arezzo 53100, Italy
{michele.tittarelli,iolanda.iacono}@glitchfactory.it

Abstract. Quietude [1] is an EU funded project that aims at creating interactive fashion accessories and jewellery for deaf women to experience and make sense of sounds. Through Participatory Design, a series of prototypes were developed to scaffold design inquiry and develop human-centred solutions. Deaf women and women with different levels of hearing impairment were involved in various activities throughout the design process, from in depth interviews, inspirational workshops, and co-design activities, through to body storming with experienciable prototypes. Each design iteration consolidated the theoretical grounding and the definition of new forms of design support. The latest suite of accessories addresses a number of needs of deaf people, from functional needs like ambient awareness and safety, to hedonic needs like aesthetics, curiosity, possibility to express a personal sense of style when accessorizing the body.

Keywords: Interactive jewellery · Disability · Deaf women · Co-design Participatory design

1 Introduction

Disability can represent a tremendous opportunity for wearable design. In Design Meets Disability, Pullin [2] shows how design and disability can inspire each other. By discussing insightful design cases, he states that disability can force some new questions onto the agenda that can actually open up new ways of thinking from subjective viewpoint, and not just in terms of better accessibility. Balancing the tension between a functional approach to disability with a more ethical and aesthetic exploration of technologies supporting disabilities is therefore quintessential.

This is the challenge of Quietude [1], an EU funded project within H2020 WEAR Sustain, which develops jewellery products addressing the complex tangle of functional, ethical and aesthetic needs of women with hearing impairment.

Quietude aims to "change stigmas into desirables" [3] by designing smart jewels to counteract the negative impact of disability. In the project, disability is not seen as a problem to solve or an impairment to hide [4]. It is regarded as an opportunity to bring

A. L. Brooks et al. (Eds.): ArtsIT 2018/DLI 2018, LNICST 265, pp. 429–438, 2019.

mindful attention to aesthetic, ethical and cultural values in designing solutions for hearing impairment.

In fact, the proximity of jewels to the human body emphasises aspects of materiality which go beyond the visual, involving ergonomics (e.g. weight and tactility), personal meaning, style and expression.

2 Related Work

There is a growing interest in the design community for wearables for deaf people. Vibeat [5] is an interactive jewellery for deaf and hearing impaired people which translates different musical tracks into specific vibrations. This design offers a parallel sensory experience of music conveyed by the sense touch.

Neosensory's Versatile Extra-Sensory Transducer (VEST) [6] is a garment designed to map information stream such as sound, vision, or data (e.g. stock market data or state information of an aircraft) to a wearer's sense of touch, using vibration in real time. While functionally effectively, VEST's aesthetics remains limited. Cute Circuit's Sound-Shirt [7] allows a deaf person to feel music on their skin at live symphonic concerts. The wearable device maps instrument groups to body locations through light. Vibrohear, is a bracelet designed for deaf blind to communicate to the wearer the volume and distance of the sound [8]; Music For Deaf People, is a concept collar designed by Frederik Podzuweit that converts auditory input into vibrations [9].

None of the above mentioned designs widely explores the full potential of accessory design: materiality, aesthetics, relation to the body and personal values remain in the background.

3 Design Process

A mixed group of experts including deaf women, designers, ethicists, technology experts and a psychologist joint the design process. Participatory design activities [10] like inspirational workshops, in-depth interviews, co-design and body storming with experienciable prototypes unfolded throughout the design process to elicit needs, envision and reflect upon solutions, incrementally develop and refine prototypes.

The initial inspirational workshop took place in a Fab Lab, and involved four deaf since birth women, two sign language interpreters, an ethicist, and a mixed group of designers, technology experts and makers [11]. The group of deaf participants was composed by an architect (40 years old), a psychotherapist (41 years old), a special education teacher (30 years old), a university student (21 years old). The workshop aimed at inspiring each other and stimulating an empathic understanding of deafness. Initially participants were prompted to reflect on feelings of deafness which were mapped on body maps using simple post-it notes (see Fig. 1 left).

The activity continued with an exploration of materials with different visual, tactile and behavioural features which were paired to the feelings identified on the body maps (see Fig. 1 left). Some participants located "frustration" around the ears and under the armpits to mean that deafness is considered as something to hide.

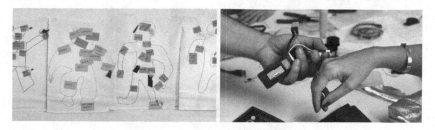

Fig. 1. Body maps and technology exploration

The discussion about the positioning of the post-it notes stimulated the participants to make needs and desires emerge during the exploration.

The next phase regarded a technology exploration (see Fig. 1 right). Participants experimented with simple vibration circuits including transducers and vibration motors. This exploration was inspiring to appreciate the sensitivity of participants to vibration and micro-movements in different parts of the body. From this phase we learnt that deaf people have very different sensitivity to vibration. Some of them are not sensitive to vibration around the wrist, some others are very sensitive on the neck and the bones around the ears.

The workshop disclosed complex needs of deaf women and contributed in knowledge to the design inquiry.

- There is a clear need of awareness about meaningful personal sounds (e.g. pet, doorbell, name, etc.) and public notifications, such as alarms, announcements in public spaces, police whistles, and more.
- Safety is fundamental to avoid that sounds requiring a quick response (e.g. a car horn from behind) go unnoticed by a deaf person with negative consequences.
- Jewellery products should be adaptable to individual preferences. As said above, during the workshop our deaf experts showed different sensitivity to vibration. The position on the body and the behaviour of the jewellery should be defined according to individual preferences and sensitivity.
- Deaf people are curious about the quality of sounds and would like to experience them with other senses (e.g. sight, touch, on-body vibrations).
- Medical aids usually conform well to medical needs, but they neglect complex aesthetic needs of the individual. Hearing aids should be beautiful, smart and comfortable to wear.

A co-design session followed involving one deaf participant, the university student who participated to the previous workshop. Staring from the outcomes of the inspirational workshop, the co-design session was based on hands-on activities and rapid prototyping.

A preliminary set of jewellery prototypes was developed (see Fig. 2). It included:

- A bobby pin with interchangeable parts that move according to the ambient sound detected by directional microphones embedded in a brooch. This object signals deafness to others and crucial sound events to the wearer.

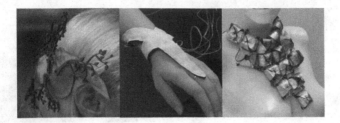

Fig. 2. Bobby pin, armband and 3D shape-change necklace

- An armband that translates different sonic qualities of the ambient environment, including range, volume and direction into vibrations.
- A 3D shape-change necklace that expressively enacts live or recorded sounds, translating the sounds into physical expression.

These prototypes were a vehicle for materialising questions and creating a common ground that resonated with design inquiry and human-centred research. In this activity of thinking-through-making [12] participants designed solutions which inspired one another in an incremental generation of forms and interaction behaviours.

3.1   In-depth Interview

Low-fi prototypes developed during the co-design session were incrementally refined toward the development of working prototypes. Some of them were abandoned, some others were transformed. For example, the bobby pin was not developed further since it created interferences with the hearing aid; the brooches were not implemented as single accessories since the microphone was embedded in the necklace. The design team decided to concentrate on refining the necklace and developed other accessories like a ring with embedded LEDs that light up to represent the frequency of incoming sounds.

A new and more advanced jewellery collection was exhibited at the 2017 Florence Biennale of Contemporary Art. This included a necklace, a ring and a number of interactive single modules which could be assembled to encourage visitors to envision scenarios of use and provide us with additional feedback. Several people with hearing impairment visited the stand. A deaf lady with a cochlear implant accepted to be interviewed. The interview took about 1 h and was video recorded. The lady said that hearing loss shouldn't define people in any negative way, making them stupid or disengaged. *"I think that Quietude would help because, when you think of hearing loss, you don't think of fun, you don't think of pretty. You think of ugly. And I wanna change that. I don't like that....So, this is what I like about Quietude. It infuses hearing loss with something friendly and something beautiful. If my hearing loss were to be visible, well - the beauty of what you're doing is that you're making it visible from a beautiful and fun way. And that's what I love."* Another theme concerned communication and the quality of hearing. *"I think people with hearing loss want to be able to hear. They want to be able to communicate, they want to be a part of... the world!"*.... *"I really, really hear wrong. In fact, if you're in the hearing world, you're in the hearing world. If you're deaf, you can communicate by signing. If you're having hearing loss, you're kind of in between: not really in the heart hearing world because you don't hear perfectly, but you're not in the deaf world, because you don't know how to sign.... And there's a big difference between people who are deaf and cochlea implants......* (pointing at her implant) *"So, this is a processor. Every cochlea implant is a surgical procedure. This is a magnet, on the inside of my skull there's another magnet, which connects and the inside magnet is attached to the electrons that go over my cochlea. And it's an electrical, it's, it's electronic. I'm actually a computer... You see in cochlea implants you hear electronically, you don't hear acoustically".*

The lady suggested to define our target community in a clearer way, adapting the jewellery system to the different needs of deaf people and people with different levels of hearing impairment. People with hearing loss live in the hearing world. They use hearing aids or cochlear implants or assistive listening devices. Sometimes the hearing devices do not allow a clear comprehension of sound, e.g. it might be difficult for some people to distinguish between the door bell and the interphone at home. Our jewels could support people with hearing impairment providing means to tag sounds of interest whose occurrence could be notified by the jewellery system through vibrations, light, or kinetic modifications. On the other hand, deaf people have little or no comprehension of words and generally communicate with sign language. Our system could support their curiosity about sounds, letting them to experiment with sound through other senses, like touch and sight.

4   Jewellery System Design

Building upon the new input, our design process evolved with additional prototyping sessions and participatory design activities. From the feedback received at Florence Biennale, we started improving our jewels by introducing new features. The accessories were designed as a modular system which can be configured in different forms and on-body use.

The modules embed sensors and actuators allowing self-actuation and kinetic modifications in presence of particular sounds. The system's behaviour can be defined and fine-tuned through a smart phone app that works with the accessories. The app allows personalisation of both input and output, and the construction of a personal library of sounds that can be monitored for and replayed on demand through the accessories.

The concept design phase was inspired by a powerful metaphor that emerged during the initial inspirational workshop. One of the participants used the expression "feeling under water" to describe deafness as a hushed feeling of the perception of sound. Coherently with this metaphor, the suite of jewels was inspired by the sea world. The modules resemble sea-urchin shells and the palette of colours reflects images of sand, deep ocean and coral. The jewels were conceived as modular structures which can be assembled to create personal jewels. Modularity addresses the need emerged during the workshop of placing and playing out the jewellery on parts of the body which are more sensitive to vibrations and micro-movements.

Modules are realized using laser cut regenerated leather, felt or fabric petals which are folded and sewed to create a shell-like shape. The jewellery system was assembled in a craftsmanship way: modules were sewn by hand, connectors were fabricated recycling flat connectors of obsolete computers, and most of all no glue or binders were used. An innovative design was studied to connect the modules through 3D printed interlocked supports. The electronic components are placed in an octagonal shaped PCB that keeps the modules fixed and stable in horizontal position. Some modules contain electronic boards and sensors (e.g. the Bluetooth communication board and the microphone), some others contain actuators (e.g. LEDs, servo-motors, vibration motors), some other are empty and are used to enrich the aesthetics of the system. This modular system allows the creation of a variety of fashionable jewellery including necklaces, armbands, brooches etc.. We developed three necklaces with different behaviours: kinetic transformations, light patterns and vibrations (see Fig. 3).

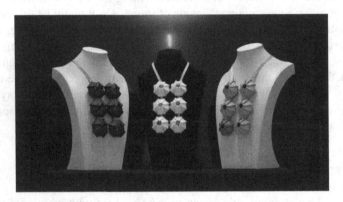

Fig. 3. 3D shape-change fabric modules (left), felt necklace with light patterns (center), regenerated leather necklace with vibration (right).

The jewels sense sounds in two modalities: in real time continuous monitoring, to notify the wearer of the frequencies and the amplitudes of surrounding sounds; at the occurrence of specific sounds defined by the wearer through the mobile app.

The 3D shape-change necklace provides micro-movements in response to external sounds, whilst the necklace embedding LEDs and the one with vibration motor use light patterns and vibration respectively to represent incoming sounds. The actuators embedded in the three necklaces are directly mapped to the intensity and amplitude of incoming sounds.

The design of the 3D shape-change necklace was probably the most complex. Shape-change modules contain a servo motor that changes the orientation of the petals bending them towards the lower center of the module.

The combination of the micro-movements of the petals of different modules results in a coordinate and expressive movement of the overall structure. Incoming sounds are filtered by a bandpass filter to detect their intensity and amplitude.

The system detects three frequency bands each one actuating micro-movements of a module. The same implementation is used also for the other two necklaces, which differ only for the type of actuators used to represent incoming. This solution allows to create a rich and expressive behaviour of the necklaces representing nuanced qualities of sounds. Several tests were made in indoor/outdoor, public and private contexts to identify the most significant frequencies to detect. After testing, we decided to use low-mid, mid, and high-mid frequency bandpass filters. We decided not to filter low and high frequencies because, in real contexts, theses frequencies rarely occur.

The jewellery system is connected to a smartphone application (see Fig. 4) which allows personalisation of sound recognition in input and kinetic transformation and shape change in output.

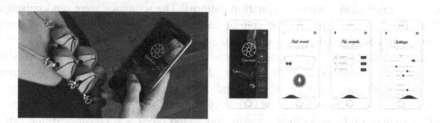

Fig. 4. Smartphone app.

Key features of the application are the management of the kinetic, light or vibration output on the basis of a comprehensive sound recognition process; and the setting up of a personal library of sounds. The user can create a library of sounds by recording personal meaningful sounds through the microphone embedded in the jewels. After-wards, sounds are labelled and stored in the app to allow real time sound monitoring and on demand playback.

5   Experimenting with Experienciable Prototypes

The three necklaces were presented in a public event. About 50 deaf people attended the presentation and some of them tried out the prototypes in body storming scenarios.

Some people pretended to dance in a disco following the light patterns emitted by the necklace. Other participants envisioned scenarios at home or in the car where sounds like the doorbell or the horn where notified through vibrations. A deaf lady was fascinated about the behaviour of the jewels. She was amazed to see and feel her voice through the necklaces and tried out the system several times having fun.

The vibrating necklace was the most appreciated and the most personalised since people showed very different sensitivity to vibration. The app was considered extre-mely simple to use and easy to manage.

The aesthetics of the accessories was recognised as a paradigm shift in the design of hearing aids. Fun and beauty were considered a way to dignify deafness and a step forward in overcoming the stigma of disability.

Other experiments were conducted with 4 hearing impaired persons and an Italian sign language interpreter to understand how the jewels can expressively enact live or recorded sounds through cross-modal associations with light and vibration patterns [13]. 6 short scenarios were presented to the participants, each one depicting a story containing a particular sound (alarm, ambulance, home appliance, policeman whistle, doorbell, car horn). The sounds selected as stimuli were defined during interviews with deaf women who identified the most useful sounds to be notified in indoor and outdoor daily life situations. The association between sounds and light/vibration patterns was implemented following Harrison et al. [14] who assessed potential expressive forms in which information might be conveyed.

Just after reading story, the deaf women were invited to watch three different light patterns and to associate one of them to the sound described in the scenario. The procedure was repeated with the vibration patterns. The scenarios were randomised as well as the light patterns. At the end of each session, an in-depth interview was conducted to collect qualitative comments.

The most recognised light patterns were the alarm, the doorbell and the car horn. 1 person correctly associated all patterns, 2 persons answered correctly 4 (alarm, doorbell and car horn and ambulance) and 3 (alarm, doorbell and car horn) times respectively and 1 person found the task very difficult.

The association between light patterns and sound types was considered interesting to explore and potentially effective to use. The ladies, including the one who found the association task difficult to perform during the experiment, felt confident to be able to learn the correct associations between light patterns and sounds after a training period. The app can help in this respect.

The most recognised vibration patterns was the home appliance which was recognised by all persons. The alarm, the ambulance, the car horn and the police whistle were recognised by 3 over 4 persons. The doorbell was recognised by 2 over 3 persons.

During the post-test interviews, participants agreed to consider the vibration patterns easier to understand than light patterns. Vibration was considered more discrete and comfortable even if it should be customisable since the intensity we set was considered a bit invasive. People would prefer a subtler vibration corresponding to incoming sounds that could not be detected otherwise.

The light behaviour was considered less practical in everyday life situations but suitable as a "public display" for environmental sound awareness. For example, in transit centres, people heading in myriad directions, with varied intentions, may be unexpectedly influenced at any moment by varied factors to which they must constantly attend. A deaf person can overlook the challenges that a hearing person might be experiencing due to distracting noises in this kind of scenarios. Social situations can bring a minefield of challenges.

Further experiments with deaf persons regarding the 3D shape-change necklace, as well as the design of cross-modal associations between sounds and other sensorial modalities than hearing are ongoing. The current version of the jewellery system offers a versatile platform to experiment with and engage deaf people in envisioning a more sustainable future.

6   Reflections and Lesson Learnt

Disability has its own stigma, pervasive in every society, which generates profound social barriers. One of the goals of Quietude is to contribute to mitigate the stigma of hearing loss by leveraging in ethic and aesthetics.

Participatory design was adopted to explore our vision about disability considered as an opportunity for design rather than a problem to solve and confront it with the real experience of people with disability. The design team promoted the project to develop aesthetically sophisticated objects that draw inspiration from deaf women's personal experiences; acknowledging that personal expression, visibility and discretion can be intertwined.

The approach is a combination of design research, participatory design and making, which employs rational judgments and empathic concerns with the goal of creating prototypes that clearly communicates the research contribution. The project demonstrated that disability can enlarge our vision of human variation and difference and can put forward new perspectives for design.

Our prototypes have been constantly imagined, assessed, improved, and enriched together with the deaf women [13]. Their responses to the prototypes were multilayered and insightful. There were slight differences in each person's perceptions to the jewels, but each individual expressed a perceived resonance with demand a common appreciation of the importance of supporting the need of beauty and individual style that any person, including hearing impaired persons, has when accessorizing and clothing the body.

Working closely with deaf women we learnt that technologies should be experiential and respectful [15], that is they have to respectfully address all human skills, including the social ones through rich, natural, and meaningful interaction possibilities. This vision requires societal, cultural and aesthetic sensitivity to be achieved [11]. Medical aids can be elegant and smart to wear as any other accessory which adorns our body, so to minimize the social stigma.

Acknowledgments. The authors would like to thank the women that joined the workshop and the experimental session and the Siena Art Institute for their precious collaboration. We would like also Simone Guercio for his help in designing the illumination and vibration patterns; Adria Nicula, Alice Comacchio and Elena Ranicchi for their support in conducting the experiments.

References

1. Quietude: www.quietude.it. Accessed 28 June 2018
2. Pullin, G.: Design Meets Disability. The MIT Press, Cambridge (2009)
3. Norman Donald: http://www.jnd.org/dn.mss/design_meets_disability.html. Accessed 28 June 2018
4. Cherney, J.: Deaf culture and the cochlear implant debate: cyborg politics and the identity of people with disabilities. Argum. Advocacy **36**, 22–34 (1999)
5. Vibeat: http://www.designindaba.com/articles/creative-work/wearables-helping-deaf-feel-beat. Accessed 14 Apr 2018

6. Vest: https://www.redbull.com/us-en/neosensory-vest-interview. Accessed 28 June 2018
7. Cute Circuit's Sound-Shirt: http://cutecircuit.com/soundshirt/. Accessed 28 June 2018
8. VibroHear: http://www.abledata.com/product/vibrohear. Accessed 28 June 2018
9. Music for Deaf People: https://www.fastcompany.com/1653578/how-collar-could-help-deaf-people-hear-music. Accessed 28 June 2018
10. Bjerknes, G., Ehn, P., Kyng, M., Nygaard, K.: Computers and Democracy: A Scandinavian Challenge. Avebury, Farnham (1987)
11. Wilde, D., Marti, P.: Exploring aesthetic enhancement of wearable technologies for deaf women. In: 13th ACM SIGCHI Conference Proceedings Designing Interactive System. ACM, Hong Kong (2018)
12. Ingold, T.: Making: Anthropology, Archaeology, Art and Architecture. Routledge, London (2013). ISBN 978-0-415-36723-7
13. Marti, P., Iacono, I., Tittarelli, M.: Experiencing sound through interactive jewellery and fashion accessories. In: Bagnara, S., Tartaglia, R., Albolino, S., Alexander, T., Fujita, Y. (eds.) IEA 2018. AISC, vol. 824, pp. 1382–1391. Springer, Cham (2019). https://doi.org/10.1007/978-3-319-96071-5_140
14. Harrison, C., Horstman, J., Hsieh, G., Hudson, S.: Unlocking the expressivity of point lights. In: Proceedings of the SIGCHI Conference on Human Factors in Computing Systems, Austin, Texas, USA (2012)
15. Overbeeke, C.J., Djajadiningrat, J.P., Wensveen, S.A.G., Hummels, C.C.M.: Experiential and respectful. In: International Proceedings on Proceedings of the International Conference 'Useful and Critical'. UIAH1999, Helsinki (1999)

Design, Learning and Innovation in Developing a Physical Activity Training Network: L.U.C.A.S Project

Eva Brooks[✉] and Anthony L. Brooks

Aalborg University, 9000 Aalborg, Denmark
eb@learning.aau.dk

Abstract. This paper introduces a seven-country international partner consortium project carried out under the Erasmus+ Program of the European Union. The project was titled L.U.C.A.S. (Links United for Coma Awakenings through Sport). Targeted user-group was acquired brain injured, spinal cord injury, and patients recovering from coma – many being profoundly impaired some being vegetative state. Elaboration and sharing of rehabilitation models to consider best practices targeting physical exercise, especially adapted sports, was catalyst of the project theme investigating a posited methodology. L.U.C.A.S. ran from January 2015 to December 2016 and was built upon an earlier Lifelong Learning European Program funded five-country project titled L.U.C.A. - Links United for Coma Awakening having its focus on learning and dissemination of good practices.

The specific focus of the contribution is to briefly share both the Scandinavian research element of the project as well as the holistic outcomes to enable others to use, reflect, and critique the methodology. The paper also introduces the annual European Day of Awakenings that emerged under the L.U.C.A.S. project.

Keywords: Acquired Brain Injured (ABI) · Spinal Cord Injury (SCI)
Physical training methodology · International network development
Design · Learning

1 Introduction and Background[1]

Brain Injury is a huge problem such that Traumatic Brain Injury (TBI) is forecast to surpass many other diseases as major cause of death and disability by the year 2020 [1]. It is estimated that approximately ten million people are affected annually by TBI and the burden of mortality and morbidity that this condition imposes on society makes it a pressing health and medical problem [2]. Acquired brain injury (ABI) is the single greatest cause of permanent acquired disability in our society [3, p. xi]. It affects body, brain, life, status, and future and it is said that these people do not 'get better', 'recover' or 'return to a normal state of health, mind, or strength' [4]. Independent of what is 'known' about the prevalence of brain injury; far less attention has been paid to self-

---

[1] NB: Selected text abridged/cf our overall project report documentation as url linked

© ICST Institute for Computer Sciences, Social Informatics and Telecommunications Engineering 2019
Published by Springer Nature Switzerland AG 2019. All Rights Reserved
A. L. Brooks et al. (Eds.): ArtsIT 2018/DLI 2018, LNICST 265, pp. 439–449, 2019.

awareness of those with brain injury: This self-awareness is a complex issue as pointed out in [5, p. 3]. The L.U.C.A.S. project, by targeting adaptive designed sports and physical exercise (PE) activities, offered a platform for those with TBI/ABI and Spinal Cord Injury (SCI) to learn self-awareness. Innovatively, the project also targeted those in regular contact (e.g. family members, caregivers, or health-providers) to participate in the same adaptive designed sports and physical exercise (PE) training and activities to potentially give opportunities to improve shared experiences toward optimizing well-being and quality of life via shared participation. This aligns with [5, p. 5] who posited how self-awareness is discovered for themselves, through participation, things they could do to help themselves. Further, it is posited that adaptive designed sports and physical exercise (PE) – as tailored physical activities – supports a whole person approach offering possible reconstruction potentials and their lives [ibid, p. 6]. Self-awareness can also be supported via knowledge gain from reading about the injury and related issues e.g. books or acknowledged Internet sites such as that created by Dr. Glen Johnson, Clinical Neuropsychologist - http://www.tbiguide.com.

Within this context, the project L.U.C.A.S (Links United for Coma Awakenings through Sport), funded by the Program Erasmus + Sport Collaborative Partnerships and co-funded by the European Commission, was initiated to create a stable European network for sharing information, expertise and good practices on rehabilitation through sport for people with Acquired Brain Injury (ABI) (in particular after a coma) and Spinal Cord Injury (SCI), including families, caregivers etc. The Danish partners of the consortium carried out a pilot study including children with multiple disabilities, including ABI and SCI. This pilot study was based on the L.U.C.A.S methodology and applied a specific technical tool, which enabled the children to move, dance, and jump in a playful way. This pilot study is presented after sharing the L.U.C.A.S methodology and the overall outcomes of the interventions through this methodology.

2 L.U.C.A.S Methodology

The L.U.C.A.S collaborative partnerships developed and tested a multidisciplinary experimental methodology of rehabilitation through sport and physical activity training, with specific objectives for the final beneficiaries (people with ABI and/or with SCI and their families, caregivers, etc.):

- To facilitate physical rehabilitation through the improvement of motor aspect
- To improve perception of quality of life and psychophysical well-being
- To facilitate social reintegration and to help to reduce loneliness
- To improve quality of relationship between ABI person and family/caregiver
- To improve awareness and self-awareness of the disability
- To give the opportunity for the ABI person to practice adapted sports.

Activities:

- Adapted sport activity for persons with acquired disability;
- Physical and motor activity for caregivers;
- Motor, physical and sport activity for the 2 groups together.

2.1   Implementation of the Methodology

L.U.C.A.S. consortium of seven countries initiated eighteen adapted sports/physical exercise activities (Fig. 1): Methods implemented aligned with [1]. Evaluations were pre- and post- the activity periods using indicators described in the following, however, these methods were flexibly applied and other methods/tools supplemented as necessary. As "L.U.C.A.S. Methodology" included activities that affected various and different fields of a person's life (physical, psychological, relational, emotional, environmental, well-being perception, social, etc.,) no specific questionnaire was used, rather a set of evaluation tools already validated to analyze action indicators of the activities were used.

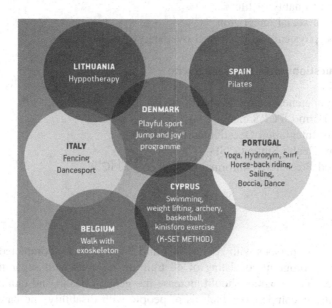

Fig. 1. Seven partner countries and LUCAS activities © L.U.C.A.S. report document

2.2   L.U.C.A.S Tools

To assess the holistic approach of the L.U.C.A.S methodology including the participants with ABI and SCI as well as their caregivers (e.g. parents, siblings, assistants), we identified a set of indicators for each of the targeted participants and, moreover, used different types of established and validated questionnaires. The tools covered different areas of well-being, such as quality of life, psychophysical well-being and social integration. The following indicators and questionnaires were used:

Indicators for People with Disability:
- Disease awareness and functional abilities
- Perception of quality of life and psychophysical well-being
- Perception of social integration.

Validated Questionnaires for People with Disability:

- Patient Competency Rating Scale (PCRS)
- Patient Form ("PCRS-patient")
- Activities of Daily Living Scale ("ADL scale")
- Short Form Health Survey ("SF-36")
- Community Integration Questionnaire ("CIQ").

Indicators for Caregivers:

- Disease awareness about his/her relative
- Perception of quality of life
- Perception of social integration
- Caregivers' physical and emotional overhead of assistance.

Validated Questionnaires for Caregivers:

- Patient Competency Rating Scale (PCRS)
- Caregiver Form ("PCRS-caregiver")
- Community Integration Questionnaire ("CIQ")
- Short Form Health Survey ("SF-36")
- Experienced Pressure by Informal Caregiver ("EPIC").

3   Results

87 participants (49 persons with ABI or SCI and 38 caregivers) completed a 24-week physical activity program consisting of 48 training sessions with separate and combined activities. The program should increase the general health and quality of life of the participants. A comparative analysis of people with disability and caregiver characteristics across all partner countries indicated that an overall pre- versus post-intervention comparison was allowed. This means that the characteristics between persons with ABI or SCI and caregivers, but also between the partner countries were similar. Consequently, all data were pooled into one large data-set. As such, the effect of the 24-week physical activity programs was analyzed for all participants. An additional analysis on the effect of the intervention on people with disability and caregivers separately was completed to provide a more complete understanding of the results. Statistical analysis (Pearson χ^2 with significance level $p < 0.05$) revealed the following findings:

Quality of Life (SF-36):
- Physical Functioning: No significant improvement
- Role Limitations due to Physical Health: Significant improvement for persons with ABI or SCI, not for caregivers
- Role Limitations due to Emotional Problems: Significant improvement for persons with ABI or SCI, not for caregivers

- Energy/Fatigue: Significant improvement for persons with ABI or SCI and caregivers
- Emotional Well-Being: Significant caregivers improvement, not for persons with ABI or SCI
- Social Functioning: Significant improvement for persons with ABI or SCI, not for caregivers
- Pain: No significant improvement
- General Health: Significant improvement for persons with ABI or SCI, not for caregivers.

Competency (PCRS):

- No significant improvement.

Community Integration (CIQ):

- Home Integration: Significant improvement for persons with ABI or SCI and caregivers
- Social Integration: Significant improvement for persons with ABI or SCI and caregivers
- Integration into Productive Activities: No significant improvement for persons with ABI or SCI, not for caregivers.

Activities of Daily Living Scale (ADL): For Participants Only

- No significant improvement.

Experienced Pressure by the Informal Caregiver (EPIC): For Caregivers Only

- No significant improvement.

The results of the study suggest that a 24-week physical activity program increases the general health and quality of life of persons with ABI or SCI, as well as their informal caregiver(s). The increased quality of life of people with disability (ABI or SCI) seems to be manifested in physical, psychological and social aspects of quality of life, whereas in caregivers, the improvements are mainly situated in psychological and social aspects. The latter can be expected given the physical consequences of brain injuries or spinal cord injuries versus the unchanged physical abilities of care- givers. Furthermore, the results also suggest a positive effect of physical activity on the social (re-)integration of people with disability and caregivers. On the other hand, no significant improvements could be demonstrated based on this study with respect to pain treatment, functioning in ADL, and experienced pressure by the caregiver(s).

In conclusion, physical activity improves the physical, psychological and social well-being of persons with ABI or SCI, as well as their informal caregiver(s). Further interventions are necessary to optimize the nature and content of the L.U.C.A.S methodology.

4 L.U.C.A.S Pilot Study: Jump and Joy (Scandinavia)

The L.U.C.A.S methodology was adapted to a specific technical tool i.e. Jump and Joy [Hoppolek], targeting joyful physical training for children with disabilities - see Fig. 2 and [6].

Fig. 2. Jump and Joy [Hoppolek] device © Dalén with permission

The Jump and Joy device is developed by Ylva Dalén, who is graduated as a physio- therapist and has a degree in special pedagogics at the Swedish School of Sport and Health Sciences in Stockholm, Sweden. Furthermore, she has a licentiate degree from the doctoral students program at the Department of Neurobiology, Care Sciences and Society, Division of Physiotherapy, at Karolinska Institutet, Stockholm, Sweden. Dalén has functioned as an expert in the Danish L.U.C.A.S. methodology pilot case study and she has set up the field studies carried out within this pilot case study.

5 Physical Activity as 'Sport' in the Context of Children

In line with the definition of the term sport applied within the LUCAS methodology, sport can be considered as an activity involving physical activities and skills where individuals or teams are involved for pleasure and enjoyment. In line with this, related studies (c.f. Physical Activity During Youth Sport Practices, 2011; U.S. Department Health and Human Services, 2008) states that the most common reasons for why children initially choose to play sports are: having fun, learning new skills, making friends and to be challenged. Yet, free play has shown to produce higher levels of physical activity than organized sports. In addition, a genre of sports is termed "mind sports", where minimal physical activity is involved. Aligned with this, this pilot case study considers the participants' self-agency [7, 8] as significant. In line with this, we argue that the Jump and Joy device intentions, i.e. to create conditions for the child to be in control of own physical activity, is essential and an integral tool in the child's self-agency in creating a meaningful physical activity for play and development. Drawing upon the concept of Zone of Proximal Development (ZPD) [7], this pilot case study views the physical activity by means of Jump and Joy as a situated activity involving negotiation of meaning between the child and the operator guiding the child during the activity.

5.1 Pilot Study Methods

In contrast to the L.U.C.A.S methodology study, the pilot study applied qualitative methods within a case study framework. Interviews, video observation, and note taking were used to identify the children's experiences when using the Jump and Joy technical tool. The study included 12 children between 5 and 14 years of age and 12 special teachers and physiotherapists.

5.2 Jump and Joy Tool

The height of Jump and Joy is 150–180 cm, depending on the adjustment of the stand (a form of upright spine that parts lock onto); the weight of the base is 43.5 kg; and the stand with knee, pelvic and trunk supports and maneuverable arms weighs 10–12 kg. The length of the platform is 74 cm and the width is 65 cm. Manufacturing mate- rials consist of steel plate; platform 4 mm, and the other details 2–3 mm.

The tool includes a control panel with yellow, red, green, blue, and black buttons. By pressing these buttons, it is possible to experience vibrations, bounces, and rotations – either individually or together (i.e. 1, 2, or 3 feedbacks simultaneously). The vibration is oscillating motion around a horizontal axis simulating a sine wave with peak-to- peak displacement being 0.2 mm, with frequency of 40–42 Hz, and acceleration of 33.35 m/s^2. The dynamic bounces are 3 cm, numbering 77 bounces/min with an acceleration of 17.65 m/s^2 (1.8 G). The rotation has a load on the base of 67 kg: 8.5 revs/min and without any load 10 revs/min. Furthermore, a CD player can be connected for child-control by a button press. The device is patented.

The child stands on a round platform (Fig. 3), with or without standing shell, and is strapped in a safe way. By pressing the above-mentioned buttons, the child controls the feedback vibrations, bounces, and rotation and can, thereby, carry out activities such as spinning, jumping, dancing, and at the same time physically train and strengthen the skeleton [6]. Based on this, the aim of Jump and Joy is to offer children with disabilities possibilities to joyful physical activity on their own premises.

5.3 Procedure

The Jump and Joy activity session started with the operator, sometimes assisted by a colleague, placing the child in the device and adjusting the stand with the knee, pelvic, and trunk supports to fit the height of the child. When this is done, the operator secures the straps so that the child is safely positioned to start using the Hoppolek by him/herself (see example Figs. 3 and 4).

Fig. 3. (Left) operator secures the straps to support the child's trunk and knees.

Fig. 4. (Right) two operators adjusting the knee and pelvic support

5.4   Pilot Study Results

Childhood acquired brain injury has impact on cognitive, physical, language, social and behavioral functioning as well as on participation in home and school activities. Furthermore, it has impact on the child's play, in particular a child's playfulness and ability to approach play. Play is an important childhood activity as it contributes to meaning and quality of life and provides opportunities for skill development. By limiting the child's engagement in play and playful activities where such skills are practiced it may further impact the child's quality of life.

This pilot study used the Jump and Joy device to explore children's actions when they are enabled to, through the device, move on their own premises. As mentioned, the device has a control panel with buttons, which the child uses to push forward movements from the platform. These movements charge the child's skeleton and stimulate balance organs: jump, spin and vibrations. The child can choose if (s)he wants to utilize one movement at the time or all together. It is also possible to press for music and experience dancing.

A theme analysis was applied, identifying three themes: *I am able to...*; *I can express myself...*; and *The child's desire as a starting point*.

'I am able to...'

- Ability to initiate activities and actions
- Increased degree of being awake
- Be in charge; to be able to take own decisions
- Keep doing; forgetting that the activity/actions are tedious and/or painful.

NB: A child has a natural need and desire to jump, spin and move: When the children started to spin and jump, and could do as much as they wanted to, first one direction and then another one – they experienced that they were able to be in control of their own actions = Cause and effect.

'I can express myself...'

- Initiating communicative and playful activities (for example, dancing, hiding, running after, spinning towards... and away from...)
- Shaping inter-play where all participants can influence the situation
- Child-child
- Child-parent
- Child-facilitator
- Medical results.

The child's desire as a starting point

When having the child's desire as the starting point, playfulness emerges and other outcomes develop as an added value. In other words: If we want to train the child's hand motor skills, this is not the starting point, but play and playful frameworks enabling play. Then, hand motor skills develop as an added value. For example, the study has shown that the children, by using the Jump and Joy buttons to initiate e.g. spinning, also started to use hands in ADL situations.

In Conclusion

- The importance of focusing not only on self-care activities and productivity, but to enable play and opening up for playfulness.
- Play as foundation for physical activity builds confidence and imagination.
- Play as foundation for physical activity makes children (any human being) happy.
- Play as a foundation for physical activity initiates interactions and develops skills – in a joyful and playful way.

Implications and Suggestions for Future Interventions

Experiences from L.U.C.A.S, including the pilot study, resulted in an evolved flexible, open and all-encompassing methodology, that, whilst context and case dependent, innovates by being inclusive of caregiver\families alongside people with disability. Optimization of engagement, fun, play and social interactions is targeted in method-based activities toward participants' benefits, thus advancing the field. NB for others who want to apply this methodology to be aware of the following:

- Be flexible
- Context and case specific
- Pay attention to participants' needs (inclusive of caregivers/family members)
- Optimize engagement fun and play (involvement)
- Promote a multidisciplinary approach
- Feel free to use any adapted sport and motor/physical activity.

Closing

Terms inclusion and accessibility are increasingly heard wide and far in contemporary society. Media channels are active in improving awareness of people with dysfunctional differences. Reports of adversities and corresponding achievements and courage to overcome are apparent. Sporting activities are especially effective in bringing home awareness and none more so than the Paralympics, Special Olympic World Games, and others. Through projects like L.U.C.A.S, the wider meanings of the terms inclusion and accessibility ring loud so that even those with profound impairment can participate.

A sustained outcome of the L.U.C.A.S project is a common program of events and initiatives in nine countries to raise awareness on the coma awakening and the problems of people with acquired brain injuries and their families, namely the establishment of the yearly "European Day of Awakenings", that obtained the High Patronage of the European Parliament, which involves partners' joint actions in their own countries and takes place in October every year. The activities highlight the L.U.C.A.S. project of Casa dei Risvegli Luca De Nigris through social themes as well as clinical research issues and the topic of therapeutic alliance between health professionals, non-health operators, families and volunteers.

Notes (please also see end notes):

- All images are used with permission or are covered by author 1 ©.
- Consortium partners conducted investigations in their own country –this is apart from the authors who are based in Denmark but were unable to establish Danish collaborating partners. The Scandinavian element of L.U.C.A.S. was therefore carried out solely in Sweden as a pilot project.[2]
- *Outcome booklets were produced in each partner's language: See English at: https://ec.europa.eu/programmes/erasmus-plus/project-result-content/9a3fda1d-3edf -4222-b028-bb42b0772583/LUCAS_Methodology_EN.pdf
- Note: A summary of the L.U.C.A.S. project was presented to the European Parliament by the coordinator organization March 2018. A video in Italian is available for viewing at YouTube https://www.youtube.com/watch?v=AnkDq99j5xQ
- A panel of experts from the Directorate-General for Education, Youth, Sport and Culture of the European Commission selected LUCAS as a "success story" under Erasmus+ Programme for Education, Training, Youth and Sport, Stakeholder Engagement and Programme Impact. "Success stories" are finalized projects that have distinguished themselves by their impact, contribution to policy-making, innovative results and/or creative approach and can be a source of inspiration for others. The award was made on the basis of a selection process according to rigorous criteria regarding the quality, relevance and results of the project. As a consequence of this selection, visibility and acknowledgement was given to the project, for instance on EU websites, social media, and when preparing documentation for conferences or other events with high-ranking attendance.

Acknowledgements. To other LUCAS collaborator/partner personnel, namely: Francesca Natali, Federica Ragazzi, Elena Vignocchi (Futura Soc. Cons. r. l., Italy); Fulvio De Nigris (Casa dei Risvegli project - Municipality of Bologna/Gli Amici di Luca Onlus Association, Italy);

---

[2] http://www.cfp-futura.it/PubblicaAmministrazione/ProgettiEuropei/Progetti/ProgettoLUCAS.aspx.

Elena Boni, Georgia Murtas (CSI - Centro Sportivo Italiano, Italy); Lieven Demaesschalck, Ingrid Knippels, Joeri Verellen (MOBILAB – Multidisciplinary Expertise Centre of the Thomas More University College, Belgium); Veronika Georgiadou, Onisiforos Hadkionosiforoy, Chrysis Michaelides, Mikela Michaelidou (European Social Forum Cyprus, Cyprus); Estrella Durá Ferrandis, Maria Teresa Ferrando García, Victoria Ibars Guerrero (SEAS - Spanish Society of Social and Health Care, Spain), Josep Francesc Sirera Garrigós (Dependentias - Asociación Estatal Para El Desarrollo De Servicios Y Recursos, Spain); Vaida Ablonske, Ilona Dobrovolskyte, Lina Miliuniene, Daiva Mockeviciene, Liuda Radzeviciene, Agne Savenkoviene (Siauliau University, Lithuania); Sara Fernandes, Fabiana Gomes, Filipe Neto, Rui Rebelo, Catarina Soares, Inês Teixeira (PODES - Desenvolvimento Sustentável, Portugal).

References

1. Global Recommendations on Physical Activity for Health, Geneva, Switzerland, World Health Organization (2010)
2. Hyder, A.A., Wunderlich, C.A., Puvanachandra, P., Gururaj, G., Kobusingye, O.C.: The impact of traumatic brain injuries: a global perspective. NeuroRehabilitation 222(5), 341–353 (2007)
3. Rees, R.J.: Interrupted Lives: Rehabilitation and Learning Following Brain Injury. IP Communications, Melbourne (2005)
4. Oxford dictionaries: Oxford University Press (2010)
5. Durham, C., Ramcharan, P.: Insight into Acquired Brain Injury: Factors for Feeling and Faring Better, pp. 1–29. Springer, Singapore (2018). https://doi.org/10.1007/978-981-10-5666-6
6. Dalén, Y.: Standing with and without vibration in children with severe cerebral palsy. Licentiate thesis, Stockholm, Karolinska Institutet (2011)
7. Vygotsky, L.S.: Mind in Society: The Development of Higher Psychological Processes. Harvard University Press, Cambridge (1978)
8. Vygotsky, L.S.: Thought and Language (revised edition). The Massachusetts Institute of Technology, Cambridge (1986)

Head-Mounted Display-Based Virtual Reality as a Tool to Teach Money Skills to Adolescents Diagnosed with Autism Spectrum Disorder

Ali Adjorlu[✉] and Stefania Serafin

Multisensory Experience Lab, Aalborg University Copenhagen,
Copenhagen, Denmark
{adj,sts}@create.aau.dk

Abstract. In this paper, we present a study conducted to investigate the feasibility and effectiveness of Virtual Reality (VR) for teaching money skills to adolescents diagnosed with Autism Spectrum Disorder (ASD). Through a user-centered design, in collaboration with teachers at a special school for adolescents with mental disorders, a VR money skills training application was developed. A pre- and post-VR training evaluation was conducted on five students diagnosed with ASD using real coins and bills. The data triangulated with observations during the VR training sessions illustrates some potentials and benefits in using VR as a mean to teach money skills to adolescents diagnosed with ASD.

Keywords: Virtual Reality · Autism Spectrum Disorder
Everyday living skills training · Learning money skills

1 Introduction

Autism Spectrum Disorder (ASD) describes a spectrum of lifelong neurodevelopmental disorders that affect the social and everyday living skills of individuals diagnosed with it [1]. These deficits result in a dependence on support from parents or social agencies upon adulthood. A study conducted by Howling et al. measured the adult outcome of 68 individuals diagnosed with ASD with IQ above 50 [2]. The results show that only 3 out of the 68 individuals did not live with their parents and only 8 were independently employed. Another more recent study on 48 adults diagnosed with ASD and above the age of 24 showed similar results [3]. The study showed that 44 out of the 48 participants lived with families or in shared homes with caretakers. Furthermore, the study also showed that only one of the participants was independently employed

Special thanks to Sune Buch-Sloth from Rødovre Municipality and the teachers Thor Jønsson, Tina Johansen, and Majken Jacobsen as well as the students from STUEN for their contribution to this study.

© ICST Institute for Computer Sciences, Social Informatics and Telecommunications Engineering 2019
Published by Springer Nature Switzerland AG 2019. All Rights Reserved
A. L. Brooks et al. (Eds.): ArtsIT 2018/DLI 2018, LNICST 265, pp. 450–461, 2019.
https://doi.org/10.1007/978-3-030-06134-0_48

while 48 % of the participants had never been engaged with work of any sort (part-time, voluntarily etc.).

Impairments in daily living skills (DLS) such as bathing, cooking, cleaning, and handling money can decrease individuals' chance for an independent adulthood. A study conducted by Farley et al. [4] on 41 adults diagnosed with ASD indicated that there is a direct correlation between daily living skills and independent adulthood. This confirms the importance of teaching DLS such as money management to children and adolescents diagnosed with ASD. Interventions designed to teach DLS might also help reduce the socioeconomic costs of individuals diagnosed with ASD [5]. This socioeconomic cost is estimated to be around 1.4 million dollars in the United States of America and 0.9 million pounds in the United Kingdom [6], consisting mainly of adult care services and loss of productivity. Furthermore, Leigh and Du estimate a significant rise in the annual medical- and non-medical economical cost of ASD in the United States of America from 268 billion dollars in 2015 to 461 billion dollars in [7]. The high prevalence of ASD (1 out of 50) [8] further emphasizes the agency for interventions to teach DLS to children and adolescents diagnosed with ASD.

Results from a literature review on interventions to teach social and everyday living skills to children and adolescents diagnosed with ASD illustrate that video modeling is a particularly effective method [10]. Video Modelling is a method that involves watching a video that illustrates the correct performance of the targeted DLS to be learned. Individuals diagnosed with ASD are better at processing and remembering visual information compared to verbal information [9], which can explain the high effectiveness of the video modeling interventions. Furthermore, Christy and Daneshvar argue that the reason why children diagnosed with ASD attend to video models more than real people is due to their social skills' deficits, making them uncomfortable around real people compared to video models [11]. In their review of intervention to increase the independence of individuals diagnosed with ASD [12], Hume et al. further underline the importance of DLS teaching interventions that do not require direct interaction with teachers.

Virtual Reality (VR) can be used to train daily living skills within relevant, interactive and immersive virtual environments. VR fulfills some of the above mentioned requirements for effective DLS training intervention such as mainly relying on visual information and not requiring direct interaction with the teachers. Furthermore, the advantages of computer-based learning interventions for individuals diagnosed with ASD over human-mediated interventions have been reported in several studies [12–14]. One of the first studies investigating the potentials of VR to help children diagnosed with ASD was conducted by Strickland et al. in 1996 [15]. Two case studies were conducted in order to discover whether children diagnosed with ASD would accept and tolerate VR head-mounted displays and respond meaningfully to the virtual environment. The virtual environment consisted of a street setting including moving cars with disguisable colors. The child's task was to locate the cars in the scene and say out loud the color of each car. The results of the study showed that both participants accepted the VR head-mounted display while being able to fulfill the tasks within the virtual environment. Since then, there has been a number of studies investigating the effectiveness of VR to teach a variety of social and everyday living skills to children and adolescents diagnosed with ASD. Adjorlu et al. conducted a study investigating the potentials of VR to teach social skills to children diagnosed with ASD [16]. A virtual classroom was developed with a number of interactive social scenarios with the purpose of teaching the children about sharing toys. The training sessions were facilitated by a teacher who controlled a virtual avatar using a microphone and keyboard. According to post-session interviews with the teachers, the children were able to have a productive discussion about sharing with the teachers after training with the VR application, showing their capability to relate to the social situations they experienced. In another study, Adjorlu et al. investigated the effectiveness of VR to teach shopping skills to children diagnosed with ASD [17]. The children could navigate in a virtual supermarket and pick up items listed on a virtual shopping list. Navigation was done via walking within the VIVE base station area. The user held a real shopping basket with a sensor attached to it in one hand and an HTC Vive controller in the other hand. The grabbing of items from the shelves was done using the HTC Vive controllers and they were then placed in the virtual shopping basket which was controlled with the real shopping basket. The intuitive interaction scheme was developed to increase the ecological validity of the VR training intervention. Ecological validity refers to the degree of similarity between an intervention and the real world 's counterpart. The virtual supermarket, its shelves, and the products on the shelves were designed to look like a real-world supermarket in order to increase the ability of transferring the skills trained in VR to the real supermarket. An in-between subject study was conducted, with the experiment group having seven VR training sessions while the control group received traditional lectures. Pre- and post measurements of all of the participants' shopping skills were done in a real supermarket. The experiment group performed worse in the pre-VR measurements compared to the control group while they performed better in the post-VR measurements. This study also illustrated the potentials of VR to train DLS, helping children diagnosed with ASD towards an independent adulthood. In this paper, we present a study investigating the potentials of VR and whether it can be used to teach money management skills to adolescents diagnosed with ASD. Purchasing skills and the ability to understand the concept of money and set personal budget is an essential step towards independent adulthood for children and adolescents diagnosed with ASD [18–20]. Through user-centered design via cooperation with teachers from a special school for adolescents with mental disabilities in Denmark, a VR application was designed and developed with the purpose of money skills training in adolescents diagnosed with ASD.

2 Method

2.1 Participants

The study was conducted at a special school for adolescents diagnosed with mental disorders at Rødovre municipality in Denmark. A total of nine students attend this school while five of them participated in this study. The five participants age ranged from 18 to 22 years old. All five participants were diagnosed with ASD while one of them was also diagnosed with Aphasia. The participants IQ ranged from 40 to 61, and all five participants were male.

2.2 The VR Intervention

The VR money training intervention was developed through a user-centered design aimed at understanding the teachers' current context and needs when performing money skills training. Four teachers participated in an unstructured focus group interview. All four teachers worked at the special school for adolescents with mental disorders and all four had experience performing money skills training sessions with their students. During the focus group session, the teachers explained that they currently perform money skills training using role-playing sessions. Pictures of daily products are cut out from supermarket catalogs while the students receive fake money from the board game Monopoly. The roleplay training sessions involve the teachers showing the student one of the products and saying an imaginative price out loud that can be paid with the Monopoly money available to the students. Role-playing has been described as one of the important steps in practicing money skills in children with mental disorders, helping them to generalize their money skills to other contexts [21]. Cichak and Grimm evaluated the effectiveness of money skills training in a classroom setting by pretending that the teacher was the cashier and the students were going to buy something [22]. The results indicated that this role-playing combined with a variety of teacher instructions during the session was a successful method to teach money skills to children diagnosed with ASD. Therefore, the main part of the VR money training intervention will involve role-playing having to pay for a variety of products using virtual money that looks similar to real money. Furthermore, the teachers involved in the focus group session explained that they also perform simple exercises such as matching real coins and bills with different numbers to gain an understanding of the difference values of the coins and bills.

Based on the focus group, the VR intervention was divided into three levels:

1. Matching virtual coins and bills with the right image illustrating each specific coin or bill.
2. Matching virtual coins and bills with numbers illustrating the value of each specific coin and bill.
3. Practicing purchasing a variety of daily items by paying the right amount of money using the virtual coins and bills.

The VR money training intervention was developed using Unity 3D and C# scripting. The application was developed to run on the HTC Vive VR hardware. The virtual coins and bills were designed using textures from images of real danish money (see Fig. 1) and included 50 Øre, 1 Dkk, 2 Dkk, 5 Dkk, 10 Dkk, 20 Dkk coins as well as 50 Dkk and 100 Dkk bills. All of the coins and bills were placed on a table in the virtual environment. The coins and bills could be grabbed by the player using the grab button on the HTC Vive controller and released again by releasing the same button. A simple cartoonish low polygon park was designed as the surrounding environment for the VR money training application.

Fig. 1. The virtual money available to the student placed on a table on a table next to the users' starting position. The student can grab the coins and bills on the table using the grab button on the HTC Vive controller

For the first two levels, eight smaller tables were placed in the VR environment each representing a specific coin or bill either with a picture (level one) of that specific item or the number representing it (level two) (see Fig. 2).

The player's task in the two first levels was to grab one of the coins or bills and place it on the appropriate table. If the right coins or bill was placed on the correct table, a short positive earcon sound clip would play as a reward for the successful execution of the task. No negative earcon for failure was included in this iteration of the application. Feedback to wrong coin or bill placement was provided via a visual sign that would turn red in case of wrong answer and green in case of right answer. A clapping sound would play once all the coins and bills were placed on the appropriate table followed by the player surroundings changing to the next level.

For the final level, a bazaar stand was placed in the virtual environment. A variety of supermarket products would appear on the bazaar stand table, each having a different price. A cash register machine was also placed on the bazaar stand table, illustrating the price of the products via written text. A rigged 3D model of a salesman was placed behind the bazaar stand table (see Fig. 3). He

Fig. 2. <u>Left</u>: Level one within which the student must place the right coin or bill on the table with a image illustrating each coin and bill. <u>Right</u>: Level two. The student must place the right coin or bill on the table with the same number written on top of it. Green lights indicate correct answer. Red light indicate wrong answer. (Color figure online)

was programmed to ask out loud how much the product on the table would cost. A number of cues were programmed in the application. If the students did not successfully place the right amount of money on the table after 60 s, a voice cue would play telling the student the amount needed to be added or removed from the table in order to pay the correct amount of money for the product. Furthermore, if the student still had trouble placing the right amount of money on the table, another voice cue would be activated informing the player exactly which coins and bills should be placed on the table. The audio aids could also be activated by the student via the the trigger buttons on the HTC Vive controller. The teacher could also activate the audio guide by pressing the S and G buttons on the keyboard when she felt it was necessary. All the voice acting was done by one of the authors of the paper.

Once the correct amount of money was placed on the bazaar stand table, the 3D salesman would say "Thank you" out loud while performing one out of five animated dance moves to provide some positive feedback to the student (see Fig. 3). A total of 25 products to pay for were included in the VR money training application.

2.3   Evaluation

The participants went through a total of five VR training sessions within a period of two weeks. Each VR training session lasted from 10 to 15 min. One moderator was present in the room, helping the students to start the developed VR DLS training application as well as taking observation notes during each training session. Screen video recording data was also gathered during each session. The moderator was well known by the students due to time spent working on the VR

Fig. 3. The bazaar stand and its salesman. Each time the correct amount of money was placed on the bazaar stand, the 3D model would start dancing one out of the five animated dance moves

application in the school's computer lab. Pre- and post-VR training measurement of the participants' money skills was done by presenting the students with a total of 30 price cards, similar to the study conducted by Cihak and Grim [22]. These price cards were divided into three groups: ten price cards ranging from 0 to 50 Dkk, ten price cards ranging from 50 to 100 Dkk and ten price cards ranging from 100 to 150 Dkk. The student would have a collection of Danish bills and coins in front of him. The researcher would verbally state the price while presenting the written price card to the student. The researcher would then give the student 10 s to pay the right amount of coins and bills.

3   Results

The goal of this study was to investigate whether a VR money management training application can be designed to teach money management skills to adolescents diagnosed with ASD. Pre- and post measurements of the students' money skills were conducted and triangulated with observation data gathered during the training session to shed some light on the potentials of the VR application as a DLS training tool.

3.1   Pre- and Post Measurements

The results of the pre- and post measurements of the students' money skills are reported in Table 1. Student D and E failed to pay the right amount of coins and bills for any of the 30 prices during the pre-VR training evaluation with real money. During the post VR evaluation session, student E once again failed to pick out the right coins and bills during all 30 attempts while student D managed to pick out the right answer twice. Both of these students have an IQ below 50. Student C paid the right amount of money three times during the pre-VR evaluation while the right amount was paid eight times during the post VR evaluation session. Student C is diagnosed with both ASD and Aphasia with an IQ of 55. Student B answered correctly to nine of the prices presented to him in the pre-VR training evaluation while student A answered correctly to 19 of the prices. After five sessions of VR training, both of the students answered correctly to all 30 out of 30 prices. Both of these students have an IQ above 50 and below 61.

Table 1. Number of correct purchases made by each student before and after five VR money training sessions

Participant	Before	After
Student A	19	30
Student B	9	30
Student C	3	8
Student D	0	2
Student E	0	0

3.2   Observation Results

Student A

During the VR money training sessions, student A seemed extremely comfortable, solving all of the tasks while he seemed to enjoy the process. He would pick up the coins and start juggling with them by throwing them up in the air and grabbing them again using the other controller/hand. He also enjoyed trying to throw the appropriate coins on the right table as if he was playing a game of basketball. He mentioned that he was expecting a feedback sound each time he put the wrong coin or bill on a table. He continued to effortlessly completing all the levels during the next four sessions while he seemed a bit bored with the training application on the 4th and 5th session, wanting to get it over without much juggling and throwing of the coins.

Student B

During his first attempt at completing level one in the VR training application, student B seemed to have problems distinguishing between 50 Øre, 5 Dkk, and 50 Dkk. After a number of trial and errors, he reacted to the positive feedback provided to him via the earcon and the visual green light on top of the table. After that, he finished most of the tasks without any issues. The only tasks that caused him some confusion were at level three where he was asked to pay 10.50 Dkk. He again first tried to place a 5 Dkk coins instead of the smaller 50 Øre coin. However, he eventually managed to place the right amount on the table. During the second training session, he once again had issues with the 50 Øre coin during level three. However, this was the last time he had an issue with any of the tasks, completing all of them effortlessly during sessions three, four, and five.

Student C

Student C had issues distinguishing between 1 Dkk, 2 Dkk, and the 5 Dkk coins. Level one proved to be challenging again during the second VR training session. Level one was no longer an issue during session three, four, and five. Level two pose the same challenges as level one during the first, second and third training session. Level three where the user had to pay for a different variety of products was the most problematic level for student C. During first VR training session when asked to pay 3 Dkk for an item, he starts by placing a 10 Dkk coin on the table, or when he was asked to pay 10 Dkk he started by placing a 2 Dkk on the table, waiting for a respond from the seller. The audio guide was frequently activated, telling him exactly how much was needed to be added or subtracted from the table for him to complete each task. Some improvement in his level three performance was observed during the third VR training session where he managed to place the right amount of money when asked for simple prices such as 60 Dkk or 110 Dkk. He enjoyed throwing the coins and bills at the product, looking pleased each time he managed to hit the product from a distance. The coins and bills he threw were often the correct ones.

Student D

Student D struggled a bit with the control schemes of the VR training application in the beginning. However, after a short time, he got comfortable with the grabbing and placing of the coins and bills in the VR training application. The first two levels never seemed to cause him any trouble. Each time he picked up a coin or bill, he would say out loud the number on the coin or bill. He would then place it on the right table. On the contrary, level three seemed to be more challenging for him. While managing prices such as 3 Dkk, 10 Dkk, and 10.5 Dkk without any issues during his third VR training session, he consistently struggled a lot with prices such 65 Dkk, 25 Dkk or 15 Dkk throughout all of the training sessions. Whenever the 3D model of the virtual salesman danced (after the student had placed the right amount of money on the table) student D laughed out loud stating "He is dancing, he is dancing!".

Student E

Distinguishing between the 1 Dkk and the 2 Dkk coins was a problem for student E during level one in his first two VR training sessions. After a number of trial and errors, he managed to get used to the coins and place them on the correct tables. Level one and two was completed without any issues during his third, fourth, and fifth VR training session. He consistently struggled with level three during the first and second VR training sessions. The audio guide was activated for every single product, telling him on several occasions how much money needed to be added or removed from the table. During the third session, he started showing some improvement in level three, managing to place the right amount of money on the table for a number of prices without much effort. However, prices such as 65 Dkk, 85 Dkk, and 25 Dkk was still a big challenge, taking a long time and a number of trials before getting it right during all five sessions.

4   Discussion and Conclusion

The purpose of this explorative study was to examine whether VR can be used as a tool for adolescents diagnosed with ASD to train money skills. Pre- and post-VR training measurements of the participants' money skills was conducted, counting the number of correct purchases done by the students using real money. Four out of the five participants showed some improvement in their money skills after five training sessions with the VR application. Student E did not show any improvement, failing to complete any correct purchases during both the pre- and post VR evaluation sessions. Furthermore, students C and D illustrated very small improvements (from 3 to 8 and 0 to 2 correct purchases). However, noticeable improvements were observed in these three students performance during the VR training sessions. During the first two VR training sessions, none of these three students were capable of independently completing a single purchase with virtual money. During the third session and thereafter they all managed to occasionally place the right amount of money on the bazaar stand table without the need of trial and error or any of the audio guides. Future studies should, therefore, measure the students' performance during the VR training sessions, triangulating the data with the pre- and post-VR measurements using real money. This could shed some further light on whether the students lack the ability to generalize skills they trained and learned in the virtual environment to a real-world context. It has been suggested that individuals diagnosed with ASD have a reduced ability to generalize knowledge from one context to another [23]. According to behavioral analysts Stoke and Bear, it is essential to include as many common stimuli in the training environment as there is in the environment within which the child diagnosed with ASD is suppose to perform the trained task [24]. The VR money training application developed for the purpose of this study included a number of common stimuli. As an example, the movement required to grab coins and bills and place them in front of a salesman is the same as in the real world thanks to the HTC Vive hardware. Another explanation for the inability to make a single correct purchase during the post-VR session with real money by student E might be him feeling uncomfortable performing in front of a real person compared to the 3D model of a salesman. Future iterations of the VR training application might include virtual environments such as supermarkets and shops in order to further close the gap between the training environment and the real world. Two of the students went through the post-VR evaluation with real money without making a single wrong purchase, showing that there is some potential in the VR money training application. Despite one of the students looking to be bored during his fourth and fifth VR training sessions due to the repetitive nature of the current version of the application, the students mostly showed that they enjoyed the experience, wanting to continue beyond the 15 min limit. Including gamification to some extent in the future iterations of the application might further increase the participants' motivation, which will be measured during future studies.

References

1. DSM-5 American Psychiatric Association. Diagnostic and Statistical Manual of Mental Disorders. American Psychiatric Publishing, Arlington (2013)
2. Howlin, P., et al.: Adult outcome for children with autism. J. Child. Psychol. Psychiatry **45**(2), 212–229 (2004)
3. Eaves, L.C., Ho, H.H.: Young adult outcome of autism spectrum disorders. J. Autism Dev. Disord. **38**(4), 739–747 (2008)
4. Farley, M.A., et al.: Twenty-year outcome for individuals with autism and average or near-average cognitive abilities. Autism Res. **2**(2), 109–118 (2009)
5. Järbrink, K., et al.: Cost-impact of young adults with high-functioning autistic spectrum disorder. Res. Dev. Disabil. **28**(1), 94–104 (2007)
6. Buescher, A.V.S., et al.: Costs of autism spectrum disorders in the United Kingdom and the United States. JAMA Pediatr. **168**(8), 721–728 (2014)
7. Leigh, J.P., Du, J.: Brief report: forecasting the economic burden of autism in 2015 and 2025 in the United States. J. Autism Dev. Disord. **45**(12), 4135–4139 (2015)
8. Xu, G., et al.: Prevalence of autism spectrum disorder among US children and adolescents, 2014–2016. JAMA **319**(1), 81–82 (2018)
9. Quill, K.A.: Instructional considerations for young children with autism: the rationale for visually cued instruction. J. Autism Dev. Disord. **27**(6), 697–714 (1997)
10. Wang, P., Spillane, A.: Evidence-based social skills interventions for children with autism: a meta-analysis. Educ. Train. Dev. Disabil. **44**, 318–342 (2009)
11. Charlop-Christy, M.H., Daneshvar, S.: Using video modeling to teach perspective taking to children with autism. J. Posit. Behav. Interv. **5**(1), 12–21 (2003)
12. Hume, K., Loftin, R., Lantz, J.: Increasing independence in autism spectrum disorders: a review of three focused interventions. J. Autism Dev. Disord. **39**(9), 1329–1338 (2009)
13. Chen, S.S.A., Bernard-Opitz, V.: Comparison of personal and computer-assisted instruction for children with autism. Ment. Retard. **31**(6), 368 (1993)
14. Zarr, M.: Computer-aided psychotherapy: machine helping therapist. Psychiatr. Ann. **24**(1), 42–46 (1994)
15. Strickland, D., et al.: Brief report: two case studies using virtual reality as a learning tool for autistic children. J. Autism Dev. Disord. **26**(6), 651–659 (1996)
16. Adjorlu, A., et al.: Head-mounted display-based virtual reality social story as a tool to teach social skills to children diagnosed with autism spectrum disorder. In: 2017 IEEE Virtual Reality Workshop on K-12 Embodied Learning through Virtual & Augmented Reality (KELVAR). IEEE (2018)
17. Adjorlu, A., et al.: Daily living skills training in virtual reality to help children with autism spectrum disorder in a real shopping scenario. In: 2017 IEEE International Symposium on Mixed and Augmented Reality (ISMAR-Adjunct). IEEE (2017)
18. McDonnell, J., et al.: Impact of community-based instruction on the development of adaptive behavior of secondary-level students with mental retardation. Am. J. Ment. Retard. **97**, 575–84 (1993)
19. Burckley, E., Tincani, M., Guld Fisher, A.: An iPad^{TM}-based picture and video activity schedule increases community shopping skills of a young adult with autism spectrum disorder and intellectual disability. Dev. Neurorehabil. **18**(2), 131–136 (2015)

20. Hughes, C., et al.: Student self-determination: a preliminary investigation of the role of participation in inclusive settings. Educ. Train. Autism Dev. Disabil. **48**, 3–17 (2013)
21. Browder, D.M., Grasso, E.: Teaching money skills to individuals with mental retardation: a research review with practical applications. Remedial Spec. Educ. **20**(5), 297–308 (1999)
22. Cihak, D.F., Grim, J.: Teaching students with autism spectrum disorder and moderate intellectual disabilities to use counting-on strategies to enhance independent purchasing skills. Res. Autism Spectr. Disord. **2**(4), 716–727 (2008)
23. Arnold-Saritepe, A.M., Phillips, K.J., Mudford, O.C., De Rozario, K.A., Taylor, S.A.: Generalization and maintenance. In: Matson, J. (ed.) Applied Behavior Analysis for Children with Autism Spectrum Disorders, pp. 207–224. Springer, New York (2009). https://doi.org/10.1007/978-1-4419-0088-3_12
24. Stokes, T.F., Baer, D.M.: An implicit technology of generalization 1. J. Appl. Behav. Anal. **10**(2), 349–367 (1977)

A Theory Based Dialogic Learning Architecture for Sustained Innovative Collaborative Learning Across Diversity and Professional Borders

Elsebeth Wejse Korsgaard Sorensen[(✉)] [iD]

Aalborg University, Kroghstraede 3, 9220 Aalborg Oest, Denmark
elsebeth@learning.aau.dk

Abstract. This paper addresses theoretically the challenge of establishment of a networked learning architecture appropriate for the sustained design of both continuing and professional education. Bringing in theoretical concepts, together with affordances of digital technologies, and using an action research meta-methodology of critical research, the paper attempts to elucidate make transparent the type of considerations and discussions needed as a prerequisite for forming a general concept/model for pedagogic design for professional and continuing education. The study finalizes with a suggestion for a conceptual model for producing innovative learning processes within professional and continuing education.

Keywords: Learning design · Learning as negotiated identification
Collaborative dialogue · Virtual environments · Innovation · Creativity
Digital Dialogue (DD) · Collaborative Knowledge Building (CKB)
Agency · Meta-learning · Networked learning · Empowerment

1 Introduction

Today's continuing and professional education curricula focus on teaching/learning of subjects and competencies. At the same time, increasingly, they emphasize *creative* and *innovative* construction and implementation of *new knowledge*, new processes and new production:

> Within professional education a recent shift has taken place. Professional education has moved from specialized education and update of professional knowledge, over competence-based education, to, recently, education with goals such as creativity, innovation, intrapreneur- and entrepreneurship. OECDs Centre for Educational Research and Innovation (CERI) reveals this tendency. The core idea here is that education, in a very goal-directed way, supports initiatives, which - in turn – results in added-value to society. [1:22]

Learners are expected to learn *something*, *learn-to-learn*, and learn to *produce and implement the new* in their professional practices.

Existing educational concepts, pedagogies and methodologies, as we know them, are not in sync with this need of our current and future society [2]. Their loyalty is directed towards the past. They rely too heavily on "conservative thinking" in that they

A. L. Brooks et al. (Eds.): ArtsIT 2018/DLI 2018, LNICST 265, pp. 462–471, 2019.

are almost entirely informed by and based on the knowledge society has already acquired, and not on visions of a modern society casting a glans to the future. Novel, sustainable concepts need to incorporate strategies, which not only generally fit a modern society, but also more specifically allow data from the future to be incorporated – continuously as they emerge [3, 4].

However, digital technologies, including Networked Learning, Open Educational Resources (OERs) and social software, make it possible to renew pedagogical thinking and learning designs and envision the scope of action of learners [2, 5], during their education not only as *producers of knowledge*, but also as *consumers of the same* [6]. In particular, Virtual Learning Environments (VLEs), are often characterized as having a non-hierarchical infrastructure in the communication process [7]; In any case, as confirmed by Dalsgaard [8], the educational potential of digital technologies and environments cannot be disputed. One clear and concrete design potential of e.g. VLEs is their ability to enable and provide structure to a communicative process that transcends physical borders.

Nor can it be easily overlooked, as also noted by [9] that the ability of VLEs for facilitating communicative interactivity amongst participants, is an essential feature that invites and supports *learner empowerment* and *learner agency* – provided the learning design as well as the underlying pedagogic values and techniques [9] are also inclusive and widening participation [10]. The possible initiatives of learners are strengthened in two ways: *Dialogic participation* and *democratic negotiation*, and *creation and sharing* of knowledge and digital resources [11].

This paper shares these values. It is based on a view of "learning as negotiated identification", a learning concept, launched by Oestergaard and Sorensen [1]. The concept entails/comprises a learner identity as an active democratic-oriented citizen as a meta-learning output of the learning process [12], and is associated with (1) agency and communicative initiative, (2) digital dialogue and collaborative knowledge construction, (3) open educational resources.

The intention of this paper is to take the concept of "learning through negotiated identification" one step further and provide a theoretical argument for an inclusive learning design for the future, aiming at facilitating negotiation and inclusive collaboration between stakeholders and thus involving the say and perspective of all stakeholders involved. The paper concludes with a suggestion for promoting an understanding of networked teaching and learning as, essentially, situated processes of negotiated identification, inspired by Sorensen and O'Murchu [4] and Sorensen and Brooks [11] and suggesting a conceptual model in the form of a digital learning architecture, adapted to and directed towards sustaining innovative networked teaching and learning within professional and continuing education.

2   Methodology

This methodological approach of this study is qualitative and situated within the constructivist paradigm. Building on the experience and insights from earlier research, the paper explores an identified problem that becomes elucidated through a theoretical lens - a kind of overarching theoretical umbrella, which provides a framework for the theoretical discussion and argumentation: The research framework of Skovsmose and Borba [13].

2.1　Skovsmose and Borba

Skovsmose and Borba present a kind of action research, "participatory research", in which they incorporate a theory of "critical research that investigates alternatives". In other words, research that is directed towards hypothetical situations (in contrast to, for example, grounded theory):

> "Critical research designates the analytical strategy aiming at investigating imagined educational situations based on studies of particular arrangement, representing the imagined situation" [13:17]

Skovsmose and Borba underlines that action research is a cyclical process, which evolves through "acting-observing-reflection-change-planning-acting" [13:8-9]. Their framework (Fig. 1) operates with three different situations: "current situation" (CS), "imagined situation" (IS), and "arranged situations" (AS). CS describes the status of the situation as it appeared before the initiative; IS describes a hypothetical ideal situation that provides future directions and wished intentions, and AS the situation that gets arranged with IS in mind. In between the three corners/situations (CS = current situation, IS = imagined situation, AS = arranged situation) of the model, the lines indicate processes (PI = pedagogical imagination, PO = pedagogical organization, CR = critical reasoning).

Pedagogical imagination (PI) – the key focus in a learning design - is concerned with what is captured within the dotted line in the model. What remains outside the dotted line, could potentially be the focus of a Design Based Research (DBR) project [14] with imagined situation (IS) in mind. In the present study, the research momentum is situated in *"Critical reasoning" (CR),* where arranged situation (AS) is compared with IS and simultaneously viewed in the light of PI and PO that underpin the two situation.

The model of Skovsmose and Borba (Fig. 1) constitutes a way of structuring pedagogical development and research work. Departure is taken in the situation in question, which needs to be changed, and the implementation of the change is facilitated by incorporating the people affected by the implementation. The process of change is guided, partly by a vision, and partly by the contextual pragmatic conditions for change.

The remaining theoretical terms and concepts of the study that are chosen as a background for the discussion, underpin the author's understanding of education as something, which should be constructed and re-constructed on the basis of accompanying reflection. They are also an indication of the view that learning entails an inherent socio-cultural aspect.

This study does not address the entire model. It zooms in on the part of the model captured by the dotted line (Fig. 1):

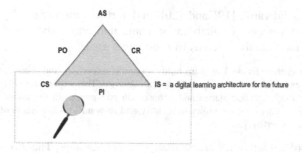

Fig. 1. A model for the development of learning designs (13:11)

"Pedagogical imagination may express a historical sensitivity acknowledging what has happened in education; an anthropoligical sensitivity, acknowledging what else has been done in education; and a critical sensitivity which means not taking the current situation as given." (13:13)

Along the lines of the study by Oestergaard [15], it aims to argue for the construction of a new innovative learning design model for professional and continuing education, which explores the rationale of pedagogical imagination (PI) as a pending process between the current situation (CS) and the envisioned conceptual model (IS).

3   Theoretical Perspective

This section gives an account of some of the main theoretical concepts, views and ideas involved in building up the discussion of the suggested digital architecture (Fig. 3) and its association with a view of "learning as negotiated identification" [1]. The idea is to generate a model for stimulating the creation of useful "prosumers" [6] of our social society. Through processes of negotiation and sharing of creative ideas and co-creating knowledge results to form citizens that potentially may be of value to other people and to society at large [16].

More concretely, the section will present and argue theoretically for the quality and virtues of the envisioned model through views on learning design characteristics that – from a theoretical perspective – invite an engaged learning behavior.

3.1   Agency and Communicative Initiative

Edwards and Mackenzie [17] introduced the concept of *relational agency,* resting on the idea of multivoicedness [17] and [18]. The term is further applies by Sorensen and Brooks [11], to understand online communicative behavior. They all agree that the term to denote "working alongside others toward negotiated outcomes". This invites another route of understanding for professionals who "are given significance through their ability to work independently" [19:61]. Each professional individual or team has a social language and its own way of representing reality. Therefore, collaborating and achieving a shared understanding requires a negotiation that "involves drawing on the resources of others and being a resource for others" [17:9].

According to Edwards [19] and [20], and further emphasized by Sorensen and Brooks [11], two aspects of collaboration come into play, when professionals work across different individuals or teams to negotiate a goal.

The first is that each individual or team holds a specific expertise, and second, they combine both their core expertise and develop a *relational expertise*. This expertise stems from working across individual or team boundaries and is based on engaging with the knowledge of one's specialist practice as well as the ability to identify and respond to what others offer from their local systems of expertise [20:33).

In other words, boundaries create dialogic opportunities. Therefore, for relational agency to develop, an architecture for negotiation of diversity and collaborative meaning is inevitable, - that is, if collaborative learning and inclusive knowledge production across differences and professional borders are to be aimed for and facilitated.

3.2   Digital Dialogue and Collaborative Knowledge Construction

In the present perspective, "dialogue" is understood as a tool for negotiation of meaning, and *as a way of knowing*. A kind of epistemology [12], in which there are no fixed meanings to be learned. Meaning is always situated and expressed in a dialogic context, which is always open to new reflective and re-assessing comments. With reference to the insights of Bakhtin [18], Wegerif [20, 21] and Edwards (2011) takes this view to the extreme when concluding that there is neither a first nor a last word, and that there are no limits at all to the dialogic context, as it extends retrospectively into the "boundless past" and ahead into the "boundless future". In essence, the requirement for supporting *meta-communicative awareness* involves the wider concept of mutuality and relational agency, with significant implications for the design of learning.

For several decades Sorensen has worked with digital dialogues and co-creation of knowledge in online learning, (e.g. [4, 9, 11]). She argues that many virtual learning designs still fail, when unfolding in a virtual context, to let go on methodologies specifically inherited from face-to-face teaching/learning paradigms, many of which fail to stimulate learner-initiated democratic online interaction. This includes meta-interaction, a vehicle for supporting awareness, and it includes the birth of innovative learning. With the obtained insight and practical experience from many years of practical use and research studies, Sorensen and O´Murchú [4] presented a learning model for co-construction of knowledge *through learner dialogue and meta-learning* (Fig. 2).

The model (Fig. 2) produced the concept of "dialogic tapestries" and operates with a multimodal and very wide and diverse concept of resources [4], and the use of it continuously spawned new investigations, insights and resources. The latter may be of any kind of nature, ranging from traditional literature and readings of research papers, pieces of software, personal/mutual experience, and expert knowledge, to "meta-resources" like, e.g. previous dialogue and other plays of learning (Fig. 2). This wide resource concept adds to the openness of the model. Minimizing the determination of the script of the play of learning (the predicted frame of the future process), it leaves the actors with a freedom to establish ownership, to improvise, and thereby excerpt influence in a meaningful collaborative knowledge building (CKB) process (the actual situated unfolding process). In principle, any type of resource that enhances the CKB

Fig. 2. Learning and collaborative knowledge building through online digital dialogue. Involved interaction (learners-learners and teachers-learners), and reflective meta-interaction (teacher-learners and learners-learners) [4:235].

process may be identified and pulled into the discussion and meta-discussions by the participants. Teacher and learner roles are equalled out and subverted dynamically. The strongest collaborative energy of a learning group manifests itself in the "Now" [4].

Through more than a decade, this model (Fig. 2) has been successfully implemented in practice contexts of Master programmes in higher education in both Denmark and Ireland[1].

Acknowledging the accumulated insights from both theory and practice on digital dialogues for learning of Sorensen [4], Wegerif [21], as well as the work of Darsoe [16] on innovation and learning designs for the emerging future, it makes sense to take these insights one step further and develop a learning architecture, which not only incorporates empowering learner dialogue and interaction, but actually puts an essential focus on the facilitation of *the collaborative and dialogic co-construction of NEW knowledge together with others*.

3.3 Open Educational Resources (OER)

The OER movement originated from developments in open and distance learning (ODL) and in the wider context of a culture of open[2] knowledge, open source, free sharing and peer collaboration, which emerged in the late 20th century[3]. A too tight definition of OER would exclude a large numbers of content representations that may still have been perceived, and/or used as OER.

---

[1] The model has generated not only extensive data through educational practice (see e.g. Sorensen and Brooks [11], but has over the years also given birth to several scientific papers, the latest being Sorensen and Brooks [9]. Moreover, further research has explored digital learning dialogues, using Wittgenstein's Language Game theory [4].

[2] The word "open" has physical, psychological, narrative, and moral or value related implications. Openness also refers to various states of mind, including not having a secret agenda; being open to more angles, methods or theories; willingness to accept more than one possible conclusion and so forth. In respect of OER there is no doubt of the "Open" term meaning "free").

[3] Wikipedia: https://en.wikipedia.org/wiki/Open_educational_resources#cite_note-expert-meeting-17.

"Open" implies the idea of inclusiveness and that the content is completely accessible, easy to find, visible for the public and useful for somebody. The content can eventually be changed or reconfigured by the user(s). OER information and/or tasks can stand alone - that is to say, content which has been made for one context may potentially be used in a new context.

"Educational" suggests that one can learn something new at a qualitative formal level, which is different from knowledge sharing, peer-to-peer learning, or apprenticeship learning, implying that education is something that happens when one or more educated persons (with formal qualifications on a subject) teach their knowledge or skills on the subject. OER then refers to content that is formally qualified, and the content is meant as a possible help for learning the subject or topic in question. This content may be purely informational, training or exercises, self-tests or simulations, or it may be combinations of two or more of the above.

OERs may be viewed in a knowledge generating perspective in relation to learners recitation, knowledge sharing, knowledge selection, knowledge arrangement and, not least, meaning-making. But more importantly in relation to learning as a construction process and resources for knowledge sharing, see Harlung [5].

Learners may thus be characterized as both *consumers* of knowledge and *producers* of knowledge, the so-called "prosumers" [6]. These prosumers may thus incorporate OERs in order to produce new knowledge, but may also be seen as innovative producers of OERs. From this point of view there is an expectation to learners in professional and continuing education to learn something, to learn-to-learn [23], to produce something new, and implement the new" in their professional practices.

In a learning architecture for a sustainable future it makes sense to incorporate mechanisms of "openness", not only in terms of access to resources of all kinds, but also when we are aiming at a sustainable and yet innovative learning architecture prepared for the unforeseen future:

- Openness to the new. When learning processes are unpredictable it is not possible to know in advance which resources are relevant. This means that access to open and flexible learning resources is necessary in other to create, participate and reify the learning process.
- Openness in relation to the surrounding society, with a possibility for engaging in actual authentic dialogue and in order to align set of values and strategies.
- Openness in order to continuously be in contact with various human networks.
- Openness provides opportunity for timing and intervention.
- Openness within and outside the formal learning community invites inter- and transdisciplinarity.

Summing up, the author has argued for the importance of the three areas elucidated, "agency and communicative initiative", "digital dialogue and collaborative knowledge construction", and "open educational resources". They are all pertinent ingredients, of a learning design model and architecture in an innovative professional and continuing education design context. The model that the author proposes, incorporates the idea of "being innovative in relation to the future, while moving into the future". The model is outlined and presented in the next section.

4   A Sustainable Empowering Democratic Learning Architecture for the Future (SLAF)

The envisioned SLAF learning and negotiation model (Fig. 3) integrates the successful netbased dialogical model for collaborative knowledge building from Fig. 2. SLAF then becomes a communicative melting pot, in which all stakeholders – across hierarchical positions and disciplines - in a "modus 2" setting [3] participate, create and innovate in a collaborative knowledge building process without walls. All participants (including researchers) are both contributors (provide input) and learners (gaining output). Everyone involved (i.e. perspectives and areas of the various knowledge areas represented), may be characterized as "prosumers" [6]. All stakeholders from the four main areas of society (Fig. 3) contribute as *input* their insights and expertise to the collaborative work and negotiated identification/learning process, and likewise every stakeholder takes away, as *output* from the collaborative learning and negotiation process, exactly that which makes sense to him/her and is useful from his/her individual position and perspective. In the wording of Edwards [24]:

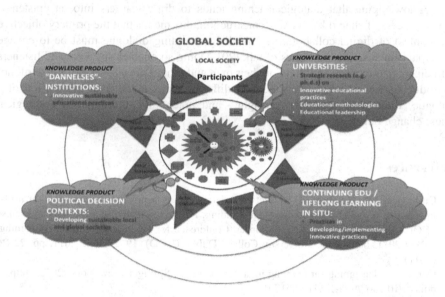

Fig. 3. The SLAF model. Innovative learning and collaborative knowledge building across positions and disciplines. Innovation and data generation in situ.

(...) boundaries as spaces where the resources from different practices are brought together to expand interpretations of multifaceted tasks, and not as barriers between the knowledge and motives that characterize specialist practices. Importantly, the learning that occurs in these spaces is not a matter of learning how to do the work of others, but involves gaining sufficient insight into purposes and practices of others to enable collaboration [25:34]

5 Conclusion

This paper has addressed the challenge of establishing a networked learning design or architecture appropriate for the sustained design of both continuing and professional education. Bringing in theoretical concepts, together with the affordances of digital technologies, and using an action research methodology of critical research in a meta-perspective [13], the paper has attempted to elucidate the type of considerations and discussions needed as a prerequisite for forming a general concept/model for pedagogic design for professional and continuing education.

In a wider perspective the architecture may serve as a model for associating education with research in a way that ensure research-based teaching and learning. The two contexts share the same need for being able to work in environments for connecting and engaging in dialogue and collaboration across diverse professional contexts. This invites the interactive, inter-connective, collaborative, and reflective potential of digital technology – for creating the social networks (open to the data, processes and products of the future) and for reifying a genuine innovative collaborative process, suited and sustained for the unknown future.

Acknowledging that dialogic teaching tends to draw learners into an epistemological process of shared knowledge construction, this means that the primary objective in a context of digital collaborative knowledge building dialogue must be to engage participants in sustained stretches of talk [20]. Doing so enables speakers and listeners (participants) to explore and build on their own and others' ideas – in the course of, not re-producing, but collaboratively holding different ideas together in the tension of a dialogue, while producing NEW insight - and potentially, through this ontological focus, change our reality.

References

1. Oestergaard, R., Sorensen, E.K.: Networked learning as a process of identification in the intersection of collaborative knowledge building. Fostering creativity, awareness and re-use of OER. In: Proceedings of the European Conference for Open and Distance E-Learning, EDEN 2011, held at the University College Dublin (UCD), 19–22 June 2011, pp. 22–26 (2011)
2. Conole, G.: Designing for learning in an Open World. Springer, New York (2013). https://doi.org/10.1007/978-1-4419-8517-0
3. Nowotny, H.: Cultures of Technology and the Quest for Innovation. Berghahn Books, New York (2006). ISBN 9781845451172
4. Sorensen, E.K., O'Murchú, D.: Identifying an appropriate, pedagogical, networked architecture for online learning communities within higher and continuing education. In: Sorensen, E.K., O'Murchú, D. (eds.) Enhancing Learning Through Technology, pp. 226–251. Idea Group Inc., Hershey (2006)
5. Harlung, A.H.: Open Educational Resources in Denmark. Status report 2010, Center for IT and Learning, Aarhus University, Denmark (2010)
6. Helms, N.H., Agerbæk, L.: Nettets læringstopografi. Et anslag til didaktisk kortlægning af metaverse, i Onedge 2_10, Knowledge Lab, University of Southern Denmark (2010)
7. Dalsgaard, C., Sorensen, E.K.: A typology for Web 2.0, pp. 272–279. ECEL (2008)

8. Dalsgaard, C.N.: Internettet som personaliseret og social medie. Læring & Medier (LOM) **3** (5) (2010). ISSN: 1903-248X
9. Sorensen, E.K., Brooks, E.I.: Promoting agency and identity building in dialogic learning communities online. Submitted for the Networked Learning conference to be held in Zagreb, Croatia, 14–16 May 2018 (2018)
10. Andersen, H.V., Sorensen, E.K., De Lopez, K.J., Jensen, R.H.S. (eds.): It-baseret inklusion af elever med udviklings- og opmærksomhedsproblemer i folkeskolen. Aalborg:Aalborg Universitetsforlag, 194 p. (2017)
11. Sorensen, E.K., Brooks, E.I.: Designing Inclusive Reflective Learning with Digital Democratic Dialogue Across Boundaries and Diversities. Published in the Proceedings of the Design, Learning and Innovation (DLI) Conference, held in Heraklion, Crete, Greece, 30–31 October 2017 (2017)
12. Sorensen, E. K (2008). Design of dialogic eLearning-to-learn: metalearning as pedagogical methodology. Int. J. Web Based Communities **4**(2), 244–252 (2008)
13. Skovsmose, O., Borba, B.: Research Methodology and Critical Mathematics Education. Res. Socio-Polit. Dimens. Math. Educ.: Issues Power Theory Methodol. **2004**, 207–226 (2004)
14. Barab, S., Squire, K.: Design based research: putting a stake in the ground. J. Learn. Sci. **13** (1), 1–14 (2004)
15. Østergaard, R.: Master thesis: Professionsuddannelse i et fremtidsperspektiv, p. 2004. Aalborg Universitet, Brobygning mellem teori og praksis i fysioterapeutuddannelsen (2004)
16. Darsø, L.: Innovationspædagogik: kunsten at fremelske innovationskompetence. Samfundslitteratur, Frederiksberg (2011)
17. Edwards, A., Mackenzie, L.: Steps towards participation: the social support of learning trajectories. Int. J. Lifelong Educ. **24**(4), 287–302 (2005)
18. Bakhtin, M.M.: Speech Genres and Other Late Essays. University of Texas, Austin (1986)
19. Edwards, A.: Being an Expert Practitioner: The Relational Turn in Expertise. Springer, London (2010)
20. Edwards, A.: Building common knowledge at the boundaries between professional practices: relational agency and relational expertise in systems of distributed expertise. Int. J. Educ. Res. **50**, 33–39 (2011)
21. Wegerif, R.: Dialogic education: what is it and why do we need it? Educ. Rev. **19**(2), 58–67 (2006)
22. Wegerif, R.: Applying dialogic theory to illuminate the relationship between literacy education and teaching thinking in the context of the Internet Age. Contribution to a special issue on International Perspectives on Dialogic Theory and Practice, edited by Sue Brindley, Mary Juzwik, and Alison Whitehurst. L1-Educational Studies in Language and Literature, 16, p. 1–21 (2016). http://dx.doi.org/10.17239/L1ESLL-2016.16.02.07
23. Bateson, G.: Steps to an Ecology of Mind: Collected Essays in Anthropology, Psychiatry, Evolution, and Epistemology. University of Chicago Press, Chicago (1976)
24. Edwards, A.: Relational agency in professional practice: a CHAT analysis. An Int. J. Hum. Act. Theory **1**, 1–17 (2007)
25. Edwards, A.: Cultural Historical Activity Theory and Learning: a relational turn. TLRP Annual Conference Keynote Address, University of Warwick (2005)

What Prevents Teachers from Using Games and Gamification Tools in Nordic Schools?

Eva Brooks[1(✉)], Salvör Gissurardottir[2], Bjarki Thor Jonsson[3],
Skulina Kjartansdottir[2], Robin Isfold Munkvold[4], Hugo Nordseth[4],
and Helga Isfold Sigurdardottir[4]

[1] Aalborg University, Kroghstraede 3, 9220 Aalborg, Denmark
eb@learning.aau.dk
[2] University of Iceland, Saemundargata 2, 101 Reykjavik, Iceland
{salvor,shk}@hi.is
[3] The Comprehensive College at Armuli, Armuli 12, Reykjavik, Iceland
bjarki@fa.is
[4] Nord University, Kongens Gate 42, 7713 Steinkjer, Norway
{robin.munkvold,helga.d.sigurdardottir}@nord.no,
hugo.nordseth@nord.so

Abstract. This study is based on a survey study distributed in the fall of 2017 in Norway, Denmark, and Iceland. The study was designed by a group of researchers from the Nordplus Horizontal project: Digital Computer Games for Learning in the Nordic Countries, to uncover teachers' perceived obstacle in regard to using digital game-based learning in teaching situations. The results indicate that the teachers included in this study did not have enough information and knowledge about games and gamification tools to be used in teaching. The findings show that technical obstacles are the most experienced hurdle among the respondents in all three countries when it comes to applying games or gamification tools in teaching activities. There are not many differences to be observed gender wise. A common difference that is worth noticing, is the difference between women and men regarding their reporting on the obstacle 'knowledge/skills', where more women claim this to be an obstacle. From these results, the paper proposes three types of digital game-based learning guidelines, namely (1) *rhetoric framing of usability and learnability*, (2) *engagement* and (3) *creating a guidance area – building a DGBL infrastructure*. In conclusion, the paper calls for further empirical studies on the actual situation presented in this paper, to reach an informed discussion about questions that are of real concern for many parties, including teachers, school leaders, children and researchers.

Keywords: Nordic countries · Computer games · Digital game-based learning Educational games · Obstacles of using games in schools

A. L. Brooks et al. (Eds.): ArtsIT 2018/DLI 2018, LNICST 265, pp. 472–484, 2019.

1   Introduction

This paper addresses the current limitation of research studies on digital game-based teaching and learning, in particular focusing on obstacles that still prevent teachers in the Nordic countries from using computer games in school settings. From a perspective of educational history, digital game-based learning (DGBL) has only been around for a short while, and research into the field is therefore relatively new. In spite of this, much of early debates in this field seem to be put to rest, such as questions regarding whether significant learning can take place during game use in educational practices [1, 2].

Representatives from educations in the Nordic countries seem to be more positive wards DGBL compared to their European counterparts and seemingly above the global average. While, in 2015, others assumed that DGBL would not be a topic for mainstream use in schools until approximately two or three more years, the Nordic panel reported seeing games and gamification as a "near-term horizon topic" [3]. Similarly, in the 2017 NMC report for the Nordic countries it is acknowledged that these countries have a stronghold in the gaming industry and that time of adoption of games is a year or less. Gamification of learning environments is said to be gaining support among educators that recognise that effectively designed games can encourage engagement, productivity, creativity and authentic learning [4].

1.1   Use of Digital Games in Schools in the Nordic Countries

Norway. In 2010, the Norwegian Ministry of Education and Research founded the Center for ICT in Education. The Center aims to contribute to increased quality in teaching with use of ICT for children in preschools, pupils in compulsory education and students of teachers- and preschool teacher studies [5]. To fulfil this aim, the Center initiated different ICT directed projects. An example of such a project is Digital Games in Schools (Dataspill i Skolen) targeting a mapping of good examples of educational digital games, as well as stimulating and contributing to good practice through creating networks of schools and other stakeholders [6]. In this sense, the project provides articles, lesson plans, and general practical information about digital game-based learning (DGBL). Another governmental institution, The Norwegian Media Authority, has established an entire website dedicated to digital games in school (see [7]).

A survey from Norway [8] related to the digital condition in Norwegian schools, reports that 99% of the teachers are agree that Information and Communication Technology (ICT) can have effect on possibilities for varying teaching and learning activities. 95% of the teachers who participated in the study use ICT for motivating pupils and 89% of the teachers experience that ICT makes the teaching more explorative and experimental. Further, 33% of the teachers expire that use of ICT disturb pupils learning activities, and 98% point out that there has to be explicit rules for acceptable use of ICT in classrooms. The survey also showed that ICT equipment in Norwegian schools contains an acceptable capacity (91% of the participating teachers), acceptable internet capacity (81%) and availability (72%). For digital competence among teachers, 43% reported enough skill for integrating digital learning resources for teaching their specific subject. Lack of competence was acknowledged as a challenge for using software and games in teaching and learning activities.

Denmark. While not specifically acknowledging digital game-based learning or digital/educational games as examples of learning material, the Danish Agency for Digitization underlines that digital tools and learning materials should support good didactic practices and high-quality teaching. In particular, they underline that digital tools and learning materials can raise the didactic and academic level, motivate children, young people and college and university students, as well as ensure they take a more active role in their own learning [9]. Similarly, the Danish Ministry of Education generally put efforts to introduce strategies and directions towards strengthening pupils' technological understanding, digital learning, and computational thinking, rather than specifying digital game-based learning as a tool for teaching and learning. An example of these actions is a report from 2014, where the Danish Steering Group for IT in Elementary Schools, carried out an evaluation of digital teaching materials in schools, where the effects of using digital teaching materials were measured [10]. As a result of the analysis, the report offers some recommendations including characteristics of digital tools that can facilitate learning, contextual conditions that can influence pupils' digital learning, and other special needs identified through teachers' experiences of using digital tools in educational activities. Regarding characteristics of digital tools that can facilitate learning, direct feedback, game-like elements such as different levels, prices, and game universes. Contextual issues identified as potentially influencing an increased use of digital teaching materials were, among others, the IT infrastructure, the school culture, and upgrading of teachers' digital competencies. Special needs identified were digital tools to support crafts and design, and digital tools to facilitate implementation of cross-disciplinary learning activities. In regards to the latter issue, the Danish Agency for Digitization state that there during 2018–2020 will be efforts to support an implementation of a shared user portal for pupils, teachers, and parents to offer them a digital access point for learning materials, communications and other information regarding teaching in primary and lower-secondary school [9]. Furthermore, the agency states that there will be special efforts to enhance digital teaching skills for school teachers and pedagogues.

Iceland. Although there is no mention of computer games as learning materials in the Icelandic national curriculum guide for compulsory schools the curriculum does indeed emphasise the importance of play in learning and games in the context of several subjects [11]. Playing is considered to be fundamental to education at the lower grades but also a dominant factor at levels for older pupils (p. 293). Playing is furthermore considered as a means to encourage students interest. This can possibly support teachers' intension to use digital games for learning. There are few course options for teachers to learn about educational games or use of computer games in education, one DGBL-course is given every other year and mostly teaching of game-based learning is integrated into ICT courses in teacher training at the university level or made available by interested teachers through their websites. Teachers in Iceland are trusted to choose the educational material they use in teaching, providing that it is used to achieve the objectives of learning and teaching (p. 47), and computer programs, internet material and media content are remarked on in this context. Access and use of computers in the compulsory schools has been limited, especially to students, often to just one computer in a classroom for the teacher [12]. Changes occurred with implementation of tablets, that provide access to a plethora of tools and games through online web stores and other internet resources. These conditions have affected game-based learning in Iceland and primarily inspired the use of internet game-based learning, through websites or apps. There is, however, evidence that teachers that are using games at schools report on their websites and in social media [13].

Aim and Research Questions. When implementing and engaging in DGBL, previous research has shown that teachers face several obstacles. These can vary between the Nordic countries, according to legal framework, national curriculum, educational contexts and variations in teacher education and training.

The aim of the present study is to contribute to the academic discussion of the use of digital game-based learning in school and to relate this to the identification of obstacles hindering the use of digital game-based learning. In teaching activities. The research questions posed in this study are:

- What kind of obstacles do teachers experience in regard to using digital game-based learning in teaching activities?
- How do the obstacles relate to gender?

On the basis of the findings, we will propose guidelines for developing a digital resource that can facilitate teachers in their efforts to implement digital game-based learning.

2   Research on Digital Game-Based Learning

Game studies, the study of computer games as an aesthetic, cultural and communicative form is a relatively new phenomenon, but expanding in the new millennium (Game Studies, 2018). Research into use of computer games in education is also a growing field within game studies [14, 15], that have a practical value for education and teachers, and can support their efforts in choosing, implementing and evaluating games and their potential benefits for learning. This is a necessary effort, as many computer games are not produced specifically for educational use and these, as well as educational games have to be tested and found fit for obtaining specific educational objectives. This can be an arduous task for teachers and a time consuming one, when adopting new games for learning as well as their teaching methods.

Egenfeldt-Nielsen [16] identified areas of difficulty for teachers using computer games in education settings in study of a two month history course, as being time schedule, physical setting, class expectations, teacher background, genre knowledge, technical problems, experience with group work, teacher preparation, perception of games, class size and priority issues. He concluded that these factors added up to a tremendous workload on teachers that want to engage with educational computer games and demand that the teacher possesses a variety of skills.

Rice [17] carried out a qualitative review of scholarly papers exploring the use of computer games in the classroom, with focus on barriers to implementation. He identified six major barriers, negative perceptions of video games as educational components; the difficulty of providing a state-of-the-art graphics in educational video games; a lack of adequate computing hardware in the classrooms for running advanced video games; a school day divided by short class periods which hindered long term engagement in complex games; a lack of real world affordances; and a lack of alignment with state standards. The analysis included implications for each barrier and suggestions for future research.

Among identified hindrances are teacher's own concerns about possible negative effects of gaming [18], prejudice and various scepticism towards digital games, on behalf of other stakeholders, such as fellow teachers, leaders and parents [19, 20], and even the pupils may have some reservations or tensions regarding the use of ICT and/or games in school [1, 21, 22].

Technical issues have also been identified as obstacles in the way of implementing DGBL in schools, such as resources, access to adequate technical equipment, obtaining administering rights and technological support. A variety of other practical issues such as budget issues, inflexible curricula, students not being prepared, keeping up with rapid developments in the gaming world, finding games that fit for educational purposes, shortage of supporting materials, fixed class schedules, inclusivity, and various challenges related to differences between curriculums and game contents [18, 23–25]. Whereas Takeuchi and Vaala [25] reported insufficient time as the most commonly identified obstacle, Baek [18] reported inflexibility of the curriculum to be the strongest hindrance factor.

3   Theoretical Framework

Nousiainen et al. [26] defines game-based pedagogy as a pedagogy that is grounded on different implementations of four game-based approaches: using educational games, using entertainment games, learning by making games and using game elements in non-game contexts, named gamification. Educational games have clearly defined didactic goals and objectives and broader skills like collaboration, problem solving and communication [27]. Further, entertainment games are not intended for educational purposes, but have relevant subject-related content and broader skills like collaboration. For the approach of making games, the learner construct new relationships with knowledge for making content by using technology. Gamification turns a non-game activity into a game to make it more attractive and motivating, and to engage learners. Common gamification tools in schools in the Nordic countries are quiz tools like Kahoot and Quizlet.

Dondi and Moretti [28] categorise three types of teachers in terms of integrating games in education: (1) those who use games as an integral part of their teaching and have a good understanding of their potential, (2) those who have discovered one game or one type of games that they find useful but are reluctant to venture beyond this comfort zone, and (3) those who are not at all interested in trying games and do not see games as a serious approach to learning.

Nousiainen et al. [26] defines four main area of competence in game-based pedagogy:

1. Pedagogical competence related to curriculum-based planning, tutoring and assessment according in connection to use of games and gamification.
2. Technical competence for analysing games and technical tools and for overcoming technology-related obstacles.
3. Collaborative competence for sharing and co-development within the schools and networking and collaboration beyond the school.
4. Creative competence for playful stance, ability to explore and improvise and creative orientation to self-development.

4 Method

The present study is based on a survey study distributed in the fall of 2017 in three Nordic countries, namely Norway, Denmark, and Iceland. The study was designed by a group of researchers from the Nordplus Horizontal project: Digital Computer Games for Learning in the Nordic Countries, to uncover teachers' perceived obstacle in regard to using digital game-based learning in teaching situations. The survey was administered by partners in each of the three countries. Relevant groups or associations related to digital game-based learning (DGBL) was contacted in respective country and invited to the online survey consisting of 26 questions including multiple-choice, ratings, and free-form space for elaborating on answers. The participation varied considerably between the involved countries.

In *Norway*, the survey was spread through e-mailing principals and teachers in all schools in the areas of Nord-Trøndelag and Sør-Trøndelag (161 schools). Furtermore, e-mails was sent to principals in all upper secondary schools in the area of Nordland (20 schools). In addition, the survey was spread through various Facebook pages in groups were many Norwegian teachers are members (approximately including 50.000 teachers). Finally, 220 Norwegian teachers responded to the survey, where 165 completed the survey.

In *Denmark*, the survey was initially distributed via relevant Facebook groups to localise as many potential respondents as possible. In total the administrators of 24 Facebook groups were addressed. A broad group of participants was targeted, from early primary school level up to secondary school level. 13 of the 24 administrators responded and approved the questionnaire, which thereby was sent out through the Facebook group site. In addition, 22 primary and lower secondary schools were contacted. As a result, 93 teachers responded to the survey, where 65 of them fulfilled the questionnaire and 28 did not, but chose to interrupt their participation.

In *Iceland*, the survey was emailed to all pre-school teachers (N = 2270) and primary and lower secondary teachers (N = 4717) by their professional unions. It was furthermore emailed to 70% of upper secondary school teachers (N = 1550) by their school principals. In total 8063 Icelandic teachers received the survey, of those 270 responded (3,34%). In Iceland, 181 respondents (67%) completed the survey, but 89 (33%) did not complete.

All in all in the three countries, 583 participants responded to the survey, of which 411 completed all questions in the survey and 172 did not fully complete it. Clearly, the survey was implemented with different approaches in the different countries. This may be regarded as a weakness in the methodical process, but at the same time it can be regarded as a strength as the results are based on a more varied approach toward the population.

Disadvantages of online survey studies are related to the risk of non-responses and the challenge of accessing the relevant participants. Thus, there is a risk that the participants represent a limited sampling and respondent availability. However, an advantage is that the collection of data is convenient for the respondents and takes less time for the investigator compared to a traditional survey. Furthermore, it offers an automation in data input and handling.

5   Results

The results section is divided in two sub-sections, where the first describes the respondents reasons for not using digital games or gamification tools in their teaching activities. The second sub-section presents obstacles that respondents experienced when they used digital games or gamification tools in classrooms. This section also describes gender differences related to experienced obstacles.

5.1   Why Not Using Games or Gamification Tools in Classroom Settings?

Table 1 shows an overview of reported reasons teachers give on why they are not applying games or gamification tools in the three involved countries. The respondents have different reasons for not using games or gamification tools in their classrooms, and some of the respondents report several reasons. In all the three countries about 1/3 of the respondents claims that the schools have not resources for this. Reasons connected to available games are higher in Norway (22%) and Iceland (17%) than in Denmark (7%). Also reasons connected to that games do not fit the subject area(s) or age group are higher in Norway (28%) and Iceland (22%) than in Denmark (4%).

Table 1. Reasons for not applying games or gamification tools in classrooms.

Why are you not using games or gamification tools in your teaching?	Denmark	Iceland	Norway
# of respondents	*27*	*76*	*64*
My school does not have resources for this	33.3%	31.6%	34.4%
There are no good games available in the market	7.4%	17.1%	21.9%
I do not believe that games can advance learning	0.0%	3.9%	9.4%
Games do not fit with my teaching style	3.7%	13.2%	12.5%
Games do not fit with the subject area(s) or age group i teach	3.7%	22.4%	28.1%
Other	59.3%	32.9%	21.9%

In response to this question, 59.3% (n = 17) of the Danish, 32.9% (n = 26) of the Icelandic teachers and 21.9% (n = 18) of the Norwegian teachers cite other reasons for not using games in their classrooms, giving more detailed responses through the open-ended response possibility.

Statements on themes like "Lack of competence" and "Do not know any relevant game" are the main reasons for not applying games or gamification tools in the classroom. 14 of 18 Norwegian teachers, 13 of 26 Icelandic teachers and 10 of 17 Danish teachers post this type of statement.

In summary, the results indicate that the teachers included in this study do not have enough information and knowledge about games and gamification tools to be used in teaching.

5.2 Experienced Obstacles When Using Games or Gamification Tools

Many teachers report on different obstacles when they use games and gamification tools in the classroom. In Iceland, 158 respondents claim to having applied DGBL (out of 239 responses). Further, 111 respondents answers the question if they have experienced obstacles, where 61 (54.9%) claim to have experienced obstacles. In Norway, 128 respondents claim to having applied DGBL (out of 194 responses). Further, 108 respondents answer the question if they have experienced obstacles, where 60 (55.5%) claim to have experienced obstacles. In Denmark, 58 respondents claim to having applied DGBL (out of 87 responses). Further, 43 respondents answers the question if they have experienced obstacles, where 30 (69.7%) claim to have experienced obstacles.

We can read from the table that Technical obstacles is by far the most experienced obstacle when applying games or gamification tools (73.3%–86.7%), whilst obstacles regarding broadband issues are more often reported in Denmark (37%) and Iceland (31%) than in Norway (22%). We also see that time/management obstacles (49–55%) are fairly equal in all countries.

The table below (Table 2) shows what teachers report on obstacles experienced when applying games or gamification tools.

Table 2. Typical obstacles experienced when applying games or gamification tools.

Obstacles	Denmark	Iceland	Norway
# of respondents	*30*	*61*	*60*
Technical obstacles	73.3%	82.0%	86.7%
Social/organizational obstacles	6.7%	14.8%	25.0%
Knowledge/skills obstacles	50.0%	39.3%	26.7%
Time/management obstacles	50.0%	49.2%	55.0%
Lack of digital games	46.7%	32.8%	45.0%
Broadband issues	36.7%	31.1%	21.7%
Other obstacles	10.0%	8.2%	8.3%

The findings show that technical obstacles are the most experienced hurdle among the respondents in all three countries when it comes to applying games or gamification tools in teaching activities.

From the category "Other obstacles", the following statements exemplify what was mentioned: "PEGI rating being too high", "Many pupils are not interested in gaming", "System updates are challenging", "Parents", Internet connection problems", "Some children get too attached to the game", "Not enough iPads", "Children are too young".

We further looked for possible gender differences in regards to the reporting of obstacles. The table below (Table 3) shows what teachers report on obstacles experienced when applying games or gamification tools.

Table 3. Obstacles and gender

Obstacles	Denmark		Iceland		Norway	
# of respondents	Females 24	Males 6	Females 46	Males 15	Females 32	Males 27
Technical obstacles	71%	83%	83%	80%	81%	78%
Social/organizational obstacles	8%	0%	11%	27%	25%	22%
Knowledge/skills obstacles	63%	17%	43%	27%	41%	11%
Time/management obstacles	54%	33%	43%	67%	50%	48%
Lack of digital games	46%	50%	33%	33%	44%	33%
Broadband issues	38%	33%	30%	33%	28%	15%
Other obstacles	8%	17%	4%	20%	0%	15%

There are not many differences to be observed gender wise. The difference that is worth noticing, which seems to be common for all countries, is the difference between women and men regarding their reporting on the obstacle 'knowledge/skills', where more women claim this to be an obstacle. As we can read from the table, 41% of the Norwegian female respondents say that Knowledge/skills is an obstacle, vs. 11% of the male respondents. From the Icelandic responses, 43% of the female respondents say that Knowledge/skills is an obstacle, vs. 27% of the male respondents. The pattern is even stronger amongst the Danish responses, showing that 63% of the women report Knowledge/skills as an obstacle, vs. 17% of the men.

6   Discussion and Conclusions

The present study makes a contribution to the discussion about the use of games and gamification tools in Nordic schools (Denmark, Iceland and Norway). Through a survey, we investigated what kind of obstacles teachers experience in relation to using digital game-based learning in teaching activities. Moreover, we examined how such obstacles related to gender. The study shows that the main reason for not using games or gamification tools in Danish, Icelandic and Norwegian classrooms has to do with that teachers consider themselves not having enough resources or knowledge to apply a game-based learning approach. When it comes to the teachers' experience of obstacles when using games or gamification tools, the results indicate that technical obstacles was the most experienced reason across the three countries. Furthermore, the findings show that the females included in this study experience lack of knowledge about the topic as a major obstacle to a higher extent compared to the males. In general, the results were similar in the three countries.

When the teachers experience barriers they, above all, experience a lack of pedagogical and technical capacity to consider whether, how, and when digital games and gamification tools can be applied in an teaching activities. When it comes to technical barriers, infrastructural hurdles were emphasised rather than the teachers' own technical skills. The latter was primarily related to pedagogical obstacles, i.e. the lack of pedagogical competences to use technical tools. Furthermore, the teachers put forward various scepticism towards digital games referring to parents and children's potential reservations for using games in a school setting. It is interesting to notice that collaborative and creative competences were not put forward as barriers. From this results, how would it be possible to promote the use of digital games and gamification tools in teaching activities? This section summarises three types of digital game-based learning guidelines emerging from the empirical study, namely (1) *rhetoric framing of usability and learnability*, (2) *engagement* and (3) *creating a guidance area – building a DGBL infrastructure*.

6.1   Rhetorical Framing of Usability and Learnability

Many of the teachers are not using digital games or gamification tools in teaching activities due to experiencing technical infrastructure hurdles. Thus, the leadership of the school district should improve usability and learnability issues of the technological infrastructure and make it easier for the teachers to apply digital games and gamification tools as an alternative to traditional learning material. A rhetorical approach [29] places a broader focus on the pedagogic role of the teacher, which shifts the focus away from technical reasons that can be solved elsewhere in the organization. Thereby, a focus on rhetorical (i.e. pedagogical) strategies offers an account of the overall organization of the implementation of digital game-based learning in teaching activities and emphasizes a pedagogical entrance for teachers to learn about digital games in education.

6.2   Engagement

Engagement, involvement, interest, and motivation are all concepts used to describe aspects of a user's experience, mostly in the context of digital games. In line with Price and Falcão [30], we stress that it is necessary to move beyond engagement as something that is fun or enjoyable as it does not reveal the activities or thoughts that teachers have when trying to understand the pedagogical value of using digital games or gamification tools in teaching activities. We suggest that there is a need for a deep pedagogical analysis to disclose the educational value of digital game-based learning.

This includes giving teachers the opportunity to develop such competences and, thereby, capacity to make informed decisions about how, when, and why to apply game-based learning as a tool for their teaching activities. Through the questionnaire, it is obvious that no intrinsic educational effectiveness of digital game-based learning can be assumed.

6.3   Creating a Guidance Area – Building a DGBL Infrastructure

Yelland [31] states that learning requires more than teachers providing children with materials (such as digital games). Teachers need guidance in choosing how to use such materials. Directions from peer teachers can help newcomers to become familiar with digital game-based learning materials. In this regard, an online community resource as a guidance surface for the teachers would be helpful. However, building such a DGBL infrastructure, needs to be carefully designed as many members of online communities are passive users, regularly logging in but seldom posting. The organization of a specific DGBL focused guidance area to promote high level teacher-teacher online knowledge sharing and dialogues in relation to building competence is, also, a matter of building a DGBL attitude. A study by Amichai-Hamburger [32] shows that creating conditions for such an attitude is something that is important for maximizing the DGBL opportunities available to teachers within online communities.

6.4   Concluding Remarks

Further studies are needed to explore the mechanism of digital game-based learning (DGBL) barriers from pedagogical perspectives. Furthermore, the influence of experienced obstacles for using new kinds of educational media in teaching activities should be discussed. Moreover, the effectiveness of engaging and guiding strategies should be further evaluated, and suggestions are needed for methods to select suitable strategies to engage teachers in contributing in online knowledge sharing communities. Based on this, we call for further empirical studies on the actual situation presented in this paper, to reach an informed discussion about questions that are of real concern for many parties, including teachers, school leaders, children and researchers.

References

1. Barab, S.: Introduction to section III. In: Barab, S., Squire, K., Steinkuehler, C. (eds.) Games, Learning, and Society: Learning and Meaning in the Digital Age, pp. 269–278. Cambridge University Press, Cambridge (2012)
2. Van Eck, R.: Digital game-based learning: still restless, after all these years. EDUCAUSE Rev. **50**(6), 13–28 (2015)
3. The New Media Consortium: 2015 NMC Technology Outlook > Scandinavian Schools, p. 4, April 2015. http://www.nmc.org/publication/2015-nmc-technology-outlook-scandinavian-schools/. Accessed 24 Aug 2018
4. The New Media Consortium: 2015 NMC Technology Outlook > Scandinavian Schools, p. 10, April 2015. http://www.nmc.org/publication/2015-nmc-technology-outlook-scandinavian-schools/. Accessed 24 Aug 2018

5. Senter for IKT i Utdanningen, n.d., para. 1 Senter for IKT i utdanningen (n.d.). *Om oss*, paragraph 1 (2015). https://iktsenteret.no/om-oss. Accessed 24 Aug 2018
6. Medietilsynet. Dataspill i skolen, paragraph 1 (2009). http://dataspilliskolen.no/last-nebrosjyren. Accessed 01 Sept 2018
7. Medietilsynet. Dataspill i skolen. http://dataspilliskolen.no/last-nebrosjyren. Accessed 01 Sept 2018
8. Egeberg, G., Hultin, H., Berge, O.: Monitor skole 2016, Skolens digitale tilstand. Senter for IKT i utdanningen (2016)
9. Agency for Digitization: A stronger and more secure digital Denmark. The digital strategy 2016–2020. Danish Ministry of Finance, Local Government Denmark and Danish Regions (2016)
10. Ramboll, BCG: Anvendelse af digitale laeremidler. Effektmåling (Udarbejdet til Styregruppen for it i Folkeskolen). Ramboll, Copenhagen (2014)
11. Ministry of Education, Science and Culture. The Icelandic national curriculum guide for compulsory schools - with subject areas. Ministry of Education Science and Culture, Reykjavik (2014)
12. Sigurgeirsson, I., Björnsdóttir, A., Óskarsdóttir, G., og Jónsdóttir, K.: Kennsluhættir. Óskarsdóttir, Í.G.G. (ritstj.), Starfshættir í grunnskóla við upphaf 21. Aldar Reykjavík (2014)
13. Friðriksson, B.R.: Minecraft í kennslu Gunnlaugs (2016). http://www.snjallskoli.is/2016/09/mincraftikennslu/. Accessed 12 Sept 2018
14. Egenfeldt-Nielsen, S.: Overview of research on the educational use of video games. Nord. J. Digit. Lit. 1(3), 184–214 (2006)
15. Tobias, S., Fletcher, J.D.: Computer Games and Instruction. State University of New York, Albany (2011)
16. Egenfeldt-Nielsen, S.: Practical barriers in using educational computer games. Horizon 12 (1), 18–21 (2004). https://doi.org/10.1108/10748120410540454
17. Rice, J.W.: New media resistance: Barriers to implementation of computer video games in the classroom. J. Educ. Multimedia Hypermedia 16(3), 249–261 (2007)
18. Baek, Y.K.: What hinders teachers in using computer and video games in the classroom? Exploring factors inhibiting the uptake of computer and video games. Cyberpsychol. Behav. 11(6), 665–671 (2008). https://doi.org/10.1089/cpb.2008.0127
19. Kneer, J., Glock, S., Beskes, S., Bente, G.: Are digital games perceived as fun or danger? Supporting and suppressing different game-related concepts. Cyberpsychol. Behav. Soc. Netw. 15(11), 604–609 (2012). https://doi.org/10.1089/cyber.2012.0171
20. Steinkuehler, C.: Digital literacies: video games and digital literacies. J. Adolesc. Adult Lit. 54(1), 61–63 (2010)
21. Øygardslia, K.: 'But this isn't school': exploring tensions in the intersection between school and leisure activities in classroom game design. Learn. Media Technol. 43(1), 85–100 (2018). https://doi.org/10.1080/17439884.2017.1421553
22. Sigurðardóttir, H.D.I.: Concern, creativity and compliance - the phenomenon of digital game-based learning in Norwegian education. Ph.D. dissertation, Norwegian University of Science and Technology. Norwegian University of Science and Technology, Trondheim (2016)
23. Dicheva, D., Dichev, C., Agre, G., Angelova, G.: Gamification in education: a systematic mapping study. J. Educ. Technol. Soc. 18(3), 75–88 (2015)
24. Sigurðardóttir, H.D.I., Sørensen, K.H.: Mediating and managing: envisioning and imagining digital game-based learning. Unpublished manuscript (2016)
25. Takeuchi, L.M., Vaala, S.: Level up learning: a national survey on teaching with digital games. The Joan Ganz Cooney Center at Sesame Workshop, New York (2014)

26. Nousiainen, T., Kangas, M., Rikala, J., Vesisenabo, M.: Teacher competencies in game-based pedagogy. Teach. Teach. Educ. **74**, 85–97 (2018)
27. Nousiainen, T., Vesisenaho, M., Eskelinen, P.: Let's do this together and see what we can come up with teachers' views on applying game-based pedagogy in meaningful ways. eLearning Pap. **44**, 74–84 (2015)
28. Dondi, C., Moretti, M.: A methodological proposal for learning games selection and quality assessment. Br. J. Educ. Technol. **38**(3), 502–512 (2007)
29. Kress, G., Jewitt, C., Ogborn, J., Tsatsarelis, C.: Multimodal Teaching and Learning. The Rhetoics of the Science Classroom. Bloombury, London (2001)
30. Price, S., Falcão, T.: Where the attention is: discovery learning in novel tangible environments. Interact. Comput. **23**, 499–512 (2011)
31. Yelland, N.: Reconceptualising play and learning in the lives of young children. Early Childhood Aust. **36**(2), 4–12 (2011)
32. Amichai-Hamburger, Y., et al.: Psychological factors behind the lack of participation in online discussions. Comput. Hum. Behav. **55**, 268–277 (2016)

Evolving Playful and Creative Activities When School Children Develop Game-Based Designs

Eva Brooks[1](✉) and Jeanette Sjöberg[2]

[1] Aalborg University, Kroghstraede 3, Aalborg 9220, Denmark
eb@learning.aau.dk
[2] Halmstad University, Kristian IV:S Väg 3, 302 50 Halmstad, Sweden
Jeanette.Sjoberg@hh.se

Abstract. The presence of digital technologies in classroom settings is relentlessly getting stronger and has shown to have powerful playful qualities. In recent years, digital game-based learning (DGBL) have been introduced in schools. In this paper we investigate an innovative approach to game-based learning, namely to use game design activities as motivators for developing children's creative and social skills as well as other kinds of learning scenarios, e.g. computational. It is based on two cases, where game design activities by means of a narrative approach were applied in both analogue and digital form. The unit of analysis is game design activities. Hence, game design activities with the participating children (3rd graders, 9–10 years of age), creative materials and technologies, and children's actions as well as interactions are analyzed. The research questions posed in this study are: (1) What activities develop when school children design games in two cases, as an analogue activity, and as an activity including technology?; and (2) How do the learning environment, including the artefacts, employed mediate these activities? The outcomes of the study indicate that the game design workshop session which included both creative material and technology unfolded more combinational activities, which indicate that the inclusion of technology facilitated a more critical design decision making. However, the game design workshop session including only creative material exhibited a more thorough knowledge about what the material could do and what the children themselves could do with the material, which seemed to result in more playful interactions between the children.

Keywords: Playfulness · Creativity · Game-based design activities
Learning environment · Learning resources · Primary school children
Exploratory activity · Transformative activity

1 Introduction

The presence of digital technologies in classroom settings is relentlessly getting stronger and has shown to have powerful playful qualities [1]. Research into educational potentials and affordances of digital technologies in designs for learning indicate promising results in facilitating communication [2] and increasing feelings of presence, participation and achievement in teaching and learning processes [3]. This is supported by international research, which has shown that children's skills and comfort should be

A. L. Brooks et al. (Eds.): ArtsIT 2018/DLI 2018, LNICST 265, pp. 485–495, 2019.

better supplied by a focus on their lifelong, social and personal competencies [4–7]. In recent years, digital game-based learning (DGBL) have been introduced in schools [8]. Based on Van Eck [8], Nousiainen et al. [9] have identified four different approaches for game-based learning, namely: using *educational games*, using *entertainment games*, learning by *making games*, and using game elements in non-game contexts (i.e. *gamification*). The authors explicate that *playfulness* is defined as a mindset and cross-cuts all the four game-based approaches. In this paper we argue that there is another approach to game-based learning that has great educational potential, namely to use game design activities as motivators for developing children's creative and social skills as well as other kinds of learning scenarios, e.g. computational. In keeping with this conceptualization of game-based learning, the present study explores playful game design activities, to unfold collaborative and creative actions and interactions among the participating children (3rd graders, 9–10 years of age).

A way of incorporating creativity in game-based design activities is by using narratives as an interactive approach to learning essential life skills [4, 5] such as collaboration and problem solving, in a meaningful context [10]. Narrative is a form of human thinking [11] that is fundamental in making sense out of a person's social experience and, as such, in a person's cognitive and emotional developments [12, 13]. Thus, a narrative method can be implemented with creative materials and non or varying degrees of technology to create a playful learning environment, where children can explore, experiment, discover and solve problems in imaginative and playful ways and, at the same time, stretch their learning to higher levels [12, 13].

The aim of the present study is to contribute to the contemporary debate on the increased use of digital game-based learning in schools and to relate this to the potential of such a game design approach to game-based learning. It is based on two cases, where game design activities by means of a narrative approach were applied in both analogue and digital form. The unit of analysis is game design activities. Hence, game design activities with the participating children (3rd graders, 9–10 years of age), creative materials and technologies, and children's actions as well as interactions are analyzed. The research questions posed in this study are:

1. What activities develop when school children design games in two cases, as an analogue activity, and as an activity including technology?
2. How do the learning environment, including the artefacts, employed mediate these activities?

The following sections start with a description of the theoretical framing of the project, where creativity in relation to the design activities are conceptualized as a playful learning practice. Next, the methods are outlined, primarily based on video observations and thematic analysis. Based on three identified themes, the paper, then, presents the outcomes of the study: exploratory activities; combinational activities; and transformative activities. Finally, a discussion and conclusions end the paper.

2 Playful Creativity

Playfulness in learning situations are not only connected to individual interests and desires, but also to the material artefacts involved in such situations. In this sense, the artefacts refer to the potential uses of a given medium, based on the perceivable features of this medium [14] and how these affordances are actualized in concrete social practices [15]. Conceptualizing creativity as a playful learning practice entails, among others, the following propositions:

- Creativity and playful learning is mediated by artefacts and results in a transformation of the physical world. Artefacts provide essential resources for children to communicate, store, catalyze, evaluate and reflect on ideas while trying to overcome indeterminate situations. Artefacts, from this perspective, are not mere carriers of information, but enable and constrain a child's actions [16, 17].
- Creativity and playful learning goes along with the generation of new knowledge. As creative practices attempt to act upon a hitherto undetermined situation, the outcomes of this attempt necessarily add to a child's body of knowledge either in that assumptions about the situation are contested or supported. Creative practice hence can be understood as a form of inquiry [18–20].

The focus of this study, how game-based design activities creatively can be used in playful learning situations, hence is based on the assumption that such situations should be deliberately structured and cultivated [17] Already in the 1970s Abt [21] proposed that a game design process should be considered as a crucial learning activity. Our design of the game-based design activities was structured so that the participating children should experience and learn about different creative material and technologies involved in a game-design process where the content creation in the form of a narrative was at the core. In addition, they should also experience the group dynamic and interactions involved in a collaborative and playful activity. In this way and inspired by Abt [21], our approach is not about creating a game per se, rather the interest is related to the design activity, which should allow the children to put ideas and critical thinking into practice. In other words, our concern is to provide conditions for a playful and creative design process that is based on both analogue and digital form allowing the children to create game ideas according to their own imaginations. This requires a stimulating and allowing learning environment in which the children can experience material outcomes of their collaborative design decisions.

3 Method

The study is based on two creativity workshop cases designed to provide a playful and creative atmosphere inspiring children to collaborate to create ideas for new games. The workshops were carried out in two research laboratory settings, where the participants were supplied with a wide range of analogue materials (in both cases) (Fig. 1). One of the cases also included digital technology for creating stop-motion videos of the children's game design solution (Fig. 1 – to the right). The intention was to create a workshop setting offering an infinitive number of opportunities, inviting the children to feel inspired to explore and 'just go for it'.

Fig. 1. To the left: Case 1 experimenting with different creative materials to represent their game design idea. To the right: Case 2 experimenting with the tablet to record the stop-motion video representing their game design idea.

Case 1 included 28 children from a third grade school in north Jutland, Denmark, north Jutland. The participant were divided between 19 males and 9 females between 9–10 years of age. Case 2 included 22 children from a third grade school in south-west Halland, Sweden. Here, the participants included 16 males and 6 females between 9–10 years of age. The children's teachers participated in the activity, which helped to create a safe learning environment; in Case 1, there were three teachers and in Case 2, there were two teachers. In addition, the two authors of this paper participated in both cases together with three assistants who assisted when the children needed help, kept an eye on the cameras, and supplied the children with water and fruit during the session. Case 1 the workshop session took place in one room (approximately 90 m²), which created a lively and slightly loud environment. In Case 2, we divided the groups in two rooms, which created a more calm atmosphere compared to the other case.

The two cases were carried out in the form of a design experiment [22] in the sense that it was designed to control some variables emphasizing the availability of resources that the children can draw on and use, as well as allowing for situated interpretations related to the chosen theoretical framing. The authors of this paper designed the set-up of the study and the sessions were conducted by two research assistants to make it possible for the authors to observe the game design activities (the procedure is further elaborated below, Sect. 3.1). The empirical data consist of video observations, observer notes by the two authors. Video recordings offer opportunities to review actions and interactions and to discern minute details that otherwise can be missed out [23]. The teachers had on beforehand divided the children into six groups of approximately five children and each group had their own work station. Each of these work stations was equipped with a video camera, recording the whole game design session; what happened around the table as well as between the group members, other members and material available (Fig. 2). Accordingly, both cases used six cameras, which were operated by the research assistants, and produced empirical data consisting of 12 video observations (in total 25.8 h).

Fig. 2. A typical workshop environment representing the initial phase of the children's game design idea generation. Video cameras can be seen to the left on the pillar and on the wall (far left)

All teachers and parents were informed about the study in writing and the parents agree to let their child participate by signing informed consent forms. The children were informed that they could withdraw from the game design sessions at any time if they e.g. felt uncomfortable in any way. In line with ethical guidelines, all names of the schools and of the children are anonymized and, thereby, no identifying information is provided.

3.1 Procedure

To enhance creativity, the game design workshop was structured in an easy to understand manner offering spontaneity. In other words, rather than suppress playfulness and creativity, the structure was there to motivate the participants' minds to exercise the creative game design process (see also [17]). The workshop ran for half a day between 09:00–12:00 h and was divided into two distinct creative periods following the timings and activities depicted in Table 1.

Table 1. Overview of workshop activities and timetable.

Time	Activities undertaken
09:00–09:15	Introduction. Establishing creativity framework and climate
09:15–10:45	Exploratory activity using analogue and digital tools
10:45–11:30	Transformative activity focusing of children's presentations of their narrative game design representations (analogue form [Case 1] and digital form [Case 2])
11:30–12:00	Joint lunch and informal discussions about the activity

In both cases, the research assistant introduced the game-based design activities to the children by telling them that they were going to be game designers and in teams create games based on a specific theme. The above-mentioned controlled variables [22] are grounded in a narrative approach, where the authors, on beforehand, prepared six different themes locating the game design in different settings: Desert; Jungle; Woods; City; Under water; Space (one theme to each of the groups). The narrative as such, i.e. the game design, was developed by the children and, here, we also framed the activity for them. Each group received an A4 sheet of paper where the theme was written together with open space for the children to develop classical narrative content [24, 25], namely the plot, characters involved in the gameplay, and objects/props (Fig. 2, left). The children were then introduced to the creative material (Fig. 3, mid and right), for instance foam clay, modelling clay, crayons, markers, LEGO, cardboard, different kinds of papers, yarn, glue, tape, scissors, and post-its. The Case 2 children were also introduced to the stop motion equipment. The children were told that they were free to explore and use all materials at hand; there were no rights or wrong. This is important in order to establish trust among the participants [26].

Fig. 3. A4 sheet for the Desert gameplay theme and space for the children to specify the plot of the gameplay, characters, and objects and/or props (left). Mid and right pictures show a variety of the creative material available for the children.

The analysis method applied for this study is theme analysis [27, 28]. The transcripts were reviewed of both authors to find patterns in verbal and non-verbal actions and interactions between the children and the analogue and digital game-based design activities. From this analysis we identified three overall themes: (1) Exploratory activities; (2) Combinational activities; and (3) Transformative activities, which are presented in the next section.

4   Results

In the following sub-sections, we present the outcomes of our analysis under three headings following the above-mentioned identified themes.

4.1   Exploratory Activities

The creative material as well as the stop-motion technology used for the analogue and digital activities were familiar to all participants, and as such there was not much basic functionality for the them to discover and interpret, leaving room for playful creativity through lots of exploration of what the children themselves could do with the different materials and technology. Brooks and Petersson [29] make a distinction between exploration and play. Where exploration gave way to playfulness, the emphasis changes from the question of 'what does this object do?' to 'what can I do with this object?'. We argue that this reflects an important openness, which is similar to what happens in play opening up for the participants to take creative risks by experimenting with the material. Both mediums allowed for instances of peer learning, where the children, for example, instructed each other and showed each other how to get sound into the stop motion video (Fig. 4).

Fig. 4. An example of children's exploratory activities, where they are exploring possible game designs (left) and where the girl to the right in the right image is showing her group members how to get sound into the stop motion video.

4.2   Combinational Activities

Combinational activities represent the creation of new ideas from combination and synthesis of children's existing ideas. These combinational activities emerged from the A4 sheets of paper where the children should structure the game design's plot, characters, and other objects, and the more open-ended way of representing these game design ideas through the available creative materials. This activity contributed to the children's elaboration and combination of creative ideas without constraining the creative process. In other words, the children were able to combine ideas together in the sheet of paper and elaborate the notes by means of the creative material. These combinational activities were characterized by children's imagination and free, often humoristic, associations (Fig. 5). This example is characterized by an improbability and surprise of the combination, where it would have been more probable that the monkey should fail to escape from the tiger.

Fig. 5. An example of children's combinational activity, where a 'game over' scenario was represented by a tiger hunting a monkey (Fig. 5, left), but where the tiger fail to catch the monkey and, thereby, died and caused game over for the player who represented the tiger and victory for the player representing the monkey. The dead tiger is represented by a red spot (Fig. 5, right). (Color figure online)

Another example is when the groups should add musical or sound features to their stop motion video. This was often caused by uncertainty where the children either repeatedly tried out different music or sound combinations or compared the kind of music/sound to their game design solution. Combinational activity was also applied to create new ideas based on the ideas previously generated. This is exemplified by a group of boys who finished their game design quite quickly and when they looked at their design, they found out that they could do better and started a re-design of their original idea.

It was notable that the Case 2 workshop, including both creative material and stop motion technology, offered more opportunities for combinational activities compared to Case 1, which only included creative material.

4.3 Transformational Activities

During the game-based design activities in groups, we could identify that the children changed their ideas or solutions in a way that things that from the beginning were considered as impossible changed to become possible. This was demonstrated in one of the groups designing a space game, where the group members initially could not agree upon the game content. They were, then, encouraged by the research assistant to start materialize their idea by means of the creative material. They started to map out their idea through making space representations in foam clay and through this materialization, they changed and extend their initial solution space and knowledge about the material's opportunities (Fig. 6). This is what we conceptualize as a transformational activity.

Fig. 6. An example of children's transformative activity, where an impossible solution to a space game through materialization was transformed to a possible game design.

It was notable, particularly in Case 1, that the children's physical ideas generated more structured outputs that aligned with, not only the use of different creative material, but with the knowledge they developed through experimenting with the materials. Furthermore, children's friendship constituted a shortcut to transformative actions. This was visible through the children's way of challenging each other, for example by saying that "this is not possible". This was also seen through the way the children identified each other's strengths and encouraged each other to keep on trying, or allocated work to each other in a supportive manner, which positively determined the interaction between the group members. Finally, we could identify that transformative actions had collaborative dependencies within the team.

5 Discussion and Conclusion

The present study makes a contribution to the discussion about the use of game-based learning activities in school settings. We have investigated what kind of activities develop when school children design games in two cases; as an analogue activity, and as an activity including technology. Furthermore, how learning environments including such artefacts mediate these kind of activities.

In the game-based design activities it was apparent that the children made the creative contribution they wanted to create, with little to no consideration of their own ability to carry out the work – they simply 'went for it'. Their depicted design decisions was clearly inspired by the structure offered by the A4 sheets which detailed the specific theme and overall features to be included in a game design; plot, characters and objects/props. It was also clear that the participants benefit from the two creativity focuses included in the design of the activities; exploratory and transformative activities. Hence, Biskjaer et al.'s [17] statement about structured creativity was apparent since the children through this structure seemed to experience a framed openness facilitating playful and creative actions and interactions. It was identified that the Case 2, including both creative material and stop motion technology, offered more opportunities for combinational activities compared to Case 1, which only included creative material. However, the Case 1 children's physical ideas generated more structured outputs that aligned with, not only the use of different creative material, but with the knowledge they developed through experimenting with the materials. In this way, both cases reflect Abt's [21] suggestion about conceptualizing a game design process as a learning activity. We argue that it is crucial that this learning activity should include a diversity of material promoting children's creativity and hence offering an environment where playfulness is deliberately cultivated.

It was visible that game-based design activities not only nurture children's creativity, but also collaboration and communication. In both cases, collaboration between the group members was observed to foster children's development of mastery with material and technology as well as of group dynamics. We observed that the children developed a necessary awareness of what different kinds of material and digital tools can do (exploration) and, what the children themselves could do with it (transformation) [29].

In sum, the Case 2 game design workshop session showed more combinational activities, which indicate that the inclusion of technology facilitated a more critical design decision making. On the other hand the Case 1 game design workshop session exhibited a more thorough knowledge about what the material could do and what the children themselves could do with the material, which seemed to result in more playful interactions between the children.

References

1. Camilleri, D.: Minding the gap. Proposing a teacher learning-training framework for the integration of robotics in primary schools. Inform. Educ. 16(2), 165–179 (2017)
2. Sorensen, E.K., Andersen, H.V.: Learning together apart – the impact on participation when using dialogic educational technologies for kids with attention and developmental deficits. In: Brooks, Anthony L., Brooks, E. (eds.) ArtsIT/DLI -2016. LNICST, vol. 196, pp. 264–271. Springer, Cham (2017). https://doi.org/10.1007/978-3-319-55834-9_31
3. Sorensen, E.K., Andersen, H.V.: Amplifying the process of inclusion through a genuine marriage between pedagogy and technology. In: Proceedings of the European Distance and E-Learning Network 2016 Annual Conference. EDEN, Budapest (2016)
4. OECD: The Future of Education and Skills. Education 2030. Paris, France (2018)
5. UNESCO: A Guide for Ensuring Inclusion and Equity in Education. Education 20130. Paris, France (2017)
6. Spires, H., Turner, K., Lester, J.: Twenty-first century skills and game based learning. In: EdMediaL World Conference on Educational Media and Technology. Association for the Advancement of Computing in Education (ACCE) (2008)

7. Bellance, J., Brandt, R. (eds.): 21st Century Skills: Rethinking How Students learn. Solution Tree Press, Leading Edge (2010)
8. Van Eck, R.N.: Digital game-based learning: it's not just the digital natives who are restless. EDUCAUSE Rev. **41**(2), 16–18 (2006)
9. Nousiainen, T., Kangas, M., Rikala, J., Vesisenabo, M.: Teacher competencies in game-based pedagogy. Teach. Teach. Educ. **74**, 85–97 (2018)
10. Gjedde, L.: Designing for motivational immersive learning through narrative role-play scenarios. In: E-Learn: World Conference on E-Learning in Corporate Government, Healthcare and Higher Education. Association for the Advancement of Computing in Education (ACCE), Chesapeake (2015)
11. Bruner, J.: Acts of Meaning. Harvard University Press, Cambridge (1990)
12. Bruner, J., Haste, H. (eds.): Making Sense: The Child's Construction of the World. Methuen, New York (1987)
13. Eagle, S.: Learning in the early years: social interactions around picturebooks, puzzles and digital technologies. Comput. Educ. **59**(1), 38–49 (2012)
14. Gibson, J.J.: The Theory of Affordances. In: Shaw, R.E., Bransford, J. (eds.) Perceiving, Acting, and Knowing: Toward an Ecological Psychology, pp. 67–82. Lawrence Erlbaum Associates Inc., Hillsdale (1977)
15. Van Leeuwen, T.: Introducing Social Semiotics, pp. 219–247. Routledge, London (2005)
16. Petersson, E., Brooks, A.: Virtual and physical toys: open-ended features for non-formal learning. Cyber Psychol. Behav. **9**(2), 196–199 (2006)
17. Biskjaer, M.M., Dalsgaard, P.: Toward a constraing oriented pragmatism understanding of design creativity. In: Proceedings of the 2nd International Conference on Design Creativity (ICDC 2012), Glasgow, UK, 18–20 September, pp. 65–74 (2012)
18. Dewey, J.: Democracy and Education. The Free Press, New York (1966)
19. Schön, D.A.: The theory of inquiry: Dewey's legacy to education. Curriculum Inq. **22**(2), 119–139 (1992)
20. Sullivan, F.R.: Serious and playful inquiry: epistemological aspects of collaborative creativity. Educ. Technol. Soc. **14**, 55–65 (2011)
21. Abt, C.: Serious Games. Viking Press, New York (1970)
22. Krange, I., Ludvigsen, S.: The historical and situated nature of design experiments: implications for data analysis. J. Comput. Assist. Learn. **25**(3), 268–279 (2009)
23. Knoblauch, H.: Videography: focused ethnography and video analysis. In: Knoblauch, H., Schnettler, B., Raab, J., Soeffner, H.-G. (eds.) Video Analysis: Methodology and Methods, pp. 69–84. PeterLang, Frankfurt am Main (2009)
24. Greimas, A.J.: Actants, actors, and figures. on meaning: selected writings in semiotic theory. In: Theory and History of Literature, vol. 38, pp. 106–120. U of Minnesota P, Minneapolis (1973/1987)
25. Propp, V.: Morphology of the Folktale, 2nd edn. University of Texas Press, Austin (1928/1968)
26. Heath, C.H., Hindmarsh, J., Luff, P.: Video in Qualitative Research. Sage, London (2010)
27. Fereday, J., Muir-Cochrane, E.: Demnonstrating rigor using thematic analysis: a hybrid approach of inductive and deductive coding and theme development. Int. J. Qual. Methods **5**(1), 80–92 (2010)
28. Braun, V., Clarke, V.: Using thematic analysis in psychology. Qual. Res. Psychol. **3**(2), 77–101 (2006)
29. Brooks, A., Petersson, E.: Raw emotional signalling, via expressive behaviour. In: Proceedings of the 15th International Conference on Artificial Reality and Telexistence, Christchurch, New Zealand, pp. 133–141 (2005)

Effectiveness and Usability of a Developed Collaborative Online Tool for Children with ADHD

Doaa Sinnari[1]($\boxtimes$) (iD), Paul Krause[1], and Maysoon Abulkhair[2]

[1] Faculty of Engineering and Physical Sciences,
University of Surrey, Guildford, UK
{d.sinnari,p.krause}@surrey.ac.uk
[2] Information Technology Department, King Abdulaziz University (KAU),
Jeddah, Kingdom of Saudi Arabia
mabualkhair@kau.edu.sa

Abstract. This study evaluated the effectiveness and usability of a developed collaborative online tool (chit-chat) for children with Attention Deficit Hyperactivity Disorder (ADHD). We studied whether this tool influenced children's Knowledge and experience exchange, motivation, behavioral abilities and social skills while using another learning tool, ACTIVATE. A total of seven Saudi children with ADHD aged from 6 to 8 years were assigned to the collaborative intervention using iPads. They were asked to play mini games that positively affect children with ADHD cognitively and behaviorally, then chat using our developed collaborative online tool, for three sessions. Progress points were measured and quantitatively analyzed before and after the intervention, thematic analysis was applied on the qualitative data. Participants showed improvements in overall performance when using the learning tool ACTIVATE. E-collaboration was found to be effective to children with ADHD and positively influencing their knowledge, experience, motivation and social skills.

Keywords: ADHD · E-collaboration · Effectiveness · Usability

1 Introduction

There is a lack of research on the effectiveness of using online collaborative closed-communities designed especially for children with ADHD that might have an effect on their abilities, skills, and performance in educational activities. Moreover, in our previous work, we investigated an e-game developed to enhance abilities and skills of children with ADHD, and positive results were reported (Sinnari et al. 2018). Yet, one of the important issues that arose was not having any kind of live interaction or collaboration between the children who played with it, as each child played individually. According to the reviewed literature, collaboration is one of the most effective learning strategies. It reinforces motivation and knowledge exchange and builds social skills (Huang et al. 2017). Children learn by communicating, interacting, and imitating. By letting them work closely together, they will experience high levels of engagement, motivation, and enjoyment (Xie et al. 2008). Thus, to add a missing component to the

A. L. Brooks et al. (Eds.): ArtsIT 2018/DLI 2018, LNICST 265, pp. 496–507, 2019.

evaluated e-game, we developed and evaluated a collaboration tool, Chit-Chat, as an add-on for user engagement. The overview of Chit-Chat, the research methodology, and the results are reported in this study.

1.1 Research Questions

This experimental study investigated the following question:

- How does the use of the collaboration tool by children with ADHD in school settings affect their motivation, knowledge and experience and social behavior towards e-learning activities and environment?
- Is the developed collaboration tool interface usable and subjectively pleasing for children with ADHD?

2 Related Work

Evidence showed the optimistic impact of applications that support collaborative work among students on their motivation to learn, engagement with others, knowledge sharing, social skills and problem solving (Järvelä et al. 2015). Therefore, many researchers, developers, and healthcare specialist were encouraged to extend their work, during last decade, by developing special applications and serious games that target and promote some of healthcare students' weaknesses. But still few of them explored the impact of e-collaboration and actually integrated this strategy in their studies. There was a study found on the effect of collaborative intervention using different tools for children with dyslexia (Vasalou et al. 2017) which found emphasizing their social engagement; another one was explored with autistic children (Holt and Yuill 2017), in which they used double-iPad approach to encourage and facilitate communication with peers and adults. For younger children, a study found a promising benefit of a collaborative experience for kindergarten children with Learning difficulties (Drigas et al. 2015), this strategy helped them learn simple math in a fun way. Another study, targeted autistic children, developed a collaborative game that encouraged social interaction and cognitive abilities (Barajas et al. 2017). There was only one study, to my knowledge, that investigated the effectiveness of a collaborative serious game "plan it commander", on children with ADHD (Bul et al. 2015). The game included three mini games that offer neurocognitive and behavioural training tasks. Children collaborate with their parents only on some behavioural daily-life tasks such as: planning, time management, responsibilities, and problem solving. "Plan it commander" focused on resolving cognitive, behavioural, and social, as real-life problem-solving, issues.

3 Chit-Chat Overview

The Chit-Chat tool is a web-based application that offers a chatting panel, which is managed and monitored by teachers, for children with ADHD. The Chit-Chat interface was designed and developed to complement an e-game "ACTIVATE" (i.e. an add-on feature to help children interact between mini games). We used the 15 guidelines proposed by McKnight (2010) to design usable interfaces for children with ADHD. It contains two portals: one for teachers with more control and the other for children. Each user has to log in to the system using a unique user name and password (Fig. 1).

Fig. 1. Teacher portal with controls (right) and children portal (left).

In the student account, they can chat, send emojis, view their achieved progress scores in ACTIVATE, view their friends' progress scores, change their character avatar, and convert text to audio by tapping posted text/chat. The teacher account provides controls to activate or deactivate chat, clear/delete chat, change the character avatar, create multiple-choice challenges with timer options, print chat history, and generate progress reports for each child showing accuracy and speed averages in challenges.

4   Experiment Design and Methodology

One of the issues was the inability to develop a chatting feature within ACTIVATE itself due to a limitation from the developing company. Therefore, we decided to build an add-on application. The idea was running ACTIVATE games synchronously with the Chit-Chat application to make the students feel that they were using a single application.

Relying on our research objectives, we designed a qualitative and quantitative experimental study. The independent variable was the e-collaborative activity tool (the Chit-Chat application), and the dependent variables were all the following behaviors, which were measured and assessed in the experiment: Motivation to complete tasks, socializing, knowledge, and experience.

The experiment included three mini interventions. A pilot study was done three weeks prior to the actual experiment to test the study design to understand the time needed for each session and to test the wording of the tasks. A usability test was done during the intervention to study the interface design and discover more usability issues.

Before we started the intervention experiment, a baseline session was prepared to allow participants play with ACTIVATE alone for 20 min. Then, the intervention sessions were held on three days for 35 min each in total: 20 min for ACTIVATE and 15 min for the Chit-Chat application.

ACTIVATE contains four mini games per session. Each game takes only five minutes to complete. Thus, our idea was to slot in the Chit-Chat application for five minutes after each ACTIVATE mini game. There will be three sub-sessions of Chit-Chat in a single intervention. Children used the iPad as the tool of study.

In the first chatting sub-session, participants were asked to do certain usability tasks. In the second sub-session, the teacher initiated the chat by introducing himself and asked the participants to do so and to talk about themselves a little bit. Using this activity, the researcher studied the effect of a collaborative activity on the children's socialization. In the third sub-session, after playing the third ACTIVATE mini game, the teacher asked about the ACTIVATE games. The teacher asked: What is the best game? How can one get a higher score? What are some secret hints to share with other participants? We wanted to know to what extent the collaborative activities encourage children to exchange their knowledge and experience about given tasks.

In the second intervention, the teacher revealed the game scores for all the participants on the chatting panel. The chatting remained locked, and the children were given the chance to see their scores and their friends' scores for about one minute. We wanted to investigate the effect of seeing their peers' scores regarding whether it would motivate them to do better or worse in the next tasks.

In our last intervention, the researcher used the same experimental design for the first intervention. The only difference was that the teacher did not interfere in all three sub-session chats. We wanted to investigate whether the teacher's presence and participation affected this collaborative activity positively or negatively.

5 Participants

Seven children, all diagnosed with ADHD (three females and four males), were recruited to participate in this study. The students were from Grades 1, 2, and 3 from Al-Nojood International Private School. Pre-intervention demographic questionnaire and Conner rating were used to identify the type of ADHD, level of severity, and social skills for the participants, which were filled in by parents (Table 1). They were all familiar with the iPad and used it regularly in playing online games and viewing YouTube clips. However, the students had never used any chatting applications before.

6 Data Collection and Analysis

There were two types of data collected: quantitative and qualitative. The quantitative part was provided by ACTIVATE system, which measures each participant's overall progress in mini games against their peers. We used the baseline and the post-intervention progress measures for each participant to check their performance before and after the intervention. To statistically analyse their progress points, we used the paired t-test to evaluate the significance by calculating the p-value.

For the qualitative part, some of the participants' behavioural responses were recorded (written) by the researcher while interacting with the application, such as body and hand movements and interacting with each other. Video recording was prohibited due to school policy, but we had approval from the head of the school to take pictures without showing participants' faces. Moreover, we managed to get approval to record audio tracks of post-intervention interviews with the participants to capture their experience with the collaboration tool.

Table 1. Participant demographic data, ADHD type, and sociability

Participants	Age (years)	ADHD type	Academic level	On treatment?	Sociability?
Bader	7	Combined	Medium	No	Limited friends
Firas	6	Combined	Low	No	Social
Galia	6	Hyperactive	Medium	Yes (medication)	Shy–no friends
Obaid	7	Inattentive	Medium	No	Social
Sarah	7	Inattentive	Low	No	Shy-few friends
Suhaib	8	Combined	Low	No	Shy–few friends
Talia	8	Inattentive	Medium	No	Limited friends

Thematic analysis (Clarke and Braun 2014) was applied to the qualitative data gathered from participants' chat history, observational notes, and audio recordings of post-intervention open questions. This process allowed us to interpret the gathered raw data and present it in a more intensive construction of themes. To test usability and satisfaction, a usability test was done in the first session of the intervention. For the user experience, an open-ended interview was used. These feedback items were included in the thematic analysis as part of our gathered data.

7 Usability Test

In designing the Chit-Chat interface, we used some of the guidelines suggested from literature for children with ADHD and applied usability guidelines (McKnight 2010). The main idea was to keep it as simple and easy as possible and less distracting. Therefore, we asked the participants and a teacher to do the usability tasks on the Chit-Chat portal. As Nielsen (2000) stated, a usability test carried out by only five participants will disclose 85% of the usability issues.

The teacher completed all the tasks with no difficulties. However, some students raised issues, and we dealt with them accordingly.

8   Findings and Discussion

8.1   Effectiveness of the Collaboration Tool

For our quantitative data, we measured the effectiveness of our tool by comparing the participants' performance before and after the intervention. The statistical significance was determined by a paired t-test using GraphPad PRISM (v. 5.0, GraphPad Software, Inc.). A p-value of less than 0.05 was considered significant.

Table 2 shows the progress points scored by each participant before and after the intervention. Each progress point is a measure of the levels completed and the speed within the e-game. The distribution of the progress points differences was fairly normal. As our baseline measures, the pre-intervention mean was M = 15.57, with a standard deviation SD = 2.30. After intervention, they were M = 21.57, and SD = 1.27.

Table 2. Progress points by participants before and after the intervention.

Participants	Progress points per session			Percentage of improvement
	Baseline	Post-intervention		
Bader	17	18	37	58	12%
Firas	12	11	26	47	25%
Galia	14	20	42	63	57%
Obaid	16	14	33	55	19%
Sarah	14	15	31	51	14%
Suhaib	18	18	42	64	41%
Talia	18	20	41	65	17%

The two-tailed p-value was less than 0.0001 (p $\leq$ 0.05); thus, we rejected the null hypothesis. By conventional criteria, this difference was statistically significant. The mean of the baseline minus the post-intervention is −6.00 (95% confidence interval (CI) [−7.60, −4.40]). As a conclusion, participants' performance in ACTIVATE was positively affected by applying the online collaboration tool (Chit-Chat; t (6) = 9.165, p $\leq$ 0.05).

There was some stability in the performance between the baseline and the first intervention session; participants have earned nearly the same amount of points. However, in the second session, we spotted a progressive increase in performance. By computing the difference in performance between the first and second sessions of intervention, we found an improvement in performance at an average of 26%.

Theoretically, one of the reasons was due to motivating them by displaying participants' scores for all of them on the collaboration tool. Regarding the literature, many studies encourage posting scores for all students, so that each student can be positively motivated by others' scores (Klingberg et al. 2005; Ali and Puthusserypady 2015). Another reason is that participants in the first session exchanged some of the playing techniques and hints that helped them personally increase their scores, such as speed, concentrating on the monkey with fingers close to the screen, easy games versus hard games, and making fewer mistakes the higher the mouse goes up. By the second session, some of them were actually applying these techniques while they were playing. The observational notes and chat history demonstrate the positive effects of exchanging knowledge and experience on improving performance. This was in line with the findings of a study (Fiers 2017) that utilized peer tutoring and information exchange among students with emotional and behavioral disorders. It showed growth in cognitive skills and gains in problem-solving proficiency. As motivation and knowledge exchange were dependent variables in our study, more details and qualitative results are reviewed in the next section.

8.2   Thematic Analysis Results

In the second part, our qualitative results were built upon the thematic analysis. All the transcribed information was translated from Arabic to simple English, considering the same simple expression level. Next, will discuss the most important and prominent codes.

Knowledge and Experience Exchange
At the opening five minutes, participants (n = 3) were very shy to contribute in the chat, they told the researcher that they do not know how to spell the words correctly. The researcher expressed to them that there was no need to worry about perfectly spelled words; just write it in any way and try your best. Participants were encouraged one by one to chat (n = 4). It was clear that the participants were able to use the chatting panel in exchanging what they knew and learned.

Our findings were in contrast with an earlier study that found negative effects of an online collaborative experience on children with behavioral disorders (Lipponen et al. 2003). Our findings showed positive conversations, socialization, and information exchange. Another study explained that low progress students struggle to ask for help (Kroesbergen et al. 2004). Again, in our study, a good number of help requests were raised from some of the low progress participants.

Yet, many studies were in line with our findings (Rief 2016). It has been shown that the peer-tutoring approach has promising effects on children with learning and behavioral disorders (DuPaul and Stoner 2014). Another finding confirmed exchanging information stimulates students' abilities (Tsuei 2014). Moreover, Vasalou et al. (2017) evaluated the experience of students with learning difficulties in exchanging knowledge, which resulted in improvements on their academic achievements.

Returning to our second finding, we noticed another interesting aspect; participants were giving positive feedback to each other (n = 4). These kinds of reactions would increase their self-esteem and confidence and encourage others to improve their performance (Van Popta et al. 2017). A different form of feedback was observed – a sort of a light and respectful criticism was introduced.

Our outcome was in line with a study that specified that children with ADHD are affected by positive feedback yet are less considerate of negative feedback (Bul et al. 2015). Another study found that written peer-interaction with supportive talk increases learning and improves social skills (Genlott and Grönlund 2016).

Motivational Influence

This theme was mainly detected by the observed behavior and reactions of the participants. The second intervention was designed specifically to post game scores attained by all participants. Participants were able to see their scores and their peers' scores. Few studies have emphasized exposing group scores to reinforce motivation and to improve performance (Klingberg et al. 2005; Ali and Puthusserypady 2015). Participants (n = 6) showed excitement by moving their hands quickly up and down, jumping, and saying 'yes' or 'yay!!'. Another sign of motivation was noticed by the researcher; after score posting, some participants (n = 3) were taking a bit more time thinking about the task, concentrating, and progressing well. In addition, two participants (n = 2) shared how many reward stars they received.

Another factor that helped the researcher validate motivation was the level of engagement and activity in the chatting tool. To motivate the children's engagement in any game with others, factors such as challenge, competition, and interaction must be applied (Yee 2006). To my knowledge, there was no study found on the relation of the engagement level with the motivation for children with ADHD while using collaboration tools. Yet, we found one study (Ronimus et al. 2014) that showed that there is no significant effect on children's engagement by challenge level or reward system. From our point of view, the factors of peer interaction and competition were not presented in their work.

Socialization

One of the main symptoms of children with ADHD is having some difficulties in their social skills and interaction with peers (Wilkes-Gillan et al. 2017). Our objective in this study was to help them develop these skills by engaging them in a close collaborative online community. This assisted in reducing the fear of confrontation and encouraged them to release their feelings and opinions about certain games. In the first session, a few participants (n = 3) talked about their classes, favorite subjects, and things they like to eat. Others (n = 2) were too shy to write anything. They were observers rather than participators. In fact, they were only posting emojis as a way of interacting, but they were eventually encouraged by feedback from their peers who commented and interacted with their input. By the third intervention, some participants (n = 2) were sharing short jokes, and others (n = 2) were planning to play in the playground after the intervention. From the observation, we found that this experience has reflected positively on their prosocial relation outside the playing sessions. The concepts of indirect learning, emotional feedback, and facilitating mastery of given tasks, which are the fundamental elements of behavior development in the social cognitive theory (Bandura 1989), were executed in the intervention design.

A study done by McHale (2010) revealed that children with ADHD normally encounter difficulties in public online social communities owing to lack of safety and differences in reaction speed, cognitive abilities, and social skills. Children with this disorder usually are segregated and downgraded in social life; therefore, providing them a safe monitored online community will positively support them. Another study that was in line with our findings investigated an online communication system designed for children with ADHD. They found that children are more confident, open to self-identity, and seek support if needed from their peers more easily online than in real-life situations (Raskind et al. 2006).

8.3   Chit-Chat Usability and Satisfaction

One of our essential goals in this study was to evaluate the Chit-Chat interface in terms of usability and satisfaction. As we stated earlier, a usability test was done on the first session of the intervention with the same group of participants (n = 7). They were given certain tasks to perform, and they were encouraged to talk aloud during the test. Detected usability issues were fixed on the same day, and a post-intervention open-ended interview was done to assess their experience with the tool.

Nielsen (1994) identified usability using five quality components that must be applied, to any system in which humans might interact. Thus, any system interface would be considered usable if it was efficient, learnable, memorable, and satisfactory and has a small error rate.

The quantitative results showed that Chit-Chat is an effective collaboration tool for children with ADHD. We found fairly significant improvement in the participants' performance after comparing their achievements in ACTIVATE before and after using the tool. From these findings, the Chit-Chat collaboration tool is *efficient*.

The remaining quality components were measured by seeking the participants' feedback and experience with the tool, combined with our observational notes while they were using the application. A post-intervention interview was conducted with each participant individually. We did not use the questionnaire type due to their young age and probable struggle of reading, comprehending, and writing well-constructed and explanatory sentences. Therefore, we used interview-like questions with the aid of five printed smiley's that ranged from strongly agree to strongly disagree to help them show their emotions about a specific question, and then talk about the 'why?' afterwards.

The interview took approximately ten minutes with each participant. They were asked multiple questions that relate to each quality component. All participants (n = 4) strongly agreed and (n = 3) agreed that the system was simple and easy to use from the first time they interacted with the interface. Two participants (n = 2) found that the chat deactivation feature was confusing in the beginning, but in less than a minute they noticed the statement 'the chat is locked by the teacher' and immediately understood and waited until the teacher unlocked the chat. Regarding the avatar icon, and after changing it from a gear (⚙) that resembles settings to a small human character (👤), they easily knew how to change their avatar character. The participants did not face any problems with converting text to audio. Most of them (n = 5) tapped the text directly when we asked them to hear what they wrote on usability test and recognized the left-hand side when they were asked about scores. From these user experiences with the tool, Chit-Chat is *learnable*.

On the third intervention, all the participants (n = 7) remembered how to reach all the features within the Chit-Chat interface. They were using the tool with confidence and skill. The features were few, easy to reach, and all on the same page; therefore, the Chit-Chat interface is *memorable*.

As expected, due to its nature as a chat-only tool, the error rate was nearly none. There was no wrong way of doing something. All the participants completed the tasks they were asked to do correctly and chatted through the panel without mistakes. They knew the use of each icon, and no multi-steps nor multi-levelled tasks were required. For that reason, the Chit-Chat interface has *no error rate*.

The design was kept simple and easy with less distraction. All participants (n = 7) strongly agreed that they liked the theme, colors, and icons in the interface. A few of them (n = 2) suggested that they want to customize their pirate avatars and dress them up, and one (n = 1) asked about whether they could have more control of the text in terms of changing the color, font, and size. All these suggestions will be taken in consideration when modifying the tool in the future for another evaluation. Therefore, the participants agreed that Chit-Chat was *subjectively pleasing*, and they were satisfied with the overall interface design.

From these previous findings and feedback, Chit-Chat is efficient, learnable, memorable, and satisfactory with no error rate. Thus, the Chit-Chat collaboration tool is considered usable and satisfactory.

9 Conclusion

The outcomes of the current study fit into the forthcoming projects of online collaborative interventions for children with ADHD. The online tool Chit-Chat was designed and developed to validate the 'e-collaboration' concept through providing a chatting panel to engage participants. The intervention took place in an international primary school in Jeddah, Saudi Arabia. Seven students with ADHD aged between 6 and 8 years participated in the study. The intervention involved three mini interventions, each with four ACTIVATE mini games, and a chatting session after each game. Children showed fairly significant improvements in their performance while playing ACTIVATE. Chit-Chat, the online collaboration tool, was found to positively influence children's knowledge and experience exchange, motivation, and social skills. In addition, the Chit-Chat tool was effective, usable, and subjectively pleasing. The results did not reveal improvements in the following participants' cognitive abilities: attention, processing speed, and working memory. This could be clarified by the fact that the developed collaboration tool did not aim to target these types of abilities by itself. It was developed to be integrated with another system, ACTIVATE, that works on improving those abilities. No direct nor noticeable effects on the children's behavior were found. As for future work, it is recommended to repeat the evaluation with a larger sample size and longer duration, perhaps including a control group to explore how does diversity affects the interaction with the tool.

References

Ali, A., Puthusserypady, S.: A 3D learning playground for potential attention training in ADHD: a brain computer interface approach. In: 2015 37th Annual International Conference of the IEEE Engineering in Medicine and Biology Society (EMBC), pp. 67–70. IEEE, August 2015

Bandura, A.: Human agency in social cognitive theory. Am. Psychol. **44**(9), 1175 (1989)

Barajas, A.O., Al Osman, H., Shirmohammadi, S.: A serious game for children with autism spectrum disorder as a tool for play therapy. In: 2017 IEEE 5th International Conference on Serious Games and Applications for Health (SeGAH), pp. 1–7. IEEE, April 2017

Bul, K.C., et al.: Development and user satisfaction of "Plan-It Commander", a serious game for children with ADHD. Games Health J. **4**(6), 502–512 (2015)

Clarke, V., Braun, V.: Thematic analysis. In: Michalos, A.C. (ed.) Encyclopedia of Critical Psychology, pp. 1947–1952. Springer, New York (2014). https://doi.org/10.1007/978-94-007-0753-5

Drigas, A., Kokkalia, G., Lytras, M.D.: ICT and collaborative co-learning in preschool children who face memory difficulties. Comput. Hum. Behav. **51**, 645–651 (2015)

DuPaul, G.J., Stoner, G.: ADHD in the Schools: Assessment and Intervention Strategies. Guilford Publications, New York (2014)

Fiers, J.: The effects of peer tutoring on math fact fluency of elementary students with emotional and behavioral disorders. Doctoral dissertation, Western Illinois University (2017)

Genlott, A.A., Grönlund, Å.: Closing the gaps – improving literacy and mathematics by ICT-enhanced collaboration. Comput. Educ. **99**, 68–80 (2016)

Holt, S., Yuill, N.: Tablets for two: how dual tablets can facilitate other-awareness and communication in learning disabled children with autism. Int. J. Child-Comput. Interact. **11**, 72–82 (2017)

Huang, C.S., Su, A.Y., Yang, S.J., Liou, H.H.: A collaborative digital pen learning approach to improving students' learning achievement and motivation in mathematics courses. Comput. Educ. **107**, 31–44 (2017)

Järvelä, S., et al.: Enhancing socially shared regulation in collaborative learning groups: designing for CSCL regulation tools. Educ. Technol. Res. Dev. **63**(1), 125–142 (2015)

Klingberg, T., et al.: Computerized training of working memory in children with ADHD-a randomized, controlled trial. J. Am. Acad. Child Adolesc. Psychiatry **44**(2), 177–186 (2005)

Kroesbergen, E.H., Van Luit, J.E., Maas, C.J.: Effectiveness of explicit and constructivist mathematics instruction for low-achieving students in the Netherlands. Elementary Sch. J. **104**(3), 233–251 (2004)

Lipponen, L., Rahikainen, M., Lallimo, J., Hakkarainen, K.: Patterns of participation and discourse in elementary students' computer-support collaborative learning. Learn. Instr. **13**, 487–509 (2003). https://doi.org/10.1016/s0959-4752(02)00042-7

McHale, T.J.: Delayed maturation of neuropsychological abilities in ADHD: a developmental comparison between children, adolescents, and adults. Doctoral dissertation (UMI No. 3449435), Fielding Graduate University, Santa Barbara, CA (2010)

McKnight, L.: Designing for ADHD in search of guidelines. In: IDC 2010 Digital Technologies and Marginalized Youth Workshop (2010)

Nielsen, J.: Why You Only Need to Test with 5 Users. NNGroup, Nielsen Norman Group, USA (2000). https://www.nngroup.com/articles/why-you-only-need-to-test-with-5-users/. Accessed 02 Jan 2017

Nielsen, J.: Usability Engineering. Elsevier, Amsterdam (1994)

Raskind, M., Margalit, M., Higgins, E.: "My LD": children's voices on the internet. Learn. Disabil. Q. **29**(4), 253–268 (2006)

Rief, S.F.: How to Reach and Teach Children and Teens with ADD/ADHD. Wiley, Hoboken (2016)

Ronimus, M., Kujala, J., Tolvanen, A., Lyytinen, H.: Children's engagement during digital game-based learning of reading: the effects of time, rewards, and challenge. Comput. Educ. **71**, 237–246 (2014)

Sinnari, D., Krause, P., Abulkhair, M.: Effects of e-games on the development of Saudi Children with attention deficit hyperactivity disorder cognitively, behaviourally and socially: an experimental study. In: Antona, M., Stephanidis, C. (eds.) Universal Access in Human-Computer Interaction. Methods, Technologies, and Users. LNCS, vol. 10907, pp. 598–612. Springer, Cham (2018). https://doi.org/10.1007/978-3-319-92049-8_44

Tsuei, M.: Mathematics synchronous peer tutoring system for students with learning disabilities. J. Educ. Technol. Soc. **17**(1), 115–127 (2014)

Van Popta, E., Kral, M., Camp, G., Martens, R.L., Simons, P.R.J.: Exploring the value of peer feedback in online learning for the provider. Educ. Res. Rev. **20**, 24–34 (2017)

Vasalou, A., Khaled, R., Holmes, W., Gooch, D.: Digital games-based learning for children with dyslexia: a social constructivist perspective on engagement and learning during group game-play. Comput. Educ. **114**, 175–192 (2017)

Wilkes-Gillan, S., Cantrill, A., Cordier, R., Barnes, G., Hancock, N., Bundy, A.: The use of video-modelling as a method for improving the social play skills of children with attention deficit hyperactivity disorder (ADHD) and their playmates. Br. J. Occup. Ther. **80**(4), 196–207 (2017)

Xie, L., Antle, A.N., Motamedi, N.: Are tangibles more fun? Comparing children's enjoyment and engagement using physical, graphical and tangible user interfaces. In: Proceedings of the 2nd International Conference on Tangible and Embedded Interaction, pp. 191–198. ACM, February 2008

Yee, N.: Motivations for play in online games. Cyberpsychol. Behav. **9**, 772–775 (2006)

Learning Basic Mathematical Functions with Augmented Reality

José Cerqueira[1]([✉]) , Cristina Sylla[2] , João Martinho Moura[1] ,
and Luís Ferreira[1]

[1] Instituto Politécnico do Cávado e do Ave, Barcelos, Portugal
cerqueirajm@gmail.com, {jmoura, lufer}@ipca.pt
[2] Research Centre on Child Studies (CIEC), Universidade do Minho,
Braga, Portugal
cristina.sylla@ie.uminho.pt

Abstract. This article presents the development of a serious game targeting secondary school students, that uses Augmented Reality (AR) to visualize, manipulate and explore mathematical concepts, particularly linear, quadratic, exponential and trigonometric (sine and cosine) functions. The motivation behind the development of the AR application was to provide students with learning materials that facilitate the exploration of a mathematical subject that is often considered difficult to learn. Whereas traditional resources for teaching and learning mathematics use manuals and scientific calculators to solve problems, the application, named FootMath, simulates a 3D football game, where the users can manipulate and explore the different functions using parameters with different values to score goals. Additionally, we discuss the potential of AR games as educational and engaging tools that can be used to facilitate learning, especially problem based learning and logical reasoning.

Keywords: Augmented Reality · Education · Math · STEM · Functions
Game based learning

1 Introduction

The motivation to develop an AR application to visualize, manipulate and explore mathematical functions emerged out of the knowledge that many students have difficulties to understand and mentally visualize abstract concepts. This capacity is particularly important for learning mathematics, as it demands logical and problem-solving abilities. When confronted with such difficulties, the students often feel frustrated and lose interest in the learning subject. Therefore, and specially in fields that demand a high degree of logical reasoning and abstract thinking, as it is the case in mathematics, one of the great challenges in the process of teaching/learning, is the use of adequate tools that have the potential for engaging students with the learning subject while facilitating learning [1].

The decision to address mathematical functions emerged from the relevance that functions have within the mathematics curriculum, and the complexity of the subject area, which poses great difficulties for many students. According to literature "*the*

A. L. Brooks et al. (Eds.): ArtsIT 2018/DLI 2018, LNICST 265, pp. 508–513, 2019.

*concept of function is central to understanding mathematics, yet students' under-
standing of functions appears either to be too narrowly focused or to include erroneous
assumptions*" [2:747]. Besides, it is considered that week graphing skills compromise
the understanding of mathematics and science [3].

Previous research has claimed the need for changing the way mathematics are
taught, in order to promote the development of relevant competencies, as well as to
promote the enjoyment and appreciation of a subject field that is highly present in
uncountable daily activities. Effective learning can take place when the students are able
to visualize, explore and manipulate the learning content, being able to construct their
own knowledge [4]. Ideally, such tools should provide a *low floor, high ceiling and wide
walls* [5], this is, they should be easy to start with, allow different approaches and
support the exploration of different levels of difficulty. Recent technological developments such as AR have the potential to create rich and engaging learning scenarios.
However, in order to achieve a change of paradigm in the learning/teaching process it is
also important to support and encourage teachers to use these new technological
developments promoting students' active participation in the learning process [6].

Outgoing from the notion of transformative education technology [7] the FootMath
application uses AR technology to manipulate, explore and visualize mathematical
functions, thus, potentially contributing to a better understanding of the subject.

Given the lack of adequate tools that are aligned with the secondary school
mathematics' curriculum, and that can potentially contribute to the student's engagement and learning achievements, FootMath aims at providing the students with
opportunities to think, explore and reflect on previously learned concepts while promoting meaningful learning of new more complex concepts, thus supporting a
"Backward Transfer" of knowledge [8].

2 Background and Related Work

The development of FootMath follows a *Game Based Learning* approach. According
to literature, digital games can be successfully used as complementary learning tools
[9]. Further, the use of digital games for learning has the potential to result in new
teaching/learning paradigms, as digital games have certain advantages over traditional
learning materials, such as encouraging decision taking and experimentation of different solutions to solve problems [10]. Particularly regarding STEM (Science, Technology, Engineering and Mathematics) educational digital games seem to be an
adequate tool for facilitating learning [11].

As previously referred, new technological developments have the potential to create
innovative learning/teaching scenarios, e.g., by enabling the combination of various
media, and providing a set of potentialities for the implementation of different learning
methodologies in physical and virtual environments.

2.1 Virtual, Augmented and Mixed Technology

Virtual, Augmented and Mixed Reality bring together different environments and degrees of immersion. The Augmented Reality (AR) technology combines physical artefacts with digital content, offering the possibility to physically interact with these virtual elements. Virtual Reality (VR), is another technology that also allows the virtual re-creation of reality, consisting of a computer-generated artificial simulation that allows the representation of a real-life environment or situation. The VR technology allows the user's immersion in the virtual environment, specially by stimulating the visual and auditory senses. Mixed Reality (MR) is a technology that brings together Virtual and Augmented Reality. The latter has recently gained attention in educational settings. Billinghurst and Dünser [12] refer the following potentialities of the use of AR technology in the classroom: (i) mediation between the real and the virtual environment with a more fluid interaction, (ii) the possibility of using metaphors through tangible artefacts for object manipulation and (iii) an easy transition between reality and digital visualizations. As they refer: *"AR educational media could be a valuable and engaging addition to classroom education and overcome some of the limitations of text-based methods, allowing students to absorb the material according to their preferred learning style"* [12:60].

The use of AR in the classroom context can be particularly advantageous for exploring innovative methodologies, e.g., by creating different scenarios and simulations, taking advantage of tangible interaction and promoting and supporting exploration and experimentation. Some examples of browser-based applications for mathematics are Geogebra Classic[1] or Desmos[2]. Examples of virtual environments for learning mathematics are GeoGebra Augmented Reality[3], which includes several examples of 3D mathematical objects that the users can place on a flat surface. The VR Math[4], is an interactive educational application for learning 3D geometry, graphs and vectors, with Virtual and Augmented Reality. The VR Math website presents examples of VR technology use in the context of mathematics. [1] uses tangible interaction mediated by AR technology to visualize and manipulate platonic solids.

3 The FootMath Application

FootMath employs tangible interaction mediated by AR Technology. The aim of the game is to score goals using mathematical functions. To do so, the player has to choose the correct function and modify its parameters depending on the position of the ball in the game area.

---

[1] https://www.geogebra.org/classic.

[2] https://www.desmos.com/calculator.

[3] https://itunes.apple.com/us/app/geogebra-augmented-reality/id1276964610.

[4] https://vrmath.co/.

3.1   Technical Development

FootMath was developed in UNITY[5] 2017.3.0f3 (64-bit) and AR Vuforia[6] and runs in Windows and Android. The application uses 2D physical markers for triggering the different mathematical functions. The physical markers were created using the Vuforia platform and then printed on cardboard. The Vuforia platform indicates the quality and degree of accuracy of each marker classifying them on a given scale. For a good detection of the physical markers it is necessary that each marker has a high number of visual characteristics. To achieve this, we have applied different colors to the various markers, which were classified with a degree of accuracy over 90%, on the rating scale of the Vuforia platform. This degree of accuracy also allows detecting two markers simultaneously and the visualization of the corresponding functions. This way, allowing the comparison of various functions and its simultaneous exploration on the football field.

3.2   Exploring Functions with FootMath

FootMath[7] uses 2D physical markers to start the game and to trigger the various functions. The game starts by showing the physical marker that represents the football field to the camera (see Fig. 1, left).

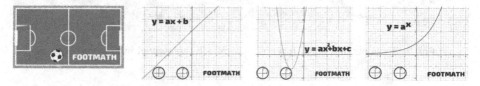

Fig. 1. (from left to right) Marker to start the game, makers with following mathematical functions: Linear, $y = ax + b$; Quadratic, $y = ax^2 + bx + c$ and Exponential, $y = a^x$.

When the camera detects a marker, the application displays a 3D football field with a menu on the left with five (selection) buttons (see Fig. 2). The buttons show the following functions: $y = ax + b$ (linear); $y = ax^2 + bx + c$ (quadratic); $y = a^x$ (exponential); $y = a \sin (bx + c)$ (sine) and $y = a\cos (bx + c)$ (cosine). Each physical marker presents the graph associated to the respective function. Besides using the physical markers for each function, the user can opt to choose the functions by clicking any of the five buttons displayed on the screen. This option can be particularly helpful when the detection conditions of the physical markers is not ideal, e.g., intense light conditions or incorrect handling of the physical marker.

After selecting a function using a physical marker, the function appears on the football field. The interface menu comprises two joy sticks for manipulating the

---

[5] https://unity3d.com/.

[6] https://www.vuforia.com/.

[7] Video at https://drive.google.com/open?id=1VE3fHCsdynd9ajGDkctXvWmFvvWoXlif.

function's parameters (a, b, c, d). The joystick on the bottom right hand corner allows manipulating the a and b parameters, the joystick on the bottom left hand corner allows manipulating the parameters c and d. Each equation button shows the parameters that the user can manipulate. The visualization of the parameters when the user changes the values with the joystick is displayed on the top hand right corner of the menu.

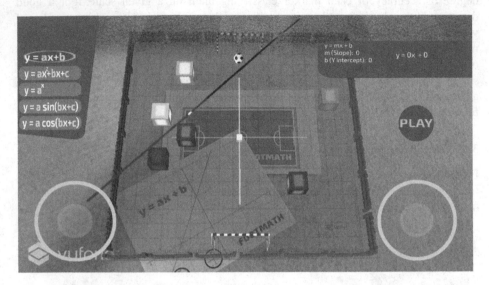

Fig. 2. Example of a linear function, $y = ax + b$ represented in the game area.

By using the right and/or left joystick the user can change the parameters of the function, triggering its plotting on the virtual environment. After defining the right position for scoring by manipulating the function according to the position of the ball, the user kicks the ball by pressing the Play button. When this happens, a small cube, located on the left side at the beginning of the function begins its trajectory along the function, when the ball is in the same trajectory as the function the cube collides with it and scores goal.

In order to increase the difficulty level to score a goal, there are cubes moving around in the football field that can influence the trajectory of the ball. Therefore, and depending on the position of the ball and the cubes, the user needs to decide which mathematical function is the best to use in order to score a goal.

4   Conclusion and Future Work

In this paper we have described FootMath, an AR application that can be used to visualize and explore mathematical functions. The application aims at facilitating the student's exploration and visualization of linear, quadratic, exponential and trigono-metric (sine and cosine) functions as well as to promote the student's interest and involvement with the subject. As the application is still under development, we carried out a first informal evaluation with a group of 24 eight graders. The students explored the different functionalities of FootMath during a mathematics class and expressed their enjoyment over using Augmented Reality to explore mathematical functions. In future work, we intend to implement more functions and different levels of difficulty addressing the different school years. Further, we plan to extend the existing functionalities of the physical markers, to allow using them to explore and manipulate the functions visualizing them from different angles and distances. The application will be tested at school with classes ranging from 8th to 12th grade. This work will be planned and carried out in collaboration with the mathematics teachers and will involve a pre- and post-test of students' knowledge regarding the different mathematical functions. Further, we expect to integrate the markers into the school manuals as a complementary learning resource.

Acknowledgments. Cristina Sylla acknowledges the funding from the FCT (Portuguese Foundation for Science and Technology) and the European Operational Programme Human Capital (POCH), grant SFRH/BPD/111891/2015.

References

1. Cerqueira, J., Cleto, B., Moura, J., Sylla, C.: Visualizing platonic solids with augmented reality. In: Proceedings of the 17th ACM Conference on Interaction Design and Children (IDC 2018), pp. 489–492. ACM, New York (2018). https://doi.org/10.1145/3202185. 3210761
2. Clement, L.: What do students really know about functions? Math. Teacher **94**(9), 745–748 (2001)
3. Lapp, D., Cyrus, V.: Using data-collection devices to enhance students' understanding. Math. Teacher **93**(6), 504–510 (2000)
4. Papert, S.: The Children's Machine: Rethinking School in the Age of the Computer. Harvester Wheatsheaf, New York (1993)
5. Resnick, M.: Lifelong Kindergarten: Cultivating Creativity Through Projects, Passion, Peers, and Play. MIT Press, Cambridge (2017)
6. Wright, G.: Student-centered learning in higher education. Int. J. Teach. Learn. High. Educ. **23**, 92–97 (2011)
7. Hess, F.M., Hochleitner, T., Saxberg, B.: E-Rate, Education Technology, and School reform. American Enterprise Institute, 22 October 2013
8. Hohensee, C.: Backward transfer: an investigation of the influence of quadratic functions instruction on students' prior ways of reasoning about linear functions. Math. Think. Learn. **16**(2), 135–174 (2014). https://doi.org/10.1080/10986065.2014.889503
9. Drigas, A., Pappas, M.: On line and other game-based learning for mathematics. Int. J. Online Eng. (iJOE) **11**, 62–67 (2015). https://doi.org/10.3991/ijoe.v11i4.4742
10. Griffiths, M.: The educational benefits of videogames. Educ. Health **20**, 47–51 (2002)
11. Kelley, T., Knowles, J.: A conceptual framework for integrated STEM education. Int. J. STEM Educ. **3**, 11 (2016). https://doi.org/10.1186/s40594-016-0046-z
12. Billinghurst, M., Dunser, A.: Augmented reality in the classroom. Computer **45**(7), 56–63 (2012)

A Tangible Constructivist AR Learning Method for Children with Mild to Moderate Intellectual Disability

Filip Černý[✉], Georgios Triantafyllidis, and George Palamas

Aalborg University, A. C. Meyers Vænge 15, 2450 Copenhagen, Denmark
fcerny16@student.aau.dk, {gt,gpa}@create.aau.dk

Abstract. This paper explores augmented tangible user interfaces (ATUIs) as a new educational paradigm for teaching special need children concepts from abstract domains. Case study being presented focuses on learning concepts of musical notation through constructivist multisensory AR experience utilizing TUI. The study was conducted in collaboration with Speciální Základní Škola Vysoké Mýto (Czech special needs school), where the experiment with such learning method using proposed ATUI called ARcomposer was held. In a user study with 22 participants, it was found that ATUIs are not only useful for children with intellectual disabilities, but that most of the children also yield great educational gains. The results of the study were concluded in a form of quantitative research in cooperation with pedagogues specialized in teaching students with intellectual disabilities.

Keywords: Augmented reality · Tangible user interface
Constructivist learning · Special education · Music education
Manipulative learning · Multisensory

1 Introduction

With rapid pace at which today's media technology is evolving, education is also being affected. Due to recent advances in technology such as virtual reality (VR), augmented reality (AR) and low-cost educational robotics, an ongoing debate between supporters of traditional and progressive learning approaches has been amplified, bringing the topics of hands-on learning and tangible user interfaces (TUIs) back to life. While the first group supports instructivist education - structured, scripted, standardized learning environments and materials, the latter stresses the importance of exploration, construction, and discovery – the constructivist model. A number of researchers [1, 10] suggest interaction models based on embodied knowledge as tools able to support children's learning in abstract domains.

The premise of the constructivist learning utilizing ATUIs is that the students who discover various learning topics by hands-on exploration create deeper and more meaningful knowledge structures [2, 12] especially when it comes to abstract domain concepts [1] utilizing higher cognitive processes such as mathematical operations, some topics from geometry, physics and the topics that require more profound imagination such as writing music. While constructive learning approach is theoretically

A. L. Brooks et al. (Eds.): ArtsIT 2018/DLI 2018, LNICST 265, pp. 514–519, 2019.

sound, it was proven rather challenging to mediate such experience in real-world classrooms that would suit all the students, hence, it is necessary to develop new tools and approaches and aforementioned technologies seems like a promising direction [7].

Although learning experiences utilizing multisensory TUIs, multi-touch table-tops, and AR/VR applications have been a focus of many recent studies, according to Javier Marco et al. [5], studies that combine augmented tabletop technology and tangible interaction applied to children with intellectual disabilities (IDs) remain scarce and pre-liminary. Learning disabilities of ID children vary broadly, however, they all share common difficulties such as lack of abstract thinking which prevents them from com-prehending higher-order cognitive concepts as spatio-temporal reasoning, logical oper-ations, etc. [9], however, methods utilizing progressive and constructivist learning approaches seem to work better for conveying such concepts than the traditional ones [6].

1.1 Project Goals

The aim of this work is to explore augmented tangible user interfaces (ATUIs) as a new educational paradigm for children with intellectual disabilities (ID). The level of usability and potential educational gains of the aforementioned learning method must be verified. Furthermore, this work researches how learning methods utilizing ATUIs help maintain attention and motivation of such students. In this context, it was decided to design a multisensory, tangible, AR learning experience for music classes in special needs schools (SNS) and explore the benefits this technology offers to ID.

2 Design and Implementation

The TUI of ARComposer consists of five blocks tagged with image-based markers which the users are allowed to compose into a simple melody of up to five tones (See Fig. 1). Those physical blocks are then augmented with a audio-visual information - no different

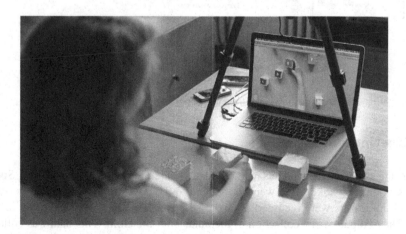

Fig. 1. One of the participants playing with ARComposer. Both, tangible interface and augmented content is visible in the figure. Different tones are defined by a step of 4 units on Y-axis.

from the relative positions of the notes in the standard musical notation. Finally, the composed arrangement of the blocks can be played as a melody in the looped.

2.1 Application Development

ARComposer application was developed using Unity Game Engine and Vuforia SDK for augmented reality features (See Fig. 2).

2.2 Application Logic

The user controls a maximum of 5 image-based markers during the experience. Serial placement of the markers defines the order of the tones being played. Y-axis position of the markers defines the sound (tone), the color of the augmented etiquette and the name of the tone dynamically displayed on the marker. The first marker being introduced is a "base marker". Positional data of this marker are retrieved from Unity scene and compared with all non-base image-targets. If current Y-distance between two tones changes by 4 units (virtual size of the marker) all the variables are set accordingly. The updates are executed on every frame so all the feedback is live. The user can press the space bar on the keyboard to play the melody of the tones in a looped sequence in intervals of 0.7 s.

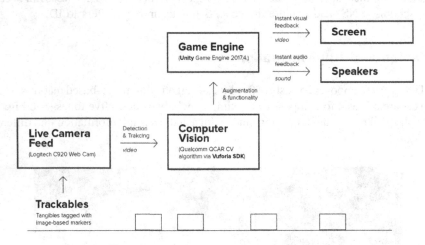

Fig. 2. Diagram showing different components of ARComposer system.

3   Experimental Procedure

During the experiment, students with mild to moderate ID (IQ 36-69) from Special needs school in Vysoké Mýto were introduced to the ARComposer application one by one and the results were recorded after the sessions. The data were collected in May 2018. The first part was a collection of the data about the child. This data was collected from special pedagogue who had the diagnosis cards of every test subject. The data collected were mainly gender, age, grade, level of ID (IQ range) and other possible disabilities. Following was the data collection of musical history of every child before the experiment, which was collected directly from the children.

The second part was the introduction to the game setup and tangible mechanics following a pre-written script which was carefully consulted with the special pedagogues. The experiment consisted of several tasks that the children tried to accomplish, practicing concepts of lower/higher pitch, serial placement of the notes in the notation etc.

The last part was the data collection in form of a questionnaire. The questioner was asking the questions and recording the answers to the Google Form document for further analysis.

3.1 Experimental Setup

Evaluating with ID children is difficult and specific conditions must be met in order to achieve smooth experiment such as familiarity with the environment and persons being present during the sessions. Children with ID can keep their attention for a limited time, hence, it is necessary to design the experiment in a short time frame. It is also crucial to formulate instructions or questions in the most straightforward manner for them to be fully understood, preferably in a pre-written script.

Furthermore, favorable lighting conditions are necessary for successful AR experience as well as a neutral working surface that would not confuse the CV algorithm. The application was running on 15' Apple MacBook Pro 2014. The camera was installed at a distance of roughly 1 m above the surface.

4 Evaluation and Results

The usability test consisted of observational methods which were complemented by the adapted DEVAN (DEtailed Video ANalysis) method originally proposed by Vermeeren [11]. In order to assess the educational potential of proposed ATUI, the active intervention method with questions formulated in advance was used together with usability testing. Information about the children and learning outcomes were then analysed from the questionnaires. Expert evaluation method was used in cooperation with pedagogues specialized in teaching children with ID. The data from 22 subjects were collected for further analysis. Twelve of these children were females and 10 males in age from 9 to 13 years. Almost ¾ (68%) of the participants were over 12 years. All participants were attending 3rd–9th grade of the SNS in Vysoké Mýto. Distribution of mild/moderate intellectual disability was three-quarters mild ID and ¼ moderate ID with 4 autistic children.

4.1 Usability

Usability tests revealed several shortcomings. Among the biggest issues was marker occlusion problem and subsequent loss of the tracking and augmentation when children accidentally covered the tangibles with their hands. Another poor design decision was use of analogous color scheme for the augmented etiquette. Using colors that are next to each other on the color wheel unfortunately resulted in insufficient color contrast between various tones and thus degraded orientation for those children who were orienting rather by the colors.

4.2   Educational Impact

When it comes to declarative knowledge gains, participants were tested on the number of the tones they remembered shortly after the experiment. Compared to the number of the tones they knew from before the experiment, the gains were significant since most of the children (20%) before the test did not know any tones, while right after the experiment 21 students (96%) remembered at least one tone from which 19 participants (86%) were able to recall at least 3 tones by their names.

In regards to procedural knowledge gains, the results were even more satisfying. All the children except for one autistic (96%), did understand the concept of arranging the tones on the vertical axis in order to influence the resulting pitch of the tone. Average percentage of the positive answers about procedural and declarative knowledge was 86,5% of successfully answered questions which is considered significant.

5   Conclusion

No decisive performance differences were found between the groups of students with mild/moderate IDs. It was helpful to consult the questions in the questionnaires and pre-written script with special pedagogue before the actual experiment as it unveiled the importance of correct formulations.

While usability tests uncovered several shortcomings, it turned out that constructivist learning methods using ATUI are well-suited for the education of ID children. The hands-on experience where the children have to physically manipulate the tangibles kept the children attentive during the whole session. Furthermore, due to the naturality of the tangible interface, the controlling of the application was usually effortless from the very beginning of the session. The live feedback helped the children to orientate between the tones considerably and they got the grasp of the TUI very quickly. Furthermore, their motivation has increased significantly after initial successes and after hearing the melody they composed in the looped sequence, they were notably very proud. All the children apparently enjoyed the experience very much and the educational gains seemed almost like a bi-product of a children play.

Constructivist learning approach using ATUI turned out to be not only completely usable for ID children, but also yield great educational gains in both procedural and declarative knowledge domains. Successfully conveying such abstract concepts as composing music by arranging high-pitched or low-pitched tones or placing the tones serially to create the sequence was one of the main goals of the proposed system, thus such results can be considered as very rewarding.

6 Further Development

Most of the shortcomings revealed by the usability test can be easily fixed. Occlusion problem can be fixed by placing the marker on the bottom of the graspable object which would be tracked by the camera installed beneath the transparent surface. When it comes to future research, long-term effects of such application need to be studied. Furthermore, there is a need of a comparative study in order to confirm or disprove the hypothesis that the constructivist approach using ATUIs helps ID children grasp abstract concepts faster and with less effort than the standard instructivist approach.

Potential evolution of the ARComposer might bring more features such as different blocks with varying note values such as a half note, quarter note or even rests. Such features would make the application more complex, hence suitable more for regular children in elementary and music schools than ID children.

Another interesting update might be a gamification of the application. Furthermore, this research initiated a conversation with the pedagogues with further suggestions and potential areas of research, such as: Preparatory classes of music schools; Sensory education (up, down, before, behind, below); Listening practice for children with impaired hearing; Gripping objects (especially for children with cerebral palsy); Melodic/rhythmic exercises; Practicing a song and Concentration.

References

1. Bakker, S., Antle, A.N., Van Den Hoven, E.: Embodied metaphors in tangible interaction design. Pers. Ubiquit. Comput. 16(4), 433–449 (2012)
2. Bara, F., Gentaz, E., Colé, P.: Haptics in learning to read with children from low socio-economic status families. Br. J. Dev. Psychol. 25(4), 643–663 (2007). https://doi.org/10.1348/026151007X186643
3. Laine, T.H.: Mobile Educational Augmented Reality Games: A Systematic Literature Review and Two Case Studies (2018)
4. Likert, R.: A technique for the measurement of attitudes. Arch. Psychol. (1932)
5. Marco, J., Cerezo, E., Baldassarri, S.: Bringing tabletop technology to all: evaluating a tangible farm game with kindergarten and special needs children. Pers. Ubiquit. Comput. 17(8), 1577–1591 (2013)
6. McLinden, M., McCall, S.: Learning Through Touch: Supporting Children with Visual Impairments and Additional Difficulties. Routledge, Abingdon (2016)
7. Schneider, B., Blikstein, P.: Flipping the flipped classroom: a study of the effectiveness of video lectures versus constructivist exploration using tangible user interfaces. IEEE Trans. Learn. Technol. 9(1), 5–17 (2016). https://doi.org/10.1109/TLT.2015.2448093
8. Simonetti Ibañez, A., Paredes Figueras, J.: Vuforia v1. 5 SDK: Analysis and evaluation of capabilities. Master's thesis, Universitat Politècnica de Catalunya (2013)
9. Švancarová, I.: Mentální retardace. Praha: Portál, ISBN 80-7178-821-X (2003)
10. Ullmer, B., Ishii, H.: Emerging frameworks for tangible user interfaces. IBM Syst. J. 39(34), 915–931 (2000)
11. Vermeeren, A.P.: DEVAN: a tool for detailed video analysis of user test data. Behav. Inf. Technol. 21(6), 403–423 (2002). https://doi.org/10.1080/0144929021000051714
12. Zuckerman, O., Arida, S., Resnick, M.: Extending tangible interfaces for education: digital Montessori inspired manipulatives. In: Proceedings of CHI 2005, pp 859–868. ACM Press (2005)

'Portugal Without Fires', A Data Visualization System to Help Analyze Forest Fire Data in Portugal

Duarte Gonçalves$^{(\boxtimes)}$ ⓘ, Bruno Lima ⓘ, João Martinho Moura ⓘ,
and Luís Ferreira ⓘ

School of Technology, Polytechnic Institute of Cávado and Ave (IPCA),
Barcelos, Portugal
{al5146,a6838}@alunos.ipca.pt, {jmoura,lufer}@ipca.pt

Abstract. The year 2017 was relatively tragic concerning the fires in Portugal. The scourge that settled in the country and the loss of countless human lives were engraved in the Portuguese memory. Due to extraordinary weather conditions and a lack of powerful means to immediately respond to the tragedy, more than a hundred citizens lost their lives in forest fires, some of them in severe conditions, in the middle of the forest and without a chance of escape, burned in cars as they fled. This paper presents the development of an integrated visualization system, exploring data acquired over the period of last ten years of Portuguese Forest Fires. The data was extracted from multiples of official public sources and formats, analyzed and classified accordingly. Advanced graphics and data-intense processing techniques provide distinct outputs, results, and correlations on acquired sources. This project contributes to innovative data analysis and reports perception, and it is intended to fit the expectation and needs of forest fires experts in crisis scenarios, representing an add-value for transformative co-decision.

Keywords: Data visualization · Data analytics · Big data · Wildfires
Interaction · Co-decision

1 Introduction

Decision making in environments characterized by the uncertainty and unpredictability of several variables is a very demanding task. If, on the one hand, this decision can be hampered by the lack of data, on the other hand, if the data exist, the ability to process and handle it and to get the expected answers, in a timely and efficient manner, also requires considerable effort and expertise. Interactive data visualization facilitates this process by allowing users to navigate, select, and display data via an easy-to-use interface [1]. Indeed, being vast and dynamic data sets, most of the times dispersed in multiple sources and formats, collecting, interpreting and analyzing it, requires time and complex processes. The capacity to quick and easy visualize such data, extract useful knowledge and information timely, represents a critical service of enormous interest and usefulness in contexts where rapid and agile decisions are required.

A. L. Brooks et al. (Eds.): ArtsIT 2018/DLI 2018, LNICST 265, pp. 520–525, 2019.

Scenarios of natural disasters or accidents are examples of such cases. Near real-time continuous multidimensional data analysis, discover and explore existing correlations and predicting results, are effective services that must be supported. According to experts on wildfires, the uncertainty caused by (i) the quantity and types of involved resources (persons, technicians, vehicles) and (ii) the amount, variance and variety of influencing data (time, humidity, temperature, wind, orography), the existing and used integrated strategies of experts, communications and information systems are not sufficient to support timely and right decisions.

This work intends to develop a set of novelty services for data processing and useful visualization, applied to Portuguese forest fires events, of the last ten years. It intends to contribute to demonstrate that collecting and processing scattered hetero-geneous data, using advanced analysis and processing mechanisms such as Big Data, exploitable with advanced visualization data-intense graphics libraries, provides operational near-real-time context-aware information for simulation, monitoring, management and assessment of fire risk and impact scale. The ability to make timely decisions based on available data is crucial to disaster management [2]. It is thus critical to investigate and establish connections of different order among the acquired data, to promote awareness of its correlated information, as exploring large collections of data becomes increasingly difficult as the volume grows [3].

The project presented here also aims to enable the public, in general, to become aware of and establish interconnections between the various fire incidents occurred in Portugal, understanding bonds of causality, through an interface that is desired to be functional and useful for civil protection authorities.

2   Background and Related Work

Wildfire is a global problem that put forward several studies and developments for analysis, prevention, detection, and reacting against these kinds of problems. Existent technologies and solutions like satellite-based systems, embedded integrated systems, sensors networks, high processing data capacity, give us almost near real-time data from fires and climatic conditions [4, 5]. Since 2007, the Council for Scientific and Industrial Research (CSIR) developed the Advanced Fire Information System (AFIS) that provides almost in real-time information for the prevention, monitoring, man-agement and assessment of wildfire as a risk or hazard to society on a local, regional and global scale, as well as Europe, that works towards the European Forest Fire Information System (EFFIS), a Global Wildfire Information System (GWIS) [6]. Among others, both initiatives show that this still is a severe problem.

Portuguese scenario is characterized by scattered data in distinct formats and multiple sources and not integrated information systems (IPMA [7], ICNF [8], POR-DATA [9], APA [10], MAI [11]). Collect and analyze this data is not easy, as our ability to generate information now far exceeds our capacity to understand it [12]. The existence of integrated processes and visual systems to display correlated information is essential to support quick and efficient responses, as visual displays provide the highest bandwidth channel from the computer to the human [13].

3   Portugal Without Fires

The solution explored in this work represents a responsive data visualization service, following a cloud pattern architecture with (a) a no-relational database (NoSQL) repository to store the multiple structured data (JSON) collected from varied sources [7–11]; (b) an API of REST services to explore the repository; and (c) an interactive visualization graphical system that behaves as an integrated interface to support analysis and perceptions of past and present scenarios, and helps predicting future occurrences.

4   Technical Development

The data was extracted from multiples official public sources and formats, analyzed and classified accordingly, following complex ETL processes and several scripts processing. The application was developed using Processing, MongoDB as a repository and RESTful services in PHP7. The frontend dashboard was developed from the scratch, integrating several existing libraries. Particular emphasis to library ControlP5[1] that lets the user visually filter the information and decide what to see, giving a personal experience while using the application, and library ANI[2] that offers animations on transactions and information display. This demo represents fires, between 2007 to 2017.

5   Data Visualization

The application was thought to be used by generical public and was produced with a simple and minimalist interface. Usability heuristics, proposed by Jacob Nielsen [14], were highly considered [15]. The application starts with the explicit links to the main sections with direct access to national statistics, an interactive map, meteorological section and an obituary (Fig. 1).

Fig. 1. The visualization's main screen.

---

[1] http://www.sojamo.de/libraries/controlP5/.

[2] http://www.looksgood.de/libraries/Ani/.

After filtering, a second graphic offers a visual comparison of the results for selected criteria. At the same time, the map on the left of the screen changes the color of the districts. If the user crosses over the district area on the map, the graphical information about the burned area appears (Fig. 2).

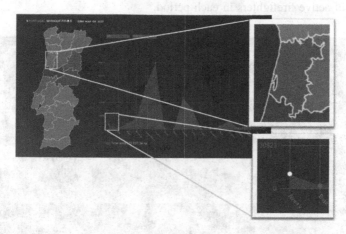

Fig. 2. Data visualization frontend. By selecting districts on the left, fire information appears on the right side.

To have a detailed perspective about a region is possible to click on and jump to another screen with more detailed data of the municipalities in the selected district. It is possible to analyze the causes of fire and check the areas of Portugal with more damage.

2017 was a dramatic year in Portugal [16]. To demonstrate this impact, we created a screen that shows the number of deaths of civilians and operational professionals by the fires (Fig. 3).

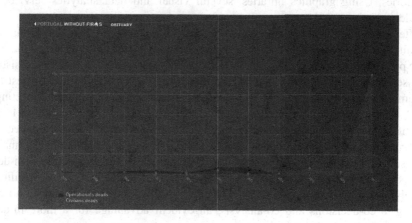

Fig. 3. Obituary section on data visualization frontend.

Because the project involved the research of different sources of information, in the proposed visualization system we collect graphically, and through a timeline, different information that, when combined, provide a perception of the problem and indicates the possible associated causes. Figure 4 represents the comparison of the total burned area with the number of occurrences. Having these results, it was possible to associate the number of active firefighters in each period.

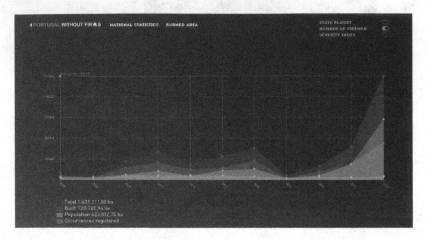

Fig. 4. Comparing data from different sources of information.

6   Conclusions

This paper describes an integrated data visualization interface that offers a set of innovative analysis services over forest fires occurrences data, bringing a new perspective about the fires in Portugal in the period of 2007–2017. Several distinct data sources were selected and processed; extraction processes were implemented and applied, and acquired data was preserved and classified accordingly in non-structured repositories. Using graphics libraries, several visual and data analytics services are possible to explore, and many results can be correlated, easily.

After some public presentations, the application results and knowledge that was transmitted made a significant impact on the audience's sensibility. During the MSc public presentation of the proposed solution, occurred in April 2018 at IPCA, assistants witnessed a set of information that offered them a new perspective on the forest fires problematic in Portugal. The project was then presented in an institutional meeting at ANPC - Portuguese Authority for Civil Protection, in May 2018. According to that institution, the most relevant result of this visualization system is the existence of a global and integrated data visualization tool and the possibility to dynamically analyze any result in multiple perspectives, in such fluent way, towards a more in-depth analysis of the fire problem and causes. They further strengthen the possibility to remotely analyze distinct contexts, providing real indicators for authorities and contributing to co-decisions and co-analysis, an evident advantage for a more in-depth analysis of the fire problem and causes.

A video demonstration of the data visualization system can be observed at: http://web.ipca.pt/mei/portugal-without-fires_papper-assets/video.mp4.

Acknowledgements. We thank the Civil Protection Service of the Municipality of Esposende, especially in the person of Engineer Carlos do Carmo, who facilitated access to the data that served as the basis for this work. To our families, while we were working on this project. We also dedicate this research to all the families that lost their relatives in the tragic forest fires in Portugal, in 2017.

References

1. Janvrin, D.J., Raschke, R.L., Dilla, W.N.: Making sense of complex data using interactive data visualization. J. Account. Educ. **32**(4), 31–48 (2014). https://doi.org/10.1016/j.jaccedu.2014.09.003. ISSN 0748-5751
2. Keim, D., Qu, H., Ma, K.-L.: Big-data visualization. IEEE Comput. Graph. Appl. **33**(4), 20–21 (2013). https://doi.org/10.1109/mcg.2013.54. ISSN 0272-1716
3. Shneiderman, B.: The eyes have it: a task by data type taxonomy for information visualizations. In: Proceedings 1996 IEEE Symposium on Visual Languages, pp. 336–343. https://doi.org/10.1109/vl.1996.545307. ISBN 0-8186-7508-X
4. Alkhatib, A.A.A.: A review on forest fire detection techniques. Int. J. Distrib. Sens. Netw. **10** (3) (2014). https://doi.org/10.1155/2014/597368. ISSN 15501477
5. Molina-Pico, A., Cuesta-Frau, D., Araujo, A., Alejandre, J., Rozas, A.: Forest monitoring and wildland early fire detection by a hierarchical wireless sensor network. J. Sens. **2016** (2016). https://doi.org/10.1155/2016/8325845. ISSN 16877268
6. San-Miguel-Ayanz, J., Barbosa, P., Schmuck, G., Libertà, G.: The european forest fire information system. In: Proceedings of the 6th AGILE, pp. 27–30 (2003)
7. Instituto Português do Mar e da Atmosfera. https://www.ipma.pt/pt/index.html. Accessed 15 June 2018
8. ICNF - Instituto da Conservação da Natureza e das Florestas. http://icnf.pt/. Accessed 15 June 2018
9. PORDATA - Estatísticas, gráficos e indicadores de Municípios, Portugal e Europa. https://www.pordata.pt/Homepage.aspx. Accessed 16 June 2018
10. Agência Portuguesa do Ambiente. https://www.apambiente.pt/. Accessed 15 July 2018
11. Portal da SGMAI. https://www.sg.mai.gov.pt/Paginas/default.aspx. Accessed 15 July 2018
12. Lima, M.: Visual Complexity: Mapping Patterns of Information. Princeton Architectural Press, New York (2011). ISBN 978-1568989365
13. Ware, C.: Information Visualization: Perception for Design. Morgan Kaufman (2004). http://dl.acm.org/citation.cfm?id=983611. ISBN 1558608192
14. Nielsen, J.: Usability inspection methods. In: Conference Companion on Human Factors in Computing Systems - CHI 1994, pp. 413–414 (1994). https://doi.org/10.1145/259963.260531. ISBN 0897916514
15. Nielsen, J., Molich, R.: Heuristic evaluation of user interfaces. In: Proceedings of the SIGCHI Conference on Human Factors in Computing Systems Empowering People - CHI 1990, pp. 249–256 (1990). https://doi.org/10.1145/97243.97281. ISBN 0201509326
16. Jones, J., Chavez, N., Narayan, C.: Portugal wildfire: 62 killed, victims burned in cars as they fled - CNN, CNN (2017). https://edition.cnn.com/2017/06/18/europe/portugal-fire/index.html. Accessed 10 June 2018

Development of a Pervasive Game for ADHD Children

Jesús Gallardo[1]([⊠]), Carmelo López[2], Antonio Aguelo[3],
Belén Cebrián[1], Teresa Coma[3], and Eva Cerezo[1]

[1] Departamento de Informática e Ingeniería de Sistemas,
Universidad de Zaragoza, Zaragoza, Spain
jesus.gallardo@unizar.es
[2] Departamento de Ingeniería de Diseño y Fabricación,
Universidad de Zaragoza, Zaragoza, Spain
[3] Departamento de Psicología y Sociología,
Universidad de Zaragoza, Zaragoza, Spain

Abstract. The field of pervasive games is gaining importance in the last times. These games are characterized by exceeding the usual dimensions of time, space and social component that are present in traditional games. These games are usually played in an interactive space, in which several user interfaces following a multimodal approach work together to obtain the pervasive game experience. Pervasive games have proven to be useful in several fields, including the educational one. Here, we introduce *The Fantastic Journey*, a pervasive game directed towards children with Attention Deficit Hyperactivity Disorder. The game has been designed with the help of pedagogues so that it really matches some educational goals. The game is made up of some *missions* that integrate different kinds of interaction: gestural, tangible, etc. The game has been developed following a methodological approach developed as a previous work. In this paper, the main features of the game, focusing on its different missions and their educational goals, are explained.

Keywords: Pervasive game · Interactive space · ADHD

1 Introduction

Usually, games have been played out in the physical world, where they have made use of real-world objects and properties. However, human activities and relationships are migrating from the physical world to the virtual world. So, a new type of games has appeared. The term *pervasive game* is the usual way to refer to this new kind of games. Usually, the idea in pervasive games is that they overcome the limitations of traditional games in the spatial, temporal or social dimensions. In a previous work, we have defined pervasive games as *"a way to deliver a new gaming experience to the player through an evolution of the dynamics of the game, enriching the gaming space by means of the information provided by the context where it is played. This allows breaking the boundaries of the game, making reality part of it and that the elements in that reality have an influence during the game."* [1].

© ICST Institute for Computer Sciences, Social Informatics and Telecommunications Engineering 2019
Published by Springer Nature Switzerland AG 2019. All Rights Reserved
A. L. Brooks et al. (Eds.): ArtsIT 2018/DLI 2018, LNICST 265, pp. 526–531, 2019.

Video games have proven to be useful to work with children and adolescents with special educational needs [2]. In this work we have focused on children with ADHD (Attention-Deficit Hyperactivity Disorder). Attention deficit hyperactivity disorder (ADHD) is a mental disorder whose symptoms include attention and concentration difficulties, lack of emotional auto-regulation, and a high level of impulsivity [3]. Interactive games are stimuli that can help to improve the attention and planning skills and could perform mediation functions encouraging children to explore, generate questions, and reflect. As far as we now, the game presented here is the first pervasive game aimed to ADHD children.

Pervasive games can be potentially played at any place. One possibility is to play them at an Interactive Space. Interactive Spaces are distributed user interfaces that support collaborative work in digitally augmented rooms or workplaces [4]. In our work we will work with pervasive games played in an interactive space.

This work is framed within a project for the development of multimodal pervasive games for children. In the scope of this project, we have developed a methodological proposal for the development of pervasive games [5]. One of the relevant elements in the proposal is the use of a Game Experience Design Document (GEDD) specific for pervasive games.

Taking all the aforementioned into account, in this paper we introduce a pervasive game named *The fantastic journey*. The game is intended to be played in an interactive space placed in the Cesar-Etopia labs in Zaragoza, Spain. The game is directed towards children with ADHD, and it has been developed with pedagogues that have helped us to establish the educational goals of the game.

This document is structured as follows: in Sect. 2, educational video games for ADHD are presented. Section 3 is about our previous work that has been used in the development of the game. In Sect. 4 we introduce the game with its main features. Finally, Sect. 5 is about conclusions and future work.

2   Related Work: Technologies and Applications for Children with ADHD

Several works that make use of technologies specifically developed for children with ADHD can be found in the literature. The applications can be classified considering different contexts: desktop applications, augmented reality applications and tangible interfaces. We are going to mention an example of each context.

In the context of desktop applications, ACTIVATE™ [6] is a program that combines cognitive brain training with physical exercise. It is composed by several neuroscience-based games specifically designed to increase and strengthen your child's ability to concentrate and focus, to work memory, to acquire speed in information processing, cognitive flexibility, etc. It has a real time data module that collect children results and interactions, generating reports, alerts and statistics available for parents and educators.

In the context of augmented reality, Rizzo et al. have developed a virtual classroom in order to work attention deficits [7]. They make use of a head mounted display and different tracking devices to immerse children in the classroom. Children interact with the system through a virtual teacher, who assigns them different tasks to work the different types of attention (classified in: focused, sustained, selective, alternating and divided) while several distracters are taking place.

Lastly, in the context of tangible interfaces, TangiPlan [8] is a system composed of six tangible objects whose objective is to help children work their executive functions. Each object represents a task that the child has to carry out in the morning. The child situates the objects at the places where the tasks have to be performed and select the time that they have to devote to every task.

3 Gaming Space and Development Methodology

The interactive space where the game will be played is an indoor space of around 70 m^2. It includes a real-time localization system, Kinects, microphones, and projectors. One of the most remarkable user interfaces it includes is the set of four tangible tabletop devices which allows working with the approach of tangible user interfaces. These devices are tables capable of both displaying images and tracking objects placed on them. We have used the devices (NikVision tabletops) in previous works with children with very satisfactory results [9].

Regarding the development of the game, in a previous work we developed the GeoPGD methodological proposal for pervasive game development [5]. This proposal evolves from the classic approach of game development, adapting it to the features of these games. The four components of GeoPGD should be defined in order to specify a pervasive game. This is done in the Game Experience Design Document (GEDD). Those four components are (i) pervasive narrative, (ii) game world, (iii) rules and (iv) pervasive dynamics.

4 The Fantastic Journey

In this section, we are going to provide the details of the game making use of the most relevant information included in the GEDD of the game.

4.1 Justification and Goals

The game is directed towards children with ADHD, who have problems of attention and concentration. The game helps to work these aspects in a fun way by means of the combination of different goals, devices and technologies. The educational goals of the game are the following:

- The development of selective, focused and maintained attention.
- The development of abilities of creation, organization and selection of the best strategy depending on the task.
- The planning of paths and processes linking space and time with the efficacy of the task.
- Listening in an active way.
- Solving problems using both oral and written information.
- Collaborating in an active and respectful way to achieve a common goal.
- Self-regulation of behavior in order to achieve the tasks in an effective way.

4.2   Features, Gameplay and Story

The game is an adventure game, in which the protagonist has to progress over the story interacting with different characters and objects. It is multiplayer, as players will interact among them in a collaborative way to achieve a goal. The game is played between the real world and the virtual game. This implies that the game is pervasive mainly in the physical dimension, as players can freely move throughout the interactive space. It also could have some kind of social pervasiveness, as players can interact with other people in the space and ask them for help.

The story is about a girl called *Pipo*, who has a dream in which she puts on a magic hat. With the hat on, she flies into the space, where she meets the *Comet of laughs*, which delivers laughs all over the universe. During the encounter, Pipo gets lost with the *bag of laughs*. Then, she decides to travel through the space to find the comet and return the bag. This story is an evolution of the one defined in [10].

The game uses the technologies present in the interactive space explained in Sect. 3. The target players of the game are between 7 and 12 years. The children will be accompanied by one of more *mediators*, which will supervise them, help them if they need it, or manipulate the progress of the game if the children find any difficulty. Before the start of every mission, a video with instructions is projected on the walls. The mediator has the option to replay it if needed.

4.3   Elements of the Game

The main elements that are present in the game are the following: the *protagonist*, the *friends* that will interact with her, the *stars* where the *missions* (challenges) take place and the *sound*, made up by a main theme and sound effects.

The physiognomy and visual style of the protagonist have been designed by a product designer following the recommendations of the pedagogues related to which would work best with ADHD kids: smooth and round shapes, smooth and not loud colors, visually powerful but without adornment. The final appearance of the character is shown in Fig. 1.

4.4   Missions

Magic Words. Here, children have to pay attention to the lyrics of a song and then, order the words that make up the chorus. This is made in the tabletop devices.

The Sun and The Moon. In this mission, children have to make up the shapes of the sun and the moon (projected on a wall) by placing themselves (localization) in the interactive space.

The Search for the Suitcase. Here, players have to find a suitcase and a key. The suitcase is physically hidden, whereas the key can be obtained by playing Starloop [4], a game that we have developed to improve computational thinking in kids.

Fig. 1. Appearance of the protagonist of the game. In the right side of the figure, the main anatomy of the protagonist, made up of 5046 polygons.

Keyword. This mission allows working attention in both selective and global levels. Children will listen to a story in which a word is constantly repeated. Then, they will have to find the word in an alphabet soup that will appear on the tabletop devices.

Indians. Here, children have to follow patterns, so successive processing and selective attention are worked. Each tabletop device will represent a color and a shape (Fig. 2 left). First, players have to touch the table when it matches the element shown. Afterwards, they will have to touch the table repeatedly when it is required.

Fig. 2. Indians (left) and Butterflies (right) missions.

Freeing the Stars. Here, the goal is to free three stars that have been trapped in a spider web. Selective attention and simultaneous processing are the abilities developed. The player has to select the elements required by means of gestural interaction.

Meteorite Attack. This mission is about destroying a set of meteorites. It helps to work on selective attention and planning of time-space paths. The meteorites get destroyed by interacting with the tabletop devices.

Butterflies. In this game, players must stay quiet so that the butterflies that are projected on the walls are placed on the flowers (Fig. 2 right). The idea is to work on the inhibition of impulsive behaviors and on self-control. When the players have been quiet for two minutes, the mission finishes.

Encounter with the *Comet of Laughs*. The last phase of the game consists of a projection of the last scene, in which the protagonist meets the *Comet of laughs*, and of the playing of the song of the game, which will be sung and danced by the children.

5 Future Work

In this paper we have introduced *The fantastic journey,* a pervasive game for children with ADHD to be played in a multimodal interactive space. The game has been developed following a methodological approach which is specified in a Game Experience Design Document. The game is designed to achieve some educational goals. Thanks to the research project, we have been collaborating during the last two years with an association of children with ADHD and their families; in fact, they have help us to establish the educational goals of the game. Thanks to this collaboration, we will be able to evaluate the complete game, which will be our next step.

Acknowledgments. This work has been partly funded by the Spanish Government (contract TIN2015-67149-C3-1R). We would like to thank Marian Garrido and Ana Cristina Blasco for their help in the definition of the missions and Jorge Moreno for the design of the scenarios.

References

1. Arango, J., et al.: Pervasive games: giving a meaning based on the player experience. In: Proceedings of Interacción 2017 (2017)
2. Durkin, K., Boyle, J., Hunter, S., Conti-Ramsden, G.: Video games for children and adolescents with special educational needs. Zeitschrift für Psychologie **221**, 79–89 (2013)
3. Barkley, R.A.: Attention-Deficit Hyperactivity Disorder: A Clinical Workbook, vol. 2. The Guilford Press, New York (2006)
4. Marco, J., Bonillo, C., Cerezo, E.: A tangible interactive space Odyssey to support children learning of computer programming. In: ISS 2017, pp. 300–305 (2017)
5. Arango, J., et al.: GeoPGD: proposed methodology for the implementation of geolocated pervasive games. In: Proceedings of Interacción (2018)
6. ACTIVATE™. http://www.c8home.com. Accessed May 2018
7. Rizzo, A., et al.: The virtual classroom: a virtual reality environment for the assessment and rehabilitation of attention deficits. CyberPsychol. Behav. **3**(3), 483–499 (2000)
8. Weisberg, O., et al.: TangiPlan: designing an assistive technology to enhance executive functioning among children with ADHD. In: Proceedings of the 2014 Conference on Interaction Design and Children, pp. 293–296. ACM (2014)
9. Marco, J., et al.: Bringing tabletop technologies to kindergarten children. In: Proceedings of the 23rd British HCI Group Annual Conference on People and Computers: Celebrating People and Technology, pp. 103–111 (2009)
10. Aguelo, A., Carrera, M., Coma, T., Gómez, M., Ortiga, M.: El Viaje Fantástico. Aula Libre N° 58, Ed. Movimiento de Renovación Pedagógica "AULA LIBRE", pp. 12–15 (1993)

What Is It Like to Be a Virtual Bat?

Anastassia Andreasen[✉][iD], Niels Christian Nilsson[iD],
Jelizaveta Zovnercuka[iD], Michele Geronazzo[iD], and Stefania Serafin[iD]

Multisensory Experience Lab, Aalborg University Copenhagen,
A. C. Meyers Vaenge 15, 2450 Copenhagen, Denmark
{asta,ncn,mge,sts}@create.aau.dk,jzovne13@student.aau.dk,
https://melcph.create.aau.dk/

Abstract. Virtual Reality (VR) might give us a glimpse of what it
feels to have a different from human shaped body and how to orientate ourselves in virtual environment (VE) with it. Bats' wings structure
has anatomical similarities to a human hand; yet would it be possible
to achieve a compelling illusion of virtual body ownership (VBO) over
bat's avatar is questionable. Hence our main aim of research is to imitate
bat's sonar system and achieve embodiment of anatomically similar but
morphologically different body – a body of a bat. Test results showed a
possibility to achieve VBO illusion using bat's avatar. VBO was significantly higher when steering through VE, as opposed to steering without
a virtual body and exposing to involuntary movement through VE. With
our research prototype, users will be able to navigate with echolocation
system and fly through a virtual cave.

Keywords: Virtual Reality · Virtual Body Ownership · Echolocation

1 Introduction

If it would be possible to answer such philosophical question as "What is it like
to be a bat" [5] it might be easier to understand and simulate any life form as we
would perceive surrounded environment as bats do. In order to elicit objective
cognitive embodiment of a bat it will be useful to provide people with the experience of "seeing" the world through bat's eyes and allow them to inhabit a bat's
body. As bat's anatomical structure of the wing, for example, is very similar to
human's hand, it might give us an opportunity to do so. In attempt to create
bat's simulator the following challenges arise: (1) providing users with the sense
of ownership of the bat's body; (2) enabling users to control the bat's body in a
way that is both intuitive and mimics real bat's behaviour; (3) providing users
with impression of how the world "looks" when experienced through bat's senses.
In order to imitate bat's basic physiological ability to flight – by inhabiting its
body, and orient in the environment – by using echolocation system, we would
apply virtual reality (VR) technology to allow users to navigate with a virtual
avatar. A commonly held view is that the virtual body should have resemblance

A. L. Brooks et al. (Eds.): ArtsIT 2018/DLI 2018, LNICST 265, pp. 532–537, 2019.
https://doi.org/10.1007/978-3-030-06134-0_57

to human morphological structure in order to create a compelling illusion of virtual body ownership (VBO) [4]. Furthermore, VR allows to inhabit not only morphologically modified virtual human bodies [3] but also bodies with additional virtual limbs [7]. This research prototype presents the system intended to produce an illusion of being a bat and navigate inside the virtual environment (VE). The system is a part of ongoing research seeking to address three questions related to this illusion: (1) To which extent can user get the sense of VBO? (2) How can VR be used to replicate the perceptual experience of being a bat? (3) How to navigate with the virtual body using echolocation inside the VE? In order to answer all these questions, the system enables users to control the body of a virtual bat, fly through the VE and simulate the experience of echolocation. The body of the virtual avatar used in the experiments is presented in Fig. 1.

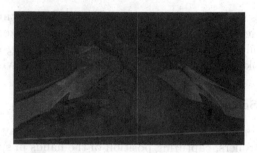

Fig. 1. Virtual bat's position from first person perspective

In the ongoing research, we are exploring the amount of VBO illusion that participants experience over a virtual bat's body through visuo-tactile stimulation of their arm while seeing an object touching their virtual wing [2]. Furthermore, we research agency [1] as voluntary limbs movement and navigation through the environment. The last study indicated a linear relationship between agency and VBO. The higher agency was the more VBO was experienced, which suggests that felt and seen motor activity generated VBO as well as regulated its extent. Asynchronous mapping used for controlled movements produced the illusion of synchronous actions.

Series of pilot tests have been conducted in order to make use of real-time sound spatialization algorithms in VR (see [6] for a recent review on this topic) using appropriate parameters for providing echolocation cues as in a natural environment. The first couple of tests investigated which sound qualities enhance the ability to echolocate. The first experiment included a pre-recorded mouth click 13 ms long [9]. The second one used an expert mouth click [8], generated in Matlab with the length of 2 ms. Both tests involved the following conditions: vision, early reflections without vision, reverberation without vision and finally early reflections together with reverberation but without vision. To measure accuracy and speed performance, time and distance traveled as well as the number of mouth clicks produced by the participants were noted. Test results showed that musicians were more sensitive to perception of audio stimuli and therefore showed a better performance than non-musicians. Based on the comparison of audio behaviour in the real world through impulse response measurements to the obtained results from the first two experiments we were able to modulate realistic sound behaviour and spatialization when echolocating in the VE. The final study is still currently in progress.

The novel aspect of this research demo is an attempt to simulate echolocation with the help of delay-based effects using expert-generated mouth clicks and navigate through the VE while inhabiting a virtual avatar that is morphologically different from a human shape structure.

2   System Demonstration

Locomotor kinetics (vertical lift to overcome gravity and thrust to overcome drag) and kinematics were considered together with wing size and shape (bat's wing is ideal aerofoil), air density and angle of the attack. Flight locomotion was divided into upstroke and downstroke, which produced one wingbeat cycle.

2.1   Hardware Setup

The system consists of an Oculus Rift head-mounted display (HMD) and two motion Touch controllers, capturing position of the hands in space. Headset resolution is 2160×1200 at refresh rate of 90 Hz. Two cameras are used – one for positional tracking of HMD, another one for touch controllers. For the echolocation system, Oculus left-hand Touch controller (button "X") is used for generating mouth click and as a result, an output signal is transmitted through Bose AC35 headphones. Overall system setup is presented in Fig. 2.

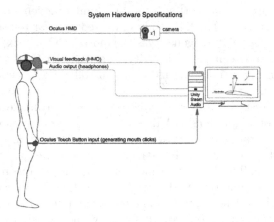

Fig. 2. System set-up

2.2   User Interaction

Users will be able to control their flight with their hands through Oculus Touch controllers. Before users would be able to proceed with the system, calibration is applied. During the calibration phase that lasts for 5 s, users have to keep their hands in T-pose (or in front and slightly to the sides for convenience), and press down PrimaryThumbstick button of the left-hand Touch controller. The users are notified about application start through a screen message when calibration is done. Navigation requires the constant unified hand movements (up and down passing the "zero" angle acquired from the T-pose) to generate physical forces and to avoid falling down, since if the attack angle would be negative (hands down) gravity and drag forces would eventually make the virtual body to fall. Direction of the flight is computed in the direction of the hands. Users will be able to experience echolocation by pressing the button generating expert mouth clicks and listening to the audio feedback from the virtual space through their headphones. The duration and volume of the feedbacks will allow users to determine primarily the distance to the objects in virtual space, the size of the VE and, theoretically, provide additional information on the shape, size and material of the objects.

2.3   Software Architecture

To meet the requirements for natural sound propagation in VR, Steam Audio engine was used. As soon as the users' press "X" button generated mouth click audio sample is processed through Steam Audio in real-time. Steam Audio casts multiple rays from the sound source within the defined radius (radius = 7 m) that imitate sound propagation as in the real world with multiple real-time reflections that could be controlled in the program, and finally level and decay time of reverberation is also calculated by Steam Audio in real-time. User's movements are mapped to the virtual avatar also in real time. Linear mapping is used for this purpose, tracking one "hand beat" cycle (hands up and hands down) in a virtual representation of one wingbeat cycle (upstroke and downstroke) through animation.

Gesture Detection. Bat's animation is synchronized with real-time data acquisition from users' input gestures imitating bat's locomotive cycle. The system would register hands movements, following along Y-axis: positive α, when hands go up above "zero" angle, and negative α, when hands go down below "zero" angle, equivalent to upstroke and downstroke of bat's biological locomotive cycle. A certain position on the Yaxis is capturing a specific a. Finally "zero" angle interval passes highest/lowest positional values of a into the system.

Velocity Estimation. The faster the users imitate flying movements (passing "zero" angle) the faster bat flies through VE. Stroke duration computes the amount of time passed, depending on the up- or down stroke of the cycle. It keeps track of the stroke speed allowing to control the speed of the bat, depending on the positive or negative α, which in its turn differs depending on the calculated aerodynamic forces.

Heading Direction. Touch controllers (hands) position are responsible for the direction of movement through the environment. This is done in order to "free" HMD from being responsible for the direction of the flight and give users full control over the bat's body. Direction of the flight is calculated in the direction of the unified movement of the hand controllers. E.g. if the users would want to change direction they would need to rotate/move their body to the desired direction and new direction for the virtual body will be calculated. It is realized by creating a forward directional vector, using position of the Touch controllers in space.

Echolocation. In order to properly simulate echolocation, raycasting is used to calculate distances from the virtual bat to virtual objects in the VE space. This information provides the proper delays parameters for input clicks as it would occur in real life taking into consideration sound speed. Head-Related Transfer Function (HRTF) provides further spatial information about the direction of arrivals of echoes reflecting from objects (azimuth and elevation). For stimulating more realistic reverberation succeeding parameters are adapted: bilinear HRTF interpolation, physics-based attenuation, air absorption, direct mix level $= 1.0$ (where minimum is 0 and maximum is 1), frequency dependent transmission occlusions using partial method, e.g. casting multiple rays from the sound source within the radius of 7 m, real-time reflections with indirect mix level $= 1.0$ (where minimum is 0 and maximum is 16). The system is able to perform real-time calculations of sound impulse reflections and reverberations depending on the user position and head rotation. The following audio shaders are applied to the objects in the VE: "Rock" for the walls, "Wood" for the trees, roots and vegetation and "Glass" for crystals.

3 Conclusion

The discussed system is built to support learning echolocation during flight locomotion. In the ongoing research, we create a new compelling illusion of VBO over anatomically similar but morphologically different virtual body of a bat, which can be achieved during navigation and orientation through VE. Navigation is performed by specific gestural inputs imitating flight in combination with echolocation using expert-generated mouth clicks, imitating sonar signals in the VE. Flying algorithm was computed using bat's locomotor kinetics and kinematics.

4 Video

Video is hosted by Youtube and could be seen on the following url: https://youtu.be/uB2ApqoNzzU.

References

1. Andreasen, A., Nilsson, N.C., Serafin, S.: Agency enhances body ownership illusion of being a virtual bat. In: IEEE Virtual Reality 2018. IEEE Press (2018)
2. Andreasen, A., Nilsson, N.C., Serafin, S.: Spatial asynchronous visuo-tactile stimuli influence ownership of virtual wings. In: IEEE Virtual Reality 2018. IEEE Press (2018)
3. Kilteni, K., Normand, J.M., Sanchez-Vives, M.V., Slater, M.: Extending body space in immersive virtual reality: a very long arm illusion. PLoS ONE **7**(7), e40867 (2012)
4. Maselli, A., Slater, M.: The building blocks of the full body ownership illusion. Front. Hum. Neurosci. **7**, 83 (2013)
5. Nagel, T.: What is it like to be a bat? Philos. Rev. **83**(4), 435–450 (1974)
6. Serafin, S., Geronazzo, M., Nilsson, N.C., Erkut, C., Nordahl, R.: Sonic interactions in virtual reality: state of the art, current challenges and future directions. IEEE Comput. Graph. Appl. **38**(2), 31–43 (2018)
7. Steptoe, W., Steed, A., Slater, M.: Human tails: ownership and control of extended humanoid avatars. IEEE Trans. Vis. Comput. Graph. **19**(4), 583–590 (2013)
8. Thaler, L., et al.: Mouth-clicks used by blind expert human echolocators - signal description and model based signal synthesis. PLOS Comput. Biol. **13**(8), e1005670 (2017)
9. Zovnercuka, J., Konovalovs, K., Andreasen, A., Geronazzo, M., Serafin, S., Paisa, R.: Navigate as a bat. Real-time echolocation system in virtual reality. In: Proceedings of 15th International Sound and Music Computing Conference (2018)

CodeCubes - Playing with Cubes and Learning to Code

Bárbara Cleto[1]([⊠]) [iD], João Martinho Moura[1] [iD], Luís Ferreira[1] [iD], and Cristina Sylla[2] [iD]

[1] Escola Superior de Tecnologia,
Instituto Politécnico do Cávado e do Ave, Barcelos, Portugal
al3993@alunos.ipca.pt, {jmoura,lufer}@ipca.pt
[2] Research Centre on Child Studies (CIEC),
Universidade do Minho, Braga, Portugal
cristina.sylla@ie.uminho.pt

Abstract. We present the concept, design and first prototype of CodeCubes, a hybrid interface that combines physical paper cubes with Augmented Reality (AR) for promoting computational thinking. Additionally, we reflect on the potential of combining digital games with new interaction paradigms in the context of the classroom for introducing students to programming concepts in a playful, engaging way, this way promoting student's interest and engagement for STEAM (Science, Technology, Engineering, Art and Math).

Keywords: Tangible interfaces · Interaction · Co-learning
Augmented Reality · Computational thinking

1 Introduction

In recent years the video/digital games industry has grown exponentially playing an increasingly important role in entertainment. A few successful video games have even been adapted and released as films, e.g., Tomb Raider or Resident Evil. At the same time there is also a trend for integrating real and virtual environments (augmented and virtual reality) using optical sensors (present in mobile technologies) and the convergence of several gaming platforms, allied to a new type of interaction, based on gestures. The enormous success of digital or video games lead to a new learning approach [1], named Game Based Learning (GBL) in which games are used to motivate and involve the students with the learning subject [2], as is the case of Serious Games (SG). A more recent trend considers that the students can create their own games and by doing so developing problem solving as well as programming skills.

In this paper we present CodeCubes, a hybrid interface for learning basic programming concepts. The combination of physical and virtual objects aims at assessing the impact that the addition of a tangible component to a digital game can have in the teaching/learning process, as well as at investigating whether a hybrid interface motivates the students to collaboratively solve problems. The development of Code-Cubes is being carried out with two classes of 8th graders following a Design Based Research methodology [3]. Following this methodology, we have carried out several

A. L. Brooks et al. (Eds.): ArtsIT 2018/DLI 2018, LNICST 265, pp. 538–543, 2019.

design sessions with the students in which we have tried out different possibilities for the design of the interface. After several iterations where we imagined different forms, materials and objects we decided to use physical paper cubes as interface for learning basic coding. Paper cubes are easy to craft and handle and provide a good metaphor for representing data.

In the following section we discuss relevant work in this area.

2 Related Work

There are various kits and digital platforms for children and young adults that aim at promoting the development of logical reasoning and programming skills. These tools have been developed both in commercial and academic contexts and can be classified in three main groups: (i) physical (all the components are tangible), (ii) virtual (all the components are virtual e.g., PC and/or mobile-device based applications without physical components), (iii) hybrid (combining physical and virtual components) [4].

An aspect that is particularly important specially for children is the kind of inter-action supported by the materials. This is, the physical or the virtual features of an interface, strongly influence the way children perceive and use it [4]. Previous research has shown that tangible interfaces are especially adequate for supporting and promoting collaboration [5, 6]. Some authors consider that hybrid interfaces that combine physical and graphical elements are also advantageous as they allow changing between two interaction modalities. Here the tangible component can be used for exploration whereas the graphical component can be used for rapid prototyping [7].

In line with this last approach CodeCubes combines Augmented Reality (AR) with physical blocks for promoting the learning of basic programming concepts. Some relevant examples of interfaces that use AR to promote computational thinking are the AR Scratch [8], Code Bits [9], AR-Maze [10] or Paper Cubes [11].

The AR Scratch is an extension that adds an Augmented Reality functionality to the Scratch programming environment, displaying virtual objects on a real-world space seen through a camera, where the virtual world can be controlled by physical markers. The AR-Maze, is a tangible programming tool for children, that uses physical pro-gramming blocks and mixes virtual and real elements. Children can create their own programs by manipulating the programming blocks and debug or execute the code with a mobile device. Code Bits is a tangible paper kit that students can use to create programs. The code is then processed in the Code Bits mobile application. Paper Cubes aims at teaching basic computational skills as well as more advanced programming skills in the field of Artificial Intelligence (AI) or Machine Learning (ML) using AR. Cubely [12], is an immersive Virtual Reality (VR) programming environment in which novice programmers solve programming puzzles within a virtual world.

CodeCubes combines affordances from Paper Cubes (the physical paper cubes) and from Code Bits, however CodeCubes allows users to program and process the code on the virtual environment without having to change environments like in Code Bits. In the following section we present the CodeCubes interface.

3   CodeCubes

CodeCubes builds on the Classic Maze game [13], in which the users use visual programming blocks that they can drag and drop to program and overcome various challenges. However, instead of using virtual programming blocks e.g. as in the Scratch platform (see Fig. 1, top), CodeCubes uses physical paper cubes that can be easily crafted by the users and serve as interface to manipulate the virtual elements (see Fig. 1, bottom).

Fig. 1. The scratch programming environment (top), the CodeCubes environment (bottom)

CodeCubes was developed in the Unity 2017.4.0f1 (64-bit) game engine [14] and the Vuforia AR platform [15], which allows the virtual simulation of the tangible programming cubes. Each face of the cubes has an AR marker that represents one of the basic programming instructions: start, forward, right, left, back and end. To improve the detection of the physical cubes and to minimize possible recognition errors, mainly in poor light conditions, the markers present text labels and patterns.

CodeCubes presents the users a labyrinth with various paths along which there are cubes and pyramids scattered. The application allows the users to create their own labyrinths, which they can print on an A4 sheet of paper. The printed labyrinth displays the area for placing and moving the physical cubes.

To start the game, the users show the face with the start marker of a physical cube to the camera. Once the camera detects the start marker a 3D virtual cube appears over the physical paper cube. The users can visualize both the virtual cube and the path that they need to program with the physical cubes to follow a certain route. After programming the virtual cube using the physical programming blocks, by clicking the play button, the user visualizes the programmed actions (see Fig. 2). This is the virtual cube moves along the programmed path.

Fig. 2. Interface and game interaction

To fulfil the game the user needs to program the virtual cube to follow a certain path in order to pick the different cubes and pyramids that are scattered over the play surface. When the users are successful they can start creating buildings, e.g., by pilling up cubes and pyramids on the play field (see Fig. 3). The aim of the game is to create different building constructions, resulting in a small town at the end of the game. To achieve this, the users use the physical paper cubes to program the path of the virtual cube. As previously referred each face of the cubes has an AR marker that represents one of the basic programming instructions: start, forward, right, left, back and end. In order to program a sequence of actions that the virtual cube must follow, the user places each paper cube in front of the camera of a mobile device showing the respective face, and then hits the play button to execute the programmed actions.

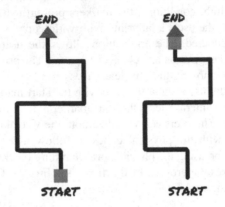

Fig. 3. Example of a path to be programmed

The goal of the game is that the students collaboratively create their own labyrinths as well as different building construction. A possible scenario could be building constructions with different heights (pilling up different number of cubes) and using the pyramids for building the roof or even incorporate them on the buildings.

4   Conclusion and Future Work

In this paper we have presented CodeCubes, a hybrid interface for collaboratively learn basic programming concepts. The combination of physical and virtual elements aims at supporting and promoting social interactions between the students themselves as well as between the teachers and the students. Therefore, potentially increasing students learning motivation and achievements. CodeCubes, is still in an early development stage, in the next design iterations we will explore together with the students the inclusion of different construction elements that the users can use to create their buildings in a more creative way. Another thought is to enable the users to create their own physical markers and the physical objects to manipulate the virtual game content. The resulting upgraded prototype will be tested in the classroom environment to investigate the impact that the addition of a tangible component to a digital game can have in the teaching/learning process as well as the extent to which it promotes collaborative problem solving.

Acknowledgments. Cristina Sylla acknowledges the funding from the FCT (Portuguese Foundation for Science and Technology) and the European Operational Programme Human Capital (POCH), with the grant SFRH/BPD/111891/2015.

References

1. Prensky, M.: Digital game-based learning. Comput. Entertainment (CIE) 1(1), 21 (2003)
2. Confessions of an Aca-Fan Homepage. http://henryjenkins.org/2011/03/how_learners_can_ be_on_top_of.html. Accessed 30 Sept 2018
3. Sylla, C.: Developing and evaluating pedagogical digital manipulatives for preschool: the case of TOK-touch, organize, create (2014)
4. Yu, J., Roque, R.: A survey of computational kits for young children. In: Proceedings of the 17th ACM Conference on Interaction Design and Children (IDC 2018), Norway, pp. 289–299. ACM Press, New York (2018)
5. Sylla, C., Branco, P., Coutinho, C., Coquet, M.E.: TUIs vs. GUIs: comparing the learning potential with preschoolers. Pers. Ubiquit. Comput. 16, 421–432 (2012)
6. Horn, M.S., Solovey, E.T., Crouser, R.J., Jacob, R.J.: Comparing the use of tangible and graphical programming languages for informal science education. In: Proceedings of the SIGCHI Conference on Human Factors in Computing Systems, Boston, MA, USA, pp. 975–984. ACM Press, New York (2009)
7. Horn, M.S., Crouser, R.J., Bers, M.U.: Tangible interaction and learning: the case for a hybrid approach. Pers. Ubiquit. Comput. 16(4), 379–389 (2012)
8. Radu, I., MacIntyre, B.: Augmented-reality scratch: a children's authoring environment for augmented-reality experiences. In: Proceedings of the 8th International Conference on Interaction Design and Children (IDC 2009), Milano, Como, Italy, pp. 210–213. ACM Press, New York (2009)
9. Goyal, S., Vijay, R.S., Monga, C., Kalita, P.: Code bits: an inexpensive tangible computational thinking toolkit for K-12 curriculum. In: Proceedings of the TEI 2016: Tenth International Conference on Tangible, Embedded, and Embodied Interaction (TEI 2016), Eindhoven, Netherlands, pp. 441–447. ACM Press, New York (2016)
10. Jin, Q., Wang, D., Deng, X., Zheng, N., Chiu, S.: AR-Maze: a tangible programming tool for children based on AR technology. In: Proceedings of the 17th ACM Conference on Interaction Design and Children (IDC 2018), Norway, pp. 611–616. ACM Press, New York (2018)
11. Fuste, A., Amores, J., Ha, D., Jongejan, J., Pitaru, A.: Paper cubes: evolving 3D characters in augmented reality using recurrent neural networks. In: Workshop in Machine Learning for Creativity and Design. NIPS 2017. http://annafuste.com/portfolio/paper-cubes/. Accessed 30 Sept 2018
12. Vincur, J., Konopka, M., Tvarozek, J., Hoang, M., Navrat, P.: Cubely: virtual reality block-based programming environment. In: Proceedings of the 23rd ACM Symposium on Virtual Reality Software and Technology, Sweden, p. 84. ACM Press, New York (2017)
13. Code.org - Classic Maze - Studio Code.org Homepage (2018). https://studio.code.org/hoc/1. Accessed 30 Sept 2018
14. Unity (game engine) Homepage. https://unity3d.com. Accessed 30 Sept 2018
15. AR Vuforia Homepage. https://www.vuforia.com. Accessed 30 Sept 2018

Author Index

Printed in the United States
By Bookmasters